# THE END OF AMBITION

## AMERICA IN THE WORLD

*Sven Beckert and Jeremi Suri, Series Editors*

Mark Atwood Lawrence, *The End of Ambition: The United States and the Third World in the Vietnam Era*

Roberto Saba, *American Mirror: The United States and Brazil in the Age of Emancipation*

Stefan J. Link, *Forging Global Fordism: Nazi Germany, Soviet Russia, and the Contest over the Industrial Order*

Sara Lorenzini, *Global Development: A Cold War History*

Michael Cotey Morgan, *The Final Act: The Helsinki Accords and the Transformation of the Cold War*

A. G. Hopkins, *American Empire: A Global History*

Tore C. Olsson, *Agrarian Crossings: Reformers and the Remaking of the US and Mexican Countryside*

Kiran Klaus Patel, *The New Deal: A Global History*

Adam Ewing, *The Age of Garvey: How a Jamaican Activist Created a Mass Movement and Changed Global Black Politics*

Jürgen Osterhammel and Patrick Camiller, *The Transformation of the World: A Global History of the Nineteenth Century*

Edited by Jeffrey A. Engel, Mark Atwood Lawrence & Andrew Preston, *America in the World: A History in Documents from the War with Spain to the War on Terror*

Donna R. Gabaccia, *Foreign Relations: American Immigration in Global Perspective*

Thomas Borstelmann, *The 1970s: A New Global History from Civil Rights to Economic Inequality*

Rachel St. John, *Line in the Sand: A History of the Western U.S.-Mexico Border*

Ian Tyrrell, *Reforming the World: The Creation of America's Moral Empire*

Andrew Zimmerman, *Alabama in Africa: Booker T. Washington, the German Empire, and the Globalization of the New South*

For a full list of titles in the series, go to:
https://press.princeton.edu/catalogs/series/title/america-in-the-world.html

# The End of Ambition

## THE UNITED STATES AND THE THIRD WORLD IN THE VIETNAM ERA

MARK ATWOOD LAWRENCE



PRINCETON UNIVERSITY PRESS
PRINCETON & OXFORD

Published by Princeton University Press
41 William Street, Princeton, New Jersey 08540
6 Oxford Street, Woodstock, Oxfordshire OX20 1TR

press.princeton.edu


ISBN 978-0-691-12640-1
ISBN (e-book) 978-0-691-22655-2

British Library Cataloging-in-Publication Data is available

Editorial: Brigitta van Rheinberg, Eric Crahan, Priya Nelson and Thalia Leaf
Production Editorial: Jenny Wolkowicki
Jacket design: Layla Mac Rory
Production: Danielle Amatucci
Publicity: Alyssa Sanford
Copyeditor: Joseph Dahm

Jacket image: AP Images / Bob Daugherty

This book has been composed in Arno

Printed on acid-free paper. ∞

Printed in the United States of America

10 9 8 7 6 5 4 3 2 1

CONTENTS

# PREFACE

THIS BOOK originated with a simple question: How did the Vietnam War alter the broad contours of American foreign policy in the 1960s? Although the war has drawn a staggering amount of attention from scholars, journalists, and memoirists, few authors have focused on this subject over the years despite its conspicuous importance. Appreciating the ways in which the U.S. embroilment in Southeast Asia redirected the grand patterns of history promised to help us understand what has unfolded ever since. Above all, I aimed to explore how U.S. frustrations in Indochina affected perhaps the most striking policy departure of the early 1960s—Washington's bold assurances of support for democratization and economic progress in the emerging nations of the Third World.

Answering my question not only revealed a crucial dimension of the Vietnam War but also cast light on one of the most profound transformations in U.S. foreign policy during the twentieth century. The first half of the 1960s marked a high point of U.S. power and confidence in American political and economic ideals. Almost any problem, abroad as at home, seemed tractable through the application of U.S. resources and know-how. Within a remarkably short time, however, these aspirations lay in shambles. The United States unquestionably remained a superpower as the 1960s gave way to the 1970s, but the failure of ambitious liberalism confronted U.S. leaders with the challenge of refashioning American policy for a new era of disillusion, a challenge that in many ways lingers to the present.

Indeed, I did not fully realize as I began this project how strongly my story echoed in the twenty-first century. Just like American leaders in the early sixties, I came to see, President George W. Bush had responded to surging problems in the Global South after the turn of the millennium by promising to promote democracy and prosperity on a worldwide scale. Yet those ambitions, which coexisted with old doubts about the efficacy of American power, crumbled under the weight of costly wars in Iraq and Afghanistan. U.S. foreign policy grew increasingly militarized, and Washington deepened its reliance on cooperative regional powers. Commentators noted similarities in the foreign policies of Richard Nixon and Barack Obama. Despite sharp differences in political style, the two presidents aimed to reduce American commitments amid waning popular support for international activism and demoralizing military commitments that devoured U.S. resources. As a candidate and then president, Donald Trump took this approach to a new level, unapologetically calling for a foreign policy rooted in a narrow conception of national interest. The result was, among other things, closer relationships with antidemocratic regimes that stirred consternation across much of the political spectrum.

*The End of Ambition* aspires neither to predict the outcome of new controversies nor to offer explicit judgments about the twenty-first century. But the book does aim to show that the United States, shaped by competing impulses to remake the world and to serve its self-interests, has passed through similar moments before. Recognizing the ways history reverberates—the extent to which the past "rhymes" with the present, as Mark Twain put it—can help us discern the pitfalls and opportunities that lie before us. And it can, hopefully, enliven discussion of the best choices for the future.

---

One of the greatest pleasures of completing a book is the opportunity to reflect on the journey and express gratitude for the help I received along the way. In the early stages of this project, I benefited from a Cassius Marcellus Clay Fellowship at Yale University. I was delighted to be part of the remarkable group of scholars at Yale's International Security Studies program and to have a new chance to learn from John Lewis Gaddis, Paul Kennedy, and Ben Kiernan, three exceptional historians and mentors. I am grateful as well to the University of Texas at Austin, my home for most of the past two decades. For this project, I was fortunate to receive a Humanities Research Award from the College of Liberal Arts and a research fellowship from the Institute for Historical Studies. My thanks go particularly to Alan Tully and Jacqueline Jones for making so many opportunities available to me and my colleagues. I am also indebted to Williams College, where I had the good fortune to hold the Stanley Kaplan Visiting Professorship in American Foreign Policy and to work alongside James McAllister for a memorable year.

I appreciate invitations to present parts of this project to symposia focused on the study of international history. Thanks especially to Frank Costigliola at the University of Connecticut, Daniel Sargent at the University of California, Berkeley, Kurk Dorsey at the University of New Hampshire, Mitch Lerner and Robert McMahon at Ohio State, Michael Allen at Northwestern, Fredrik Logevall (then) at Cornell, and the late Marilyn Young at New York University. I learned a great deal from these eminent historians as well as the extraordinary communities of students they have nurtured.

Several other experts contributed to this book by generously sharing ideas and feedback. I am indebted to Nate Citino, David Cole, Greg Daddis, Susan Ferber, James Galbraith, Jim Hershberg, Tanvi Madan, Tim Naftali, Wen-Qing Ngoei, Andrew Preston, Elizabeth Saunders, Tom Schwartz, Kate Weaver, and the late Jon Persoff. Ryan Irwin deserves special thanks for sharing troves of archival material from South Africa. Daniel Sargent, who read the entire manuscript, provided immensely valuable comments. I also wish to thank an anonymous reader whose incisive critiques helped me sharpen the manuscript.

At UT-Austin, I am lucky to be part of an extraordinary team of international historians who have unfailingly supported my work. It is a privilege to work alongside Bill Brands, Will Inboden, Aaron O'Connell, Bat Sparrow, Michael Stoff, and Jeremi Suri. It has been my pleasure as well to work with innumerable talented undergraduates and graduate students at the University of Texas. Joe Parrott, Mark Battjes, and Brian McNeil in particular pushed me to think hard about U.S. foreign relations in the 1960s. Special thanks go as well to my research assistants, Kayleigh Berger and Marcelo José Domingos.

At Princeton University Press, Brigitta van Rheinberg expressed enthusiasm for this book at a pivotal point in my career and showed a perfect blend of support and patience thereafter. I am grateful, too, to Eric Crahan and Priya Nelson for their consummate professionalism and to Thalia Leaf for deftly shepherding the manuscript to publication. I benefited from the expertise of Joseph Dahm and Jenny Wolkowicki in the final stages. For help with the photos, I am grateful to Jay Godwin and, for creating the chart, to Alexis Schrubbe. I am also pleased to acknowledge the generosity of the Herblock Foundation for permitting me to publish two cartoons.

Finally, I owe a massive debt to the friends and family who provided sounding boards, encouragement, and welcome distractions. For all of the above, I am especially grateful to Michael Anderson, Doug Hood, John Merriman, Jennifer Siegel, Bat Sparrow, Alan Tully, and Mark Updegrove. My deepest thanks go, too, to Priscilla, Patrick, Elizabeth, and Jane MeLampy for their exceptional generosity and good cheer. My parents, Elizabeth Atwood and Robert Lawrence, did not live to see this book, but it owes much to the enthusiasm and love they showered on me for years and years. Most of all, I am grateful to Steph Osbakken and our daughters, Maya and Bryn, who (along with Hamley) created a household where serious pursuits mingle effortlessly with boundless joy. This book is dedicated to Steph, Maya, and Bryn.

# ABBREVIATIONS

| | |
|---|---|
| CF | Country Files |
| FCO | Foreign and Commonwealth Office |
| FRUS | *Foreign Relations of the United States* |
| JCS | Joint Chiefs of Staff |
| JFKL | John F. Kennedy Presidential Library and Museum |
| LBJL | Lyndon B. Johnson Presidential Library and Museum |
| NARA | National Archives and Records Administration |
| NAUK | National Archives of the United Kingdom |
| NSAM | National Security Action Memorandum |
| NSC | National Security Council |
| NSF | National Security Files |
| PPC | Policy Planning Council |
| RNL | Richard Nixon Presidential Library and Museum |
| WHCF | White House Central Files |

# THE END OF AMBITION

# Introduction



AS THE PRESIDENTIAL RACE heated up in the summer of 1960, few politicians embodied the spirit of the moment so well as Frank Church. The Democrat had been elected Idaho's junior senator just four years earlier, handily defeating Republican incumbent Herman Welker, an old-school conservative known for fervent anticommunism. Church left no doubt of his own hostility to the Soviet Union. No viable contender for high office could have done otherwise at a time when anticommunism, even if it had cooled since the Red Scare of the early 1950s, remained an American preoccupation. But Church, like other liberals in his party, promised to wage the Cold War with greater subtlety, vision, and vigor than the Republicans had done in the Eisenhower years. Like his friend John F. Kennedy, the thirty-six-year-old Church exuded youthful vigor and intellect, precisely the qualities that Democrats were eager to contrast to Eisenhower's elderly torpor. And, like Kennedy, Church spoke passionately of the need for a fresh, activist brand of leadership prepared to mobilize the nation's prodigious power, wealth, and know-how to meet rapidly metastasizing challenges at home and abroad.

Church was especially concerned with the Cold War in regions variously called the "underdeveloped," "less-developed," or "third" world. Asia, Africa, the Middle East, and Latin America were, Church believed, undergoing an epoch-defining transformation that required Washington's urgent attention. Colonialism and other forms of oppression that ensured Western dominance over much of the globe appeared to be crumbling, and nonwhite peoples were asserting themselves in international affairs as never before. "The prevailing order of the last three centuries has been destroyed," Church declared in his keynote address at the 1960 Democratic National Convention in Los Angeles. Nothing less than the outcome of the Cold War seemed to hinge on whether the democratic West or the communist East responded more effectively. "These underdeveloped and uncommitted nations are the 'no-man's land' on which the destiny of the human race will be decided," Church told the convention delegates and a nationwide television audience. Castigating the

Republicans for propping up colonialism, coddling friendly dictators, and furnishing military equipment to help suppress popular demands for justice, the Idahoan promised that his party would do things differently. Under a Democratic administration, he pledged, the United States would work with, rather than against, the forces of progress; it would build democracy and craft ambitious programs not to equip authoritarians with the latest weaponry but to fill stomachs and fuel development.[1]

A little more than a decade later, Church ruefully admitted that all of this—the grand aspirations to cultivate democracy, promote prosperity, and align the United States with the yearnings of people struggling against oppression—had come to nothing. "Ten years ago," Church declared in a Senate speech on October 29, 1971, "the leaders of the United States—and to a lesser degree the American people—were filled with zeal about their global goals." With "supreme confidence both in our power and capacity to make wise and effective use of it," he added, Americans had proclaimed the dawning of a new era for the "impoverished masses of mankind." Nonetheless, Church lamented, "we have not only failed to accomplish what we set out to accomplish ten years ago; we have been thrown for losses across the board." The United States had watched as "free governments gave way to military dictatorships in country after country." Worse, Church added, ten years of voluminous economic aid had failed to raise up impoverished nations, while disparities of wealth between rich elites and the masses in many nations had widened. Calling American aid programs a "proven failure," Church urged that they be ended. The larger lesson he drew from this dismal record could hardly have contrasted more starkly with his optimism just a few years earlier. "Even with enormous power and the best of intentions," he asserted, "there are some things we cannot do, things which are beyond our moral and intellectual resources."[2]

Church's two speeches neatly capture the trajectory of U.S. policymaking toward the Third World during the 1960s. In the first part of the decade, many Americans—not least their dynamic young president—joined Church in viewing the transformation of Asia, Africa, the Middle East, and Latin America as their nation's biggest foreign policy challenge and embraced the tasks of promoting political and economic change. "To those peoples in the huts and villages of half the globe struggling to break the bonds of mass misery," Kennedy declared in his grandiloquent inaugural address, "we pledge our best efforts to help them help themselves, for whatever period is required."[3] Committed to the quintessentially liberal idea that the nation's power must be mobilized to solve problems at home and abroad, Kennedy aimed to pump resources into the Third World and promote political and economic change in areas that had seldom ranked very high in American priorities.

Within a few years, however, much of this energy and ambition had drained away. Enthusiasm for foreign aid dwindled, as did efforts to spread democracy. The election of 1968 signaled the collapse of the earlier vision, bringing to office a new president, Richard Nixon, who showed little interest in the transformation of poor nations. "For years, we in the United States have pursued the illusion that we alone could re-make continents," Nixon declared in a speech on Halloween 1969. "We have sometimes imagined that we knew what was best for everyone else and that we could and should make it happen. Well, experience has taught us better."[4] Speaking privately with an aide, Nixon made clear where he wished to focus his efforts. "The only thing that matters in the world," said the president, "is Japan, China, Russia, and Europe."[5] Nixon's top foreign policy lieutenant, Henry Kissinger, felt the same way. "The Third World has not proved to be a decisive arena of great power conflict," Kissinger wrote in 1969.[6] Under what the media took to calling the Nixon Doctrine, Washington aimed merely to promote pro-American stability in the Third World, even if it meant bolstering unjust political and economic arrangements.

Why did American leaders reverse their approach to the Third World in such a short span of time? Answering this question promises to contribute new insight into U.S. history during one of the nation's most tumultuous and consequential eras. Historians have long written of the sixties as a time when large numbers of Americans, inspired by a surging sense of moral purpose and technical know-how, worked to address their society's abundant imperfections, including poverty, racism, materialism, and ignorance. Equally, the sixties stand out for the disappointments and divisiveness that engulfed much of this high-minded agenda in the latter half of the decade. Far less appreciated is how the trajectory of efforts to address problems within U.S. borders ran parallel to foreign policy. Exploring the history of decision making toward the Third World during the 1960s highlights continuities between America's domestic and international experiences and contributes to a more complete understanding of the process by which American liberalism fractured and gave way to a new political era that took shape in the 1970s. The United States still commanded monumental power, but the 1960s clarified the limits on Americans' ability to transform their own society or the wider world.

Appreciating the shift in U.S. foreign policy during the 1960s also helps to explain the broad contours of global history in the years since 1945. The Second World War accelerated the disintegration of colonial empires and energized nonwhite peoples of the world by weakening the imperial metropoles and stirring appeals to the principles of self-determination, human rights, and unfettered economic exchange. Old hierarchies persisted in some areas, but starting in the late 1950s the independent nations of Asia, the Middle East, and Latin America asserted themselves as never before, while numerous colonial territories, especially in Africa, claimed their independence. This epoch-defining process—a watershed arguably more profound than either the start or the end of the Cold War—redrew the map of the world and confronted the great powers with a host of new challenges. The reaction of the United States, by far the world's most powerful nation, to this revolution in global affairs was bound to shape both the way in which the process played out and the nature of the new international order that emerged.

In the early 1960s, American leaders such as Kennedy and Church responded to ferment in the Third World with determination, at least rhetorically, to reorient U.S. foreign policy toward winning the loyalty of emerging nations and integrating them into the American-led order that prevailed outside the communist bloc. Their inability to achieve those goals marked a singular failure of U.S. policy, with implications for international relations long after the Cold War ended. Rather than aligning the United States with bold sociopolitical change, Washington increasingly sought to bolster existing sources of stability, whether colonial regimes or postcolonial governments that promised to prioritize partnership with the West above other objectives. Following this course, the United States often tied itself to repressive political forces and alienated itself from governments that refused to toe the U.S. line.

American leaders lost opportunities to establish a world order more amenable to U.S. leadership over the long term—and perhaps more just and peaceful—than the one that came into being after the rush to independence and self-assertion that peaked in the 1960s. To be sure, this shift in American policy was hardly unreasonable or driven by malevolent designs. The turn away from dynamic engagement with the Third World made eminent sense amid the turmoil of those years and the staggering demands on U.S. resources from nations that often defied U.S. policy preferences. Still, with the benefit of hindsight, American decisions stand out for engendering doubts, both abroad and at home, about the morality of U.S. foreign policy and Washington's claims to global leadership. Making sense of those doubts may help us appreciate the global position of the United States, so often vexed by tensions with poor nations of the Global South, in the later twentieth and even twenty-first centuries.

Given the pivotal importance of the Third World's transformation during the 1960s and the American response to it, the contours of U.S. decision making have attracted surprisingly sparse analysis over the years. One reason is the paucity of U.S. documents until the 1990s and early twenty-first century, when the bulk of American records from the later 1960s became available to researchers. A second reason is a notable aversion among historians, including those studying international affairs, to examine global trends and generalize about U.S. foreign policy. Such caution emerges at least in part from laudable concern that geographical breadth might come at the expense of appreciating distinctions between foreign societies and exaggerating the centrality of the United States. Accordingly, historians have usually focused on bilateral interactions between the United States and individual nations—a tendency that has yielded valuable insights and deeply researched studies on particular relationships but less analysis of global trends.[7]

Another reason for the lack of attention to American policymaking toward the Third World is the overwhelming amount of attention that one small part of it—Vietnam—has attracted. By one reckoning, the Vietnam War has been the subject of more than thirty thousand nonfiction books.[8] This outpouring is surely justified by the war's momentous significance to the social, political, and cultural history of the United States, not to mention the larger international history of the twentieth century. But controversies about the war have distracted attention from other aspects of U.S. foreign policy that also had a great—perhaps greater—impact on the global position of the United States over the long run.[9] The trajectories of Brazil, India, and other major countries of the Third World turned out to be at least as significant to American policymaking as the expansion of communism in Indochina. Even if the Vietnam War was the central geopolitical event of the 1960s, though, widening the geographical lens to examine what else was happening throughout the world reveals how the U.S. preoccupation with Vietnam affected Washington's relationships with other nations of Asia, Africa, the Middle East, and Latin America—one of the few consequences of the war to remain largely unexamined.[10]

*The End of Ambition* takes up the challenge of examining U.S. policymaking toward the Third World in the 1960s, arguing that the Vietnam War played a crucial role in leading U.S. leaders to abandon their liberal preoccupations in favor of a more cautious approach aimed at ensuring stability. The war had this effect partly because it demanded so much of America's military and economic resources, making politicians and policymakers wary of assuming additional burdens and anxious to minimize risks in other areas of the world. As the war in Vietnam dragged on, mounting frustration sapped much of the confidence about development and democratization that informed American policymaking at the start of the decade. The war also undermined the liberal agenda by fueling sharp criticism of the United States in many parts of the Third World, making it difficult for sympathetic officials in Washington to defend generous policies toward areas that increasingly seemed to defy American desires. All of these trends grew more evident as the Johnson presidency advanced and came to a head in the Nixon years, when U.S. leaders explicitly turned away from the policies embraced a few years earlier.

Unquestionably, memoirists and scholars have contended over the years that the war left little time for other international challenges. LBJ's deputy secretary of state, George Ball, made the point deftly in his memoir, noting that U.S. leaders' obsession with Vietnam "progressively constricted their vision" everywhere else. "The metaphor I thought most apt," added Ball, "was that of a camera, focused sharply on a small object in the immediate foreground but with no depth of field, so that all other objects were fuzzy and obscure."[11] Scholars have tended to make the point more bluntly. Because of the Vietnam imbroglio, American policymaking toward other regions "ground to a virtual halt" by 1968, claims historian Thomas J. Noer.[12] Historian H. W. Brands agrees, asserting that by the end of his presidency LBJ had "given up on most of the world," while Stephen Graubard goes so far as to say that "after 1965, there was no United States foreign policy; there was only a Vietnam policy."[13] This book is the first to examine such claims by exploring in detail how the preoccupation in Southeast Asia affected other American relationships in the Third World.

It is too simple, though, to argue that the war by itself caused the transformation that this study explains. At least three other developments would have driven significant change in U.S. policy even if no American troops had set foot in Southeast Asia. These developments—changes in American leadership, the rapidly shifting political landscape within the United States, and accelerating polarization in the Third World—were already visible by 1965, when Johnson dramatically escalated U.S. involvement in Vietnam, and their course after that fateful year was not shaped solely by the war. Rather, the conflict in Vietnam acted as a powerful accelerant, energizing the other trends leading the United States to reappraise its foreign policies and ensuring that the total effect of those changes came to more than the sum of their individual potentials. The effect of the war on the liberal underpinnings of U.S. foreign policy thus ran in parallel to its impact on domestic affairs, where controversy over Vietnam intensified social and political upheaval that steadily eroded policy initiatives that had been embraced by a broad swath of Americans at the start of the sixties.

The first trend catalyzed by the war was the declining influence of U.S. policymakers sensitive to sociopolitical change in the Third World and the rise of others with far less interest in the issue. Understanding this pattern depends on appreciating the outlooks and decision-making styles of leaders at the pinnacle of the U.S. bureaucracy. This book offers fresh appraisals of the three presidents who, along with their senior aides, compose its core dramatis personae. It argues that John F. Kennedy genuinely sought to grasp the political and economic transformation playing out in much of the Third World and sincerely aspired to recast U.S. policy to swim with what he regarded as the inevitable tide of history. But Kennedy, like the advisers who surrounded him, never settled on a coherent approach and left behind an inconsistent and even confusing record. For his part, LBJ lacked both Kennedy's interest in the Third World and his patience for debate about American policy. Although a committed reformer in the domestic arena, LBJ had no such impulse in the international domain. He abandoned much of JFK's agenda and, particularly as the Vietnam War became a major preoccupation, sought to ensure stability in the Third World in order to minimize distractions from his higher priorities. In this way, Johnson anticipated, more than scholars have acknowledged, the approach embraced by Nixon and Kissinger after they moved into the White House in January 1969. Indeed, this book argues that the Nixon administration did not so much conceive innovative policy departures, as both admirers and detractors have long credited it with doing, as articulate ideas that had been embraced during the Johnson years.[14]

This book thus highlights the predilections of individual presidents, underscoring how personal experiences and idiosyncrasies drove policy choices. The differences among the men in the Oval Office mattered a great deal. The book also, however, assigns importance to the outlooks of the subordinates who often decisively shaped policy. More specifically, it views U.S. decision making as the product of debate among competing factions of policymakers. Although U.S. officials during the Kennedy and Johnson years broadly accepted that the Third World presented momentous challenges, they differed markedly in their sense of how the United States should respond. Conflict was particularly acute during the JFK years but, as the latter chapters of this book show, persisted into the Johnson period. To be sure, this study demonstrates that presidents set the parameters within which conflict occurred. The predispositions at the top of the decision-making hierarchy constrained the jockeying at lower levels by empowering some factions and weakening others. Yet second- and third-tier bureaucrats often exerted significant authority, not least because presidents only intermittently paid attention to the details of policy toward Third World nations.[15] There was thus ample opportunity for lower-level officials to control day-to-day policy implementation.

The second trend that drove U.S. policymaking toward the Third World was the transformation of American domestic politics during the 1960s. During the first half of the decade, Americans backed liberal reform projects as never before, targeting racial segregation, poverty, and other problems whose solutions seemed within reach for a nation endowed with limitless purpose, prosperity, and knowledge. Yet the 1960s also yielded a powerful surge of conservatism as the pervasive optimism of the early years gave way to disappointment and division. By 1965 or so, large numbers of Americans were growing weary of liberal reformism and coming to fear that rapid social change threatened their livelihoods and social mores, trends that only intensified under the pressure of political controversies stirred up by the U.S. escalation in Vietnam.[16] This book argues that this transformation—as dramatic as any that played out in so short a period of time in all of American history—had profound consequences. As urban unrest, antiwar protest, and backlash against the perceived excesses of the Great Society fueled hostility to the Johnson administration, policymakers became increasingly wary of costly policies that seemed to invite even greater criticism of the administration if they were not scaled down. Fully cognizant of the shifting political tide, LBJ abandoned what enthusiasm he still had for efforts to revamp U.S. policy toward the Third World, diverted funds from aid programs that had been hallmarks of Kennedy's New Frontier, and grew notably tolerant of authoritarians who promised to serve U.S. interests. Richard Nixon, free of any attachment to the ambitious goals laid down by JFK or the Democratic Party more generally, completed the reorientation of policy after taking office, especially by explicitly avowing policies that had already been adopted in practice.

The third trend that contributed to the transformation of U.S. policy in the Third World was the marked decline of sympathy for the United States across much of the globe during the 1960s. Mounting hostility to U.S. involvement in Vietnam was one major cause of this tendency. Across the Third World, many nationalist leaders castigated the United States for wreaking destruction on an impoverished society and backing an unsavory autocracy in Saigon. Washington was guilty of "all types of crimes including genocide" in Vietnam, asserted one declaration of Third World leaders in January 1966.[17] Even among Third World nations that remained aligned with the United States, leaders such as the shah of Iran and the fiercely anticommunist military officers who wielded power in Brazil sometimes sniped at U.S. decision making and permitted criticism of Washington as a way of demonstrating their independence from the United States.

But other factors, some of them visible before Washington became consumed with Southeast Asia, contributed as well to rising anti-Americanism. Most importantly, the accelerating Sino-Soviet competition for leadership among the revolutionary movements in Asia, Africa, the Middle East, and Latin America drove both communist powers to emphasize their radical commitments and to step up support for anti-Western forces in various places. The benefits of hindsight reveal the limits of Soviet and Chinese capabilities to expand their influence around the world. Above all, the start of China's Cultural Revolution in 1966 significantly blunted Beijing's ability to project power beyond its borders. But the communist powers' revolutionary rhetoric, along with the rise of Third World governments inspired by their support and examples, fueled anti-Western militancy in many places.[18]

Meanwhile, the non-aligned impulse that had once inspired some Third World leaders to seek a genuine third way outside the Cold War blocs lost traction. Polarization flowed partly from a series of coups that jolted several countries sharply to the right during the 1960s. Various forces, meanwhile, led other nations in more radical directions, tilting Third World forums against the United States and encouraging cooperation among anti-Western forces in societies as varied as North Vietnam, Cuba, and Angola. The death or downfall of charismatic Afro-Asian leaders such as India's Jawaharlal Nehru and Ghana's Kwame Nkrumah, towering figures who led their nations to independence and championed the non-aligned ideal, opened the way to more confrontational alternatives. So too did frustration with the slow rate of economic progress within newly independent nations and festering geopolitical tensions among them. Conflict between India and Pakistan, Iran and Egypt, and Indonesia and Malaysia shattered the notion of a united Third World operating independently of the great powers. By the mid-1960s, U.S. leaders saw few indications of the political moderation that they had sought to encourage through patient cooperation. The Johnson administration distanced itself from governments hostile to the United States and warmed up to friendly regimes that promised partnership in an increasingly hostile world. The distinct possibility that some Third World nations might soon acquire nuclear weapons only heightened U.S. determination to find more reliable ways to exert control.

Developments within the Third World thus did much to shape Washington's agenda. A global history of international affairs during the 1960s unquestionably requires deep analysis of Third World governments, political movements, and international organizations. This book, however, focuses on the deliberations and behavior of U.S. presidents, cabinet secretaries, members of Congress, military officers, diplomats, and national security bureaucrats—the American leaders who struggled to craft U.S. responses to an unusually momentous set of challenges. These officials frequently voiced frustration about the ways in which foreigners limited their options and confronted them with vexing dilemmas or faits accomplis. But their choices emerged first and foremost from the shifting political, bureaucratic, and intellectual contexts within which they made policy.[19] Accordingly, the chapters that follow draw largely on U.S. source material—reports, memoranda, telegrams, letters, opinion polls, and others kinds of documents from numerous repositories around the United States—supplemented by material from foreign archives.

To tell the story of U.S. policymaking toward vast swaths of the globe across a decade exceeds the limits of a single volume. To cope with this limitation, this book follows a distinct strategy designed to strike a productive balance between breadth of coverage—both geographical and chronological—and depth of analysis. It begins with a broad-brush treatment of the Kennedy years and concludes with a brief overview of policy departures undertaken early in the Nixon presidency. The aim in these sections is to identify general patterns of behavior and lay out the interpretive arc of the book. In between, the book follows a different approach, offering five case studies chosen to highlight decision making during the Johnson presidency, a crucial period of transition. These chapters permit close examination of U.S. policymaking with respect to places that posed especially serious challenges. The areas in question—Brazil, India, Iran, Indonesia, and the British territory of Southern Rhodesia—were selected for their sheer importance to international affairs in the 1960s and their representativeness of broad challenges that the United States confronted in the 1960s and beyond.[20] All of them captured headlines and commanded the attention of U.S. leaders for much or all of the decade, largely because they seemed to be key battlegrounds of the Cold War and to play crucial roles not only in their regions but in the Third World more generally.

A risk of this approach lies in exaggerating the extent to which such diverse countries represented global trends or embodied core aspects of the nebulous entity that this book calls the Third World. The existence of such a "third" grouping of nations is, admittedly, problematic at best.[21] For one thing, "Third World" implies that its component territories held only tertiary significance. That implication is misleading not only because these areas were foremost to the hundreds of millions of people who lived there but also because, at least for a time during the 1960s and 1970s, they arguably became the primary arenas of conflict in the Cold War rivalry involving the mightiest industrial powers. But the notion of a Third World is even more questionable because of the extraordinary diversity of the nations that composed it. Politically, countries generally categorized as parts of the Third World ran the gamut from U.S. allies such as Iran and the Philippines to communist nations including North Vietnam and Cuba and perhaps China, which sought to keep a foot in both the communist and Third World camps for much of the Cold War. Economically, the diversity is at least as pronounced. In the middle decades of the twentieth century, South American nations conventionally assigned to Third World status had, in some cases, per capita incomes on par with Western nations such as Greece, Finland, and Italy and considerably higher than those of many Eastern European nations belonging to the "second" world.[22]

Yet "Third World," for all its shortcomings, holds value for thinking about the international history of the Cold War. In the first place, American leaders had little doubt that such an entity existed, even if terms like the "underdeveloped" and "less developed" world sprang more readily to their lips during the sixties. U.S. officials were well aware of the political, economic, cultural, historical, and other kinds of distinctions among the relatively poor, mostly nonwhite nations. On the whole, though, most of them had little trouble buying into the idea, objectionable as it may seem in retrospect, that this mélange of nations shared much in common and that the United States confronted a distinct set of political and economic problems in dealing with them. Historian Jason C. Parker argues compellingly, in fact, that U.S. public diplomacy—official rhetoric, propaganda, broadcasting, and the like—did much to create the concept of the Third World by projecting a vision of unity and shared interests onto diverse societies.[23] But if Americans envisioned a Third World in their public rhetoric, U.S. policymakers at the highest levels of government also embraced the concept behind walls of secrecy. The documentary record is rife with examples of American officials making sweeping generalizations or drawing lessons from one part of the Third World and applying them to another. Just as important, leaders of Asian, African, Middle Eastern, and Latin American countries embraced the idea that, for all their differences, they were bound together by certain experiences and interests, even by a shared "consciousness," distinct from other segments of the globe. By the late 1960s, these leaders, like outsiders shaping and observing their behavior, were increasingly comfortable with the concept of a Third World, even if the precise meaning varied from usage to usage. Indeed, the permeability of the category and the ability of different leaders to invoke what historian Vijay Prashad calls the Third World "project" for divergent purposes at different times do much to explain how the term became so pervasive and durable.[24]

One reason U.S. and foreign leaders alike promoted the term is one of the same reasons the term is especially useful in this book to describe the collection of nations about which it generalizes. Whereas "underdeveloped" and "less developed" suggest economic criteria for belonging, "Third World" indicates the primacy of nations' political status vis-à-vis the democratic West and the communist East. For American leaders of the 1960s, it was this political stance outside the Cold War blocs—or potentially outside of them in the case of volatile Latin American or Middle Eastern nations formally aligned with the United States—more than any other characteristic that defined the problem and fueled the urgency of dealing effectively with them. Additionally, Third World is a more useful category than "non-aligned" world (or movement) since American officials saw no sharp distinction between nations that explicitly kept clear of the Cold War blocs and others that were affiliated with one side or the other but were generally presumed to have only weak and changeable commitments. To be sure, American leaders were attentive to the particular challenges posed by the principle of non-alignment starting in the mid-1950s and then by the Non-Aligned Movement after its formal establishment in 1961. For the most part, however, they saw far fewer meaningful distinctions between the aligned and non-aligned nations of Asia, Africa, the Middle East, and Latin America than they did between that broad collection of nations, on the one hand, and the industrialized areas that had definitively chosen sides in the Cold War, on the other. Americans, to put it differently, thought about Indonesia and Brazil in fundamentally similar ways even though one was a strong adherent to non-alignment and the other was formally aligned to the United States.

Accordingly, this study accepts a basic geographical conception neatly articulated by economic historian William Easterly in describing, though surely not applauding, the worldview of U.S. policymakers during the Cold War. "The First World was the United States and its rich, democratic allies," Easterly writes. "The Second World was the Soviet Union and its eastern European satellites. The Third World was simply defined as what was left over, the areas of the world where the United States desperately wanted to deny the Soviets additional allies."[25] This category clearly included even strongly Western-leaning nations in Asia and Latin America, which Americans believed to be vulnerable to revolutionary subversion and political reorientation if the United States did not play its cards right. Historians of the Third World movement undoubtedly have reason to focus on non-alignment per se as an important strand of the larger phenomenon, but historians of U.S. foreign relations do so at their peril. What counted for American officials was their sense of a nation's vulnerability to the temptations of anti-Western radicalism or procommunist sympathies rather than their membership in a vaguely defined and changeable international grouping.

Given the array of countries meeting this capacious definition of the Third World, another major challenge of the case study approach employed in this book lies in choosing among the bilateral relationships that were both important to Washington and representative of broad patterns of U.S. behavior. One relatively easy decision was to omit U.S. policymaking toward Cuba, North Vietnam, and China, countries that seemed irrevocably committed to the communist side even if they hardly marched in lockstep with Moscow. In addition to being heavily researched by other scholars, these nations do not lend themselves to exploring how American leaders interacted with nations whose political and economic destinies seemed up for grabs.[26] Another decision was to draw case studies from an array of regions that stirred concern in Washington. Accordingly, the book's central chapters span the arc of territories girdling the Sino-Soviet landmass—undoubtedly the focal point of American concern about communist expansion—as well as sub-Saharan Africa and Latin America. A final important decision was to choose cases that highlight the various paths that American foreign policy followed in the Third World. In two cases, those of Brazil and Indonesia, Washington backed coups that brought to power right-wing regimes promising to reinforce pro-Western stability in turbulent regions. In Iran, the United States reconfigured and tightened its commitment to an existing regime generally aligned with the West. In India and sub-Saharan Africa, meanwhile, the United States distanced itself from a government (India) and a cause (vigorous opposition to the illegal white regime in Rhodesia) that seemed likely to draw the United States into draining commitments at a time when U.S. leaders aimed to cut costs and lower risks.

Taken together, these shifts conform to a cyclical pattern that runs through the twentieth century if not the entire history of U.S. relations with the outside world. At times, the United States acted boldly on its universalizing impulse to remake the international order. In due course, however, Americans rediscovered the limits of their power and reverted to a hardheaded determination to defend narrow U.S. interests in an inhospitable world. The 1900s, 1920s, and 2010s—moments when Americans backed away from the ambitions that had once seized their imaginations—offer striking parallels to the late 1960s. In all of these cases, American leaders, making decisions in the shadow of draining wars in faraway lands, lost confidence in expansive schemes to impose U.S. political and economic models on the wider world. Yet the 1960s were an especially consequential phase of this interplay of competing impulses. The disintegration of the European colonial empires and the assertiveness of Third World nations generated an exceptionally fluid moment in world history. The 1960s, even more than the "Wilsonian moment" following the First World War, yielded nothing less than a rupture in the basic composition of international society and global consciousness about who was entitled to a voice in geopolitics. The U.S. response to such a moment was sure to have profound implications not only for the pace and extent of change but also for the ways in which foreign societies viewed the United States and Americans understood themselves.

By the early 1970s, the United States indisputably remained a globe-straddling superpower with enormous political, economic, and military influence. But the experiences of the previous decade had shattered the confidence and ambition to refashion the global order that had grown since the Second World War and peaked in the early 1960s. In different ways, the stories in this book reveal Washington trying and mostly failing in the Kennedy years to promote constructive change through the power of its example and know-how. Fully confronting the limits of its capabilities for the first time since 1945, American leaders thereafter resorted to different methods of exerting control over a world rife with troubles. Those new methods sometimes succeeded in shoring up American influence while reducing costs, as architects of the changing policies intended. Yet Washington's altered approach to the Third

World was hardly a clear-cut success. The new regimes cultivated by U.S. leaders often made heavy new demands of Washington even while asserting their independence of American leadership. Over the longer term, some of those regimes brought discredit to the United States and ultimately collapsed. The policy innovations of the 1960s yielded not the stability and security that U.S. officials hoped for but a world of uncertainty and a host of new dilemmas that would beset the United States in the 1970s and beyond.

# 1

# The Liberal Inheritance



WHAT SORT OF PRESIDENT would Lyndon Johnson be? The question reverberated throughout the United States—indeed throughout the world—in the hours following the assassination of John F. Kennedy on November 22, 1963. The *New York Times* editorial page saw reason for optimism about the new commander in chief but conceded, "No one can really know his qualities as a leader until he has had a chance to demonstrate them in an assignment more difficult than any other on earth."[1] The Associated Press captured another reason for uncertainty: the sheer complexity of the enigmatic Texan. "He has been called self-centered and considerate; a humanitarian and power-hungry; a shrewd opportunist and a political genius; tough and yet vulnerable; vain, friendly, sensitive, flamboyant," the AP observed.[2] Who knew which qualities would shine through when he occupied the Oval Office? The British ambassador, Sir David Ormsby Gore, fretted that nothing would become clear until after the 1964 election, when American voters would give shape to an uncertain political environment. "The internal political situation," he advised the government in London two days after the assassination, "has been thrown into the melting pot."[3]

Eager to allay pervasive anxieties, LBJ projected purpose and confidence, above all by staking himself to the record of his predecessor. In his speech to a joint session of Congress on November 27, essentially Johnson's presidential debut before the nation, he hammered away at the theme of continuity. Unquestionably, the gray, bespectacled southerner, who appeared older than his fifty-five years, offered a stark contrast to the youthful, urbane Kennedy. LBJ's colorless delivery featured little of the soaring eloquence that Americans had come to expect of JFK. In its substance, though, the speech left no doubt that Kennedy's priorities lived on. The nation's challenge at an agonizing time of transition, asserted LBJ, was "not to hesitate, not to pause, not to turn about and linger over this evil moment, but to continue on our course so that we may fulfill the destiny that history has set for us." In his celebrated inauguration speech back in January 1961, Kennedy had laid out an ambitious program of domestic and international reform, urging, "Let us begin." Now LBJ echoed those words, declaring, "Let us continue." Indeed, Johnson used the verb "continue" five times in his address and highlighted his dedication to JFK's agenda in virtually every paragraph.[4]

Johnson's reassuring message served its purpose. Around the world, the *Washington Post* reported, LBJ's words went a long way toward easing concern that the transition to a new leader would bring "uncertainty and confusion."[5] But LBJ's words were, in various senses, misleading. In the arena of domestic policy, Johnson undoubtedly embraced Kennedy's priorities but was eager to go far beyond anything JFK had contemplated in connection with civil rights, education, poverty, and an array of other issues. Six months later, Johnson's appeal for nothing less than a "great society" rooted in bold government-led reform would make clear just how much LBJ's aspirations exceeded those of his predecessor. In the arena of foreign affairs, Johnson's assurances of continuity were problematic in a different way. Kennedy bequeathed no clear-cut agenda, and Johnson himself had few strong predilections. To be sure, Johnson spoke of his dedication to existing U.S. commitments abroad, maintenance of a military "second to none," continued cooperation with the United Nations, and support for ongoing economic assistance programs. But such bland promises, affirming the broadest contours of U.S. foreign policy, revealed little about how LBJ understood his predecessor's approach or how he would cope with complex international problems.

With the benefit of hindsight, it is easy to see continuity between Kennedy and Johnson in connection with Washington's most dangerous foreign policy challenge: managing the nuclear-tinged rivalry with the Soviet Union. Following the Cuban Missile Crisis of October 1962, perhaps the most perilous moment of the entire Cold War, JFK had reoriented U.S. policy toward Moscow and worked to reduce the likelihood of nuclear war. In partnership with similarly chastened Soviet leaders, the Kennedy administration had lowered the temperature of superpower tensions—the start of what some historians have dubbed the "little détente"[6]—and achieved tangible successes, above all the Limited Test Ban Treaty of 1963, the first important arms control agreement of the Cold War. Johnson endorsed this bid for improved U.S.-Soviet relations, not least so that he could focus on his domestic ambitions. Under Johnson's guidance, the United States played a leading role in negotiating the Treaty on the Non-Proliferation of Nuclear Weapons and laid the groundwork for talks aimed at limiting the superpowers' stockpiles of ballistic missiles, efforts that would culminate in treaties signed during the Nixon presidency.

In other domains of foreign policy, however, it is difficult to assess the extent to which Johnson sought or achieved continuity in any meaningful sense. One major reason is that Kennedy, despite a propensity for bold rhetoric, often failed to establish clear policies that his successor could reasonably hope to perpetuate. With regard to Western Europe, Kennedy proposed an ambitious "Grand Design" to establish a more productive partnership with America's most important allies and trade partners. As historian Thomas Schwartz demonstrates, however, Kennedy's achievements fell far short of his ambitions, leaving an ambiguous inheritance for Johnson.[7] Much the same can be said about U.S. policymaking toward the Third World. Kennedy and his team spoke boldly of their determination to remake the U.S. relationship with the emerging nations of Asia, Africa, the Middle East, and Latin America by throwing American support and resources behind their aspirations for development and a greater voice in global affairs. Yet, as this chapter demonstrates, the Kennedy administration conceived no consistent or coherent approach to the Third World generally or to specific challenges that arose on its watch. When LBJ gained the presidency, he inherited a muddled set of policies that offered no blueprint for the future.

Appreciating this murkiness is the starting point for understanding Lyndon Johnson's approach to the Third World during his sixty-two months in office. To be sure, the attitudes that LBJ and his aides brought with them to the Oval Office—the subject of chapter 3—are important as well. But looking backward to the peak years of liberal ambitions in the Third World helps reveal the ways in which decision making during the Johnson years was shaped by what came just before. This chapter exposes the indeterminacy of U.S. policymaking by examining the broad lines of intellectual and bureaucratic debate that swirled within the Kennedy presidency with respect to a set of issues that took center stage during the early 1960s.

## "The Most Powerful Single Force in the World Today"

As he campaigned for the presidency in 1960, John F. Kennedy dwelled on the shortcomings of U.S. foreign policy. Above all, he declared in speech after speech that the United States had failed under Republican leadership to cope with the profound transformation sweeping across much of Asia, Africa, the Middle East, and Latin America. Unsophisticated, unimaginative men—not least Vice President Richard Nixon, now the Republican presidential nominee—had done little to shore up American power, leaving these vast areas "on the razor's edge of decision" between East and West, vulnerable to neutralism or, much worse, absorption into the communist bloc.[8] "Never before have we experienced a more critical decline in our prestige, driving our friends to neutralism and neutrals to hostility," the Massachusetts senator scolded in one campaign appearance, pointing to dangerous leftward swings in Cuba, Laos, and the Congo. "Never before has the grip of communism sunk so deeply into previously friendly countries."[9] Under Eisenhower, Kennedy insisted in his speech accepting the Democratic nomination, "Communist influence has penetrated further into Asia, stood astride the Middle East and now festers some ninety miles off the coast of Florida." What was needed, he declared, was youthful and energetic leadership capable of appreciating the aspirations of young and vigorous peoples clamoring for a place in the sun. "More energy is released by this awakening of these new nations than by the fission of the atom itself," added Kennedy in a statement that suggested both the scale of the problem and the stakes of failing to solve it.[10]

Unquestionably, such words were chosen partly for their political effect. Numerous studies undertaken by the Democratic Party before the 1960 vote found that the Republicans held an edge in perceptions of their determination to stand up to Moscow but that Kennedy stood to gain by projecting youthful dynamism in confronting new kinds of problems and reassuring voters about declining American influence around the world. A typical assessment of Kennedy's appeal in 1958 pointed out that voters tended to see the young senator as a "forward-looking and vital new force" who offered "new and progressive approaches."[11] After Kennedy won the nomination in 1960, his political advisers stressed the need to stick with that theme, which seemed to register with Americans unsettled by the Cuban revolution and other setbacks around the world. A study of the political situation in New York, for example, urged "constant reiteration" of Kennedy's "promise of rebuilding our position in the world, of moving ahead."[12]

Yet Kennedy's words did not reflect only political calculation. Despite a lackluster performance in Congress, JFK had demonstrated unusual interest in the dynamics of social and political change in the Third World and made a name for himself through his strong views on the subject long before 1960. Kennedy's interest may have flowed from his Irish American heritage, which generated sensitivity to the effects of colonialism, or a sense of noblesse oblige inculcated by his father. But a tour of the Middle East and South Asia in 1951 seems to have cemented his conviction that rising nationalism would play a major role in global affairs in the years to come. Following that trip, Representative Kennedy spoke of nationalism "sweeping with forest-fire fury" across the Middle East and Asia and, with nuanced appreciation of the underlying social dynamics rare in the heyday of the Red Scare, listed an array of problems that spelled trouble for the United States: "exploitation by foreign countries of the resources and manpower of backward nations"; widespread "illiteracy, misery, and starvation"; domination of local administrations by "venal and corrupt politicians"; "massive and inefficient" bureaucracies unresponsive to their people's needs; and "a new and self-conscious proletariat" arising in many places. It was time for Americans to

"You Think You Can Get My Bandwagon Going Again?"
J.F.K.
U.S.A.
HERBLOCK
©1960 THE WASHINGTON POST CO.

FIGURE 1.1. During the 1960 presidential race, Democratic candidate John F. Kennedy capitalized on a widespread perception that U.S. foreign policy had lost its vitality under Republican leadership. Herbert Block captured the mood in this cartoon published in the *Washington Post* on July 15, 1960. A 1960 Herblock Cartoon, © The Herb Block Foundation.

abandon a "weak and vacillating approach" that had too often prioritized stability over change, he asserted in a speech to Massachusetts constituents. "We have been anti-communist," he declared. "We have been 'Pro' nothing. That puts us in partnership with the corrupt and reactionary groups whose policies breed the discontent on which Soviet Communism feeds and prospers."[13] It was insufficient, he believed, to defend American interests merely by manipulating the highest echelons of power in Third World territories; enduring stability could be achieved only by promoting economic and political progress that served the ordinary people who lived there.[14]

Kennedy returned to these themes in a widely noted 1957 speech on the Senate floor criticizing Eisenhower for passivity in the face of French repression in North Africa and demanding that Washington back Algerian independence. "The most powerful single force in the world today," he declared, was not communism or capitalism or even nuclear weapons. Rather, it was "man's eternal desire to be free and independent." The biggest enemy of that desire, Kennedy continued, was "imperialism"—both the Soviet and Western varieties. He hastened to add that the two must not be "equated," an essential proviso to keep his comments within the parameters of acceptable debate. But he nevertheless distanced himself from the sitting administration's emphasis on slow, deliberate change carefully managed by the colonial powers. "The single most important test of American foreign policy today," he asserted, lay in responding to these imperialisms and determining "what we do to further men's desire to be free." The uncommitted nations of the Third World were watching, as were peoples trapped behind the Iron Curtain. Alas, he concluded, the United States, committed to Eisenhower's "head in the sand policy," was "failing to meet the challenges of imperialism—on both counts—and thus failing our responsibilities to the free world."[15]

In his inauguration speech three and a half years later, Kennedy hit many of the same notes in unprecedentedly grandiose language. First, he made clear that his administration would tolerate non-alignment. Addressing "new states whom we welcome to the ranks of the free," the president vowed that the United States would not always "expect to find them supporting our view," though he expected them to defend their freedom from the communists. He also declared that the United States would be guided by moral purpose in putting its resources to work for poor nations. In the breathtaking boldness and open-endedness of this promise lay Kennedy's sharpest break from the previous administration. "To those people in the huts and villages of half the globe struggling to break the bonds of mass misery," he avowed, "we pledge our best efforts to help them help themselves, for whatever period of time is required—not because the communists may be doing it, not because we seek their votes, but because it is right." The challenge amounted to nothing less than a test of the new generation's abilities to secure the nation's claim to global leadership in a new age. "If a free society cannot help the many who are poor," Kennedy said, "it cannot save the few who are rich."[16]

## Contradictions

Many Americans responded enthusiastically to Kennedy's call to energize America's role in the Third World.[17] What precisely his grandiose words meant in practice was, however, anything but clear as the Kennedy era began in

January 1961. The president's rhetoric suggested new priorities and a dedication to innovate. Yet JFK neither articulated nor possessed any detailed blueprint for coping with the problems he so often described in colorful and urgent ways. How would the administration convince Congress and the public to dedicate more resources to remote, unfamiliar parts of the world? How would Kennedy and his team balance the interests of Washington's European allies against the demands of nationalists in the Third World? How far could a non-aligned nation stray from U.S. policy preferences before overstretching Washington's tolerance? How high a priority would the United States attach to democratization, particularly in nations where authoritarian regimes promised to promote economic development along paths preferred by Americans and to assure a more fertile field for American trade and investment? Precisely which tools and resources would U.S. leaders draw on to effect positive change? These were among the innumerable dilemmas that lurked just beneath the surface as the new administration confronted the challenge of converting its words into practice.

During their years in office, Kennedy and his advisers showed little consistency in their answers. At times, the administration lived up to its promises of meaningful change. Kennedy showed striking tolerance for non-alignment, cultivated productive relationships with independently minded leaders in numerous Third World nations, and backed expanded U.S. resources for promoting economic and political development around the world. JFK even made quiet efforts—revealed in detail only in the twenty-first century—to wind down costly commitments to defend South Vietnam and overthrow Fidel Castro's regime in Cuba, partly out of conviction that hawkish U.S. policies in those places ignored the reasonable grievances of ordinary Vietnamese and Cubans.[18] At other times, however, Kennedy and his advisers responded in more conventional ways to problems in the Third World. He showed hostility to nationalist leaders in many instances and tolerated, if not actively supported, a variety of unrepresentative regimes that served American interests. Moreover, whatever his misgivings about U.S. policies regarding Vietnam and Cuba, he unquestionably expanded the U.S. commitment in Southeast Asia and persisted for years in his often-macabre attempts to get rid of Castro.

How can such variability be explained? One possibility is that one of these tendencies represented the authentic disposition of the "real" John F. Kennedy. Numerous historians, journalists, and memoirists have pursued this line of thinking over the years, giving rise to a vast body of contentious work claiming, in various ways, to have uncovered the core of JFK's approach to the Third World. Some of these authors describe JFK as a forward-thinking president who sincerely questioned Cold War verities, even if he occasionally conceded to unimaginatively hawkish advisers or public opinion that remained wedded to conventional wisdom.[19] Other authors, meanwhile, view Kennedy as a prototypical cold warrior who understood the political value of bold rhetoric but lacked principled commitment to anything beyond waging the anticommunist struggle more aggressively.[20] For commentators of this sort, Kennedy's reputation as an innovator was largely the fabrication of loyalists who cleverly reshaped perceptions of his presidency following his death to make him seem far more visionary than he really was. A third possibility, suggested by historians looking for a middle ground, is that Kennedy changed over the course of his presidency, transitioning from the flat-footed cold warrior of his early months to a more sophisticated, confident, and innovative policymaker by the end of his life.[21]

But there is at least one other way of explaining JFK's contradictions: the president and his administration had no central guiding principles as they made policy. They were neither innovators nor dyed-in-the-wool cold warriors. They were both—and, at times, various gradations in between. This is not to say that Kennedy and his advisers did not genuinely believe in the importance of the problems they confronted in Asia, Africa, the Middle East, and Latin America or aspire to a coherent set of policies that would achieve the desired reorientation of U.S. policy. Nor is this to suggest that Kennedy lacked a guiding belief, shared with other U.S. presidents, that American activism on the world stage was necessary to shape an international order conducive to a thriving capitalist economy on a global scale. Rather, the administration, like the larger society from which it sprang, encompassed divergent, even contradictory ideas about how to achieve these objectives. These competing outlooks jockeyed for position during the Kennedy years as the United States confronted disparate challenges in different places amid constantly shifting political and international contexts. Appreciating the Kennedy administration as a conglomeration of tendencies, rather than executor of a core set of ideas, provides fresh perspective on high-level U.S. decision making and, more broadly, on the nature of the ambitious liberalism that resonated so powerfully within American society in the early 1960s, a tumultuous period that hardly lent itself to one-size-fits-all solutions. Kennedy and his advisers disagreed constantly about how best to put American power to use and left behind a bewilderingly mixed record that offered little guidance when Lyndon Johnson assumed the presidency.

## "The Center of the Political Cobweb"

The variability of behavior during the Kennedy presidency stemmed in part from the character of the president himself. Despite his frequently bold words—and despite the persistent efforts of historians and biographers to describe a president as holding a clear set of ideas—Kennedy is best understood as a pragmatist who possessed a general sense of objectives but no fixed convictions about methods or timetables. Such flexibility should come as no surprise given Kennedy's formative experiences. Biographers have repeatedly noted that his drive for public office was motivated not by any particular policy agenda but by such pedestrian forces as sibling rivalry and the desire to impress a domineering father. Across his congressional career, moreover, JFK moved among different strands of the Democratic Party, at times emphasizing his fiscal conservatism and wariness of extending the New Deal, at other times avidly backing public housing, federal support of education, and other typically liberal agendas. Even as a presidential candidate, Kennedy was not easily identifiable with any particular constituency within his own party.[22] Detractors were apt to see him as an unprincipled dilettante, whereas supporters tended to view him as a new kind of liberal who believed, in the words of an admiring campaign biography published in 1959, that liberalism "must be rethought and renewed."[23]

But the most perceptive commentary has emphasized that Kennedy, for good or ill, defied categorization. "Kennedy had a dozen faces," wrote author Norman Mailer in the November 1960 edition of *Esquire*. JFK's expression "rarely changes," but his "appearance seems to shift from one person into another as the minutes go by," added Mailer, who likened Kennedy to the actor Marlon Brando.[24] Others saw the same quality. There were "many president Kennedys," observed military aide Maxwell Taylor. Kennedy's secretary of health, education, and welfare made the point differently, allowing that the president possessed a core but was a "very introverted man" who "only exposed different facets of himself to different people."[25]

Kennedy's decision-making style reflected this adaptability. In contrast to many other presidents, Kennedy deliberately surrounded himself with advisers holding divergent views and relished debate. To some extent, this tendency reflected Kennedy's keen awareness of political necessity. As economic adviser Paul Samuelson noted many years later, the president was "an extremely hesitant person who checked the ice in front of him all the time."[26] JFK had good reason to act this way. Having won the White House by the smallest margin in nearly a century, he felt pressure to solidify his standing with as much of the political spectrum as possible and especially the center-right, a tendency that annoyed his liberal supporters. Political calculations were especially evident in Kennedy's appointments. He named Republican C. Douglas Dillon, a former undersecretary of state in the Eisenhower administration, to be secretary of the treasury even as he chose the prominent liberal economist Walter Heller to be chairman of his Council of Economic Advisers. In the domestic policy arena, Kennedy reappointed conservative FBI director J. Edgar Hoover even as he named the ultraliberal law professor Harris Wofford to be his top adviser on civil rights. Foreign policy was no different. Kennedy selected Republicans Robert S. McNamara and McGeorge Bundy to be secretary of defense and national security adviser, respectively, while keeping the Eisenhower-era holdover Allen Dulles as director of the Central Intelligence Agency. But Kennedy surrounded these men with liberals such as economist Walt W. Rostow as deputy national security adviser, former Connecticut governor Chester Bowles as undersecretary of state, former Democratic presidential nominee Adlai Stevenson as U.S. ambassador to the United Nations, and Pulitzer-winning historian Arthur Schlesinger Jr. as presidential adviser.

Kennedy's cultivation of diverse points of view also flowed from sources deeper than partisan calculation. For one thing, his approach carried the unmistakable benefit of ensuring that final decisions would be left to JFK himself—no small thing for a president anxious about the possibilities of small conflicts escalating into general war in the nuclear era. Throughout his presidency, Kennedy exerted strong personal control over the most important foreign policy questions and, when all others had left the room, sometimes consulted only his brother, Robert F. Kennedy, who was equally averse to fixed positions and driven by single-minded dedication to JFK's political success. In many cases, JFK used his control of the policy process not to make bold choices but to defer decisions, thereby dodging pressure from his aides. Kennedy's approach also flowed, though, from a genuine intellectual suppleness and desire to consider a variety of viewpoints on difficult problems. He liked, in David Halberstam's apt phrasing, to "ventilate" issues before coming to a decision by listening to advisers, including younger ones from the middling levels of the bureaucracy, debate before him.[27] "The last thing I want around here is a mutual admiration society," Kennedy exclaimed to his press secretary, Pierre Salinger. "When you people stop arguing, I'll start worrying."[28] Biographer Robert Dallek speculates that Kennedy's devotion to his acerbic aide Kenny O'Donnell owed much to the latter's ability to stir productive argument among senior advisers.[29]

Some aides disliked this approach. Undersecretary of State George Ball complained in a 1965 interview that Kennedy had been "almost too tolerant" of conflicting points of view and too little disposed to consider dilemmas "within the framework of any larger policy" providing overall guidance.[30] But others admired Kennedy's intellectual curiosity and his ability to keep control despite the flurry of competing viewpoints. The president maintained "more reliable bilateral human relations than any man I have ever known" but always remained "the center of the wheel," recalled Walt Rostow, adding, "It was always the same pattern: spokes out from himself."[31] Biographer James MacGregor Burns, writing in 1959, used a different metaphor. JFK was, to Burns, a "master broker" who operated "at the center of the political cobweb."[32] Kennedy's ambassador to Yugoslavia, George Kennan, who served several presidents across his long diplomatic career, called JFK "the best listener I've ever seen in high position anywhere."[33]

Unsurprisingly, Kennedy appointed as his national security adviser a man with similar nondoctrinaire sensibilities about major policy issues, including policymaking toward the Third World. In this arena, McGeorge Bundy shared the president's broad concern about the changes sweeping much of the globe but did not hold fixed ideas about how U.S. policy should be reoriented. Much like JFK, Bundy's policy preferences were hard to categorize. Undoubtedly Bundy's status as a registered Republican appealed to Kennedy for the political balance it brought to his administration, but Bundy's Republicanism was notably understated. He remained mostly quiet on hot-button political controversies of the 1940s and 1950s, preferring instead to be seen as "the latest scion of a prestigious lineage of bipartisan statesmen" going back to the Second World War, in the words of historian Andrew Preston.[34] Bundy prided himself, that is, on agility of mind, talent for managing conflicting opinions, and comfort with nuance. "Gray," Bundy averred in a 1967 speech, "is the color of truth."[35] These traits inspired any number of colleagues and admirers to praise him as one of the most capable minds of his generation and account for his appointment in 1953, at the tender age of thirty-four, as the dean of the Faculty of Arts and Sciences of Harvard University. One classmate at Yale in the 1930s aptly described Bundy as "a chess master" with a genius for moving "the pieces (human beings) around."[36] To Robert Komer, who served under Bundy on the National Security Council, Bundy was the "high priest of feasibility."[37]

Bundy filled out his National Security Council staff with like-minded men committed to the rhetoric of the New Frontier but lacking precise commitments. These appointments unquestionably reflected JFK's goal of revamping the NSC as the central institution driving the energized and creative foreign policy that he hoped to craft, a desire that grew even more intense after the Bay of Pigs debacle. Whereas Kennedy often dismissed the State Department as a hidebound institution with nothing of value to contribute, he looked to his team in the White House for the vigorous debate and forward thinking that he prized.[38] Key NSC aides were predictably cut from the Bundy mold—men lacking deep experience with the issues they handled but brimming with confidence in their problem-solving abilities. In connection with the Third World, easily the most influential figure was Robert Komer, Bundy's top aide for the Middle East and Asia. Komer frequently took the lead in urging American sensitivity to Third World points of view, but he did so more from a sense of pragmatic necessity than any dogmatic views about socioeconomic change. Indeed, Komer, who had risen to prominence in the late Eisenhower years as the CIA's liaison to the NSC, disliked the grand rhetoric of Kennedy inauguration speech, espousing instead a more pedestrian vision of how the United States should use its power internationally. "Unless you can disassociate the practical hard facts with which you must deal, or the attitudes with which you must deal, from the emotional biases and prejudices of one kind or another," he warned in a 1964 speech about the Middle East, "you cannot have a sensible approach [to foreign policy]."[39] Perhaps most strikingly, Komer led the way in suggesting that Washington ease its relationship with China at a time when American domestic political pressures made any such step unlikely.[40]

Nondoctrinaire flexibility at the highest levels did not mean, however, that debate within the Kennedy administration proceeded without reference to the wide range of ideas circulating in Washington and throughout American society about how the United States should respond to rapid change in the Third World. On the contrary, the administration's pragmatism coexisted with vigorous debate inspired by proponents of particular ideas about how to confront burgeoning problems. Indeed, the administration's devotion to debate and pragmatic choice ensured that the president and his advisers would carefully consider strong views backed by eloquent and often influential, if sometimes second-tier, participants in the policymaking process. Since problems in the Third World, with the notable exceptions of Cuba and Indochina, only intermittently commanded sustained attention in the Oval Office, in fact, opportunities abounded for highly motivated officials to shape the way problems were understood and the choices that were made. Such policymakers drew upon—and to some extent embodied—four patterns of thinking that swirled within Washington as well as the academic and journalistic communities. No official represented any of these patterns perfectly. Yet it is possible nevertheless to discern four clusters of like-minded policymakers whose ideas flowed from particular historical experiences and bureaucratic responsibilities. Understanding the differences among these tendencies is essential to appreciate the ebb and flow of debate within the Kennedy administration, the variability of its policy choices, and the mix of options that Lyndon Johnson inherited upon assuming the presidency.

## Currents of Thought

One strand of thinking that shaped U.S. policy during the Kennedy years might be called "globalist." This outlook was embodied most prominently by individuals such as Undersecretary of State Chester Bowles, UN ambassador Adlai Stevenson, Assistant Secretary of State G. Mennen "Soapy" Williams, and economist John Kenneth Galbraith, who served as Kennedy's ambassador to India. All of these men had deep roots in the progressive wing of the

Democratic Party, and the older ones had cut their policymaking teeth during the FDR years, especially as functionaries in wartime agencies responsible for managing the domestic economy. All held an idealist vision of social uplift at home and abroad. In the domestic arena, they championed civil rights; overseas, they similarly backed policies tolerant of diversity and equality. They believed that oppressed masses were throwing off their chains in both realms and that the duty of the U.S. government, for both altruistic and self-interested reasons, was to support them.[41]

At the heart of the globalist outlook lay three interconnected ideas about the sort of international order that the United States should seek in Asia, Africa, the Middle East, and Latin America. First, advocates backed quick decolonization and full autonomy for Third World nations, an attitude that flowed from hostility to colonialism and confidence about the ability of young nations to participate responsibly in global affairs. Although globalism clearly aspired to an integrated global economy, it tolerated nationalization of economic resources as a near-term option for nations emerging from decades, if not centuries, of colonial plunder. Second, globalist thinking was notably tolerant of political diversity among Third World nations. This view was especially manifest in acceptance of non-alignment as a legitimate posture for governments whose priorities lay in economic and political development rather than in choosing sides in a dispute among the industrial powers. Third, globalism, notwithstanding its eagerness for self-determination, envisioned an integrated world order in which self-determining nation-states would be anchored in regional and international organizations. In this way, policymakers hoped for a new set of norms and principles to reintegrate the world once the bonds of colonialism had been sundered.

These ideas found eloquent expression in a series of reports prepared by the incoming administration in late 1960 and early 1961, exercises in which globalist thinking often predominated. Typical was a study drafted by Stevenson in November 1960, just after Kennedy's election. The report urged that the United States devote huge new resources to the Third World but also that Washington guard against the temptation to demand obedience in return. "In offering this opportunity for economic development, I think it important that we not try to impose our own political or economic ideas," Stevenson wrote. "Our objective should rather be to establish the conditions under which the emerging peoples can exercise a broad freedom of choice with respect to the varying types of political and economic systems, free from the direction of the major powers." Writing specifically about Africa, Stevenson went so far as to suggest that "for the foreseeable future a policy of non-alignment is best" for both the newly established nations and the industrial West. "There is excellent reason to believe," he asserted, "that the surest way

FIGURE 1.2. Liberal policymakers such as Adlai Stevenson, the two-time Democratic nominee for president, saw overlap between the quest for civil rights at home and the drive for decolonization abroad. Stevenson was photographed with President Kennedy and civil rights leader Martin Luther King Jr. at the White House on December 17, 1962. AP photo.

to alienate Africans from the West would be to insist that they participate actively on our side in the cold war."[42] The way to encourage moderation and cooperation, globalist thinking held, was not to impose U.S. preferences but to respect the sovereignty of foreign nations and build multilateralism through the United Nations and regional organizations. One report imbued with these ideas made the point explicit with respect to Latin American countries that had gained their independence many decades earlier but were powerfully asserting their autonomy for the first time. "The United States is neither omnipotent nor omniscient," asserted a task force of experts assembled to advise the incoming president. Their paper warned that Washington "cannot solve, but can only help the Latin Americans to try to solve, most of the problems of their highly diversified region in their own way."[43]

A key tool to achieve U.S. goals was, then, Washington's enormous political clout, but only if that influence was used in measured ways that respected the diverse sensitivities of newly assertive societies. Part of this challenge lay in resisting the temptation to rely on the former colonial powers to manage Western interests, especially in Africa. When international action seemed necessary, it should be carried out as much as possible through international institutions that conferred broad legitimacy.[44] The other important tool was development assistance. A pivotal challenge seemed to lie in establishing new mechanisms for distributing aid, a concern that would result in the establishment of the U.S. Agency for International Development within the State Department and the creation of the Peace Corps. To be sure, bureaucratic procedures for administering economic aid had been periodically updated and expanded since the start of President Harry S. Truman's Point IV program in 1949. In 1954, Congress had passed the Agriculture Trade and Development Act, under which massive quantities of American food were sent abroad, and three years later set up a Development Loan Fund to provide long-term, low-interest loans for poor nations. By the dawn of the Kennedy years, however, these innovations seemed to many U.S. officials to be inadequate to the complexity and scale of the assistance that the new era demanded.[45]

A second strand of thought that ran through the Kennedy administration—what might be called the "nation-building" line of thinking—has received considerable attention from scholars in recent years and has sometimes been singled out as the dominant intellectual current.[46] Given this tendency, it is perhaps surprising that only a small number of U.S. officials, mostly in the second tier or below, clearly bought into the nation-building vision. The most prominent was the prolific economist Walt W. Rostow, who joined the administration as deputy national security adviser and assertively advanced his ideas throughout the Kennedy and Johnson presidencies. Others closely linked to Rostow's policy ideas include Roger Hilsman, the director of the State Department's Bureau of Intelligence and Research and later assistant secretary of state for Far Eastern affairs; David E. Bell, the director of Kennedy's Bureau of the Budget who became head of the U.S. Agency for International Development in 1963; and academic social scientists Max F. Millikan and Edward S. Mason, who consulted for the Kennedy administration on problems related to economic development in the Third World.

Most of these men had been military officers or had held positions in the Office of Strategic Services during the Second World War, focusing their intellectual powers on the challenges of using American military prowess to maximum effect. Several remained active in government during the Truman and Eisenhower years, but their most significant commonalities were the academic credentials that they amassed during the 1950s. They all published influential academic studies that conveyed exuberance for bringing social-scientific insights to bear on policy problems and confidence about the possibilities of using American power and know-how to shape foreign societies.

The core nation-building ideas flowed most elegantly and ambitiously from the pen of Rostow, who had already taught at the Massachusetts Institute of Technology for a decade and become one of the world's foremost economists before joining the Kennedy administration.[47] In his 1960 treatise *The Stages of Economic Growth,* Rostow advanced the notion, later labeled "modernization theory," that human societies inevitably advanced through five "stages" from economic backwardness ("traditional society") to full industrial development ("mass high consumption"). A few advanced nations had already reached this end state, and one of them, the United States, had achieved such a remarkable level of comfort that the population was, according to Rostow, showing signs of forgoing further increases in income in favor of larger families, perhaps the ultimate indication of a society's level of economic satisfaction. But Rostow left no doubt that most nations were passing through the difficult middle phases of the modernization process, working toward the all-important "take-off" that would launch them toward "maturity" and then "mass consumption."[48]

Rostow's confidence that the United States embodied the predestined end point of history coexisted with anxiety about the effect of the Cold War on the ability of less advanced societies to follow the same trajectory. Historically, he contended, many underdeveloped areas had benefited from the intrusion of more advanced societies, which disrupted stagnant social relations and provoked innovation. But Rostow worried that poor nations were now subject to a different kind of intrusion—a communist variant that, by promising a false route to progress, threatened to knock immature societies off the upward pathway toward prosperity and political stability. Communism was, Rostow explained in 1958, "a disease of the transitional process from a traditional to a modern society."[49] The Soviets believed, he added in a speech three years later, "that they can exploit effectively the resentments built up in many of these areas against colonial rule and that they can associate themselves effectively with the desires of the emerging nations for independence, for status on the world scene, and for material progress." Communists were mere "scavengers of the modernization process," said Rostow, asserting that nations would become invulnerable once that had achieved sufficient progress. But in the short term, the risks were grave.[50]

To ensure that Third World nations moved in the right direction, Rostow and other like-minded officials urged that the United States act resolutely to help establish robust nation-states capable of resisting communist subversion, making progress toward economic takeoff, and ultimately participating in the Western-oriented global economy. As for proponents of globalist thinking, development aid stood out as a crucial tool of U.S. policy. But the nation-builders differed by pursuing this point with scientific precision. In *The Stages of Economic Growth*, Rostow insisted on a specific amount of external aid—$4 billion per annum, with 1.5 percent increases each year for the foreseeable future—that was necessary to put all of Africa, the Middle East, Latin America, and noncommunist Asia on a path to predictable growth.[51] Nation-builders also differed from globalists in their aversion to nationalization of resources. Although national control over resources fit in some ways with the vision of robust and autonomous nation-states, advocates of nation-building saw trade and foreign investment as key drivers of economic uplift.

Proponents of nation-building also differed from globalist thinking in their emphasis on another tool—military aid. Although globalists generally backed military assistance for Third World societies, they often criticized the Eisenhower administration for going too far. "Our emphasis on military spending . . . represents a degree of waste of public funds," asserted Chester Bowles in 1959, insisting that such aid often empowered "disruptive internal forces" within recipient nations and diverted "governments faced with pressing problems of internal economic development into a strident military escapism."[52] The nation-builders viewed such opinions as naïve given the alarming spread of communist-backed subversion in many parts of the world and urged stepping up both military and economic assistance. Waging guerrilla war against communist insurgents was, Rostow declared in 1961, "a terrible burden to carry for any government in a society making its way toward modernization." The United States, he added, bore "special responsibilities" to help weak nations build up military forces, infrastructure, and expertise sufficient to police their borders, deter aggression, and, if necessary, mount effective counterinsurgency campaigns.[53]

The sharpest distinction between the globalist and nation-building sensibilities, though, had to do not with notions of the most useful policy tools but with ideas about how political change should ideally unfold in Third World nations. Globalists envisioned a world of diverse nation-states that embodied the desires of their populations and cautioned against any U.S. effort to demand political or economic homogeneity. The nation-builders also sometimes spoke of their tolerance of—even enthusiasm for—political diversity.[54] In fact,

Rostow insisted that it was the Soviet Union, not the United States, that demanded its allies march in lockstep. Yet Rostow's words contradicted a core tenet of modernization theory: every nation was moving along the same road toward the same end state. Both the underlying forces of history and the natural preferences of rational people defied geographical variation and inevitably led toward a world of market economies, materialist values, and mass consumption. Critics of modernization theory often fixated on this tendency to overgeneralize. Like his colleagues, Rostow "made absolutely no distinctions between countries with completely different historical experiences" and were "completely impervious" to advice from officials possessing deep knowledge of distinct societies, complained Paul Kattenburg, a State Department official focused on Vietnam. "He'd figured out how to build nations, you know, so what's good for Peru is good for Vietnam."[55]

The nation-builders' attitude toward democracy also illuminates this lack of interest in, or tolerance for, diversity. Democracy, in this view, would become possible only at a late stage in the development process, once the economic transformation was well advanced. Modernization entailed breaking down outmoded social identities, loyalties, and conventions, an enormously disruptive process likely to be led by unrepresentative yet enlightened political vanguards capable of glimpsing larger forces and eager to engage in entrepreneurship beneficial to the larger society. Implicit in the nation-building idea was the expectation that the United States must rely on these like-minded elites in nations receiving American aid and that those elites need not be committed to democracy except as a general goal for the indefinite future. What counted most was that governments resist communism and embrace an American vision of development, not that they represent the will of their people. The people would, in a sense, catch up with their more enlightened leaders at some later point.[56]

The third strand of thinking within the Kennedy administration might be called the "strongpoint" outlook.[57] This pattern of thought generally acknowledged the growing importance of the Third World but held that, on balance, Washington's relationships with traditional allies—the strongpoints in the global order crafted by the United States since the Second World War—must take precedence. This point of view, which had mostly predominated in U.S. deliberations ever since the colonial problem had emerged after the Second World War, did not mean simple acceptance that imperial structures, whether old-fashioned colonial control or new postimperial federations, invariably provided stability or that the United States should never take the initiative in promoting change in the Third World. Nor did it mean adherents always opposed U.S. accommodation of Third World demands. Rather, this view reflected wariness of overstating the priority that should be placed on the autonomy of Third World societies and thereby sacrificing Washington's interests with its most powerful allies, which remained the cornerstones of U.S. foreign policy even if new problems in the Third World generated headlines.

Predictably, the most influential advocates of this outlook were policymakers who had spent their careers focused on the most important region of longstanding U.S. interest, Western Europe. For example, Dean Acheson, who advised Kennedy on foreign policy after turning down the president-elect's invitation to become ambassador to the North Atlantic Treaty Organization, had been a key architect of the alliance and other transatlantic initiatives during his tenure as secretary of state in the Truman years. Another powerful voice in favor of the needs of U.S. allies in Europe was George W. Ball, Kennedy's undersecretary of state for economic affairs. Although sixteen years younger than Acheson, Ball had played central roles in negotiations that produced the Marshall Plan and European integration in the early years of the Cold War. Moreover, both men had cultivated close relationships with Western European elites during the spectacularly successful legal careers they pursued when not serving in government positions.[58]

But not all strongpoint thinking was focused solely on Europe. Secretary of State Dean Rusk undoubtedly joined Acheson and Ball in the importance he attached to transatlantic relations, but he also prioritized the interests of Japan more than many of his colleagues. These tendencies may have flowed from a vanilla intellect that made Rusk, in the words of journalist Walter Lippmann, "a profound conformist" or, in John Kenneth Galbraith's biting assessment, "a passionate and indiscriminate exponent of all the Establishment clichés."[59] They also stemmed, though, from Rusk's formative educational experiences in England and a career built largely on expertise in Far Eastern affairs. Rusk served as an army officer in Southeast Asia during the Second World War and then as a senior State Department official charged with the restoration of Japanese power after 1947 and the creation of a regional order that would sustain Japan as a robust ally of the United States.[60]

Broadly speaking, these men recognized the complexity of trends unfolding in the Third World and, as Ball put it in his memoir, regarded Kennedy's desire for innovation as "certainly an improvement over the two-dimensional thinking" characteristic of the "Manichean crusade" waged by Eisenhower's secretary of state, John Foster Dulles.[61] In the late 1940s, for example, Acheson had shown some willingness to accommodate surging nationalism in Indonesia and the Middle East, where the communist danger was small and American long-term interests immense. Yet these men left no doubt where they believed the most important American interests lay. Acheson, who scorned Kennedy's soaring rhetoric about the Third World, made clear in 1958 that he had little admiration for liberal ideas circulating within the Democratic Party.

Kennedy's well-known speech criticizing French colonialism in Algeria amounted to "impatient snapping of our fingers" and a needless affront to a valued ally, Acheson wrote.[62] The former secretary of state was, Ball noted three years later, a dedicated "Europeanist" who cared "nothing for Africa."[63] Acheson "saw the Atlantic as the center of everything," concurred McGeorge Bundy.[64] Journalist David Halberstam drew the inverse conclusion: "The underdeveloped world was not," in Acheson's thinking, "a serious place."[65]

Rusk similarly had a hard time seeing beyond the Cold War order he had helped to create. "He tried to take a less rigid view," noted his onetime subordinate, Chester Bowles, "[but] he never succeeded in seeing any international conflict in terms other than those of the Cold War."[66] For this reason, Rusk particularly disdained the globalists, whose intellectualism seemed to distract them from the sheer malevolence of communism. In Rusk's view, writes Halberstam, liberals like Schlesinger and Galbraith were "quick, glib men dancing around Georgetown cocktail parties," intellectuals empowered by direct access to the president but lacking in real understanding even as they were afforded the opportunity of "testing their theories on the world." Rusk believed that foreign affairs were "filled with pitfalls for well-meaning idealists" who often failed to see the moral stakes in the East-West confrontation, adds Halberstam, who sums up Rusk's Manichean view of the United States and the Soviet Union in a single sentence: "We wore the white hats and they wore the black."[67]

Ball was even more explicit about U.S. priorities. Although he refrained from commenting on JFK's words, he scorned colleagues who espoused ambitious new approaches to the Third World, castigating champions of nation building in particular for "overblown nomenclature and faddish reliance" on social-science theory. "Hubris was endemic in Washington," he wrote in his 1982 memoir, adding dismissively that the "prospect of leading the Third World into the twentieth century offered almost unlimited scope for experimentation not only to economists but also to sociologists, psychologists, city planners, agronomists, political scientists, and experts in chicken diseases."[68] Whereas Rostow had insisted that the United States would be "better served by accepting the risks of leaning forward towards more modern groups than the risks of clinging to familiar friends rooted in the past," Ball believed nothing fundamental had changed because of the growing ambitions of the Third World. The North-South divide was hardly "our number one danger and hence not our number one problem," Ball wrote in 1968, suggesting that geopolitical calculations must not be driven simply by growing awareness of problems besetting parts of the world that had not previously drawn Washington's attention. "Priorities have not been changed by improved communications or even a more active social conscience; our first need is to maintain an effective balance between East and West," wrote Ball.[69] All in all, he asserted on another occasion, the United States must not waste its energies on obscure nations "with names like typographical errors."[70] At the core of Ball's outlook, writes Halberstam, lay a simple maxim: "do not dissipate power in a situation where it is not applicable."[71]

Unlike champions of the nation-building and globalist perspectives, advocates of strongpoint thinking did not generate studies or assertively tout their ideas in the run-up to the 1960 election or in the early days of the Kennedy presidency. The reason for their quiescence is not difficult to see. These men had little interest in the dynamics of social change in the Third World at a time when the political advantages for the Democratic Party lay on the side of demonstrating fresh ideas. Officials attached to strongpoint ideas were, in short, out of step with the New Frontier ethos that pervaded Washington at the administration's outset, even if they were well represented within the new team that would make foreign policy. Moreover, there was no mystery about the logic of long-standing Cold War thinking that prioritized U.S. alliances in Western Europe and East Asia and emphasized the preservation of stability elsewhere, including via the maintenance of existing patterns of trade and foreign investment. Nor was there any mystery about the methods that such an approach implied. Officials who leaned this way advocated working closely with allies and even relying on the old colonial powers to take the lead on problems in still-colonized parts of Africa. Only when Washington faced challenges that could not be managed in partnership with allies, most obviously in Vietnam and Cuba, did the strongpoint position lose its resonance. Acheson frequently advocated hawkish positions, most notably during the Cuban Missile Crisis and the early stages of U.S. escalation in Vietnam, in order to end conflicts decisively on U.S. terms. By contrast, Ball often advocated more dovish approaches aimed at deescalating crises without unnecessary diversion of American resources to relatively inconsequential parts of the world.

The final strand of thinking—what might be called "unilateralism"—was especially prevalent within the U.S. military, though civilians such as CIA director Allen Dulles also frequently espoused this outlook. Such men were often hostile to colonialism in principle and generally advocated a U.S.-led global order of autonomous nation-states. But they had little interest in, or appreciation for, the social and political transformation taking place in Asia, Africa, the Middle East, and Latin America and stood outside the liberal consensus that, with varying emphases and intensity, ran through the other currents of thinking. Unilateralism entailed minimal enthusiasm for the idea of government-led reformism in either the domestic or international sphere, embracing instead a view of government as a relatively blunt instrument whose responsibility in the national-security arena lay entirely in achieving decisive results in defense of U.S. interests. However dissonant their views may have been amid the general tenor of the new administration, however, the military and CIA nearly always had seats at the table when important decisions were made. Indeed, President Kennedy's caution about antagonizing these bureaucracies—institutions with thinly veiled contempt for the inexperienced commander in chief—probably ensured that such views were taken more seriously than they might otherwise have been.[72]

Unilateralist tendencies flowed partly from the distinct niches that proponents tended to occupy in the national-security apparatus. Unlike officials of the National Security Council or State Department, whose responsibilities entailed coordinating different policy tools, leaders of the intelligence agencies and military had direct control over discreet elements of national power—covert operations in the case of the CIA and armed force in the case of the military. Budgetary and careerist pressures pushed officials of these bureaucracies to advocate using what they had to offer and to protect their prerogatives.[73] Yet the unilateralist viewpoint also stemmed from the particular personalities and experiences of many key military and intelligence men who surrounded Kennedy. To be sure, the president aspired to appoint military advisers who thought creatively about Third World problems and most notably advanced the career of General Maxwell Taylor, whose 1960 book *The Uncertain Trumpet* called for a thorough rethinking of American military doctrine in order to prepare for limited warfare.[74] Yet the top military brass whom JFK inherited—Joint Chiefs of Staff chairman Lyman Lemnitzer of the Army, Admiral Arleigh Burke of the Navy, Air Force generals Curtis LeMay and Thomas Powers—were gruff veterans of the Second World War who prided themselves on their ability to use America's massive power to crushing effect. CIA director Dulles, though far more urbane in his demeanor, shared this confidence in U.S. capabilities and, having managed networks of spies during the Second World War and then led the agency during the heyday of its covert operations in the 1950s, strongly advocated such clandestine activities, especially in the Third World.[75]

Certain of American might, the unilateralists shared neither the strongpoint advocates' concern for the interests of U.S. allies nor the desire manifested by both globalists and nation-builders to deploy power in relatively subtle ways aimed at bolstering independent nations rather than asserting American power directly. In a meeting with Kennedy just a month after the new president took office, Marine Corps commandant David M. Shoup characteristically questioned the administration's proposals to help train indigenous forces in Latin America to resist Cuban subversion. The Marines, said Shoup, "would rather go in and do the job themselves."[76] Some military leaders even dragged their feet on proposals backed by Kennedy and many of his civilian advisers to give U.S. forces greater resources to fight guerrilla wars in the jungles and mountains of the Third World. The Kennedy administration was "oversold" on the idea of reforming the military for new missions, complained Lemnitzer, who voiced confidence that the nation could cope with peripheral challenges even while sticking with its accustomed focus on large-scale conventional war.[77] Such attitudes naturally rankled officials with different ideas. Presidential aide Arthur Schlesinger Jr. complained in his memoir that Chief of Naval Operations Burke "pushed his black-and-white views of international affairs with bluff naval persistence." International cooperation and promotion of economic development seemed to have little importance in such a worldview. "For men of Burke's persuasion," Schlesinger lamented, "talk of an alliance for progress could only seem bleeding-heart, do-good globaloney."[78]

Allen Dulles, a key proponent of unilateralism at the CIA, similarly bucked prevailing tendencies within the Kennedy White House by championing not subtle uses of American power to shape emerging nations but bold covert actions to achieve what in the twenty-first century would be called "regime change." Dulles had helped engineer coups in Guatemala and Iran in the early stages of the Eisenhower presidency and, emboldened by these successes, championed similar projects elsewhere. "Where there begins to be evidence that a country is slipping and communist takeover is threatened," Dulles declaimed, "we can't wait for an engraved invitation to come and give aid."[79] Covert operations appealed because they were "easier, less messy" than the techniques preferred by other advisers, wrote Halberstam, an acute observer of U.S. decision making in the 1960s. Dulles and like-minded colleagues were enamored of the idea, added Halberstam, that they were the "real players in the real world" of power politics who bypassed the academic policy debates that unfolded in newspapers, universities, and Congress.[80]

## Ebb and Flow

The interplay among these currents of thinking suffused policymaking deliberations as the Kennedy administration confronted numerous challenges in the Third World. Virtually every major decision generated disagreement, rivalry, and uncertainty. Tensions were most obvious between those who attached high priority to problems in the Third World and called for ambitious solutions—officials who leaned toward the globalist and nation-building impulses—and others who remained wedded to relatively conventional thinking about how to wage the Cold War. These were, in the words of the famed journalist Halberstam, the "two main cords" running through American policy debates. One consisted of those who questioned simplistic assumptions about communism and self-consciously attached themselves to the New Frontier; the other was made up of "hard-nosed" Cold War realists who were mostly unimpressed with calls for innovation.[81] Yet disagreements were sometimes just as fierce on either side of this fundamental cleavage, where subtler difference sometimes made for sharper clashes.

Kennedy's discomfort with simple solutions flowing from any one of the main strands of thought became abundantly clear during his first year in office. His differences with the military and intelligence officials inherited from the Eisenhower presidency were most obvious, driven in part by Kennedy's resentment about the dismal advice he received in connection with the Bay of Pigs invasion, a humiliating failure rooted in wild overconfidence among military and intelligence officials about the likelihood of overthrowing the Castro government. Tensions with the military chiefs boiled anew after the Cuban Missile Crisis in October 1962, when senior commanders lambasted the president for failing to act decisively against Cuba. McGeorge Bundy speculated that the president "would never feel really secure" about the military until "young generals of his own generation in whom he has confidence" occupied key positions.[82] Unsurprisingly, Kennedy promoted his confidant in military affairs, General Taylor, to increasingly important roles and ultimately, in October 1962, the chairmanship of the Joint Chiefs of Staff. The president moved even more quickly to replace Allen Dulles, naming a new CIA director in November 1961 (though the new appointee was another Republican, businessman John McCone). Still, JFK's distrust of these bureaucracies persisted, and he appreciated subordinates who defied the military. He also frequently distanced himself from advocates of the strongpoint approach, whom he viewed as insufficiently attuned to emerging global trends. Above all, JFK shared a pervasive view of Rusk as a dull, unimaginative policymaker at the head of a bureaucracy, the State Department, hopelessly wedded to the status quo. As for Acheson, the president found him sometimes "worth listening to" but on many occasions "worthless," according to Robert F. Kennedy.[83]

JFK kept his distance as well from appointees who most obviously seemed to share his desire for innovation in the Third World. Perhaps fearing the political costs of close association with the liberal wing of his party, he rebuffed Stevenson's desire to be secretary of state, instead giving him the ambassadorship to the United Nations, and dispatched John Kenneth Galbraith to faraway New Delhi as U.S. ambassador to India. Indeed, Kennedy viewed ambassadorships as the best posts for liberals eager to reorient U.S. policy in the Third World. He was unquestionably enthusiastic about innovators like William

Attwood (assigned to Guinea), John Badeau (Egypt), and Howard Palfrey Jones (Indonesia), but he conspicuously deployed them all to distant posts and tolerated less innovative diplomats such as Julius Holmes in Iran. Closer to home, Kennedy risked his standing with the progressive wing of his party by unceremoniously demoting the most highly placed official with globalist views, Undersecretary of State Bowles, in November 1961 after Bowles leaked word of his opposition to the Bay of Pigs operation. JFK gave Bowles the grand title of "special representative and adviser for Asian, African, and Latin American affairs," but there was no disguising the president's agreement with Acheson's sense that Bowles was a "garrulous windbag and ineffectual do-gooder."[84] For troubleshooting in the Third World, in fact, JFK often called on W. Averell Harriman, the veteran diplomat and former governor of New York who exuded a pragmatic approach to problem-solving.

Nor was JFK always favorable to the nation-building impulse, despite his enthusiasm for innovations such as the Green Berets and the Peace Corps. Just ten months after Walt Rostow joined the administration as Bundy's deputy at the National Security Council, Kennedy transferred him to the State Department as part of the same shake-up—the "Thanksgiving Day Massacre," as it came to be known—that had brought Bowles's demotion. The problem was the hawkishly doctrinaire tenor of Rostow's advice. "Walt is a fountain of ideas," said Kennedy. "Perhaps one in ten of them is absolutely brilliant. Unfortunately six or seven are not merely unsound, but dangerously so."[85] Bundy held a similar view, noting that he could not stop Rostow from writing reports but insisting that he did not have to read them.[86]

Shuffling of personnel diminished as the Kennedy administration progressed, but stability among his advisers did not result in more definitive policy outcomes. To the final days of his life, as the next chapter demonstrates, the administration showed contradictory tendencies. Sheer instability and the complexity of local dynamics in diverse parts of the world defied any one-size-fits-all approach and ensured that U.S. policy would take different forms in different places. So too did the ever-shifting political context within which the administration maneuvered. Steadily climbing approval ratings presumably gave Kennedy more confidence to pursue relatively innovative and risky approaches, but he remained keenly sensitive to the political dangers of challenging deeply ingrained assumptions about the need to prioritize anticommunism above all else. Tellingly, historians who have most assertively credited Kennedy with sincere hopes to ease Cold War hostilities with Cuba or North Vietnam or to reorient U.S. policy toward the non-aligned world have relied heavily on speculation rooted in mere shards of evidence about JFK's intentions. The political constraints of the early 1960s clearly did not permit him to speak openly about such objectives without risking his prospects for reelection in 1964. In the end, of course, LBJ would sit in the Oval Office when that election took place. Johnson's inheritance consisted of a favorable political position and high expectations for the use of U.S. power at home and abroad. In the Third World, however, he inherited contradictory impulses and innumerable unresolved dilemmas that had beset JFK across his thousand days in office and would bedevil LBJ for two thousand more.

# 2

# A World of Dilemmas

THE VARIABILITY and indecisiveness of U.S. foreign policy during the Kennedy presidency is visible in any number of diplomatic problems that beset Washington from 1961 to 1963. Throughout Asia, Africa, the Middle East, and Latin America, American interests seemed imperiled by rapid political, economic, and social change. Kennedy and his advisers struggled to balance the need to accommodate such change with the requirements of safeguarding American interests and maintaining the support of Congress and the public. The result was different approaches in different places and pervasive uncertainty. This chapter charts the broad patterns of U.S. policymaking toward the five nations whose stories sit at the heart of the book. The purpose is not to provide exhaustive narratives of these interactions. Rather, the objective is to reveal how geopolitical problems elicited a range of ideas and sparked debate. In each case, administration officials acknowledged that their decisions carried heavy implications for U.S. interests in crucial parts of the world. But they failed to achieve the coherence or consistent innovation that JFK's rhetoric so often seemed to promise. Perhaps Kennedy's assassination in 1963 deprived him of the opportunity to achieve more impressive results. There is simply no way to know what he might have done in the following five years, assuming his reelection in 1964. What is clear is that Lyndon Johnson inherited a world of dilemmas and no clear guidance for solving them.

## "A Zoo with All Types of Specimens"

Brazil encapsulated one type of problem that confronted the United States in the Third World and was particularly prevalent in Latin America: a historically pro-U.S. nation that, under the strains of accelerating social and political change, threatened to break away from Washington as it asserted itself more energetically. Indisputably, Brazil was a nation on the rise whose political choices would influence the hemisphere if not the wider world. "Brazilians are convinced that their country is fast becoming a world power, and as such is entitled to a voice in international affairs commensurate with its stature," the CIA advised the new administration in March 1961.[1] No longer, added a study by the National Security Council, could the United States treat Brazil as "just another of the Latin American 'banana republics.'"[2] So dynamic and ambitious was Brazil that Kennedy's aides sometimes noted parallels to the New Frontier ethos that they cultivated so eagerly for themselves, a tendency reinforced by the fact that the forty-four-year-old Jânio Quadros became president of Brazil in January 1961, just eleven days after the forty-three-year-old JFK took the oath of office in Washington. The two youngest chief executives in their nations' histories came to power amid enthusiasm for national renewal.

But anxiety about Brazil's distressing blend of political and economic instability far exceeded enthusiasm for its rising power. In the political realm, Quadros, a left-leaning populist with strong ties to Brazil's labor movement, seemed dangerously fond of Fidel Castro and determined to lead his country away from its long-standing partnership with the United States. Indeed, Quadros seemed to champion a new political orientation for the hemisphere as a whole, praising Castro for contributing to nothing less than "the construction of a New World that is awakening now in America."[3] U.S. officials took note in 1961 when the head of the Brazilian delegation to the United Nations General Assembly asserted that Brazil was taking India's place "as the democratic leader of the underdeveloped and peace-loving nations."[4] That claim far exceeded any plausible overhaul of Brazil's global role in the near term, but Washington could hardly miss the point: the Brazilian government aimed for something more like the non-alignment that prevailed in much of the Afro-Asian world than the perpetuation of Brazil's close partnership with the United States.

At times, administration policymakers expressed tolerance for the drift of Brazilian policy. Following a visit to Brasilia, presidential aide Arthur Schlesinger Jr. suggested that Quadros's "semi-neutralism" was "tactical rather than principled"—designed, that is, more to bolster him politically with a restive population than to signal a true realignment.[5] To the extent that Brazilian non-alignment was genuine, moreover, it might even pay dividends for the United States. The CIA speculated that Brazil's market-oriented vision of economic development had a constructive influence in Africa, where nationalists were often drawn to the Soviet and Chinese models of economic and political progress.[6] For the most part, though, U.S. officials feared Brazil's tilt away from Washington, especially as it became clear that "independence" would entail deeper relationships with the communist world. It was one thing for a historically non-aligned nation such as India to cultivate ties with the communist powers but quite another for a nation within the Western Hemisphere to flirt with U.S. adversaries. The Monroe Doctrine still shaped the attitudes of U.S.

leaders, as did their keen awareness of the political cost to be paid if a piece of Latin American flew out of Washington's orbit. U.S. officials watched with horror as Brazil restored diplomatic relations with the Soviet Union, sent a trade mission to Eastern Europe, and refused to fall in line behind Washington's efforts within the Organization of American States to punish Cuba for cozying up to Moscow.

The other problem that preoccupied the Kennedy administration was Brazil's ever-deepening economic crisis. In some respects, Brazil's woes seemed to be tied to the country's rising ambitions. Under the slogan "Fifty years progress in five!" President Juscelino Kubitschek had borrowed extensively abroad and run up huge deficits in the late 1950s in order to finance industrial development and construction of a grand new capital city, Brasilia. Among the consequences were rampant inflation running to 35 percent per year and massive public debts owed to the International Monetary Fund, the U.S. Export-Import Bank, and other creditors.[7] Meanwhile, Brazil, like many developing nations, struggled with low commodity prices, widespread corruption, poor public services, and yawning disparities between regions undergoing rapid modernization and others virtually unaffected by economic change. Most glaringly, Brazil's vast northeast suffered from endemic poverty, illiteracy, disease, and malnutrition.[8]

As so often during the Cold War, U.S. leaders feared that economic crisis, combined with rising expectations among the Brazilian population, provided fertile soil for communist subversion. Brazil's flirtation with non-alignment might be just the start of a slide into the Soviet bloc. Washington officials understood that the tiny Brazilian communist party, like its counterparts in other Western Hemisphere countries, posed little threat and that the left was badly fragmented. (Brazilians quipped that their nation had not a "left" but "lefts.")[9] But few Americans doubted Schlesinger's assessment that, in conditions like those prevailing in Brazil, ordinary people "tend toward Communism both as an outlet for social resentment and as a swift and sure technique for social modernization."[10] Cuba and the Soviet Union, meanwhile, seemed poised to pounce on a weak and poorly led Brazil and pull the nation into the communist bloc, a catastrophe that might dwarf the implications of the Cuban revolution.

Washington's solution, as throughout much of the Third World, was to promote a "middle class revolution" by providing economic aid to empower moderate urbanites committed to constitutional government, a stable party system, and economic austerity sufficient to overcome the nation's vast problems.[11] These ideas, broadly shared within the Kennedy administration, underpinned JFK's signature initiative in Latin America, the Alliance for Progress. Announced on March 13, 1961, and then given substance at a summit meeting of

FIGURE 2.1. U.S. fears that Brazil would follow the revolutionary path blazed by Cuba ran high during the Kennedy years. This cartoon by Ed Valtman was published in the *Hartford Times* on August 31, 1961, a few days after President João Goulart came to power. The Library of Congress.

Western Hemisphere leaders at Punta del Este, Uruguay, five months later, the program promised to distribute $20 billion of U.S. assistance, a massive figure amounting to more than $100 billion in twenty-first-century terms, over the ensuing decade. Factoring in an additional $80 billion in commitments from Latin American nations, architects of the alliance aimed for 2.5 percent annual increases in per capita income across the recipient nations, eradication of inflation, and more equitable distribution of land and other resources.[12] Nowhere did these goals seem more urgent than in Brazil.

The alliance did little to reverse worrying trends, however. Widespread illiteracy, rapid population growth, and low levels of education seemed likely to frustrate even the most dedicated efforts to address the fiscal and monetary crises.[13] Yet Quadros appeared to move further away from the austerity measures that U.S. policymakers believed urgent. In the political realm, the Brazilian leader sometimes voiced appreciation for U.S. assistance but also defied Washington by, for example, giving Cuban revolutionary Ernesto "Che" Guevara a warm reception during his visit to Brazil and sending a Brazilian "observer" to the 1961 meeting of non-aligned nations in Belgrade.[14] On August 25, 1961, Quadros confirmed the worst American suspicions about political volatility in Brazil by abruptly resigning the presidency. He probably hoped that the Brazilian Congress would quickly reinstate him with enhanced powers, but, if so, his gambit failed. The Congress instead elevated Vice President João Goulart, another left-leaning populist, to the presidency in September after he agreed to cede some of his powers to the legislature.

The next two years brought a few periods of relatively harmonious U.S.-Brazilian relations. Goulart's visit to Washington in April 1962 went smoothly, resulting in new U.S. promises of alliance aid. The Cuban Missile Crisis also seemed to affirm the warming trend. Although the Brazilian left mounted pro-Castro street demonstrations and labor unions threatened to boycott U.S. ships in Brazilian ports, Goulart quietly endorsed the U.S. quarantine against Cuba and even suggested that the Brazilian Air Force would help enforce it. Impressed, the Kennedy administration saw him as a constructive force during the crisis. Officials welcomed his proposal to denuclearize Latin America as a way to end the confrontation and his willingness to use Brazilian diplomats to mediate covertly between Havana and Washington.[15]

On balance, however, U.S.-Brazilian relations deteriorated during 1962 and 1963. The independence that made Goulart a plausible intermediary with Castro also made him suspect in U.S. eyes. Indeed, U.S. diplomats sometimes likened Goulart to Charles de Gaulle, the mercurial leader of a nation formally allied to the United States who delighted in defying Washington's leadership.[16] More commonly, they worried that Goulart, whether deliberately or inadvertently, was becoming more like Castro. Neutralism among Western Hemisphere nations, after all, seemed just a short step from outright hostility to the United States, a view that gained substance as Goulart's regime deepened its ties with the Soviet Union and stood back when the government of the state of Rio Grande do Sul expropriated property of the American-owned International Telephone & Telegraph. Just as alarming was Goulart's refusal to distance himself from the far left or to commit to an economic program of the sort that U.S. officials considered essential. In December 1962, an exasperated President Kennedy exclaimed that he worried more about Brazil than about Cuba.[17]

The Kennedy administration applied intense pressure on the Brazilian government to mend its ways. In the months leading up to Brazil's October 1962 legislative elections, the president authorized covert support for Goulart's political opponents.[18] In December, the president's brother and closest adviser, Attorney General Robert F. Kennedy, flew to Brazil to urge Goulart to reverse the government's leftward drift and to deal seriously with the economy. "The U.S. wanted to aid Brazil's development and social progress but could not do so if steps were not taken to get the economic and financial house in order," RFK threatened.[19] The administration meanwhile distributed Alliance for Progress aid in smaller tranches in order to maximize U.S. leverage. In June 1963, the Kennedy administration cut off the Goulart regime altogether and began sending assistance directly to Brazil's state governments, which Americans dubbed "islands of sanity" in the roiling sea that was the nation as a whole.[20]

Meanwhile, U.S. Ambassador Lincoln Gordon and the Pentagon began pushing another option: a military coup against Goulart. Reports piled up during 1962 about growing restiveness within the Brazilian officer corps as economic chaos worsened and the government moved more openly to the left. Amid speculation that a *golpe de estado* might come before the end of the year, the Defense Department appointed a new military attaché, Army Colonel Vernon Walters, to deepen U.S. contacts with Brazilian officers. Walters, who arrived in Brazil in October 1962, seemed the perfect man for the job. An old acquaintance of Gordon's, he spoke fluent Portuguese and had friendly ties to numerous Brazilian officers stemming from his service as a liaison to the Brazilian expeditionary force in Italy during the Second World War.[21] With Walters on the job, the United States was well positioned to bolster the confidence of pro-U.S. elements of the Brazilian military, monitor coup plotting, and, if the time came, provide U.S. support. The possibility of backing a coup received another boost in November, when a committee appointed by Kennedy to study the situation in Brazil came out unequivocally on the issue. The Draper Report, named for retired U.S. Army general William H. Draper, who chaired the commission, advised cultivating contacts with potential leaders of a "friendly alternative regime" and making preparations "to act promptly and effectively in support of such a regime, in case the impending financial crisis or some other eventuality should result in the displacement of Goulart."[22]

The possibility of a military solution sparked debate within the Kennedy administration that endured for the remainder of the presidency. Even as economic conditions worsened and Goulart seemed to veer leftward, U.S.

policymakers were well aware of the principled commitment to democracy that had pervaded the Alliance for Progress at its inception. The Western Hemisphere's "unfulfilled task," Kennedy had declared in his soaring 1961 speech unveiling the alliance, "is to demonstrate to the entire world that man's unsatisfied aspiration for economic progress and social justice can best be achieved by free men working within a framework of democratic institutions." The alliance, added Kennedy, was nothing less than a "plan to transform the 1960s into an historic decade of democratic progress."[23]

During 1962, U.S. tolerance for military coups in Argentina and Ecuador suggested that the administration was backing away from this sort of commitment. But some officials resisted the idea of a military solution in Brazil. In November 1962, Walt Rostow, hardly a consistent defender of democracy, contended that it was too soon to give up on Goulart, who was more an inept opportunist than ideologue. In any case, Rostow predicted new problems after a coup. "I am not confident," he wrote, "that the outcome of his overthrow would be orderly and effective, if autocratic, military rule."[24] The best move, Rostow and others conjectured, would be simply to hold on until the next presidential election in Brazil, scheduled for October 1965, and hope that the democratic process would yield a tolerable government. Wariness of military regimes ran so deep in May 1963 that Rostow and National Security Adviser McGeorge Bundy, along with committed globalists such as Assistant Defense Secretary Adam Yarmolinsky and NSC aide Gordon Chase, quietly toyed with the idea of tolerating a leftist government in the hemisphere as long as it was independent of the communist bloc, an idea that JFK himself was secretly entertaining in connection with Cuba during his final months.[25]

On the other side of the debate, champions of a coup insisted that a military takeover, far from destroying democracy, might be the best way to shore it up over the long term.[26] The March 1962 coup in neighboring Argentina and the quick restoration of civilian rule suggested that something similar might be possible in Brazil. Indeed, U.S. policymakers were accustomed to describing the Brazilian military in favorable terms. Perhaps the most influential proponent of this view was Ambassador Gordon, who cut a sharp distinction between the repressive role played by the military in most Latin American countries and the situation in Brazil. There, Gordon wrote in August 1962, the army was widely regarded as the "guardian of [the] constitution and of institutional and public order." The army was, he added, the "most effective stabilizing force in [the] country" and lacked "extreme rightist or reactionary" tendencies.[27]

A rough division within the Kennedy administration grew increasingly visible in 1963. Foreign Minister Francisco Clementino de San Tiago Dantas, for one, had little difficulty discerning tension between, on one side, a "tough line" advocated by RFK and Ambassador Gordon and, on the other side, a "co-operative line" backed by Bundy and Rostow.[28] To be sure, the divide was not always clear, with even Goulart's fiercest critics in the United States sometimes doubting that the situation was ripe for bold action to remove him. In March, Secretary of State Rusk conceded that conditions were not so bad in Brazil that all "non-communist or non-totalitarian Brazilians would understand or participate in an effort to overthrow the present regime." The United States, Rusk added, did not yet have "the basis for a clear break" with Brazil "that would be understood throughout the hemisphere" and therefore must, at least for the time being, continue down the road of pressing Goulart to move in a "more wholesome direction" politically and economically.[29]

Some of those reasons for delay dissolved later in 1963. In a steady drumbeat of reports from Brazil, Ambassador Gordon dismissed Goulart's occasional promises of "reform" as cynical maneuvers to keep his adversaries at bay. Meanwhile, reported Gordon, Goulart grew more dependent on a motley array of leftist advisers, labor activists, and cabinet officers sympathetic to communism—"something of a zoo of all types of specimens," the ambassador dismissively wrote.[30] During a meeting with Kennedy in October, Gordon stated his opinions still more bluntly. Goulart's early departure would be a "very good thing for both Brazil and Brazilian-American relations," asserted the ambassador, who urged the president not to be squeamish about sending aid to post-coup Brazil. He advised simply "doing what we ought to do, which is to welcome [Goulart's ouster]." To ensure that the "right side" prevailed in any fighting that might result from a coup attempt, Gordon urged that the administration study the possibility of U.S. military intervention, a suggestion that Kennedy approved while also insisting that channels to Goulart remained open.[31]

Perhaps the surest sign of momentum in favor of a coup was the State Department's decision in October 1963 to announce a new attitude toward military regimes in the hemisphere. That statement came in the form of an op-ed by Assistant Secretary of State Edwin Martin in the *New York Herald Tribune*, but the State Department circulated it to diplomatic posts throughout the hemisphere, noting that it "constitutes U.S. policy." Without specifically mentioning Brazil, Martin began by affirming U.S. dedication to democracy and asserting that coups were to be resisted "with all the means we have available." He left no doubt, though, that Washington increasingly acknowledged the weakness of democratic regimes in the face of rising nationalism and social tensions. "In most of Latin America, there is so little experience with the benefits of political legitimacy that there is an insufficient body of opinion, civil or military, which has any reason to know its value and hence defend it," added Martin, denigrating advocates of democracy as "impatient idealists."[32]

None of this meant, however, that the administration had reached a decision. Although Kennedy had approved contingency planning to provide U.S. support for a coup and never directly challenged Gordon's enthusiasm for that possibility, he categorically expressed his hostility to military coups during the final weeks of his life. In his last statement about military takeovers in Latin America, JFK downplayed the significance of Martin's op-ed, asserting that he had not relaxed his commitment to democracy and rejecting the idea that military regimes be counted on to bring about progressive reform and to restore democracy. In fact, the president stated in a news conference on October 9 that military governments had often proved to be the "seedbed" for the very outcome they were supposed to prevent: communist takeover. "We are opposed to coups because we think that they are . . . self-defeating," insisted JFK, who also invoked the U.S. commitment to democracy under the Alliance for Progress.[33] Was Kennedy being fully honest? Which way was he leaning in connection with Brazil? The president's contradictory behavior makes it impossible to answer these questions with any certainty. All in all, it was classic Kennedy: entertaining a range of views and keeping his options open as the situation evolved.[34]

## "The Most Important of All the Uncommitted States"

More than any other nation, India was the epicenter of Kennedy's determination to reshape American policy toward the Third World. The president and his team viewed that country as exceptional—"the most important of all the uncommitted states," JFK declared—because of its sheer size and democratic aspirations but also because of its stature among newly emerging non-aligned nations. What occurred in India promised to reverberate from "Casablanca to the Celebes," Kennedy declared.[35] Unquestionably, the Eisenhower administration had also recognized India's importance and made a determined effort in its last years to improve relations, above all by showing greater tolerance for non-alignment and boosting U.S. development assistance. But Kennedy, first as a senator and then as president, sought to go much further, even at the cost of antagonizing Pakistan, America's ally in the region. In March 1958, Senator Kennedy delivered an eight-thousand-word speech, written by Rostow and other MIT economists, proposing that the United States drastically increase assistance to shore up the faltering Indian economy. Ensuring the success of such a pivotal nation, Kennedy urged, easily trumped any concern about India's non-alignment. "Our friendships," declared the senator, "should not be equated with military alliances or 'voting the American ticket.'"[36]

Kennedy's proposal failed but offered a glimpse of what was to come during his presidency. While reassuring Pakistan that Washington remained true to its alliance commitments, the new administration took immediate steps to open a new era of cooperation with India. Kennedy's personnel appointments made his intentions clear. If the president's political sensitivities made him reluctant to have John Kenneth Galbraith by his side in Washington, he was eager to appoint his friend U.S. ambassador in Delhi. Kennedy also appointed two men well known for their pro-India views—arch-globalist Chester Bowles and the former journalist Phillips Talbot—as undersecretary of states and assistant secretary of state for Near Eastern and South Asian affairs, respectively. Policy changes came quickly. The new administration pledged $500 million for each of the first two years of India's five-year economic plan due to begin in 1962—roughly a tripling of U.S. development assistance over the final year of the Eisenhower presidency—plus an additional $500 million per year in food aid.[37] Galbraith soon proposed going even further by funding major public works projects central to the Indian government's economic ambitions, a steel mill at Bokaro and a nuclear power plant near Mumbai.[38]

Gestures of friendship abounded. In an exchange of letters, Kennedy praised Indian leader Jawaharlal Nehru's efforts to "create a peaceful world community" and held up Indian economic progress as "an example for the whole world of the achievements possible to a free society." In reply, Nehru heaped praise on the "goodwill and generous assistance" of the United States.[39] Perhaps the most revealing indication of U.S.-Indian comity was the warm relationship between the austere Nehru and the folksy Lyndon Johnson when the vice president visited New Delhi in May 1961. LBJ's report on his trip noted an "affinity of spirit" and pointed out that although India was "neutral" in its geopolitical outlook, its neutrality leaned "in favor of the West."[40] For evidence of such a tilt, Americans looked to the Congo, where India disregarded the preferences of many non-aligned nations and provided a five-thousand-man brigade to help implement the UN plan to stabilize the strife-torn country that had gained its independence in 1960. U.S. aircraft carried some of the Indian force into the Congo in early 1961, and the two nations coordinated their political and military activities.

The warming trend of 1961 signaled not the start of a new era, however, but the apex of a relationship that fell short of Kennedy's hopes. In retrospect, it is clear that American aspirations rested on illusions about Nehru's appetite for bold departures and his willingness to cooperate with Washington. For one thing, Americans failed to appreciate how worn out the seventy-one-year-old Nehru had become. The Indian leader's decline became especially evident in November 1961 during a state visit to Washington. U.S. officials expected that the meeting would affirm "converging trends" between the two nations.[41] Instead, Americans encountered a leader unwilling to make commitments of any kind. "I had the impression of an old man, his energies depleted, who heard things as at a great distance and answered most questions with indifference," recalled presidential aide Arthur Schlesinger Jr.[42]

Particularly annoying to Kennedy was Nehru's unresponsiveness about Indochina. Administration officials had hoped that India would bolster U.S. efforts with the prestige that it commanded as a leading non-aligned nation. More specifically, U.S. officials pressed Indian counterparts to use India's chairmanship of the International Control Commission (ICC)—the three-nation body set up in 1954 to monitor implementation of the Geneva peace agreements for Indochina—to help call attention to communist aggression in Laos and Vietnam. At the November 1961 summit with Kennedy, though, Nehru offered only "remote silence" when the subject arose, according to Schlesinger.[43] Indian ambivalence deepened in the months that followed. Far from using its influence, the Indian-led ICC virtually suspended its activities, failing to produce a single official report on conditions in Indochina over the next three years.[44]

Indian passivity stemmed from a basic reality that no amount of U.S. effort could alter. Much as Indian leaders welcomed U.S. aid, they saw no reason to shift closer to U.S. international priorities. For one thing, they wished to maintain constructive relations with the Soviet Union, whose long-standing friendship with India and support for statist models of development made it an attractive partner for New Delhi. In fact, heightened cooperation with the United States accentuated Indian leaders' determination to cultivate good relations with Moscow in order to balance the two superpowers against one another and keep open multiple channels of support. India's purchase of Soviet MiG jets in mid-1962, a stark counterpoint to the flow of American development assistance, made this approach clear.

Meanwhile, Nehru remained committed to the principles of non-alignment and anticolonialism that had shaped his nation's foreign policy since independence in 1947. Unquestionably, he championed a relatively moderate vision of Third World solidarity dedicated to a genuine third way separate from West and East, and U.S. leaders were gratified by his determination to oppose what he called "extremists"—advocates of revolutionary activism hostile to the West—when Third World governments gathered at Belgrade to establish a non-alignment movement in September 1961.[45] But Americans learned that moderation did not mean that India would embrace U.S. points of view. Indeed, growing anti-Western radicalism within the Third World movement created powerful incentives for India to bolster its non-aligned credentials by demonstrating independence. Under such pressures, the Indian government provoked American anger during the summer and fall of 1961 by criticizing U.S. nuclear testing and policy toward Berlin. Tensions soared higher when Nehru's forces suddenly seized Goa, a slice of India's west coast that had

FIGURE 2.2. Indian prime minister Jawaharlal Nehru addresses reporters just after arriving at Andrews Air Force Base outside Washington, D.C., on November 6, 1961. Nehru is surrounded by (left to right) John Kenneth Galbraith, the U.S. ambassador to India; State Department chief of protocol Angier Biddle Duke; Army general Lyman Lemnitzer, the chairman of the Joint Chiefs of Staff; B. K. Nehru, the Indian ambassador to the United States; Secretary of State Dean Rusk; Vice President Lyndon Johnson; and President John F. Kennedy. Abbie Rowe / John F. Kennedy Presidential Library.

remained under Portuguese control despite New Delhi's demands to put an end to the glaring vestige of colonialism. While Soviet and non-aligned leaders applauded India, U.S. officials lamented the seizure as a dangerous precedent that might encourage unilateralism elsewhere and an unwelcome affront to Portugal, a NATO ally of the United States.[46]

This string of disappointments stirred debate in Washington about whether the United States had bet too heavily on India and should lean back toward its long-standing ally, Pakistan. Pressure for change came partly from Congress, where critics of Kennedy's policy complained that U.S. generosity had produced little but Indian defiance and urged slashing U.S. aid by as much as 25 percent. Meanwhile, within the State Department, where attachment to the alliance with Pakistan ran strong, a sweeping study made the case for restoring balance in U.S. policy toward South Asia. While acknowledging that India's enormous weight in international affairs could "do more to help us or harm us than can Pakistan's," the report insisted that choosing between the two would be a "failure of policy," concluding simply, "We need both."[47]

Within the White House, however, champions of the administration's India policy resisted pressures for change. "If we must choose among these countries," wrote NSC aide Robert Komer, a strong proponent of engaging India and other non-aligned nations, "there is little question that India (because of its sheer size and resources) is where we must put our chief reliance." Komer dismissed Pakistan's obligation under the Southeast Asia Treaty Organization (SEATO) and the Central Treaty Organization (CENTO) as a "paper commitment," while heralding the geopolitical benefits of a "strong neutralist India" whose interests largely coincided with those of the United States.[48]

Komer's view seemed vindicated in the fall of 1962, when dramatic events along the Sino-Indian frontier appeared to demolish remaining obstacles to close U.S.-Indian collaboration. China and India had enjoyed a brief period of harmony in the mid-1950s, but Beijing's reversion to a confrontational foreign policy at the end of the decade ignited long-simmering tensions. With the U.S. and Soviet governments preoccupied by the Cuban Missile Crisis, Chinese forces launched attacks against disputed border areas on October 20, 1962, and overwhelmed Indian defenses. Moscow's grudging support for China, a byproduct of Soviet insecurity about losing its leadership of the international revolutionary movement, left India no alternative but to ask the United States for help. Komer welcomed the war as a "golden opportunity for a major gain in our relations with India."[49] All of Washington's goals suddenly seemed within reach. Chinese perfidy and Soviet complacency would drive India closer to the United States, leading New Delhi to relax its non-aligned commitments if not entertain some form of alliance with the West. Meanwhile, military aid would give the United States leverage over India that could be deployed to push Nehru into a settlement of the long-running dispute with Pakistan over Kashmir, a key irritant in Indian-Pakistani relations. In this way, the United States could keep both South Asian rivals within the Western fold.

American optimism soared as Indian leaders seemed to recognize the need for a fundamental rethinking of their nation's geopolitical position. Nehru hinted at the bankruptcy of past policies, telling his nation that India had been "living in an artificial atmosphere of our own creation."[50] He also gratified Washington by ousting Defense Minister Krishna Menon, his cabinet's most outspoken critic of the United States. With the Kennedy administration providing transport aircraft and supplies for ten Indian mountain divisions, the U.S. embassy in New Delhi became a scene of jubilation. Indians hanged Mao Zedong and Zhou Enlai in effigy.[51] A new round of Chinese attacks starting on November 14 drove India even further toward the United States. With Indian forces buckling in places and fears mounting of Chinese attacks on major cities, Nehru asked for a dozen squadrons of U.S. fighter jets and sophisticated radar equipment. Most remarkably, the Indian leader asked that Americans pilot the jets until Indians could be trained to take their places. Although the Chinese halted their advance before Kennedy could reply, this request for direct U.S. intervention on Indian territory marked a stunning departure from Nehru's cherished non-alignment.

American optimism dissipated in 1963, however, as U.S. leaders once again confronted the limits of their influence in South Asia. To be sure, U.S. emissary W. Averell Harriman, joining forces with British Commonwealth Relation Secretary Duncan Sandys, convinced Nehru to accept a new round of talks with Pakistani leader Mohammad Ayub Khan over the status of Kashmir, an Indian concession encouraged by $120 million in Anglo-American military aid to meet India's short-term needs. Both sides quickly advanced unreconcilable positions, however, and the talks ground to a halt. Ambassador Galbraith quipped that U.S. efforts had brought about rare agreement between India and Pakistan: "Both have joined in denouncing our proposals."[52] Meanwhile, Nehru's non-aligned principles proved dormant rather than dead. Once the crisis of fall 1962 had subsided, Nehru resumed constructive relations with Moscow and reasserted his independence from the West. It may be, as Walt Rostow insisted many years later, that much of the Indian foreign policy bureaucracy quietly leaned toward the United States after the 1962 war.[53] But Nehru's investment in non-alignment was too profound to permit any break in India's basic geopolitical disposition. Non-alignment, Nehru insisted in January 1963, was not only a "moral issue" but also crucial to the Indian people's sense of self-reliance and a key asset in India's efforts to play a peacemaking role in the Cold War.[54]

With India resisting U.S. pressure on Kashmir, Indochina, and other issues, American leaders confronted anew the question of whether to adjust their hopes. In practical terms, the dilemma boiled down to the size and ambition of U.S. military aid in the aftermath of the border war with China. A large, long-term package might deepen the U.S.-Indian partnership but would also do lasting damage to Washington's relationship with Pakistan, which staunchly opposed U.S. military support for India. The question thus amounted to a test of U.S. confidence in India's potential as the foundation of U.S. policy in South Asia. A meeting of the president and key advisers in April 1963 revealed deep divisions. Bowles, Kennedy's choice to replace Galbraith as ambassador, expressed sympathy for India and proposed $500 million in U.S. assistance over five years, the closest any U.S. official came to India's exorbitant $1.3 billion request. On the other side, Secretary of State Rusk and Secretary of Defense McNamara argued for a much smaller figure. For these men, the old U.S. alliance with Pakistan seemed the safer bet as returns on the investment in India seemed increasingly meager. McNamara worried in particular about continued American access to the U.S. airfield at Peshawar, a launching point for U-2 reconnaissance flights over the Soviet Union.[55]

The continued deterioration of U.S.-Indian relations intensified differences among U.S. officials. First, Nehru canceled an agreement allowing the United States to install a Voice of America transmitter in eastern India. Nehru then withdrew a request for U.S. funding of the Bokaro steel mill when it became clear that the Kennedy administration could not muster the necessary votes in Congress, where hostility to public-sector development projects ran high. Quick Soviet agreement to fund the project put a demoralizing cap on the whole affair and highlighted persistent Indian determination to avoid overreliance on the United States. As in the past, some Americans hoped U.S. aid would lure India away from the Soviet Union; for India, however, such aid made alternative sources even more desirable, not least because U.S. aid came with pressure—sometimes explicit, sometimes implied—to resolve tensions with Pakistan and to limit overall military spending. The Soviets delivered a few MiG jets to India in the spring of 1963 and, over the course of the year, advanced plans to help India develop the capacity to manufacture Soviet-designed jets, missiles, radar equipment, and other military gear.[56]

Did all this mean that Kennedy's oft-stated ambitions in India were dead? Bowles hoped not, reaffirming his support for a large arms package and chastising others in the administration for "devot[ing] the last few months almost entirely to the Pak problem."[57] Komer took a more measured view, recommending only that Americans set their sights "a little lower and more realistically" with respect to India and test the possibilities of gaining Indian concessions in return for substantial aid.[58] As usual, the Pentagon showed deep skepticism about India, reducing its arms proposal to just $50 million per annum over five years in order to minimize the impact on Pakistan.[59] Bowles wrote later there was "no doubt in my mind" that JFK was prepared to support a much higher number when he discussed the long-delayed assistance package with his aides, a conversation scheduled for November 26, 1963.[60] Komer was less certain but noted that JFK seemed "favorably impressed in principle" with Bowles's proposal for a five-year deal.[61] The decisive meeting never took place, however, making it impossible to know how Kennedy would have coped with growing bureaucratic divides. When these issues next arose for discussion, Lyndon Johnson occupied the Oval Office.

## "A Low Grade Chronic Fever"

Outwardly, the political situation in Iran bore little resemblance to faraway Brazil. While Brazilian leaders seemed to wobble away from the United States, Iran's undisputed leader, Mohammad Reza Shah Pahlavi, consistently declared his fealty to the Western camp. That stance was no surprise given that the shah had consolidated his rule in 1953 thanks to a British- and U.S.-backed coup that ousted his nationalist rival, Mohammad Mosaddegh. By the late 1950s, however, the shah ruled with such iron-fisted disregard for the grievances of his restive population that American leaders feared rebellion. Iran seemed poised to follow in Brazil's footsteps toward a dangerous destination: collapse of a pro-American political order under the weight of popular unrest and the rise of a new regime prone to non-alignment if not accommodation with the Soviet Union. As in the Brazilian case, the solution for Washington appeared to lie in promoting sociopolitical change necessary to anchor the nation in the Western camp over the long run. But precisely how should this be done? The Kennedy administration struggled throughout its years in office to find answers.

U.S. officials never wavered about Iran's importance in the Cold War. From Kennedy's first days in office, policymakers shared an apocalyptic vision of the consequences if Iran left the U.S. fold. "Loss" of Iran, noted the Joint Chiefs of Staff, would threaten U.S. access to Middle Eastern oil, "drive a wedge" between Western alliance networks in Europe and Southeast Asia, and destroy the Central Treaty Organization (CENTO), which Americans regarded as a pillar of U.S. security in southwestern Asia even though the United States did not fully belong.[62] For his part, Rostow worried that Iran's defection from the Western order might cause the whole U.S. effort to promote economic development to "crack up."[63] American military planners fretted that Iran was indefensible against a Soviet attack, much as a Soviet-controlled Mexico would be in the face of U.S. invasion.[64] But the far more realistic nightmare scenario for the West was the country's political and economic collapse. "Profound political and social change in one form or another is virtually inevitable," concluded an intelligence report in February 1961. Possibilities included everything from a coup by senior military officers to an uprising against the shah by nationalists whose vision of non-alignment and economic reform harkened back to Mosaddegh's rule a decade earlier. In any case, the report concluded, tensions had reached a point where it was "unlikely that this change will be evolutionary."[65]

So dire had the shah's position become that U.S. officials floated the possibility of backing a change of government in hopes of exerting influence as a new political order took shape. As recently as November 1958, the National

Security Council had concluded that the United States must cultivate ties with groups opposed to the regime, and the Kennedy administration deepened contacts after coming to office in 1961.[66] Although opinions differed, one State Department study contended that the nationalists were generally "neutralist along Indian lines" and were not strongly hostile to the United States.[67] The shah himself feared such a reorientation of U.S. policy and dispatched the chief of his security services, General Teimur Bakhtiar, to seek reassurance just after Kennedy's inauguration. In fact, the shah's anxiety was probably misplaced. Although the idea of abandoning the shah continued to percolate through U.S. policy discussions, administration officials generally concluded that the shah remained the best bet to maintain a pro-American political order in Iran and, if pushed to embrace political and economic reforms, could yet put his country on the road to enduring stability in partnership with the West.

American leaders did not relish the task of convincing the shah to play his part in such a transformation. Kennedy administration officials, like those who served President Eisenhower in previous years, viewed Mohammad Reza Shah Pahlavi as an unpredictable, neurotic, and craven autocrat whose occasional promises of reform came to nothing. A blunt CIA report written in 1958 noted the persistence of "near feudal economic and social conditions" created in part by the royal family's "predatory economic activities," indulgence of "flagrant corruption," and tolerance of wild economic inequities that left just 2 percent of the country's land in the hands of the peasants who worked it.[68] Even as his popularity declined over the ensuing years, he showed little interest in addressing his country's economic conditions. By contrast, complained the State Department in 1961, he was "almost obsessed" with increasing the size and sophistication of his military, which he viewed as "a tool of personal power" that ensured his rule and Iran's international stature.[69]

The key question that divided American officials was how much pressure to apply on the shah to undertake the reforms necessary to head off a political explosion.[70] On one side stood risk-averse State Department officials who consistently expressed caution about pushing the shah too hard. For one thing, insisted officials in the Bureau of Near Eastern and South Asian Affairs, "reform" was no easy matter. Corruption was "a part of Iranian culture" that could not easily be stamped out, while free elections were bound to create a parliament (Majles) so starkly divided between traditional elites and clergy on the one side and urban nationalists on the other as to raise the specter of civil war. At the same time, the bureau added, proposals to lean on the shah erred in assuming that the Iranian leader was "a creature of the United States and the United Kingdom" when, in fact, his geopolitical loyalties remained unpredictable. The shah was an "emotionally insecure" man liable to interpret pressure for reform as a threat to his control so dangerous that he might swing suddenly toward neutralism or even the Soviet Union. The riskiest course of all seemed to lie in exerting pressure to divert resources from the military to the civilian realm. "To ask the Shah to de-emphasize the military element in the Iranian Government would be to attack his most sensitive personal quirk, and would completely dishearten him," asserted the bureau in February 1961.[71]

On the other side of the debate were officials who advocated a more confrontational approach. This view rapidly gained strength in the spring of 1961. Amid worsening social unrest in Iran, journalist Walter Lippmann reported an interview with Nikita Khrushchev in which the Soviet leader spoke confidently about Iran's revolutionary potential. Then, in early May, tens of thousands of Iranian teachers took to the streets to demand improved working conditions, triggering a violent crackdown that left one Iranian dead and two badly injured. With the pro-Mosaddegh National Front threatening a nationwide strike, the shah dismissed his cabinet and named Ali Amini, a onetime member of the National Front, as prime minister in a new government. This appointment represented a concession to Washington's desire for a new political tone in Tehran. Over the following fourteen months, Amini, in the face of opposition from both the National Front to his left and entrenched political and religious elites to his right, initiated programs to promote economic austerity, redistribute land, and fight corruption. But the shah was mistaken if he believed these steps would relieve U.S. pressure. In fact, the political crisis and Amini's appointment—easily understood as a desperation move—focused attention on the shah's drawbacks and emboldened U.S. officials critical of his rule. Prominent members of Congress lambasted the shah and questioned the scale of U.S. aid. "There is a limit to the amount of money that this country can give to those people who are unwilling to do what they ought to do," declared Democratic senator Hubert Humphrey of Minnesota.[72]

In the White House, the National Security Council assembled an interdepartmental task force to consider options. Although State Department officials served in prominent roles, the task force brought together an array of opinions and injected new vigor in U.S. policymaking. Undersecretary of State Chester Bowles welcomed Amini's appointment but also, in contrast to the Near Eastern bureau, insisted that U.S. ambassador Julius Holmes take a more confrontational tone by conveying "home truths" to the shah about the need for economic and political reforms.[73] NSC aide Robert Komer concurred, complaining that the State Department bureaucracy had "perennially been reluctant to press the shah very hard, with the result that not much has been accomplished." Now the United States needed to use every carrot and stick to ensure the success of the Amini "experiment," which he described as possibly the "last good chance of forestalling Iran's slippery slide into chaos." Komer urged that the United States end its practice of paying "military baksheesh"—a Persian term connoting bribery—to the shah and channel funds instead toward economic reforms that the task force judged necessary to head off a political revolution. Most strikingly, Komer recommended to JFK that continued U.S. aid of any sort must be "conditional on prompt and effective Iranian action to carry out these and related measures to resolve Iran's basic political and economic problems."[74]

In practice, neither side of the debate carried the day. To be sure, from mid-1961 until Amini's ouster in July 1962, U.S. officials consistently emphasized the need to divert Iran's resources from military to civilian purposes. The shah resented U.S. pressure and, a few years later, called 1961 and 1962 the "worst period" of U.S. interference in his country. Kennedy's policies, he charged, amounted to "more or less an American coup directed against him," orchestrated by eggheaded idealists whom the shah dismissed as "Harvard men."[75] Yet Washington continued to send vast military assistance—$60.7 million in 1963, down just 25 percent from levels at the end of the Eisenhower presidency and only a little below aid for SEATO ally Pakistan[76]—and to demonstrate understanding of the shah's anxieties about threats he perceived from the Soviet Union as well as Arab nationalists across the border in Iraq. Amid mixed signals from Washington, the shah and Amini, bound together in awkward embrace, kept the regime afloat and, for a time, seemed to tamp down the most urgent threats. All in all, Iran resembled an "individual who was consistently subject to a low grade chronic fever," as Assistant Secretary of State Lewis Jones put it in spring 1961. "Each time you took a new look at the patient there was no clear evidence of a crisis but sometimes the temperature was down a little, sometimes it was up a little."[77]

Predictably, many State Department officials, including most conspicuously Ambassador Holmes, expressed optimism about the flow of events in Iran and counseled against new pressure. Acknowledging that he might be criticized as a defender of the status quo, Holmes advised his superiors in Washington that Amini was making good progress despite huge obstacles. Among the latter, he wrote in August, were not only monumental economic and social problems visible to Washington but also limitations peculiar to Iranian culture. "I need not dwell," Holmes advised, "on those aspects of their character which make it so hard for Iranians to work together, to plan for the future, and to take drastic action when drastic action is necessary." On the whole, Holmes wrote, Amini was proceeding with "determination and courage and a good deal of skill," helping make it "inevitable" that the middle class would eventually take control of the country.[78] Holmes cautioned against stringent cuts in military assistance and urged that Washington accede to the shah's desire for a face-to-face meeting with JFK.[79]

Other officials doubted that Iran was achieving any meaningful progress and worried that the United States remained too dependent on the shah. As usual, Komer made the case most forcefully. Noting worsening economic trends, the NSC aide warned Kennedy that the "continued slide toward chaos in Iran could result in as great a setback as in South Vietnam"—hardly reassuring words at the moment of growing crisis in Southeast Asia.[80] Most troubling to Kenneth Hansen, assistant director of the Bureau of the Budget, was growing wariness in Washington about leaning on the shah for fear that he might abdicate or abandon his partnership with the United States if pressure grew too strong. Such anxiety, complained Hansen, a leading participant in policymaking toward Iran, risked subordinating the obvious need for bold reforms to "the previous preoccupation with the dangers of displeasing the Shah."[81] So dire was Iran's situation by early 1962 that Attorney General Robert F. Kennedy, whose taste for regime change far exceeded that of his brother, mused about an "inspired revolution"—a U.S.-backed coup—to bring new leaders to power.[82] Komer and Hansen, however, saw no good alternative to redoubled efforts to get the State Department to lean on Tehran more forcefully ("butting our heads against the stonewall of State," Komer despaired) and tying U.S. aid more explicitly to specific economic reforms and reduction in the size of the Iranian army.[83] To apply "all the pressure and persuasion we can muster," Hansen suggested appointing a new ambassador to Tehran in place of the annoyingly pro-shah Holmes and proposed several outspoken globalists—Chester Bowles, Arthur Schlesinger Jr., and John Kenneth Galbraith among them—with close ties to the president.[84]

Little was resolved during the shah's state visit to Washington in April 1962. JFK publicly praised the shah as "the keystone to the arch in Iran," a leader without whom "Iran and then the whole Middle East would crumble."[85] For his part, the shah spoke in terms calibrated to the administration's broader approach to the Third World. Iran was determined to pursue "positive nationalism," declared the shah, contrasting his constructive approach to the West with the "hatred" underpinning nationalism in Africa, a reference to the vociferous anticolonialism of the shah's bitter rival in the Middle East, Egyptian leader Gamal Abdel Nasser.[86] Yet tension bubbled just under the surface. The shah repeatedly pressed for military assistance necessary to transform Iran into a "showcase" that would enable other countries to see "that it is possible to work with the West." The president, meanwhile, stressed the need to focus on economic challenges and pointed to budgetary limitations making it impossible to turn Iran into any kind of "showcase."[87] Secretary of Defense McNamara presented a blueprint for U.S. military aid over the following five years, but the shah—"piqued" because he had not been involved in drafting the plan,

U.S. interlocutors surmised—left Washington without indicating whether he would accept it.[88]

Any goodwill generated by the summit dissipated amid renewed upheaval in Tehran. Exhausted by his exertions over the previous year, Amini confronted yawning budget deficits that imperiled his reform plans. But Amini's bigger problem was the shah's anxiety about his prime minister's popularity. Fearing a challenge to his own stature, the shah replaced Amini in July 1962 with the more pliable Asadollah Alam. Although Alam's appointment suggested a swing away from Amini's ambitious reforms, it became clear over the following months that the shah intended not to abandon Amini's agenda but to co-opt the reform program for his own purposes. In January 1963, the shah announced a sweeping array of initiatives that he labeled the White Revolution and declared his intention to hold a referendum to secure popular backing for the effort. Announcing his dedication to economic modernization and social progress, the shah unveiled six major programs focused on land distribution, nationalization of forests and grazing lands, sale of state-owned factories, profit sharing for urban workers, literacy promotion, and enfranchisement of women.[89]

The shah's proposals, apparently rooted in the belief that his long-term prospects would be ensured best by cultivating the nation's peasantry as well as the urban middle class, inspired enthusiasm among U.S. officials predisposed to view him sympathetically. Gratian Yatsevitch, the Ukrainian-born CIA station chief in Tehran, offered a favorable assessment of the shah's motives, noting the Iranian leader's sensitivity to conditions in the Iranian countryside.[90] Meanwhile, the State Department praised the shah for initiating "fundamental and irreversible change" that would tear down Iran's outmoded social order and confer a new status as "savior and hero" of the peasantry.[91] At last, the monarch seemed to be reckoning seriously with the living conditions endured by the vast majority of his people, even at the cost of alienating traditional elites. Secretary of State Rusk took this view to the president in April 1963. Drawing selectively on intelligence reports that noted the shah's growing popularity, Rusk predicted that, barring assassination, he would remain in power indefinitely and continue his alliance with the United States. Rusk advised that the United States should back the shah's efforts politically and materially, including by expanding development assistance.[92]

Predictably, others cast doubt on almost everything that Rusk had to say. In this view, the shah's sudden embrace of reform was merely a ploy to tighten his own control by heightening his appeal in the countryside. Dangers abounded, not least the risk that the monarchy's traditional sources of support—landowners and the clergy—might sour on the shah, warned

William R. Polk, a Kennedy appointee to the Policy Planning Council who bucked the general trend of thinking within the State Department.[93] In any case, CIA analysts observed, the shah's activism would make him "the single focal point" of criticism and therefore more vulnerable to overthrow.[94] In Komer's view, the stability achieved in the second half of 1962 was just a "lull before the storm" for a country that remained "as serious a crisis area as any we confront." So dangerous was the situation that Komer revived the possibility of throwing U.S. support behind the nationalists or another alternative leadership and, while conceding that such a course was "not yet" realistic, urged that the United States "keep actively looking." For the time being, the best Washington could do was, as usual, to back the existing regime while "simultaneously mak[ing] every effort to enhance its effectiveness by actively pushing, prodding, and cajoling it in directions we favor."[95] Komer reserved his sharpest vitriol for Rusk, blasting the secretary of state for failing even to mention economic reform during a recent meeting with the shah.[96] Little changed in Komer's outlook as the shah forged ahead with the White Revolution. Endorsing proposals from the Bureau of the Budget to apply more pressure, Komer urged that the entire U.S. bureaucracy "push hard to get our ideas across" to the Iranian government on budgetary priorities, political reform, and military restraint.[97]

Differences among U.S. officials intensified in 1963 amid evidence that the White Revolution had done little to quell social tensions. In June, demonstrations and street riots erupted across the country, a powerful display of hostility to the shah instigated by religious leaders including a charismatic Shia cleric later known in the West as the Ayatollah Khomeini. The shah's forces responded by brutally suppressing the demonstrators, killing hundreds. Some U.S. officials drew the lesson that the United States must help Iran improve its repressive apparatus. U.S. military planners recommended expedited help to train and equip Iranian security forces, while U.S. embassy officials in Tehran counseled quicker resort to force in the future. "It was a mistake to delay the use of weapons by the troops on the first day," noted Deputy Chief of Mission Stuart W. Rockwell, who added, "This mistake will not be repeated on future occasions."[98] Indeed, Ambassador Holmes and the Joint Chiefs of Staff credited U.S. military cooperation for the general improvement in Iran's internal security and welcomed the presence of U.S. aircraft carriers in the Persian Gulf as an additional assurance for the shah.[99] The State Department, meanwhile, entertained proposals to squelch anti-shah opinion in the United States by deporting outspoken Iranian students who backed the National Front.[100]

Other officials thought differently in the waning weeks of the Kennedy administration. At a meeting of key decision makers on October 17, even Vice

President Johnson, generally sympathetic to the shah, worried about Washington's "heavy reliance" on his leadership. From the Policy Planning Council came a discordant report bitingly critical of Ambassador Holmes and other diplomats who wanted to be "left alone" by Washington. Far from stabilizing the situation in Iran, insisted the report's author, William R. Polk, the shah had become dependent on an ever-narrower segment of the Iranian elite. If he were assassinated, in fact, political order would totally disintegrate and the United States would have virtually no leverage in the country. Polk recommended a thorough policy review carefully managed to avoid provoking the embassy in Tehran.[101] Komer was less concerned about antagonizing the State Department and hoped JFK and Holmes could meet face to face sometime in December 1963.[102] More importantly, Komer concurred on the urgency of a major review of policy throughout the Middle East, where, he noted, the need to bolster short-term stability conflicted with the necessity of facilitating long-term change. The United States, Komer noted ten days after Kennedy's death, was "in for a time of trouble throughout the Middle East." Even if his prediction was "half right," Komer added, "President Johnson will be faced with a series of tough policy problems . . . at a time when he'd prefer tranquility—if not a few successes—as the 1964 elections draw near."[103]

## "On a Silver Platter for the Bloc"

Southeast Asia posed as many dilemmas as any part of the world for the Kennedy administration, whose decision making toward Laos and Vietnam has drawn massive scholarly interest. But another nation—Indonesia—ranked alongside those territories as a focal point of the administration's concern. The problem was hardly new when JFK took office. U.S. leaders had struggled—and mostly failed—to woo or coerce Indonesia into a cooperative relationship ever since it had gained independence from the Netherlands in 1949. Like Nehru in India, Indonesian president Sukarno vigorously espoused nonalignment and a brand of anticolonialism that ruled out close cooperation with the West. Far more than Nehru, though, Sukarno leaned toward the communist powers, becoming the largest recipient of their assistance outside the Eastern bloc. Meanwhile, he tolerated a huge communist party that composed the single biggest political movement in his nation. So dangerous had the situation become by 1961, warned the U.S. ambassador to Jakarta on JFK's fifth day in office, that Indonesia stood on the brink of "falling under Communist control."[104] It was a frightful prospect for the whole Kennedy team, which readily agreed on Indonesia's vital importance to U.S. economic, political, and military objectives throughout Asia. The country not only possessed the world's fifth largest population and massive natural resources but also commanded shipping lanes between the Pacific and Indian oceans and wielded influence throughout the Afro-Asian world.

The question for U.S. policymakers during the Kennedy years was how to cope with a leader who consistently antagonized Washington but enjoyed broad support in his own country. The issue inspired vigorous disagreement within the administration, exposing conflicting outlooks as clearly as any problem in the Third World. In the administration's first year and a half, debate centered on how to handle Sukarno's insistence on absorbing the western half of the island of New Guinea, also known as West Irian, into his nation. The status of that obscure territory, populated mostly by indigenous Papuans, had provoked controversy since 1949, when the Netherlands retained colonial control even as it granted independence to the rest of Indonesia. But the problem surged anew in 1961, at least partly on the strength of Sukarno's calculation that JFK's sympathy for Third World nations might lead Washington to back Indonesian demands.[105] The territory, which one U.S. diplomat dismissed as a "a conglomeration of mountains and swamp land half a world away," carried little tangible value to either Indonesia or the Netherlands.[106] But the prestige of both nations was heavily engaged, and a war pitting a close U.S. ally and a vital Third World nation threatened as Kennedy settled into office. Fighting promised not only to confront the administration with an impossible choice between its NATO commitments and its assurances of sympathy for Third World nationalism but also to stoke a new crisis in Southeast Asia at a time when Washington faced insoluble problems in Laos and Vietnam.

U.S. officials agreed that Dutch colonialism must be ended, but they differed about how to accomplish that goal. On the one hand, the United States could promote an international trusteeship that would set West Irian on a path to eventual self-determination. That solution catered to Dutch sensitivities by denying Indonesian control. Alternatively, the United States could work toward absorption of the territory into Indonesia. Secretary of State Dean Rusk consistently championed the former view, as did the State Department's European branch and other advocates of strong-point thinking who prioritized U.S. relations with a NATO ally. This view had roots stretching back to the Second World War, when many American policymakers had become accustomed to viewing nationalist challenges in Southeast Asia as dangerous threats to the interests of European nations on whose cooperation U.S. security would depend in the postwar era. By 1961, Dutch leaders seemed open to relinquishing colonial control over West Irian but hardly enthusiastic about transferring the territory to Indonesia, a humiliation the Hague had bitterly resisted for a dozen years. A trusteeship would, in the words of Rusk, permit the Dutch to "retire gracefully."[107] The CIA's deputy director of plans, Richard Bissell, came to a similar conclusion. Indonesian absorption of West Irian, wrote Bissell, would only embolden Sukarno to throw his weight around in the region and to deepen his ties to the Soviet Union.[108]

On the other side stood key National Security Council aides, including Robert Komer; the U.S. ambassador in Jakarta, Howard P. Jones, a Kennedy appointee who shared little in common with Julian Holmes in Tehran; and Washington-based policymakers in the State Department's Far Eastern division. These officials expressed frequent exasperation with Sukarno but consistently held that U.S. interests lay on the side of accommodating Indonesia. For one thing, Komer argued, the United States could not stop Sukarno from getting his way through military action. But he insisted as well that Washington had a "positive interest" in convincing Sukarno that the United States was not hostile to an objective so close to his heart. Resistance would only drive the Indonesian leader closer to the communist bloc, whereas cooperation would give him an incentive to find a formula for transferring sovereignty that would allow the Dutch to save face. Komer and other advocates of a pro-Indonesian position asserted that Sukarno was not irretrievably lost to the communist bloc and, with the right mix of political support and material aid, might still be pulled back from the brink. In the best case, argued Komer, concessions would open a "new chapter" in U.S. relations with Sukarno. At a minimum, catering to his desires would enable the United States to mount a "holding operation" to keep him away from the communist bloc long enough for the Indonesian army or other pro-Western elements to assert themselves.[109]

Debate between these two points of view ran hot and cold across 1961 and much of 1962 as Dutch-Indonesian tensions mounted and small-scale military posturing threatened to grow into major fighting.[110] Rusk and other champions of trusteeship showed sympathy for Dutch sensitivities, while their bureaucratic opponents chastised them for counterproductive ideas that would only fuel communist influence and drive Sukarno into China's hands. In early December 1961, National Security Adviser McGeorge Bundy took his concerns directly to the president, asserting that Rusk's "dislike of Sukarno" fed into policy proposals that, if implemented, "can only help the Communists" while weakening Indonesian moderates who were Washington's best hope over the long term.[111] In a remarkable indication of how bitter the internecine feud had become by that point, Komer overtly welcomed the UN General Assembly's rejection of a State Department–backed proposal aimed at advancing the trusteeship idea. "We've just been saved from the worst consequences of our recent attempt to walk down the middle," wrote Komer. "Inevitably West Irian will go sooner or later to Indonesia," he insisted. "The only question is will it go with our help, and in such a way that we get some credit for it, or will this issue be left on a silver platter for the Bloc?"[112]

FIGURE 2.3. President John F. Kennedy and Indonesian leader Sukarno ride together during arrival ceremonies at Andrews Air Force Base outside Washington, D.C., on April 24, 1961. Ensuing meetings failed to resolve the growing controversy over the status of Western New Guinea (West Irian). Abbie Rowe / John F. Kennedy Presidential Library.

So contentious did the issue become in the middle of 1961 that NSC aide Robert H. Johnson feared the policymaking process had bogged down in a hopeless muddle that yielded no clear alternatives for the president. Within the State Department alone, Johnson complained, differences had become "so considerable that any paper produced by the normal coordination process is likely to be quite lacking in clarity of purpose or direction of action."[113] With the benefits of hindsight, historian Robert Rakove imposes order on the tangled deliberations that played out within the U.S. bureaucracy, suggesting that policymaking passed through four phases from early 1961 to mid-1962 as the balance of influence shifted from one side to the other.[114] In any case, a key juncture in the debate arrived in fall 1961, when Rusk's failure to win UN support for an internationalization scheme sparked new efforts by proponents of Indonesian control. "It is the feeling of all of us on your staff that the Western world has got to consider this problem somewhat less in terms of the pure diplomacy of West Irian and more in terms of a common interest in frustrating communism in Indonesia," Deputy National Security Adviser Rostow wrote to the president on November 30 in a thinly veiled critique of Rusk.[115]

Such appeals led Kennedy to focus on the issue as never before and to tilt toward his NSC team. To blunt Rusk's initiatives, JFK appointed W. Averell Harriman, a veteran diplomat known to sympathize with the desires of Third World nationalists, as assistant secretary of state for Far Eastern affairs.[116] Next, as Sukarno engaged in a new round of saber-rattling, Kennedy made clear to British prime minister Harold Macmillan that the Dutch could expect no support from the United States if war broke out over West Irian. Finally, Kennedy dispatched his brother Robert to Jakarta in February 1962 to bolster relations with Indonesia. The attorney general played to Indonesian sensitivities, telling one audience that Sukarno was "the first of the new young leaders" transforming the world. "Today," RFK proclaimed, "President Kennedy follows in that tradition."[117] In private, RFK gratified Sukarno by telling him that Washington was prepared to take an active role in facilitating negotiations between Indonesia and the Netherlands. Underlying all this movement was a clear-eyed calculation that Kennedy bluntly communicated to Dutch prime minister Joseph Luns in early March 1962. Although the United States had "no confidence" in Sukarno, said JFK, pushing him into a war over West Irian would drive Indonesia into the communist bloc. "This would be a disaster for the free world position in Asia and would force us out of Viet Nam," Kennedy declared.[118]

Direct U.S. involvement in negotiations between the Dutch and Indonesian governments began in March 1962 and played a decisive role in bringing about a settlement five months later. The negotiating process was rocky throughout, not only because of hostility between the two contending governments but also due to simmering disagreements among U.S. officials. Komer consistently complained that the State Department refused to apply necessary pressure on the Netherlands, leading to a "wavering and inconsistent" U.S. position that encouraged Dutch foot-dragging.[119] On August 15, however, Indonesian and Dutch negotiators reached agreement on a formula crafted earlier in the year by U.S. mediator Ellsworth Bunker. The deal called for the Netherlands to cede control to a UN-organized "temporary executive authority" on October 1. Indonesia would assume control on May 1, 1963, when Indonesian officials would start replacing UN personnel. Although the agreement called for a plebiscite no later than 1969 to enable the Papuan population to express its desires, it required little imagination to see that provision as a face-saving gesture to soothe Dutch sensitivities about abandoning the Papuans. Indonesia would obviously control what diplomats vaguely called a "self-determination exercise" and had no obligation to respect the outcome in any case.[120]

The resolution of the West Irian problem emboldened officials sympathetic to Sukarno to try to build on the accomplishment by opening new channels of cooperation with Jakarta. "Capital of the sort we've gained is a transitory asset to be used while it's still good," Komer wrote to the president on the day the West Irian deal was signed. "Having invested so much in maneuvering a [West Irian] settlement for the express purpose of giving us leverage in this competition, we'd be foolish not to follow through."[121] Above all, officials aimed to expand U.S. aid for Indonesia in order to demonstrate the value of strong ties to the West but also to help resolve the monumental economic problems widely assumed to invite communist influence. From Jakarta, Ambassador Jones optimistically noted that the West Irian settlement reduced the Indonesian government's eagerness for Soviet help and sparked new interest in American assistance. But he warned that a "sharp turn to the left" was possible if the United States did not act to affirm the trend. Although U.S. observers continued to view Sukarno as an unpredictable leader susceptible to radical influences, they pinned their hopes on a growing cohort of Western-trained military officers, bureaucrats, professionals, and businessmen that, in Jones's words, "gives us all confidence in the long run."[122]

Shards of evidence suggest that the CIA explored the possibility of assassinating Sukarno. The scheme progressed as far as identifying a potential assassin "who it was felt might be recruited for this purpose," CIA deputy director of plans Richard Bissell remembered later.[123] But Kennedy did not authorize any such scheme and, on the contrary, banked on increased U.S. aid to keep Indonesia out of communist hands and strengthen pro-Western elements over the longer term. In pursuit of a "new and better relationship," Kennedy approved National Security Action Memorandum 179, an appeal to all federal agencies to consider new aid initiatives.[124] A long list of proposals was ready by mid-October 1962. The Joint Chiefs of Staff urged expanded aid to the Indonesian military in order to diminish Jakarta's reliance on the Soviet bloc, embolden anticommunist elements of Indonesia's officer corps, and intensify "civic action" initiatives giving the military a key role in rural modernization projects. The Pentagon also proposed to expand the number of Indonesian officers enrolled in U.S. military training institutions, a program that U.S. leaders believed had paid dividends in earlier years.[125] Outside the military realm, various agencies recommended development assistance totaling up to $62 million in grants and $110 million loans over a three- to five-year period, as well as immediate deliveries of food and grants to fund purchases of desperately needed spare parts and raw materials. American officials also agreed that Indonesia must accept a program of budgetary austerity and monetary reform to be drafted by the International Monetary Fund.[126]

In late 1962 and early 1963, Americans saw reason for optimism. With the resolution of the West Irian problem, Sukarno spoke publicly of his desire to focus on his nation's economic woes. He even surprised Washington by accepting, at least in principle, the need for an IMF-crafted stabilization plan, a gesture that opened the way for discussions between U.S. officials and a cluster of Western-trained economists in the Indonesian government. Americans understood the pain that such a plan, entailing cuts to state subsidies for basic consumption, might cause in Indonesia and sought to avoid pressing the matter too hard.[127] Still, Komer exulted in July 1963, the new U.S. approach to Indonesia was "gathering speed in the right direction, if we can only stick it out."[128] To keep things moving, Washington dangled the possibility that President Kennedy might repay Sukarno's 1961 visit to the United States by meeting with Sukarno in Jakarta in 1964.

The warming trend petered out, however, in the final months of Kennedy's presidency, and old dilemmas returned with a vengeance. For one thing, Congress balked at the administration's plans for Indonesia. Members of both parties had consistently criticized Kennedy's desire to assist non-aligned nations uncooperative with American priorities and managed to slash the 1963 aid budget by 20 percent. Indonesia became a particular sore point during and after the West Irian negotiations, which Kennedy's opponents regarded as appeasement of a hostile nation at the expense of a NATO ally. Senator Richard Russell, the powerful Democratic chairman of the Senate Armed Services Committee, spoke for many when he blasted Sukarno as a "tin dictator" whose professions of neutralism masked an "open affection for Communism and the world-wide Communist movement."[129] The administration's desire to expand American aid after the settlement stirred fresh outcries in Congress and heightened concern in the White House about the dangers of pressing too far, too fast.

Just as troubling for the administration were new signs of Indonesian hostility to Western interests, painful reminders that Sukarno could bend only so far toward the West without alienating the communist party that sustained his rule. Indonesia's coziness with the communist bloc became clear in early spring 1963, when Soviet defense minister Rodion Malinovsky and Chinese Communist Party chairman Liu Shaoqi paid high-profile visits to Jakarta. Around the same time, negotiations between the Indonesian government and American oil companies over the terms of foreign involvement in the nation's vast oil industry broke down rancorously. Although those talks concluded successfully in June 1963, the dispute inflamed opinion in Congress and soured U.S.-Indonesian relations by leading Washington to deploy its economic aid as leverage to promote the interests of American companies.[130]

Most damagingly of all, Sukarno provoked a new regional crisis in the fall of 1963 by refusing to accept the British government's momentous decision to fuse its Southeast Asian colonies into a new nation, Malaysia, on Indonesia's western doorstep. Americans sympathized with their British ally, which aimed to reduce its commitments in Southeast Asia by creating a robust multiethnic nation. But Sukarno, after initially waffling on the British plan, strongly opposed establishment of Malaysia, which he castigated as a vestige of Western colonialism and an affront to Indonesian leadership in the region. With diplomatic hostility threatening to break into armed conflict, the United States was once again torn between loyalty to an ally and determination to cultivate cooperation with a pivotal emerging nation.[131]

As crisis mounted in the first half of 1963, the Kennedy administration hoped to prevent the issue from jeopardizing the aid plan on which its ambitions in Indonesia now hung. The United States followed through with much of its proposed assistance for Indonesia's military and police forces, making the country the second largest recipient of U.S. "public safety" assistance in the world.[132] The Kennedy administration also delivered food aid and emergency loans to cover purchases of raw materials and industrial spare parts. But Washington's dilemma became immeasurably more difficult in September, when Indonesia responded to the official proclamation of Malaysian independence by unleashing mobs to attack the British embassy in Jakarta and stepping up guerrilla activity in Sabah and Sarawak, Malaysian territories abutting Indonesia. Meanwhile, the Indonesian leader lashed out at the United States, complaining on November 4 that the CIA was actively attempting to overthrow him.[133]

Ambassador Jones denied that allegation, but there could be little doubt that U.S.-Indonesian relations, so carefully nurtured over the previous two years, were plummeting toward a new low. Exasperated administration officials saw no choice but to suspend most ongoing aid programs and to halt consideration of a large U.S. loan to support the IMF stabilization program.[134] Ambassador Jones hoped that Washington and Jakarta could get their relationship back on track and used an Oval Office meeting with Kennedy on November 19—just four days before JFK's assassination—to argue for a "package deal" exchanging resumption of aid and a presidential visit to Indonesia for Sukarno's agreement to negotiate a peaceful solution to the crisis over Malaysia.[135] The fate of those ideas remained uncertain, however, when the president set out for Dallas.

## "A Sea of Developing Hate"

Kennedy's challenges in India, Brazil, Iran, and Indonesia broadly resembled problems that had bedeviled his predecessors. Even if some officials hoped to go in new directions, the basic options were familiar. Sub-Saharan Africa was different—a remoter region that had drawn little sustained attention from Washington. For years, Washington had managed its interests in the region mostly via its relationships with the colonial metropoles that had dominated the region since the nineteenth century. As late as 1958, the United States stationed more diplomats in West Germany than in all of Africa.[136] By the dawn of the 1960s, however, a new era was at hand. The combination of nationalist agitation, European weakness, and rapidly intensifying global intolerance of colonialism brought nationhood within reach for numerous territories. Starting with Ghana's independence from Britain in 1957, nineteen sub-Saharan nations came into existence by the time JFK assumed the presidency, most of them during the landmark year of 1960; another seventeen followed over the remainder of the decade.

For Kennedy, this transformation brought good news and bad. Independence validated the administration's oft-expressed certainty that the world was passing through momentous change inspired by a universal quest for justice that Americans believed to be consistent with their own nation's purposes. Yet the birth of so many unpredictable new countries, most with valid historical reasons for hostility to the West, also seemed to open a huge new arena for communist advances. The continent was, in fact, "probably the greatest open field of maneuver in the world-wide competition between the [Soviet] Bloc and the non-Communist world," observed one State Department study in 1962.[137] This blend of opportunity and risk fired the administration's enthusiasm for innovation.

To be sure, Kennedy's interest in Africa was always "marginal" compared to other international preoccupations, as one of his diplomats observed later.[138] But, relative to the attention that the continent had previously received, Kennedy displayed notable concern. Aiming to show sensitivity for the non-aligned tendencies of the new nations while steering them down paths of political moderation, the administration expanded U.S. aid programs and dispatched capable ambassadors who projected sympathy for the countries to which they were accredited.[139] To run the State Department's Africa office, a job JFK described as "second to none" in importance for his administration, the president appointed former Michigan governor G. Mennen "Soapy" Williams, a prominent liberal aligned with the surging civil rights movement within the United States.[140] Kennedy also demonstrated his interest in the continent by receiving a steady stream of African leaders at the White House, gestures of good will that yielded affection for Kennedy lasting well beyond his death. JFK received eleven African heads of state in 1961, ten in 1962, and seven in 1963.[141]

Most revealing of the administration's approach to the region was, however, its response to acute policy dilemmas. The most alarming of these concerned the Congo, where Belgium's concession of independence on June 30, 1960, brought chaos and uncertainty. The province of Katanga, epicenter of the Congo's copious mineral deposits, declared its intention to secede from the nation and curried favor with European industries that stood to gain from privileged relations with the breakaway region. Meanwhile, Belgium airlifted troops into the country to protect the white minority from the African population. The Congo's new leaders demanded intervention by the United Nations to evict the Europeans but also feuded among themselves. For anxious U.S. officials, a nightmare scenario appeared to be unfolding: as sources of authority crumbled, the Soviet Union seemed poised to capitalize, especially after the unpredictable new premier, Patrice Lumumba, accepted Soviet military aid and advisers. By the time JFK became president, U.S. leaders feared that the Congo, with its huge territory and massive natural resources, was teetering on the brink of falling into the communist camp.

How could the United States demonstrate its support for Congolese nationalism while keeping the nation within the Western fold? The question provided what one member of the incoming national security team, Roger Hilsman, would later call "the Kennedy administration's first sustained test."[142] Secretary of State Rusk urged members of a task force assembled to study the problem to "take the ceiling off your imaginations," and in short order the bureaucracy offered an array of possibilities.[143] The U.S. ambassador to the United Nations, Adlai Stevenson, backed proposals by UN Secretary-General Dag Hammarskjöld to encourage formation of a coalition government and to give multinational peacekeeping troops authority to suppress factional fighting. The idea amounted to a striking vote of confidence in the United Nations and Afro-Asian nations, especially India, that contributed soldiers to the UN force. Meanwhile, the CIA cultivated the pro-Western Army chief of staff Joseph Mobutu as the next leader of the Congo and welcomed the assassination of Lumumba, an act carried out by Lumumba's Congolese adversaries on January 17, though news did not reach Washington for almost a month.[144] Other U.S. policymakers including George Ball, a prototypical advocate of strong-point thinking who played a leading role in the crisis, took more nuanced positions, often backing a role for the United Nations but only on the condition that European nations with strong economic stakes go along with any scheme to reestablish order.

During Kennedy's years in office, these approaches ebbed and flowed as Washington struggled to establish a unified Congo aligned with the West. The administration consistently worked with the United Nations, throwing its weight behind various UN efforts to broker peace and providing logistical support for the multinational force working to hold the nation together under moderate leadership. On more than one occasion, JFK and his aides even entertained the possibility of sending U.S. troops to strengthen the UN contingent, though JFK also fired the U.S. ambassador to the Congo in 1961 for making too assertive use of a U.S. Navy task force. At the same time, the administration took heavy account of European interests, repeatedly adjusting U.S. cooperation with the United Nations in order to minimize discord with allies. Even as Washington struggled to preserve a moderate Congolese leadership, however, the Kennedy administration nurtured alternatives. Above all, the military and CIA hedged American bets by providing political and material support for Mobutu, and the Department of the Army flew him to the United States in May 1963 to visit American military bases and meet President Kennedy. By the time of Kennedy's assassination in November, U.S. policy remained a work in progress, beset by conflicting impulses to disengage from a messy situation, promote an effective moderate government, and tighten links to a reliable authoritarian. Johnson inherited, in the words of one leading historian of the crisis, a "confused legacy."[145]

Desire to balance competing goals also suffused U.S. policymaking in connection with another issue that beset the administration farther south: the determination of white minorities to hold onto power despite surging Black nationalism. In the Portuguese territories of Angola and Mozambique, the Lisbon government refused to cede its authority, leaving in place an old-fashioned colonial apparatus. Meanwhile in independent South Africa, which fully broke from Great Britain in 1961, the white minority defied international condemnation by tightening the long-standing system of racial separation known as apartheid. The dangers inherent in white recalcitrance became all too clear in March 1960, when South African police fired on Black protesters, killing sixty-nine and injured more than two hundred others in what became known as the Sharpeville Massacre. Less than a year later, confrontations between Black nationalists and colonial authorities in Angola erupted into full-scale war.

Americans had good reason to fear still more problems as Britain moved ahead with its plan to grant independence to the Central African Confederation (also called the Federation of Rhodesia and Nyasaland), which comprised Nyasaland (modern-day Malawi), Northern Rhodesia (Zambia), and Southern Rhodesia (Zimbabwe). Britain had formed the federation in 1953 in order to promote economic integration. By 1960, however, pressures for decolonization threatened the arrangement. Britain negotiated new constitutions for all three territories and in 1964 granted independence to two of them, Malawi and Zambia, under principles of majority rule. But Southern Rhodesia's status remained uncertain. Due to historical patterns of European settlement, that territory possessed a notably large white population—8 percent of the total, compared to 3 percent in Northern Rhodesia and less than

1 percent in Nyasaland. Additionally, Southern Rhodesia had historically enjoyed more autonomy from Britain than the other two territories, holding the status of self-governing colony rather than protectorate. There could be little doubt in the early 1960s that the European-derived population intended to exploit its numbers and authority to hold onto power.[146]

The prospect of white rule in a fully independent Southern Rhodesia offended the moral sensibilities of American liberals, but it also stoked geopolitical anxieties. As in other parts of the world, Americans assumed that frustration of nationalist ambitions would provide fertile soil for radicalization, a trend that Moscow seemed well positioned to exploit. "Blacks face Whites across a sea of developing hate," warned a 1962 study by two State Department officials eager to move African issues higher up the U.S. agenda. Across the southern part of the continent, whites were "taking up a defensive position along a rampart from which they feel there is no retreat," while Black demands steadily grew. "The possible collision of these rival forces in a world already full of racial hatreds is highly dangerous," asserted the State Department paper. A serious effort to discourage further Black-white polarization was urgent, concluded the study, adding ominously, "In all areas time is running out."[147]

But a separate set of considerations dictated that the United States could go only so far in pushing for majority rule. For one thing, the key European powers in the region were NATO allies of the United States. Pressuring Lisbon to decolonize or London to move boldly to establish a new racial order in its territories carried the risk of creating friction with implications that went far beyond Africa. Kennedy and his aides feared in particular that Portugal would retaliate against American pressure for decolonization by limiting U.S. access to military bases in the Azores, a crucial mid-Atlantic waystation for American forces. With respect to Britain, Americans worried about provoking resentment by insisting too stridently on objectives that British leaders largely shared.[148] But U.S. leaders also feared taking steps that would alienate the very white Africans who so staunchly resisted change. While only a few officials, notably Dean Acheson, showed outright sympathy for racial attitudes of the European-derived populations, many policymakers appreciated their staunch anticommunism and pro-Western economic orientation. The benefits for the United States were most tangible in South Africa. U.S. mining companies profited from access to the nation's vast mineral reserves. Meanwhile, U.S. military planners valued strategically important waterways around the Cape of Good Hope and access to South African ports. Strategic dependence on South Africa only increased during Kennedy's presidency with the expansion of the network of U.S. missile-tracking stations in the country.[149]

For most policymakers, the solution to the conflicting pressures was to find a middle ground that would maintain pro-Western stability while facilitating a gradual transition to majority rule. But agreement on this broad proposition left plenty of space for debate. Precisely how should the United States strike such a balance? Opinions varied greatly. The Pentagon leaned toward the white governments, noting that sub-Saharan Africa held only "secondary importance," as the Joint Chiefs of Staff put it in one memorandum, compared to American interests in NATO.[150] The Chiefs and Defense Secretary McNamara urged that Washington continue to voice objections to racial injustice in principle but avoid punitive steps such as economic sanctions, arms embargoes, or expulsion of South Africa from the United Nations.[151] Secretary of State Rusk also opposed such measures, noting that U.S. relations with "half of the existing community of states" would be jeopardized if Washington began sanctioning nations because of the injustice of internal political arrangements.[152]

Williams, Stevenson, and others sympathetic to Black Africa tilted the other way, arguing that the United States had stronger interest in aligning itself with political forces certain to prevail in the long run. NATO had survived differences among its member nations in the past and should "no longer be regarded as an excuse for not developing a new and independent posture" toward Africa, where "volcanic forces could be ignored only at great peril," asserted Senator Frank Church, a close ally of the administration, in April 1961.[153] McGeorge Bundy advised the president in 1963 that the United States could withstand the loss of missile-tracking capabilities based in South Africa, noting that he remained "quite favorable" to Black African demands for stiffer U.S. condemnation of the Pretoria government.[154]

The result of such differences was a mix of policies toward southern African problems that sometimes veered in one direction, sometimes in the other. A good barometer of such variation was U.S. behavior in the United Nations, where Washington occasionally criticized white rule and, in 1963, accepted a voluntary embargo on arms sales to South Africa, a measure that did not impinge appreciably on South African military capabilities but amounted to a significant political gesture. At many points, however, Washington resisted pressure from African nationalists and steered clear of the most strident efforts to promote majority rule.[155] This pattern of tacking back and forth is especially clear with respect to South Africa and the Portuguese colonies. It is also evident in connection with Southern Rhodesia, a problem that steadily climbed the administration's list of concerns and would erupt as a major crisis in Johnson's presidency.

At first, administration officials saw a glimmer of hope. The constitution negotiated by Britain and Southern Rhodesia in 1961 set aside fifteen of the territorial legislature's sixty-five seats for Black members, an unprecedented step to involve Blacks in the territory's political life. U.S. officials welcomed that move, along with other efforts to relax the most draconian forms of racial segregation, as evidence that the government in Salisbury was making "earnest efforts to promote [a] multi-racial society," as Rusk put it.[156] Americans hoped for further conciliation and even offered U.S. mediation. Hoping that compromise was still possible, Rusk leaned on London for assurances that Britain would not grant full independence to Southern Rhodesia until it had reached agreement on a formula for majority rule. He also urged Britain to use its influence in Salisbury to end a ban on Southern Rhodesia's most powerful nationalist movement, the Zimbabwean African People's Union, in exchange for ZAPU's disavowal of violence and to win the white government's assurance that the fifteen African legislators would never be overruled on matters directly related to the welfare of the Black population.[157]

Americans hopes were dashed, however, in December 1962, when general elections in Southern Rhodesia revealed a sharp backlash by the white population in the form of a sweeping victory for a new right-wing party, the Rhodesian Front. Almost immediately, American fears of violence soared. After a trip to the region in early 1963, Assistant Secretary Williams concluded that Southern Rhodesia was "the new African time bomb."[158] Among the most troubling prospects was that the Salisbury government, under the hardline leadership of Prime Minister Winston Field, would unilaterally declare its independence from Britain and thereby take total control over the nation's political and racial order. Such an illegal regime might then inflame racial tensions by forming an economic or even military partnership with other white governments in the region.

Undersecretary of State Ball recommended an "urgent reassessment" of U.S. policy in light of the election, but administration officials of all stripes quickly recognized a problem with implementing any ideas that might emerge:[159] whatever influence the United States had once wielded to facilitate a moderate outcome was quickly eroding amid the rapidly polarizing situation. In Southern Rhodesia, empowered white radicals condemned Washington for encouraging political turmoil and demanded to be left alone.[160] One of the few Americans to win praise was the segregationist senator Allen Ellender of Louisiana, who created a public relations nightmare for the Kennedy administration by denigrating Africans' capacity for self-government during his trip to southern Africa in late 1962.[161] Meanwhile, the election result sparked African and Asian nations to demand debate of the Southern Rhodesian situation in the United Nations, where U.S. officials feared radical voices might predominate and the Soviet bloc might gain a bigger role in African affairs. The middle ground was rapidly crumbling.

U.S. leaders retreated to a more passive role geared to avoid antagonizing either side. Within the United Nations, the epicenter of international controversy over Southern Rhodesia, the U.S. representative to the committee focused on decolonization abstained on a resolution, backed by many African governments, demanding that Britain throw out the 1961 constitution and begin the process over again. Three months later, Americans similarly abstained on a Security Council measure condemning London's plans for officially dissolving the Central African Confederation and especially for giving the Salisbury government most of the federation's military supplies. Concluding that the resolution would only harden white intransigence if it passed, the Kennedy administration worked eagerly—unsuccessfully, as it turned out—to line up sufficient abstentions from friendly European and Latin American governments to defeat the measure.[162]

Mostly, though, U.S. officials placed their bets on the British government as the only moderating force with sufficient clout to defuse the crisis. That approach seemed vindicated in March 1963, when London surprised many Americans by vigorously rejecting Salisbury's formal request for independence and laying down conditions that Southern Rhodesia had to satisfy before independence would be possible. Among these conditions were direct political participation by Black Africans, abolition of discriminatory laws, and clear evidence that a majority of all residents of the territory favored independence. All in all, asserted a State Department report, the British showed "a marked sense of responsibility."[163]

Still, doubts persisted, and some U.S. officials sought to apply greater pressure on London to drive home the need for a new political order in Southern Rhodesia before granting independence. Sidney R. Yates, the U.S. representative to the UN committee in charge of decolonization, urged that London play an "active role" in the issue and exert the "special influence" it wielded not just because of its legal responsibilities but also due to its cultural and historical role in southern Africa. More specifically, Yates proposed precisely the solution on which the United States, anxious to show outward support for Britain, had abstained in UN deliberations: pressure on Britain to call a new constitutional conference. To make that approach palatable to Salisbury, Yates suggested that Britain offer generous development aid targeted at ensuring Southern Rhodesia's economic viability over the long term.[164]

Debate over how hard to push the British reflected growing concern by the fall of 1963 that the United States was failing in its effort to balance competing objectives in southern Africa. NSC staffer William H. Brubeck captured American frustrations in October. The United States, he wrote in a memorandum for National Security Adviser Bundy, had "sailed an improvised, often erratic course between the antagonists" in Portuguese Africa and South Africa. This was, he added, "the most sensible—indeed the only sensible—course open to us." Still, he concluded that Washington was "beginning to run out of sailing room" and needed "some basic reconsideration and clarification of policy at this point."[165] Among the uncertainties was the relationship that Washington should seek with the African nationalist movements that were gaining clout throughout the region, including in Southern Rhodesia. "I gather that we really don't have much of a policy or we are just beginning to develop one," complained Attorney General Robert F. Kennedy just two days before his brother's assassination, urging Bundy to put the issue on the agenda for the high-level NSC Standing Group where RFK had a powerful voice. "It seems to me these areas are going to be extremely important in the future and that some serious thought should be given to what we are going to do," asserted Robert Kennedy. "As usual," he added, "there seems to be some strong differences of opinion."[166]

# 3

# Lyndon Johnson's World

FROM THE OUTSET of his presidency, Lyndon Baines Johnson made abundantly clear where his priorities lay. Behind closed doors and in the public spotlight, the new president urged passage of an array of ambitious social and economic reforms, including a major tax cut, meaningful civil rights legislation, and a raft of antipoverty measures. LBJ invoked the need to honor John F. Kennedy, who had backed all of these initiatives, but Johnson also left no doubt of his desire to go beyond what his predecessor had proposed. LBJ's rhetoric soared as he described his sweeping vision of social change. In his State of the Union speech just six weeks into his presidency, Johnson called for nothing less than an "unconditional war on poverty in America" and vowed not just to ameliorate the problem but to "cure it." In the realm of civil rights, he promised to "abolish not some, but all racial discrimination."[1] Thus dawned the era of the Great Society, the remarkable years of domestic innovation that saw Congress destroy Jim Crow, extend voting rights, establish Medicare and Medicaid, pump federal resources into education, revamp U.S. immigration laws, and much else. For all of these accomplishments, historians have little difficulty judging Johnson one of the most—if not *the* most—transformative presidents in the second half of the twentieth century.

LBJ had no such ambitions in the realm of foreign affairs, as the 1965 State of the Union address also made clear. The president turned to the international scene in the closing sections of the speech and made headlines only with assurances that he would keep going with efforts to lower tensions with the Eastern bloc. All in all, as the *New York Times* editorial page put it, LBJ's foreign policy "continues as expected, along familiar lines."[2] This low-key approach reflected Johnson's desire to keep Congress and the American public focused on his domestic ambitions, but it also flowed from a fortuitous set of circumstances that prevailed in the months around LBJ's ascension to the Oval Office. The new president benefited from a lack of major international distractions, a trend that dated back to the relaxation of superpower tensions following the Cuban Missile Crisis. To be sure, problems festered beneath the surface of events, including the dilemmas described in the previous chapter. For the moment, though, those and other concerns could mostly be deferred or managed by the bureaucracy.

That moment would not last long. Starting in the spring of 1964, Johnson and his advisers confronted the inescapable need to make policy choices toward not just Vietnam but also Brazil, India, Iran, Indonesia, southern Africa, and numerous other places. Their decisions gradually revealed a distinct approach to the Third World that largely resolved the ambiguities of the Kennedy presidency and set down policies that would persist after Johnson had left office. Confronting a growing array of problems and eager to protect his highest priorities, LBJ and his advisers chose again and again to lower American ambitions in the Third World, to reduce risk of setbacks, and to shore up Washington's control over global affairs by establishing or bolstering regimes that promised to cooperate with the United States. Unquestionably, Johnson did not wholly abandon his predecessor's desire to promote constructive change in the Third World, and LBJ frequently spoke of his dedication to roughly the same goals that had animated Kennedy's rhetoric in earlier years. But Johnson's preference for stability over all other ambitions brought a new approach to the Third World that departed in crucial ways from the Kennedy years and laid the tracks on which Richard Nixon and Henry Kissinger would drive American decisions after coming to office in 1969.

This chapter sweeps across the Johnson presidency to highlight four principal reasons why U.S. policymaking toward the Third World underwent this transformation between 1964 and 1969. First, Lyndon Johnson brought a different set of experiences and intellectual tendencies into the presidency. Whereas Kennedy viewed the transformation of the Third World as perhaps the most important development of the era and advocated new methods for coping with it, Johnson saw the problem in less grandiose terms and believed that relatively conventional policy responses were adequate to the challenge. Second, in contrast to JFK, Johnson's decision-making style closed down the vigorous, if inconclusive, debate that had prevailed during the Kennedy years. Like Kennedy, Johnson preferred informal decision-making procedures, but his dislike of dissent tended to exclude viewpoints that he did not readily embrace. Third, the rapidly evolving political scene within the United States discouraged the experimentation and risk-taking that Kennedy and his advisers sometimes pursued in connection with the Third World, especially their tolerance of non-alignment. Simply put, the growing backlash against Johnson's domestic agenda after 1965, combined with his mounting unpopularity due to the Vietnam War, discouraged foreign policy initiatives that might invite additional criticism. Finally, growing international turmoil after 1965 accentuated Johnson's wariness of unpredictability and risk in the geopolitical realm.

Above all, the expansion of the Vietnam War heightened Johnson's determination to bolster reliable regimes and thereby lessen the need to expend American resources in other places.

## Core Beliefs

Contemporaries of LBJ as well as later commentators have sometimes charged that Johnson's performance in the foreign policy arena reflected inexperience with international affairs and ignorance of the wider world. Johnson "always felt a little limited in the field of foreign policy," noted longtime aide Walter Jenkins.[3] The outgoing British ambassador put the matter more bluntly after observing LBJ's first fifteen months in office. "He has little sensitivity to the attitudes of foreigners," David Ormsby-Gore wrote in March 1965, decrying LBJ's tendency to believe that people he encountered abroad would "prefer to be Americans."[4] Historians have often pointed out that LBJ, despite his Texas roots and cosmopolitan connections, learned neither Spanish nor any other language and never took an obvious interest in the wider world. Moreover, LBJ barely ever traveled abroad before becoming vice president. "Lacking a detached critical perspective," writes historian Waldo Heinrichs, "he was culture-bound and vulnerable to clichés and stereotypes about world affairs."[5] Historian H. W. Brands agrees, writing of LBJ's "dogged lack of imagination" in international affairs.[6]

There is some merit in these judgments. As numerous commentators have pointed out, LBJ's career soared mostly on the strength of an uncanny knack for persuading people who operated within his own social and political milieu and sputtered when he confronted the need to understand political movements—whether Vietnamese guerrillas half a world away or African Americans in U.S. cities—driven by historical experiences different from his own. He was, as David Halberstam put it, "a man of Washington more than of the nation."[7] Yet it is too simple to view LBJ's foreign policy as solely the product of ignorance. He had ample experience with foreign and defense affairs, after all, by the time he became president. During his long tenure in Congress, he served on numerous committees with responsibilities in these domains, and as Senate majority leader in the 1950s he cooperated closely with President Eisenhower in crafting bipartisan policies during critical years of the Cold War. As vice president, he traveled more extensively than anyone who had ever held the position. During his presidency, moreover, Johnson occasionally showed remarkable ingenuity. For instance, he spearheaded negotiations that resulted in the Non-Proliferation Treaty and broached the idea of bridge-building with China.[8] Close analysis of these experiences and Johnson's performance as president reveals that his approach to international affairs was rooted not so much in ignorance as in distinct intellectual tendencies that JFK did not share and therefore stand out in bold relief by comparison with what had prevailed just before LBJ entered the White House. These proclivities require careful attention in order to appreciate the directions in which Johnson steered U.S. foreign policy from 1963 to 1969.

A key to understanding Johnson's performance in the international arena lies in his belief that the United States could manage its relationships with other nations mostly through interactions with their most senior leaders. Far more than JFK, LBJ possessed an elitist vision of geopolitics, a tendency with especially heavy implications for decisions toward politically unstable parts of the Third World. As political scientist Elizabeth N. Saunders argues in an astute study of Cold War presidents, Kennedy was remarkably open to the notion that political instability sprang from the grassroots grievances of ordinary people and could be addressed only through policies that encouraged the establishment of more effective institutions capable of delivering meaningful social, economic, and political progress. In this sense, to use Saunders's terminology, JFK had a "transformative" vision of political change needed in the Third World in order to serve U.S. interests over the long term. Only by accommodating the desires of people emerging from long periods of exploitation, according to this view, could the United States secure the genuine cooperation of Third World nations and thereby defeat the danger of communism, which tended to feed on economic and political injustice. From this outlook sprang some of the distinctive patterns of thinking that informed, if not always drove, decision making in the Kennedy years: willingness to tolerate annoying but popular nationalists such as Goulart and Sukarno, desire to assist ordinary people through person-to-person programs such as the Peace Corps, acceptance of non-alignment in places where that policy seemed to reflect a broad popular consensus, and determination to pump U.S. resources into nations that distanced themselves geopolitically from Washington in hopes of generating stability that would work to the U.S. advantage over the long run.[9]

By contrast, Johnson had a distinctly "non-transformative" approach, according to Saunders. What mattered to LBJ was the disposition of the leaders who held power at the highest levels in nations with which the United States interacted. Leaders who aligned with Washington in the Cold War won his favor, whereas he frowned on those who refused to cooperate closely in the East-West struggle. In contrast to Kennedy, Johnson cared little about the internal workings of those nations, discounting the ways in which social change, economic desperation, and weak institutions drove unrest and increased the likelihood of radical outcomes. For LBJ, it was enough to exert U.S. influence at the highest echelons of foreign governments. From this approach emerged distinctive patterns of policymaking in the LBJ presidency: impatience for non-alignment, tolerance of authoritarian regimes, diminished enthusiasm for U.S. aid programs, and attentiveness to the interests of American firms operating abroad.[10] Although LBJ was only slightly more inclined than Kennedy to consider the interests of specific companies, he was far more likely to view American investment as an important source of stability and economic progress in poor nations.

None of this is to say that LBJ did not sincerely sympathize with the plight of downtrodden peoples in the world's poorest nations or back development assistance in principle. Indeed, LBJ spoke genuinely in late 1963 when he told the UN Security Council he had seen "too much of misery and despair in Africa, in Asia, in Latin America." His rhetoric consistently revealed visceral concern akin to the sentiments he expressed in connection with poverty in the United States. Too often during his travels as vice president, he lamented, he had observed "the ravages of hunger, and tapeworm and tuberculosis, and the scabs and scars on too many children who have too little health care and no hope."[11] In his attention to the very broadest of global challenges—disease, food scarcity, and environmental degradation—LBJ was arguably even more forward thinking than JFK, displaying awareness of problems that transcended the ability of individual nations to manage and would fully emerge on the international agenda in the twenty-first century.[12]

In other ways, however, Johnson's outlook on foreign aid was more limited than that of Kennedy. For one thing, LBJ had little inclination to resist congressional pressure to cut development assistance and, in a throwback to the Eisenhower period, hoped to achieve results as much through enhanced trade and multilateral mechanisms as through direct U.S. contributions. Johnson also differed, as Saunders argues, in seeing relatively little direct connection between broad social disgruntlement in the Third World and geopolitical instability capable of menacing U.S. interests. Kennedy viewed U.S. aid as a vital method of shaping the internal institutions of developing societies; steering nationalism, including the urge to nationalize resources, in nonthreatening directions; and weakening the appeal of communism. For LBJ, the internal problems of Third World countries were "largely separate from the ongoing Cold War struggle," Saunders writes.[13] Indeed, in one of his most eloquent appeals for development assistance, Johnson insisted that poverty, disease, and resource depletion did "not spring from the cold war or even from the ambitions of our adversaries" and would "persist beyond the cold war."[14] If U.S. aid had value in prosecuting the Cold War, it lay, for LBJ, in the leverage it conferred over the decision making of leaders who benefited from American largesse. Much more than Kennedy, Johnson believed that the United States was entirely justified in expecting something in return. "To the extent that we need foreign aid to serve our national interest," asserted Johnson, "the recipients must be brought to see that they too have an interest in conducting themselves as to justify our help. I have in mind not only their making the most effective use of our assistance but of their posture on issues where the US feels deeply and—in elementary prudence—of their avoiding provocations which outrage US sensibilities."[15]

Why did Johnson place so much emphasis on leaders rather than the internal dynamics of foreign societies? One answer lies in LBJ's tendency to view politics principally as the art of interacting with and influencing other powerful men. This trait and the rewards he reaped from it are easy to see in LBJ's long political career. In the House, Senate, and White House, he gained a well-earned reputation for getting his way through the "Johnson treatment," an array of persuasive techniques that he wielded with uncanny skill in his interpersonal interactions. He was an "unbelievable man in terms of sizing people up: what they would do, how they would stand up under pressure, what their temperament was," recalled Hubert Humphrey, LBJ's Senate colleague and later his vice president. "This was his genius," said Humphrey, who called Johnson a "master of human relations."[16] Unsurprisingly, LBJ's understanding of how to accomplish his goals carried over into the international sphere. "Johnson thought all problems could be solved by making a deal with a leader," wrote Ted Sorensen, a close adviser of Kennedy's who briefly served LBJ before leaving the new administration in early 1964.[17] LBJ believed the way to achieve results was to "deal with men at close combat, man to man," writes Halberstam. "Since he was not a contemplative man, a man who read books, and since he had little belief in the rhythms and thrusts of history," Halberstam continues, "he was convinced that you could accomplish things by reasoning with leaders, by moving them to your goal, manipulating them a little, and that, finally, all men had a price."[18]

Johnson's "instinct to personalize," to use Halberstam's phrase, also flowed from his historical experiences.[19] For one thing, he believed that meaningful change domestically and abroad would be accomplished best through the work of strong national leaders and centralizing governments capable of channeling national will and resources, just as it had been in the United States during the New Deal. Unlike Kennedy, who fashioned himself as a new brand of liberal capable of transcending old categories, LBJ lost few opportunities across his political career to highlight his loyalty to Franklin Roosevelt and the vision of reform that be embodied. The slogan of LBJ's 1941 campaign for a seat in the Senate—"Franklin D. and Lyndon B."—boosted the young Texan's prospects at a time when his state and much of the South embraced New Deal programs.[20] By contrast, JFK, eight and a half years younger than Johnson, won his first political races at a moment of conservative resurgence after the Second World

War. But LBJ's affinity for the New Deal stemmed from more than political calculation. He shared FDR's desire for bold action as well as the president's sense of the methods by which it should be carried out. Starting as early as 1928, when Johnson became principal of a small school in the impoverished Texas town of Cotulla, he imbibed a paternalistic view of reform, holding that activist elites were best positioned to marshal expertise and resources to create beneficial change for the less powerful. The New Deal, embodying a similar top-down ethos, meshed well with Johnson's outlook and reinforced his confidence about the capacity of an inspired and empowered government to accomplish momentous things. When LBJ ascended to the presidency, he possessed what historian Daniel Sargent has aptly called a "New Deal psyche" that informed his approach to any number of policy challenges.[21]

Among these challenges was policymaking toward the Third World. To the extent that he valued social and political change in other nations, he counted almost instinctively on fellow elites to manipulate the levers of governmental power to promote reform via top-down development schemes. Most strikingly, Johnson drew on the example of the Tennessee Valley Authority in backing the scheme to promote economic development along Southeast Asia's Mekong River by building dams that would generate power and improve conditions for agriculture. Central to LBJ's concept was the notion that government institutions, whether those of the United States or of the nation receiving aid, would drive the development process. NSC aide Robert Komer later paraphrased Johnson's aspirations: "We're going to provide them with rural electricity. We're going to provide them with roads and water, and we're going to improve the rice crop."[22] By "we," Johnson clearly meant government authorities. Compared to Kennedy, this outlook left little space for the possibility of ordinary people exerting agency over their conditions or the functioning of their governments and, during Johnson's presidency, helped rationalize reliance on nondemocratic regimes as the most efficient purveyors of economic development. So powerfully did the state-building impulse of the 1930s run through LBJ's vision of global progress that one scholar has suggested he aimed for nothing less than a "New Deal for the world."[23]

Johnson's focus on the role of elites also sprang from his experience of international affairs during the early years of his political career, when he formed core ideas about how threats to the United States were likely to emerge and how Washington should best cope with them. During the late 1930s and Second World War, the young congressman watched rapacious powers in Europe and East Asia conquer their neighbors while the United States and its allies struggled to find the will to resist. Like many members of his generation, he drew lessons that endured for decades to come. Above all, he internalized the ideas that geopolitics were driven by the ambitions of powerful leaders and that security could best be obtained by resisting the temptation to appease or accommodate them. Only personal toughness by determined elites could hold aggressors at bay. "From the experience of World War II," Johnson later recalled, "I learned that war comes about by two things—by a lust for power on the part of a few evil leaders and by a weakness on the part of the people whose love for peace too often displays a lack of courage that serves as an open invitation to all the aggressors of the world."[24] LBJ carried these ideas into the Cold War, personalizing the communist threat in much the same way he had earlier described the danger of fascism. "One thing is clear," Johnson said in a 1947 speech. "Whether communist or fascist or simply a pistol-packing racketeer, the one thing a bully understands is force and the one thing he fears is courage." He continued on another occasion: "If you let a bully come into your front yard, the next day he'll be on your porch, and the day after that he'll rape your wife in your own bed."[25]

Two key aspects of LBJ's attitude toward challenges in the Third World resulted from this way of thinking. First was his relative lack of patience for leaders who refused to line up firmly alongside the United States in the East-West struggle. To LBJ, accommodation of irresolute or hostile governments carried the implication of U.S. weakness that could only embolden aggressors and endanger the United States over the long term. Second, as Elizabeth Saunders argues, LBJ's tendency to view geopolitics as a contest among powerful elites discouraged interest in the internal dynamics of the societies that they led. The key danger to the United States, writes Saunders, lay in a "Soviet-directed elite takeover" of a nation rather than internal weaknesses that might render a nation vulnerable to radicalism or communist insurgency.[26] In Johnson's view, weak nations could be straightforwardly assessed based on their governments' willingness to align themselves with Washington and to use their limited capabilities to resist communist aggression that originated in the machinations of "coldly thinking men in Moscow and Peiping," as he put it in a 1958 Senate speech. LBJ noted that the United States confronted challenges in places as varied as North Africa and Latin America. But he characteristically warned against any temptation to see problems as arising from dynamics distinct to particular countries or regions. These hot spots, he insisted "are not widely separated" in the minds of communist leaders determined on "world domination."[27]

## Decision-Making Dynamics

If Lyndon Johnson's habits of mind help explain shifts in American foreign policy with respect to the Third World after he rose the presidency, so too did the decision-making dynamics that prevailed within his administration.

As demonstrated in chapter 2, John F. Kennedy assembled an intellectually and politically diverse array of advisers and encouraged vigorous debate. The continuity of personnel from the Kennedy presidency into the Johnson administration may suggest that not much changed. Yet in crucial respects Johnson proceeded in a different manner, surrounding himself with like-minded team players and prizing loyalty to a chosen course of policy over intellectual exchange. The combination of these traits reinforced the policy-making tendencies that flowed from the core ideas that LBJ brought with him into the presidency: an inclination for nation-building and strongpoint ideas along with disdain for the globalism of men like Stevenson and Bowles. Egotistical by nature and firmly rooted in his foreign policy convictions, he closed out subordinates who voiced dissenting views, leaned on advisers who catered to his style, and gradually appointed new officials whose thinking meshed with his own.

In the arena of domestic policy, Johnson permitted, if not enthusiastically encouraged, debate and allowed his advisers to solicit additional opinions in universities and other institutions outside of government. Rivalries between boldly ambitious progressives and old-guard liberals unquestionably shaped the president's agenda in productive ways, and Johnson allowed his aides a strong hand in crafting and implementing key legislation.[28] But in the domestic realm, Johnson could count on the fact that everyone he consulted was determined to move in the same direction. Debate was tolerable because it mostly concerned tactics and the finer points of policy. In connection with foreign policy, where viewpoints among U.S. officials tended to be much more varied, the administration proceeded in a different way. Johnson showed little interest in debate and relied on a small circle of aides who shared both his aversion to freewheeling discussion and his policy predilections. He called meetings of the full National Security Council infrequently, preferring, in the words of historian Andrew Preston, "to deliberate and decide policy in front of, and with the participation of, as few people as possible."[29] When he did stage meetings with larger groups of advisers, he often did so to ratify decisions he had already made.[30]

LBJ's convictions about foreign policy, rooted in his experiences in the 1930s and 1940s, help account for this tendency. To Johnson, there was little to be gained from wide-ranging discussion since the core necessities of foreign policy were clear. But his decision-making style also flowed from elements of his character. For one thing, Johnson's immense ego meant that he possessed minimal tolerance for dissent or wide-ranging deliberation. LBJ's narcissism, writes Blema S. Steinberg, a psychoanalyst who has studied presidential decision making, made him "determined to avoid situations that would demonstrate his vulnerability to being shamed."[31] This trait, argues Steinberg, was especially limiting in connection with diplomacy and national security, where Johnson suffered from insecurity about his lack of experience and expertise. He was wary of challenges from foreign policy intellectuals and area specialists—"the Harvards," he called them—both inside and outside the administration.[32] To be sure, he formed close bonds with a few foreign policy experts, especially those at the most senior levels, who affirmed his inclinations. But he showed little interest in viewpoints that conflicted with his basic outlook on international affairs. "He cannot stand criticism of any kind and reacts very badly to it," noted a 1965 British assessment of LBJ's decision-making style in connection with foreign policy.[33] National Security Adviser Bundy later called LBJ "the wariest man about whom to trust that I have ever encountered."[34] When confronted with information that did not mesh with his preferences, Johnson was not, in fact, above simply conceiving an alternative reality. "He had a fantastic capacity to persuade himself that the 'truth' which was convenient for the present was the *truth* and anything that conflicted with it was the prevarication of enemies," remembered longtime aide George Reedy.[35]

But he mostly revealed his intolerance of inconvenient points of view through a near-obsession with loyalty among his staff. As numerous colleagues and acquaintances recalled in later years, LBJ despaired of being alone. "He had to have people around him," remembered Vice President Hubert Humphrey. "And if he couldn't get you physically, he'd pick up the phone and get you." His objective, though, was rarely meaningful give-and-take. Rather, he demanded single-minded service to his agenda and to himself personally. "One time he told me that there were ten principles of politics, and that they were, in order of importance, loyalty, loyalty, loyalty, loyalty, loyalty, loyalty, loyalty, loyalty, loyalty, and loyalty," recalled Larry Temple, who served LBJ as a White House adviser in the administration's final year.[36] When shown proper deference, Johnson was often warm and generous. Numerous onetime aides felt strong affection for their boss.[37] Failure to show proper loyalty, though, sometimes elicited verbal abuse and ostracism from the inner circle. Perhaps most strikingly, Johnson marginalized Humphrey in 1965 after the vice president dared to send him a memo advising de-escalation in Vietnam. "Ultimately," recalled *Washington Post* publisher and LBJ confidant Katherine Graham, "[Johnson] cut himself off from all but about four people who agreed with him" on the Vietnam issue.[38]

As Graham's comment suggests, LBJ's decision-making proclivities narrowed the number and range of voices participating in deliberations at the highest levels. This transition carried heavy implications for U.S. policymaking toward the Third World, an arena where policymakers were especially prone to disagreement. One consequence of LBJ's rise to the presidency was the marginalization of the globalists, whose outlook on problems in Asia, Africa, the Middle East, and Latin American differed most sharply from the preferences of the new president. Unquestionably, Johnson leaned on Kennedy aides such as Ted Sorensen, Adlai Stevenson, Richard Goodwin, and Arthur Schlesinger Jr. to remain in their positions as a way to demonstrate continuity, and he largely succeeded, a notable accomplishment of LBJ's first days in office.[39] Yet Sorenson and Schlesinger soon resigned, at least partly out of conviction that Johnson had little sympathy for their outlooks on a range of issues. Other globalists, including Stevenson and G. Mennen Williams, remained in their positions but discovered that their influence had waned considerably. John Kenneth Galbraith followed a different path, forging a close friendship with Johnson, but his role in foreign policy deliberations largely evaporated after the end of his ambassadorship to India in 1963. The only globalist to retain a significant voice in policymaking throughout the Johnson presidency was Bowles, but his position—the ambassadorship to New Delhi, more than seven thousand miles from Washington—makes clear that LBJ valued his counsel little more than had JFK.[40]

Whether globalists left or stayed was not, however, decisively important given Johnson's heavy reliance on only his most senior aides. His preference probably sprang from a combination of intellectual insecurity, a top-down notion of politics forged in the early years of his career, and a belief that power had to be earned through experience and promotion. But the implication for policymaking was crystal clear: decisions lay mostly in the hands of Secretary of State Rusk, Secretary of Defense McNamara, and National Security Adviser Bundy, officials appointed by Kennedy and kept on by Johnson in order to project continuity. The losers were lower-ranking foreign policy officials, the military, and the CIA. "He still meets with the NSC," noted *Time* magazine in 1965, "but when he really wants to speak his mind—or hear others speak theirs—he summons the Big Three." In Kennedy's presidency, noted one unnamed official quoted in the *Time* article, "a lot of people kibitzed who didn't have operational responsibility." But now, according to the magazine, "to a remarkable degree, [Johnson] has come to rely on the Big Three to help focus his thinking not only on Viet Nam but also on a wide range of problems involving both military and diplomatic considerations."[41] For their part, Rusk, McNamara, and Bundy, whether because of naked ambition or principled dedication to the presidency as an institution, adapted to the new decision-making environment and transferred their loyalty to LBJ without the qualms that beset some lower-ranking officials with strong affinities for Kennedy.

This concentration of decision-making authority was especially meaningful for Rusk. The secretary of state had wielded little power under JFK and had been especially disliked by globalists who saw him as the embodiment of an outmoded set of attitudes toward the Third World. Asked on one occasion why he relied on Rusk rather than lower-ranking officials within State Department bureaucracy, as JFK had done, Johnson replied simply, "He's my secretary of state."[42] The position alone carried enormous weight. But Johnson's faith in Rusk rested on deeper affinities: humble socioeconomic origins, boldly liberal instincts in the domestic arena, and a broadly similar belief that the United States must use its power first and foremost to buttress allies and preserve positions of strength, including in the turbulent Asian theater. This convergence goes far to explain why Rusk was the only senior aide of JFK's who lasted in office all the way to the end of Johnson's presidency. By contrast, Bundy and McNamara, whose greater flexibility of mind contributed to their growing despair over U.S. struggles in Vietnam, left the administration in 1966 and early 1968, respectively.

The narrowing of views within the Johnson administration also resulted from LBJ's promotions and appointments. The most significant promotion went to Walt Rostow, the onetime deputy national security adviser whom Kennedy had demoted to the State Department's Policy Planning Staff in late 1961. When Bundy resigned in February 1966, the outgoing national security adviser recommended Komer for the post, while McNamara suggested Bill Moyers, a longtime aide to Johnson with a reputation for nuanced thinking. But Johnson was drawn to Rostow's loyalty and hawkishness at a moment when the president increasingly resented advisers who had grown wobbly on Vietnam. On that issue, LBJ appreciated Rostow's enthusiasm for force even while keeping the military and CIA—institutions that LBJ often mistrusted since they enjoyed a measure of independence from the White House—at arm's length. He also appears to have appreciated Rostow's broad ideas about the uses of American power to bolster friendly regimes, which Johnson saw as a welcome departure from the liberal impulses that had swirled around Kennedy and that Bundy had sometimes embraced. "He's not Bundy's intellectual. He's not Galbraith's intellectual. He's not Schlesinger's intellectual," declared LBJ. "He's going to be my goddam intellectual and I'm going to have him by the short hairs."[43]

Two other notable appointments—Thomas C. Mann as assistant secretary of state for Latin American affairs and director of the U.S. Agency for International Development at the end of 1963 and William Raborn as director of the CIA in 1965—sprang from similar desires to ensure loyalty and craft simpler policy. To be sure, as the most authoritative study of Mann's career makes clear, his policy ideas were more complex than his liberal critics usually allowed. Yet, compared to Schlesinger, Goodwin, and other officials who shaped the Alliance for Progress and other initiatives in Latin America during the Kennedy years, he represented a long step away from the democratizing ambitions of the alliance.[44] Above all, Mann, an old acquaintance of LBJ's with similar Texas roots, showed greater tolerance for U.S. reliance on authoritarian regimes in the hemisphere and saw U.S. business, more than U.S. aid, as the key driver of development. Johnson's elevation of Raborn, a fellow Texan who had campaigned for him in 1964, in place of CIA director John McCone, an outspoken adviser prone to pessimism on Vietnam and forthright assessments of other policy problems, grew from LBJ's desires for loyalty and advice hewing closer to his own geopolitical outlook. Raborn's loyalty was not, however, accompanied by bureaucratic acumen. In 1966, Johnson replaced him with Richard Helms, a career CIA officer who gained LBJ's trust by shaping his input to mesh with his boss's inclinations on Vietnam and other matters.[45]

## Domestic Politics

Lyndon Johnson's calculations about domestic politics strongly affirmed his desire to minimize disagreement over policy and prioritize stability in the Third World. Innumerable memoirists and biographers have made clear that LBJ possessed exceptionally ambitious plans for reforming American society even before he entered the Oval Office, the massive agenda that he dubbed the Great Society. Not without reason, Johnson told confidants that Kennedy was too cautious for his taste in domestic affairs and that he would not only implement his predecessor's aspirations but go far beyond them. LBJ went to work almost immediately and, through skillful manipulation of Kennedy's legacy and his own legendary mastery of the legislative process, won passage of a long-stalled tax cut, along with the landmark Civil Rights Act and Economic Opportunity Act, in 1964. Amid these legislative battles, Johnson had little time for, or interest in, the complexities of foreign policy. The looming 1964 presidential election compounded this desire to keep international affairs out of the headlines and off his agenda. Crises, he feared, would distract Congress and the American public from his priorities, call attention to his lack of experience in international affairs, and embolden conservative critics whose hawkishness in international affairs might put pressure on the administration to act more boldly abroad than it cared to do.

When the administration had no choice but to respond to foreign policy challenges, it prioritized firmness in order to bolster American power and keep critics at bay. Such tendencies became obvious in the first international crisis that Johnson faced after assuming the presidency, a confrontation between the United States and Panama that sets the administration's general approach in bold relief. On January 9, 1964, rioting erupted along the edges of the Panama Canal Zone, a ten-mile-wide strip of territory that the United States had controlled as a colony within Panama since the canal's construction in the early twentieth century. The spark was Panamanian outrage that American students had raised the U.S. flag in violation of complicated agreements negotiated by the Kennedy administration governing where the flags of the two countries could be flown. But the larger problem was burgeoning Panamanian resentment over American domination of the zone and Washington's failures to deliver on promises to renegotiate the treaties governing control of the canal. The flag incident mushroomed into major clashes, and by the time the smoke cleared on January 13, twenty-one Panamanians and four Americans lay dead. Panamanian president Roberto Chiari broke diplomatic relations with the United States, insisting that ties would be restored only when Washington agreed to negotiate a new treaty.[46]

Although midranking officials expressed a degree of sympathy for Panamanian demands, Johnson and his senior advisers jumped to the conclusion that the United States must reject Panamanian demands and show unbridled toughness. This view rested in part on Johnson's characteristic assumption that, despite the obvious role of Panamanian nationalism in generating the confrontation, communists were ultimately responsible for the crisis. "Kids started it and [then] the communists got into it," Johnson insisted. If the flag dispute had not occurred, he added, communists "would have kicked [the rioting] off in some other way, some other time."[47] Conceding to Panamanian demands in any way seemed a recipe for further trouble in Panama or elsewhere in Latin America. But LBJ's political calculations also encouraged firmness. Democratic congressman Danial Flood of Pennsylvania, one of the most outspoken defenders of U.S. control over the canal, had already indicated the risks for any administration that gave ground, accusing Kennedy of presiding over "another Munich" in 1962 by allowing the Panamanian flag to fly in the Canal Zone.[48] Democratic political analyst Richard Scammon drove the point home a week after Panama broke relations. Scammon informed Johnson he was "more than a little concerned with the potential trouble which Panama could cause us in November," warning that any concessions would create the impression of the United States "getting pushed around by a small country" and would give Republicans their "first real solid muscled hit at the Administration."[49]

Scammon's warnings were rooted in abundant evidence of political risk. Of 64 percent of Americans who were aware of the crisis a month after it started, almost half urged a "firm policy," whereas only 9 percent favored concessions to Panamanian demands.[50] Similar views rippled through Congress, where a State Department analysis detected a "general consensus" for a "firm U.S. stand" while noting that some members even favored a "U.S. show of force."[51] Key Republicans spoke out in terms certain to resonate with LBJ. His likely Republican opponent in the 1964 presidential contest, Arizona senator Barry

Goldwater, declared, "That canal is ours, and we can't have other governments taking our property away." The United States, Goldwater demanded, must not "back down an inch."[52] Meanwhile, Senate majority leader Everett Dirksen charged, "We are in the amazing position of having a country with one-third the population of Chicago kicking us around. If we crumble in Panama," Dirksen declared, "the reverberations of our actions will be felt around the world."[53]

Johnson's firmness paid off in April, when the Panamanian government, under growing U.S. economic pressure, accepted an agreement to restore relations without any explicit assurances from Washington about opening negotiations on the canal. But that victory, though widely praised by Republicans, did little to lessen LBJ's worry about the political costs of setbacks abroad. With the November vote hovering in the distance and landmark Great Society legislation within reach, LBJ continued to calculate throughout 1964 that his ambitions would be best served by a firm approach that would keep national attention where he wanted it and deny the hawkish Goldwater any opportunity to change the conversation.

Johnson's preferences became especially clear in early August, when he responded to suspected North Vietnamese attacks on U.S. warships in the Gulf of Tonkin by ordering airstrikes on the Vietnamese coast and obtaining congressional approval for a resolution giving him the go-ahead to use American military power whenever he chose—a deft blend of military and political action that conveyed firmness while also permitting the immediate crisis to die down. To be sure, LBJ probably had little to worry about. Polls showed him with commanding leads throughout the spring, summer, and fall, including large edges over Goldwater in approval of his management of foreign policy. Yet Johnson aspired to win by a big margin and had no tolerance for risk. He had "difficulty enough" in pursuing his domestic agenda, noted one British diplomat who astutely predicted a mere "holding operation" in international affairs. Compared to the energy and innovation that Kennedy had shown, the diplomat added, U.S. leadership in foreign policy would likely be "reluctant, deficient, or lacking in important fields" until after the election.[54]

When Johnson achieved the massive victory that he had hoped for—the biggest presidential landslide in American history to that time—some aides urged that the moment had come for greater risk-taking in foreign policy, especially in the myriad problems confronting the United States in the Third World. Most strikingly, Vice President Humphrey urged LBJ to rethink U.S. policy in Vietnam, insisting that 1965 was "the year of minimum political risk for the Johnson Administration."[55] Yet Johnson, whose ambitions in the domestic realm grew as a consequence of his electoral triumph, gave little ground and, in fact, punished Humphrey by excluding him from the administration's inner circle.[56] Only in a few instances did he show greater flexibility. In

Panama, for instance, he announced in December 1964 that the United States was prepared to renegotiate the terms under which it operated the canal, a notable concession to widespread hostility among Latin Americans to U.S. dominance of the Canal Zone.[57] Revealingly, though, that decision rested on confidence that concession would secure U.S. interests by dampening unrest and bolstering conservative political forces aligned with Washington, a set of calculations that did not apply elsewhere. Indeed, Johnson's decision to send U.S. Marines—ultimately twenty-two thousand—to prevent leftist political forces from taking power amid civil unrest in the Dominican Republic showed his inclination to perceive complex political situations in Manichean terms. In a case where LBJ showed genuine ingenuity—his flirtation in 1965 and 1966 with small steps toward rapprochement with China—he ultimately lost interest as other priorities crowded in on him.[58] In all of these cases, the president viewed firmness as the best way to protect American interests globally and to bolster his prospects for winning major domestic reforms. As Johnson told Senator Richard Russell in 1964, voters like those in Russell's home state of Georgia would "forgive you for everything except being weak."[59]

If Johnson was anxious about the political implications of international instability in the good times of 1964 and 1965, he was bound to become even more so as trends turned against him from 1965 until the end of his presidency. At the root of LBJ's problems lay growing social unrest within the United States, which fueled a backlash against LBJ's domestic program. The benefit of hindsight reveals not just pushback against the innovations of the Great Society, however, but a major watershed in American history—the "hinge of the twentieth century," political scientist Robert Putnam calls it—marking the end of the liberal era that stretched back to the turn of the century.[60] Rioting in the Watts neighborhood of Los Angeles in August 1965, resulting in thirty-four deaths and hundreds of injuries, signaled the turn, calling into question LBJ's ability to hold a broad coalition of Americans behind his agenda of top-down reform. Subsequent events further eroded the commanding political position that LBJ had once held. Racial unrest fueled far more destructive riots in numerous American cities during 1966 and 1967, culminating in the massive disturbances following the murder of Martin Luther King Jr. in April 1968. Meanwhile, LBJ confronted growing antiwar activism as he escalated the U.S. commitment in Vietnam between 1965 and 1968. LBJ's approval ratings tumbled, while polls showed growing skepticism about reform efforts that had commanded broad popularity not long before.[61]

Central to the backlash was the notion that the pace and extent of change had dangerously weakened old social norms, unleashing intolerable licentiousness, disrespect for authority, and crime. The rhetoric of social uplift, a political winner as recently as 1965, gave way to a new emphasis on law and

"Where I'm In Charge, There's Absolutely No Danger Of Democratic Government Being Subverted"
U.S.
ANTI-DEMOCRATIC RULERS
©1965 HERBLOCK
THE WASHINGTON POST

FIGURE 3.1. This cartoon by Herb Block was published in the *Washington Post* on May 3, 1965, a few days after U.S. Marines landed in the Dominican Republic to bolster a friendly regime. The cartoon hints at the Johnson administration's attraction to reliable authoritarian leaders across the Third World. A 1965 Herblock Cartoon, © The Herb Block Foundation.

order in 1966 midterm election season. "How long are we going to abdicate law and order—the backbone of any civilization—in favor of a soft social theory that the man who heaves a brick through your window or tosses a fire bomb into your car is simply the misunderstood and underprivileged product of a broken home," asked Gerald Ford, the Republican leader in the House of Representatives.[62] From this sort of language, it was but a short step to the idea that domestic unrest ran parallel to—and was perhaps intermingled with—burgeoning challenges abroad, where many American observers also saw a growing number of brick throwers eager to undermine the United States. Radicals such as Stokely Carmichael fueled conservative fears by celebrating the global revolutionary movement and urging American leftists to see themselves as part of a single worldwide struggle against oppression. But conservatives in the United States hardly needed Carmichael's words to suspect that foreign radicals were spurring domestic tensions. The arch-segregationist governor of Alabama, George Wallace, spoke for many when he claimed that rioting resulted not from poverty or racism but from the plotting of "world guerilla warfare chieftains" based in Havana.[63] In 1967, amid rioting in Newark and Detroit, the conservative *Chicago Tribune* similarly drew links between domestic and foreign problems when it blamed the Johnson administration for "subsidizing local 'wars of liberation' in cities all over the country" by pumping War on Poverty funds into inner-city neighborhoods.[64]

Against a backdrop of growing fears of radicalism and turmoil, Johnson felt new pressure to project toughness abroad, especially in nonwhite parts of the world, which fell down the list of U.S. priorities as the atmosphere of crisis intensified. LBJ's responses can be seen in the case studies explored in the remaining chapters of this book. But they can also be seen in the administration's positions in debates over foreign aid, an issue that, as much as any, encapsulated U.S. attitudes toward the emerging nations of Asia, Africa, the Middle East, and Latin America. During his years in office, Kennedy had worked hard—with mixed results—to protect foreign aid against congressional opposition and to discourage strings on American assistance. LBJ attached a lower priority to the issue, and unsurprisingly U.S. aid dipped during his years in office as political support for liberal initiatives weakened. In his first budget, Johnson signaled his changed approach by requesting just $3.52 billion in foreign aid for the 1965 fiscal year, a full $1 billion less than Kennedy's proposal to Congress the year before. In January 1966, LBJ's $3.39 billion request was the smallest in the history of the program.[65] Amid changing political winds, U.S. foreign aid disbursements declined over the rest of the decade.[66] But the shift from JFK to LBJ lay as much in the uses of U.S. money as in the total expenditures. To the dismay of Komer, "Soapy" Williams, and other supporters of Kennedy's approach to development assistance, Johnson dragged his feet on new aid for India, Indonesia, Egypt, and other non-aligned nations while redirecting assistance to nations that consistently cooperated with the United States. Johnson's approach was no doubt part and parcel of an outlook on politics that prized hard bargaining and quid-pro-quo thinking. But Johnson also drew back from legislative battles as the public and Congress turned against largesse for nations that defied Washington.

Opinion polls made clear there would be no reward for taking risks on the issue. Across the decade, Americans showed declining interest in foreign aid. Even in the optimistic year of 1964, one Gallup poll showed that 59 percent of Americans believed that the United States should reduce or end economic assistance to foreign countries, while only 32 percent favored maintaining current levels or increasing aid. In August 1967, the numbers grew even more lopsided. Fully 68 percent of Americans favored "cutting down" spending on foreign aid, whereas a mere 20 percent opposed that step. A February 1966 Gallup survey demonstrated that Americans had particularly strong views when it came to U.S. aid for nations that bucked Washington on political questions. Asked their attitude about aid for any country that failed to support the United States "in a major foreign policy decision such as Vietnam," only 16 percent backed continuation of American assistance. Thirty percent supported a reduction of U.S. aid, while 45 percent backed a total "cut-off." Still other polls indicated that declining public enthusiasm for foreign aid was directly connected to LBJ's overall political standing. In August 1964, 58 percent of Americans believed that Johnson was doing an "excellent" or "pretty good" job on foreign aid; two years later, that number had dropped to 38 percent, while Congress won high marks for its efforts to trim American aid programs.[67]

Some of the best evidence of just how seriously Johnson took the shifting political climate lies in the widening rift that opened between himself and the liberals who had played a significant, if not always decisive, role during the Kennedy administration. Within the administration, Chester Bowles, the U.S. ambassador to India and an adamant globalist despite the changed tenor of American politics, reflected liberal frustrations in 1966, confiding to his diary a suspicion that Johnson's stingy approach to aid resulted partly from the president's "sadistic pleasure in the display of power."[68] In public, Johnson faced mounting criticism from congressional liberals who objected to what they saw as the administration's unimaginative reversion to conventional Cold War thinking. Much of that criticism focused on Johnson's pursuit of the war in Vietnam, but some of it ranged beyond Southeast Asia and amounted to a broader questioning of American foreign policy toward problems of development and democratization. One of the most vociferous critics was Senator J. William Fulbright, the Arkansas Democrat who chaired the Senate Foreign Relations Committee. Fulbright welcomed Johnson's rise to the presidency in 1963 and expressed confidence about a fruitful partnership. Within three years, however, Fulbright was using his high-profile position to hold hearings and deliver speeches censuring U.S. foreign policy for narrow-minded overconfidence and lack of imagination, a critique at the heart of Fulbright's 1966 best-seller *The Arrogance of Power*.[69] Fulbright denied any intention to attack Johnson personally and did little to extol JFK, but his appeals for modesty about Washington's ability to control foreign societies and for a new commitment to multilateralism clearly flew in the face of Johnson's reorientation of U.S.

foreign policy. For LBJ, such criticism was deeply wounding, and he increasingly railed against Democrats whom he accused of abandoning him on Vietnam and other issues. But he gave little ground to his detractors in his bid to secure the political rewards of pursuing stability and lowering American ambitions in the wider world.

## The Toll of War

The Vietnam War contributed to LBJ's preference for stability in the broader Third World largely because of its effect on domestic politics. Controversy flowing from the war, combined with the erosion of public support for the Great Society, made LBJ eager to squelch other potential sources of political unpredictability and turmoil. A striking irony of the Johnson presidency is that, as the political winds shifted after 1964, LBJ's prospects of winning liberal advances at home seemed to depend increasingly on closing down liberal possibilities abroad. But the war in Vietnam also affected the Johnson administration's calculations about the Third World in ways unrelated to domestic politics. Indeed, as it intensified between 1965 and 1968, the war strongly reinforced the administration's risk aversion in at least three ways. First, the war fueled hostility to the United States across much of the Third World, making it more difficult for Washington to strike a pose of constructive moderation than had been plausible earlier in the decade. Second, the war proved enormously costly in economic terms, making the administration wary of other international commitments that might generate an additional drain on the U.S. budget. Third, the war created a huge burden on U.S. military resources. Heavily committed in Southeast Asia, the administration wanted no part of international controversies that might require U.S. intervention of any sort.

The dramatic escalation of U.S. involvement in Vietnam did not at first carry heavy implications for Washington's relationships with the wider Third World. As historian Robert Rakove argues, various non-aligned governments issued pro forma protests against U.S. intervention but, with the exception of Indonesia, avoided strong positions. Most, after all, were focused on controversies closer to home and saw little advantage in antagonizing the United States on a secondary issue.[70] When Third World governments gathered at Cairo in October 1964, they paid little attention to Vietnam and, in their final declaration, issued a generic appeal for a peaceful settlement.[71] To the extent that Third World nations, individually or collectively, took positions on the Vietnam problem in 1964 and the first half of 1965, they usually put themselves forward as potential peacemakers. Seventeen non-aligned governments responded to the initiation of the U.S. bombing campaign against North Vietnam in March 1965 by issuing a joint declaration appealing for peace, offering to mediate, and conspicuously refraining from criticizing the United States. U.S. officials cautiously welcomed the proposal, which they hoped might help sway world opinion in Washington's favor.[72]

Those hopes were dashed, however, as the war escalated. To be sure, American intervention in Southeast Asia was not the only reason why numerous Third World governments grew more critical of the United States in the second half of the decade. Intensification of the fighting coincided with trends that weakened prospects for constructive relations between Washington and non-aligned governments while giving the Johnson administration new incentive for bolstering ties with nations strongly aligned with the United States. For one thing, Jawaharlal Nehru's death in 1964, combined with the dramatic weakening of Gamal Abdel Nasser's stature as a consequence of Egypt's defeat in the 1967 Arab-Israeli War, eliminated two leaders who prioritized a third way between the Eastern and Western blocs. Although American officials were frequently frustrated by the two men, they nevertheless often regarded Egypt and especially India as relatively moderate voices in Third World circles that promised some degree of cooperation.

The declining influence wielded by those two nations fed into another trend of the later 1960s: the surging influence of a more radical, anti-Western variant of Third World solidarity. Internal tensions had beset the Third World movement since its inception at the 1955 Bandung Conference, with nations prioritizing non-alignment in the Cold War often at odds with more radical nations dedicated to revolutionary anticolonialism above all else, even when that position entailed close association with the communist powers. The latter point of view gained strength in the later 1960s, fueled by the dynamics of the Sino-Soviet split as well as spreading outrage about white rule in southern Africa, polarization flowing from the Arab-Israeli confrontation, Cuba's revolutionary ambitions, and the war in Vietnam.[73]

Washington's diminishing prospects to exert influence in the Third World were notably clear in January 1966, when more than six hundred representatives of governments, liberation groups, and political parties met in Havana to announce a new global revolutionary movement explicitly aligned with the communist bloc. Unquestionably, Johnson and his aides drew confidence from recent coups against Algerian leader Ahmed Ben Bella and Sukarno in Indonesia, which eliminated two of most outspoken voices of Third World radicalism and diminished Chinese influence globally. Those advances coincided, however, with diminished traction in other areas as polarization in the Third World shrunk the political middle ground where Kennedy had hoped to make his mark. Worrying trends were especially evident at the Havana "Tricontinental" conference, which embraced a sharply anti-U.S. agenda and aimed to extend networking among radical governments and movements by building new links between the Afro-Asian and Latin American revolutionaries. Predictably, the conference resounded with anti-U.S. rhetoric and readily connected the war in Vietnam to a larger pattern of U.S. behavior around the world. The "aggressive war against Vietnam" and against "other peoples in Asia, Africa, and Latin America," along with the "crimes committed by the North American aggressors" revealed that the United States was "the number one enemy of the peoples of the three Continents and of all mankind," announced one declaration adopted at the conference. More threatening to the United States, participants created new bureaucracies, including a Tricontinental Committee for the Support of the Vietnamese People, to coordinate political and material aid for revolutionary efforts around the world.[74] U.S. officials hoped to blunt such efforts through denial of U.S. aid to regimes that avowed revolutionary purposes and by exploiting persistent divergences between more and less radical participants in the Third World movement. But no longer could Washington pin its hopes on exerting influence through constructive relationships with major non-aligned nations.[75]

The sheer cost of the war in Vietnam, in both financial and military terms, also discouraged risk-taking by the Johnson administration in the conduct of foreign policy. From the outset of his presidency, Johnson had appreciated that achieving his overall agenda, especially the Great Society, depended on careful handling of the Vietnam problem, which threatened to consume his political capital, eat up the federal budget, and fuel debilitating inflation. Undoubtedly, he believed that failure to prevent a communist takeover of South Vietnam would expose him to withering political attack and kill any chance that Congress or the public would back his highest priorities. But he also concluded that he had to downplay the crisis in Vietnam in order to prevent alarm about a looming war in Southeast Asia from eclipsing all interest in his goals. The implication was clear: Johnson needed to walk a tightrope, escalating in Vietnam but doing so with as little fanfare as possible. For a time, the administration succeeded in this balancing act, in part by deliberately obscuring the actual costs of the war. The introduction of American combat forces in Vietnam blunted communist military gains without disrupting LBJ's political effectiveness at home. He signed the landmark Voting Rights Act in August 1965 even as U.S. ground forces went into action, and more legislative victories followed in that peak year of the Great Society. Rhetorically, Johnson insisted that the nation did not have to choose between guns and butter. The fighting in Vietnam must not come at the expense of "the hopes of the unfortunate here in a land of plenty," LBJ declared in his 1966 State of the Union address. "I believe that we can continue the Great Society while we fight in Vietnam."[76]

Behind the scenes, however, pressure mounted for tax increases to pay for expensive initiatives at home and abroad and to hold down inflation. In

Congress, if not the White House, the implications of soaring costs in both the domestic and international realms were impossible to ignore. The breaking point came with the midterm congressional elections of November 1966. Amid surging criticism of the war and urban unrest, Democrats lost forty-seven seats in the House and three in the Senate, while Republicans scored a net gain of seven governorships. Johnson's Democrats still controlled both houses of Congress, but the setback weakened the liberal faction that had most eagerly backed the Great Society and restored power to a coalition of Republicans and conservative southern "Dixiecrats" critical of much of LBJ's agenda and anxious about budget deficits. As the cost of the war soared toward $2 billion per month, LBJ could no longer avoid a reckoning. In his State of the Union speech on January 10, 1967, Johnson proposed a 6 percent surcharge on individual and corporate taxes to pay for the war and expanding social programs. But the proposal only stirred new acrimony over the nation's priorities. Wilbur Mills, chair of the House Ways and Means Committee and a staunch critic of the Great Society, immediately demanded deep cuts in domestic spending before any tax proposal would be considered. From the left, too, came unwelcome attention to the links between war and other budgetary priorities. Above all, Reverend Martin Luther King Jr., who had previously been quiet about the war, used a high-profile speech on April 4 to berate U.S. leaders for a conflict that, like a "demonic, destructive suction tube," pulled "men and skills and money" away from urgent tasks at home.[77]

The vice tightened over the following months. In August 1967, revised estimates of U.S. expenses in Vietnam and likely budget deficits led LBJ to increase his surcharge proposal to 10 percent and to accept for the first time that he would have to give ground on spending. After months of deliberation with an increasingly hostile Congress, Johnson signed legislation on June 28, 1968, imposing the 10 percent surcharge and requiring $6 billion in cuts to domestic programs.[78] These changes naturally heightened the administration's wariness of new spending commitments abroad, as did another trend that dramatically worsened in the late 1960s: the balance of payments crisis. Americans had worried about the outflow of U.S. dollars since the beginning of the decade, when the dollar's extraordinary strength led foreign bankers to accumulate as many as possible. The war in Vietnam drastically heightened the danger to the economy by eroding confidence in the United States, leading foreign dollar holders to demand exchanges for gold and eventually causing the temporary closure of the international gold market in March 1968.

The problem led the Johnson administration to impose limits on foreign investment by U.S. companies and even to request that Americans postpone "unessential" travel for two years. It also did much to intensify the

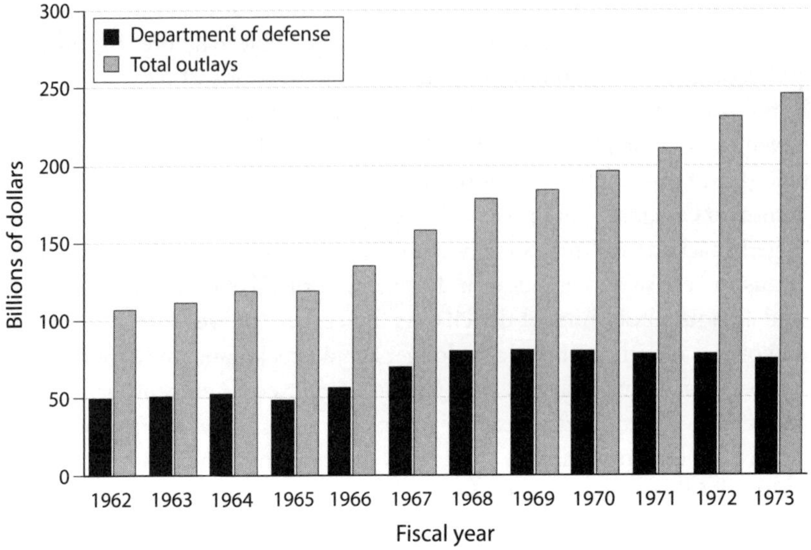


FIGURE 3.2. U.S. spending soared across the 1960s, driven by the twin costs of the Great Society and the war in Vietnam. Source: Office of Management and Budget Historical Tables, https://www.whitehouse.gov/omb/historical-tables/.

administration's caution about foreign aid, an attitude rooted in deteriorating political support for liberal ambitions abroad but increasingly affirmed by economic realities. Unsurprisingly, U.S. development aid—both the administration's requests and especially the terms approved in Congress—declined amid the new budgetary climate. The Senate Foreign Relations Committee's Democratic majority captured the prevailing mood in explaining its decision to trim $28 million from LBJ's proposal for 1967 and to insist that U.S. aid go to a smaller number of recipient nations. The war, wrote the committee's majority faction, "cast a very long shadow" and led many members to "feel that the United States is overcommitted, or in danger of becoming overcommitted, in the world at large."[79]

A similar sense of overextension suffused U.S. calculations about the nation's ability to meet its military commitments around the world as the Vietnam War consumed more and more resources. Simply put, American leaders concluded that the war in Vietnam left scant resources for any new commitments elsewhere. In 1964 and 1965, U.S. leaders had hoped to avoid trade-offs between U.S. commitments in Vietnam and other areas of the world by limiting the embroilment in Southeast Asia and trimming American defense spending globally. They also hoped to manage the drain on U.S. resources by securing substantial military contributions from other nations for the war effort in Vietnam. Eager to get "more flags" flying alongside the stars and stripes in Vietnam, Johnson used a news conference on April 23, 1964, to share his hope that an array of nations "could all unite in an attempt to stop the spread of communism in that area of the world."[80] U.S. diplomats posted to numerous nations worked strenuously thereafter to secure military or, if necessary, nonmilitary contributions for what Johnson hoped would become a broad international effort, much as the Korean War had been. The administration clearly hoped for significant military commitments from major allies, including NATO nations with strong interests in maintaining U.S. military power in Europe, but also wanted at least token contributions from Third World nations, including non-aligned countries, as a means of demonstrating a broad global determination to resist communist advances.

In the end, just five East Asian and Pacific nations—South Korea, Australia, New Zealand, Thailand, and the Philippines—contributed combat forces. Numerous others sent nonmilitary aid, but most of these contributions were meager in size and given only under U.S. pressure.[81] Meanwhile, the U.S. troop deployment quickly soared to levels unimaginable when Johnson decided to commit the nation to combat. The problem of paying for the escalating war naturally drew most attention in congressional and public debate. But maintaining U.S. obligations outside of Southeast Asia—just a small segment of the global chessboard, after all—stirred mounting concern among U.S. policymakers and military commanders. For many critics of the war such as Senate Foreign Relations chairman Fulbright, the solution lay in rethinking the extent of America's responsibilities, which were impossible to maintain and perhaps even counterproductive to U.S. interests. In the short term, though, critics and supporters alike worried that the United States would not be able to maintain interests that were at least as important as Vietnam to overall U.S. interests.

The drain on U.S. military resources was especially worrisome in connection with the defense of Western Europe, the focal point of U.S. global strategy. As the U.S. commitment to Vietnam escalated dramatically in 1964 and 1965, Secretary of Defense Robert S. McNamara promised that no U.S. troops or equipment would be moved from Europe to Southeast Asia. The Pentagon reneged on that commitment, however, after the United States embraced a full combat role in Vietnam. As early as September 1965, the senior U.S. commander in NATO, Army general Lyman Lemnitzer, warned that diversion of ammunition and other combat equipment from the European theater might damage U.S. credibility with European allies. The risk of stirring political trouble seemed particularly grave given the Johnson administration's simultaneous efforts to convince NATO allies to modernize and build up their national forces.

Yet LBJ's refusal to enhance American troop strength by calling up reserve units left McNamara with few choices but to degrade forces dedicated to Europe. In the second half of 1965, needs in Vietnam led the Army to divert 130,000 U.S.-based personnel whose main mission had been to reinforce Europe-based troops in an emergency. Commanders warned that such reductions would degrade the ability of U.S. forces to resist a Warsaw Pact attack in Europe, raising the likelihood that Washington would have to resort quickly to nuclear weapons. Before long, however, growing demand in Vietnam led McNamara to go even further by tapping 30,000 Army personnel stationed in Europe, a move that reduced the Army's Europe-based force to 8 percent below U.S. commitments to NATO and substantially lowered its combat capabilities. McNamara tried to keep declining U.S. military capabilities in Europe secret from the American public but could not deceive the Joint Chiefs of Staff, who insisted repeatedly during 1967 and 1968 that current budget ceilings did not allow the United States to wage the war in Vietnam effectively while maintaining other global commitments.[82]

Johnson administration officials naturally denied that the war in Southeast Asia was badly compromising American influence elsewhere, but it required little imagination to see a pattern of U.S. caution and recognition of limits as new international problems emerged in the later 1960s. "Rich and powerful though we are," Stuart Symington, an influential Democrat on the Senate Foreign Relations Committee, asserted in May 1967, the United States could no longer maintain peacetime obligations, much less entertain new commitments abroad. "Under current plans and programs," Symington added, "there is little chance of maintaining adequately trained personnel, military personnel, to handle our present world commitments even if those commitments do not involve us in further trouble in some other parts of the world."[83] The veracity of Symington's words became clear as confrontation between Israel and its Arab neighbors escalated toward the outbreak of the Six-Day War in early June, a crisis sufficiently dire to provoke the risk-averse LBJ to consider action. Following Egypt's decision to close the Straits of Tiran, an important waterway linking Israel to the outside world, Johnson toyed with the idea of assembling a U.S.-led naval task force to escort Israeli ships and push Egypt to back down. But the president soon discovered problems. For one, the idea had no support in Congress, which, in the words of Secretary of State Rusk and Secretary of Defense McNamara, had a bad case of "Tonkin Gulfitis." Many legislators, in other words, believed Congress had made a grievous mistake four years earlier by giving the president a blank check to wage war in Vietnam after U.S. warships appeared to come under attack in the Gulf of Tonkin. There was another problem, too. American action seemed certain to provoke Egypt's Arab partners to retaliate by cutting off the flow of oil to the United States and its allies.

An embargo would unquestionably imperil Western economies, but Johnson and his aides had a more specific reason for worry: military operations in Vietnam depended on the flow of oil—as much as 200,000 barrels a day—from the Middle East.[84]

In the end, LBJ's naval-escort plan came to nothing, killed in part by the implications of a draining war on the other side of the world. The Middle East crisis of 1967, which mushroomed into a major war, was just the most serious of myriad challenges that the United States faced in the Third World in the second half of the 1960s. "You are certainly getting more than your share of crises," Senator Claiborne Pell, a Democrat from Rhode Island, told Secretary Rusk at a congressional hearing in 1967.[85] Pell might well have listed Brazil, India, Indonesia, Iran, and Rhodesia among the numerous parts of the world that had demanded urgent U.S. attention in the period since LBJ had become president. In each of those places—and in numerous others—Johnson's behavior was shaped by his own distinct predilections as well as shifting political and geopolitical circumstances, the sum total of which led the administration to back away from the ambitions that Kennedy and at least some of his aides had entertained for U.S. relations with the Third World earlier in the decade. Increasingly, American leaders regarded political change in Asia, Africa, the Middle East, and Latin America as a threat that might not only invite communist advances but also place burdens on the United States that its population would be unwilling—and its national security institutions unable—to bear. In some places, this tendency drove the administration to bring to power or tighten relations with reliable, often authoritarian, regimes that promised to cater to U.S. interests. In others, it widened rifts between Washington and Third World nations that refused to align themselves more closely with the United States. Overall, the effect was to suppress the uncertainty and malleability of the early 1960s and help usher in a world more neatly divided between friends and foes.

# 4

# Brazil

## THE ALLURE OF AUTHORITARIANISM

ONE OF THE more awkward diplomatic encounters of Lyndon Johnson's presidency occurred at the end of January 1967, when the president-elect of Brazil paid a visit to the United States. Johnson, consumed with Vietnam and other problems, had cut back on White House audiences with Latin American leaders since the heyday of the Alliance for Progress under John F. Kennedy and had little enthusiasm for this meeting. General Artur da Costa e Silva, due to assume the presidency of Brazil a few weeks later, was in many ways the embodiment of a Latin American dictator whose close relationship with the United States contradicted U.S. claims to support democracy abroad.

Undoubtedly, Costa e Silva projected a more congenial image than the austere Field Marshall Humberto de Alencar Castelo Branco, who had served as Brazil's president since he and other military officers had overthrown the democratically elected government in April 1964. National Security Adviser Walt Rostow saw reason to hope that Costa e Silva would dispense with his customary dark glasses—the signature look of the Latin American strongman—and engage with LBJ as a "fellow civil statesman" about education, housing, and other matters close to Johnson's heart.[1] Costa e Silva apparently aimed for something similar, even tacking on a trip to Disneyland to show his softer side.[2] But U.S. officials knew there was only so much either government could do to downplay the harsh authoritarianism of the Brazilian regime. In the months preceding Costa e Silva's trip, the military had tightened its grip on power, and many Johnson administration policymakers predicted that the incoming president, despite his benign exterior, would soon cave in to hardliners around him and do away with the remaining vestiges of democracy.

But LBJ and his closest aides saw no alternative to working with Costa e Silva. Brazil's military regime was too important an ally for the United States to snub the junta or to apply meaningful pressure to reverse the momentum toward dictatorship. "Brazil holds the key spot in our hemispheric policy," Secretary of State Dean Rusk reminded the president, echoing conventional wisdom that had circulated among U.S. policymakers for years.[3] Despite the political turmoil that had beset the country since the start of the decade, Brazil clearly possessed disproportionate influence in the hemisphere due to its sheer population and size. Moreover, the country stood out from the rest of Latin America in the desire of its leaders—the military men who came to power in 1964 just like the democratically elected populists who had preceded them—to play a major role in regional and even global affairs. Brazil was, in short, an aspiring great power with the resources and will to be a valuable partner for Washington in promoting stability beyond its borders. U.S. officials looked to Brazil to back Washington's preferences in the Organization of American States, to help manage instability in Portuguese-speaking Africa, and to support the United States in Vietnam. Given these stakes, Rusk urged a friendly reception for Costa e Silva. "If he were to feel slighted for any reason," advised the secretary of state, "it could cost us support from one of our staunchest allies."[4]

The administration's anxieties ebbed quickly. Costa e Silva's visit affirmed the U.S.-Brazilian partnership without causing embarrassment to either side. Best of all for Johnson, the meeting drew little public notice in the United States at a time when controversies connected to the Vietnam War gave the administration enough to worry about. The *New York Times* relegated its story on the summit to page 13, while the *Washington Post* ignored the event entirely.[5] The administration could comfortably resume the posture it had endeavored to maintain—low-key cooperation in the interest of regional stability—ever since helping the generals take power in April 1964.

At that time, Brazil had momentarily taken center stage for Johnson, who resolved the uncertainties that had bedeviled the Kennedy administration by throwing U.S. support squarely behind a military coup. Thereafter, U.S. officials fell into a pattern that would prevail through the end of the Johnson presidency: Washington lodged rhetorical objections each time the Brazilian regime lurched further to the right, but those concerns faded once the immediate shock had passed. In this way, the United States settled into a close association with a regime that ran afoul of its principles but clearly served the Johnson administration's geopolitical preferences. On the whole, the repressive character of the Brazilian government bothered LBJ far less than criticism of the U.S.-Brazilian partnership from his political opponents within the United States and mounting evidence that his enthusiasm for the government in Brasília was not always reciprocated by the generals.

U.S. policymaking toward Brazil differs in some respects from other cases analyzed in this book. Far more than in any other part of the world, American leaders of all stripes appreciated the limits on how much risk they could run by tolerating non-aligned tendencies or indulging nationalism in Latin America. Assumptions of U.S. predominance in the Western Hemisphere went at least as far back as the 1823 Monroe Doctrine and thoroughly pervaded congressional and public opinion. Given this long history and heightened American anxiety after the Cuban revolution, Americans were less likely to sympathize with political movements that challenged U.S. geopolitical priorities. Even as Kennedy agonized over American commitments to democracy in the hemisphere and kept his options open, momentum for a coup was gaining strength throughout the U.S. bureaucracy. Revealingly, however, it was Johnson who presided over the transformative events and constructed a new U.S.-Brazilian relationship that endured—and sometimes thrived—even as the generals steadily dismantled Brazilian democracy. In doing so, LBJ revealed patterns and priorities that would inform his policymaking toward the Third World more generally over the years that followed. Johnson's behavior reflected his tolerance for authoritarianism, his belief that economic progress depended far more on cooperation with like-minded elites than the legitimacy of U.S. aims at the grassroots, and his desperation for international support of his policy in Vietnam.

## "The Best Friend in the White House"

For a moment, John F. Kennedy's assassination on November 22, 1963, breathed new life into relations between the United States and João Goulart's administration in Brazil. Tensions between Washington and Rio de Janeiro had mounted in recent months as Goulart seemed to veer dangerously to the left. Although Kennedy and some of his aides had held out hope of preserving democracy, others increasingly favored a coup. Still, many ordinary Brazilians viewed the charismatic Kennedy, along with his wife Jacqueline and their children, "as if they were part of their own family," U.S. ambassador Lincoln Gordon later recalled.[6] The president's death inspired an outpouring of sympathy in Brazil, leading both sides to see value in an exchange of letters between Goulart and President Johnson as a way of testing the possibility of rapprochement. Goulart acted first, sending a warm letter of condolence on December 13. The missive struck even Gordon, one of Goulart's strongest American critics, as a step forward since it lacked the "carping" tone of previous Brazilian communications and offered new efforts to resolve disagreements about Brazilian debt payments and constraints on foreign investment.[7] LBJ followed up a week later with a cordial letter that went over well with Goulart. The Brazilian president expressed hope that Johnson's expressions of friendship would help him resist the demands of the far left, including left-wing proposals for a moratorium on all debt payments to the United States and other creditors.[8]

The constructive mood faded quickly, however, and the relationship plummeted to new lows. Encouraging developments in Brazil proved "more of a sedative than a cure," wrote Acting Secretary of State George Ball in mid-December 1963. So far had the economic and political situation deteriorated that Goulart, whatever urge he might feel to gratify Washington, was "bound to be harassed by a progressively worsening inflation, increased political turbulence, and the cacophony of extremist pressures for drastic action."[9] A move to the left by Goulart seemed increasingly possible, if not likely—a development that would place Brazil "on the road toward at best a Yugoslav and at worst a Cuban type of orientation," speculated John G. Mein, Gordon's deputy in Rio de Janeiro.[10] Gordon deployed a different analogy sure to resonate with policymakers whose careers had taken off during the Red Scare era. A leftist takeover might make Brazil "the China of the 1960s," Gordon advised, a prediction that strained credulity but demonstrated the lengths to which Goulart's strongest critics were prepared to go in championing U.S. support for action against him.[11] Meanwhile, U.S. intelligence detected evidence of preparation for armed subversion by the extreme left. The danger seemed not to come from the Brazilian Communist Party, committed as it was to "peaceful revolution." Rather, the CIA noted in early 1964 that Peasant Leagues—radical groups concentrated in the impoverished northeast—were busily expanding their paramilitary capabilities, as were armed groups organized by the far-left Popular Mobilization Front and backed by Cuba.[12]

Making these trends still more menacing to U.S. officials was a general deterioration of the political situation across Latin America. Nearly everywhere, rising demands for quick economic progress were at odds with rampant inflation and other economic problems that fueled unrest to the point where, contended the CIA, democracy was no better than a "tender plant" in most countries where it existed at all.[13] The potential for political explosions seemed born out in Panama, where large-scale rioting erupted in January 1964, rupturing U.S.-Panamanian relations and imperiling U.S. control over the Panama Canal. At the same time, other Latin American governments increasingly toyed with "independent" foreign policies amounting, in the words of the CIA, to a "special brand of non-alignment" that in practice often meant "taking a position opposite to, or at odds with the United States."[14] Such questioning of U.S. leadership peaked in July, when Chile, Bolivia, Uruguay, and Mexico refused to go along with all or parts of U.S.-led efforts within the OAS to isolate Cuba.

Personnel changes in Washington ensured that these distressing developments would enhance the appeal of a military solution in Brazil. Most

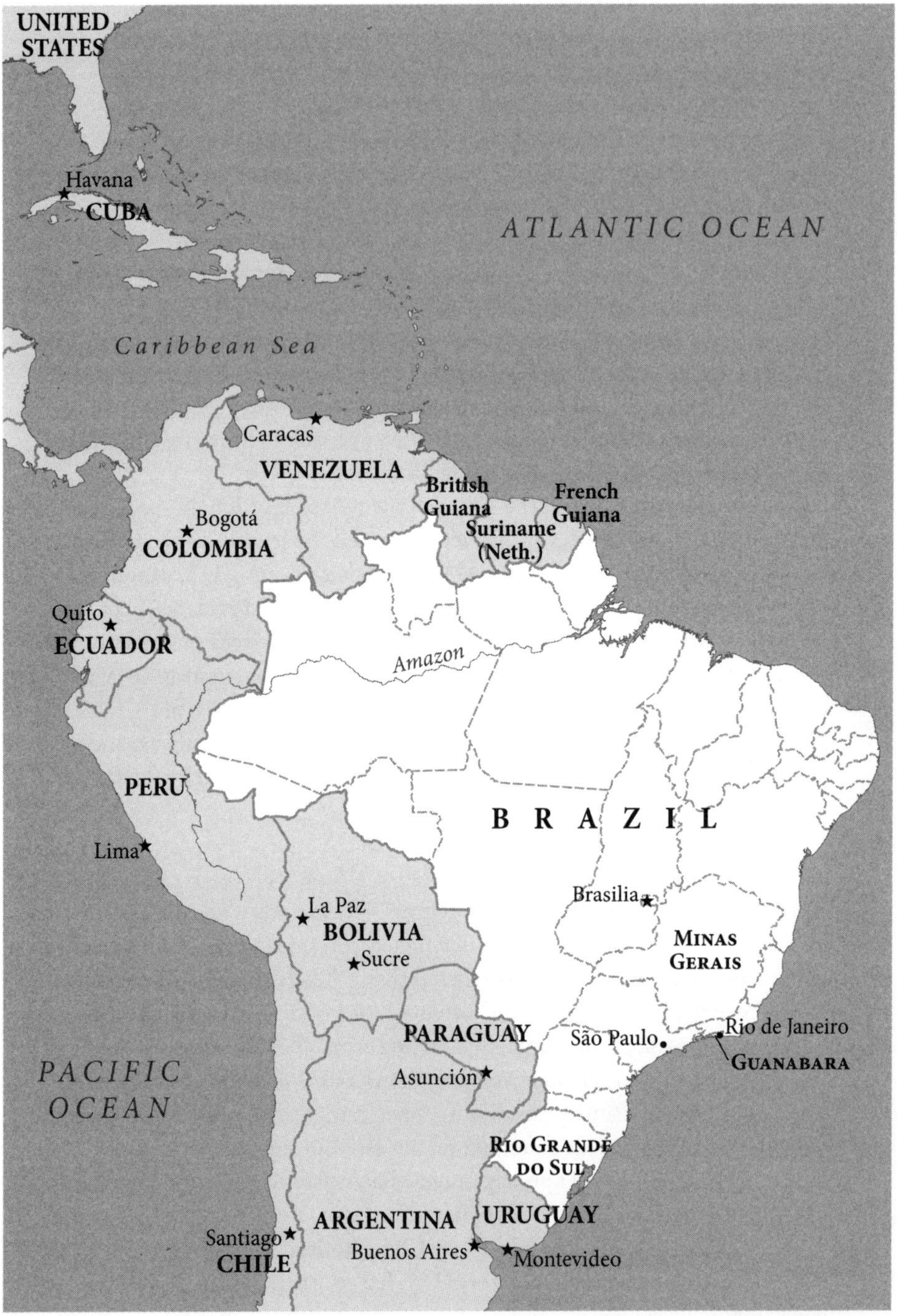


MAP 4.1. Brazil and neighboring regions around the time of the 1964 coup. Mapping Specialists, Ltd., Madison, WI.

important, of course, was the new man in the Oval Office. Kennedy's approach to Brazil had oozed with ambiguity and indecision. He had never taken a clear position and gave contradictory signals to the end of his life. Johnson showed none of this ambivalence, exuding instead a sense of blunt certainty about Latin America in general and Brazil in particular. LBJ's heavy focus on his domestic agenda helps account for his tendency toward clear-cut decisions, as does his conviction that he—a Texan who had lived alongside Latinos for much of his life—understood the region better than any previous president. Latin America had, he insisted a week after taking office, "the best friend in the White House that they'd ever had, one that was raised with them, that knows them and loves them."[15] In the Brazilian case, LBJ readily viewed the crisis in black-and-white terms. Brazil was "going completely leftist," he remarked to Senate majority leader Mike Mansfield in December.[16] At no point between his assumption of the presidency and the coup against Goulart on April 1, 1964, did LBJ insist on a careful exploration of Goulart's motives or express concern about the extinction of Brazilian democracy. One astute British diplomat stationed in Washington, the Latin America specialist Iain Sutherland, noted in December 1963 that Johnson had no interest in the opinions of "the young intellectuals of the New Frontier" such as Arthur Schlesinger and Richard Goodwin, White House appointees who had sometimes played key roles in policymaking toward the Western Hemisphere during the Kennedy presidency. Instead, Sutherland predicted that Johnson would rely on the "higher echelons of the State Department," including Secretary of State Dean Rusk and Undersecretary of State George Ball.[17]

Sutherland's prediction proved accurate. Goodwin lost influence over Latin American affairs, and Schlesinger resigned from the White House staff in January 1964. Later that year, Johnson fired Kennedy's administrator of the Alliance for Progress, Teodoro Moscoso, whose sweeping promises of democratization and development seemed to the new president to be unmatched by tangible results. Most importantly, LBJ replaced Edwin Martin with Thomas C. Mann, a Latin America specialist who had served presidents of both parties since joining the Foreign Service in 1942, as assistant secretary of state for Inter-American Affairs. Martin's October 1963 op-ed indicating greater U.S. tolerance for authoritarian regimes undoubtedly tarnished him in the eyes of Kennedy's more liberal advisers, but his larger record reflected Kennedy's approach to Latin America and a nuanced view of political change in the region. By contrast, Mann shared LBJ's foreign policy predilections.[18]

Above all, Mann's outlook meshed with Johnson's belief that political and economic development must take place gradually and under the careful control of political elites. For Mann, part of the problem with the alliance was the tendency of Kennedy's aides to speak in terms of fostering a "revolution" in social and economic arrangements throughout the hemisphere. "I never believed that we should compete with the revolutionaries," Mann declared in a 1968 interview. "To a Latin American," he added, "I'm convinced that revolution means blood in the streets and shooting." By contrast, his goal for the alliance was to "avoid large scale internal disorders" and to "bring about progress without bloodshed."[19] To achieve such controlled progress, Mann's highest priority upon assuming his new post was to impose order on the unwieldy decision-making procedures that had taken root in the freewheeling atmosphere of the Kennedy administration, which he believed had raised expectations of dramatic change while failing to deliver results. Complaining that under Kennedy "rivalries developed where there should have been teamwork," Mann took pride in streamlining decision-making processes, with the result that more alliance money flowed to Latin America in the first half of 1964 than in the entire previous year.[20]

Fundamentally, however, Mann believed that U.S. aid, even if distributed more efficiently, could accomplish only so much. While conceding that Latin Americans needed "spirit, optimism and hope" in order to tackle the enormous problems besetting their societies, he insisted that "what the Americans need is more realism."[21] Among the implications of this outlook were two features of Mann's thinking that coincided with Johnson's approach to development and democratization: tolerance for authoritarian regimes and confidence that American trade and investment, rather than direct infusions of U.S. aid, would pay off best in the long run. The latter view, a reversion to ideas that had prevailed in the Eisenhower presidency, reflected Mann's and Johnson's skepticism about the possibility of using aid to promote structural reforms with the capacity to improve everyday life in societies that received American largesse.

Liberals who had worked with Kennedy were aghast. Mann was "a little too insensitive to the need for reform," complained Bundy in an understated note to President Johnson.[22] The more outspoken Schlesinger charged that Mann was "not only out of touch with the vital forces of contemporary Latin America" but "actively opposed to them."[23] This was not the sort of criticism that bothered LBJ, however, and he stood by his appointee. Johnson made it known "far and wide that when Mann said something it was the president talking, and he didn't want Mann taking any guff from the rest of the bureaucracy," Pat Holt, the chief of staff to the Senate Foreign Relations Committee, recalled later.[24]

While serving as U.S. ambassador to Mexico in 1962, Mann displayed his Johnson-esque view that economic development driven by sound policy undertaken at the highest level must precede the achievement of social justice. "As we say at home," Mann told a Mexico City audience, "it is necessary to make a mighty big pie before one can distribute large pieces to every member of a large family."[25] But it was a second speech in March 1964, just after Mann's appointment as assistant secretary, that more fully laid out his sense of U.S. priorities. Addressing a closed-door meeting of senior American diplomats gathered for a high-level briefing in Washington, Mann emphasized U.S. dedication to economic growth and the protection of $9 billion in direct investment by U.S. companies in Latin America. The latter represented a shift from the Kennedy administration's emphasis on government-to-government aid rather than the role of private American business in promoting economic development. The more striking change came in the part of the speech dedicated to military regimes. The United States, declared Mann, still advocated democracy, but it "could not impose this system on Latin American countries." Noting that the "anti-dictator policy" had failed to prevent military takeovers, Mann declared that the United States would no longer involve itself in "domestic political situations" by threatening to withhold recognition or aid from military regimes. Indeed, Mann insisted that the United States must be careful to avoid close association with any political groups in the region, where, he complained, democrats and dictators—"good guys" and "bad guys"—were often difficult to tell apart.[26]

The extent to which Mann's statement—quickly dubbed the Mann Doctrine—marked a break with U.S. policy in the late Kennedy administration is a matter of debate among scholars and memoirists, just as it was among U.S. officials at the time. Many commentators have suggested that American leaders had been backpedaling for so long from the original promises of democratization enshrined in the Alliance for Progress that Mann was merely stating what had become widely accepted. Yet there is little question that Mann's statement resolved uncertainty swirling within the Kennedy administration and marked the first time that a senior U.S. official had explicitly given voice to the fact that the United States would no longer use its power to deter military coups. Mann did not, that is, betray or reverse Kennedy's policy so much as throw his weight behind one of the strains of thinking that had competed for influence. The effect, clear for all to see since the speech was immediately leaked to the *New York Times*, was to strip the alliance of its political ambitions, leaving in place only the economic objectives.

Although it is impossible to know with any certainty, the message presumably registered in Brazil, where new indications of Goulart's leftist sympathies and ever-advancing preparations for a coup made for a combustible mix. In any case, the final phase of Goulart's tumultuous presidency began on March 13, when his supporters staged a huge demonstration in Rio de Janeiro. Appearing before the crowd, Goulart waved off cries to disavow the constitution, but he gave the left what it wanted by announcing his decision to nationalize all oil refineries that were not yet in the hands of Petrobras, the government-owned petroleum company. Conservative fears intensified over the following days amid signs of Goulart's unwillingness to suppress agitation among left-leaning enlistees in the Brazilian navy. Fearing threats to military discipline, the generals went into action. On March 31, the commander of Brazilian forces stationed in the influential province of Minas Gerais, just northwest of Rio de Janeiro, denounced the government and ordered his troops to round up political opponents. Other generals soon joined in.[27]

## "The Good Guys Are in Control"

Although U.S. officials had encouraged coup plotting since 1962, Washington did not know the precise timing or play a direct role in sparking action in the last days of March. American leaders responded cautiously to evidence that the generals had begun to move. To be sure, Gordon urged an "affirmative" U.S. response, and President Johnson was excited about the possibility of scoring what he knew would be praised as a major foreign policy success.[28] The United States, LBJ told his aides on March 31, must "take every step we can" and even "stick our necks [out] a little" to ensure Goulart's overthrow.[29] Some senior aides were not so sure, but their concerns reflected worry about appearances rather than the desirability of a coup. Rusk cautioned against bold moves, warning that Washington might be "branded with an awkward attempt at intervention" if it staked out a strongly anti-Goulart position before the outcome was assured.[30] Ball echoed that concern even as the coup gathered momentum. "We don't want to get ourselves committed before we know how the thing is going to come out," Ball advised the president.[31] Accepting this view, the State Department instructed Gordon to make no commitment of U.S. support for the time being.

The most concrete U.S. response to events in Brazil split the difference between the impulse to act and concern about going too far, too fast. On the morning of March 31, the administration approved a plan—an outgrowth of the military contingency studies undertaken in earlier months—to send a U.S. naval task force, accompanied by four tankers laden with petroleum, to Brazilian waters. Dispatch of the task force, which included an aircraft carrier and four destroyers, would be passed off as "normal naval exercises," though the obvious intention was to show American muscle in the event of fighting in Brazil. The tankers had a more concrete purpose. Given the Brazilian government's dominance of the country's energy industry, U.S. military planners worried that the coup might falter due to lack of fuel for vehicles and aircraft. Supplies from the United States might therefore be needed to tip the balance in favor of the *golpistas* if hostilities broke out and continued for any period of time. Still, LBJ's aides repeatedly emphasized that these plans did not commit the United States to any particular action. They advised that it would take all the ships several days to reach Brazilian waters, leaving plenty of time for consideration of whether to make use of them. Similar considerations surrounded a separate scheme approved by the administration to stockpile arms and ammunition for possible delivery to Brazil via air if the situation seemed to warrant such a move.[32]

In the event, material support for the coup proved unnecessary. Despite lack of coordination among the conspirators, key military units joined the rebels and the generals tightened their grip without significant opposition. Calls for popular resistance fizzled, as did appeals by labor leaders for a general strike. Meanwhile, no evidence of a communist conspiracy dedicated to Goulart—long a source of anxiety among conservatives—came to light. A pivotal moment came in the late morning of April 1, when the fence-sitting general Amaury Kruel threw his support behind the coup after Goulart refused to disavow his links to the Central Geral dos Trabalhadores, a major communist-led labor organization.[33] Later that day, Goulart left Rio and the whole undertaking was "about 95% over," Gordon cabled Washington. "It looks," added the ambassador, "as though the good guys are in control."[34] The Pentagon ordered the naval task force to stop, engage in "some kind of limited exercise to provide cover," and then turn around.[35] Goulart fled into exile in Uruguay on April 4.

None of this meant that U.S. anxieties were at an end. On the contrary, the coup's success raised new questions that would preoccupy U.S. leaders for years to come: What was the nature of the new Brazilian regime? How much influence would the military wield? To what extent was it committed to constitutional government, and what difference should the answer make to U.S. policy? Unquestionably, U.S. leaders had moved away from the outspoken support for democracy that had infused the Alliance for Progress at its inception. Yet significant pressures still operated on the Johnson administration to maintain a semblance of constitutional rule in Brazil and thus, as Rusk put it, "some color of legitimacy" for a government likely to cooperate closely with the United States.[36]

U.S. leaders seldom articulated their reasons for supporting at least the veneer of constitutionalism, but at least three factors weighed in their thinking. For one thing, Johnson and his advisers, for all their relief over Goulart's ouster, saw themselves as defenders of democracy and progress. Even as they backed a military coup, U.S. leaders searched for plausible ways to reassure themselves that they were preserving freedom in the longer term. Internationally, Washington's claim to leadership in the hemisphere rested in part on its ability to distance itself from a long history of heavy-handed behavior, including a marked tendency to exercise power through friendly autocrats who had gained authority via dubious means. The trend toward independent foreign policies in the hemisphere made some U.S. officials wary of alienating more Latin Americans through extraconstitutional regime changes that could be attributed to U.S. machinations. Domestically, meanwhile, the administration had reason to project moderation in policymaking toward Brazil, even if its highest priority was to squelch the danger of leftist takeover. Although American public opinion strongly backed assertive defense of U.S. interests in the hemisphere, LBJ and his aides were aware that the liberal wing of the Democratic Party, backed by the editorial pages of the *New York Times* and *Washington Post,* opposed a hardline policy in Latin America.[37] To the extent that the administration relied on Congress to support its foreign policy preferences, Johnson and his aides felt pressure to tout their democratic purposes.

No matter their mix of motives, a broad array of administration officials wanted the new government in Brazil to appear as legitimate as possible. They drew confidence from the fact that the elected civilian governors of states with more than half of Brazil's population had come out against Goulart within the first two days of the coup.[38] Mostly, though, they welcomed evidence that the transfer of power was proceeding along a path that could plausibly be construed as consistent with the Brazilian constitution. Undersecretary of State George Ball advised Johnson on April 2 that anti-Goulart elements of the Brazilian Congress had played their part by declaring the presidency vacant and promoting Ranieri Mazzilli, the president of the Chamber of Deputies, as acting president of the republic. "There is some question as to whether or not this is legal," Ball acknowledged, and he urged LBJ to hold off on any decision to recognize Mazzilli until the issue was cleared up. But he had no doubt about the ultimate implications for Washington. "We will treat this government," Ball said of Mazzilli's interim administration, "as a continuation of the old one."[39] Johnson quickly accepted the idea. Later that day, LBJ sent a note offering Mazzilli "warmest good wishes" on his "installation as President of the United States of Brazil."[40] Secretary of State Rusk publicly declared his support for the new government the next day, contending that the succession had taken place "as foreseen by the Constitution" of Brazil and that therefore no difficult questions about recognition had arisen.[41]

Rusk's affirmation of the new government obscured doubts, however, that persisted out of public view. Even Gordon, who had urged quick recognition, acknowledged the dubious legality of Mazzilli's ascent to power, noting that neither a majority of the Brazilian Congress nor the country's highest court had endorsed the transition. More worrying still was the behavior of the Brazilian officers who had engineered the coup. Senior generals declared their respect for the constitution and denied any intention to bring "pressure tactics" to bear on civilian leaders, but it was easy to see something very different playing out.[42] The CIA reported on April 4 that the military aimed to remove leftists from all levels of government and to establish a "junta" that would "control the government."[43] The accuracy of that prediction became clear in the following days. First, General Costa e Silva, who had proclaimed himself head of a new Comando Supremo Revolucionário (Supreme Revolutionary Command), reached agreement with supportive civilian politicians on a measure that became known as the First Institutional Act. The measure, promulgated on April 9, distorted the intent of Brazil's 1946 constitution by giving the president authority to declare a state of emergency, remove elected officials from office, dismiss civil servants, and annul the political rights of citizens deemed to have committed subversion, with no possibility of appeal. Second, Congress, disregarding constitutional constraints on the role of military officers in politics, elected General Castelo Branco to replace Mazzilli and serve the remainder of Goulart's term as president.

Washington's anxieties intensified as the full implications of these measures became clear in the following weeks. Under the new government's Operação Limpeza (Operation Cleanup), police and military units arrested as many as fifty thousand people in the first three months after the coup, a roundup that sometimes degenerated into "ugly brutality," in the words of *Time* magazine. "Brazil today," reported the magazine shortly after the coup, "is an armed camp, astir with hate and fear."[44] Reports of torture by security forces became so widespread that the government ultimately succumbed to pressure to launch an investigation. (Unsurprisingly, investigators found no proof.) Meanwhile, military courts were established to root out officials who had supported Goulart or otherwise engaged in subversive activities. Castelo Branco's regime went to work dismissing leftists from the Congress.[45] In all, 122 military officers, several state governors, and forty members of Congress, including popular ex-president Juscelino Kubitschek, were removed from their posts.[46]

Concerned that the new government was going too far, U.S. officials quietly urged that the junta moderate its behavior. Gordon considered the purging of forty members of the Brazilian legislature to be "grossly excessive" and warned leaders of the new government that such actions might jeopardize U.S. support. "We are happy with the results of the revolution," Gordon assured the Brazilian minister of war on April 8. But U.S. backing of the new regime, Gordon added, depended on the opinion of congressional and public opinion in the United States, "which is very sensitive to anything which smacks of an old-fashioned reactionary Latin American military coup." Military attaché Vernon Walters made a similar point in conversation with Castelo Branco.[47] U.S. worries mounted as Operação Limpeza went forward. In

Washington, the State Department objected especially to procedures that denied suspected subversives any rights to know the charges against them, to defend themselves, or to appeal. Rusk instructed Gordon not only to protest the regime's behavior but also to suggest specific changes to Brazilian law to require speedy trials and permit appeals. "I am sure you will appreciate," Rusk wrote to Gordon, "that the failure on the part of the Brazilian Government to follow due processes of law and to proceed in a democratic manner will increase our difficulties in responding to Brazilian requests for economic assistance."[48]

In practice, though, officials driving policy toward Brazil showed little interest in carrying out their threats when the junta failed to comply with their demands. At first, U.S. tolerance of the junta's behavior flowed largely from a sense that, for all its blemishes, the new regime had crushed a serious danger of communist takeover and scored a major Cold War victory for the West. Whatever their distaste for the regime's repression, advised Gordon, U.S. leaders must recognize that Brazil had had "a very narrow escape from [a] communist-dominated dictatorship"—a view that the Brazilian government worked strenuously to reinforce as it resisted U.S. pressure to moderate its behavior.[49] The new foreign minister, Vasco Leitão da Cunha, boasted to reporters, in fact, that the coup had done no less than save all of Latin America from communism.[50]

Such claims became increasingly far-fetched during the spring and summer of 1964, when virtually no evidence came to light to suggest that the coup had rescued Brazil, much less the region, from a leftist power grab. But U.S. policymakers readily fell back on a broader set of rationales for standing by the generals despite the repression they unleashed. For one thing, they concluded that the coup dealt a major setback to long-term Soviet and Cuban ambitions throughout Latin America. For the Soviets, reported the CIA, the coup marked a stinging defeat of Moscow's strategy to use nonviolent infiltration of Latin American governments and labor unions to expand communist influence and weaken U.S. interests. To the extent that communists remained active in Brazil, the CIA predicted a damaging power struggle between elements loyal to Soviet preferences and the smaller pro-Chinese faction that advocated armed struggle. Meanwhile, Goulart's ouster seemed to crush Fidel Castro's best hope of overcoming his government's isolation in the hemisphere. Brazil broke diplomatic relations with Cuba in May.[51]

The Johnson administration certainly had no complaints about the junta's realignment of Brazilian foreign policy. True, the new leadership, eager to discourage any impression of subservience to Washington, insisted that it would pursue an "independent" foreign policy. But Castelo Branco used the occasion of a state visit by French president Charles de Gaulle in October to make clear that Brazil was uninterested in the French notion of a "third force" between West and East. Brazil was "firmly a part" of the Pan-American system led by the United States, declared Castelo Branco in remarks widely reported in the Brazilian press.[52] The new regime also demonstrated its pro-U.S. orientation by breaking diplomatic relations with Cuba, backing a strict economic embargo of the island, asserting a renewed commitment to the Alliance for Progress, and practicing what one admiring U.S. report called a "new attitude of coolness and correctness" toward the Soviet Union, China, and other communist nations.[53] All in all, avowed Leitão da Cunha in July, the overriding goal of Brazilian foreign policy was to "strengthen all the ties to the United States, our great neighbor and friend to the north."[54]

That pledge acquired new significance for U.S. leaders in early August, when Johnson ordered air strikes against North Vietnam in retaliation for suspected attack on U.S. warships in the Gulf of Tonkin. Castelo Branco quickly praised the U.S. action in a note to Johnson. LBJ, frustrated about the lack of international enthusiasm for his policies in Indochina, responded warmly to Castelo Branco. Linking communist subversion in South Vietnam and Brazil, LBJ insisted that "there comes a point at which countries such as the United States and Brazil, firmly committed to the peaceful solution of problems, must exercise their basic rights of self-defense."[55] The Brazilian response to the Gulf of Tonkin episode was even more favorable than U.S. officials fully realized. Noting that Southeast Asia was "distant and remote" from Latin America, the State Department cautioned against any expectation that Brazil would provide tangible support for the war effort in Indochina. Western Hemisphere governments, noted a study completed in late August, had "more pressing needs for their limited resources at home."[56] In fact, however, the exchange of letters sparked a flurry of speculation in the Brazilian press indicating that senior air force and especially naval officers, apparently eager to demonstrate their fidelity to Washington's leadership, were weighing a contribution to the U.S.-led war.[57] The idea came to nothing in the short term but laid the groundwork for further discussion of the issue as the war in Vietnam expanded in the months to come.

The administration also tolerated the new government's authoritarianism because of its satisfaction with the economic reforms embraced by the generals. To be sure, points of disagreement persisted between Washington and the new Brazilian government, including a long-simmering dispute over U.S. demands that Brazil purchase an unprofitable U.S.-based utility company generally known as AMFORP (the American & Foreign Power Company).[58] Eager to apply pressure for a solution to that problem and uncertain at first of the new government's determination to address the country's massive economic woes, Washington, like other potential foreign creditors, took a wait-and-see approach. Only in June 1964 did the United States finally announce a $50 million aid package. That delay did not mean, however, that the Johnson administration disliked what it saw from the new regime. Although the government favored a gradualist approach over the "shock treatment" preferred by the International Monetary Fund, it vowed its commitment to major changes of the sort long demanded by Washington. Brazil was "seriously proceeding on reform measures" despite having to make "disagreeable economic decisions" that pinched many ordinary Brazilians and risked the regime's credibility with the population at large, noted a National Security Council assessment as U.S. aid began to flow in June.[59] Among the initiatives that won approval in Washington were measures to fight inflation and stabilize the economy by slashing "nonessential" government spending, to reduce the yawning federal budget deficit, to simplify the tax code, to enforce payment of taxes, to restrict private-sector credit, to control wages, and to empower federal authorities to enact these innovations. Even as the World Bank and IMF remained cautious about new help for Brazil, the United States committed close to $1 billion in the final seven months of 1964, cementing its status as the military regime's most avid supporter.[60]

The Johnson administration's willingness to tolerate the Brazilian regime's authoritarian ways flowed as well from the same consideration that had eased American minds about the possibility of a coup many months earlier: a sense that the military was apolitical and would, once it had implemented necessary reforms, restore democracy. To some extent, U.S. optimism in this regard stemmed from officials' high regard for Castelo Branco, a well-educated and thoughtful sixty-three-year-old associated with a moderate group of officers who seemed committed to the restoration of democracy in due course. To many Americans, he seemed to be "above party interest" and mostly concerned with the restoration of order.[61] He was "basically centrist" in his orientation and "makes a point of denouncing extremists on both sides," concluded the CIA.[62] All in all, contended McGeorge Bundy, Castelo Branco was turning out to be "quite a fine fellow."[63]

Americans had some reason to view Castelo Branco in this way. As leader of the so-called Sorbonne group of officers—a faction of relatively cosmopolitan military men connected to the Escola Superior de Guerra (Higher War College)—he distanced himself from the "hard line" wing that favored a thorough purge of Brazilian society and had fewer scruples about violating constitutional processes.[64] Yet American confidence in Castelo Branco also reflected willful blindness about the likelihood that he and his fellow moderates would restore democracy. For one thing, U.S. officials, though well aware of factionalism within the Brazilian military and the fragility of Castelo Branco's hold on power, devoted little study to the question of what would happen if the right wing secured control. In late July 1964, for instance, a wide-ranging CIA assessment noted that hardline pressure could lead Castelo Branco "to resort to more forceful methods" but failed to develop the point in any way.[65]

Nor did the U.S. bureaucracy, which tended to equate the regime with the behavior of its preeminent leader, delve much into the ideological underpinnings of the new government as a whole. In fact, since the late 1950s, military officers had been developing a set of ideas known as the National Security Doctrine, which provided a blueprint for Brazil's transformation over the following years. At the heart of this outlook, which the new regime proclaimed publicly as the government's official position in November 1964, lay a starkly Manichean view of the Cold War and the place of Brazil within the global struggle. This dogma held that nothing less than the fate of Western civilization and Christianity was at stake in the East-West struggle, which, given the pointlessness of war between the two nuclear-armed superpowers, was certain to take place in peripheral areas such as Brazil. Under these perilous circumstances, the generals insisted that the state must hold indisputable power to marshal the nation's resources, enhance its power, and ensure unity of purpose. Under the banner of "Security and Development," the regime viewed not just acts of subversion but even mere expressions of dissent as threats to the state that must be stamped out. Nowhere in this bundle of ideas did the regime attach importance to the return of democracy except as a far-off goal that would affirm the innovations wrought by the military.[66]

## "Unwritten Alliance"

Events in 1965 and 1966 forced U.S. officials to recognize that their hopes for moderation were misplaced. Brazilian politics lurched to the right as Castelo Branco came under pressure from officers who championed the *linha dura*. This unmistakable trend stirred new concerns in Washington and tested the Johnson administration's tolerance for a regime whose promises of democratic restoration were increasingly far-fetched. Washington's fundamental attitude toward Brazil was never a matter of serious doubt, however, and the Johnson administration reciprocated the regime's desire for an "unwritten alliance," as Foreign Minister José Magalhães Pinto put it during a meeting with Dean Rusk in September 1966.[67] The Johnson administration, having shed the voices of dissent that might have resisted, lined up squarely behind the Brazilian regime, even as their blinders about the nature of the government dropped away. In this period, then, lay U.S. policy decisions every bit as consequential as the decision to support a coup in the first place. Americans rationalized authoritarianism in Brazil no longer as a short-term expedient certain to lay the foundation for the restoration of democracy but as an end in itself.

Castelo Branco's rightward shift reflected recognition among Brazilian conservatives in mid-1964 that they could not achieve their economic and political goals in the time remaining before the next presidential election, scheduled for November 1965. Indeed, supporters worried that the government might lose popularity as *brasileiros* coped with the full effects of its economic austerity program without seeing any of the benefits that would presumably follow in due course. In July 1964, Castelo Branco caved in to pressure to accept a constitutional amendment postponing the election to November 1966 and extending his presidency until March 1967. Four months after accepting that arrangement, Castelo Branco removed the governor of the state of Goiás due to suspicions about his leftist sympathies. The retreat from democracy accelerated in the middle months of 1965. First, in March, an antigovernment candidate won an election for mayor of São Paulo, stirring outrage among military hardliners and fear about potential setbacks in upcoming gubernatorial elections in eleven Brazilian states. Castelo Branco and Congress responded in July with measures to tighten eligibility requirements for aspiring candidates. Right-wing anxiety intensified four months later, though, when moderate opposition candidates won the governorships of Minas Gerais and Guanabara, two of Brazil's most populous and politically influential states.[68]

Fearful that his right-wing critics would mount a new coup aimed at establishing a full-fledged dictatorship, Castelo Branco took his most definitive steps away from democracy. Undoubtedly, he successfully resisted demands that he block the inauguration of the two governors and even assemble military tribunals to investigate them. But he conceded that steps must be taken to prevent such political setbacks in the future. On October 27, 1965, Castelo Branco proclaimed the Second Institutional Act, which gave the government powers to manipulate what remained of Brazil's democratic procedures. More specifically, the measure dissolved all existing political parties and replaced them with two new ones: the government-backed Aliança Renovadora Nacional and an officially approved opposition, the Movimento Democrático Brasileiro. The act also bolstered the president's powers to strip citizens of political rights and remove officeholders from their positions, extended the jurisdiction of the military courts, and replaced the popular election of the nation's highest officials, including state governors, with new processes that concentrated power in the hands of federal authorities. Castelo Branco and other moderates may have hoped that these measures would facilitate the restoration of democracy by assuring conservatives of reliable outcomes when the military stepped back. But it was not hard to see that these measures might just as well mark an open-ended retreat from democracy of any sort.[69]

These developments, supplemented in February 1966 by a Third Institutional Act giving state governments authority to appoint mayors of state capitals and other "national security" cities, generated alarm in the U.S. embassy and in Washington. Although the act seemed to fall "well short of outright dictatorship," Gordon condemned it as a "severe setback" to U.S. hopes for Brazil and expressed alarm that the government had made "much greater than necessary concessions to the hard line." The measures seemed likely to fuel further polarization of Brazilian politics by simultaneously emboldening the extreme left and right, while, internationally, disrupting hemispheric unity by sparking other Latin American governments to condemn Brazil.[70] In Washington, State Department spokesmen insisted that the Institutional Act was a domestic matter on which the Johnson administration would not comment, but behind the scenes, senior officials shared Gordon's assessment. National Security Adviser Bundy speculated in a memo for the president that the act would weaken support for Castelo Branco within Brazil and the United States, where he had enjoyed a "generally good image." In order to distance the United States from the Brazilian government and demonstrate displeasure, Bundy suggested that the administration might do no less than "take a fresh look at our assistance to Brazil."[71]

Bundy's suggestion, which harkened back to debates within the Kennedy White House about right-wing regimes in the Third World, went nowhere. Although Gordon and other U.S. officials denounced the Institutional Act in conversations with Castelo Branco, Secretary Rusk, possibly in consultation with the president, rejected the ambassador's proposal that the administration issue a public statement criticizing Brazil's retreat from democracy. To take even that mild step, noted an NSC summary of the matter, risked laying the United States open to the charge of interfering in Brazil's internal affairs.[72] But a larger array of considerations lay behind the continuity in U.S. policy as the Brazilian regime shifted to the right. As with the initial decision to support a coup and to back Castelo Branco's regime in the spring of 1964, U.S. policy in the months surrounding the Second Institutional Act resulted from calculations about Brazilian politics, the status of Brazil's economy, and the dynamics of the Cold War in the Western Hemisphere.

Washington's support for Castelo Branco still rested in part on the notion that he could be relied upon more than any other potential leader to guide Brazil down a moderate path. As the Brazilian leader steadily moved to the right, however, the U.S. definition of moderation shifted in subtle but consequential ways. Americans looked to Castelo Branco not so much to restore constitutional practice as to resist the installation of a full-fledged dictatorship under the control of hardline generals. This shift proved uncomfortable for many U.S. officials, especially Gordon, who bought more fully than any participant in the policymaking process into the idea that Washington could count on Castelo Branco to restore democracy. That expectation was mostly extinguished by the Second Institutional Act. The measure not only marked a "substantial retrogression" from the political goals long espoused by Castelo Branco's regime, Gordon noted on November 14, but also demonstrated that the United States should "have no illusions regarding our ability greatly to influence [the] course of political developments in Brazil."[73] No one knew better than Gordon how much effort U.S. leaders had expended to shape the new government, and yet, he acknowledged, it had all amounted to little.

Gordon attributed Washington's difficulties to the sheer "size and complexity" of Brazil, but he and other U.S. officials also blamed the rightward lurch on Castelo Branco's leadership, which they viewed with an increasingly critical eye.[74] A man who had once been described as introspective and serene now seemed aloof and uninspiring. Instead of rallying Brazil's centrists, noted an NSC report, he had failed to "develop a political base" on which a stable political order could be built. "This failure reflected the technocratic character of the cabinet and the President's inexperience and distaste for political leadership," the report noted. The government handled organized labor "ineptly," while students and intellectuals were "positively antagonized," the NSC complained.[75] The CIA observed, meanwhile, that Castelo Branco had mishandled the all-important relationship between the military and elected officials who supported the government, the nexus on which any hopes for the restoration of constitutionality rested. Some members of the Brazilian Congress had lost faith in the president, contended the CIA, while hardline junior officers displayed "growing disdain" for the government and civilian politicians alike.[76] All in all, U.S. agriculture secretary Orville Freeman wrote President Johnson after a tour of Brazil in the spring of 1966, only about 20 percent of Brazilians supported the government.[77]

And yet the Johnson administration readily accepted the need to continue supporting Castelo Branco's regime and found enough to like about the regime to justify that approach. U.S. officials came to terms with Castelo Branco's concessions to the hardliners and, during late 1965 and 1966, backed away from some of their harsher judgments. Numerous assessments by the embassy in Rio de Janeiro and by various Washington bureaucracies speculated, albeit with a tone of uncertainty that contrasted with firmer judgments expressed in the more optimistic days of 1964, that Castelo Branco had merely done what he needed to do to stay in power and did not intend to use the most extreme powers granted to the executive under the Second Institutional Act. Castelo Branco "probably" still hoped to steer a moderate course, the CIA concluded in November 1964.[78] Certainly Castelo Branco worked hard to encourage this belief in his interactions with Gordon, who dutifully informed Washington of the general's reassurances and expressed cautious satisfaction in early 1966 that Castelo Branco had returned to his earlier path.[79]

Mostly, though, U.S. officials judged that Castelo Branco, whatever his actual intentions, was infinitely preferable to the extreme right. As always, deeply ingrained assumptions about the desirability of democracy and the duty of the United States to oppose dictatorships suffused this judgment. But more concrete calculations also fed into the administration's determination to stand by Castelo Branco. For one thing, the Johnson administration feared that members of Congress, the press, and even the broader public might raise uncomfortable questions about U.S. policy in Brazil if the government fell into the hands of hardliners with fewer scruples about civil rights or the long-run restoration of democracy. On the whole, Johnson and his aides had good reason to be pleased with public and congressional attitudes toward the administration's handling of foreign policy in general and Latin America in particular. Even Johnson's controversial decision to send U.S. Marines into the Dominican Republic in the spring of 1965 won broad public approval, with 76 percent of Americans backing the invasion and only 17 percent opposing it, according to a poll conducted in mid-May.[80] Regarding Brazil, U.S. support for the 1964 coup and the consolidation of Castelo Branco's rule stirred little dissension in the United States, where press reports emphasized the government's moderate character.

The mood changed to a degree around the time of the Second Institutional Act, which coincided with a much broader upsurge in popular and congressional criticism of the Johnson administration in connection with Vietnam. Democratic senator Wayne Morse, chair of the Senate subcommittee on U.S.-Latin American affairs, blasted the act as a "disastrous reversal for liberty" and insisted that claims about the regime's democratic intentions "will not fool any but those who want to be fooled."[81] More worrying for the White House, Senate Foreign Relations Committee chair J. William Fulbright, a bellwether of liberal opinion about foreign policy, dramatically shifted his attitude about Brazil. On a trip to Brazil in August 1965, Fulbright had voiced strong support of the Castelo Branco government, endorsing the notion that sometimes "economic and social development must precede democracy" and that "collective discipline" permitted a country to "focus on its real problems."[82] By the following May, however, the senator, responding to the arrests of four Americans in Brazil, had changed his tune. The regime showed "clear disregard for due process," subjecting the detainees to a hearing that amounted to "a mockery and a farce," he charged.[83]

Criticism of the regime—and of the U.S. role in the coup that had brought it to power—surged anew in June 1966 during Senate hearings on LBJ's plan to promote Lincoln Gordon to be assistant secretary of state for Inter-American

Affairs. The nomination of an official deeply implicated in the overthrow of a democratically elected regime spoke volumes about the administration's attitude toward Latin America, but it elicited sharp questions from Foreign Relations Committee liberals. Senator Albert Gore of Tennessee declared that he was "quite a bit disturbed" by Gordon's apparent enthusiasm for the coup, while Senator Joseph S. Clark of Pennsylvania demanded a "right angle turn" away from the "hard Thomas Mann line" that had laid the groundwork for U.S. partnerships with authoritarian governments. As before, Morse also spoke up in no uncertain terms. "When the chips of freedom [were] down," said Morse, referring to the run-up to the coup, "we walked out." He accused Gordon of offering mere "window dressing" by insisting that Castelo Branco had acted only to defend democracy in the long run. Castelo Branco's promises, insisted Morse, would have "vanished into thin air" if he had been seriously impeded in imposing the military's power over Brazil.[84]

It would be going too far to suggest that any of these complaints reflected the emergence of a broad movement critical of U.S. policy toward Brazil. Gordon perhaps recognized the potential of widespread criticism when he pushed Castelo Branco to hew closer to democratic norms by warning him of growing disquiet in the U.S. Congress, which controlled the purse strings of U.S. economic and military assistance.[85] On the whole, though, he pushed back successfully against Senate critics by insisting as usual that Castelo Branco represented a centrist response to Brazil's political troubles that would bring satisfactory political and economic progress over the long run. "Political development is a process in time," Gordon told the Senate committee during his 1966 confirmation hearing. Reflecting broadly held ideas within the administration, he insisted that political reform necessarily "goes along with economic and social development" and should not be prioritized as a separate objective of U.S. policy.[86]

U.S. dedication to Castelo Branco also stemmed from Washington's assessment that a takeover by the far right would undermine the pursuit of the Cold War in the hemisphere. Despite its obvious weaknesses, the existing government seemed best positioned to balance competing factions and thereby strengthen the U.S. drive to promote political moderation and unity of purpose across Latin America, the NSC concluded shortly after the Second Institutional Act. A "military dictatorship," the NSC added, would be not only "unstable" but also "belligerently nationalist" in foreign policy, "[à] la Nasser"—hardly a prediction likely to produce enthusiasm among American leaders whose hostility to neutralism had led them to support Goulart's overthrow in the first place.[87] By contrast, Castelo Branco had not only proclaimed his desire to cooperate with the United States but also repeatedly delivered on that promise, transforming Latin America's largest nation into a reliable supporter of the Johnson administration's priorities around the world.

Brazilian cooperation paid off for Johnson in ways general and specific. Broadly, the eclipse of the leftist danger in Brazil contributed to a dramatically lower sense of urgency about the Cuban threat in the hemisphere—undoubtedly a tremendous relief for a president with little interest in the controversies surrounding Cuba that had so preoccupied Kennedy. Fidel Castro now recognized, reported the CIA in 1966, that "new Cubas" were "not imminent," and the Cubans had "considerably narrowed the scope of their subversive activities" while aligning themselves more closely with the cautious Soviet approach in the Western Hemisphere. U.S. officials saw new dangers in rising Chinese influence in the region as well as disturbing long-term trends such as soaring population growth and looming food shortages, but for the time being they were encouraged by trends playing out since Goulart's ouster.[88]

Reinforcing that optimism were specific policy positions taken by the Castelo Branco's government. Most spectacularly, Brazil vocally backed LBJ's decision in late April 1965 to send U.S. Marines into the Dominican Republic in order to block the restoration of a democratic regime that U.S. officials considered subservient to communist elements. Eager to avoid accusations of old-fashioned U.S. interventionism, Johnson hoped to cast the invasion as much as possible as a multilateral endeavor that reflected the will of the Organization of American States. This desire proved controversial in the weeks that followed, leading some hawkish members of Congress to insist that the United States reassert its right to act unilaterally in the hemisphere.[89] For LBJ, though, embedding the United States within a multilateral operation held obvious appeal as a way to squelch surging protest in Latin American capitals as well as mounting criticism of his administration as a result of simultaneous U.S. escalation in Vietnam. Brazil stood out as a potentially powerful supporter of U.S. moves, and the administration dispatched no less a figure than the veteran diplomat W. Averell Harriman to meet with Castelo Branco.

The outcome was everything LBJ could have wished for. The Brazilian government indicated its expectation of expanded U.S. aid in return for its support, but its backing for the U.S. operation was both ostentatious and abundant, giving credibility to the notion that the intervention amounted to a regional endeavor rather than naked U.S. gunboat diplomacy.[90] Besides providing political support, Brazil sent a battalion of troops, by far the largest among contingents from the six Latin American nations that sent forces under the OAS banner, and accepted command arrangements that placed a Brazilian general in charge of the OAS occupation force charged with securing the new political order. Both Washington and Brasília consistently touted their partnership as a clear-cut success in ensuring a satisfactory solution in the Dominican Republic and upholding the principle of hemispheric cooperation.[91] On the U.S. side, officials particularly celebrated the role of Castelo Branco and speculated that the hard right would likely withdraw the Brazilian force if it came to power.[92]

The Johnson administration also saw Castelo Branco as an important asset in connection with the foreign policy problem that increasingly pushed all others to the side: war in Vietnam. The Johnson administration renewed its "more flags" campaign in the first months of 1965, targeting seven countries in Latin America—Brazil, Argentina, Chile, Colombia, Peru, Venezuela, and Uruguay—despite their distance from the affairs of Southeast Asia.[93] For reasons both symbolic and material, Brazil stood as the most important potential contributor in the region, and U.S. leaders hoped for troops as well as a warship. Some officials were even willing to use U.S. economic aid as leverage to push the Brazilian government in those directions. In December 1965, for example, Johnson authorized a new $150 million loan "with the expectation that every effort will be made to obtain Brazilian military participation in Viet-Nam," as LBJ's emissary to Brazil, W. Averell Harriman, put it. So eager was Johnson for a military commitment—ideally a battalion-sized army or marine unit—that he was willing to absorb the financial cost of such a deployment and to increase overall U.S. aid for the Brazilian military.[94] In Brazil, Gordon made a "very strong pitch on the troops" in a meeting with Castelo Branco despite the ambassador's misgivings about creating political problems for the Brazilian government by inviting criticism from right-wing elements hypersensitive about Brazil's autonomy from the United States.[95]

U.S. pressure appears to have caused dissension among senior Brazilian leaders. Newspaper reports indicated that some Brazilian officers favored acceding to the Johnson administration's request, and at least one prominent civilian, the veteran diplomat Nelson Tabajara de Oliveira, spoke out publicly in favor of a Brazilian military contribution.[96] In the end, however, Castelo Branco, possibly under pressure from War Minister Costa e Silva and other officials worried about creating an impression of subservience to Washington, refused any sort of military contribution, invoking the urgency of domestic economic problems as well as constitutional prohibitions on the use of Brazilian forces outside the region.[97]

Yet all was not lost for the Johnson administration. Castelo Branco's government exceeded all other Latin American nations in its support of U.S. objectives in Southeast Asia. In a November 1965 meeting with Secretary Rusk, the general praised the rapidly expanding U.S. war effort as, ultimately, a defense of the "Western Hemisphere and therefore of Brazil."[98] Castelo Branco wrote to LBJ in even warmer terms in July 1966. "Our solidarity with the United States in [the] face of the Vietnam problem is complete," declared the Brazilian president.[99] Meanwhile, Brazil gratified U.S. officials by granting diplomatic recognition to South Vietnam and stationing diplomats in Bangkok and Washington to manage the relationship. More tangibly, the Brazilian regime sent nine hundred pounds of medical supplies to South Vietnam in June 1965 and another one and a half tons in the fall of 1966. A donation of one thousand bags of coffee followed in January 1967.[100] By that time, a tacit agreement seems to have taken hold, enabling the Johnson administration to list Brazil among the nations supporting U.S. policy in Southeast Asia while keeping the Brazilian contribution within tight limits: Brazil offered both rhetorical and limited material support in return for Washington's agreement to drop the idea of combat forces. Rusk accepted—apparently without serious quibble—Brazilian insistence that the question of troops be dropped from the agenda for Costa e Silva's meetings with LBJ in January 1967, and the two leaders avoided the issue thereafter.[101]

U.S. acceptance of Brazil's authoritarianism also stemmed from continued satisfaction with its economic program. Undoubtedly, the results were consistently mixed. On the positive side, reform efforts paid off in dramatically lower annual inflation rates (just 25 percent in 1967 compared to 100 percent in April 1964), stronger flows of foreign investment, and reduced public spending, which fell from 12.1 percent of Brazil's gross national product to 10.5 percent in the first two years after the coup. On the negative side, austerity measures drove a 5 percent reduction in industrial output in 1965, an alarming development certain to heighten Brazil's chronic unemployment, stir popular unrest, and weaken the government's popularity. Meanwhile, a huge coffee crop and an unexpected trade surplus exacerbated the government's problems by necessitating large payouts in order to fulfill the government's commitments to maintain commodity prices and interfering with efforts to fight inflation.[102] For U.S. officials, as for Castelo Branco and his supporters, though, good and bad news led to the same conclusion: the government was succeeding, if slowly, in stabilizing the Brazilian economy. The good news naturally spoke for itself, while officials often interpreted the bad news as evidence that progress would unavoidably incur short-term pain that would be resolved by stronger doses of the same medicine.

Although U.S. policymakers criticized Castelo Branco for failing to sell his economic reforms more effectively, they consistently praised the policies themselves and backed a steady stream of U.S. assistance. A typical U.S. study lauded the government for undertaking unpopular but necessary initiatives including wage and credit restraints, budget cuts, and withdrawal of subsidies.[103] So optimistic were State Department officials that the U.S. aspiration to convert Brazil into a net exporter of development aid by 1970 seemed plausible.[104] The World Bank and International Monetary Fund were also impressed with Castelo Branco's reforms and, starting in February 1965, announced a series of new loans. Indeed, the IMF awarded Brazil its highest credit rating.[105] But U.S. aid, driven by a redoubled sense of Brazil's centrality to the broader Alliance for Progress, flowed in even more impressive quantities. Of the $625 million promised by Washington from the start of the Alliance for Progress to Goulart's overthrow, the United States disbursed $525 million following the coup. Congress approved another $625 million between late 1964 and the end of 1967, while Brazil lengthened its lead as the biggest recipient of U.S. military aid in the hemisphere.[106]

## Setbacks and Solidarity

U.S. policymaking followed a distinct pattern in the year from the fall of 1965 to the fall of 1966. Johnson administration officials, including even stalwart proponents of the 1964 coup such as Lincoln Gordon, expressed anger over the Second Institutional Acts and seriously considered whether the United States should distance itself from a government that showed so little dedication to democratic principles. As the months passed, however, Gordon and others gradually came to terms with Castelo Branco's government and learned to live with his authoritarian ways. To some extent, this acceptance flowed from a sense that Castelo Banco and his supporters—a group increasingly known as *castelistas*—were better than the alternatives and might yet pursue a moderate course. American tolerance flowed as well, though, from broad recognition that the government, despite its shortcomings, in fact served U.S. interests in multiple ways. Once the initial shock wore off and U.S. officials had an opportunity to recalibrate their expectations and perhaps their sense of themselves as unfailing champions of democracy, that is, recognition of the regime's value to U.S. purposes in the Western Hemisphere and globally easily trumped qualms about its antidemocratic tendencies.

The same pattern played out between late 1966 and the end of the Johnson administration. In several ways, developments in Brazil tested anew U.S. confidence in the military regime. The most immediate challenge to U.S. comfort with the government in Brasília was the election of General Costa e Silva to the presidency in October 1966. That outcome was hardly surprising. Attempting simultaneously to demonstrate moderation and appease hardliners, Castelo Branco had agreed not to run for a second term. His decision left a clear path for the military's top choice, War Minister Costa e Silva, who was also aided by the opposition party's decision to boycott an election process widely regarded as rigged. The *castelistas'* fear that the new president would turn Brazil

FIGURE 4.2. President Lyndon Johnson and Brazilian president Artur da Costa e Silva, accompanied by aides, confer while walking across the White House grounds on January 26, 1967. LBJ Library photo by Yoichi Okamoto.

sharply toward the right led them to push hard for a new Brazilian constitution in the waning days of Castelo Branco's presidency, an effort that came to fruition in January 1967, just weeks before Costa e Silva's inauguration. The new constitution, drafted by legal experts appointed by the lame-duck president, essentially enshrined the Institutional Acts as the basic law of the land, thereby limiting the new government's freedom to take further steps to dismantle democracy. Even so, it was easy to see that Costa e Silva might not be so easily constrained. He had long been the chief spokesman for the *linha dura* in senior government circles, and the new constitution gave him unspecified powers to crack down on "criminal infractions against national security, the political and social order, or to the detriment of the property, services, and interests of the federal government."[107]

Uncertainty about the direction Costa e Silva would take his nation underlay American anxiety during the president-elect's visit to Washington in January 1967. While hopeful that the gregarious general known for his love of horse racing might give a more human face to the Brazilian government than the dour Castelo Branco had done, U.S. officials had no illusions about the policy positions that the new president had long championed and was likely to implement once he held the reins of power. U.S. intelligence services, for instance, viewed Costa e Silva as "more a man of action" who was likely to "resort to harsh, authoritarian measures." Just as worrying was the incoming leader's greater willingness to play on themes of Brazilian nationalism, even at the cost of causing "friction" with the United States.[108] The general worked hard to counter such views, emphasizing his moderate intentions during visits with U.S. officials and in public. His goal, he told newly appointed U.S. ambassador John W. Tuthill, was to lead Brazil "back to normalcy" through unfortunate but necessary reliance on the military, which he characterized as "essentially democratic" in orientation. Moreover, Costa e Silva affirmed his desire to preserve his country's "special relationship" with the United States.[109] Once he assumed the presidency on March 15, 1967, however, these assurances rang hollow.

For one thing, the new government confirmed U.S. suspicions that it would have even less interest than its predecessor in restoring any semblance of democracy. Undoubtedly, predictions of a sharp rightward turn proved inaccurate. U.S. officials expressed relief that Costa e Silva, despite the heavy presence of military officers in his inner circle, seemed to favor a truce among contending factions and preservation of the status quo. If U.S. officials had a complaint early in Costa e Silva's tenure, it centered on his lackadaisical leadership. But Costa e Silva's passivity increasingly appeared to indicate a drift away from any intent to restore democracy once essential economic and political reforms had been carried out. In this way, Brazil appeared to slide into a more permanent state of authoritarianism as the government abandoned assurances that had helped Americans reconcile themselves to the coup and the regime that it brought to power. "The administration may change its views in time," reported Ambassador Tuthill in June 1967, "but for the present—and probably for the next few years at least—the punitive acts as well as the system institutionalized by Castelo Branco are both considered 'untouchable.'"[110] Eight months later, U.S. assessments were even gloomier. Under strong pressure from military hardliners to clamp down on civilian criticism, Costa e Silva was actively weighing "moves of a more authoritarian nature" that might expose the administration to heightened congressional criticism for supporting military regimes, Rostow reported to LBJ in February 1968.[111]

As Rostow suggested, U.S. support for authoritarianism in Brazil and other Latin American countries was increasingly contributing to Johnson's problems with Congress and the American public. Dissent against U.S. policies in the Western Hemisphere did not come close to the scale and ardor of opposition to the war in Vietnam. Yet congressional skepticism about U.S. backing of Latin American military governments spread beyond relative eccentrics like

Oregon senator Wayne Morse to other liberals, who increasingly voiced the globalist themes that had once circulated within the Kennedy administration. In his 1966 book *The Arrogance of Power,* Senator Fulbright condemned U.S. policymakers for allowing the slightest whiff of communism in a Latin American country to drive the United States into a "stifling embrace of the generals and the oligarchs" that would prove counterproductive by emboldening the left.[112] Meanwhile, Senator Frank Church, who would lead hearings into human rights abuses by the Brazilian junta in the early 1970s, began speaking out about U.S. policy toward Latin America for the first time. Since Castro had come to power, Church told his Senate Foreign Relations committee colleagues in 1967, eight democratically elected governments had been overthrown in military coups throughout the hemisphere. "In these imprisoned lands," he added, "our identification with the garrison forces—far from augmenting our prestige—tends only to poison mass opinion against us."[113] Beyond the corridors of power, meanwhile, a grassroots movement focused on abusive regimes in Latin America sprouted up in the shadows of the much larger surge of dissent spawned by the war in Vietnam. "Slowly, imperceptibly, a loose network of individuals, collectives, and projects emerged to challenge Washington's policies" toward Brazil and other countries in the hemisphere in the mid-1960s, observes historian James N. Green.[114]

Costa e Silva's dictatorial tendencies and the unwelcome attention they drew disturbed U.S. leaders in part because of Brazil's simultaneous drift away from close partnership with the United States in foreign affairs and economic policy. In this sense, Costa e Silva's authoritarianism tested U.S. willingness to support the Brazilian regime more seriously than had Castelo Branco's. The latter, after all, had studiously catered to U.S. preferences in the expectation—certainly correct—that a cooperative approach would win aid for his regime and cushion him from U.S. pressure. Costa e Silva's willingness to distance himself from Washington threatened to unravel the basic bargain—Washington's support for the military government in exchange for close coordination on important issues—that the *castelistas* had made. The reasons for this trend were well understood in Washington. U.S. officials appreciated that hostility to reliance on the United States ran strongly in the hardline circles that most eagerly backed Costa e Silva, a view made more plausible by the declining urgency of U.S. aid as the Brazilian economy strengthened in the later 1960s. Washington also knew that the regime's reliance on nationalist themes reflected its hopes of bolstering popular support as economic austerity and political repression stoked intensifying unrest across Brazilian society. Recognition of underlying causes did not, however, make Brazilian independence easier to bear.

Perhaps most alarming to the Johnson administration was Costa e Silva's insistence on what he called a "sovereign foreign policy."[115] At first, U.S. officials hoped privately that the regime was merely trying to enhance its standing domestically by harping on nationalist themes and that the new rhetoric carried little meaning for the actual conduct of policy.[116] As time passed, however, U.S. fears were confirmed by the government's concrete steps to distance itself from Washington's preferences. "The easy, almost automatic intimacy that U.S. officials inside and outside Brazil enjoyed with their counterparts at almost every level of the Castelo Branco government is already largely a thing of the past," Ambassador Tuthill noted in September 1967.[117] The trend affected U.S.-Brazilian cooperation in numerous policy arenas. Rostow informed the president in June 1967 that Brazil was wavering in its once iron-clad hostility to Cuba and taking an annoyingly "equivocal position" toward U.S. policy in the Middle East, where the Johnson administration was struggling to restore stability after the Six-Day War.[118] These positions stemmed from a desire not just to demonstrate independence from the United States but also to associate Brazil more closely with the developing nations of Africa and Asia in order to help overcome "the division of the world between the North and South," as Costa e Silva put it in an April 1967 speech that ranked the North-South divide alongside the East-West conflict as "one of the great sources of international tension."[119]

Costa e Silva and his foreign minister, the ambitious civilian Magalhães Pinto, provoked alarm in Washington by indicating that the modernization of Brazilian society would trump the nation's alignment with the United States when those two fundamental tenets of Brazilian foreign policy came into conflict. In the arena of nuclear power, for instance, Brasília consistently opposed a draft treaty on nonproliferation that the Johnson administration had made a cornerstone of its arms-control agenda in 1967 and 1968. Although Costa e Silva disavowed any desire for nuclear weapons, he insisted that constraining Brazil's right to develop a nuclear power program would amount to "accepting a new form of dependency certainly not compatible with our aspirations for development."[120]

Similar considerations underpinned another Brazilian bid for autonomy that irritated U.S. leaders: efforts to purchase supersonic aircraft from France. The problem emerged when Washington, eager to restrain the spread of sophisticated military technologies within the hemisphere and to keep Latin American regimes focused on economic problems, rebuffed Brazilian efforts to purchase such planes, promising only to deliver a limited quantity of F-5s in 1969 or 1970. In July 1967, the Brazilian government, like its counterpart in Peru, responded by opening talks with the French government on the purchase of Mirage supersonic fighters. The Johnson administration feared French penetration of the Latin American arms market but also appreciated growing congressional opposition to U.S. arms sales, which culminated in a series of legislative amendments requiring the executive branch to limit the provision of weapons to poor nations that failed to hold down their military budgets.[121] "Arms races in other parts of the world resulting in crises (e.g., Kashmir and the Middle East) have made the American people acutely sensitive to United States military involvement overseas and the furnishing of arms to other countries which could result in situations where we might be drawn in," noted one briefing paper for Assistant Secretary of State Covey Oliver.[122] Brazil's ambassador in Washington, Vasco Leitão da Cunha, warned LBJ that U.S. obstruction could fuel a dangerous surge in Brazilian nationalism.[123] Still, boxed in by Congress, U.S. officials saw no alternative to dragging their feet and passing the issue along to the next administration.

Also disturbing to the Johnson administration was the Costa e Silva government's retreat from the support that Castelo Branco had provided for the war in Vietnam. U.S. officials expressed hope that declining Brazilian enthusiasm owed more to internal jockeying among senior officials, above all to Magalhães Pinto's desire to boost his political prospects by separating himself from the president, than to any general change of heart across the government as a whole. Yet by late 1967, it was increasingly clear that Magalhães Pinto was only the most outspoken member of a regime that had shifted significantly on the war. Political and material support for the U.S.-led war effort dried up, and, in December 1967, the foreign minister declared his country's "complete neutrality" in the conflict. Out of public view, State Department officials voiced frustration with this turn of events, declaring their intention to do "all possible" to register U.S. disappointment and to make Magalhães Pinto aware of the "potential consequences" of his words.[124] U.S. officials found, however, that they could do little to change Brazilian minds.

Indeed, the Johnson administration readily understood that it had neither the leverage nor any overriding incentive to apply strong pressure on Costa e Silva's government to hew more closely to U.S. preferences. Indeed, one of the most striking developments in 1967 and 1968 was rapidly declining U.S. confidence about the possibility of exerting influence on the Brazilian regime or other military governments in the hemisphere. A joint commission of State and Defense Department officials made this view explicit in an April 1968 report that could hardly have offered a sharper contrast to the optimism that had surrounded the unveiling of the Alliance for Progress just seven years earlier. "We cannot change rapidly the attitudes or forms of the Latin American governments and thus must carefully adapt our tactics to their characteristics," stated the report, which urged "substantial assistance" even for an authoritarian government so long as it "undertakes modernizing steps intelligently."[125]

Rooted in this logic, U.S. support for Brazil thus remained steady despite worrying developments. Even hinting at a reduction of U.S. assistance for Brazil would, Tuthill insisted in June 1967, run an "unacceptably high risk of [an] adverse political reaction" in Brazilian leadership circles, possibly causing a "breach which would destroy relationships we are attempting to build and would be very difficult to repair." At least for the time being, Tuthill advised Washington to live with the "hyper-sensitive" government in Brasília and took steps to lessen friction by sharply reducing the number of U.S. personnel in Brazil, an endeavor that ultimately reduced the number of U.S. representatives by about one-third.[126]

Underlying these steps were the same judgments that U.S. leaders had made since the early 1960s: the military was far better than the alternatives and had plausible reasons for behaving in ways aimed at securing power to carry out necessary reforms. Connected, too, was LBJ's belief that he had managed Brazil effectively during his years in office. Political adviser Harry McPherson worried in early 1968 that the administration had grown too close to Latin American military regimes and was inviting criticism from, among others, political rival Robert F. Kennedy. "Is there any way to head this off by an announcement that we are about to do something with South American liberals?" McPherson wondered.[127] But LBJ showed little interest in such a move and prided himself on the steps his administration had taken to build stability in the hemisphere, especially Brazil. "Your corn pone president didn't go to Harvard," Johnson told journalist Hugh Sidey in late 1966, "but Brazil hasn't gone communist yet."[128] He was probably right to feel confident that there were few political risks in connection with Brazil. A poll conducted in early 1968, at a time of growing criticism of U.S. support for authoritarian regimes in Brazil and elsewhere, found that 76 percent of Americans had a "favorable" opinion of the nation, making it the highest rated non-European country in the world.[129]

In any case, LBJ's crass assertion captured an indisputable geopolitical reality. Numerous analyses from 1967 and 1968 affirmed that the overall security situation in the hemisphere was reasonably strong, giving Johnson and his advisers little reason to take risks in a massively important country such as Brazil. Unquestionably, U.S. officials worried about a persistent leftist threat and detected a new trend toward guerrilla activity in Latin America's cities. Yet, in a marked contrast to the mood in Washington a few years earlier, State and Defense Department experts concluded in April 1968 that there was little chance of "any significant Castroist successes" or the emergence of any Soviet-backed communist governments in the hemisphere over the next five years. Officials expressed confidence that improving economic conditions throughout Latin America were likely to favor the United States over the long term, even if near-term social dislocations caused by the modernization process caused setbacks from time to time.[130] Implicit in this view was an assumption that played an increasingly important role in U.S. thinking as the 1960s advanced: political and social turmoil might be an indication of success, rather than failure, if it emerged from popular backlash against the efforts of authoritarian regimes to implement modernization that would inevitably impose short-term costs on impoverished societies.

Certainly U.S. officials saw the Brazilian government's management of the economy as one of the strongest reasons to stand behind Costa e Silva. At first after the new president's inauguration, it is true, U.S. officials expressed alarm about the government's intent to relax the austerity policies that Castelo Branco had enacted with strong U.S. and IMF backing. Costa e Silva appointed an entirely new cabinet and relied on a different team of economic advisers, all of which seemed to imply a lack of the seriousness that Castelo Branco had brought to the task.[131] As time passed, however, U.S. officials developed a higher level of comfort with Costa e Silva's less doctrinaire approach, which sought to lighten the burden on the Brazilian populace by lowering or postponing taxes, increasing government subsidies for coffee and other primary goods, and backing away from planned budget cuts. By the end of 1967, economic indicators satisfied Washington that Costa e Silva was still producing significant results, and the Johnson administration continued to deliver aid that averaged $303 million per year from 1964 through 1968 despite congressional efforts to trim foreign aid as the costs of the Vietnam War were pinched more tightly.[132] In 1968, Costa e Silva's first full year in office, came the most impressive gains of all. Brazil's GDP growth soared by 11 percent (up from 4.7 in 1967), while inflation held steady. Meanwhile, industrial output, agricultural production, and exports surged commensurably.[133]

U.S. officials also recognized that Costa e Silva faced a mounting array of political challenges that made his unsavory tendencies—his dependence on hardline military officers as well as his willingness to cater to Brazilian nationalism—at least understandable if not actually desirable. On the right, the government faced the usual pressure from extremists who favored a thorough purge of alleged subversives throughout Brazilian society and new steps to limit the power of civilian politicians. On the left, a fledgling guerrilla movement emerged in the Caparaó mountains north of Rio de Janeiro, and the army headquarters in São Paulo came under attack in June 1967. Dissidents targeted the United States around the same time, bombing the Peace Corps office in Rio de Janeiro and the home of the U.S. Air Force attaché. Challenges to the Brazilian regime intensified in 1968, part of a worldwide surge of antiestablishment activism in that year. The potential of the Vietnam War to stir rebellion was highlighted in 1967 and 1968, when demonstrators in Brazil and several other Latin American nations increasingly linked the war to the repressive tendencies of their own governments and attacked U.S. installations. Thus did activists register their disgust in a way that elided local and global grievances.[134] In Brazil, the military regime, despite its own skepticism about the U.S. war in Vietnam, clearly understood the connection and targeted innumerable political opponents with records of activism against the Vietnam War. Military courts consistently highlighted antiwar behavior—speaking out against the war, displaying the North Vietnamese flag, and taking part in antiwar "solidarity weeks"—as key indicators of political unreliability.[135]

As social tensions escalated, U.S. officials worried that Costa e Silva would crack down, but they also readily foresaw that he might have to do so in order to prevent dramatic lurches to either left or right and keep power in relatively moderate hands. Costa e Silva had "no desire" to impose a more authoritarian form of government, noted a CIA report in November 1968, but he might have no choice if he hoped to preserve "hierarchy and discipline" and to keep the extremists at bay.[136] In this way, U.S. officials subscribed to the same logic that had guided them through Brazil's step-by-step retreat from democracy since 1964: the government's authoritarianism was not only necessary to bring about critical reforms but essential in order to squelch new forms of political chaos that would ensue if it failed. Along the way, the Johnson administration's definition of "moderate" shifted significantly to accommodate geopolitical independence and authoritarian behavior that it once would have excoriated.

## Coda: A Final Test

Events tested the Johnson administration's attitude toward Brazil's military rulers one more time before LBJ surrendered the presidency to Richard Nixon in January 1969. Tensions within Brazil reached the breaking point in December 1968, when the federal legislature refused to lift the immunity of a deputy who had spoken out sharply against the military. On December 13, Costa e Silva gave in to hardline pressure by proclaiming a Fifth Institutional Act and other unprecedentedly draconian measures that abolished most of the remaining elements of Brazilian democracy. Most strikingly, the acts suspended Congress indefinitely, imposed tight censorship on the media, banned all demonstrations against the government, suspended habeas corpus, and affirmed the president's power to suspend any citizen's political rights. Hundreds of Brazilians, including prominent politicians and intellectuals, were arrested. Subsequent measures suspended the legislatures in several states, brought state military and police forces under the control of the central government, postponed upcoming elections, and crafted a new curriculum for Brazilian schools to inculcate students with the key tenets of the National Security Doctrine. Thus did Costa e Silva fully embrace that hard line with which he had flirted for several years, establishing the full-fledged police state whose mass arrests and systematic use of torture to punish and intimidate its enemies became exemplars of dictatorship.[137]

These developments fueled a new wave of protests in the United States, although, as always, criticism of Washington's behavior in Latin America paled in comparison to dissent against the war in Vietnam. The outcry was especially sharp from American media, perhaps no surprise given the sharp crackdown on press freedoms in Brazil. A *New York Times* editorial, for instance, blasted "a clique of hypersensitive officers who claim a monopoly on patriotism and honesty" for carrying out what "can only be called a coup." The generals had "behaved like spoiled children and put even further into the future the day Brazilians dream of when this giant of a country will assume a position of respected leadership in the Americas and the world."[138] The *Washington Post* urged that the Nixon administration reappraise U.S. relations with Brazil, insisting in an editorial that "there is no good reason to maintain a high identification with a repressive government."[139]

Facing such pressures, the Johnson administration responded by suspending both ongoing assistance and consideration of a new aid program for 1969. The harsh measures in Brazil "strike at the very heart of human rights" and placed the Johnson administration in an "extremely difficult position" because of the strong reaction they had engendered within the United States, William Belton, the second-ranking U.S. diplomat in Brazil, charged in a confrontational meeting with Brazilian counterparts.[140] At the same time, however, U.S. officials aimed to minimize the damage. Certainly, Brazilian leaders worked hard to encourage that approach, deploying old rationalizations for new decisions. Foreign Minister Magalhães Pinto told Tuthill, for example, that Costa e Silva chose the "least bad course of action" necessary to hold onto power in the face of extremist pressure and intended to use his new powers "firmly but moderately."[141] The just-appointed Brazilian ambassador to the United States urged Washington against any statement critical of the Brasília regime, requesting that both sides maintain "an atmosphere of normality" in their relations.[142] But U.S. officials hardly needed Brazilian persuasion to accord Costa e Silva the benefit of the doubt. Tuthill suggested a "wait-and-see" approach to aid over the long term while urging Washington to move ahead with existing commitments and to avoid any strong statements that could create "an aftermath of distrust" or "circumscribe our options for the future."[143] The State Department instructed its diplomats in Brazil to take a "calm, friendly and frank" approach in contacts with Brazilian counterparts and to emphasize that there was "still time and good opportunity to avoid the congealing of public opinion in the U.S.A. along lines that would make it very difficult for any administration in this country to continue [existing] degrees of cooperation and mutual assistance."[144]

The administration left it to the incoming Nixon administration to decide whether and when to resume aid disbursements. But it is not difficult to see that Johnson administration officials, before they surrendered their posts, quickly overcame their initial shock and fell back into familiar habits of mind. A month after the events of December 13, Rostow reported to LBJ with satisfaction that the State Department was maintaining normal diplomatic contacts while indicating to Brazilian leaders that Washington was "reviewing" U.S. assistance program, a "polite" way of handling the question.[145] For his part, Johnson made no mention of recent controversies in his final note to Costa e Silva, a pro forma letter thanking his Brazilian counterpart for years of cooperation and passing along a photo taken by the recent Apollo 8 expedition.[146] Underlying this posture was persistent hope that Costa e Silva, for all his flaws, could be counted on to stand up to the extremists. He was, concluded a CIA study a week after the Fifth Institutional Act, "a determined man" and was "not likely to be displaced passively." The Brazilian leader remained, in short, the best bet to resist the "narrow nationalism" of the officers who surrounded him. Under the circumstances, there seemed little to gain by publicly admonishing the regime or withholding American help. "If . . . the US reduces aid to Brazil or fails to provide requested military equipment," the CIA observed, "hurt bewilderment followed by open antagonism could well result."[147] That state of affairs was, if anything, even less appealing at the end of 1968 than it had been when Washington established its relationship with the military back in 1964.

# 5

# India

## THE PARTNERSHIP THAT FADED

THE WAR in Vietnam topped Lyndon Johnson's agenda as he jetted to Honolulu in the first week of February 1966 to consult with leaders of the Saigon government. The administration's attention, along with that of the American public, was focused ever more tightly on the faraway Southeast Asian nation, where almost 200,000 American military personnel were now stationed. Less noticed were the ways in which the war seeped into U.S. relationships with other nations far from the fighting. When the Brazilian government promulgated the Third Institutional Act on February 6, abolishing direct election of mayors in the nation's biggest cities, the Johnson administration muted its criticism of the junta in part because of the possibility the generals might help in Vietnam.[1] American officials also viewed India through the prism of Vietnam. Like President Kennedy, LBJ had hoped that shared hostility to Chinese expansion would lead to a productive partnership between the world's two largest democracies. By February 1966, however, LBJ and his advisers were rapidly losing hope, not least because of India's distinct lack of support for the U.S. role in Vietnam. Stung by Indian criticism, Johnson insisted that his vice president, Hubert Humphrey, use a February 10 meeting with newly appointed prime minister Indira Gandhi to drive home American frustrations. The United States did not expect India to "ally itself with us" or "adopt our economic system or philosophy," read Humphrey's marching orders, but it did expect consideration of the burdens it was bearing in Vietnam. "When the US is under attack in the UN or other forums," the president insisted with palpable sarcasm, "it would be immensely helpful if the Indians could occasionally at least stand up and say 'stop, look and listen—let's try to understand what the US is doing before we criticize it.'"[2]

The combativeness of Johnson's instructions reflected the trend in U.S.-Indian relations during the LBJ years. The Sino-Indian War of autumn 1962 had stoked optimism among U.S. officials about cooperation rooted in shared geopolitical concerns. The mood changed, however, by the end of Kennedy's presidency, leaving the Johnson administration with critical decisions about what sort of relationship to pursue. From the outset, Johnson had lower expectations of India, whose non-alignment and dedication to a socialist model of economic development affronted LBJ far more than his predecessor. The U.S. relationship with India deteriorated rapidly after 1965, when shifting political winds in India drove leaders in New Delhi to adopt a more critical attitude toward Washington even as the country grew more dependent on American aid, a combination certain to irritate Johnson. To be sure, Ambassador Bowles clung to his globalist outlook and, with some support from Bundy and Komer, urged that Washington be patient with a country that could yet play a central role in containing Chinese expansion. But Johnson and Rusk, who played the dominant roles in shaping policy, showed little tolerance for India's apparent indifference to U.S. geopolitical preferences. By 1969, mutual disappointment had plunged U.S.-Indian relations to a new nadir. The partnership had not quite failed, but it surely had faded into the background of U.S. priorities.

This relationship highlights the broad currents of U.S. policymaking in the Johnson presidency by offering a counterpoint to U.S.-Brazilian interactions during the same period. In the latter case, Johnson helped squelch political uncertainty by bringing to power a new regime certain to hew closely to U.S. preferences. When that government veered in authoritarian directions or refused to cooperate with Washington as closely as U.S. leaders would have liked, Johnson and his aides continued to see overriding advantages in standing by the generals, who ensured predictability at a time of growing U.S. despair about international affairs. In the Indian case, by contrast, U.S. leaders were consistently frustrated by their failures to win New Delhi over to American priorities and, far from suppressing their concerns about Indian choices, readily expressed their irritation. When Indian leaders bucked U.S. preferences, Washington responded vocally and even punitively. U.S. aid shrank, and Washington entertained few hopes beyond simply keeping India from collapsing or sliding fully into the Soviet camp.

## Searching for a New Balance

When LBJ abruptly ascended to the presidency, he confronted unresolved questions about U.S. policy toward the subcontinent. The Kennedy administration had sought to craft a new era of cooperation with India. Since 1962, however, India's dedication to non-alignment, renewed friendliness with the Soviet Union, and recalcitrance in the face of Washington's pressure to resolve long-standing hostilities with Pakistan had thrown the Kennedy approach into doubt. Champions of the tilt toward India such as Ambassador Chester Bowles and NSC aide Robert Komer, who oversaw South Asian affairs in the White House, worried that LBJ would undo everything that had been accomplished in a country that remained, as Komer put it, "the major prize in Asia."[3] Johnson had, after all, formed an obvious friendship with Pakistani leader Mohammad Ayub Khan during an exchange of visits in 1961 and dismissed Kennedy's key advisers as "India lovers."[4] To keep JFK's approach going, it seemed vital to get the new administration started in the right way. "Unless we get the new President signed on now [to new support for India] while he is still carrying out the Kennedy policy, we may lose a real opportunity," Komer wrote Bundy a day after Kennedy's death.[5]

Komer's fears were only partially borne out during the ensuing weeks. LBJ gratified pro-Indian policymakers by sharply criticizing Pakistan's preparations to receive Chinese premier Zhou Enlai on a diplomatic visit a few weeks later and warning that closer ties between Karachi and Beijing might jeopardize U.S. aid for Pakistan. No dramatic warming of U.S.-Pakistani relations appeared to be at hand. But Johnson showed little enthusiasm for new initiatives with India. The litmus test of the new administration's attitude was precisely the issue that had sparked disagreement among U.S. officials in the final weeks of the previous administration: the amount and duration of American military aid for India. For Bowles and Komer, a generous American commitment was crucial to U.S. efforts to build up India into a major bulwark against Chinese expansion in Asia. Secretary of State Rusk and the Defense Department, meanwhile, backed a relatively limited package of grants—about $50 million per annum over five years—carefully balanced against U.S. assistance for Pakistan. Eager to lower expectations, Johnson leaned toward the more modest sum and, accepting the advice of Joint Chiefs of Staff chairman Maxwell Taylor, insisted that the United States could fund no more than one year. Further assistance would depend on the attitude of Congress and the performance of both India and Pakistan on a range of issues.[6]

Skepticism about a larger aid package for India flowed from two calculations. In the geopolitical arena, Johnson feared that lavish assistance unaccompanied by commensurate aid for Pakistan would damage U.S. relations with Ayub Khan's government, which viewed American assistance for India through the lens of its bitter rivalry with its larger and more powerful neighbor. Back in 1962, the U.S. officials who supported the opening to India had expressed a willingness to risk the U.S. relationship with Karachi. By early 1964, however, the best course seemed to lie in moving forward on parallel tracks with India and Pakistan in hopes of keeping them both in the U.S. orbit. In this way, Washington sought to establish a durable new status quo that would balance new ambitions in India with old commitments to Pakistan. LBJ made this goal clear in a blunt message to Bowles on January 21, 1964. Although "fully aware" of India's importance to U.S. geopolitical objectives in Asia, the president insisted that the United States must make decisions about aid "in ways which will minimize the risks to our relationship with Pakistan."[7] Two weeks later, he formally instructed his secretaries of state and defense to request that India and Pakistan prepare "austere" five-year programs to which the United States would contribute in due course. Underscoring his lack of enthusiasm for the whole venture, he stipulated that U.S. representatives should say little about precise amounts until the two countries had drafted satisfactory plans.[8] Thus did LBJ demonstrate willingness to use aid as leverage, a trend that would cause tension with India as the Johnson presidency advanced.

In the case of Pakistan, Johnson's conditions were mostly geopolitical. He insisted that Ayub Khan's government fulfill its obligations under the SEATO and CENTO agreements and continue to permit the operation of the major U.S. intelligence-gathering installation at Peshawar. In the case of India, the administration insisted on New Delhi's agreement to limit defense spending in order to ensure sufficient resources for economic development. Underlying this demand sat the second major reason for the Johnson administration's caution about military aid for India: belief that the most urgent priority to build India into a major anti-Chinese asset in South Asia was to address the deficiencies of the nation's economy through substantial reforms directed from the highest level. Such concern reflected a subtle but important shift that, as historian Tanvi Madan observes, had taken place in U.S. perceptions of India since 1962. Hopes of an Indian "takeoff" had given way to fears of India's collapse.[9] A devastating mix of problems—accelerating inflation, mounting food shortages, worrisome indebtedness, and rapidly diminishing foreign exchange reserves—led observers in New Delhi and Washington alike to compare the situation to that of China on the verge of the communist takeover in 1949.[10] With India seeming to teeter on the brink of economic and political chaos, Johnson instructed his Defense and State departments to do everything they could to discourage "excessive" attention to military preparedness at the cost of India's development priorities.[11]

U.S. officials expressed optimism as work began on the arms deals. Although the Indian government clearly hoped for much more than LBJ was prepared to provide, New Delhi catered to U.S. sensitivities by assuring that defense spending would not interfere with development. In April, a constructive tone suffused Johnson's meetings in Washington with Indira Gandhi, the daughter of Nehru and a rising star within India's governing Congress Party. American optimism climbed further in May, when Nehru's death, an event that had been foreseen for several months, brought Lal Bahadur Shastri to the premiership. Although Shastri disappointed U.S. interlocutors by insisting that

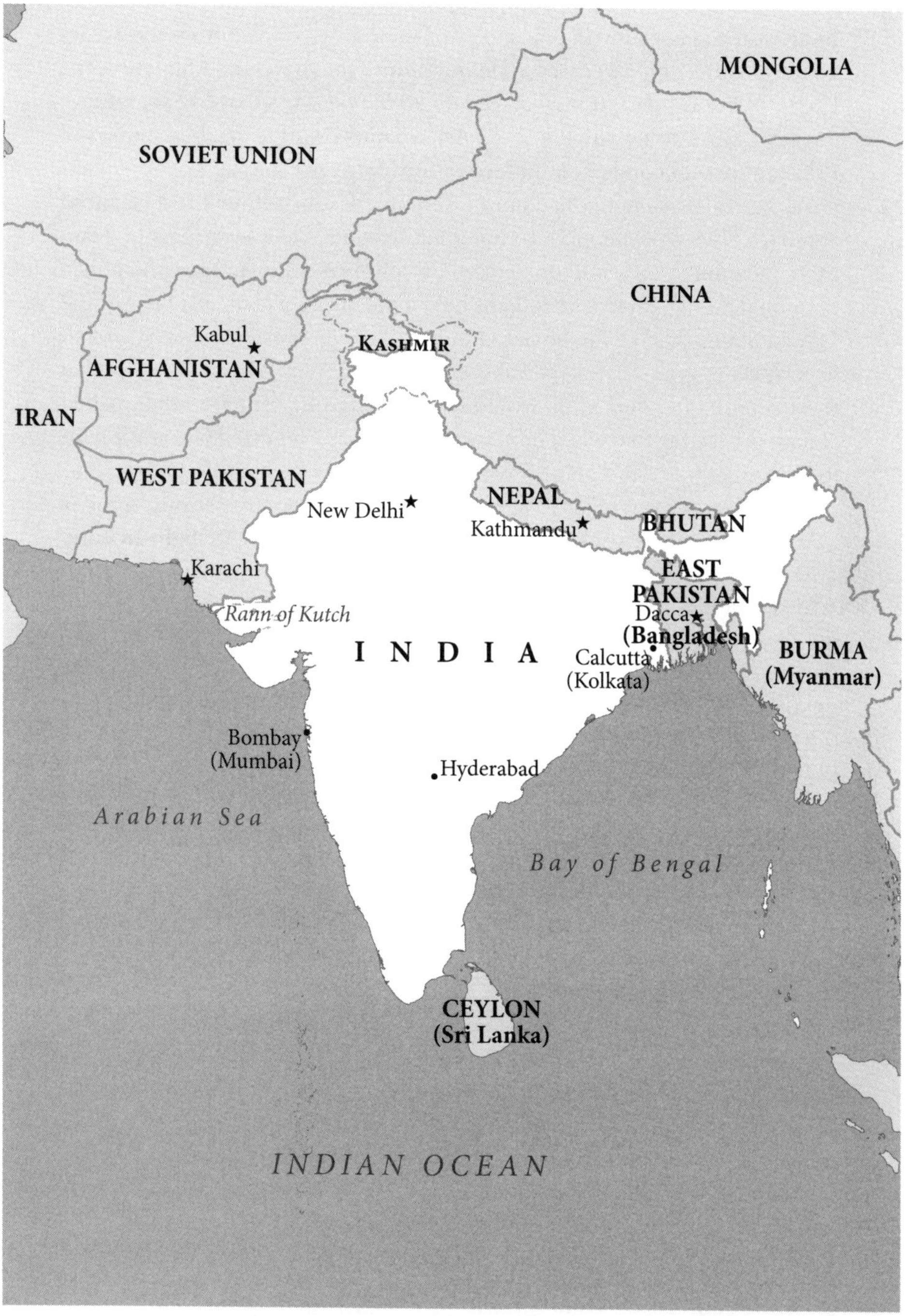


MAP 5.1. South Asia around the time of the 1965 war between India and Pakistan.
Mapping Specialists, Ltd., Madison, WI.

India would proceed with plans to purchase fighter aircraft from the Soviet Union, his rise to power was a "definite plus" for the United States, noted Komer.[12] For his part, Bundy played down the tensions that had sometimes dogged U.S. relations with the South Asian nations, noting that both India and Pakistan were making a "painful transition" from the "out and out pro-Pak" position that Washington had once taken on the subcontinent to a balanced approach.[13] Meanwhile, U.S. economic aid continued to flow in massive quantities, including a $435 million pledge at a donors meeting in May, and public opinion data suggested that Indians held a much more favorable view of the United States than of the Soviet Union.[14] Perhaps most encouraging of all from Washington's standpoint, Pakistani president Ayub seemed to accept that the United States and India would have an ongoing military relationship. "I have the feeling that while he is swallowing hard," reported General Taylor in December 1963, "it is going down."[15]

Optimism proved misplaced. Far from contributing to a satisfactory new balance, the arms deal reached by Washington and New Delhi in early June 1964 unleashed new waves of acrimony in the fraught triangular relationship among the United States, India, and Pakistan. Pakistani leaders blasted the agreement as a betrayal of U.S. obligations to an ally. "The time has come for Pakistan to undertake a reappraisal of its foreign policy and to review her political and military commitments," Foreign Minister Zulfikar Ali Bhutto told the Pakistani parliament.[16] Anti-U.S. demonstrations, including an attack on the U.S. Information Agency library in Dacca, and Pakistan's increasingly warm words about China gave substance to Bhutto's threats. In response, Johnson showed little inclination to soothe Pakistani feelings. Instead, he lashed out at Pakistan for cozying up to China, prioritizing its feud with India over larger geopolitical interests, and showing insufficient gratitude for U.S. economic aid, which he claimed amounted, on a per capita basis, to twice the assistance that the United States was giving India. Echoing Bhutto's words, the president asserted that the United States would "have to re-examine our policy toward Pakistan" if the Ayub government continued to act provocatively.[17] Softening LBJ's tone only a little, the U.S. ambassador in Karachi, Walter McConaughy, carried the message to Ayub a few days later.[18] But softer words could not disguise the fact that Washington would provide no new military aid for Pakistan until its geopolitical position clarified.

Meanwhile, the U.S.-Indian agreement on military aid hardly brought harmony between Washington and New Delhi. Tension sprang in part from a U.S. decision to delay an offer of supersonic F-104 jets, one of India's highest priorities, out of fear of intensifying the regional arms race. But antagonism also flowed from a basic element of Indian politics that Americans appreciated on an intellectual level but nevertheless struggled to accept: aid from the

United States created strong incentives for the Indian government to secure assistance from the Soviet Union as well. In part, the Indian calculations were driven by persistent doubts about the United States as a reliable source of aid. The United States, after all, had historically backed Pakistan, had entertained military assistance for India only under extraordinary circumstances in 1962, and had shown a willingness to use aid as leverage to extract concessions from the Indian government. On a deeper level, moreover, the Indian desire to diversify its dependencies stemmed from the non-aligned impulse at the core of Indian foreign policy. U.S. intelligence agencies concluded that India exercised declining influence in the non-aligned world during 1964, but that did not mean that the principle mattered any less than it had previously.[19] A poll of Indian legislators conducted in 1963 revealed that 83 percent did not want their nation to side with either Washington or Moscow.[20] The implications of this attitude were easy to see in the military arena. Even as India negotiated large-scale U.S. assistance, it obtained Soviet commitments to provide $130 million in military aid between October 1962 and May 1964, a level of support that outraged U.S. officials hopeful of weaning India off Soviet supplies.[21] Especially annoying was the Shastri government's deal with the Soviet Union, consummated at the same time as the arms deal with Washington, to build MiG jets in India.[22]

Another development in the second half of 1964—the rapidly growing salience of the American commitment to Vietnam—made Pakistani flirtations with China and Indian overtures to the Soviet Union even more objectionable in Washington. Those relationships made perfect sense, of course, in Karachi and New Delhi, where officials sought to diversify their sources of international support at a time when neither government viewed the United States as a reliable partner. The Sino-Soviet rivalry created golden opportunities for each South Asian nation to accomplish that objective by aligning itself with a major patron eager to demonstrate its interest in the region. But for Johnson and his advisers, warmer relationships with the communist giants amounted to a direct challenge to U.S. goals in Southeast Asia. Indeed, LBJ looked to both India and Pakistan to throw their support behind the deepening U.S. commitment to Vietnam, which Americans viewed as a contribution to the security of the subcontinent. Their persistent failure to comply while cozying up to Moscow and Beijing exacerbated tensions with the United States and, as much as any other issue, fed LBJ's increasing gloom about the possibility of establishing productive relationships with either India or Pakistan across the remainder of his presidency.

The Johnson administration had higher expectations of Pakistan due to its membership in two alliances—CENTO and SEATO—designed to contain communist expansion in Asia. Neither organization, it is true, carried an automatic obligation to provide military support for the burgeoning U.S. commitment in Vietnam. But the Johnson administration, which publicly launched its "more flags" campaign in April 1964, left little doubt of its expectation that Pakistan would contribute to a war effort that involved more than twenty thousand U.S. personnel by that point and created a growing drain on U.S. resources. At a time when the United States had already provided enormous economic and military aid for Pakistan, Johnson was quick to complain of Pakistani ingratitude and deploy U.S. assistance as leverage to change Pakistani minds. Following Zhou Enlai's visit to Karachi in February, Phillips Talbot, the assistant secretary of state for South Asian affairs, told Ayub that the United States had become "profoundly disturbed" by Pakistani initiatives enabling China to "make hay" in one part of the continent while the United States was trying to contain it in another.[23] U.S. anger escalated in July amid Pakistani protests against the arms deal for India. LBJ complained to his advisers that he "didn't know whether we were getting very much for our money," offering Karachi's attitude toward Vietnam as the prime example of Pakistan's distressing lack of dedication to its alliance obligations.[24]

U.S. complaints made no difference to Pakistani leaders. On the contrary, Ayub defiantly highlighted his government's refusal to contribute in Vietnam more than any other issue at a tense meeting with Ambassador McConaughy in mid-August, just after the Gulf of Tonkin episode. On the matter that mattered most to Johnson—a Pakistani contribution to the U.S.-led war effort—Ayub was categorical: there would be none. In fact, McConaughy reported, the Pakistani president intended to reexamine his nation's commitments under SEATO and "voiced a neutralist line of thinking" about the war, emphasizing the need for a negotiated compromise to end the fighting. McConaughy found this attitude "unnatural and out of character" for a leader who had once sought close relations with the United States but now seemed inclined to parrot the anti-Western themes swirling among Afro-Asian nations. Ayub at times seemed "sympathetic" to the U.S. position in connection with the Gulf of Tonkin incidents but blamed Washington for Pakistan's inability to help in Vietnam. It was impossible for Pakistan to take on commitments in Southeast Asia, said Ayub, given Pakistan's "increased vulnerability" closer to home—a thinly veiled reference to U.S. military support for India. With Washington seeming to side more openly with India on the subcontinent, Ayub continued, his people would not understand any move to side with the United States elsewhere, rejecting even the "token contribution in the nonmilitary field" that McConaughy requested. But that was not the only reason the Pakistani people opposed any role in Vietnam, Ayub insisted. He charged that Pakistanis were confused by U.S. backing for an "authoritarian" and "hard-fisted" South Vietnamese regime that commanded little support from its own population.[25]

Secretary Rusk gave voice to U.S. outrage a few days later. Although he conceded that nothing could be done about Pakistan's unwillingness to help in Vietnam, Rusk instructed McConaughy to warn Ayub that any Pakistani "reappraisal" of the country's commitments to SEATO would lead to a "similar action on our part." More specifically, Rusk pointed out that any actions "appearing to support [the] Chicom position" would stir a "profoundly adverse reaction" from Congress and the America public, jeopardizing the flow of U.S. military aircraft and other aid valued by Pakistani leaders. Summit meetings between Ayub and the U.S. president—a regular feature of U.S.-Pakistani relations in recent years—would also be endangered, Rusk declared.[26]

The full implications of the latter warning became clear in April 1965, when President Johnson abruptly postponed Ayub's scheduled visit to Washington. The administration attempted to break the news gently, claiming that LBJ was simply too busy with other issues and simultaneously postponing a scheduled visit by Indian prime minister Shastri. Behind the scenes, however, Johnson made clear that his decision stemmed largely from Pakistan's budding relationship with China at a moment when the United States was bearing heavy costs in Vietnam. LBJ took an "extremely strong stand" in favor of the postponements, noted Rusk, due to the fact that Ayub, like Shastri, would "almost certainly feel compelled" to make public statements about Vietnam during his trip to Washington, embarrassing the administration and stirring trouble in both the press and Congress. Postponement, by contrast, might provide "shock treatment" that would convince Ayub of the depth of U.S. concern about Pakistan's geopolitical drift, Rusk added.[27] Especially galling to Washington was Ayub's visit to Beijing in March. The trip that culminated in a joint Sino-Pakistani communique pledging "firm support" for "national-independence movements and struggles against imperialism and all forms of colonialism in Asia and Africa," language that resembled Chinese propaganda.[28] U.S. officials were relieved when Ayub seemed to take the postponement in stride, but U.S.-Pakistan relations had undeniably reached a new low.

The postponement of Shastri's scheduled visit to Washington was an inevitable result of the decision about Ayub, a price LBJ had to pay in order to keep alive his hope for a balanced policy toward the subcontinent. Yet LBJ hardly regarded the lost opportunity to sit down with Shastri as a setback since he feared that the Indian leader might use his trip to criticize the war in Vietnam. LBJ's wariness of India's attitude went back at least to 1961, when Nehru had refused to condemn communist activity in Vietnam as assertively or publicly as the vice president wished.[29] The Sino-Indian War of 1962, of course, fueled hope that shared hostility to China might lead Nehru to side openly with the United States in Southeast Asia. By the time Johnson rose to the presidency, however, the tide was running in the other direction, leaving U.S. officials with a renewed sense of frustration.

In private, Indian officials sometimes offered reassuring words in conversations with U.S. counterparts. For instance, Asoka Mehta, a prominent Congress Party politician, told Bowles in May 1965 that "practically all members of the cabinet basically were aware of [the] importance to India of our efforts to keep communists out of Southeast Asia, and it was hoped that this effort would be successful."[30] By the end of the year, Bowles even speculated that the Indian government might be willing to send an ambulance unit to support the U.S.-South Vietnamese war effort.[31] Even if that contribution did not materialize, some U.S. officials hoped India might help less tangibly by using its stature within non-aligned circles to advance moderate views of U.S. policy, no small thing at a time when China exerted growing influence in the Third World and anticolonial militancy was displacing non-alignment as the dominant motif of solidarity among Afro-Asian nations. Bowles credited the Indian government with working "most effectively behind the scenes" at the 1961 Belgrade conference of non-aligned nations and other gatherings of Third World governments to promote a relatively balanced view of the situation in Southeast Asia, and he expected more of the same.[32]

Even as the United States escalated the war in 1965, L. K. Jha, the secretary to Prime Minister Shastri, indicated Indian determination to continue in that role by providing the U.S. embassy a detailed run-down on Shastri's talks with Yugoslav leader Josip Broz Tito, another moderate within the global non-aligned movement. Indian policymakers understood that their effectiveness was limited by Chinese and North Vietnamese hostility to their nation, but they expressed optimism that cooperation with Third World leaders more acceptable to Beijing, especially Egyptian leader Gamal Abdel Nasser and Ghanaian president Kwame Nkrumah, might lend credibility to Indian positions. Jha assured the U.S. embassy in New Delhi that Indian leaders "would do their best to exert influence in quarters where they could."[33]

U.S. officials also voiced occasional appreciation for Indian efforts to pass along information gathered by Indian diplomats in North Vietnam, including detailed reports on military activities above the seventeenth parallel, and to promote what Washington regarded as fair-minded peace proposals. Most strikingly, Shastri responded to the start of the U.S. bombing campaign in February 1965 by calling for "immediate suspension of all provocative action" in Vietnam "by all sides" and the convening of a new Geneva conference.[34] A month later, India joined a declaration by seventeen non-aligned Third World nations blaming "foreign intervention in various forms" for the war and appealing for talks without preconditions. Then, on April 24, President Sarvepalli Radhakrishnan offered the most detailed Indian proposal yet, calling for a cease-fire and the establishment of an Afro-Asian military force to police South Vietnam's borders.[35] Even before that last of these initiatives, Secretary Rusk called the Indian role "generally helpful" to the United States, and the Johnson administration publicly welcomed the seventeen-nation and Radhakrishnan plans, which, in contrast to some peacemaking initiatives circulating at the time, seemed to hold both sides responsible for the fighting and aimed at mutual disengagement and the preservation of an independent South Vietnam.[36]

On the whole, though, Indian proposals brought no tangible benefits for the United States, and U.S. leaders grew increasingly frustrated by the Shastri government's unwillingness to lean more heavily toward the United States as the war in Vietnam accelerated. Whatever mild satisfaction U.S. leaders expressed with the Indian attitude stemmed from their low expectations of what New Delhi would provide and relief that Indian criticism was not sharper. Tensions were bound to increase as LBJ grew more sensitive to the attitudes of foreign governments and resentful of the ones that received American aid but provided nothing in return. U.S.-Indian tensions festered, above all, in connection with India's role in the International Control Commission, the bureaucracy that had been established to monitor implementation of the 1954 ceasefire in Indochina. In the aftermath of the 1962 Sino-Indian War, the Indian government had sometimes gratified Washington by joining with Canada's ICC delegation—and thereby outvoting the third member, Poland—to criticize communist aggression in Vietnam. As India struggled to recover its non-aligned posture, however, it changed its tune in the commission, retreating into what delegation chief Ram Goburdhun called "masterly inactivity."[37]

The reasons for India's reluctance to criticize either side in the expanding Vietnam conflict were not difficult to see. Dedication to non-alignment, along with the desire to obtain Soviet backing as a counterweight to U.S. aid, made Indian leaders wary of tilting toward South Vietnam and its U.S. patrons and, as military dependence on the United States increased, led New Delhi to take positions favorable to Hanoi. Understanding of India's bind did not elicit sympathy, however. Goburdhun's Canadian counterpart, Gordon Cox, blasted India for its reluctance to investigate communist violations of the 1954 treaty. "Frustration," he wrote in 1964, "is not . . . a strong enough word."[38] By 1965, U.S. officials regarded the Indian-led ICC as a "ridiculous" organization, Walt Rostow later recalled.[39]

U.S. anger also mounted as Indian leaders spoke out against the Rolling Thunder bombing campaign against North Vietnam that accelerated in the middle months of 1965. The sharpest attack on U.S. policy came from Indira Gandhi, whose position as minister of broadcasting and information belied the influence she wielded as the daughter of Jawaharlal Nehru and a rising figure within the Congress Party. In June 1965, she antagonized U.S. officials by denouncing U.S. "intervention" in Vietnam. The "whole world, except Britain, Australia, and a few other countries" was arrayed against the United States, she added, suggesting that U.S. policy invited the very Chinese escalation in Southeast Asia that Washington claimed to oppose. Moreover, Gandhi, apparently aiming to burnish her credentials as a potential challenger to Shastri, celebrated India's non-alignment and even praised Pakistan for easing its dependence on the United States and moving toward the non-aligned world.[40] Shastri, by contrast, conveyed his doubts about the U.S. bombing in restrained, private communications.[41] Yet restraint won him little favor among U.S. officials as escalation heightened Washington's sensitivity to criticism of any kind. In explaining the decision to postpone Shastri's visit to Washington, Rusk noted "substantial differences of emphasis" between Washington and New Delhi on the Vietnam issue and foresaw that the premier would "almost certainly find it necessary" to make statements that could be construed as critical of the United States if the visit went ahead as planned.[42] Even Bowles, normally quick to accentuate the positive in U.S.-Indian relations, complained of India's failure to acknowledge publicly that the United States was "fighting their battles as well as our own" by resisting Chinese expansionism in Asia.[43]

But no one expressed American disappointment with India more forcefully than LBJ, who pleaded with Shastri to recognize that communists posed the same sort of threat to Vietnam that China had posed to India back in 1962.[44] Failure to see the connection, asserted LBJ, not only damaged the anticommunist fight in Asia but also undermined Indian interests. In a July 1965 meeting with B. K. Nehru, the Indian ambassador to Washington, the president complained that New Delhi's attitude about Vietnam was undercutting his efforts to win congressional support for foreign assistance, including urgent food aid for the subcontinent. LBJ blasted Ayub for being "off receiving Chou En-lai" but also chastised Indian leaders, who, he complained sarcastically, "kept telling us how to solve Vietnam." In fact, he asserted, his administration had worked hard to find a negotiated solution to the war but had encountered Hanoi's rejection at every turn. "In view of the way the Indians seemed compelled to comment so often on Vietnam, we would certainly like to know India's solution," he exclaimed. "If Shastri knew how to settle Vietnam," Johnson added, "we wished he would tell us."[45] Joseph N. Greene, the U.S. deputy chief of mission in New Delhi, made a similar point in meetings with Indian officials, albeit in more diplomatic language. American honor was at stake in Vietnam, Greene told Shastri on one occasion, and "in such circumstances, the US cares a great deal both about what happens and what people say."[46]

## "Get Behind a Log and Sleep a Bit"

Postponement of the meetings with Ayub and Shastri provoked resentment in Pakistan and India, leaving the U.S. effort to find a satisfactory new status quo on the subcontinent in tatters by the middle of 1965. Frustrated U.S. officials across the spectrum—from champions of U.S. activism in the subcontinent like Komer to skeptics such as Rusk—lowered their expectations. "With Vietnam in the forefront of all minds," wrote Bundy at the end of April, the administration had little capacity for "constructive focus" on anything new regarding India, and the same was surely true for Pakistan.[47] Unquestionably, vast amounts of U.S. assistance continued to flow to both countries, providing leverage that administration officials aimed to exploit. In the best case, wrote Komer, both countries would draw the appropriate lessons after having a chance to "reflect on the moral that Uncle Sam should not just be regarded as a cornucopia of goodies, regardless of what they do or say."[48] Only time would reveal how to get relations back on track. In the event, however, momentous developments during the second half of 1965 and early 1966 left Washington little choice but to focus anew on the subcontinent. Still, the outcome was more of the same: the Johnson administration found little but frustration and emerged from a new crisis with even bleaker hopes for establishing a healthy balance in South Asia that would bolster U.S. interests.

One problem that focused U.S. attention on India during 1965 was the possibility that New Delhi might commit to developing nuclear weapons. The Nehru government had disavowed any intention to do so, but China's detonation of a nuclear weapon in October 1964 altered Indian calculations. China's nuclear capability seemed not only to weaken India vis-à-vis its northern neighbor but also to undermine Indian prestige in the non-aligned world, where China's technological accomplishment stoked admiration. Shastri's government left no doubt that it might initiate a nuclear program if domestic and international pressures continued to mount. That possibility alarmed the Johnson administration for various reasons. An Indian bomb might fuel an arms race with Pakistan, further undermining U.S. efforts to achieve stability in South Asia. Nuclear development also seemed likely to siphon scarce resources into the military sector and undercut the Johnson administration's aspirations—then in an early, inchoate form—to constrain proliferation of nuclear arms through a broad international agreement. Indeed, U.S. officials viewed India as a potentially crucial voice in favor of the nonproliferation principle.

The good news for Johnson administration officials, who worked hard to downplay the significance of the Chinese test, was that India seemed undecided on nuclear development and appeared open to the idea that a U.S. or U.S.-Soviet guarantee of its security could be a reasonable alternative to an Indian nuclear arsenal. The bad news was that a nuclear program seemed to lie well within India's economic and scientific capabilities and that a decision to go ahead with development depended mostly on Chinese behavior, a variable over which the United States had no control. The issue thus highlighted both the continued urgency of South Asian affairs and the declining leverage that Washington possessed in the region. Indeed, U.S. intelligence agencies concluded grimly in early 1965 that the chances were "better than even" that India would go ahead with a nuclear program in the next several years if it did not get "satisfactory" assurances from abroad.[49]

The potential stakes of nuclearization on the subcontinent became clear as a consequence of the second—and far more urgent—problem that confronted the United States in the region during 1965: a sharp upsurge in India-Pakistan tensions that culminated in war. Hostilities broke out in April in a disputed border territory along the Arabian Sea known as the Rann of Kutch. Although Pakistan instigated the crisis, Washington predictably sought to craft a balanced response that would prevent the fighting from spreading and preserve its influence with both parties. But its options amid what Ambassador McConaughy dubbed a "witches brew" of challenges were limited. In response to the most serious problem besetting Washington—bitter complaints from each side that the other was using U.S.-supplied military equipment—the Johnson administration saw no alternative but to forbid both to employ American-made gear. That decision caused fury in Pakistan, which relied far more heavily on U.S. materiel. But the U.S. position also antagonized Indian leaders, who accused Washington of doing too little to restrain Pakistan and for harping on balance despite Pakistani misdeeds. "India observes its commitments scrupulously," Ambassador Nehru angrily insisted to Rusk. "To equate it with Pakistan was wrong."[50] So badly did U.S. influence deteriorate that Washington could do little more than applaud "from the sidelines," in the words of historian Robert J. McMahon, as the British government mediated a cease-fire agreement signed by the two sides in late June.[51]

A different president, as McMahon suggests, might have redoubled his attention to the region amid such dangerous developments. But LBJ, infuriated by recalcitrant leaders in both countries and consumed by Vietnam, doubled down on his effort to extract concessions by pulling back and manipulating U.S. aid from a distance. This approach stemmed, wrote Komer, from LBJ's "deep instinct that we are not getting enough for our massive investment" in either India or Pakistan and a desire to "soften up" both countries and "make them come to us."[52] This "tough minded" approach, as Komer labeled it, consisted of various prongs. In the military arena, Washington delayed delivery of various types of materiel and continued dragging its feet on providing supersonic aircraft to India. In the field of economic aid, meanwhile, LBJ insisted that every proposal go to the White House for his personal approval, an approach the president used to stall new aid commitments. India felt the impact hardest at first, but Pakistan took the brunt of the new approach by late summer due to Johnson's decision to delay approval of the U.S. contribution to the international aid consortium focused on Pakistan's needs. Meanwhile, Washington sought to erase one of Pakistan's sources of leverage over the United States by dropping hints that U.S. intelligence services could manage without access to the satellite facilities at Peshawar.[53]

All of this carried obvious risks. India could be driven further into Soviet arms, especially for military assistance, whereas Pakistan might move further toward China. So dangerous was the administration's approach, in fact, that Komer advised the president to lean heavily on the bureaucracy to make sure his wishes were respected. Johnson did exactly that, vetoing a proposal to send high-level U.S. emissaries to both India and Pakistan and insisting that diplomats make clear the United States had "pulled up business for a while."[54]

LBJ's hope that Washington's cold shoulder would compel the South Asian nations into greater cooperation with the United States and each other came to little. The aid slowdown, coming on top of Washington's failure to stop Pakistan from using U.S.-supplied weaponry, only deepened Indian skepticism of the United States, while in Pakistan it provoked huge demonstrations throughout the country. U.S. influence in South Asia was thus declining to new lows when fighting erupted anew between India and Pakistan in the late summer. This time the focus of hostilities was Kashmir, where Ayub, apparently hoping to mount an insurgency against Indian rule, ordered infiltration by irregular Pakistani forces in August. When Indian forces responded effectively, Pakistan escalated the fighting by dispatching regular army units. American officials expressed alarm about the potential human consequences of a major war—Rusk had recently fretted about the possibility of casualties "comparable to those of a nuclear exchange"[55]—as well as the likelihood of expanded Soviet and Chinese influence in the region as India and Pakistan depended more heavily on their communist patrons.

Alarmed, Ambassador Bowles urged that the Johnson administration reopen the flow of military aid to New Delhi, essentially a proposal to turn back the clock to the Kennedy-era tilt toward India. But LBJ would have none of it, suggesting instead that the United States "get out of military aid to both

Pakistan and India."[56] The United States should, the president told his senior aides on September 2, "get behind a log and sleep a bit," while leaving the thankless job of peacemaking to UN Secretary-General U Thant. At the heart of LBJ's position lay a simple observation. "The President said he had found out over the last few months," read a summary of the meeting, "how little influence we had with the [Pakistanis] and Indians."[57] George Ball indicated that the United States might use resumption of aid as a carrot to induce cooperation with U Thant's mediation efforts, but there is no indication that LBJ was thinking the same way.[58]

The strongest test of Johnson's restraint came a few days later, when Indian forces crossed the international border with Pakistan. Some of the most intense combat the world had seen since the Second World War ensued over the following few days. The Chinese government raised the stakes still higher on September 9 and 17 by threatening to intervene if India did not back down. All of this stirred new demands for the Johnson administration to take a more proactive approach. First, Pakistan invoked its alliance with the United States in demanding that Washington lend political support, while New Delhi renewed its protests about Pakistan's use of U.S.-supplied military gear. Still greater pressure for action flowed from the fearsome prospect of Chinese intervention and the expanded Soviet role in India that would undoubtedly result. In urging that the administration take a more assertive peacemaking role, Secretary Rusk, despite his growing frustrations with the subcontinent, warned that U.S. interests "all along the Asian rim" hung in the balance. Without U.S. leadership, declared Rusk, India might "go down the drain" by abandoning its ties to Washington—a situation "in many ways as serious as the loss of China" in 1949—while countries as diverse as Iran and Japan might question Washington's dedication to its commitments and drift out of the Western orbit.[59]

Such apocalyptic fears failed, however, to shake LBJ out of his inclination to pull back from South Asia. On September 8, Johnson formally cut off all U.S. arms supplies to both India and Pakistan. Meanwhile, he rejected all Indian and Pakistani efforts to convince Washington to step up its involvement in the war, instead reiterating his support for U Thant's mediation. That support took more concrete form on September 20, when the Security Council adopted a resolution calling for a cease-fire within two days, and Ambassador McConaughy's strenuous appeals may have helped secure Ayub's grudging last-minute acceptance of the UN arrangement. On the whole, though, Johnson sought to exert influence more through withholding U.S. power than deploying it. In the final days of the war, in fact, he even dragged out approval of new food assistance for India as a way of exerting leverage, leading Ambassador Nehru to lash out at Washington for "trying to starve us out" of the war.[60] Johnson hoped that withholding aid, above all in the military arena, would bring home to both India and Pakistan "the consequences of their folly."[61]

But his decisions also reflected his sensitivity to mounting outrage in Congress over U.S. arms sales to both countries, which threatened passage of the administration's foreign aid bill for 1966. In the end, Congress stopped short of demanding a cutoff of military assistance to the subcontinent, but opinions ran strong. Indeed, Idaho senator Frank Church, a bellwether of the administration's growing problems with liberal Democrats, went so far as to propose that the United States suspend not only military but also economic aid to encourage peacemaking in South Asia. To Church, the failure of U.S. largesse to bend India and Pakistan toward U.S. policy interests encapsulated a much larger problem. "This tragic war between India and Pakistan, to which the United States has extended a total of some $12 billion in various forms of foreign aid, should, at the very least, force us to undertake a fundamental review of our continuing military assistance programs in many parts of the world," Church insisted.[62]

The ceasefire that Ayub accepted on September 22 ended the bloodshed and foreclosed the most dangerous possibilities, including Chinese intervention. But it also left behind urgent questions about the basic geopolitical orientation of India and Pakistan. Johnson had begun his presidency hoping to establish a balanced policy that would assure U.S. interests with both countries, give them each a measure of security against the other, and minimize the influence of the communist powers. As the guns fell silent, Washington had failed to achieve any of these goals. Both the Indian and Pakistani governments sharply criticized the United States, regarded each other as a threat more serious than the danger posed by international communism, and eagerly cultivated the support of Moscow (in India's case) and Beijing (in Pakistan's). So discouraged had Johnson become that he was content to leave the task of mediating a peace agreement entirely to the Soviet government. By the end of November, both Shastri and Ayub had accepted Moscow's offer to host talks at Tashkent, the capital of Soviet Uzbekistan. Bundy and Komer captured the administration's sense of resignation on December 1, noting that the maddening Kashmir issue was now in Soviet hands. If the Soviets got somewhere, which the two U.S. officials rated as a "remote chance," Washington would gain as much as Moscow. If it failed, Bundy and Komer added, "the Soviets will find themselves in the same box we've been in."[63]

This gloomy outlook did not mean that the Johnson administration had given up hope of revitalizing U.S. policy and exerting constructive influence in South Asia. Officials readily agreed, after all, that the United States had enduring interests in South Asia, above all the goal of obstructing Chinese expansionism that Washington was pursuing in Vietnam at enormous human and material cost. But how precisely to revamp American policy? A study completed by U.S. intelligence agencies in early December acknowledged a basic reality that had become evident over the two years since LBJ had assumed the presidency: "We do not believe that the basic antagonisms between the two countries can be significantly reduced by the influence of any outside powers," asserted the intelligence report. Still, it laid out an array of options to maximize the scant influence the United States possessed. One possibility was to throw support behind either India or Pakistan, essentially choosing a favorite while making some effort to keep the other in the Western orbit. The other options focused on resuming the "even-handed" approach but at different levels of commitment. At the more ambitious end of the spectrum lay the possibility of resuming aid to both countries at roughly 1963–1964 levels and actively supporting UN efforts to resolve the Kashmir problem and other sources of tension on the subcontinent. A middling alternative involved a "wait-and-see" approach that entailed approval of short-term aid but deferred decisions on longer-term assistance until the two countries took steps to resolve their differences and to make their geopolitical orientations clearer. A final choice, resting on the assumption that Indo-Pakistani tension was "so profound as to be insoluble in the foreseeable future," proposed going forward with food aid but cutting back decisively on both economic and military assistance.[64]

The final days of 1965 and the first weeks of 1966 heightened the possibility that the Johnson administration might choose one of the more generous approaches. First, Shastri and Ayub signed the Soviet-mediated Tashkent Declaration on January 10, 1966, agreeing to withdraw their military forces to prewar positions and to dedicate themselves to peaceful resolution of their differences. Although Shastri's sudden death from a heart attack the next day introduced new uncertainty, U.S. officials concluded that, on the whole, conditions had improved significantly, a sense confirmed when LBJ met with his two South Asian counterparts. Despite intense waves of anti-Americanism in Pakistan during the second half of 1965, President Ayub took a notably conciliatory approach during his trip to Washington in mid-December. The Pakistani government had "never given a thought" to an alliance with China, declared Ayub, who affirmed his nation's partnership with the United States and appealed for the restoration of U.S. aid programs.[65] For his part, LBJ gave a little ground on Pakistan's flirtation with China. Johnson insisted that Pakistan could have no "serious relationship" with Beijing if it wanted American support. "At the same time," LBJ added, "we understood certain relationships just as a wife could understand a Saturday night fling by her husband so long as she was the wife."[66]

FIGURE 5.2. President Johnson and Indian prime minister Indira Gandhi consult in the Oval Office on March 28, 1966. The two leaders struck a positive tone that contrasted with the overall decline in the U.S.-Indian relationship. LBJ Library photo by Yoichi Okamoto.

A similarly genial tone suffused Johnson's meetings in March with the newly appointed Indian prime minister, Indira Gandhi, a summit so crucial to the future of U.S. relations with the world's second most populous nation that Komer rated it the most important diplomatic encounter by a U.S. president since John F. Kennedy had met with Nikita Khrushchev in 1961. Nothing less than a "historic opportunity to settle on a new course with 500 million Asians" lay in the offing, Komer claimed.[67] So dramatically did U.S.-Indian relations improve in the run-up to the meeting that Bowles briefly entertained hopes that Gandhi might send a "symbolic civil contribution" of some type, perhaps the medical team that Americans had long wished for, to support South Vietnam.[68] Although the summit produced no such decision, American and Indian officials expressed satisfaction with the warm tone surrounding the encounter, including even on the issue of Vietnam. Both leaders spoke enthusiastically, if only in general terms, about their common dedication to peace and development. LBJ professed that he had not previously realized how much the two nations had in common and even compared the problems Indira

Gandhi faced after the sudden death of her predecessor—internal problems, international crises, and upcoming elections—to those he had faced after taking over for John F. Kennedy in 1963. In sharp contrast to the exasperation he had shown previously in connection with India's stance on the war in Vietnam, LBJ asked Gandhi to share her ideas "from time to time" about how to end the fighting in Southeast Asia.[69] For an administration consumed by Southeast Asia, there could hardly have been a stronger indication that U.S.-Indian relations were suddenly on the upswing.

## "What Are They Going to Do for the United States?"

The warming trend came to little, as so often in the past. By the middle of 1966, the U.S.-Indian relationship had settled into a pattern that essentially inverted the manner in which Washington interacted with the regime in Brazil. In the latter case, the generals periodically disappointed the Johnson administration, stirring doubt among U.S. officials about the desirability of continuing with U.S. support. Each time, however, Washington concluded that the benefits of cooperation outweighed the drawbacks, and the relationship, rooted in a common approach to the Cold War, endured. In the Indian case, relations between New Delhi and Washington periodically showed signs of improvement, only to fall anew into discord as underlying divergences in the two nations' geostrategic outlooks reasserted themselves. So it was in the six months following Indira Gandhi's visit to Washington, when the goodwill generated by the encounter gradually dissipated, leading U.S.-Indian relations into a new phase of mutual disappointment and slow-burning antagonism. The benefits of hindsight make it possible to see that the lows and highs of U.S.-Indian relations around the time of the 1965 war in no way amounted to a dramatic turning point in the relationship, as scholars have sometimes suggested. Rather, as historian Tanvi Madan argues, the war merely catalyzed existing trends toward disillusionment.[70]

Basic calculations on both sides ensured that the U.S.-Indian relationship would not break down completely. On the Indian side, leaders saw numerous reasons to cultivate ties with the United States. U.S. assistance remained vital to India's economic development, and American food aid became increasingly urgent due to a catastrophic blend of drought, population growth, and agricultural inefficiencies. Moreover, New Delhi viewed U.S. military assistance as a crucial part of its efforts to defend itself against both Pakistan and China and to avoid overreliance on the Soviet Union. As before, the Indian government sought varied sources of support for reasons both starkly pragmatic (to ensure the largest possible flow of aid) and political (to lend credibility to India's non-aligned position in world affairs). On the U.S. side, consensus prevailed on the importance of bolstering India as a bulwark against Chinese expansion, even if officials differed over how to accomplish this goal. Defense Secretary McNamara encapsulated the logic in late 1965 in a memorandum highlighting the broad contours of U.S. policy in Asia. There were three fronts in the effort to contain China, according to McNamara, who listed the "India-Pakistan front" alongside the "Japan-Korea front" in Northeast Asia and the "Southeast Asian front" dominated at the time by Vietnam. In words sure to draw the president's attention, the secretary added that "decisions to make great investments today in men, money and national honor in South Vietnam make sense only in conjunction with continuing efforts of equivalent effectiveness in the rest of Southeast Asia as on the other two principal fronts."[71]

Yet several other trends, none of them entirely new, converged in 1966 to ensure that U.S.-Indian relations, far from achieving the dramatic improvement suggested by the tone of Gandhi's visit, would fester in a state of mutual disappointment. Increasingly, the goal of U.S. policymakers became simply to prevent the worst possible outcomes. As usual, American frustration with India came to the surface in connection with questions about U.S. aid—the types and quantity of such assistance and the conditions that Washington demanded in return for its generosity. In the military arena, both India and Pakistan requested the resumption of U.S. arms deliveries in the months following the 1965 war. As had become commonplace, the U.S. ambassador in New Delhi and his counterpart in Karachi—the persistently pro-Indian Bowles and the newly appointed Eugene M. Locke, respectively—made the case for American concessions toward the nation where he served. The arguments were familiar: military assistance would bolster Washington's influence in the region while discouraging India's dependence on Moscow and Pakistan's flirtation with China. Komer leaned toward India, while Rusk, sympathetic as usual to formal allies of the United States, saw merit in the Pakistani point of view. Unwilling to choose sides and wary as ever of encouraging either South Asian nation to prioritize defense over economic reform, the Johnson administration dragged its feet in hopes of inducing India and Pakistan to ease their hostility and show more respect for U.S. sensitivities. "Neither seems aware," Undersecretary of State Nicholas Katzenbach wrote in an October 1966 statement of the administration's position approved by LBJ, "that public and Congressional reaction to last fall's tragic Indo-Pak war, diminished resources for foreign aid overall, and our bed-rock commitment to Viet-Nam could make it impossible for us to do what we believe needs to be done even in [the] area [of] economic aid (not to mention [the] security field) unless some more constructive element than now exists is introduced into Indian-Pakistan relations."[72]

Johnson responded more favorably to pressure for the resumption of economic assistance and even broached the possibility of a new five-year package for India. Yet the president's attitude was decidedly cooler than it had been a year earlier. Striking evidence of LBJ's disgruntlement about the outpouring of U.S. funds—some $12 billion in development assistance for the subcontinent since 1949—was Komer's embarrassment when he brought new Indian and Pakistani demands to the president in February 1966. Komer confessed that he could not avoid causing annoyance since he was "unfortunately the staffer responsible to you for half the beggars in the world."[73] But the president's own words and actions, despite the conciliatory tone he took in his meeting with Indira Gandhi, also made his irritation clear. Especially revealing was Johnson's telephone conversation with his agriculture secretary, Orville Freeman, at a moment of mounting Indian demands for both the resumption of development assistance and dramatically increased food aid. An exasperated LBJ blasted his bureaucracy for "Indian lover" tendencies, singling out Bowles, Komer, and Bundy—all champions of the opening to India in the Kennedy years—for special criticism.

Instead of caving to their pressure, Johnson affirmed the transactional approach to aid decisions that he had embraced as Indo-Pakistani tensions heated up in mid-1965. "It's not going to be a one-way deal," he exclaimed. "I'm not just going to underwrite the perpetuation of the government of India and the people of India to have them spend all their goddamn time dedicating themselves to the destruction of the people of the United States and the government of the United States." Before he would make any major decision on new aid, LBJ added, imagining himself in a conversation with his Indian counterpart, "I'm waiting to see what kind of a foreign policy we can have with your people."[74] A few days later, Vice President Humphrey carried the message to Gandhi during a visit to New Delhi, telling the prime minister the least her government could do "if she disagreed with some of our policies was to express that disagreement discreetly in the channels of diplomacy rather than in public statements and the press."[75]

Johnson's taste for quid pro quos was especially evident with respect to food aid provided under Public Law 480, a controversial element of U.S. assistance as the 1960s advanced. The initiative, which promised food deliveries from surplus American stocks, had originated under the Eisenhower administration, but JFK expanded it and dramatically raised its profile in 1961, touting the "Food for Peace" program as a boon to both American farmers and needy populations around the world. Characteristically, LBJ took a more skeptical view and shifted the PL 480 bureaucracy into the State Department in 1965. The program for India had already become controversial the year before, however, when LBJ, facing a decision about a new four-year commitment to India, approved only a one-year extension. LBJ's distinctive approach to India became even more evident in mid-1965. As part of his broader effort to exert

FIGURE 5.3. Lyndon Johnson consults with Deputy National Security Adviser Robert Komer on February 1, 1966, a few weeks before Komer was reassigned to work on counterinsurgency efforts in Vietnam. LBJ Library photo by Yoichi Okamoto.

leverage over South Asia, the president put India's new request on hold pending further study and took personal control over the matter. To the surprise of some aides, he even refused to move forward when advisers warned him that any interruption of deliveries could have devastating consequences in India. After a monthlong delay, Johnson finally acted, but he approved shipments of only a two-month grain supply of one million tons—just a fraction of the one-year, six-million-ton scheme that the director of the U.S. Agency for International Development had proposed to him. Thus did LBJ initiate what would later be dubbed the "short-tether" policy.[76]

Johnson's approach grew in part from his conviction that India must be incentivized to step up the efficiency of its food production in order to achieve self-sufficiency. One reason for this concern was LBJ's growing attentiveness to global population growth and resource depletion. Although he had once kept his distance from advocates of population control, he appears to have changed his mind early in late 1964 as the issue gained more prominence in Congress and the press. In his State of the Union address in January 1965, Johnson boldly promised steps to "help deal with the explosion of world population and the growing scarcity of world resources," problems that he ranked second in importance behind only the search for peace.[77] Before long, his concern for the issue had focused on one nation in particular—India—that seemed to be afflicted by a trifecta of problems: soaring population, persistent agricultural inefficiencies, and incipient natural disaster. The last of these was caused by the failure of the summer monsoons in 1965, leading to the worst drought in many years.

In the opinion of many commentators, LBJ's insistence on doling out food in relatively small increments—an approach that angered some of his aides—grew entirely from a humanitarian desire to push India into reforms necessary to feed the country's population. "It is hard to recapture how deeply Johnson felt about getting the Indians to do a better job in producing food," Walt Rostow asserted in 1990. "It was part of Johnson's fundamental concern for human beings and his hatred of poverty."[78] Added Rusk: "We weren't asking any political quid pro quo in terms of Viet Nam, or a vote on Red China in the United Nations, or anything of that sort."[79] Numerous scholars similarly emphasize that LBJ's "obsessive" oversight of food deliveries, to use historian Dennis Kux's word, stemmed from a farsighted desire to push India toward self-sufficiency.[80] LBJ's broader antipoverty agenda as well as the concurrence of many Indian officials with his insistence on reform tend to buttress this generous interpretation of his motives. Yet evidence abounds of LBJ's simultaneous determination to use food aid as leverage over Indian foreign policy, especially in connection with Vietnam.[81] To be sure, it is impossible to disentangle Johnson's humanitarian, economic, and geopolitical aspirations or to establish the precise balance among them. But the conditionality of U.S. aid was evident from the first weeks of the Johnson administration and suffused policymaking thereafter. The government of India already understood that U.S. aid deliveries depended on "a context of broad agreement on certain aspects of foreign policy," wrote Undersecretary of State Ball in February 1964. "Naturally," he continued, Washington would "expect" New Delhi to remain in "broad agreement regarding their assessment of [the Chinese communist] threat to Asia and the strategy required to meet it."[82]

The links between U.S. aid and India's performance in the geopolitical arena were just as evident in the second half of 1965, when the Indo-Pakistani war and the impending food crisis left U.S. officials groping for new ways to influence the subcontinent. American aid was not "a state of nature," wrote Dean Rusk at the peak of U.S. gloom in November 1965. Indian hopes of getting back in Washington's good graces, he added, would require not only substantial reform of Indian agricultural policies but also a serious attempt to refocus Indian foreign policy on the danger posed by China. The latter goal was "not too much for a friend interested in India's future to ask," insisted Rusk.[83] By early 1966, LBJ was openly singling out Vietnam as the issue that concerned him most. "When I put my wheat down here, and it costs me a few hundred million, I want to see what [India is] putting on the other side," he griped in his conversation with his agriculture secretary on February 2, warning of his inevitable anger if India offered just "bullshit and a lot of criticism of the President." He added, "I don't think they need to denounce us every day on what we're doing in Vietnam." A moment later, he came to the core consideration that would guide his thinking about food: "What are they going to do for the United States?"[84] Any compunction that LBJ might have felt about using food aid in this way was perhaps lessened by his sense that India was engaging in the same kind of cynical behavior. If the United States refused to provide food, LBJ complained, Indian leaders were sure to "turn loose the *New York Times* and *Washington Post* on us."[85]

American willingness to use aid, including food, as leverage over Indian foreign policy became still more evident in early 1966 amid confidence that this approach was paying dividends. Even Komer, initially a skeptic of the short-tether approach, concluded at the beginning of the year that the policy was working "remarkably well."[86] U.S. leaders were encouraged by Indian reforms spelled out in the Treaty of Rome, an agreement reached between Agricultural Secretary Freeman and his Indian counterpart, Chidambaram Subramaniam, in December 1965. Gandhi's warm tone during her March 1966 visit to Washington and indications of India's progress in implementing reforms later in the year seemed to provide additional assurance that U.S. policy was succeeding. Undoubtedly, Komer worried that India's commitments to nonalignment and to its partnership with Moscow would prevent it from moving decisively toward the United States, but he nevertheless voiced confidence that India was becoming "increasingly serious" about the Chinese threat and that "all we need do is nudge this trend along."[87]

In a new turn of the familiar cycle, however, American hopes were badly disappointed over the remainder of the year. The problem was not so much India's agricultural reform efforts, which mostly satisfied U.S. officials and repeatedly led Washington to approve incremental food deliveries. Rather, surging Indian dependence on U.S. aid along with Washington's mounting problems in Vietnam and shifting political circumstances in India proved a toxic mix, ensuring that the flurry of good will at the start of the year would dissipate. The problem flowed partly from Gandhi's place in Indian politics. Just forty-eight years old when she became prime minister, Gandhi gained the post largely through the support of Congress Party insiders who valued not just the high profile she carried as Jawaharlal Nehru's daughter but also the pliability that they perceived as a consequence of her lack of experience or close association with any particular political faction. Characteristics that made her appealing within Indian political circles ensured tensions with the United States. Wariness of deviating from her father's non-aligned principles caused her to pull back from the flexibility and moderation that Shastri had sometimes shown in forums of Third World nations and to lean anew toward the Soviets to compensate for dependency on the United States. Moreover, Gandhi's relatively weak position rendered her more sensitive than her predecessors to charges of caving in to foreign pressure and more likely to bend with prevailing political winds, which were decidedly leftward in the second half of the 1960s.

The potential of U.S. food assistance to inflame relations between Washington and New Delhi arose briefly during Gandhi's otherwise congenial meetings in Washington in March 1966. Questioned by Secretary Rusk about the climate in the Indian legislature, the Lok Sabha, Gandhi noted she would soon be asked "have I sold the country?" to the United States in return for food.[88] With opposition parties sharpening their attacks ahead of elections scheduled for February 1967, she had reason for worry. One communist Lok Sabha member had accused her of traveling "post haste" to Washington in response to a "summons" from Johnson and succeeded in forcing the government to make public the finance ministry's correspondence with U.S. officials. The government's position hardly improved when that correspondence revealed that New Delhi had accepted American demands for stepped-up fertilizer production and liberalization of the agricultural sector.[89] Unquestionably, dramatic evidence of U.S.-Indian harmony drowned out the naysayers in the immediate aftermath of the summit. The *Times of India* proclaimed that Gandhi had "won American hearts" and steered Johnson around to her point of view.[90] A day after she left Washington, Johnson announced his support for a new 3.5-billion-ton food package, which Congress unanimously endorsed two weeks later.[91] The administration also backed a major IMF loan that New Delhi sought to negotiate in return for liberalization of its economy. Yet Gandhi's worry about the potential of India's dependency to provoke major controversy proved justified by the middle of the year.

The blowup occurred after Gandhi announced a 57 percent devaluation of the rupee on June 6. The IMF had demanded that bold move in return for expanded loans aimed at alleviating India's urgent shortage of foreign exchange—a bargain Gandhi was willing to make. Much of the ruling Congress Party was hostile to the idea, however, fearing that the devaluation, in addition to the short-term economic dislocations it would inevitably cause, would be seen as a concession to foreign pressure. Congress leaders, including party head Kumaraswami Kamaraj, feared that such a perception would badly undercut the party's prospects in the upcoming general elections and voiced opposition as the agreement took shape. Gandhi went ahead anyway. The decision gratified President Johnson, who quickly approved a $335 million U.S. contribution toward the IMF's $1.2 billion target. In India, however, it unleashed a tidal wave of discontent. Members of parliament blasted the decision as the "mandate of Washington" and "the price we have got to pay" for dependence on foreign aid.[92] Bowles reported that Gandhi risked being "swept aside" because of a perception she was an "American stooge."[93]

With her premiership in jeopardy just six months after it began, Gandhi faced pressure to distance herself from Washington. The war in Vietnam provided an obvious means of demonstrating her independence, and Gandhi jumped on the issue. Indeed, her opportunity—and political incentive—to do so increased dramatically in the first days of July, when U.S. aircraft hit oil-storage facilities in the Hanoi-Haiphong area for the first time, a significant escalation in the American air war against North Vietnam. In New Delhi, Ambassador Bowles warned of a "powerful anti-US reaction" to the attacks. "The man in the factory and the paddy fields," he noted, had little appreciation of geopolitical complexities and would inevitably view the bombings as "devastating attacks on a small brown-skinned Asian underdog." At first, Gandhi offered a relatively moderate response in keeping with India's non-aligned stance. She called for mutual de-escalation of the war, followed by a new Geneva conference to seek Vietnam's neutralization, proposals that she reiterated at a meeting in Belgrade with her Yugoslav and Egyptian counterparts. Although Bowles believed the scheme was full of "bear traps," he cautiously welcomed it, at least as a propaganda boon since Hanoi would surely reject the proposal.[94]

The U.S. mood darkened abruptly when Gandhi, having moved on to Moscow, veered sharply toward the Soviet view of the war. Abandoning the studiously balanced proposals she had made just a few days before, she agreed to a joint Indian-Soviet communique demanding a halt to the U.S. bombing of North Vietnam and decrying the growing risk of general war "as a result of aggressive actions of imperialists and other reactionary forces."[95] Whether Gandhi intended to send a message to Washington or had merely erred in agreeing to the Soviet-drafted communique, as she quickly claimed, remains a matter of speculation. But it is not difficult to see that Gandhi had good reason to distance herself from the United States and to warm up to Moscow, where Soviet leaders had watched with growing anxiety as she improved relations with Washington and embraced economic reform demanded by Western governments and the IMF. As much as her predecessors, Gandhi aimed to balance between the United States and the Soviet Union in order to ensure aid from each. She arrived in Moscow at a moment of sharply rising Soviet exasperation about U.S. policy in Southeast Asia. Indian participants were impressed by the growing Soviet inclination to back North Vietnam. Soviet premier Alexei Kosygin conceded that the United States had "floundered" into the war on the basis of misguided "idealism," but he insisted that Moscow stood ready to give Hanoi "whatever it might ask for in the way of help . . . a blank cheque," according to one account of the meetings. Gandhi offered little resistance and was apparently unable or unwilling to resist Soviet pressure for a strongly worded communique critical of the United States.[96] The bad impression among U.S. observers was no doubt heightened when New Delhi relieved its consul general in Saigon of his post after he defended the recent U.S. decision to escalate the bombing.[97]

In any case, the communique provoked a strong reaction among U.S. officials. Bowles immediately denounced a "shocking document" replete with the "familiar language of Soviet propaganda bureaus" and urged Washington to "register vigorous and immediate protest."[98] In Washington, Rostow advised that Bowles craft a "scorching personal letter" to Gandhi.[99] For his part, LBJ used part of a news conference on July 20 to assail Indian criticism of U.S. bombing in Vietnam, insisting that New Delhi, like other governments around the world, had a bad habit of ignoring what North Vietnam needed to do in order to achieve peace. "We can't talk about just half the war," declared LBJ. "We should talk about all the war, and we have not the slightest indication that the other side is willing to make any concession, to take any action that would lead to the peace table."[100] If the president's wrath reflected American anger about criticism from a broad array of governments, India's reliance on U.S. aid made Gandhi's comments particularly galling. Bowles later recalled that when he pointed out that Gandhi's position on the war was close to that of the pope and UN Secretary-General U Thant, an unnamed U.S. official retorted, "Yes, but the Pope and U Thant don't need our wheat."[101]

## A New Equilibrium

Resurgent tensions in mid-1966 set the tone for the remainder of the Johnson presidency. As always, shared concern about Chinese expansion assured that relations would never break down completely. Yet various sources of friction guaranteed that the United States and India would continue to move apart. Discord over the war in Vietnam was just one of those sources, but it assumed a central importance because of the growing political salience of the conflict in both countries. As the war dragged on in 1967 and 1968, LBJ grew increasingly bitter toward both domestic and foreign critics of his Vietnam policy. In India, meanwhile, Gandhi appears to have understood the significance of the war among Indian public opinion and therefore the possibilities of using public statements on the subject as a way to adjust the political standing of her government. In both Washington and New Delhi, leaders viewed a range of issues through a Vietnam-tinged lens.

Out of public view, it is true, the two governments—particularly officials in secondary tiers of influence—sometimes interacted constructively on the war. Indeed, India's recent tilt away from Washington may have improved the country's chance of playing a meaningful diplomatic role. On January 4, the North Vietnamese consul in New Delhi, Ngu Yen Hua, made explicit what Indian diplomats had been sensing for a few weeks. In a meeting with T. N. Kaul, the secretary general of the Indian Ministry of External Affairs, the consul stated that if the United States stopped bombing North Vietnam "unconditionally and indefinitely," the gesture would lead to a "cessation of hostilities and other steps" in the South. Optimistic about a breakthrough toward a negotiated settlement, Ambassador Nehru relayed the message to Rusk, advising the secretary that Hanoi's démarche was "more than a whisper." Rusk told Nehru that Washington was "most interested" and asked that Indian officials pursue the contact in New Delhi.[102] U.S. officials felt sufficiently confident about the new channel of communication with Hanoi to assign it a codename—NIRVANA—for easy reference.

Indian officials grew more hopeful about the initiative in the ensuing days, fueled by a belief that mounting chaos within China as the Cultural Revolution intensified was emboldening moderates in Hanoi to assert themselves. Yet the scheme came to nothing. Very likely, the initiative never had any chance of success due to persistent U.S. hostility to an unconditional bombing halt and Hanoi's demand that the National Liberation Front play a role in negotiations thereafter. Rusk indicated he was willing to "play games" with the idea of NLF participation for the purpose of exploring the North Vietnamese bargaining position but had "no illusion" that the NLF amounted to an independent entity that should be permitted to take part.[103] Hanoi, though, did more to crush Indian hopes by abruptly altering its tone as January advanced. When Indian officials pressed Ngu Yuen Hoa for details of the North Vietnamese position, he gave a "somewhat peremptory reply" and merely repeated his government's long-standing negotiating position. Indian diplomats speculated that a news leak in the Indian press may have scuttled the peace bid by exposing the dovish faction in Hanoi to pressure from China or hawks in their own government.[104]

Whatever the reason for the failure, the NIRVANA initiative, feeble though it was, represented the high-water mark of New Delhi's peacemaking efforts. When Kaul tried later in the year to reopen contact with North Vietnamese diplomats, U.S. officials, including even Bowles, quickly dismissed the possibility. "We have had from Kaul messages from Hanoi before and then been disappointed," Bowles wrote to the State Department.[105] He and other U.S. officials complained about the uncoordinated mix of views on the war within the Indian government and questioned whether New Delhi was deliberately exaggerating the significance of its contacts with Hanoi in order to raise India's profile on the Vietnam issue.[106] Those doubts aligned U.S. skepticism about India's mediatory role with the broader mood surrounding U.S.-Indian relations in 1967 and demonstrated that tensions at the most senior levels on both sides tended to swamp the efforts of subordinates to maintain cooperation on issues where U.S. and Indian interests coincided.

The potential for tension at the highest levels grew in 1967 and 1968 as the political environments on both sides grew more contentious and polarized. In the United States, Congress became increasingly skeptical about economic and especially military aid, a trend that heightened President Johnson's own desire to keep a lid on such programs. The mood in Congress became especially clear in January 1968, when a coalition of conservatives who generally disliked foreign aid and liberals who were hostile to the militarization of poor Third World nations came together around legislation constraining U.S. aid of any type for governments that refused to hold down defense spending. But the trend was evident as early as the 1966 midterm elections, when the Democratic Party lost forty-seven House and three Senate seats to the Republicans. Although it is impossible to discern the precise impact of foreign aid on these results, a nationwide poll conducted just before the November election revealed that a candidate's opposition to any further foreign aid made 46 percent of Americans more likely to vote for him or her, whereas 42 percent were more likely to vote the other way.[107]

Any chance that Johnson would resist the political logic of such numbers dwindled amid personnel changes that both reflected and affirmed the trend away from international largesse. The two senior officials most dedicated to the U.S. opening to India that originated in the Kennedy administration—men LBJ had once scorned as "India lovers"—left their posts in 1966. First, National Security Adviser Bundy stepped down in February 1966, opening the way for Rostow, a champion of using U.S. aid as leverage over India and a staunch loyalist to Johnson. Six weeks later, the president drastically altered Komer's role, placing the NSC aide in charge of interdepartmental efforts to beef up counterinsurgency efforts in Vietnam. The transfer was laden with significance easy to see in retrospect: a key official who had voiced consistent concern about the Third World beyond Vietnam was now swept up in the war.[108] Revealingly, too, LBJ replaced Komer as deputy national security adviser with Francis M. Bator, a specialist in economic and European affairs. Never again would a single NSC official wield so much influence across such a broad swath of the Third World. Komer's portfolio was increasingly divided up among various NSC officials, indicating a final break from President Kennedy's tendency to view the Third World in terms of the common challenges besetting an array of diverse societies rather than as a series of discrete regional or national problems.

In India, meanwhile, mounting political unrest emboldened Gandhi's critics and incentivized the prime minister to lash out at the United States as a way to cultivate her leftist and nationalist credentials. The nation's problems—massive poverty, inflation running as high as 15 percent annually, a rapidly growing population, separatism in various regions, and widespread corruption, overlaid with threats from abroad—were staggering to begin with and only worsened during 1966, when the monsoon rains failed for a second year. The threat of famine displaced the corrosion of democracy at the top of the nation's long list of ills, and gloomy prognostications abounded. "The Grimmest Situation in 19 Years," declared a headlined in the *Hindustan Times*, which spoke for an increasing number of Indians in expressing skepticism about the ruling Congress Party. "The future of the country is dark for many reasons, all of them directly attributable to 19 years of Congress rule," asserted the paper, decrying a dangerous mix of food shortages, strikes, and incipient social violence.[109] In the political arena, distress fed populism and nationalism, trends that favored neither the cerebral moderation of the Nehru years nor smooth relations with the United States.

Indeed, U.S.-Indian relations grew more strained as President Johnson doubled down on the "short-tether" approach as the food situation in India grew more perilous in the second half of 1966 and early 1967. Key aides including Agriculture Secretary Freeman and David Bell, the head of the U.S. Agency for International Development, backed by a bipartisan congressional commission, urged LBJ to approve large deliveries of American grain. But Johnson, as before, stood his ground, withholding approval of significant deliveries until late 1966 and then distributing food in small increments and insisting that other nations supplement the U.S. contributions. He undoubtedly acted on several considerations, including a persistent desire to press India to adopt thoroughgoing agricultural reforms and a new concern about low crop yields in the United States. It is ultimately impossible to know the extent to which he also acted out of anger about India's persistently disappointing behavior with respect to Vietnam. Rostow told an interviewer in 1990 that Johnson was "playing a long-term game to get India to feed its people" and denied that sensitivities about Vietnam played any role. Other U.S. officials, however, disagreed, suggesting that demonstrating disappointment in connection with Southeast Asia was at least a meaningful bonus in LBJ's mind, if not the primary motive of his behavior in 1966 and 1967.[110]

All of this provides crucial context for an event that strongly reinforced the growing rift between the Washington and New Delhi. In February 1967, India's fourth general election since independence in 1947 resulted in a humiliating defeat for the Congress Party. The party's share of seats in the Lok Sabha shrank from 72.8 to 54.5 percent. Meanwhile, the party lost control over the legislatures in eight of the seventeen states and saw its overall percentage of seats plunge from 60.7 percent of seats to 48.5.[111] Meticulous historical spadework over the years makes clear that this outcome had numerous causes, but the United States was clearly implicated in two of the most damaging complaints about Gandhi's government: the devaluation of the rupee in 1966—"wholesale political and economic surrender to Washington," in the words of the leftist mass-circulation weekly *Blitz*—and humiliating dependence on U.S. food aid.[112] Food shortages and the government's difficulties winning American agreement to make up the shortfall amounted to "serious setbacks" for the Congress Party, noted the *Times of India* as the voting got under way.[113]

Just as it had done when Gandhi journeyed to Moscow after the devaluation the year before, criticism of the U.S. role in Vietnam offered a means to demonstrate distance from Washington and gain favor on the restive political left. To be sure, antiwar activism never became widespread in India, and Indian newspapers did not harp on the theme. Moreover, the Indian government's dedication to a moderate position in the global Third World movement imposed limits on how far leaders would go in associating themselves with a harsher brand of anti-Vietnam activism characteristic of nations such as Algeria or Cuba. Yet anecdotal evidence suggests strong undercurrents of hostility to U.S. policy that invited attention to the issue at the highest levels. American journalist Selig Harrison detected a "broad-based antiwar consensus embracing not only diverse sectors of Indian opinion but also diverse elite groups," though the most striking evidence unsurprisingly emerged on the political left.[114] In the left-leaning hotbed of Calcutta, a theater staged weekly shows of *Invincible Vietnam*, a play that depicted U.S. servicemen torturing to death a

Vietnamese nurse, using napalm and poison gas against defenseless villages, and burning the Bible and the works of Shakespeare.[115] One of the city's central thoroughfares, Harrington Road, was renamed for the Vietnamese communist leader, making the address of the U.S. consulate 7 Ho Chi Minh Sarani.[116] In Mumbai and Hyderabad, demonstrators burned effigies of Lyndon Johnson in front of the U.S. Information Agency headquarters and the U.S. Cultural Center, respectively.[117] Meanwhile, Vietnam figured prominently alongside U.S. policy toward Southern Rhodesia and the Middle East in propaganda produced by the Indian Communist Party, which declared a "Vietnam Solidarity Week" in July 1966 to mark the twelfth anniversary of the Geneva Accords.[118]

Whatever her mix of motives, Indira Gandhi made an apparently calculated decision in May 1967 to antagonize Washington over Vietnam by sending—and making public—effusive birthday greetings for Ho Chi Minh. The note expressed hope that "the Vietnamese people will have the good fortune of having Ho Chi Minh's wise and dedicated leadership to guide them." Indian officials tried to explain away Gandhi's message as an unfortunate error while emphasizing that India regarded Ho Chi Minh as a nationalist and had sent similar greetings in earlier years.[119] But the damage was done. In Washington, Secretary Rusk instructed Bowles to lodge a protest with the Indian government. "If Mrs. Gandhi thinks that we are just good guys and will take a lot of punishment without reaction, she is underestimating the mood of the American people while we are carrying such heavy burdens," Rusk wrote to his ambassador. "The general mood in this country does not permit us to act like an old cow which continues to give milk, however often one kicks her in the flanks." Rusk professed to acknowledge that India and the United States would hardly agree on everything but insisted that "those who pretend to be non-aligned should in fact be non-aligned and stay away from questions on which they are not prepared to take any serious responsibility." No one, he added, was serving India's interest in a durable peace in Southeast Asia more than the president and "the young men in this country who are being killed in Viet-Nam."[120]

Rusk's undiplomatic language captured the mood in Washington as officials lost hope of progress on key sticking points in the relationship with India. New issues sometimes stirred fresh tensions. For instance, U.S. officials expressed anger when, hard on the heels of the flare-up over Ho Chi Minh's birthday, Indian leaders chastised Israel as the aggressor in the June 1967 war in the Middle East. Although Arab support for Pakistan two years earlier had caused disquiet in India, much of the Indian political elite sided openly with the Arabs in 1967, whether out of solidarity with nations loosely aligned under the Third World banner or due to anger over the deaths of five Indian peacekeeping soldiers killed by Israeli attacks in the opening stages of the war.[121] National Security Adviser Rostow spoke for many of his colleagues in privately criticizing India's "irritating and often stupid role in the Middle East crisis."[122] Indians also found new reasons for disgust during 1967 when it became clear that prestigious cultural and educational institutions such as the Asia Foundation and the Friends of India Committee Trust had received covert CIA funding over the years to advance U.S. interests. Intellectuals and academics blasted Washington for violating its own principles of transparency and free exchange of ideas, while the Indian left seized on the revelations as further evidence of U.S. imperialism.[123]

None of these issues produced dramatic ruptures, and U.S.-Indian relations muddled along. The new equilibrium was perhaps most evident in the military relationship between Washington and New Delhi. Persistently irritated by high defense spending on the subcontinent and the refusal of India and Pakistan to resolve their differences in order to refocus on the broader imperatives of the Cold War, the Johnson administration resolved uncertainty over the status of the arms embargo it had declared in response to the 1965 Indo-Pakistani war by essentially extending the cutoff indefinitely. There was no hope, wrote Rusk, of pushing the two nations to settle their differences "no matter how hard we try."[124] Under a policy adopted in April 1967, the United States refused to offer grants or credits for lethal military equipment to either nation and banned sales of everything except spare parts for equipment that the United States had supplied in earlier years. Giving the new policy a feeling of finality was a simultaneous decision to withdraw the advisory teams that had once supervised U.S. assistance and training in India and Pakistan.[125] Unsurprisingly, Gandhi's government responded by stepping up India's reliance on Soviet assistance, which climbed sharply in 1968. U.S. officials decried this trend, which exacerbated old anger about India's willingness to deal with U.S. adversaries even as it remained dependent on food and economic assistance. But Americans also conceded that they had virtually no leverage. Bowles expressed U.S. impotence in March 1968 when he acknowledged that if New Delhi faced a choice between conceding to U.S. demands to reduce defense spending or forgoing U.S. assistance of any type, it might well choose the latter.[126]

Alongside food deliveries, U.S. economic assistance continued to flow in 1967 and 1968, albeit in reduced quantities and with lower levels of commitment than in the past. Congressional appropriations for development aid shrank to their lowest totals since 1961 and, on a per capita basis, their lowest point since 1959.[127] At the same time, Johnson grew more insistent that other nations share more of the burden not just in delivering food aid but also in funding long-term economic programs. It was high time, he exclaimed on one occasion, for other governments to "recognize their responsibilities" in India, adding that he would welcome even Soviet contributions of food.[128] Yet Washington largely failed in its efforts to generate a greater multilateral effort. National Security Council aide Edward Hamilton pointed out the gloomy mood in August 1967, noting of potential donors around the world, "Everybody is tired; everybody is unhappy with the Indians; and everybody has budget problems."[129] The international consortium of donors assembled by the World Bank to provide economic assistance fell far short of its promises. The donors' group provided just \$295 million of India's estimated \$750 million aid requirement in 1968 and pledged just \$642 million of \$1.275 billion in needs projected in 1968–1969, according to historian Dennis Kux.[130]

Declining U.S. assistance eroded whatever influence the United States might have otherwise possessed over India's attitude toward U.S.-backed efforts for a multilateral nonproliferation agreement, a high U.S. priority during Johnson's final months in office. Although India had disavowed any plan to build a nuclear weapon in the years following China's test in 1964, American officials understood that the government might change its mind if the United States and the Soviet Union could not find a way to reassure New Delhi. U.S. officials had sought to "buy time" in order to reach such an agreement, as Rusk put it in 1966.[131] Curiously, however, the Johnson administration's urgency about the issue resulted in no bold initiative to soothe Indian sensitivities, which grew more intense after China tested a hydrogen bomb in June 1967.[132] U.S. and Soviet leaders applied pressure on India to sign the Non-Proliferation Treaty after it opened for signature on July 1, 1968. But the Indian government, wary of China and sensitive about conceding its sovereign prerogatives in return for no tangible gain, refused to go along, joining Pakistan among a small collection of holdout nations. To be sure, Indira Gandhi also refused to authorize development of nuclear weapons and avoided any categorical statement of hostility to the NPT. But American officials understood that there was little they could do to push Gandhi to sign the treaty. Withholding the latest delivery of U.S. economic aid in order to exert leverage over New Delhi would only give Indian politicians "so juicy a political plum to oppose the Treaty that it would tip the final balance against it," Rostow advised in May 1968. All in all, he asserted, the United States had little choice but to "swallow our discontent" and keep sending assistance without assurances of an Indian signature on the NPT.[133]

Amid the U.S. pullback from South Asia, there was some serendipitous good news for Washington in 1968, no doubt a welcome break from the litany of problems that Johnson and his aides confronted in the administration's final months. For one thing, the food crisis ebbed thanks to a record-setting crop, the cumulative effect of rain and reforms enacted under intense U.S. pressure during two tumultuous years. Bowles extolled India's "impressive progress" in these arenas.[134] Indeed, with the benefit of hindsight, historians would later write of a transformative Green Revolution that had taken place in India and other poor countries during the mid-1960s as a result of new technologies and economic practices. In the military realm, meanwhile, U.S. officials welcomed evidence of India's improved capacity for defending itself during major border clashes with China in September 1967. Though much of its equipment had come from the Soviet Union, India had built up "substantial" forces that would be able to "give a good account of themselves" in any future war with China, advised Undersecretary Nicholas Katzenbach. All in all, he concluded, the Indian military was a "net plus" for Western efforts to contain China.[135]

So encouraged was Katzenbach that he urged Johnson to schedule a meeting with Indira Gandhi during her upcoming trip to New York for the opening of the UN General Assembly. But the proposal, which cut against many months of growing distance between the two nations, led nowhere. Indeed, the relationship had settled into a new pattern hardly conducive to sudden upturns. In her remarks at the UN headquarters, Gandhi disavowed any "partisan spirit" but demanded an end to all U.S. bombing in North Vietnam and chastised the big powers for managing nuclear weapons in ways that undercut the "political authority" of smaller nations—positions that showed little had changed in the Indian outlook on key issues.[136] For his part, Johnson refused to decide on any new assistance for India during his final months in office, even when aides urged him to approve small loans or minor food deliveries. All decisions, insisted LBJ, would be left to the next president.[137] This immobility offered striking evidence not just of LBJ's frame of mind during his final days in the White House but also of the disengagement from India that had been under way at least since the middle of 1966, if not, in a more general sense, since 1962. Little remained of hopes that had once run high.

# 6

# Iran

## A RELATIONSHIP TRANSFORMED

A GRADUATION ceremony of sorts took place on November 29, 1967. Gathered in the John Quincy Adams Room at the State Department, the Iranian ambassador to the United States, Hushang Ansary, and Secretary of State Dean Rusk presided over a lavish luncheon to celebrate the termination of the U.S. program that had sent $605 million in economic assistance to the South Asian nation over the previous fifteen years. Now Iran, relying on its vast oil exports, could finance its own development. "What we mark today is Iran's success," President Johnson declared in a statement prepared for the occasion. "What we celebrate is Iran's economic and social progress."[1] Both governments had strong incentives to herald the significance of the moment. For Tehran, the ceremony nurtured an image of Iran's arrival as a major player in world politics. For the Johnson administration, starved for good news, there was also reason to "squeeze maximum publicity from the occasion," as National Security Adviser Walt Rostow put it.[2] The event represented just the second time that the U.S. Agency for International Development had crossed a nation off its list of aid recipients, welcome evidence that U.S. development assistance sometimes paid dividends. (Taiwan had been the first to "graduate," in 1965.)[3]

Iran still needed American food and military equipment, and no one doubted such aid would continue to flow. Yet the end of economic aid marked a real milestone—Iran's transition from a dependent of the United States to something more like a partner capable of upholding American interests in a distant but crucial part of the world as long as the United States continued providing security assistance. The most critical phases of this transformation occurred during Lyndon Johnson's presidency, when the shah's consolidation of power combined with growing U.S. tolerance of his authoritarianism to put an end to the strains that had suffused U.S.-Iranian ties during the Kennedy years. This is not to say that the relationship improved in a linear or seamless way. Indeed, the reconfigured U.S.-Iranian link evident by late 1967 came only after many months of tension and even rancor as the shah experimented with a foreign policy relatively independent of the United States and U.S. leaders struggled to come to terms with their declining leverage over Tehran. At the end of his presidency, though, LBJ spoke sincerely in assuring the Iranian foreign minister that he knew of no other country "where the leadership has been wiser or more effective" than it had been in Iran over the previous few years. The United States and Iran were, agreed the minister, "real friends."[4]

The trajectory of U.S.-Iranian relations illuminates broad policymaking trends during the Johnson presidency in ways different from the cases analyzed in the previous two chapters. Clearly, Washington's interactions with Tehran contrast sharply with patterns of U.S. decision making toward India. In the latter relationship, disappointment rooted in divergent outlooks on regional and global priorities torpedoed efforts to put the relationship on a stable new footing and culminated in failure, despite a common hostility to China. Johnson administration officials viewed India as far more hostile to American purposes in 1968 than they had in 1963. The U.S. success with Iran comes much closer to the pattern of U.S.-Brazilian relations. As in that case, American leaders concluded that Iran's authoritarian regime would serve U.S. interests by ensuring security and orderly development. But subtle differences ensured that Washington would take even more satisfaction in its relations with Iran. Greater geographical distance and shallower historical connections to Iran, along with that country's history of authoritarian government, meant that American leaders felt less squeamishness about democracy than they did in Brazil. Meanwhile, LBJ felt more comfortable with the urbane shah, a civilian who spoke LBJ's language of state-led reform, than he did with the uniformed, bemedaled generals in Brazil. The shah emerged as the quintessence of a Third World leader around whom the United States could build its foreign policy at a time of setbacks and diminishing expectations.

## Embracing the Shah

A telegram that Mohammad Reza Pahlavi, the shah of Iran, dispatched to Lyndon Johnson on November 24, 1963, struck an oddly upbeat tone considering the worldwide surge of grief surrounding John F. Kennedy's assassination. The forty-four-year-old potentate assured LBJ of his "heartfelt congratulations" and "sincere good wishes" for his presidency, while offering no words of regret about events in Dallas.[5] It is impossible to know whether these words reflected the shah's anger about JFK's ambivalence toward the Iranian regime. But it stands to reason that the shah had much higher hopes for the man suddenly thrust into the presidency. Johnson had exuded friendship for the Tehran government during his vice presidential trip to Iran back in 1962, endearing himself to the shah as well as much of the Iranian public at a time of strained relations with Washington.[6] The shah's first full-fledged letter to President Johnson in January 1964—the start of an elaborate personal correspondence between the two men during LBJ's years in the White House—extolled Johnson's "kind-hearted and affable" demeanor during that trip and solicited his understanding of Iranian objectives on a number of issues that had often provoked disagreement during the Kennedy period.

In that letter and in conversations with Ambassador Julius Holmes during the first weeks of the new administration, the shah blended assurances of his regime's dedication to social and economic progress with appeals for U.S. aid and subtle warnings that he might turn to other suppliers if Washington failed to meet his demands, themes that he would hammer on relentlessly over the years to come. Internally, the shah assured Johnson, the White Revolution had already "transformed completely the entire structure of our society," which was built on no less than the "enlightened and progressive principles of our time." Yet he warned that Iran faced urgent external threats that jeopardized all these advances. He fixated most of all on Gamal Abdel Nasser, whose growing stockpile of Soviet weaponry appeared to tilt the regional balance of power toward Egypt and its radical partners in the Arab world. Already, asserted the shah, Nasser was meddling in Yemen, Somalia, and North Africa. "I should perhaps add that even Iran does not seem to be too distant for his desires or immune from his subversive activities," the shah wrote LBJ on January 7, 1964. The most urgent threat seemed to lie in Iran's southwestern province, oil-rich Khuzestan, where the predominantly Arab population offered an obvious target for Nasserist subversion.[7] But American officials surmised that the shah also feared a broader offensive toward the Persian Gulf, where Iraq and even Saudi Arabia appeared vulnerable to Egyptian intervention.[8]

To counter such threats, the shah demanded increased access to U.S. weaponry. In September 1962, the Kennedy administration had grudgingly agreed to a five-year military assistance program that promised as much as $298.6 million worth of equipment by the middle of 1967. U.S. officials worried that an expanded military would divert Iran's resources from urgent economic priorities, whereas the shah disliked the agreement for the opposite reason: it was far too modest. With a new president in power, he appealed in no uncertain terms for a higher ceiling on U.S. aid. In virtually every category of military gear, he insisted, Iranian capabilities fell far below what was necessary to protect his nation amid the "changing situation" in the region. With its outdated tanks and meager supplies of ammunition, small arms, and much else, the army could not fight effectively either in the mountains or on the plains, the shah complained. He painted an equally grim picture of Iran's naval and air forces. Emphasizing Iran's "clear and urgent military needs," he requested additional American assistance or, as a second choice, Washington's consent to buy U.S. gear on favorable terms.[9]

The shah mostly tried to woo LBJ with the carrot of shared interests in the security of a vital region of the world. But occasionally he reached for the stick. In one encounter with Ambassador Holmes in Tehran, the shah blasted Washington for failing to treat its friends "as well as we treat those who are either our enemies or are not committed to us"—a reference to the warming trend in U.S.-Soviet relations and U.S. indulgence of India at the expense of Washington's long-standing ties to Pakistan.[10] If the United States failed to increase its military assistance, warned the shah, Iran might have no choice but to go "elsewhere."[11] Western European nations were an obvious possibility, but the Soviet Union also loomed as an option despite the history of Soviet-Iranian tensions stretching back to the eighteenth century. Even though Tehran feared Soviet-backed regimes in the Middle East, bilateral Soviet-Iranian relations had improved dramatically in recent years. Driven by a desire to extract more help from the United States and to move toward a more independent foreign policy befitting a rising power, the shah had irritated U.S. officials in 1962 by pledging never to permit stationing of foreign missiles on Iranian soil in return for implicit Soviet promises to discontinue efforts to overthrow the shah.[12] In January 1964, the Iranian leader reminded Johnson that Khrushchev was doing "his best to be friendly" and reiterated his dislike of Iran's military dependency on the West. Johnson and his aides could hardly miss the suggestion that the shah might take the incipient Iranian-Soviet détente to the next level if the United States let him down.[13]

For Americans skeptical of the shah's regime, there was nothing enticing about this latest bid for U.S. assistance. Predictably, Komer, the shah's leading critic among senior officials, scorned the new Iranian overtures. Describing the shah's January 7 letter as "ten rambling pages," Komer dismissed Iranian desiderata as "old and tired requests for military hardware that JFK had repeatedly rejected."[14] The solution, Komer wrote, was to throw a "large dose of flattery" at the shah in order to "massage" him—a favorite metaphor of Komer's in connection with U.S.-Iranian relations—while rejecting the bid for additional arms.[15] As usual, Komer regarded the request as evidence of the shah's obsession with weaponry rather than any serious danger to Iran. As usual, too, Komer worried that expanded grants or sales of American equipment would distract the shah from his internal problems, which struck many U.S. officials as by far the biggest danger to what remained, in the words of one State Department official, "the most vulnerable country on the Soviet perimeter."[16] A wide-ranging intelligence report concluded in May that the White Revolution was still a work in progress, having not yet produced any "basic

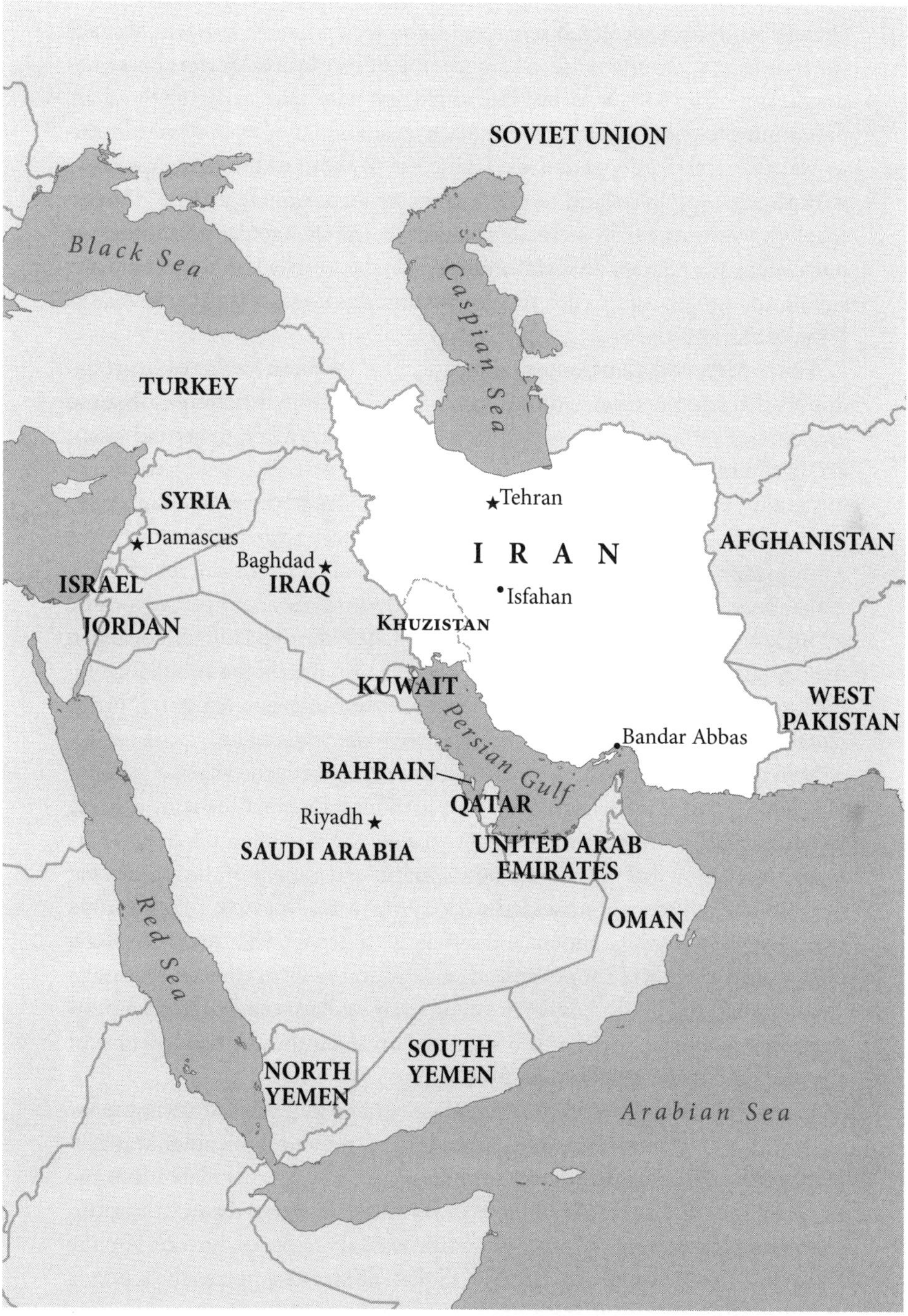


MAP 6.1. Iran and neighboring nations. Israel's borders reflect the situation before the 1967 war with its Arab neighbors. Mapping Specialists, Ltd., Madison, WI.

change" in Iranian society. It remained to be seen whether Iran would make the transition to "modern life" without "violent revolution." As for Iran's budding relationship with Moscow, U.S. intelligence agencies expected the shah, determined to enhance his international prestige and to placate domestic critics wary of excessive dependence on the West, to continue to seek cooperation with the Soviet Union and to pay "lip service" to "nonalignment." On the whole, however, the risks seemed manageable. The shah remained sufficiently pro-American and wary of Soviet ambitions in the Middle East to prevent "any significant danger" of a major shift away from the West if Washington called Iran's bluff.[17]

For a variety of reasons, however, such skepticism about Iranian overtures—doubts that had often carried the day during the Kennedy period—began to erode in 1964, the start of a trend that would play out, albeit in fits and starts, across the LBJ presidency. Gradually, the shah gained credibility and stature in Washington. One cause was the sheer persistence of the shah's champions in the U.S. bureaucracy. Undoubtedly the most important such official was Ambassador Julius Holmes, who, like Lincoln Gordon in Brazil, rejected the globalist currents swirling within the Kennedy administration and advocated strongly for the regime to which he was posted. Although Holmes conceded that the shah had a long way to go to realize the promises of the White Revolution, he urged in January 1964 that the administration recognize Iran's "legitimate concern" about acquiring sufficient weaponry and offer a "positive" response to Iranian requests, at least in connection with the shah's desire for assurances about American military support after the expiration of the existing five-year deal. Central to Holmes's point of view was not only a sense that Iran's security situation had deteriorated but also his assessment of the regime. Far from an isolated despot obsessed with military hardware, the shah was, in Holmes's view, a "self-confident and self-assured" leader who was successfully managing his country's modernization. The ambassador praised the shah's "hopeful start" on his domestic reform program and insisted that Iran was now in a much better financial and budgetary situation than in the recent past thanks to increased oil revenues.[18]

Crucial to the evolution of U.S. policy toward Iran was a growing sense among U.S. officials by early 1964 that Holmes, rather than Komer, was correct in his assessment of the country. Even as the CIA speculated that the regime still faced a meaningful risk of revolutionary overthrow, American commentary grew more positive about the stability of the shah's rule. For one thing, Iranian security forces had honed their ability to suppress the regime's enemies within Iran, showing a "high degree of reliability and increasing technical capacity" without going so far as to create an atmosphere of wholesale repression. But the best news, in the opinion of many American officials, was the shah's progress toward bolstering his legitimacy with a broader swath of the Iranian population than he had previously cultivated. In pursuit of his White Revolution reforms, noted one State Department report, the shah was loosening his customary dependence on landlords and conservative clerics, long the principal pillars of the Pahlavi regime, while forging ties with the peasantry and rising middle classes that composed much larger chunks of the nation.[19]

This process was, of course, fraught with peril for both Washington and the shah. The shah's cultivation of professionals and intellectuals, for instance, seemed likely to fuel the rise of what one NSC study dubbed Iran's "new men"—educated and ambitious urbanites with a strong sense of Iranian nationalism and a corresponding aversion to overreliance on the United States.[20] Cutting ties with the clergy, meanwhile, threatened to stir new grievances among a segment of the population whose influence had been clearly displayed in the riots of mid-1963. At the other end of the spectrum, Iran's restive student population, both within Iran and living abroad, seemed likely to grow more critical of the regime's authoritarianism. On the whole, however, U.S. assessments credited the shah with managing these problems as he moved forward with reforms that seemed to be steadily solidifying the regime. A CIA study completed in late May 1964 noted that land reform had achieved "substantial progress" in the countryside while the shah's enemies, ranging from the conservative mullahs to the communist Tudeh party, were so fragmented that no meaningful opposition was remotely likely.[21] Indeed, Iran's steadily improving economic situation suggested that the shah's position would strengthen. As in so many U.S. assessments of Third World nations, economic progress seemed the surest ticket to pro-Western political stability.

President Johnson appears to have shared this upbeat view of Iran. To be sure, he left no record of his thinking in the early days of his administration, and he did not even mention the country in the memoir of his presidency that he later published.[22] But the warm bond LBJ established with the shah back in 1962 suggests a predisposition toward the more positive view, as does his general appreciation of strong leaders dedicated to ambitious programs of top-down reform. For these reasons, writes James A. Bill, a leading scholar of U.S.-Iranian relations, the shah was, from the outset, "an extremely attractive and important figure to Johnson," who seems to have appreciated the Iranian leader's toughness in the face of threats from inside and outside his country.[23] Armin Meyer, who served as U.S. ambassador in Iran for most of LBJ's presidency, later recalled Johnson's feelings of "deep friendship and respect" for the shah.[24] That sentiment was evident before and during the shah's visit to

Washington in June 1964, an encounter that left little doubt the U.S. attitude had changed markedly since the JFK years. In a letter to the shah in March, LBJ went so far as to declare Iran "the brightest spot in the Middle East these days," a remarkably bold statement at a time when some of his officials disagreed.[25] Johnson repeated precisely those words when the two leaders met at the White House on June 8, while praising the shah's reform initiatives and—perhaps the strongest indication of Johnson's approval of the shah's program—likening the Iranian reform effort to the "never-ending" process of modernization that he was trying to nudge along in the United States.[26]

More concretely, Johnson and his aides abandoned much of the caution that Komer had urged about new military assistance for Iran, indicating that Washington was prepared to meet at least some of Iran's demands. Unquestionably, the president and like-minded aides stressed their concern that the shah's plans for expanding the Iranian military would divert valuable resources from his reform projects. U.S. officials also cautioned that the shah was exaggerating the military threat posed to his country by Nasserism. Yet growing American sympathy for the shah's internal and geopolitical priorities, combined with mounting confidence that Iran's financial position enabled the United States to shift from grants to sales of military gear, produced a fundamental change in the U.S. outlook. During the shah's visit to Washington, administration officials agreed to provide credits for the sale of four C-130 transport aircraft and dozens of sophisticated tanks (although the model remained a matter of discussion), all of which went well beyond the five-year military assistance program dating from 1962. W. Averell Harriman, the senior diplomat whom LBJ would increasingly entrust with managing relations with the shah, assured the Iranian delegation of "continued U.S. assistance in strengthening Iran," suggesting an open-ended willingness to consider new Iranian requests.[27] The generosity of the evolving American position became clear in July, when Washington agreed to extend a $200 million line of credit for the period from 1965 to 1969 as well as a $50 million grant for immediate purchases of planes and tanks.[28]

The shifting balance within the U.S. bureaucracy was most obvious in the changing role played by Komer. On the eve of LBJ's meeting with the shah, the NSC aide struck much the same tone that he had sounded ever since the start of the Kennedy presidency. The meeting, he urged, should be regarded mostly as an "exercise in political massage" designed to soothe the "moody monarch's" ego by talking with him about "the military toys he loves." Komer advised that U.S. interlocutors should rebuff the shah's demands for more military aid and keep "his nose to the grindstone" on political reform.[29] When Johnson proved amenable to the shah's new requests, however, Komer backed off. In early July, he not only dropped his resistance to the new arms deal but also abandoned his fallback proposal that Washington demand Iran's agreement to a firm ceiling on total military spending.[30] Thereafter, Komer lodged relatively few objections against arms sales and held a less prominent role in policymaking toward Iran than he had previously played, while Rusk, Assistant Secretary of State Phillips Talbot, and W. Averell Harriman (and eventually Rostow and NSC aide Hal Saunders) exerted stronger influence.

The administration's preferences also became clear with the appointment of Armin H. Meyer, a career foreign service officer whose experience in the Middle East stretched back to the Second World War, to replace Julius Holmes as U.S. ambassador in Tehran in early 1965. Over the following four years, Meyer proved an even more outspoken champion of the shah than his predecessor had been, consistently depicting the Iranian leader in glowing terms and discouraging his staff from developing contacts with opposition elements. In the words of political scientist James Bill, Meyer's actions "approached those of a public relations officer for the Persian king."[31] If Komer had managed to battle Holmes to a stalemate in the Kennedy period, he rapidly lost ground amid the changing bureaucratic landscape of the Johnson administration.

The flow of events during 1964 played into the hands of U.S. officials inclined to a more favorable view of the shah. Pakistani leader Ayub Khan's flirtations with China clearly underscored the value of Iran's pro-U.S. orientation. In the worst case, closer U.S.-Iranian cooperation could compensate for the loss of Pakistan as a major ally in southwest Asia; in the best case, the shah could play a helpful role in convincing Ayub, a fellow Muslim leader with a penchant for U.S. military gear, to recommit to CENTO and to the United States. The shah also stood out as a potential source of help in connection with another worrying part of Asia: Vietnam. Just before his June 1964 trip to Washington, the shah, who had publicly endorsed U.S. policy in Indochina, gratified Washington by deciding "in principle" to support the rapidly growing American commitment.[32] A few weeks later, Tehran promised a thousand tons of petroleum products along with veterinary services that were ultimately declined by the government in Saigon. Even more encouraging, the State Department's intelligence division concluded that the Iranian government would probably agree "under U.S. urging" to provide still more help. Further generosity, State Department officials concluded, hinged above all on Tehran's satisfaction that it did not face urgent threats from Nasserist adversaries closer to home and could safely divert its resources to Vietnam.[33] At a moment when few allies of the United States were offering even vague assurances in response to LBJ's requests for help, it is not difficult to imagine that the president was eager to do whatever it might take to get the metaphorical, if not the real, Iranian flag flying in Vietnam.

FIGURE 6.2. President Johnson and Secretary of State Dean Rusk (with his back to the camera) consult with Julian Holmes (left), the former U.S. ambassador to Iran, and his replacement, Armin H. Meyer, at the White House on April 15, 1965. LBJ Library photo by Yoichi Okamoto.

The tightening U.S. bond with the shah became clearer still on October 13, 1964, when the two governments agreed on new legal provisions for the growing number of U.S. personnel stationed in Iran—an ostensibly technical matter that held outsize importance on both sides. The Pentagon had long applied pressure on Iran to agree to diplomatic immunity for U.S. military personnel and their dependents, essentially meaning that Americans would be subject to U.S. rather than Iranian law. The Defense Department regarded the measure as a routine part of the U.S.-Iranian "status of forces agreement" (SOFA), even though it differed from Washington's arrangements with most other allied governments in one respect: it refused to allow Iranian authorities to prosecute Americans even if U.S. courts declined to do so. The shah and his ministers understood that accepting this provision was likely to provoke widespread opposition within Iranian society, where memories of control by foreign powers resonated bitterly, and successfully dragged their feet for many months. But the Pentagon, rejecting efforts by the State Department to soften the U.S. position, clung to its approach. With final approval of the $200 million U.S. loan still pending in Washington, the Majlis voted 70–62 with numerous abstentions to pass the measure. Twelve days later, the Majlis voted unanimously to authorize acceptance of the U.S. loan, and on December 9 Tehran and Washington exchanged formal notes on the status of U.S. military personnel.[34]

Thus, in a flurry of activity in late 1964, did Washington and Tehran cap a remarkable year during which a new American president and the shah overcame much of the uncertainty that had surrounded bilateral relations in earlier years and charted the way toward a deeper partnership. All of this did not, however, mark the end of a simple transition from ambivalence to cooperation. Paradoxically, U.S.-Iranian ties entered a newly contentious phase just as the pieces seemed to be falling into place for a harmonious relationship rooted in collaboration in the security and military domains. The cause was precisely the sort of development likely to generate discontent at the highest levels of the Johnson administration. As the shah grew more confident and cultivated the support of a shifting array of social groups, he increasingly aimed to demonstrate his regime's independence of the United States and to bolster his nation's claims to regional leadership. It would take more than two years for the Johnson administration and the shah to resolve the resulting tensions.

## "Sometimes Friends Let You Down"

With hindsight, it is easy to see the SOFA controversy as a significant moment in the rise of opposition to the shah. Across the political spectrum, Iranians viewed the measure as a shameful infringement of Iranian sovereignty. The narrow margin by which the Majlis—a body blatantly subservient to the shah—approved the measure speaks volumes about the nationalist sensitivities and anti-Americanism that rippled through the country as the regime tightened its bond with Washington. The "new men" empowered by the White Revolution and cultivated by the regime were, it turned out, precisely as skeptical of the United States as American officials sometimes feared. Outside of the urban population, the SOFA also proved to be a lightning rod for another influential part of the population far more hostile to the regime, the Islamic clergy. A day after the Majlis approved the $200 million loan, the dissident religious leader Ayatollah Ruhollah Khomeini delivered a fiery speech that affirmed his status as one of the nation's most outspoken opponents of the regime. "Our dignity has been trampled underfoot; the dignity of Iran has been destroyed," declared Khomeini, who described President Johnson as "the most repulsive member of the human race today because of the injustice he has imposed on our Muslim nation." Linking the status of forces agreement to the new U.S. aid, he insisted that Iran had "sold itself to obtain these dollars" and reduced itself "to the level of a colony." But Khomeini hastened to point out that it was the government and the legislature, which had "nothing to do with the people," that had made this bargain. "What can a Majlis that is elected at bayonet-point have to do with the people?" asked Khomeini, who blasted supporters of the SOFA as "traitors to Islam" and urged overthrow of the shah's regime.[35]

To American relief, the Iranian government quickly suppressed Khomeini's activism and managed to avoid dangerous unrest. The regime arrested the cleric, who had been under close surveillance, on November 4 and sent him to Turkey, the start of a fifteen-year exile that ended only with the Iranian Revolution of 1979. Authorities in Tehran also put special forces on standby in case they were needed to cope with demonstrations and dispatched an army battalion to Qom, the holy city of Shi'a Islam where Khomeini had lived. Yet no "serious trouble" emerged, in the estimate of the U.S. embassy in Tehran, which praised the "relative moderation" of the regime's decision to exile Khomeini in comparison to the harsh punishments meted out to other political opponents for expressing similar sentiments.[36] The shah, it seemed, had weathered the storm.

To be sure, some midlevel State Department officials viewed Khomeini's hostility to the shah and the United States with alarm despite the lack of overt protest. A prescient report prepared by the State Department's Bureau of Intelligence and Research noted that Khomeini enjoyed "widespread support" in the "traditional world of bazaar, village and small city." But he also seemed to be tapping into dynamic trends running through Iranian society. The report urged Americans to recognize that Islam was "capable of change and adaptation." Most alarming, Khomeini had inspired resistance among portions of the Iranian population that had not previously opposed the regime. All in all, the shah's efforts to modernize Iran in ways anathema to the clergy was a "dangerous course of political action" that not only imperiled his regime but also "tarnished" the United States in the minds of a broad swath of ordinary Iranians. "The Shah and the United States," warned the report, "have been branded as both anti-nationalist and anti-religious," sentiments that posed a threat to U.S. interests in Iran and "will certainly make our task there far more difficult."[37]

Such warnings did not, however, resonate broadly within the U.S. bureaucracy or at the highest levels. Unquestionably, studies and memoranda continued to invoke the need for the shah to broaden political support for his rule by channeling resources into his domestic reform agenda. Yet numerous analyses around the same time emphasized the regime's basic stability and described the opposition as weak and divided. Remarkably, U.S. observers affirmed this view even after Iranian prime minister Hassan Ali Mansur was assassinated on January 21, 1965, by a young man reportedly holding a Koran and a picture of Khomeini.[38] A State Department assessment completed a few days later found "no evidence" that the assassin and his accomplices were part of a "larger movement." Indeed, the report offered an upbeat assessment of the security situation in Iran, contending that the regime had prevented the formation of "broadly based political or religious opposition movements" and concluding that the assassin had succeeded largely because the "fragmentation" of anti-regime elements made low-profile zealots hard to monitor.[39]

Americans reached a similar conclusion in April, when the shah himself survived an assassination attempt by a machine-gun-wielding member of his Imperial Guard, a bloody episode that left two body guards and the assailant dead. Meyer reported to Washington that the attempt, while highlighting the extent to which the Iranian political order depended on the survival of a single man, did not significantly alter his positive assessment of the shah's hold on power. The regime, he insisted, was capable of "dealing with any disorders that might be fomented by opposition groups."[40] The CIA concurred, asserting that the opposition was "so disorganized and fragmented as to be powerless."[41] The State Department's Bureau of Near Eastern and South Asian Affairs went still further in May. Security in Iran, it contended, had "vastly improved" in recent months.[42] So much had the situation seemed to brighten by the fall, in fact, that Ambassador Meyer recommended removing Iran from the list of countries whose internal security problems demanded high-level attention. Although "small groups of fanatics" remained, Meyer insisted there was no potential for broad-based resistance to the regime.[43]

What worried the Johnson administration most in 1965 and 1966 was not internal dissent but a new and, from the U.S. perspective, more disturbing development that seemed to flow from the shah's growing confidence: Iran's penchant for defying Washington's geopolitical priorities. U.S. officials disapproved of the shah's continued insistence—irrational harping, as Americans saw it—on obtaining still more U.S. weapons despite Washington's persistent efforts to discourage him. In his first meeting with Ambassador Meyer in late April, for instance, the shah requested quick delivery of the equipment to be purchased under the loan agreement reached the previous autumn. He also lodged new requests for advanced equipment such as the newest kinds of jets to roll off American assembly lines and "bullpup" air-to-surface missiles, the latter as a substitute for torpedo boats that Washington had previously refused to supply. Tehran subsequently asked Washington to expand the $200 million loan to $230 million. The shah justified his requests in part by pointing out long delays between American commitments of military gear and actual delivery. Adequate training and planning, he insisted, depended on knowing far in advance what Iran would obtain in the future. But the shah mostly rationalized his requests as necessary to Iran's defense against the ever-mounting threat of Arab nationalism. The successes of the White Revolution, he contended, made Iran's Arab enemies only more desperate.[44]

American annoyance was immeasurably heightened by the shah's new willingness to seek political, economic, and even military help from nations besides the United States, including the Soviet Union. Soviet-Iranian ties had improved steadily since the 1962 agreement barring missile bases on Iranian soil, but the shah showed sudden interest in 1965 in developing the relationship. During a trip to Moscow in June, he assured Soviet leaders that his country would never participate in aggression against the Soviet Union. For their part, the Soviets, showing what the Iranian delegation judged "unusual warmth," offered to fund construction of a massive steel mill near Isfahan, sign a two-hundred-year nonaggression pact, and provide MiG aircraft.[45] Moscow's friendly gestures apparently made a deep impression on the shah, who had good reason to seek improved relations with the Soviet Union. A détente promised not only to ease the threat of Soviet meddling but also to discourage Arab nationalist regimes, which relied heavily on Soviet political and military support. Diversifying Iran's sources of support and supply, moreover, appealed as a way to compensate for declining U.S. economic aid and for the U.S. shift from grants to credits in the military arena. In the domestic realm, meanwhile, ties with the Soviet Union promised to dampen hostility from the political left while also catering to rising anti-Americanism among the emergent class of urban professionals, civil servants, and intellectuals.[46]

U.S. studies sometimes showed appreciation for these rationales. As early as January 1965, a State Department paper noted that the shah's growing confidence coupled with declining U.S. material aid would inevitably mean the United States would be "drawn less closely into the government's future decision-making process and shall probably adopt more nearly the role of trusted ally rather than that of responsible senior partner." Washington, in sum, needed to recognize that it was entering a "transitional period" in its relations that would culminate not in Iran's defection from the U.S. side of the Cold War but in greater Iranian autonomy within a reconfigured alliance.[47] Americans also sometimes conceded that the shah had reason to complain about the long delays that affected deliveries of U.S. military equipment and to worry about overreliance on the United States as his sole benefactor at a time when the United States clearly aimed to cut back on economic aid and to demand repayment for military goods. The irreverent Komer even speculated that the shah might view the overthrow of South Vietnamese president Ngo Dinh Diem in November 1963 as a lesson about the dangers that could befall a leader who depended entirely on the United States while pursuing his own priorities. "He doesn't want to become another Diem," wrote Komer.[48]

These considerations did not lead, however, to broad acceptance of the shah's diplomatic moves. In the opinion of some American observers, the Iranian leader's insistence on more weaponry, fear of Arab machinations, and dalliance with the Soviet Union stemmed largely from his fundamentally erratic personality. A stream of U.S. commentary during 1965 contended variously that the shah was in "one of his periodic moods that the US doesn't love him enough," that he was in a "glum," "blue," or "gloomy" funk, and that his "state of mind" led him to conjure up "all sorts of spectres."[49] For evidence of his irrational tendencies, Americans often pointed to the shah's anxiety about the activities of Khaibar Gudarzian, an Iranian national living in the United States who persistently attempted to undermine relations between Washington and Tehran and to embarrass the royal family by alleging corruption in the distribution of American assistance. U.S. officials acknowledged that Gudarzian's charges were almost certainly groundless, but they also expressed frustration about the shah's obsession with the matter. The shah was "clearly overreacting," asserted one U.S. assessment, while another noted that the regime had responded "almost pathologically" to the Johnson administration's failures to shut down congressional and judicial investigations that Gudarzian's charges had helped inspire.[50] The best explanation, noted Ambassador Meyer, seemed to be the shah's "pure moodiness" and "brooding" over perceived American slights.[51]

In any case, U.S.-Iranian relations took a turn for the worse in the second half of 1965. Apparently eager to change his reputation as an "American stooge," the shah was opting for an "independent foreign policy more consonant with [the] mainstream of Afro-Asian nationalism," Meyer reported from Tehran. There was, the ambassador added, a strong trend in "government circles, press, and public opinion [to] treat Western interests much more critically and coolly."[52] Among other indications of this change was the regime's tolerance of press commentary critical of the rapidly increasing U.S. role in Vietnam.[53] During a meeting in late November, the shah and Meyer readily agreed that U.S.-Iranian relations were shrouded in an "uneasy feeling [of] growing estrangement." By way of itemizing his grievances against Washington, the shah revived old complaints about President Kennedy's meddling in Iranian politics but zeroed in on Washington's misapprehension of Iran's military needs as well as U.S. efforts to "dictate in [the] minutest detail what his military establishment may and may not have," according to Meyer's account. On the whole, complained the shah, the United States accorded much fairer treatment to numerous nations far less supportive of Western positions in the Cold War. More hypocritically still, the shah complained, the United States had pursued its own efforts to ease hostilities with the Soviet Union, culminating in the

1963 Test Ban Treaty, while criticizing Iran for seeking its own rapprochement with Moscow and pursuing aid, above all the Isfahan steel mill, that Washington was unwilling to offer.[54]

The downturn in U.S.-Iranian relations caused anxiety within the Johnson administration as 1965 advanced. U.S. leaders had no doubt, after all, that Iran remained crucial to Washington's global strategy for waging the Cold War. Indeed, new reasons to prize the connection with Iran emerged even as relations soured. For one thing, Iran grew more important to U.S. purposes in South Asia as U.S.-Pakistani relations deteriorated and then seemed to collapse amid the Indo-Pakistani war in September 1965. The shah was clearly shaken by the Johnson administration's unwillingness to back Washington's ally against India and toyed with the idea of sending a token Iranian force to bolster Pakistan, a fellow Muslim nation and CENTO partner. To U.S. relief, however, the shah backed away from that idea as the fighting continued on the subcontinent, earning American appreciation for his restrained approach and support for a negotiated settlement.[55] The shah, it was clear, could play a constructive role in managing one of Washington's thorniest foreign policy problems. Closely related was another calculation that heightened appreciation of Iran: if Pakistan refused to allow the United States to continue operating intelligence-gathering installations based in that country, Iranian territory would be the next best thing. Starting in August 1965, the Johnson administration officials attached what they called "super-priority" to exploring the feasibility of expanded intelligence operations in Iran.[56]

U.S. leaders also appreciated Iranian support for pro-Western positions in conferences of Third World nations at a time when the United States often came under sharp criticism from governments dedicated to revolutionary anticolonialism. If Washington valued the Indian government for the nonaligned attitude that sometimes helped blunt the sharpest anti-Western attacks, U.S. officials regarded Iran as a wholly supportive voice. American confidence in Iran's ability to defend U.S. positions was most visible in the spring of 1965 as numerous Third World nations planned for a major conference in Algiers, a gathering billed as a follow-up to the Bandung meeting that had launched the Afro-Asian movement in 1956. In a brief telephone conversation with the shah on May 18, President Johnson confessed he was "very concerned" that the Algiers meeting would "degenerate" into an "anti-U.S. operation unless some responsible delegation like Iran stands up against these steamrollers." The shah replied that Iran would "do its duty," an assertion that "delighted" LBJ, according to the U.S. record.[57] Indeed, the State Department urged Ambassador Meyer to spare no effort in informing the shah of U.S. gratitude for Iran's efforts to make sure that the "responsible voices of Asia and Africa may have a full and effective hearing at Algiers."[58] In the event, the meeting was postponed at the last minute and then canceled, a casualty of a successful coup against Algerian leader Ahmed Ben Bella and bitter Sino-Soviet tensions over the future course of the Third World movement. But expressions of mutual confidence between Washington and Tehran nevertheless indicated a genuine overlap of interests.[59]

Johnson and his aides appreciated Iranian foreign policy on no issue, however, so much as the expanding war in Vietnam. Even as the shah grew critical of the United States and tolerated anti-American voices within Iranian society, he voiced strong support of U.S. policy in Southeast Asia, both in direct contacts with American officials and in meetings with leaders of other nations. The State Department was pleased, for example, by the shah's outspoken support of U.S. military operations in Vietnam and the Dominican Republic during visits to Brazil and Argentina in spring 1965, a welcome instance of Third World governments backing the United States without direct U.S. mediation.[60] Even more gratifying was the shah's defense of U.S. policy in Vietnam during his otherwise troubling visit to Moscow in June, a position that "made the Russians very angry," according to the Iranian account of the meetings.[61] All in all, Washington had no reason to doubt that Iran supported the United States "heart and soul," as the acting Iranian foreign minister put it.[62] So steadfast was the Iranian position, in fact, that Johnson and his aides speculated Tehran might go beyond the material assistance—a thousand tons of fuel—the shah had promised the year before and faithfully delivered in July 1965. Indeed, the Iranian government offered later in the year to send a medical team consisting of two surgeons and twenty nurses affiliated with Iran's Red Lion and Sun Society, Iran's equivalent of the Red Cross. In a letter to the shah, Johnson praised the proposal as a "measure of the free world's determination" in Southeast Asia.[63] Ambassador Meyer cut to the heart of what Americans liked best about the Iranian proposal, contrasting Tehran's generosity to the "sheepishness of other Afro-Asian countries" when it came to Vietnam.[64]

The central question for the Johnson administration by the fall of 1965 was how to manage the U.S. relationship with Iran in order to minimize tensions and to maintain as much as possible of the two nations' strategic partnership. The leading idea at first was to cope with the shah through a combination of personal reassurance—what Komer continued to call "massage"—and small concessions. The reassurance came relatively easily. In a stream of correspondence, LBJ consistently praised the shah's leadership and expressed appreciation for his support on Vietnam and other issues. Meyer did likewise in Tehran, but the ambassador urged that Washington dispatch a more senior emissary to convey the president's high regard for Iran directly to the shah. The idea won approval, and from mid-1965 to the end of 1967 roving diplomat W. Averell Harriman met the Iranian leader four times. Concessions were much harder to deliver. As Meyer reminded the shah, many American believed that the United States was already doing a great deal for the shah at a time when Congress was imposing tighter constraints on aid and U.S. military power was focused on Vietnam. Still, in his communications to Washington, Meyer warned that U.S.-Iranian relations were approaching a "crossroads" and recommended various helpful steps that the Johnson administration might take. These initiatives included more serious efforts to suppress Gudarzian's harassment of the royal family, timely delivery of promised military equipment, and assurances that Tehran would benefit from the best possible terms for its military purchases.[65] Through such steps, the ambassador counseled, Washington could still hope to "repair Iran's position" as a key player in securing American foreign policy objectives.[66]

Meyer's modest proposals stood no chance of acceptance in Washington at a time when the shah appeared determined to keep pushing what he called his "independent national policy." American frustrations mounted sharply in January 1966, when the Soviet Union agreed to extend $286 million in credits to help Iran build a massive steel plant; in return, Iran would pipe natural gas to the Soviet Union in a new line to be constructed with Soviet assistance. Although U.S. intelligence concluded that Iranian negotiators did not get everything they wanted from the deal, the shah attached great importance to the signal that it sent internationally. Indeed, the agreement was just one part of a stepped-up effort in late 1965 and 1966 to demonstrate Iran's growing autonomy. In an interview with the *New York Times* just before the deal was finalized, the shah voiced appreciation for U.S. support but left no doubt of his intentions to forge "friendly, if prudent, cooperation with the Soviet Union." The goal, he indicated, was to diversify Iran's international connections. "Sometimes friends let you down," asserted the shah, adding, "And besides, it is neither manly nor intelligent to depend entirely on others."[67] The shah delivered much the same message in a speech to the Majlis in March 1966, asserting that Iranians could not "subject our destiny entirely to decisions of others who can one day help us and another day not help us."[68] By that time, the Tehran regime had also struck similar deals exchanging Iranian oil for industrial equipment from Romania ($100 million), Czechoslovakia ($15 million), Poland ($15 million), and Hungary ($10 million).[69]

The shah's willingness to provoke Washington did not mean any diminution of his desire to keep U.S. support flowing. In two letters to LBJ in March, he left no doubt of his determination to assert Iranian autonomy. "We are strongly determined to stand on our own feet and to undertake the responsibilities of an independent and peace-loving nation with vital interests in the security and stability of this area—a policy which should be welcome to our friends," wrote the shah. But he also risked American anger by asking for two types of help from Washington. First, he leaned on Johnson to approve still more arms sales in order to bolster Iran against "real dangers" in this part of the world." The Majlis had approved another $200 million line of credit—over and above the $200 million loan agreed in 1964—to obtain weapons, and the shah asserted that he hoped to make the purchases in the United States. Second, the shah urged the Johnson administration to push the consortium of oil companies that controlled Iran's vast petrochemical industry—a combination established in 1953 as part of a broad deal between the young shah and the West—to increase production and therefore the income that flowed into Iranian coffers. U.S. leaders had consistently advised the shah that the U.S. government could not dictate policy to the consortium since it was essentially a combination of private companies. But the shah thought otherwise and pressed the issue—an irritant in U.S.-Iranian relations for many years—with new vigor. Higher income from oil, he insisted to LBJ, would enable Iran not only to advance its economic modernization programs but also to fund necessary military purchases.[70]

## Reconfiguring the Relationship

The shah's behavior in late 1965 and early 1966 kicked off the most difficult phase of U.S.-Iranian relations during the Johnson presidency. Meyer noted in March 1966 that the shah's tone was "getting shriller" while his air of both "self-satisfaction and grievance" grew stronger. The shah resented what he regarded as the "'papa knows best' attitude of Americans toward Iran's military requirements," which came across as "an affront to national dignity," advised the ambassador. Worse still for Washington, Iranian leaders seem to have concluded that the best way to "deal with Uncle Sam is to make a public scene," hardly an enticing prospect for the Johnson administration as the Vietnam problem weighed more heavily.[71] In public and behind the veil of diplomatic protocol, the Iranian regime ratcheted up pressure on Washington, articulating a growing list of complaints while threatening to obtain weapons from the Soviet Union.

Yet even as relations soured, a more salubrious trend played out simultaneously in the pivotal months from early 1966 to the middle of 1967. American officials gradually acknowledged the need to reconfigure U.S.-Iranian relations in order to account for Iran's demonstrated economic progress, declining U.S. leverage, and Tehran's potential to play a more independent but still vital role as a pro-Western bulwark. To use the terminology of political scientist Mark Gasiorowski, Washington came to understand that the enormous aid it had provided over the years had transformed Iran from a U.S. client into an "autonomous state" increasingly independent of both U.S. support and the backing of its own society.[72]

This recognition marked, in essence, a second step in the evolution of the Johnson administration's efforts to resolve the tensions and ambiguities that it had inherited from the Kennedy presidency. In 1964, the new administration tightened Washington's bond with the shah and abandoned much of the pressure that Kennedy had sought to apply in order to force the pace of social and political reform. That adjustment did not, however, produce the solidified relationship that Johnson and his aides had hoped to achieve. Profound political, economic, and social transformations occurring within Iran created irresistible incentives for the shah to distance himself from Washington while giving him the confidence to do so. This reorientation of Iranian foreign policy naturally rankled American leaders, who worked hard at first to resist it. That approach, however, caused deeper antagonism between Washington and Tehran. As time passed, key U.S. officials gradually accepted the shah's new approach. They recognized that the shah, despite his newfound independence, remained securely within the Western camp and that greater Iranian autonomy actually had considerable advantages. A more autonomous shah, that is, not only would be more secure from his domestic critics but also might serve American purposes more effectively and cheaply than he could as a wholly dependent U.S. client and proxy.

This transformation in U.S. attitudes did not come easily. Tensions escalated during 1966 as the Iranian regime pressed the Johnson administration harder than ever to lean on the American companies belonging to the consortium that controlled Iran's oil production. Prime Minister Amir Abbas Hoveyda criticized production levels as "unacceptable," and the Iranian government seemed certain to become more "intransigent" on a number of issues if it did not get its way, warned the State Department.[73] No issue poisoned relations, however, as much as American reluctance to provide weapons in the quantities that the shah desired, whatever Iran's capacity to buy them. Tension peaked in July as U.S. officials became increasingly aware of the shah's desire to purchase weapons—especially anti-aircraft guns and surface-to-air missiles—from the Soviet Union. In a series of blunt conversations with Ambassador Meyer, the shah blasted the United States for its "misguided" unwillingness to meet his demands. Similar U.S. foot-dragging, he insisted, had driven Pakistan into the "arms of [the] Chinese and also Russians," he asserted, noting that a Pakistani arms-buying delegation was visiting Moscow at that very moment. But the shah also insisted that Iran's desire for Soviet arms stemmed from a nonnegotiable quest for "liberty of action" in international affairs.[74] He asserted that Iran must "stand on its own feet" and, in the worst possible scenario, be able to defend itself if a "complete break in [the] US-Iran military relationship occurs."[75] Too often, the shah complained, Washington had treated him like one of its "puppets."[76] Foreign Minister Abbas Aram accused the United States of engaging with Iran as a "lackey" or "ordinary commercial client" despite Iran's steadfast loyalty over the years.[77]

Ambassador Meyer's rebuttals reflected the exasperation that ran through the Johnson administration. Meyer told Aram he was "getting tired" of Iranian complaints about Washington's mistreatment, which he labeled "grossly unfair" in light of the tremendous aid the United States had pumped into Iran.[78] If Iranian leaders felt disappointment, Meyer told the shah they must recognize that Americans were also "human" and "would be deeply hurt that [a] valued and admired friend like [the] Shah [had] decided to trade in arms with our adversaries." The wound would be especially painful, Meyer continued, "at this time when [the] whole American nation is gripped by anxiety over Vietnam." In a comment surely calculated to be especially painful to the shah given his contempt for Egyptian leader Gamal Abdel Nasser, the ambassador asserted that many people in the Western world, which considered the shah an enlightened and capable leader, would "inevitably" feel he was "becoming another DeGaulle or even Nasser." He might, in short, be viewed as a leader who had betrayed the West after strenuous efforts by the United States to cultivate friendship.[79] In return, the shah would receive only second-rate Soviet military gear, insisted Meyer, emphasizing "how incredible it is that the Shah would jeopardize so much for so little gain."[80]

Even as Meyer exchanged these sharp words with Iranian leaders, however, he and other U.S. officials were determined to preserve close cooperation with Iran and acknowledged—grudgingly at first and more energetically as time passed—a new basis on which collaboration could proceed. They came to believe that the United States could live with a more independent Iran and that there might even be some advantages in a revamped relationship. Meyer's uncomfortable exchanges with the shah marked, in a sense, the dying moments of U.S. efforts to bolster the relationship that Johnson administration officials believed they were establishing after coming to office—a relationship rooted in Iranian subservience to Washington—and the beginning of something new. American willingness to accept Iran's more independent foreign policy rested on three calculations. First, U.S. officials concluded that the shah's efforts to diversify Iran's international connections and sources of aid were genuinely popular among key segments of his population. The shah had won plaudits for his 1965 trip to Moscow, as he did for each successive step to deepen ties with Moscow. Even as U.S.-Iranian relations reached their nadir during 1966, the CIA noted that the Iranian population "warmly welcomed" the deal for the steel mill and concluded that the shah's image would likely be enhanced by an arms deal with Moscow.[81] Americans did not, of course, like this state of affairs, but it hardly made sense to try to block initiatives that bolstered the position of the man around whom American ambitions in Iran obviously revolved.

Indeed, U.S. officials appreciated that the shah's position continued to strengthen in 1966. Certainly, that was Ambassador Meyer's view. In October, he reported that Iran was more politically stable than it had been in years. Meyer conceded that political repression had something to do with that situation but also highlighted the shah's economic and diplomatic initiatives. Stability was, he reported to Washington, "in large measure attributable to economic prosperity and to the Shah's success in giving the impression that a reorientation has taken place in Iran's international position."[82] In January 1967, Meyer reported with satisfaction that the chief of Iran's secret police, known as the SAVAK, was complaining he had "few challenges" to keep his agency busy.[83] This view also found expression outside of administration circles when the *Washington Post* published a series of articles extolling the shah's accomplishments. Just like Meyer, *Post* correspondent Alfred Friendly noted that the shah was an "autocrat" who brooked no opposition but also praised him for nurturing the "sturdy beginning" of an urban middle class unique in the Middle East outside of Lebanon.[84] Just four years earlier, Friendly wrote, Iran had been beset by rioting students, a recalcitrant landowning class, and a "reactionary" clergy "preaching what amounted to a jihad against the King"—an array of opponents that appeared "invincible." Now the shah was "firmly in the saddle" thanks to an "astonishing series of social, economic and political successes."[85]

Reinforcing American tolerance of Iran's geopolitical reorientation was a second consideration. Despite the shah's occasionally bitter words, he had no interest in any real break with the United States and remained firmly wedded to the West. Without a doubt, U.S. officials sometimes indulged worst-case fears. In one conversation with the shah, Meyer complained that Iranian overtures to the Soviet Union amounted to a "virtual stampede in [the] direction of [the] Soviet Bloc."[86] The CIA worried that an arms deal with Moscow would mark a genuine "turning point" in the U.S.-Iranian relationship. Most U.S. commentary, however, ran in the other direction, affirming that the shah would never allow his bid for "independence" to damage the fundamentals of his link to Washington. Much of the shah's brinksmanship could be attributed to his penchant for "traditional Persian bargaining," advised National Security Adviser Rostow, rather than any real temptation to abandon his association with the United States.[87] U.S. assessments cited abundant evidence of Iran's essentially pro-U.S.-orientation. So strongly did Tehran back U.S. policy in Vietnam that Secretary Rusk saw fit to ask for an additional Iranian contribution to the war effort—ideally Iranian help training constabulary forces in South Vietnam.[88] U.S. officials also appreciated Iran's strong backing in Third World forums, where Tehran resisted the "anti-American wolf pack," as Ambassador Meyer put it.[89]

Americans also took pleasure from the shah's assurances that he would never accept an arms agreement with Moscow that carried any strings damaging to Iran's relationship with the United States. More specifically, he indicated that he would refuse any Soviet demand to oust U.S. military advisers, to withdraw from CENTO, or to station Soviet technicians on Iranian soil.[90] In August 1966, the shah took another step to demonstrate the moderation of his outreach to Moscow, promising U.S. officials that he would not purchase surface-to-air missiles, as he had originally intended. Indeed, he affirmed his eagerness to "maintain maximum US procurement," especially with respect to the most sophisticated types of military hardware, and that his air force would rely strictly on American equipment.[91] All in all, asserted Rostow, there was little to fear from Iranian purchases of what he called "a few minor Soviet items," mostly anti-aircraft guns and trucks. Iran, that is, seemed to be finding a middle ground that Washington could accept. "Some independence is to be expected and is healthy," Rostow conceded. But he expressed confidence that the shah recognized reasonable limits and would not "go too far too fast."[92]

Closely connected was a third calculation that encouraged American tolerance of the shah's geopolitical choices: acceptance that Iran's geopolitical orientation made sense in view of the array of dangers confronting the nation. For years, U.S. officials had doubted Iranian claims about imminent threats posed by Arab nationalism and struggled to keep Tehran focused on the Soviet Union. During 1966, however, they increasingly agreed that the shah had a point. Early in the year, a U.S. military survey team dispatched to evaluate Iran's needs confounded expectations by concluding that the nation's needs actually ran as high as $328 million, far above the new $200 million request that the shah, to deep American annoyance, had floated in late 1965.[93] A CIA study completed in May 1966 similarly suggested the need for a fresh look at Iranian demands. The shah's concern about Nasserist inroads in the southwestern part of his country and in the Persian Gulf were, asserted the CIA, "not groundless"—a clear understatement considering the problems that the report went on to describe. Oil facilities in Iran's southwestern Khuzestan province, which generated almost three-quarters of all Iran's foreign-exchange earnings, were in fact "extremely vulnerable targets for sabotage," as the shah had long insisted. Meanwhile, Iran's shipping routes were vulnerable to threats from Iraq and the Arab sheikdoms bordering the Persian Gulf. Even if Nasser's threat to Iran was only "indirect" at present, the report noted several worrying developments: the presence of Egyptian troops in Iraq, recent border skirmishes between Iranian and Iraqi forces, clandestine Nasserist support for dissidents within Iran, and escalating Arab nationalist propaganda broadcast into Iran and the Persian Gulf sheikdoms.[94]

Adding immeasurably to the shah's worries—and American sympathy for his outlook—was the British government's plan to reduce its military presence in the Gulf as part of a general drawdown of costly military commitments "east of Suez." Earlier in the decade, the British government had avowed its intention to hold onto its traditional positions of strength in the Middle East, the Indian Ocean, and the Far East. But a review of British defense policy completed in 1965 pointed to the unsustainability of those commitments and sparked planning for dramatic reductions over the next several years. The precise implications of that policy remained murky in 1966, but U.S. officials, like the shah, had no doubt of the growing potential for instability in the oil-rich region where Britain had long played a dominant role in maintaining order. Given Nasser's obvious ambitions, it was increasingly plausible to imagine threats to Bahrain, Kuwait, and other areas. This unpredictability led National Security Adviser Rostow to look at the shah's drive for expanded military capabilities—so often dismissed as evidence of a personal obsession with prestige—in a new light. "I'm not sure he isn't right," Rostow wrote to LBJ using words nearly unimaginable a year earlier.[95]

American officials even began to accept the idea that U.S. purposes might be served by a relatively autonomous and emboldened Iran capable of exerting influence in its region. To some extent, Americans recognized that they had no choice but to concede this status to Iran. It was already clear that economic aid would be phased out completely during 1967, and U.S. officials understood that the expanding war in Vietnam made it impossible for Washington to supply all the military gear that Tehran wanted and perhaps needed.[96] Hints abound in the decision-making record that Americans were gradually coming around to the idea that Iran could in fact be what the shah claimed: a cornerstone of Western influence in the Middle East and southwest Asia. As early as May 1966, Assistant Secretary of State Raymond A. Hare acknowledged that the United States was steadily shedding its "client relationship" with Iran and must seek a "modified" relationship that would preserve a high degree of cooperation.[97] Meyer made the same point a few months later but used different—and exceptionally revealing—terminology. Iran, he wrote, was passing from an era of dependence on "large-scale aid" to a "more normal" relationship with the United States.[98] Dependence, in short, was an anomalous state of affairs, whereas a more equal relationship would be healthier and sturdier and even an indication that U.S. aid over the years had played its intended role of enabling Iran to stand on its own feet in international affairs.[99] For his part, Rostow attributed improved relations with the shah to Washington's "explicit recognition" of the need for stability in the region and the role that a more autonomous Iran could play in securing it.[100]

For all of these reasons, the Johnson administration took a more conciliatory approach to the shah in the last months of 1966 even as Tehran neared a major arms agreement with Moscow. Without question, disagreement persisted within the administration but only on technical issues such as the pace at which American credits should be extended and the interest rate charged. In contrast to earlier years, reservations about new aid sprang mostly from concerns about Iran's actual needs and the availability of American funds given the drain in Southeast Asia rather than political objections to the shah's rule or even his flirtation with Moscow. Indeed, Defense Secretary Robert McNamara, the strongest high-level critic of generous U.S. terms, indicated in July 1966 that he did not believe it would be "the end of the world" if the shah obtained military assistance from the Soviet Union.[101] Rusk, Rostow, Meyer, and the Joint Chiefs of Staff bridled against McNamara's terms, contending that the sheer importance of bolstering ties with the shah made it vital not to quibble over details. In the end, McNamara won on the technicalities, but he joined a broad consensus in favor of a new package of U.S. credits totaling $200 million to be distributed between 1967 and 1970. Assistant Secretary of Defense Townsend "Tim" Hoopes formally extended that offer during an August 1966 trip to the see the shah on the shores of the Caspian Sea, a mission aimed first and foremost at reassuring the Iranian leader of American friendship. Although the shah complained that the plan did not go far enough, both sides expressed satisfaction about the broad contours of their relationship.[102]

American adaptation to Iran's new autonomy in international affairs became evident in January 1967, when Tehran reached the long-discussed arms deal with the Moscow. The deal provoked none of the outrage that the sharp exchanges of mid-1966 between U.S. and Iranian officials might have predicted. One reason was undoubtedly the shah's decision to avoid provoking Washington by obtaining highly sophisticated military equipment from the Soviets. While the Johnson administration prepared to sell Iran F-4 Phantom jets, a technology so advanced that it had so far been sold abroad only to Great Britain, Tehran purchased low-tech jeeps and anti-aircraft guns from Moscow.[103] U.S. officials were perhaps consoled as well by Prime Minister Hoveyda's promises that Iran had made no political concessions to Moscow and had rejected Soviet overtures to help with civilian "prestige projects" like a new subway system for Tehran.[104] A CIA assessment of the Soviet aid package—ultimately estimated at about $110 million—offered still more reassurance by noting that the shah clearly regarded the Soviet gear as a mere "supplement" to U.S. assistance and expressing a degree of understanding of Iranian motives given the limitations on American aid. The Soviet equipment, asserted the CIA, would likely fill "several gaps in the Iranian arsenal which would otherwise remain open for some time under present schedules in the US military assistance program." In fact, the biggest problem that the CIA detected was the difficulty the Iranian military would have to integrate and maintain the new items.[105]

The only significant outcry came from Congress, criticism that deeply irritated administration officials who had made their peace with the new tenor of U.S.-Iran ties. The most outspoken congressional critic was J. William Fulbright, the chair of the Senate Foreign Relations Committee and, by 1967, a persistent annoyance to the administration on a range of foreign policy matters. Fulbright's opinions caused a minor blowup in U.S.-Iranian relations in early May when the senator reportedly averred in a closed-door committee meeting that Iran had purchased weapons from the Soviet Union "largely to maintain [the] shah on his throne" and that the United States was following an "unwise" course by encouraging him to maintain total political control. The inevitable result, Fulbright speculated, would be upheaval and revolution. Predictably, Iranian leaders exploded and threatened to cancel the shah's trip to Washington scheduled for early June. More revealing of the evolving state of U.S.-Iranian relations was the response from the Johnson administration. Meyer immediately sought an audience with the shah aimed at bringing him "down from the chandelier."[106] Rusk also moved quickly to limit the damage, dispatching a note to the shah emphasizing the president's confidence in the Iranian regime and the executive branch's rejection of Fulbright's views. The secretary of state expressed hope that the upcoming meeting in Washington would go ahead as planned and provide a powerful display of U.S.-Iranian solidarity.[107]

## "The High Water Mark"

Points of friction remained in the last two years of the Johnson presidency. The shah continued to complain of insufficient U.S. attention to his country's military requirements—he was a "broken record" on this issue, charged Meyer—and to threaten new approaches to the Soviets to get what Washington was unwilling to provide.[108] To American annoyance, Iran and the Soviet Union agreed in late 1967 to a new arms deal under which Moscow sent hundreds more military vehicles to Iran in exchange for natural gas.[109] The shah further antagonized the Johnson administration by visiting Moscow in August 1968, a time when Johnson and other Western leaders canceled trips to the Soviet Union in order to protest Soviet suppression of liberal reform in

Czechoslovakia.[110] Tensions flared as well over the Tehran government's "off-take" from sales of Iranian oil. The shah persistently demanded that Washington back higher levels of production, while the Johnson administration protested that decisions were a matter for the international consortium of private companies, not for the U.S. government. From time to time, too, Iranian leaders expressed anger about what they perceived as Washington's indulgence of the regime's enemies. The shah especially resented U.S. unwillingness to crack down on dissident students living in the United States and even suspected that the CIA was paying subsidies to some of them.[111] For a time during 1968, he worried that U.S. officials were secretly cozying up to Ali Amini, the onetime prime minister whose reformist agenda had pleased Americans back in 1961. Seven years later, the shah suspected Amini of cultivating American support to regain the premiership.[112]

There was, however, something increasingly routine about these problems by 1967. Moments of acrimony came and went, but underlying U.S.-Iranian harmony dominated the relationship following the reconfiguration that played out largely in the pivotal year of 1966. This fundamental good will was especially evident in a series of meetings between President Johnson and senior Iranian leaders, including the shah himself, during the final eighteen months of the LBJ administration. U.S. advocates of a close partnership with Iran had long urged the president to take a more active role in cultivating the shah. With hindsight, it is easy to see that they were correct in foreseeing benefits of closer contact at the very top. The shah clearly welcomed attention from the U.S. president, while LBJ did much to diminish the significance of remaining irritants in the U.S.-Iranian relationship by lavishing praise on the Iranian leader, whose rhetorical commitment to social reform echoed his own domestic priorities. But harmony between the two leaders grew as well from comfort throughout the U.S. bureaucracy with Iran's new status as an autonomous but reliable bastion of pro-Western strength in a tumultuous part of the world, a nation weaning itself off American support and capable of maintaining order in its neighborhood.

The administration's desire to consecrate the transformed relationship was clear in the run-up to the shah's visit to Washington scheduled for early June 1967. The CIA surely overstated the significance of the moment in one report labeling the summit a "critical point in the history of our relations with modern Iran."[113] Few U.S. officials appear, in fact, to have believed that the basic orientation of U.S.-Iranian relations was any longer at stake. NSC aide Hal Saunders, for example, acknowledged that ongoing Soviet aid might enable Moscow to "bore from within" in Tehran but insisted nevertheless that Iran was "soundly anti-Communist" and a reliable partner of the United States.[114] The State Department credited Iran with "placing prudent limits" on its associations with the communist bloc.[115] The goal for Washington was no longer to dissuade the shah from charting an independent course but to demonstrate acceptance of the revamped partnership.

The solution seemed to lie partly in showing generosity in connection with Iran's unceasing pressure for military assistance. Senior administration officials agreed in May 1967 to approve disbursement of a new $50 million installment of the $200 million in credits for arms purchases approved the year before and to show flexibility on the interest rate to be charged. They hoped to impress the shah as well by accepting Iran's aspiration to use these funds to purchase a second sixteen-aircraft squadron of F-4 fighters.[116] The Johnson administration also aimed to show its friendship for the Iranian regime in less tangible ways. While officials reassured Iranian interlocutors that the administration had no sympathy for Fulbright's opinions, Rostow, recognizing the potential value of deepening the president's personal connections with the shah, recommended that LBJ add a second one-on-one session with his Iranian counterpart during their upcoming meetings in Washington—an unusual format for an encounter that neither side regarded as a full-fledged state visit.[117] In any case, U.S. planning papers made clear that the main purpose of the meetings, whatever their number, was to convey recognition of the shah's status as an important international player. The goal, asserted one State Department study, was to convince the shah that the United States regarded him as "an intimate, valued and trusted friend." Most of all, the visit should show the shah "that we believe Iran has a valuable role to play in helping to preserve peace and promote stability with progress in the Middle East generally and the Persian Gulf area in particular."[118]

Events in the Middle East deprived Johnson of his chance to impress the shah in the spring of 1967. The outbreak of the Six-Day War on June 5 led the shah, having made it only as far as Paris, to postpone his trip to Washington in order to return home and focus on the crisis. But the fighting proved a serendipitous boon to U.S.-Iranian relations by enabling the Iranian leader to demonstrate his nation's desire and ability to serve Western interests in the Middle East. To be sure, the shah responded to the outbreak of fighting between Israel and Egypt by chiding Washington for failing to take a stronger stand against Nasser at an earlier point. Now, he complained, Iran and other Muslim nations generally hostile to Nasserism had no choice but to provide at least rhetorical support to the fight against the common foe, Israel.[119] Yet Iranian leaders proceeded to play what U.S. observers regarded as a highly constructive role in the crisis. Quietly "pleased" that Israel had given Nasser "a black eye," in the words of one State Department report, the shah largely backed U.S. initiatives to restore stability through cooperation with moderate Arab governments and

Israel, with which Iran had long maintained de facto diplomatic ties.[120] Most crucially of all, Iran proved willing to keep oil flowing to Israel and Western Europe in the face of Arab efforts to impose a punitive embargo following the war.[121] Americans took heart as well from the fact that the fighting, by underscoring Soviet support for Nasser's regime, was likely to weaken ties between Tehran and Moscow.

Impressed by these developments, U.S. assessments of Iranian foreign policy in summer 1967, particularly briefing papers prepared in advance of the shah's rescheduled trip to Washington in August, expressed unprecedented confidence about not just Iran's support for basic U.S. policy objectives but also its ability to play a leadership role in the region. The Six-Day War, that is, powerfully reinforced the trends that had led U.S. leaders to view Iran as a reliable partner capable of serving U.S. interests at a time of declining British influence and mounting uncertainty about America's capacity to exert influence, to say nothing of regional turmoil that had culminated in war. Americans expressed satisfaction that Iran was working to bolster Jordan's autonomy and to counteract Nasserist currents in Iraq and Kuwait. But they especially appreciated Tehran's efforts to cultivate stability through cooperation with other regional powers. Iran maintained "close but publicly guarded" relations with Israel while moving closer to Saudi king Faisal and reaffirming its ties to Pakistan and Turkey.[122] At a meeting with President Ayub and Turkish president Süleyman Demirel at the Caspian Sea resort of Ramsar, the shah spoke in favor of maintaining the CENTO alliance, at least until a better arrangement for regional cooperation could be devised. On the whole, noted one State Department paper, Iran was consistently demonstrating the "stature and influence" necessary to act as a "stabilizing force" in the Middle East.[123] It was "important for the Middle East to begin acting like a region," wrote Rostow, and Iran was "a natural to help draw the [region] together" because of the shah's array of constructive relationships.[124] NSC aide Saunders paid Iran the highest compliment, suggesting that LBJ ask the shah what role the Iranian government imagined for the United States in supporting the emerging association of anti-Nasserist powers.[125]

Against this backdrop, U.S. leaders and the shah struck an unprecedentedly friendly tone when they finally met in Washington on August 22 and 23. Although the Iranian delegation conveyed Tehran's desire for yet more U.S. military aid, the theme produced no rancor, even when the shah met with Fulbright and other members of the Senate Foreign Relations Committee. Meanwhile, the president and his aides listened with pleasure as the shah praised Israel's military victory, voiced determination to keep Pakistan in the Western fold, and emphasized his desire to cultivate friendship with Saudi

Arabia in order to fill the "vacuum" that would inevitably be created as Britain moved ahead with its plan to withdraw from the Persian Gulf.[126] All of this spoke to Tehran and Washington's convergence—gradual during 1966 and then rapidly in the weeks following the Six-Day War—around a shared vision of Iran as a key pillar of international order in the Middle East and Southwest Asia as British power receded. In sum, U.S.-Iranian relations were "healthier than ever" as a result of the meetings, exulted Meyer, who used an unusual ambassadorial letter to the president to praise him, Rostow, and Saunders for leading the way to this happy result.[127] Satisfaction rippled far beyond high-level policymakers. In an editorial titled "Salute for the Shah," the *Washington Post* praised Iran for the remarkable "turnabout" it had accomplished in just five years—"a standing warning to those who judge any country by its immediate prospects"—and noted that the nation's foreign policy had now evolved as much as its domestic situation. The administration's "chief interest" in Johnson's visit with the shah was to "confirm" Iran's new international role in defending against Arab radicalism and filling the regional vacuum likely to be left by the British.[128]

The months following the summit brought still more evidence that the U.S. and Iranian governments had not only accepted but increasingly embraced their reconfigured relationship rooted in an implicit bargain: the United States would continue to provide military and political support for the shah's regime, while an emboldened and self-confident yet decidedly Western-oriented Iran would exercise increased autonomy in regional and even global affairs. On the American side, the Johnson administration showed its comfort partly by gratifying the shah's craving for recognition and prestige. One occasion came on October 26, when the shah held a lavish coronation ceremony for himself and his wife, Empress Farah, an event he had deferred during his twenty-six years on the Peacock Throne in expectation of holding it once his nation had attained sufficient economic progress and a male heir had reached a satisfactory age to indicate a clear succession plan. The Johnson administration respected the monarchy's insistence that the event was a "family affair" and issued no formal statement.[129] But observers could hardly fail to notice the presence, albeit in a private capacity, of George W. Ball, the eminent administration insider who had resigned as Undersecretary of State for Economic Affairs in 1966 and would be appointed ambassador to the United Nations a few months later. Much more fulsome indications of support for the shah's regime came a month later, when Iranian and U.S. officials gathered at the State Department to mark Iran's "graduation" from U.S. development assistance. "The similarity of needs and mutuality of purpose that Iran and the United States have long shared do not stop simply because Iran's well-being enables it to shoulder greater burdens," LBJ asserted in a statement. "Now is the time when even stronger ties become possible."[130]

As if to substantiate that promise, the administration showed greater willingness in early 1968 to cater to Iranian demands in the economic and military fields. Most remarkably, the Johnson administration applied pressure on the consortium of oil companies operating in Iran to be generous in negotiations with Tehran over production levels, a step that U.S. officials had steadfastly resisted. In a meeting with executives of six companies at the end of March 1968, the undersecretary of state for political affairs, Eugene Rostow (brother of the national security adviser), acknowledged the "delicate line" between commercial and political considerations but also insisted there was a "deep national interest" in satisfactory conclusion of the ongoing round of talks. Rostow even hinted that the administration's willingness to support antitrust privileges for the consortium rested in part on the companies' acceptance of the need to serve U.S. foreign policy objectives. The Six-Day War, Rostow added, had sowed chaos throughout the region. Syria and possibly Egypt were training terrorists on a "very dangerous scale." Jordan had a "Vietcong on its territory"—a reference to the Palestinian Liberation Organization—while Israel seemed certain to launch reprisals against its neighbors, generating a mounting risk of general war with "incalculable potentialities." The best hope of stabilizing the situation lay in bolstering Iran and Saudi Arabia and ensuring cooperation between them, insisted Rostow. But Iran, as the stronger country, was clearly the "keystone of American plans" for the foreseeable future.[131]

The Johnson administration also indicated willingness to approve still more military assistance for Iran. The country's sheer importance to American objectives in a newly chaotic Middle East drove Washington's relatively generous attitude, as did Britain's definitive announcement in January 1968 that the withdrawal from bases "east of Suez" would apply to the Persian Gulf as well as territories further east. American officials lashed out at Britain for shirking its global responsibilities and easily understood Iran's importance at a time when the United States had few resources to spare.[132] American largesse may also have flowed from concern that Lyndon Johnson's announcement on March 31, 1968, that he would not seek reelection—a decision that appeared to have deeply shaken the shah—would cause Iranian leaders to doubt the durability of U.S. commitments and therefore to lean toward the Soviet Union for military aid. The administration agreed in late 1967 to augment U.S. military credits for 1968, increasing the annual outlay to between $75 and $100 million. (During the shah's visit to Washington in June 1968, Johnson agreed to the higher amount.) The administration, responding to a new $800 million military modernization program announced by the shah in 1967, also agreed in principle to a new five-year program of military credits starting in 1969, though precise amounts and types of assistance would be worked out from year to year by the next president and Congress.[133] U.S. officials remained wary of congressional skepticism about new aid for Iran and hoped, as ever, to keep Tehran's attention focused on domestic needs. Yet the administration left no doubt during its final months in office of its intention that U.S. military assistance would continue at high levels into the early 1970s. Following the termination of U.S. economic assistance, noted Walt Rostow in April 1968, military aid was the "major concrete manifestation" of the U.S. desire for close relations with Iran, which he dubbed "a new sub-regional super-power."[134]

For its part, the Iranian government increasingly demonstrated its desire to be helpful to Washington in the months following the Six-Day War. True, Tehran continued to highlight its autonomy and to maintain its leverage over Washington, not least by deepening its economic and military relationships with the Soviet Union. The visit of Soviet warships to the Iranian port of Bandar Abbas in June 1968—the same month as the shah's final trip to the United States during the LBJ presidency—drove home the point that Soviet-Iranian relations had survived the strain of the Six-Day War. Yet U.S. officials were confident that the shah remained suspicious of Soviet ambitions in the Middle East and greatly preferred U.S. military gear to the lower-quality goods the Soviets could provide. On the whole, concluded a blunt U.S. assessment in mid-1968, Iran was "not re-orienting its policy away from closeness with the West."[135]

The Johnson administration also gained confidence from new indications that Tehran was eager to use its new stature as a regional power in ways aligned with Western interests. Farthest from its borders, the Iranian regime sought to serve U.S. purposes in Vietnam during early 1968 by initiating contacts with the Hanoi government aimed at opening serious negotiations to end the fighting, an initiative that came to little but highlighted Tehran's desire to raise its global profile.[136] With respect to the Arab-Israeli conflict, the U.S. and Iranian governments worked on parallel tracks to restrain Israeli ambitions in the occupied West Bank and to bolster the independence and pro-Western orientation of Jordan.[137] Meanwhile, Iran sided with Washington by pressing the Pakistani government not to close U.S. intelligence-gathering facilities on Pakistani soil, consistently espousing the preservation of CENTO, and even suggesting that Tehran provide weaponry to Pakistan and Jordan in order to help keep those countries in the Western orbit.[138] Concerns about the scale of Iran's defense establishment and opposition to resale of U.S.-origin equipment discouraged the Johnson administration from approving those proposals, but U.S. officials sympathized with the regime's desire to exert Iranian influence in these ways and never totally squashed the ideas.

Only in one way did Iran's regional ambitions cause concern in Washington during the final phases of the Johnson administration: Tehran's aspirations fueled rivalry with Saudi Arabia for dominance in the Persian Gulf. Following the Six-Day War, the Johnson administration, like the British government, regarded those nations as the two pillars on which a stable pro-Western order could be constructed in the Middle East generally and the Persian Gulf in particular. The 1967 war had definitively quashed American aspirations to find a modus vivendi with Nasser and affirmed that U.S. interests lay with cooperative governments that could be relied upon at a time of chronic instability, declining British influence, and falling U.S. capabilities as a consequence of the drain in Southeast Asia. Cooperation between Iran and Saudi Arabia, as National Security Adviser Rostow put it on one occasion, "could become the nucleus for stability and progress in the Persian Gulf."[139] A major weakness of this vision was the potential for tension between Riyadh and Tehran, which, far from cooperating as U.S. leaders hoped, regarded Britain's impending withdrawal from the Gulf as a risky moment when the other might extend its influence over one of the world's most valuable areas. The conflict, a complicated affair entailing disputes over the Persian Gulf seabed as well as the political status of formerly British islands including Bahrein, simmered during 1966 and 1967 but erupted in February 1968 into a full-fledged diplomatic crisis when the shah abruptly canceled a visit to Saudi Arabia.[140]

The conflict alarmed the Johnson administration, particularly when the shah, well aware that U.S. oil companies derived greater profits from their Saudi operations compared to their activities in Iran, accused Washington of siding with King Faisal. U.S. officials rejected that accusation and, in fact, eager to avoid giving any impression of wanting to replace the British in the Gulf, tried to convey the message that Iran and Saudi Arabia must manage the problem on their own.[141] Still, Americans also saw compelling reasons to end the dispute as quickly as possible and worked throughout the first half of the year to find a formula that would satisfy both sides. The U.S. ambassadors in Tehran and Riyadh cultivated moderation and floated various compromise settlements.[142] Meyer probably exaggerated by suggesting in his 2003 memoir that he sold the formula that ultimately settled the most difficult aspect of the dispute—how to apportion control over oil production in the middle of the Gulf—but was surely correct in suggesting that Washington played a constructive role in promoting the "median line" settlement that Iran and Saudi Arabia signed on October 24, 1968.[143] Meyer's hope that the deal might usher in "new era of Saudi-Iranian collaboration" seemed to be affirmed a month later when the shah made a highly successful visit to Saudi Arabia.[144]

In an otherwise grim year of setbacks around the world, Washington had worked with allies to bolster stability in a key part of the world while avoiding new costs or commitments.

Even as the Iranian-Saudi conflict played out in the final months of the Johnson presidency, American officials took an unprecedentedly upbeat view of a country that had ranked near the top of Washington's worries only a few years before. "The internal Iranian political situation has not been as stable as it is today for several decades," noted one U.S. assessment in November 1968. While conceding that the regime maintained its power through authoritarian methods, the report praised the government for securing the "cooperation of most Iranians" and building a "middle class with a vested interest in stability." The opposition, meanwhile, remained "divided and impotent."[145] Underlying this optimism lay glowing appraisals of Iran's economic growth, which had, in Walt Rostow's view, propelled the nation through "take off" and positioned it well for further movement along the developmental road.[146] For a nation-builder like Rostow, Iran provided striking evidence of what could be achieved through the right combination of top-down reform and U.S. support.

In the arena of foreign policy, meanwhile, U.S. and Iranian leaders heaped praise on each other during and after the shah's June 1968 visit to Washington. The shah regarded that meeting as a "resounding success," and U.S. officials congratulated themselves for laying the tracks on which constructive relations could continue in the years ahead. "Let us hope that the high water mark in US-Iranian relations achieved during the 'Johnson years' will carry on into the future," Meyer, who had done as much as any American to bolster the shah, wrote to the president just after the Washington meeting.[147] Perhaps the most revealing indication of how much things had changed came, however, not during the shah's stopover in the U.S. capital but up the coast in Cambridge, Massachusetts. Having once been castigated by the "Harvard men"—the reform-minded liberals who vied for control over policy toward Iran during the Kennedy years—the shah now received an honorary degree from Harvard University and delivered the spring commencement address, the principal reasons for his trip to the United States.[148] The speech made headlines mostly for the shah's proposal to establish a "Universal Welfare Legion," a new international organization modeled on the Peace Corps that would bring together volunteers from around the globe to address poverty, disease, and other forms of human suffering.[149] However miniscule its chances of gaining traction with other governments, the idea reflected the shah's soaring confidence and ambition.

To the extent that Iran generated discussion among U.S. officials in the final weeks of the Johnson presidency, they were eager to reassure both themselves

FIGURE 6.3. Reza Shah Pahlavi talks with President Johnson and the new secretary of defense, Clark Clifford, on June 11, 1968, during his final trip to the United States during LBJ's presidency. LBJ Library photo by Yoichi Okamoto.

and their Iranian counterparts that the incoming Nixon presidency would preserve and reinforce the transformed relationship. Remarkably, NSC aide Hal Saunders informed LBJ on December 4 that there were "no pressing bilateral issues" that required discussion during a forthcoming visit by Iranian prime minister Hoveyda.[150] The outgoing administration indicated its expectation that the United States would continue to provide military assistance, and officials hoped for annual credits totaling $100 million.[151] The flow of oil revenues, meanwhile, though never as high as Tehran wanted, had receded as a source of controversy as payments to the Iranian regime steadily increased. Between the mid-1960s and 1970, oil revenues increased from one-half of the government's overall income to about two-thirds.[152] U.S. officials perceived, rather, that the main challenge lay in reassuring the shah that U.S. policy would not shift again with a change of president, as the shah believed it had when Kennedy had given way to Johnson. The U.S. goal during Hoveyda's visit, wrote Rusk, was to convey U.S. determination, regardless of president or party, to maintain the "present intimate relationship with Iran."[153] To the disappointment of Johnson's aides, President-Elect Nixon declined to meet with Hoveyda to convey that message in person. But LBJ and other U.S. leaders sought to highlight not only their own satisfaction with the state of U.S.-Iranian ties but also the congruity of Johnson's and Nixon's outlooks on Iran, a point that Nixon's appointee as national security adviser, Henry Kissinger, affirmed during a brief meeting with the prime minister arranged by Johnson's team.[154] As the coming years would amply demonstrate, neither LBJ nor Hoveyda had anything to worry about.

# 7

# Indonesia

## EMBRACING THE NEW ORDER

THE PEOPLE of Jakarta could have no doubt about the state of U.S.-Indonesian relations on April 17, 1965. Indonesian leader Sukarno chose that day, the tenth anniversary of the opening of the Bandung conference of Afro-Asian nations, to mount a stunning display of anti-Americanism and to herald his leadership of what he called the New Emerging Forces, or NEFOS, the Third World peoples determined to create a new international order free of Western interference. African and Asian nations must cooperate to "root out the last vestiges of colonialism, neocolonialism, and imperialism," Sukarno declared in an hour-long speech opening the commemoration, which drew representatives from across the Third World. Speaker after speaker echoed Sukarno's appeals for unity, praise of China, and condemnation of the United States, especially for its rapidly expanding role in Vietnam.[1] If anything, the atmospherics surrounding the event conveyed Sukarno's messages even more strongly than his words. Jakarta, which the *New York Times* considered "normally one of the most disheveled Asian capitals," was festooned with tens of thousands of colored lights and miles of bunting. Working-class slums had been freshly painted. "The new world is in the Nefos' hands," proclaimed banners hung around the city, while another prominent sign showed a brown hand encircling the globe. Huge murals in front of the Information Ministry made plain which nation most obstructed this vision of human progress. One depicted a U.S. soldier throwing poison gas on the people of Vietnam. Another showed an Indonesian smashing Lyndon Johnson's head with a sledge hammer.[2]

Two and a half years later to the day, Jakarta projected a wholly different image in American minds. The Indonesian military, led by General Suharto, was now in charge, having suppressed the country's huge communist party and ousted Sukarno from public office. Sukarno was now a "forlorn figure, down to his last wife and last kidney," the U.S. ambassador to Indonesia, Marshall Green, quipped about a leader whose sexual appetites and health problems made irresistible targets. Green's crack came during a White House meeting with President Johnson, Secretary Rusk, and other cabinet members on October 18, 1967, a session that exuded self-congratulatory optimism about Suharto and the New Order that he promised to construct. Under Suharto, Indonesia not only had abandoned any claim to leadership of the Third World movement but was even showing signs of backing the U.S. role in Vietnam. Johnson and his aides acknowledged that both Suharto and his foreign champions had much work to do to solidify the new regime's prospects for the long term. But the "spectacle" of Indonesia's dramatic break with China, asserted Rusk, had been vital to the erosion of communist influence throughout Asia. All in all, boasted Green, no nation in recent history had "undergone a greater transformation than Indonesia."[3]

Green indisputably had a strong case. During the Johnson presidency, Indonesia experienced a turnabout that marked a major breaking point in the histories of Southeast Asia and the Third World more generally. When LBJ took office, Indonesia presented a frightening prospect: an increasingly defiant nation, with pretentions to Third World leadership, gravitating into the Chinese orbit. When LBJ departed the White House, the country was something entirely different: an economically weak but mostly reliable nation that, in its new authoritarian guise, promised to serve Western interests in the Cold War. As with the other countries examined in this book, change was driven overwhelmingly by internal political forces. Indeed, of the countries explored in these pages, Indonesia was probably the most impervious to U.S. leverage, both before and after Suharto's emergence in late 1965. Yet U.S. leaders worked consistently to influence Indonesian politics and sometimes succeeded in shaping developments in consequential ways.

These efforts illuminate yet another variant of American behavior with respect to the Third World during the Johnson years. The first months of the LBJ presidency reveal how the administration, despite its instinct to end the prevarications of the Kennedy period, found no good alternative to the ambiguities that it inherited with respect to Indonesia. Maintaining any influence at all in Jakarta seemed to depend on sticking with some form of the nuanced approach that JFK had pursued. But everything changed in October 1965, when a complex series of events, encouraged but not stage-managed by Washington, brought the Indonesian military to power and opened the door to evisceration of the world's third-largest communist party. Still, the Johnson administration greeted the new regime cautiously, far more so than in Brazil, where the April 1964 coup marked an abrupt transformation immediately understood as a major gain for the United States. By contrast, American leaders embraced Suharto's New Order gradually, encouraged especially by Sukarno's marginalization in March 1966 and then his final removal from power almost a year later. By mid-1967, they looked back with enormous satisfaction at Indonesia's reversal, giving themselves more credit than they probably deserved and overlooking the army's brutal destruction of the Indonesian Communist Party. Indonesia, like Brazil and Iran, stood out as a major success story for the Johnson administration at a time of diminishing resources and political clout.

## "Which Way This Cat Will Jump"

During his first days in office, Lyndon Johnson demonstrated his hostility to Sukarno and his determination to quash a pending proposal for new U.S. aid to Indonesia. "I ought to be impeached if I approve it," LBJ declared in a phone conversation with Defense Secretary McNamara on January 2, 1964. "That's just how deeply I feel," added the president, who went on to describe in typical Johnsonian language the potential consequences of appeasing an aggressor like the Indonesian leader. "When you let a bully come in and start raiding you in your front yard, if you run, he'll come in and run you out of your bedroom the next night," said Johnson. "I don't think we ought to encourage this guy [Sukarno] to do what he is doing there. And I think that any assistance just shows weakness on our part."[4] The president did not offer any specific rationale for his stance, but it is not difficult to imagine the mix of emotional, political, and geostrategic considerations that weighed in his thinking. Sukarno's well-known defiance of U.S. policy was tailor-made to trigger the president's intolerance for uncooperative foreign leaders, just as Indonesia's challenge to British policy in Malaysia offended the president's sympathy for European allies. On both counts, Johnson departed from JFK's persistent efforts to rebalance American priorities and to indulge diverse viewpoints in the Third World. Another factor in LBJ's calculations was the attitude of Congress. At a time when Johnson dreamed of winning passage for the most ambitious domestic reform agenda since the New Deal, it made little sense to antagonize legislators by preserving ties to a man broadly reviled in the United States.

Among those alarmed by Johnson's attitude was NSC aide Michael Forrestal, a Kennedy appointee who feared an abrupt end to Washington's efforts to use aid to exert leverage in Indonesia. Maintaining that approach, he observed, "requires a positive effort by the President because there are not that many people in the government who care and there are many who oppose."[5] But Forrestal's anxieties proved misplaced. Despite pervasive hostility to Sukarno, officials who advocated keeping the door open to the Indonesian regime got their way. The Kennedy administration had already cut its initial aid plan for Indonesia in fiscal year 1964 by 80 percent, leaving only small programs for food and military assistance and a smattering of aid already in the pipeline for delivery to Indonesia. But those remaining streams held enormous value in the minds of Forrestal, Komer, and Howard Jones, the U.S. ambassador to Jakarta. These men led the charge to avoid drastic steps including a total cutoff of aid or a break of U.S.-Indonesian diplomatic relations.

Taking either of those steps would, they maintained, squander Washington's influence, meager though it might have been, with a country of staggering size, wealth, and potential influence. Although Sukarno seemed increasingly friendly to the communist party, the Partai Komunis Indonesia or PKI, and determined to press the confrontation with Malaysia, U.S. assessments noted that he remained fundamentally unpredictable and potentially tractable through the right mix of carrots and sticks. After all, the CIA concluded in February 1964, Sukarno was no doctrinaire communist and might eventually come to see the PKI as more of a threat than an asset.[6] Could Sukarno still be steered away from his reliance on the party and his hostile policy toward Malaysia known locally as the Konfrontasi? It was, wrote Ambassador Jones, "too early to predict which way this cat will jump."[7] But for Jones and his allies, there was little to be gained by building U.S. policy on worst-case assumptions. Sukarno had not foreclosed the possibility of a negotiated settlement to the dispute with Malaysia and still seemed eager for contacts with Washington, especially if those links might entail a face-to-face meeting with LBJ. Hoping that Johnson would follow through on Kennedy's vague assurance of a visit to Indonesia, Sukarno told Jones in early 1964 that he wanted Johnson to be the "first guest in my new guest house" sometime that year or in 1965.[8] Cutting off U.S. aid, warned Forrestal, would only convince Sukarno of U.S. hostility, unite the Indonesian population behind his aggressive policies, escalate the conflict with Malaysia, and heighten U.S. diplomatic and military burdens at a time when Washington already had its hands full in Vietnam.[9]

These arguments carried the day during an NSC meeting on January 7, 1964, the first time President Johnson addressed Indonesia with his advisers. One reason for the consensus was the president's apparent unwillingness to indulge in the tough talk that had come so readily to his lips during his conversation with McNamara five days earlier. Surrounded by his advisers, he offered no strong opinions and allowed others to drive decisions. The meeting reverberated with condemnations of Sukarno, whom Rusk dubbed "the least responsible leader of any modern state." But every participant in the session accepted that U.S. interests would be best served by keeping aid channels open to Jakarta, at least for the moment. Even Air Force general Curtis LeMay, the acting chairman of the Joint Chiefs of Staff, set aside his accustomed disdain for diplomatic solutions, urging that the United States "keep its foot in the door" in Indonesia, as did CIA director John McCone. Both worried in particular that a cutoff would destroy any slim chance that Sukarno would go along with forthcoming efforts by Philippine president Diosdado Macapagal to mediate

FIGURE 7.1. A meeting of the National Security Council on January 7, 1964, reached consensus on the need to keep providing aid to Indonesia despite Sukarno's provocations. CIA Director John McCone sits at the far end of the table, with Budget Director David Bell to his right and Attorney General Robert F. Kennedy to his left. Around the table in a clockwise direction are Undersecretary of State W. Averell Harriman, Secretary of State Dean Rusk, President Johnson, Defense Secretary Robert S. McNamara, Assistant Secretary of Defense William Bundy, Air Force General Curtis LeMay, an unidentified official, and National Security Adviser McGeorge Bundy. LBJ Library photo by Yoichi Okamoto.

a settlement of the Malaysia controversy. Rusk agreed with that line of thinking but also, echoing Forrestal, pointed to other concerns. Antagonizing Sukarno, warned the secretary, might lead him to eradicate all U.S. influence in Indonesia by confiscating American investments valued at $500 million while deepening his ties to China and the Soviet Union, potentially devastating setbacks in a vitally important nation. Rusk underscored the latter point in a way sure to grab the attention of his colleagues: "More is involved in Indonesia, with its 100 million people," insisted Rusk, "than is at stake in Viet Nam."[10]

During the first months of 1964, the chosen U.S. course—a policy aimed at preserving what Komer called "foot-in-the-door influence"—seemed to pay off.[11] In a complicated series of negotiations, Sukarno relaxed his position on Malaysia and held out the possibility of a settlement with his counterpart in Kuala Lumpur, Tunku Abdul Rahman. Attorney General Robert F. Kennedy, dispatched by Johnson to convey U.S. policy to Sukarno (and to get the new president's political rival out of Washington in the weeks following JFK's assassination), played a vital role in this process. During meetings with Sukarno in Tokyo and Jakarta, the attorney general underscored U.S. insistence on an end to the Konfrontasi, warning that continuation of U.S. aid over the long term hung in the balance. On January 17, Sukarno agreed to a cease-fire and mutual withdrawals of troops in return for talks to be mediated by the Philippine government. Although details remained to be settled, even Rusk praised Kennedy for accomplishments that might "prove to be a major turning point in the entire position in Southeast Asia."[12] For Forrestal and other advocates of keeping channels open to Indonesia, the success seemed to demonstrate Sukarno's responsiveness to pressure, especially when it was exerted by the most highly placed U.S. officials.[13]

Still, major obstacles stood in the way of a lasting deal. Sukarno's concessions led a suddenly optimistic Komer to put the odds of avoiding "another nasty Southeast Asian crisis" at better than fifty-fifty, but he and other supporters of the diplomatic effort acknowledged that RFK had won no binding assurances.[14] It remained to be seen whether Sukarno would follow through with his promises to withdraw Indonesian forces from Malaysian territories. Also unclear was whether Macapagal would play the mediatory role assigned to him and even more so whether Tunku Abdul Rahman would agree to negotiate with Sukarno in the absence of advance Indonesian recognition of Malaysian nationhood. Just as worrying to U.S. leaders was the attitude of the British government, whose unbridled hostility to the Indonesian government clashed with Washington's efforts to cultivate Sukarno's cooperation. Even as RFK drew praise for his peacemaking, U.S. diplomats in London voiced doubts about Sukarno's reliability and opposition to any deal among Asian leaders that diminished Britain's ability to safeguard Malaysian security.

American efforts to grapple with this array of problems achieved some successes, and talks between Sukarno and the Tunku got under way in February 1964. Before long, however, American optimism evaporated amid signs that, as Forrestal put it, the basic agreement between Indonesia and Malaysia to seek a negotiated settlement was coming "unstuck."[15] Most problematically, Sukarno proved unwilling to withdraw forces operating in Malaysia, though the Malaysian leader, wary of making any concessions ahead of national elections scheduled for April, also contributed to the impasse by refusing to negotiate on political questions until the Indonesian withdrawal had taken place. The talks seemed to break down completely in early March, putting the cease-fire in jeopardy. In Washington, senior policymakers suddenly returned to basic questions of the sort that had preoccupied them a few weeks earlier: how should the United States interact with a regime that consistently defied American desires and stirred trouble in its region? On March 4, National Security Adviser Bundy regretfully informed the White House staff that cutoff of U.S. economic aid now seemed "inevitable" and proposed putting the question, which had been deferred rather than settled in January, back on the president's agenda.[16] Rusk speculated that a total "parting of ways" with Indonesia was a distinct possibility.[17]

In response, advocates of keeping the door open to Sukarno doubled down on the arguments they had made at the start of Johnson presidency, mounting a rear-guard action that would continue all the way to the rupture of October 1965. During these months, Sukarno grew steadily more defiant of U.S. preferences and the PKI continued to grow in size and influence. But at each moment of decision for Washington, advocates of engaging the Indonesian leader managed to hold their own on the basic principle of maintaining relations with Sukarno, even if they had to concede incremental reductions in remaining American aid programs. The secret to their success lay not in defusing anger about Sukarno's behavior but in persuading fellow policymakers, including Lyndon Johnson, that keeping channels open to Sukarno was the least bad alternative available for the United States. At a minimum, all agreed, preserving the link would facilitate Washington's ability to exploit any sudden changes in the balance of power among Sukarno, the PKI, and the other key player in Jakarta: the army.

Forrestal and Komer led efforts to maintain links to Sukarno as the prospect of a negotiated deal to end the Konfrontasi seemed to slip away in the spring of 1964. In a vigorous memo on March 5, Forrestal urged the United States to do everything it could to prevent a breakdown of the cease-fire. "I don't understand how we can fail to use every lever at our command to prevent the outbreak of another ugly war behind our backs while we are fighting in South Vietnam," he asserted. Particularly alarming, the NSC aide added, was the prospect that the United States might be drawn into new fighting between Indonesia and Malaysia due to Washington's close partnership with Britain and its commitments to defend Britain's two most important partners in the region, Australia and New Zealand. But Forrestal concluded with an even bleaker prospect: the loss of U.S. influence throughout Asia if Washington could not keep such a pivotal nation out of the communist camp. "The surest way to have this happen," he insisted, "would be for us to stand idly by and let events take their course."[18]

Komer had a less optimistic sense of what the United States could accomplish by engaging Sukarno but similarly urged that Washington "play out our hand as long as possible with Indonesia" by avoiding dramatic ruptures. A major concern, he wrote to Bundy, was the risk of confronting too many crises at the same time and thereby encouraging critics of the administration who believed that Johnson could not handle foreign policy and was reversing "the Kennedy line" in the Third World—politically dangerous charges in an election year. "[A] showdown with Indonesia at a time when we want to step out more on Vietnam would be quite a complication," Komer advised. But he pointed out, too, that crises in Panama, Cyprus, the Middle East, and South Asia were brewing, confronting the administration with an almost impossible array of problems.[19] Bundy left no record of his response, but neither did he press for a reconsideration of U.S. policy.

Advocates of open channels to Jakarta renewed their efforts in May, when the newly appointed assistant secretary of state for East Asian affairs, McGeorge Bundy's brother William, delivered a speech that publicly threatened Indonesia with a cutoff of U.S. aid. With the benefit of hindsight, it is clear that William's appointment in mid-March marked a significant challenge to the sort of policies advocated by Forrestal and Komer and a step toward LBJ's blunter preferences for Indonesia and elsewhere. Upon taking office, Johnson had quickly developed a deep dislike for Roger Hilsman, the assistant secretary whom he inherited. The consummate Kennedy administration insider, Hilsman had consistently raised provocative questions, offered dissenting opinions, and challenged the authority of the military. William Bundy, by contrast, was a reliable bureaucrat who shared Johnson's basic approach to the Cold War.[20] He displayed these qualities in a speech to an American advertising association on May 5. The United States, he warned, may have to "eliminate" all remaining aid programs if Indonesia persisted in the confrontation. Indonesian "aggression," he added, "must be met." This assertion, reported by the *New York Times*, caused a firestorm among Indonesian leaders, with Foreign Minister Subandrio telling Jones that relations were approaching an "all time low" and threatening that Indonesia might be inclined to beat Washington to the punch by refusing to accept any more American assistance.[21] Jones regarded the blowup as a major step backward for U.S. interests, but Forrestal registered the strongest objections in a blistering memo he dispatched to William Bundy three days after the speech. "I think we can foresee that internal pressures in Indonesia are going to get worse in the next six months and probably make Sukarno even more sensitive to our public statements than he already is," stated Forrestal. "So don't we do better by keeping our mouths shut?"[22]

In the end, Forrestal, Komer, and Jones held the line, as they had in March, not least by convincing McGeorge Bundy of the merits of their case. The national security adviser succinctly relayed his views to the president in a telephone conversation on May 1, indicating that he wanted the whole issue to "go to bed."[23] With LBJ's tolerance, the administration maintained what Forrestal dubbed the "tag ends" of its once-capacious assistance program for Indonesia—a grab bag of training for civilian administrators and military officers, food aid, a communications network for the Indonesian armed forces, and a few development programs approved in earlier years—and continued to exert pressure on Sukarno for a peaceful resolution to the confrontation. This achievement was harder than it had been earlier in the year not only because of William Bundy's appointment but also because of the growing chorus in Congress and the media criticizing U.S. aid for a regime that seemed to be moving ever closer to China. Sukarno's assertion in March that the United States could "go to hell" with its aid unleashed a barrage of charges that the administration's efforts to buy the friendship of hostile nations "seemed to be blowing up in our faces," as Senator Herman Talmadge, a Democrat from Georgia, put it.[24] The task of maintaining constructive relations with Sukarno became harder still in late July, when President Johnson, straining against the balanced policy he had ruefully accepted, offered Malaysia new U.S. military assistance during a warm meeting with the Tunku in Washington. With Malaysian leaders eagerly calling attention to U.S. largesse, Komer feared that the Tunku was becoming "cocky" and acting as if he had a "blank check" from Washington in the standoff with Indonesia.[25] All of this was bound to antagonize Sukarno, and it remained to be seen whether U.S.-Indonesian ties, such as they were, could survive.

## The Year of Living Anxiously

The chance of maintaining U.S. influence in Indonesia suffered an unprecedented series of blows in August 1965, the start of a thirteen-month period in which relations between Washington and Jakarta teetered more precariously than ever on the brink of total collapse. Exactly why Sukarno chose this period to antagonize the West and move closer to the communist bloc was a matter of speculation at the time and has remained so ever since. Rusk guessed that Sukarno judged his policy of military pressure against Malaysia had failed and, in frustration, was trying to boost his prestige in Third World circles by launching a broader attack on the West.[26] Domestically, Sukarno's choices seemed to flow from a new eagerness, for some combination of ideological and pragmatic reasons, to tie himself more closely to the PKI, which leaned increasingly toward China as the Sino-Soviet split widened. In any case, Sukarno clearly demonstrated his willingness to defy Washington. On August 10, his government granted diplomatic recognition to North Vietnam. A week later, he escalated military operations against Malaysia by ordering a small but highly provocative landing by Indonesian troops north of Singapore.

But it was Sukarno's speech on August 17, Indonesia's independence day, that most repelled American officials. Aligning Indonesia more closely than ever with Hanoi, he declared that the South Vietnamese were "not yet free" and condemned "as strongly as possible" the U.S. bombing raids against the North Vietnamese coast in response to alleged attacks on American warships in the Gulf of Tonkin. Sukarno also castigated Washington for supporting Malaysia and pledged to take over American investments in Indonesia. "I wish to confirm that basically and eventually," he declared, "there will be no imperialist capital operating on Indonesian soil." In the domestic arena, meanwhile, he explicitly embraced the label "Marxist" and emphasized his old idea of fusing nationalist, religious, and communist elements of the population into a single political movement embodying the will of the nation. He hinted too at support for Chinese-style agricultural collectivism.[27]

Sukarno titled his speech "The Year of Living Dangerously," apparently in anticipation of the rancor that his words would stir among his many adversaries domestically and abroad. If he counted Americans among those most likely to pose risks to his regime, he was certainly correct. The first assessment of the speech came not from Ambassador Jones but from his deputy, Francis Galbraith, who disliked his boss's tolerance of Sukarno and saw the address as a straightforward "declaration of enmity" that showed the Indonesian leader's true colors. The speech, he reported to the State Department, demonstrated that Indonesia not only belonged to the "camp of [the] Asian communist countries" but also opposed the United States on everything from specific issues like Vietnam and Malaysia to the essence of what the United States represented in the world—"our thought, our influence and our leadership."[28] The CIA similarly concluded that Sukarno had moved "close to the immediate objectives" of the PKI and would continue moving away from the West.[29] Indonesian hostility also stirred new waves of furor in Congress, where, even before Sukarno's speech, the Senate had passed a measure aimed at forcing the administration to close down all aid to Indonesia. Known as the Tower Amendment after its principal sponsor, Republican senator John Tower of Texas, the initiative, passed by a vote of sixty-two to twenty-eight, aimed to eliminate the president's ability to carry on with aid programs he judged to be in the national interest. It remained to be seen whether the House of Representatives would go along with the Senate, but following Sukarno's broadside

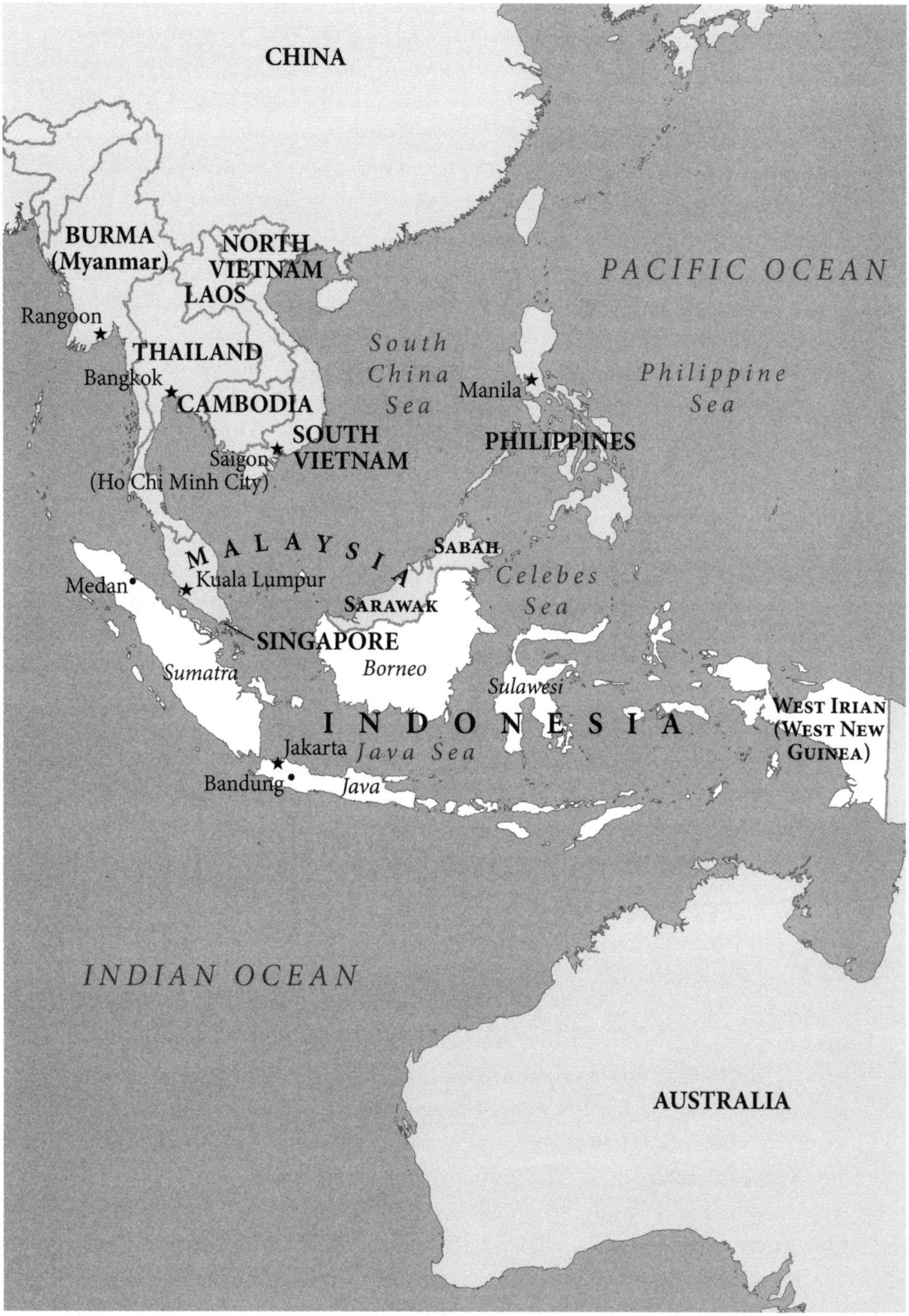


MAP 7.2. Indonesia and surrounding territories following the establishment of Malaysia in 1963. Mapping Specialists, Ltd., Madison, WI.

against the West it appeared that a cutoff of U.S. aid was once again a distinct possibility.

Amid the outrage, weary champions of engaging Sukarno went back into action within the bureaucracy. For Komer, Forrestal, and Jones, it would be a year of living anxiously amid constant fear of a rupture of relations that would surrender any chance of keeping Indonesia out of the communist camp. "We're in a fair way to lose Indonesia after all our efforts to stall off the fatal break," Komer wrote Bundy five days after Sukarno's speech. "From [a] foreign policy viewpoint it's imperative not to let [the] Indonesian tie go from bad to worse, especially when we have our hands full in Laos/Vietnam."[30] Komer floated the idea of a presidential note to Sukarno expressing U.S. disappointment and giving Indonesian leaders an opportunity to defuse the crisis by saying "they don't really mean it."[31] There was still time, urged Komer, to keep Washington's "few piddling programs" for Indonesia alive and avoid the "point of no return" for a nation that, in his judgment, remained a "far greater prize than Vietnam."[32] But an exchange of olive branches seemed unlikely in the last days of August. William Bundy's Far Eastern division at the State Department was already toying with proposing a cutoff of all remaining military assistance, and Congress was seriously weighing the Tower Amendment. Perhaps most distressing of all to Komer was the possibility that Johnson might buckle in order to protect himself during the final stages of the 1964 presidential race against Republican criticism for giving American resources away to a hostile foreign nation, a potentially damaging line of attack on the Democrats as U.S. foreign aid became less popular with the American public. "The real issue seems to be one of domestic politics vs. foreign policy," asserted Komer.[33]

In the event, Komer exaggerated the risk of the administration breaking with Indonesia. Just like earlier in the year, the arguments in favor of maintaining ties to Indonesia prevailed with the most senior U.S. leaders, including the president himself. On the State Department's suggestion, Johnson decided on August 30 to defer deliveries of equipment promised to the Indonesian military and to consider "some reduction" in military training programs. But he also approved continuation of economic assistance, aid for Indonesian "civic action programs" designed to promote development and security in the countryside, and training for police and security forces so long as it was not military in character. Rusk laid out the logic in a memorandum endorsed by LBJ: Washington must "avoid drastic or highly publicized actions" that might cause a total breakdown of relations, kill any small chance of a negotiated settlement to the Konfrontasi, and endanger American private investment in Indonesia.[34] Contributing to LBJ's attitude was growing confidence among his advisers that Congress would abandon the Tower Amendment when the measure came before a House-Senate conference committee and that the Republican leader in the Senate, Everett Dirksen of Illinois, quietly accepted the administration's rationale for maintaining ties to Jakarta and would discourage partisan attacks on the issue.[35] It may be, too, that LBJ was motivated by political calculations more complicated than what Komer supposed. While Johnson undoubtedly worried about Republican criticism for coddling a leftist government hostile to the United States, he surely also feared the political costs of seeming to lose Indonesia to the communists if he cut all links to Sukarno, an outcome that would risk U.S. investments and heighten the possibility that the United States might be drawn into escalated fighting between Indonesia and Malaysia. The best political move was thus to keep Indonesia safely on the back burner.

But another calculation also weighed in favor of avoiding dramatic breaks: by keeping links open to Jakarta, the United States could quietly cultivate relationships with Sukarno's opponents and exert its influence in the event of sudden changes in the Indonesian political landscape. Covert efforts to maintain ties to friendly political factions were nothing new in 1964. The CIA had failed miserably in its effort to foment a coup in 1958 but had continued thereafter to seek influence over Indonesian politics even as relations between Washington and Jakarta warmed up during the Kennedy administration. By the time Lyndon Johnson took office, secret efforts to curry favor with Indonesian army officers and Muslim parties hostile to Sukarno were well established in the U.S. tool kit for coping with the country. Indeed, as historian Bradley R. Simpson observes, covert operations had become such a standard feature of Washington's conduct of the Cold War around the world that it is hardly surprising that Washington entertained this option in a country as worrisome as Indonesia.[36]

The problem for proponents of a coup in Indonesia was that Sukarno seemed to have such a firm grip on power and that alternative sources of authority, especially the army, showed little interest in the idea and seemed badly divided. Ambassador Jones, hardly the keenest supporter of covert action, reflected American pessimism after a meeting with General Abdul Haris Nasution, a member of Sukarno's cabinet but also a potential dissident leader, in March 1964. The general, reported Jones, "avoided like the plague any discussion of [a] possible military takeover, even though this hovered in the air throughout [our] talk, and at no point did he pick up obvious hints of US support in [a] time of crisis."[37] In Washington, NSC aide James Thomson captured American doubts about the military's willingness to break with Sukarno and take bold action: military officers were presumably "our real pals" in Indonesia, but Thomson could suggest only that U.S. representatives in Jakarta have a "where-the-hell-do-we-go-from-here" meeting to explore the possibilities of closer collaboration.[38] Action was, it seemed, a long way off.

Sukarno's multiple affronts to the United States in the summer sparked increased U.S. efforts to achieve better cooperation. It was time, the CIA declared, to consider a new "program of covert action aimed at affecting the current trend of events" in place of the "modest" and mostly ineffectual program of clandestine operations already under way. The goal, asserted the CIA, was both to embolden the "nobler elements of Indonesian society" and to encourage "direct action" against the PKI.[39] These ideas took more concrete form as U.S. officials studied possible courses of action over the ensuing months. That process came to fruition on November 19, when Assistant Secretary of State William Bundy signed off on a CIA-State Department paper calling for secret efforts to vilify the communist party as a dangerous threat to legitimate Indonesian nationalism, to encourage "obstructive action" against the PKI, and to identify and cultivate potential leaders who could take over if Sukarno died or was overthrown.[40] The administration's interagency committee that reviewed covert operations, known as the 303 Committee, approved the plan in March.[41]

The CIA expressed no more confidence than U.S. officials had earlier in the year about the willingness of the Indonesian military to move against Sukarno. Yet it also asserted in no uncertain terms that the army—known to be far more Western-oriented than the navy or air force—was the only organized entity capable of resisting Indonesia's final slide into the communist camp, a development that Washington should expect "within the not too distant future" unless "extraneous factors intrude." The challenge ahead was clear: to nurture contacts in the army while encouraging both officers and the Indonesian population to see that institution as the defender of Indonesia's nationalist and religious traditions.[42] Indeed, U.S. officials increasingly landed on logic that would gain broad acceptance as 1965 advanced: to succeed in weakening the PKI, the army must find a way to align itself with Sukarno against the communists. The army must, in short, be seen as coming to the defense of Indonesia's nationalist icon against aggressive political forces alien to the society.

By the end of 1964, then, a broad array of U.S. officials agreed on the need to maintain Washington's channels to the Indonesian government, lowering the odds of a U.S.-initiated rupture even as tensions with Jakarta grew. The usual advocates of engaging Sukarno still held out hope for a negotiated settlement of the Konfrontasi and a relaxation of U.S.-Indonesian tensions over the long term. Another block of opinion, focused in the CIA, the State Department's Far Eastern division, and parts of the U.S. establishment in Indonesia, sought to maintain relations mostly as a way to cultivate ties to the army and other potential sources of opposition to the PKI. Admittedly, the lines between the two groups sometimes blurred. Advocates of diplomatic engagement readily grasped that a coup or other dramatic political rupture not only was a distinct possibility but also might go a long way to resolving Washington's problems in Indonesia. They accepted, too, that Sukarno's health was rapidly deteriorating due to a serious kidney ailment and that the United States must be poised to support pro-Western elements if he died or was ousted from office. (One CIA report estimated his life expectancy between one and five years.)[43] But broad agreement on the need to cultivate friends in Indonesia did not mean that American officials concurred on the best road ahead or the priority that should be attached to fomenting a dramatic break. Lively disagreement persisted even as U.S. covert operations intensified.

Secrecy of CIA documentation makes it impossible to reconstruct the details of those operations. But the available record of American decision making illuminates the ebb and flow of different policy ideas as the Johnson administration pursued what officials took to calling a "low profile" approach. Dubbing himself the "last Sukarno lover," Komer emphasized as vigorously as ever in late 1964 and early 1965 that breaking with Sukarno would only radicalize the Indonesian situation, pushing Sukarno closer to Beijing and encouraging him to escalate the Konfrontasi.[44] The latter development might, in turn, create new pressures on the United States to join Britain in the military defense of Malaysia, a distinctly unappealing prospect at a time when the U.S. military commitment in Vietnam was growing rapidly. "With so much trouble in [Southeast Asia] already," wrote Komer, "we ought to try our best to avoid more just now."[45] From Jakarta, Jones advanced concrete ideas to pursue this path. Even as he called for sharp reductions in the size of the U.S. diplomatic establishment in Indonesia, he cautioned against any major steps to punish Sukarno and urged going forward with delivery of communications equipment for the Indonesian army that had been suspended in August 1964. Perhaps most notably, Jones persistently advocated another attempt at establishing a channel of communication between LBJ and Sukarno, even a face-to-face meeting in New York or Honolulu. The United States, he advised, might still play on Sukarno's vanity and drive a wedge between him and the PKI.[46]

That idea gained little ground, however, as officials skeptical of engaging Sukarno, reinforced by vigorous British warnings that a meeting with LBJ would only embolden the Indonesian leader, grew more insistent during 1965.[47] Komer understood that he was fighting a losing battle at the end of 1964, noting that the Far Eastern division at the State Department, for one, was "tired of the game" of wielding carrots and sticks to influence Sukarno's behavior. "They keep telling me," Komer wrote gloomily to McGeorge Bundy, "we've tried all Jones' remedies before, so why mount up again[?]"[48]

Komer's challenge grew stiffer as Sukarno and the PKI became still more hostile to the West. In January 1965, Indonesia withdrew from the United Nations after Malaysia was selected as a nonpermanent member of the Security

Council. The Indonesian government seized the occasion to launch new verbal attacks against the United States and to establish a new international organization, the Conference of Newly Emerging Forces (CONEFO), designed to serve the needs of developing nations. Around the same time, Indonesian leaders declared their intention to develop a nuclear weapon and pressed the Konfrontasi by sending more troops into mainland Malaysia.[49] The tenth anniversary of the Bandung conference unleashed new barrages of anti-U.S. rhetoric, but it was attacks of a different sort—physical assaults on U.S. properties scattered around the country—that did most to heighten U.S. anger. Often expressing outrage over U.S. escalation in Vietnam, PKI-led mobs ransacked U.S. Information Agency facilities in Jakarta, Medan, and elsewhere, leading the agency to close all reading rooms in the country. Meanwhile, PKI activists attempted to seize 160,000 acres of land owned by U.S. Rubber in North Sumatra, and Sukarno informed representatives of that company and Goodyear that the Indonesian government was taking "administrative control" of their plantations. Sukarno stressed that the move was aimed at heading off demands for outright nationalization, but U.S. executives and diplomats were hardly reassured.[50]

These affirmations of Sukarno's partnership with the PKI and imperviousness to American sensitivities empowered William Bundy and other advocates of a hard line toward Indonesia while undoubtedly fueling efforts to encourage action by the army. A simple statistic suggests the turn away from diplomatic solutions: Washington reduced its embassy staff from four hundred to thirty-five between April and August 1965, while the CIA retained its full contingent of twelve officers.[51] Shifting American priorities were also clear in other developments: the idea of an LBJ-Sukarno meeting quietly died in the spring, while Jones's critics grew more assertive. Perhaps most significant was the role of Undersecretary of State George Ball, who took a more active role on the Indonesia issue as 1965 advanced. While Secretary Rusk continued to avoid a clear-cut position, his deputy showed few inhibitions in a conversation with McGeorge Bundy, labeling Jones "too soft" in his approach to Jakarta.[52]

Bundy, who doubted that covert initiatives could resolve the problem in Indonesia, indicated that he disagreed, but Ball took his case directly to President Johnson. Jones had grown "tired" after seven years in Jakarta, wrote Ball, who insisted that the ambassador's efforts to shape Indonesian behavior through his personal relationship with Sukarno were "pretty well played out." Ball stopped short of recommending any immediate hardening of U.S. policy, suggesting instead that the president dispatch Ellsworth Bunker, the diplomat who had played a key role in resolving the West Irian dispute in 1962, to meet Sukarno in Jakarta. Such a meeting could, he speculated, have a "stabilizing effect" on U.S.-Indonesian relations. But Ball left no doubt of his view that a shift in U.S. policy might be in order, warning the president of "hard decisions that may be required over the next few weeks."[53] McGeorge Bundy backed the initiative at least as a way to resolve bureaucratic differences, telling the president that Bunker's trip might help bridge divisions between advocates of a "deep freeze" with the Indonesians and others who "believe in a continued effort to win back their interest and friendship."[54]

In the end, Bunker's visit to Jakarta yielded no dramatic changes but, perhaps as Ball anticipated, tilted U.S. policy toward further curtailment of bilateral relations and heavier reliance on bonds with the army and other anticommunist political forces that might pay off in the long run. After four lengthy sessions with Sukarno, who roundly condemned U.S. behavior throughout Southeast Asia, Bunker saw no reason to believe that U.S.-Indonesian relations could be improved in the near future. On the contrary, he advised that any effort to raise the U.S. profile in Indonesia would only play into the hands of the communists. He recommended going ahead with small-scale development programs and urged completion of the much-discussed communications network that Washington had promised for the Indonesian army. Otherwise, he recommended trimming the number of American personnel in the country and putting significant resources into only those programs, including training for a small number of Indonesian military officers, that seemed likely to pay off in the long term, following some sort of sea change in the political situation.[55] On that subject, Bunker exuded optimism. More than most U.S. assessments, his report stressed that the army hoped to end the Konfrontasi in order to prepare itself for a new conflict with the PKI. Meanwhile, Bunker noted, Indonesian Muslims were growing restive and had already engaged in violent clashes with the PKI in Java and Sumatra. The main U.S. objective, the emissary asserted, should be to maintain contact with these "constructive elements of strength" and to do everything possible to create "the most favorable conditions" for them to vie for power.[56]

Bunker's report set the tone for U.S. policy over the final few months leading up to the momentous events of September 30 and October 1, 1965. Over British objections, Washington completed the sale of $3 million worth of communications gear to the Indonesian army and stopped just short of closing down the tiny programs of food and development assistance that remained. Meanwhile, the State Department replaced Jones, who had long planned to move on from his post in Jakarta, with Marshall Green, William Bundy's deputy in the State Department's Far Eastern division. The appointment removed perhaps the most persistent voice in favor of engaging with Sukarno and installed a man far more in sync with the tenor of policymaking in the State Department and the CIA. The chance that U.S. policy would diverge from this track grew still smaller as a communist takeover appeared, as Ball put it, "only

FIGURE 7.3. President Johnson meets with the retiring U.S. ambassador to Indonesia, Howard P. Jones (left), and his replacement, Marshall Green, on June 30, 1965, a few days before the latter left for Jakarta. LBJ Library photo by Yoichi Okamoto.

a matter of time."[57] Intelligence reports indicated that the PKI continued to tighten its bond with Sukarno, and Indonesian leaders antagonized U.S. officials in the summer of 1965 by reiterating Indonesian threats to develop a nuclear arsenal. Jakarta threatened, in fact, to test an atomic bomb in November following a scheduled meeting of Afro-Asian nations in Algiers. U.S. intelligence indicated that Indonesia had no such capability but held open the possibility that Indonesian authorities would either allow China to detonate a device on Indonesian territory or participate somehow in a Chinese test.[58] A more figurative bombshell landed in September, when Indonesian leaders indicated their intention to take over management of foreign oil companies, a possible first step toward nationalization.[59]

American officials were discouraged as well by a distinct lack of progress toward any sort of coup that might weaken the communists. Jones had dutifully reported rumors of forthcoming military takeover throughout the year, only to see each moment pass without action.[60] Such failures heightened American uncertainty about the army's reliability as a vigorous opponent of the PKI. Although power dynamics in Indonesia remained murky, Ball conceded in August that it was not clear the army would go "all out" against the communists. So deeply had the PKI penetrated the government and perhaps the army itself, said the undersecretary of state, that even anticommunist officers might see no alternative to establishing a "modus vivendi" with the communists after Sukarno's death.[61] U.S. intelligence agencies similarly asserted that anticommunist political forces were "discouraged and intimidated" and that the military had "all but lost the will to resist." Even if Sukarno died, asserted a wide-ranging interagency report completed in July, the military would be unlikely to risk civil war by rolling back communist influence. "Indeed," the report continued, "the Communists are already so entrenched that they could probably not be denied an important share in any successor government."[62] All in all, as McGeorge Bundy put it in a memo to the president, the United States had little alternative to "playing for the breaks" in an ever-worsening situation.[63]

## The Turn

A momentous turning point came on the last night of September 1965, when a shadowy group under the broad direction of senior PKI leaders kidnapped and executed six members of the Indonesian army's high command. Historians have long debated the nature and objectives of the so-called September 30 Movement, but recent scholarship indicates that it aimed not to overthrow the existing political order but to purge the armed forces of elements hostile to the party's growing influence.[64] In any case, the episode lit the spark that sent the Indonesian army into action against the PKI. Over the following months, the army, allied with various paramilitary forces, student organizations, and Muslim groups hostile to the communists, not only evicted the PKI from the government and banned the party's participation in the nation's political life but also carried out a brutal campaign of anticommunist repression that resulted in an estimated half a million deaths, one of the most horrific bloodlettings of the twentieth century. The army, led by General Suharto, established itself as the new center of power in Indonesia and raised hopes in the West that Indonesia's drift toward the communist bloc was over.[65]

So well did these developments serve the Johnson administration's interests that historians have naturally emphasized Washington's role in bringing them about—and with good reason. Although many details of U.S. covert operations remain classified, officials clearly concluded during 1965 that the most likely scenario for overcoming indecisiveness within the army would entail a left-wing power grab of some sort.[66] Documentary evidence also abounds of U.S. efforts to embolden the army by conveying loose promises of support if it moved against the PKI. As in the months leading up to the 1964 coup in

Brazil, the generals could hardly have failed to see the signs of American encouragement. Once the army was in the driver's seat, moreover, U.S. officials plainly knew a good deal about the massacres occurring in the countryside and abetted the anticommunist campaign politically and even materially. At least one U.S. official in Jakarta, embassy political officer Robert Martens, provided military authorities with lists of thousands of suspected communists, many of whom were killed.[67]

U.S. complicity in such horrors and the rise of the military regime that perpetrated them should not, however, be mistaken for American control over the events in question. Revelations of disturbing and immoral acts have sometimes led historians to view the U.S. role in Indonesian events as more intentional and coordinated than it probably was. In fact, available evidence demonstrates substantial confusion and indecision among U.S. officials about the nature and implications of events that unfolded during the final months of 1965 and even during 1966. Americans unquestionably saw the army's assault on the PKI as a positive development, infinitely preferable to the status quo. But the situation nevertheless appeared fraught with dangers, and it seemed possible that the political shift brought about by the army's activism would yield only incremental or even temporary change. U.S. officials differed over how best to respond, yielding tactical disagreements over how quickly, publicly, and ambitiously to back the army and its allies.

As the army moved against the communists in early October 1965, some Americans responded with unbridled optimism. Perhaps the most enthusiastic high-level appraisal unsurprisingly came from Assistant Secretary of State William Bundy and Walt Rostow, who was still serving as director of the State Department's Policy Planning Staff. "Although the resolution of recent events is somewhat obscure," they wrote to Undersecretary Ball on October 2, "we may be facing one of the potentially most favorable situations on the world scene in recent years." If the army succeeded in taking power, they added, the United States would confront no less than a "uniquely favorable moment in Indonesian history" that would permit the reopening of U.S.-Indonesian cooperation.[68] Other hopeful commentary emphasized the reliability of the army commanders who had led what Americans took to calling the "countercoup" against the PKI. A hastily prepared CIA evaluation of Suharto, who quickly emerged as the dominant figure, noted that the general possessed strong anticommunist credentials burnished over a long career.[69] Suharto's actions in the first days of October seemed to indicate nothing had changed. He quickly banned PKI newspapers and unequivocally denounced the September 30 Movement and its allies.[70]

These hopes circulated, however, alongside caution and even doubt about how big a change had actually occurred. Part of the reason was sheer confusion about what precisely had happened on September 30 and October 1, a subject of numerous studies within the CIA and the State Department for months thereafter. But the larger problem as time passed was to ascertain the extent to which the PKI had been damaged and the army was capable of exerting control. Prospects for a fundamentally transformed U.S.-Indonesian relationship seemed to hang on the answers. Ambassador Green offered a relatively pessimistic assessment on October 17 after spending more than two weeks trying to understand the new dynamics in Jakarta. Although the communists had been badly hurt, he urged Washington to recognize that there were now two "power centers" vying for control in Indonesia—the army and Sukarno. He predicted "prolonged maneuvering" and cautioned that the resolution of the competition might do "little more than paper over" lines of fracture among Indonesian elites since neither contender wanted an open break. Although Green foresaw "changes of emphasis" in political slogans emanating from the top levels of government, he warned that the "basic framework of Indonesia's domestic ideology will be retained," including Sukarno's old emphasis on unity among nationalist, communist, and religious elements of Indonesian society.[71]

Such wariness reflected both doubts about the army and concern about Sukarno's remaining strength. As for the army, U.S. officials put some hope in long-standing efforts to cultivate good relations between the American and Indonesian militaries. Thanks to training programs at Fort Leavenworth, Fort Benning, and Fort Sam Houston, there existed a "service-to-service tie between military men" and an "association founded on trust, respect, and a network of deep personal friendships," wrote David C. Cuthell, the director of the Office of Southwest Pacific Affairs at the State Department.[72] Yet Cuthell and other officials saw no obvious reason to believe that this pro-American orientation would pay off in any bold Indonesian shift toward the West. To Washington's distress, army commanders seemed determined to press ahead with the Konfrontasi. Such hawkishness put the army at odds with Washington while stirring worry that Britain might escalate the conflict in order to score a decisive victory while the Indonesian command was distracted with internal maneuvering. The army might, then, be badly weakened at just the moment when it seemed to be taking charge domestically.

Indonesian commanders disappointed Washington as well by showing no inclination to back down from Sukarno's criticism of U.S. policy in Vietnam or his desire to curry favor with elements of the global Third World movement by emphasizing anti-Western themes.[73] All in all, reported Ambassador Green, the army showed "no sign of ditching Sukarno," believing that it could hold onto power and avert civil war only in combination with a man who, in the eyes of many Indonesians, uniquely embodied the nation's nationalist traditions.[74] The CIA offered an even more discouraging assessment in late November, noting that the army remained heavily dependent on Soviet assistance and contained many officers and enlisted personnel sympathetic to communist ideology, if not to the PKI per se.[75]

Meanwhile, U.S. observers fretted that Sukarno might find ways to bolster both his own power and that of the PKI at the expense of the army and its allies. Although Sukarno's position had been badly undercut, U.S. assessments in the early days following the countercoup noted that he appeared in good health during his public appearances and, as the CIA noted in a briefing for the president, seemed determined to use his "political magic" to recover his full powers.[76] Indeed, Sukarno and Foreign Minister Subandrio, both of whom had frequently voiced suspicions of CIA plots against them in earlier months, now hit the theme even harder. They blamed the CIA for organizing the September 30 Movement and even suggested that Washington's goal was to sew confusion in Indonesia in preparation for an attack by counterrevolutionary forces from Singapore.[77] All of this seemed to be part of a concerted effort, as Green put it, to "drown internal disagreements in [a] bigger international campaign" against the West, and it even seemed possible for a time that Sukarno would try to demonstrate his power by staging a conference of Third World governments that had backed him in the past.[78] The bigger risk detected by U.S. policymakers, though, was the possibility that the PKI might survive the repression unleashed in early October and stage a comeback. Green speculated on October 19 that two such scenarios remained possible. Sukarno might be able to establish a "new-style PKI" more closely associated with Moscow than Beijing. Far worse, the party might adopt a "violent anti-government guerrilla warfare strategy," a development that might forge even tighter bonds between China and the Indonesian communists than in the past.[79]

How should the United States respond to such a tenuous situation? The Johnson administration saw much promise in the sudden reversal of the PKI's fortunes but also recognized dangers in trying to do too much, too quickly to bolster the army. Rusk expressed the split-the-difference mood in mid-October. In a missive to the Jakarta embassy, he asserted that the time might come when the United States would give the generals clear indications of its support. Accordingly, the State Department and other bureaucracies began planning behind the scenes for the resumption of large-scale military and economic aid when the right moment arrived. Yet Rusk mostly emphasized the need for caution. Too much overt enthusiasm for the army's actions risked playing into Sukarno's hands by suggesting a desire in Washington to meddle in Indonesia's internal affairs. Washington officials appreciated the powerful anti-Western opinion still circulating in Indonesia and feared weakening the army by embracing it too tightly.[80] Happily, contended Ball, the United States could rest assured that the Indonesian command had no urgent needs and knew it could rely on the United States if any developed. Years of low-key military-to-military cooperation, wrote Ball, "should have established clearly in the minds [of] Army leaders that [the] U.S. stands behind them if they should need help."[81]

Anxiety about public displays of support left open, however, the possibility of covert assistance for the army. For some Americans, even this form of aid was distinctly unappealing. When army general Sukendro, operating as Suharto's liaison to the U.S. embassy, inquired at the end of October about the possibility of getting medical supplies, communications gear, rice, and small arms from the United States, one CIA study urged rejecting the idea, at least for the time being. Skeptical agency analysts invoked uncertainties about both the army's long-range plans and the uses to which the army would put American assistance in the near term.[82] But the dominant line of thinking saw both immediate and long-term value in showing quiet support for the generals, and Washington gradually extended various types of clandestine help, the first tenuous steps toward partnership with General Suharto. In fact, small amounts of covert aid started to flow even before Washington seriously considered the whole question. Besides passing along lists of communist suspects prepared in the American embassy, U.S. operatives joined British colleagues to back the Indonesian army via an increasingly elaborate propaganda program headquartered in Singapore. This endeavor entailed radio broadcasts into Indonesia as well as efforts to feed favorable information to Singapore-based journalists reporting on Indonesian affairs.[83]

The first decision in favor of material aid came on November 4, when the administration's 303 Committee—the interagency body that reviewed proposed intelligence operations—approved medical equipment requested by the army. State Department and CIA officials agreed that the low-cost gesture seemed to offer Washington a way to "get in on the ground floor" with the new contenders for power in Jakarta, while the ostensibly humanitarian flavor of the assistance would enable the United States to dodge serious criticism if it was discovered.[84] Other decisions followed soon thereafter. Although the precise details of U.S. assistance remain difficult to reconstruct on the basis of available evidence, the Johnson administration, acting through the CIA station in Bangkok, appears to have provided small arms to support the army's operations.[85] More certain is the decision in December to satisfy the army's request for communications equipment once the CIA had settled on methods of delivery that would reliably disguise the U.S. government's role.[86] Around the same time, the administration also approved secret funding for the KAP-Gestapu, a civilian organization that Ambassador Green judged "highly successful" in abetting the army's anti-PKI program.[87] For all these reasons, it is impossible to dispute historian Bradley Simpson's assertion that the Johnson administration became a "direct and willing accomplice" in the mass killings that played out in late 1965 and early 1966.[88]

Covert assistance undoubtedly bolstered the army's anticommunist campaign, and the channels of communication established between Washington and Suharto stoked confidence on both sides that they could collaborate effectively. Limited aid to suppress the PKI did not mean, though, that the United States was prepared to resume the overt large-scale assistance programs that Washington had carried out with Jakarta in earlier years. Without question, U.S. officials, almost from the moment they first learned of the September 30 Movement and the countercoup, had been studying Indonesia's economic crisis and planning for the resumption of economic, food, and military programs. Yet numerous obstacles stood in the way of decisions. For one, the status of American investments in Indonesia, particularly in the petroleum sector, remained unclear. Additionally, tensions between the army and Sukarno made it impossible to know who spoke on behalf of the legally constituted government and whether aid would be used effectively. More generally, the army's basic political orientation remained murky, making it difficult to be certain of Indonesia's likely approach to the Konfrontasi, the communist powers, foreign investment, the terms of the country's reintegration into the international economic order, the war in Vietnam, and the Cold War more generally.

The army's obvious hostility to the PKI was, of course, gratifying, and there were other encouraging signs, including the army's quiet efforts to place officers in key positions throughout the government bureaucracy and its willingness to compensate Washington for damage to U.S. property during the mass demonstrations of earlier months.[89] But much else remained to be settled. Rusk, for one, was eager to ensure that the United States did not give aid too quickly and rejected the Indonesian army's suggestion that Washington expand its clandestine program by providing emergency deliveries of food and textiles. Doing so would, Rusk worried, not only compromise decision-making procedures in the United States but also squander the leverage that Washington possessed to encourage political concession from Jakarta in return for U.S. aid. If Washington misplayed its hand, asserted Rusk, "[the] Indonesian army and other elements friendly to us could be led to believe they can count on us whatever their posture on Viet-Nam, Malaysia and other issues important to us."[90] If the Johnson administration had resisted the temptation to insist on political concessions in exchange for the aid it had secretly provided in late 1965, it would clearly follow a different path in connection with new types of assistance that might ultimately flow in large quantities.

Only in March 1966 did a dramatic seesaw of events in Indonesia significantly alter Washington's outlook on the shape of U.S.-Indonesian relations over the long run. During the first several weeks of the new year, American pessimism grew as Sukarno seemed to mount a political comeback. Apparently emboldened by the army's unwillingness to challenge him directly, he expelled American journalists, reorganized the nation's military command system, and gave vitriolic speeches to condemn his critics and rally sympathetic Indonesians behind his leadership. These efforts culminated on February 21, when Sukarno announced his decision to evict General Nasution and seven other pro-army members of his cabinet. In Washington, Johnson administration officials struggled to agree on a response to Sukarno's bid for power. Komer, whose sensitivity to the outlooks of Indonesian leaders now morphed into relatively high respect for the generals, advocated trying to strengthen the army's hand by granting its request for covert delivery of rice and cloth, but President Johnson was apparently stymied by indecision and left it up to Ambassador Green to decide on aid questions as the situation evolved.[91] For his part, Green advised keeping U.S. options open during what he expected to be a "protracted" struggle between the army and Sukarno that could go either way.[92]

Green turned out to be wrong. Acting far more boldly than Americans anticipated, Suharto and his allies moved to reverse Sukarno's gains. The army mobilized the large student movement that it had nurtured over several months to support its program and took steps to undermine Sukarno through deliberate damage to the nation's economy. On March 11, amid mounting chaos, Suharto manipulated Sukarno into signing a landmark document later dubbed the Supersemar, which gave the general authority to restore order. Although Sukarno remained the nation's figurehead president, the document effectively consolidated executive power in Suharto's hands.[93] Within days, Suharto had banned the PKI—mostly a formality since little of its infrastructure remained—and arrested several Sukarno-appointed cabinet members who had refused to resign. At last, the CIA advised LBJ, the generals were going "their own way."[94]

No matter where they had stood in bureaucratic disputes in earlier times, American officials recognized that a major turning point was at hand. "It is hard to overestimate the potential significance of the army's apparent victory over Sukarno," exulted Komer, who saw the development as part of a "fortuitous windfall" that included a nearly simultaneous U.S.-backed coup in Ghana.[95] Friendly military officers now led two Third World nations that had recently seemed headed into the communist fold. The CIA similarly saw broad significance in Indonesian events, describing Suharto's victory as a "debacle" for China's international ambitions. "Indonesia can no longer front for the Chinese in the international arena or run interference at international gatherings," noted one agency study, adding that the PKI's destruction "may be giving Communists elsewhere second thoughts about too close identification with Peking."[96] In Jakarta, the newly empowered generals, after many weeks of waffling, seemed inclined to move toward the West on a variety of matters. Whether they did so more out of genuine pro-Western sympathies or due to recognition that significant concessions would be required in order to obtain U.S. and other Western assistance, Washington celebrated indications over the following weeks that Suharto intended to wind down the Konfrontasi, to respect American investments in Indonesia, and to take an increasingly moderate view of U.S. policy in Vietnam. The tie to China had, it seemed, been definitively broken. Green reported to Washington after a lengthy meeting with Suharto at the end of May that the general repeatedly referred to China as "the enemy."[97]

American satisfaction soared still higher when U.S. officials considered the relationship to the war in Vietnam, the administration's highest foreign policy priority in the spring of 1966. Having long feared that the collapse of South Vietnam would lead to a "domino" effect across the region, they readily viewed the evisceration of communism in Southeast Asia's biggest and most resource-rich nation as validation of the increasingly costly and controversial war in Indochina. With the benefit of hindsight, it is reasonable to ask why Indonesia's abrupt turn did not encourage Washington to deescalate the frustrating war effort to the north. After all, one of the key rationales for fighting in Vietnam—to secure Indonesia's place in the Western orbit—had been largely accomplished.[98] In fact, however, American officials were far more likely to see the connection between Indonesia and Vietnam in precisely the opposite way: the military commitment in Indochina seemed to have created conditions for virtuous developments in adjacent territories. Events in Indonesia, in short, gave U.S. leaders renewed confidence that the war in Vietnam was achieving something important even if military victory remained elusive.

The U.S. ambassador in Saigon, Henry Cabot Lodge, was one of the first to strike the theme, telling NSC members that the destruction of Indonesian communism was "a direct result of our having taken a firm stand in Vietnam."[99] The idea soon found its way into a lengthy State Department assessment of Southeast Asia. While denying that the United States had played any "direct part" in provoking the army to act in Indonesia, the paper asserted that U.S. escalation in Vietnam had "unquestionably" bolstered "the courage of the anti-Communist leaders."[100] In fact, a CIA study concluded in May 1966 that there was no such link. "We have searched in vain for evidence that the US display of determination in Vietnam directly influenced the outcome of the

Indonesian crisis in any significant way," agency analysts concluded. Rather, they contended, change in Indonesia "evolved purely from a complex and long-standing domestic political situation."[101] Revealingly, however, the CIA's conclusions made little apparent difference for U.S. officials eager for good news in Southeast Asia. Over the remainder of the Johnson administration, various officials, including ultimately the president himself, invoked Indonesia as evidence that the U.S. military commitment was bringing positive results.[102] For an administration increasingly consumed with the war, there could be no better reason to celebrate Indonesia's political turn or to work to ensure the country's reorientation was permanent.

## "A Controlled Experiment in Modernization"

A remarkable change in the tenor of U.S. decision making toward Indonesia occurred following the consolidation of power in Suharto's hands. Whereas the Johnson administration had previously fretted over tiny adjustments in the relationship between the army and Sukarno and meticulously tracked the status of the PKI, it now turned its attention to the economic crisis confronting Indonesia. The desire to secure American investments in Indonesia—a persistent concern for years, if not a decisive driver of U.S. choices—no doubt encouraged this shift. So too did the presumed connection, characteristic of U.S. thinking about numerous parts of the world during the Cold War, between political stability and economic development. Only by addressing underlying economic problems and setting Indonesia on a path toward sustained development could the West secure the political gains of 1965 and 1966 and enmesh the country into the U.S.-led international order. But the Johnson administration's aspirations for Indonesia ran higher than mere stability within Western-dominated political and economic structures. In the final two and a half years of LBJ's presidency, Suharto's government emerged as precisely the sort of regime that appealed powerfully to Johnson and his advisers at a time when so much seemed to be going against the United States. Indonesia might become nothing short of a "showcase" for the rest of the Third World, Johnson declared in August 1967.[103]

Administration officials had no doubt of the new government's authoritarian character. Suharto's regime had little patience for the "disorder of free political exchange" and "no major commitment to democratic freedoms as we know them," asserted a State Department paper handed to President Johnson in August 1966.[104] Nor did American officials hold any misconceptions about the brutality with which the very political forces now running the country had eradicated the PKI. Abundant evidence makes clear that U.S. officials were well informed about what one retrospective study called the "wholesale killings" perpetrated by the army and its allies.[105] But it required no big leap for Americans to take a positive view of Suharto and the New Order that he promised. For one thing, Americans assured themselves—disregarding the Indonesian army's vast superiority in weaponry—that a communist takeover would have been "just as bloody," as one State Department study put it.[106] Mostly, though, American acquiescence flowed from confidence that the army, though benefitting from the veneer of support from sympathetic political parties and prominent civilian politicians, was the only institution capable of imposing the discipline and order necessary to rescue the nation from economic collapse. Indeed, U.S. expectations for the army exceeded even those of the army itself. While Suharto sketched plans for elections no later than July 1968, Americans put little stock in the idea and anticipated, as Marshall Green put it, "working with an army controlled government" for years to come. "There appears to be no workable alternative short of outright military dictatorship," Green added.[107] But American policymakers hardly regretted the prospect of working with such a regime, just as they readily came to terms with the retreat from democracy in Brazil. In August 1966, CIA director Richard Helms spoke for the administration in praising the new Indonesian leadership as "the best in years."[108]

For Marshall Green, Walt Rostow, and other U.S. officials who dominated Indonesian affairs over the remainder of the Johnson presidency, one of the characteristics that made Suharto so appealing was his deference to technocrats whose ostensibly apolitical expertise seemed well suited to Indonesia's massive economic problems. Green voiced this view in July 1966 when he heralded the appointment of a new cabinet "dominated by capable technicians."[109] A year later, a State Department study for the NSC welcomed the rise of a "new post-revolutionary generation" of Indonesians relatively uninterested in the "slogans and ideology" of the Sukarno period. Instead, asserted the study, "pragmatism, rationalism, and performance have become the new watchwords."[110] No development reflected this trend in the minds of approving Americans so much as Suharto's reliance on a team of Western-educated economists who worked in advisory roles behind the scenes. While Americans grumbled that Suharto, for all his positive attributes, kept his own counsel and had unfortunate qualities of a "Javanese mystic," they had easy rapport with technocrats such as Widjojo Nitisastro, the dean of the Faculty of Economics at the University of Indonesia, and other economists later known as the "Berkeley mafia" in recognition of their graduate or postgraduate training at the University of California.[111] These "scholar-advisers," as the *New York Times* called them, moved easily among both senior Indonesian army commanders and U.S. embassy staff in Jakarta.[112] The American embrace became still warmer in June 1967, when Widjojo visited Washington. After the economist described reforms under way in Indonesia, Representative Peter Frelinghuysen, a Republican from New Jersey, joked that he would like to see Widjojo on the GOP presidential ticket. Congressman John Buchanan, a Republican from Alabama, suggested turning the Vietnam problem over to the Indonesians since they "had handled their own Communist problem with such vigor."[113]

The economists proposed reform measures tailor-made to appeal to the Johnson administration. When the reformers gained authority under Suharto, noted one State Department paper, Indonesia faced "a degree of economic collapse unparalleled for a major nation in modern times."[114] In fact, Americans readily diagnosed an interlocking array of problems similar to the situations they observed in Brazil, India, and numerous other Third World nations: out-of-control inflation, massive indebtedness, excessive public spending, shortages of food and basic consumer goods, poor transportation infrastructure, lack of foreign exchange, hostility to foreign investment, and high levels of corruption. The Indonesian technocrats earned American favor by promising the mix of remedies that Washington routinely prescribed in such conditions, including broad spending cuts, controls on credit, anticorruption measures, debt rescheduling, and reassurance of foreign investors. Suharto's evident support for austerity and the regime's insulation from public pressures suggested that conditions were optimal for a broad program of top-down reform that Marshall Green, writing in 1968, approvingly called a "controlled experiment in modernization."[115]

Just as promising to the Johnson administration were mounting indications during 1966 of Suharto's determination to reorient Indonesian foreign policy. Crucial to this process was Adam Malik, whose appointment as foreign minister in March 1966 did as much as anything to affirm Indonesia's movement toward the West. Once a close associate of Sukarno's, Malik had taken a strong anti-PKI position earlier in the decade and emerged by the end of 1964 as a key partner for Washington. As a CIA asset (the "highest-ranking Indonesian we ever recruited," one agency operative later boasted), Malik appears to have played a vital role in establishing clandestine channels of communication between the army and the U.S. embassy in the fall of 1965.[116] As foreign minister, Malik gained a reputation in American minds similar to that of Widjojo and the other economists: a highly intelligent pragmatist who enjoyed Suharto's confidence. American officials watched approvingly as Malik accelerated pro-Western trends on multiple fronts. After conceding that Britain could station troops in Singapore and abandoning long-standing insistence on a referendum to settle the status of the Borneo territories, Indonesian negotiators reached a deal with Malaysian counterparts in August 1966 to end the Konfrontasi once and for all.[117] Malik also led Indonesia back into the United Nations and restored ties to the International Monetary Fund and the World Bank.

U.S. observers understood that the new Indonesian regime would go only so far in distancing itself from the Third World movement that Sukarno had sought so energetically to lead. Once it had rejoined the United Nations, cautioned the State Department, Indonesia would "undoubtedly resume its position as one of the more militant [members] of the Asian-African bloc" and would surely oppose Washington on many issues.[118] Yet Americans saw reason to believe that this posture owed as much to the army's keen awareness of strong nationalist currents running through Indonesian society as to any genuine conviction. Even in the worst case—an assiduously non-aligned Indonesia with ties to the Soviet Union—the nation would still serve U.S. interests by serving as a "counterweight" to China.[119] As time passed, however, Americans detected welcome signs that Indonesia's international outlook was continuing to evolve. In February 1967, the CIA described Indonesia's basic international posture as "Western-leaning non-alignment" that entailed "near-total disinterest" in Latin America, Africa, or the Middle East, a remarkable abandonment of Sukarno's global aspirations. Within its own area, meanwhile, Indonesia seemed increasingly inclined to cooperate and even to play a leading role in establishing a regional grouping bound to have an anticommunist coloration, a trend that resulted in the establishment of the Association of Southeast Asian Nations (ASEAN) in August 1967.[120]

The latter transformation of Indonesian foreign policy was accompanied by shifting attitudes about the Vietnam War that American policymakers tracked with growing satisfaction. During its monthslong standoff with Sukarno in late 1965 and early 1966, the army had mostly kept quiet about the war, no doubt appreciating that the Indonesian president and the PKI had succeeded in making Vietnam a focus of popular anti-Americanism. Suharto and other officers may also have sincerely believed what they, like many Indian leaders, told U.S. interlocutors in private: that escalation in Vietnam was doing more to generate a Chinese threat in Southeast Asia than to combat it. As anti-Americanism receded, however, U.S. officials detected welcome changes, particularly on the part of Malik. The foreign minister told Vice President Humphrey in September 1966 that the American effort in Vietnam had "directly influenced" the course of events in Indonesia—an assertion no doubt deeply gratifying to Humphrey, who thereafter repeatedly emphasized the ways in which the U.S. stand in Vietnam had emboldened pro-American forces elsewhere in the region.[121] A year later, Malik went even further, voicing approval of U.S. policy and urging Washington to "keep [the] heat on Hanoi."[122] So far had Indonesian attitudes evolved, in fact, that General Earl "Bus" Wheeler, the chairman of the Joint Chiefs of Staff, saw fit in the summer of 1967 to speculate about the possibility of an Indonesian troop commitment. Unsurprisingly, he immediately dismissed the idea as far-fetched.[123] Yet the fact that he raised the prospect at all indicated changes unimaginable two years earlier. Suharto's government confined itself in 1966 and 1967 to a few low-key efforts to use its channels to North Vietnam to promote negotiations.[124]

All these favorable trends—the regime's anticommunism, its seriousness about economic reforms, and the changes it wrought to Indonesian foreign policy—combined to persuade the Johnson administration to resume large-scale aid. The myriad programs that developed over the remainder of the Johnson presidency cemented the U.S. relationship with Suharto's regime and reflected the value U.S. leaders placed on a nation with an obvious capacity to exert influence throughout its region. To be sure, Washington opened the door to aid slowly. One reason was the administration's emphasis on expanded foreign investment as the preferred method of bolstering Indonesia's economy. Another reason was the meticulousness with which Rusk insisted on using the prospect of U.S. aid to shape Suharto's decisions and monitoring the new regime's evolution. With Komer departing to his new Vietnam responsibilities, no one was left to argue for opening ties first and worrying about performance later. A third reason for the slow ramp-up of U.S. aid was lingering concern about putting Suharto and his advisers in a difficult political position with an Indonesian public accustomed to hearing that the United States was the epitome of Western imperialism. Only at the end of March 1966 did Foreign Minister Malik believe that it had become "politically possible" to receive even emergency food aid from the United States.[125] As American aid flowed in significant quantities two years later, Marshall Green still warned that Washington might trigger "long acting rejection devices" within Indonesian society if it had too high a profile or seemed to be seeking "Americanization" of the nation.[126] But perhaps the most important reason for American caution about reopening aid was a pervasive sense within the Johnson administration that American resources were tightly limited, especially because of the costly war in Vietnam and growing congressional skepticism about foreign aid.

Still, American aid flowed in amounts impressive enough to stir concern in London that Washington was cozying up to the new Indonesian regime too quickly.[127] The first step came, predictably enough, in March 1966, just after Suharto's consolidation of power and appointment of a new cabinet led by a triumvirate of himself, Malik, and the Sultan of Yogyakarta, who took charge of economic policy. Warmly endorsing these steps, Ambassador Green in Jakarta and Secretary Rusk in Washington, abandoning their previous caution, endorsed Malik's request for an emergency sale of rice. Just as significantly, Congress quickly backed the scheme, which entailed delivery of fifty thousand tons under Washington's PL-480 food aid program. NSC aide Donald Ropa called it a "turning point on the road back to cooperative relations."[128] Washington approved the sale of seventy-five thousand bales of cotton a few weeks later, and in September the Johnson administration welcomed Malik to Washington by offering to sell large amounts of food and textiles on favorable terms. An even more significant moment had come in August, when LBJ agreed to authorize the resumption of bilateral economic assistance, bypassing congressional restrictions by declaring aid for Indonesia to be in the national interest. In the short term, the administration aimed to provide raw materials and spare parts for Indonesian industry, to involve Indonesia in regional economic development projects, and to resume training programs for Indonesian students in American universities.[129]

Concerns about declining U.S. capabilities meant, however, that the Johnson administration placed heavy emphasis on multilateral solutions to Indonesia's problems. The impulse to play what one administration study called a "supporting rather than a central role" in aiding Indonesia manifested itself in numerous ways.[130] In the early months following the countercoup, Americans watched with satisfaction as other anticommunist nations—especially Japan but also West Germany, Australia, and Britain—provided emergency aid, including foreign exchange credits.[131] Administration officials also attached vital importance to Indonesia's readmission to the IMF and World Bank and welcomed IMF efforts to study Indonesia's economic needs even as Jakarta's application awaited a final decision in the summer of 1966. Similar enthusiasm for multilateralism underlay the administration's deep involvement in the work of an informal grouping of creditors and potential donor nations—the "Aid to Indonesia Club," the State Department called it—that held its first meetings around the same time.[132] By the end of 1966, the outlines of the bargain between Indonesia's creditors and the Suharto regime had become clear: the international community would reschedule Indonesian debts and extend substantial multilateral aid in return for economic austerity and new laws on foreign investment that not only abolished Sukarno-era restrictions but opened the country as never before to foreign companies.

The documentary record of U.S.-Indonesian interactions in 1967 and 1968 is riddled with anxiety among both U.S. and Indonesian leaders about Washington's failure to do as much as it might have to support this program. Suharto and other Indonesian leaders looked to Washington for far more assistance, both economic and military, than the Johnson administration supplied and made their disappointment clear on many occasions. On the American side, Ambassador Green and Vice President Humphrey in particular urged that the United States do more to support such a valuable emerging ally. With the benefit of hindsight, however, American activism and largesse at a time of expanding global demands and tightening domestic constraints stand out as the dominant patterns. The scale of U.S. involvement began to become clear in the first half of 1967. Suharto's ouster of Sukarno from the presidency in

March, the final step in the eighteen-month coup that had begun on October 30, 1965, no doubt affirmed Indonesia's growing reliability, but just as important was the ripening of plans among donor nations to build on the emergency measures taken in 1966 by embracing a larger and more concerted program. The United States took a leading role within the newly formalized nine-nation donor's "consortium" (formally the Inter-Governmental Group on Indonesia), establishing the principle that Washington would provide one-third of the total package, with Japan and Western European nations making up the rest.

The goal was to offer aid that would appear "liberal . . . but not disproportionately large" in order to ensure that Indonesia and other donors did their part, asserted guidance from the Agency for International Development.[133] This scheme entailed U.S. commitments of food and other aid totaling $85 million in 1967.[134] For 1968, Washington applied the same formula in agreeing to provide $110 million of the total international commitment, but Johnson's approval of an emergency $50 million sale of wheat and shortfalls in European contributions brought the U.S. share to 46 percent.[135] A few weeks before leaving office, administration officials grudgingly accepted that Washington, subject to congressional approval, would again have to promise close to half of Indonesia's needs in 1969 in order to reach any deal through the consortium.[136] Thus did LBJ boost U.S. assistance for Indonesia at a moment when he was cutting foreign aid to most of the rest of the world.[137]

Americans were more cautious about military assistance. Indonesian forces were clearly capable of managing any conceivable internal or external military threat to the new regime. If anything, in fact, the Indonesian military was far larger—some three hundred thousand men in uniform—and more expensive than it needed to be. As in the cases of Brazil, India, and Iran, U.S. officials worried that expansion of a force that was already the largest in Southeast Asia would divert scarce resources from economic development and might empower the generals to claim too much authority. Ambassador Green warned of "creeping militarism" in the fall of 1967 even as he welcomed a 45-percent cut in Indonesian military spending.[138] Americans possibly hoped that contraction of the Indonesian military would lessen its dependence on the Soviet Union, long Indonesia's most important military supplier, though Washington evinced surprisingly little concern about Moscow's dominant position or the possibility that it would continue into the future. As in India, Americans may have concluded that Soviet military aid was a tolerable way of lightening the burden on Washington at a time when the United States and the Soviet Union shared anti-Chinese objectives throughout Asia.

Other considerations, however, dictated that the Johnson administration take seriously the Suharto regime's requests for expanded military aid.

American officials readily accepted that the army would dominate Indonesian politics for years to come and that cultivating military commanders, above all Suharto himself, was a high priority. For evidence of the huge political payoff that could flow from military assistance, Robert McNamara pointed to the collaboration that had quickly emerged in the fall of 1965 between Washington and the Indonesian officers around Suharto, many of whom had participated in U.S. training programs.[139] Supporters of military assistance to Indonesia also pointed to another potential political benefit. By supporting military "civil action" programs aimed at bringing economic modernization to the Indonesian countryside, Washington could help put an otherwise underutilized force to work bolstering the long-term social and economic stability on which U.S. interests seemed to depend. For Rostow and other U.S. officials convinced that Third World militaries were especially well positioned to facilitate economic modernity, the Indonesian army was tailor-made for the country's precarious economic situation. The army not only exuded professionalism but also constituted the only institution capable of bridging the nation's ethnic, class, and religious cleavages and bypassing the nation's patchwork of local authorities to implement the New Order.[140]

Acting on this logic, the Johnson administration took the plunge into the military arena in the fall of 1966, endorsing $6 million in grants to fund renewed officer-training programs, support for civic action, and deliveries of spare parts and other noncombat equipment. Under an agreement with Jakarta, the money was earmarked strictly to support "a program of civil action . . . helpful to the economic and social development of Indonesia." A year later, the Pentagon judged the program a success and urged renewal for 1968. As before, urged Assistant Secretary of Defense Charles Bohlen, the United States had to maintain a "clear distinction" between desirable development programs "of direct and immediate benefit to the civilian population" and the Indonesian military's other preoccupations: gaining access to Western military hardware and mounting operations to suppress intermittent regional uprisings across the vast multiethnic archipelago. The former was no more appealing than it had been in 1966 and 1967. Involvement in the latter, meanwhile, seemed only to risk embarrassing the United States politically while diverting resources from higher priorities. In any case, contended Bohlen, well-supplied Indonesian armed forces hardly needed help with upholding the central government's authority given their "23 years of experience in counterinsurgency operations" since Indonesian independence.[141] There was, in short, nothing to worry about when it came to the basic defense and unity of the Indonesian state.

By LBJ's final months in office, American worries were focused as single-mindedly as ever on the Indonesian economy. Would Suharto's government be able to improve the nation's standard of living and thereby bolster the legitimacy of the New Order over the long term? Doubts abounded even as foreign aid flowed, Indonesia studiously complied with austerity measures imposed by the IMF and World Bank, and Americans gained confidence in Suharto's ability to learn on the job. The U.S. embassy staff in Jakarta captured the fundamental problem in a study of the Indonesian economy during 1967, when, thanks to Sukarno's final eviction from power in March of that year, the New Order seemed to bear full responsibility for the nation's performance. "The average Indonesian had no more rice in the pot at the end of 1967 than at the beginning, and what he did have cost him considerably more," the embassy reported.[142] By the fall of 1968, the Agency for International Development noted some improvement in food production and distribution but expressed concern about persistent inflation, struggles to boost exports, and overpopulation. AID's overall judgment captured the U.S. mood as the Johnson administration expired. "There are both bulls and bears on the question of Indonesia's long-term development prospects," reported the agency, asserting that even a modest rate of change would be a "sizeable achievement" over the next decade.[143]

On the broader question of Indonesia's orientation in the Cold War, however, the administration had no such mixed feelings. LBJ and his aides viewed Indonesia as a success story. American satisfaction was sometimes expressed in comparative terms. Judged against the "incredible mess" that Sukarno had created, Suharto was, for all his flaws, an immense improvement.[144] But Americans praised him not just for halting the damaging trends of the Sukarno era but also for aligning Indonesia with Western economic and strategic interests in what appeared to be an enduring way. In the economic arena, the regime showed a long-term commitment to development in ways that meshed with American preferences as well as willingness to undertake "politically difficult" programs that imposed austerity and reopened Indonesia to foreign investment, noted AID.[145] So impressive was the Suharto regime's performance that Americans inside and outside the administration began to see Indonesia as a model to be emulated elsewhere in the Third World. Walt Rostow had expressed hope as early as the summer of 1966 that Indonesia might prove a testing ground for a "new pattern of multilateral help in Asia."[146] Two years later, a widening circle of observers expressed optimism about this possibility. The New Order increasingly epitomized "model rules of behavior for backward nations," editorialized *Fortune* magazine.[147]

In the geopolitical realm, meanwhile, the Johnson administration increasingly saw Indonesia as a regional power that could be depended upon to uphold Western interests even if it remained nominally non-aligned. By August 1968, Suharto spoke with more conviction than ever about the need for

Southeast Asian nations to band together against Chinese aggression. Deterring or resisting China depended on "stronger defenses and improved bilateral defense ties," Suharto told Ambassador Green in August 1968. Suharto's words were partly an appeal for increased U.S. military aid, and he urged that Washington focus its assistance not just on the "first line" of Asian nations close to China's borders—South Korea, Vietnam, Laos, Thailand, and Pakistan—but also the second line that included Indonesia, the Philippines, and Malaysia. Yet Suharto also showed a newly expansive vision of Indonesia's role in such a broad anti-Chinese collaboration. The general, while unwilling to join a regional defense pact, urged that the nations of Southeast Asia and the South Pacific should do more to "cooperate in their own defense" and indicated that Indonesia was prepared to commit combat forces to defend neighboring countries from Chinese aggression and even to send peacekeeping forces to Vietnam once the war there came to an end. He made no mention of an Indonesian contribution to the ongoing fighting, but he gratified Washington nonetheless by "fully" supporting the U.S. role throughout the region, including in Vietnam.[148]

Inspired by these positive developments, LBJ himself took unprecedented personal interest in Indonesia during his final months in the White House. Since 1964, various advisers had been trying to convince the president to establish a direct channel to Indonesian leaders—first Sukarno and then Suharto.[149] But Johnson had hung back, in the later period no doubt due to uncertainty about the path that Suharto would travel and wariness of encouraging unrealistic Indonesian expectations of aid. As the general solidified his control in 1967 and 1968, though, LBJ took a more active role with Indonesia, not least because of the influence the country might have in buttressing U.S. policy objectives globally and especially regionally in a period of mounting American frustrations. It was in this context that the president declared Indonesia a "showcase for all the world" and began corresponding with Suharto. Johnson's missives reverberated with praise for the new regime, deploying the same sort of language used in letters to General Castelo Branco and Mohammad Reza Pahlavi. "The courage with which you and your people faced those crucial days in October 1965 is still evident in your bold and farsighted efforts to reconstruct a shattered economy," wrote LBJ on one occasion.[150]

It was also in this period that LBJ increasingly invoked Indonesia in connection with the matter that most consumed him: Vietnam. The American commitment in Indochina, he averred in the summer of 1967, justified a generous U.S. approach in Indonesia. "Our sacrifices in Vietnam avail little if we do not take strong and swift steps to foster the growth and strength which the new Indonesia can achieve," he told his cabinet.[151] He probably also accepted the inverse logic that some of his aides had already made explicit: the success in Indonesia justified the massive expenditure of blood and treasure in Vietnam. For a presidency grappling with a grueling war and other setbacks that led LBJ to call 1968 a "continuous nightmare," it was surely an irresistible notion.[152] By the time LBJ published his memoir in 1971, he was ready to come straight out with it: the "brave men" who carried out the countercoup of 1965 and defeated communism in Indonesia, he wrote, would probably never have acted if the United States had not "taken a stand in Vietnam."[153] There was little evidence to support such a claim. But LBJ, like the advisers who surrounded him by the end of his administration, was in no mood to investigate too carefully.

# 8

# Southern Africa

## SETTLING FOR THE STATUS QUO

"RIP VAN WINKLE would never understand it," declared the *Chicago Tribune*'s lead editorial on December 22, 1965. Twenty years earlier, the United States had possessed few responsibilities in Africa. But now the United States was deeply embroiled on the continent, nowhere more so than in the area south of the Zambezi River. Washington's concern for the region had mounted steadily as tensions between white and Black Africans stoked fears of political violence and communist encroachment. The risks seemed to rise to new heights in November 1965, when the white community in Southern Rhodesia unilaterally declared the territory's independence from Britain in order to sidestep London's insistence on majority rule as a precondition for decolonization. The United States had condemned the move, imposed sanctions against the breakaway Rhodesian government, and begun airlifting oil to neighboring Zambia, whose economy was endangered by the sanctions. All of this would have been thoroughly perplexing to an American who had fallen asleep in 1945, contended the *Tribune*, which speculated about some of Rip's inevitable questions. "Rhodesia? Airlift? Where and what is Zambia? And what business is it of the United States?" The upshot of the editorial was hard to miss: the United States had become too deeply involved in obscure conflicts far from its shores. "How many more 'unlimited' commitments can the United States make, in its already overextended reach around the world?" asked the *Tribune*. "Is the United States the only fireman to be called when the brush fires begin?"[1]

Such questions suffused American thinking about foreign policy as the 1960s advanced and affected U.S. policymaking toward Africa in particular. To what extent should Washington assert itself in trying to manage deepening racial tensions in so remote a region as southern Africa? The Kennedy administration had aimed to raise the American profile throughout the continent but had offered no blueprint for U.S. policy toward the intertwined problems of South Africa, the Portuguese colonies of Angola and Mozambique, and Southern Rhodesia. The dilemma fell to LBJ and his advisers, who faced especially intense pressure to clarify U.S. policy toward southern Africa after Rhodesia's provocative move to solidify white rule. Predictably, opinions differed within the administration, as they did among the American public. Some voices urged Washington to take an active role in bringing about the region's transition to independence and majority rule. Others saw little to be gained by sticking out Washington's neck, preferring instead to allow London to take the lead in a part of the world where Britain had long wielded power, even if doing so meant leaving a nakedly racist regime in charge of Rhodesia. At the heart of the debate lay the question of how best to avoid a major crisis: through activism that entailed significant short-term risks or acceptance of an unsatisfactory status quo that at least enabled the United States to keep a low profile?

The debate was sometimes lively, but the overall trend of American decision making is unmistakable. Beset by the war in Vietnam and wary of new commitments anywhere else, the Johnson administration showed declining interest in a proactive policy, preferring instead to allow London to take the lead in applying pressure on the white regime in Salisbury (Harare), even after it became clear that such pressure was unlikely to bring any resolution. In this calculation, U.S. decision making paralleled Washington's choices in other parts of the world. Rejecting the activist sensibilities of officials like Robert Komer and "Soapy" Williams, the administration sought to lower risk and avoid new burdens abroad. But the southern African case stands apart in one respect. The administration faced particularly strong domestic pressures as it made policy toward Africa, where Black-white relations intersected with burgeoning controversies over race within the United States. In this way, a part of the world that held relatively little strategic value provoked more political controversy than did pivotal nations such as Iran and Indonesia. To be sure, the U.S. domestic context profoundly influenced American choices toward those places, but the connection was explicit and direct in the case of Africa. The administration's dedication to civil rights for African Americans sometimes fed into arguments in favor of U.S. activism to achieve racial justice in Africa, especially in the administration's early years. On the whole, however, the resistance to the administration's ambitious civil rights agenda after 1965 fed LBJ's aversion to an ambitious policy toward southern Africa. Facing criticism from both Congress and the American public, the administration doubled down on policies designed to reinforce the status quo, however unsatisfying it was.

## Preparing for Crisis

To what extent would U.S. foreign policy change under Lyndon Baines Johnson? Policymakers and commentators concerned with virtually every part of the globe asked the question in the months following JFK's assassination, but few areas provoked as much speculation as Africa. At a meeting with his staff in April 1964, Assistant Secretary of State Williams, the face of JFK's efforts to focus more U.S. attention on Africa, felt the need to rebut media reports that LBJ had little interest in the continent and had "down-graded" Williams's decision-making role. There was not a "shred of truth" in this idea, protested Williams with a vigor that perhaps betrayed his anxiety on the matter.[2] Other officials certainly saw things differently. A high-ranking Soviet diplomat insisted to an American counterpart in spring 1965, for example, that LBJ "did not have the same interest in the continent" as JFK had shown.[3] Anthony Lake, a State Department official who worked on African issues in the 1960s before rising to higher positions in later years, concurred, noting in a 1976 book that Johnson "did not want to be bothered with African issues."[4] Striking evidence lies in LBJ's distinct lack of interest in the Congo, a country that had consistently preoccupied JFK. Johnson attended only a few meetings devoted to that country and took an active role in none of them.[5]

At first, Johnson's relative inattention to Africa stirred little controversy or complaint. Although Robert F. Kennedy and other officials had grown concerned about the lack of clear U.S. decision making during 1963, the sense of urgency died down the following year. Policymaking toward the Congo lay largely in the hands of bureaucracies with a track record of coping with the problem, and no other crisis demanded attention at the highest levels. Meanwhile, electoral considerations discouraged bold moves in Africa. From the outset of LBJ's tenure in the White House, the president and his aides understood that developments there were intermeshed with U.S. domestic politics due to the rising salience of civil rights for African Americans. Administration officials derived satisfaction from evidence that passage of the 1964 Civil Rights Act had produced a wave of pro-U.S. sentiment throughout the continent, with even Egyptian leader Gamal Abdel Nasser lauding the bill at a meeting of the Organisation of African Unity (OAU).[6] As the election approached, however, U.S. officials showed caution about the possibility that policy choices in Africa might alienate whites, who could tip toward the Republican contender, Senator Barry Goldwater. The administration's calculations were especially evident in September and October 1964, when the South African government pressed Washington to approve sale of anti-submarine aircraft manufactured by the American firm Lockheed. Apparently wary of stoking criticism from right or left on a sensitive subject that might draw public notice, LBJ deferred any decision until after the election. (He ultimately rejected the sale.)[7]

Inattention to African affairs during LBJ's first months in the presidency owed something as well to a flurry of new studies and reports offering reassurance about the political situation on the continent. Unquestionably, U.S. officials consistently noted that racial tensions in southern Africa were worsening in a way likely to open the door for Soviet or Chinese meddling. At least for the moment, though, the threats seemed more potential than real. A CIA report circulated in early December 1964, almost exactly a year after LBJ's rise to the presidency, noted the absence of communist groups prepared to seize or wield power, making it almost impossible to imagine takeovers of any African nations.[8] Undersecretary of State W. Averell Harriman, LBJ's troubleshooter in the Third World, offered an even more upbeat appraisal of political conditions in Africa. The continent's transition to independence had been "remarkably smooth," Harriman asserted in a note to the president. Not a single nation had fallen to communism, while most were making "solid political and economic progress." In an obvious jab at colleagues prone to more alarmist views, he urged the administration to base its policy on a "firm foundation of fact."[9]

This benign view became harder to sustain, however, when 1964 gave way to 1965. Electoral considerations evaporated following Johnson's smashing political victory in November, and U.S. assessments of trends in Africa grew notably gloomier in the new year. Underlying differences within the U.S. bureaucracy came back into the open. McGeorge Bundy captured the changed mood in a March 1965 memorandum for the president that could hardly have clashed more directly with Harriman's rosy assessment in 1964. "U.S. prestige and influence on that African Continent have never been lower," asserted the national security adviser.[10] The CIA developed the point a month later in a survey of conditions in sub-Saharan Africa. Agency analysts predicted economic crises in a number of countries, creating fertile soil for communist advances. It remained unlikely that any nation would become a "full-fledged" part of the communist bloc, but the report anticipated new opportunities for the communist powers to build on the "substantial progress" they had already made in exerting influence. Many, if not most, African countries would move closer to the communist world as Moscow and Beijing, driven by their intense competition for influence in the Third World, provided higher levels of economic assistance; a few regimes "highly unfriendly" to the West seemed sure to emerge.[11] The CIA concluded that Africa offered nothing truly "essential" to U.S. security, but Bundy demonstrated his anxieties by itemizing major U.S. interests: access to military and space-tracking installations, "substantial" private American investments, and the cooperation of African nations in the United Nations.[12]

Trends seemed especially ominous in the southern part of the continent. Although communist inroads were least advanced in that region—only Tanzania and Congo-Brazzaville had established any significant relationship with Moscow—Western officials feared for the future. Four million whites, as one NSC report put it, were attempting to keep thirty-two million nonwhites in a state of "political, economic, and social subjugation," a situation containing "the seeds of a monumental race conflict" that the communist bloc was well positioned to exploit.[13] The spark seemed most likely to come in Southern Rhodesia. Negotiations between London and the white-dominated government in Salisbury aimed at reaching a formula for Rhodesian independence ground on with no end in sight. While Britain insisted on majority rule, Rhodesian authorities were determined to maintain constitutional arrangements that enabled 220,000 whites to maintain political and economic control over about four million Black Africans. Indeed, the problem grew more intractable in late 1964 and early 1965. First, the Labour Party prevailed in Britain's general election, ending thirteen years of Conservative rule and bringing to power a government certain to insist even more adamantly on the principle of majority rule. Then, in May 1965, the hardline Rhodesian Front won a sweeping victory of its own. At the party's head stood Prime Minister Ian Smith, a onetime Royal Air Force pilot whose commitment to white rule in his native Rhodesia surpassed even that of Winston Field, whom Smith and his allies had ousted a year earlier. No informed observer could doubt that chances for compromise were evaporating and that a unilateral assertion of Rhodesian independence was growing likely.

As Americans focused anew on the Rhodesian problem, they saw mounting dangers to U.S. interests. Broadly, of course, they feared that upheaval in Rhodesia would fuel racial tensions across the region, if not the continent. There were "great risks," asserted NSC aide Ulric "Rick" Haynes, that an acute crisis in Rhodesia would aggravate tensions in "potential trouble spots" such as South Africa, Angola, Mozambique, South West Africa, Zambia, and Malawi.[14] Meanwhile, the spectacle of white defiance in Rhodesia would tarnish the West in the eyes of all Black Africa, fuel radical nationalism globally, and invite communist influence. Especially frightening was the possibility that outraged African nations might defect from the British Commonwealth, thus weakening or destroying a bulwark of Western cooperation that helped lighten the global burden borne by Washington.

U.S. policymakers also worried that any effort to punish Rhodesia for declaring its independence would disrupt the economy of neighboring Zambia, one of the few Black-led African nations where American companies had extensive investments. Zambia possessed the world's largest-known reserves of copper and already produced 15 percent of supplies available to the United

States and its allies. American companies accounted for almost one-third of that output. The problem confronting the Johnson administration lay in the possibility that Western sanctions against Rhodesia following a declaration of independence would lead Salisbury to retaliate by cutting off coal and electricity supplies to Zambian mines and blocking Zambia from using railway lines along which the nation transported 95 percent of its exports. The effect would be rising copper prices on world markets as well as severe damage to American firms and the economy of Zambia, a nation generally friendly to the West.[15]

Amid mounting concern for the continent as a whole and Rhodesia in particular, U.S. policymakers focused anew on an old question: to what extent should the United States concentrate its energies and resources on Africa? LBJ's relative lack of interest in the continent, combined with mounting American commitments elsewhere in the world, strengthened the belief among some officials that the United States must rely mostly on the Europeans, an approach that Williams labeled the "leave-it-to-the-metropole" policy.[16] Predictably, such views predominated at the highest levels of the State Department and in bureaucracies that did not bear direct responsibility for Africa.[17] The United States had no interest in launching any sort of "crusade," Dean Rusk assured the South African ambassador to Washington.[18]

On the other side were those who urged that the United States deepen its involvement in Africa—in partnership with the Europeans if they were willing to act boldly and independently if the Europeans fell short. As in the Kennedy period, Williams made the case for activism most assertively. Noting that European nations were providing more than double the economic assistance coming from Washington, the ebullient assistant secretary told Congress in February 1965, "I do not want it said a decade from now that because of short-sightedness in 1965, the United States did not take the relatively modest steps that might have averted more serious troubles in Africa."[19] At the NSC, meanwhile, Bundy, Haynes, and Komer advocated that the president hew closer to JFK's approach by authorizing a two-week "friendship" tour of African capitals by either the vice president or secretary of state, engaging in increased "personal diplomacy" with African leaders visiting Washington, giving a "pep talk" to State Department personnel concerned with Africa, and delivering a high-profile speech rededicating the United States to African affairs. Too often, noted Haynes, U.S. statements on African affairs invoked positions taken by JFK, while few Africans identified LBJ "in his own right" with their interests.[20]

While this debate concerned U.S. policy toward the continent as a whole, it was especially intense with respect to Rhodesia. Some policymakers downplayed American interests and urged Washington to do no more than support British efforts—expected to be cautious and risk averse—to resolve it. Such aversion to activism was rooted partly in the belief that existing political arrangements in southern Africa, unjust though they might be, served key American interests and could not be quickly unraveled without causing serious damage. Above all, the Pentagon, Treasury Department, and NASA aimed to preserve U.S. cooperation with South Africa, a nation that would inevitably sympathize with white-led Rhodesia. For these institutions, international sanctions against Rhodesia seemed certain to fuel efforts within the United Nations to isolate and punish the regime in Pretoria. Trade sanctions against South Africa promised to worsen U.S. balance-of-payment problems and damage the flow of South African gold critical to the international economic system. Americans worried, too, that Pretoria might respond to sanctions against white southern Africa by closing down satellite-tracking stations on South African soil. Lisbon—another government likely to back a white-led Rhodesia—might deny access to vital bases in the Azores.[21]

In the State Department, skeptics about an active U.S. policy no doubt shared some of these concerns but viewed the Rhodesia problem more as the *Chicago Tribune* did in its Rip Van Winkel editorial—as a potential drain on American resources in a part of the world that did not, in the grand scheme of things, matter very much. Undersecretary of State George Ball captured the basic idea in October 1965, insisting that the administration respond to looming crisis in Rhodesia by saying to the British government, "You take the lead and we will follow to the extent we can; but we are not going to try to tell you how to do it."[22] For Ball, this approach carried multiple advantages. For one, it promised to soothe Britain's sensitivities about its prerogatives in a territory where it had long predominated. It also seemed the best way to minimize U.S. exposure to demands by Black African nations for bold Western action to overturn Rhodesia's independence, possibly by force, once Salisbury had broken from Britain.

Perhaps most important, keeping London in the lead would lower the risk of heavy burdens on U.S. resources—economic, military, or otherwise—at a time of mounting obligations around the world. In the best case, London would resolve the problem and end the crisis. More realistically, staying safely behind Britain promised to insulate the United States from a highly complicated problem that would likely defy solution no matter how much energy Prime Minister Harold Wilson's government brought to the task. Ball had been confident in the Conservative leaders who had governed Britain before 1964, but Wilson's cabinet was something different: an unpredictable government whose principled stand on white rule, combined with thin political support in Britain, made it unlikely to achieve any breakthroughs. Thus did a policy of backing London grow far less from enthusiasm about British leadership than from wariness about becoming dangerously overcommitted through a proactive

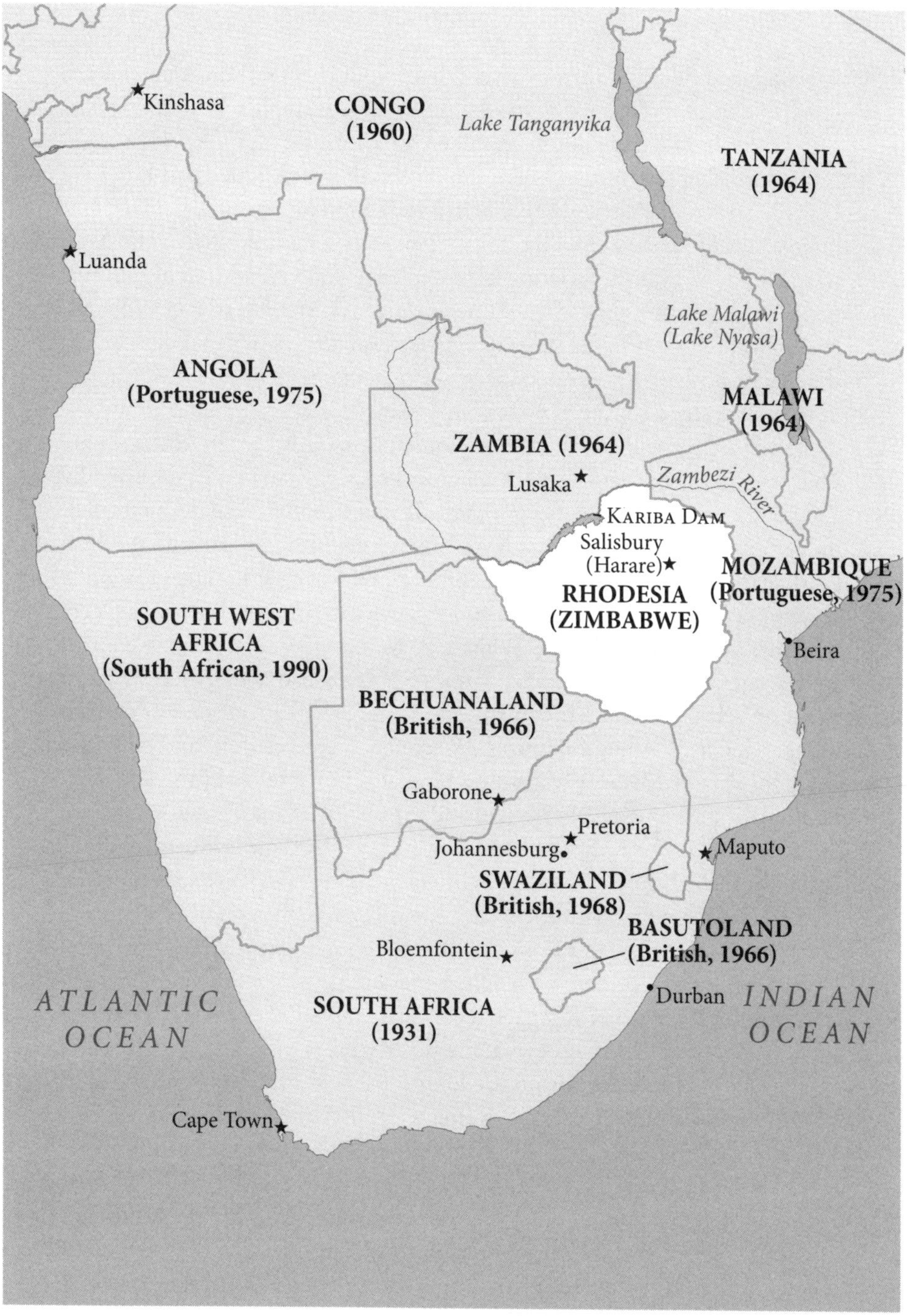


MAP 8.1. Rhodesia and surrounding territories around the time of the Unilateral Declaration of Independence. Dates of independence for each country are provided in parentheses. The nation exercising colonial authority is given for territories still under foreign control in 1965. Basutoland became Lesotho in 1966, and South West Africa became Namibia in 1990. Mapping Specialists, Ltd., Madison, WI.

approach and a desire to ensure that Britain would bear responsibility for the inevitable mess. Ball drove home the point by repeatedly insisting that U.S. support for Britain must not be mistaken for a "blank check."[23]

On the other side of the debate stood officials who worried that tying the United States to Britain would result in a weak policy that would damage U.S. interests in Africa and globally. They advocated instead proactive efforts to warn Rhodesia against declaring independence and preparation of punitive measures to be imposed if worse came to worst. Assistant Secretary Williams, backed by his deputy in the Bureau of African Affairs, J. Wayne Fredericks, led the charge. Both men possessed "deep personal commitments to the principle of majority rule in southern Africa," according to Anthony Lake.[24] But their views echoed throughout the U.S. diplomatic establishment in Africa, where officials—many of them committed globalists who had been appointed by Kennedy—focused on the danger that a Rhodesian unilateral declaration of independence (UDI) would radicalize Black regimes and damage Western prestige throughout the continent. This outlook was clear in June 1964 when Fredericks met with five U.S. ambassadors posted to African capitals. The men, who included JFK confidante William Attwood, now LBJ's ambassador to Kenya, concurred that U.S. policy toward Rhodesia had to be governed by its effect on relations with African nations. If the Smith government declared independence, Washington must immediately break relations and close the U.S. consulate in Salisbury "regardless of what action is taken by the UK."[25] In South Africa, meanwhile, U.S. ambassador Joseph C. Satterthwaite urged the State Department to authorize him to warn the Pretoria government, without reference to the British position, of vehement U.S. opposition to a Rhodesian declaration of independence.[26] At the NSC, Haynes, the son of Black immigrants from Barbados, and Komer thought in similar terms. They urged that Washington press London to recognize the seriousness of the looming crisis and consider a "*unilateral* approach" (Haynes's emphasis) to Salisbury to drive home U.S. hostility no matter what the British did.[27]

The sharp divergence within the Johnson administration was obvious to attentive observers such as J. S. F. Botha, a South African diplomat stationed in Washington. Views emanating from the "lower level" of the State Department clashed with attitudes at the "highest or ministerial level," observed Botha, who credited senior officials with recognizing "the value of a strong and ordering Western society" in southern Africa.[28] Still, conflict between these two perspectives remained relatively muted throughout 1964 and much of 1965. One reason was lingering hope throughout the U.S. bureaucracy that Britain might achieve a negotiated settlement that would head off the need for difficult choices by the Johnson administration. Another was satisfaction among most U.S. officials that Wilson's government was consistently demonstrating strong opposition to UDI, even if London did not yet seem to have a consistent negotiating strategy or clear idea of the punitive steps it would take in response to independence.

London's strong position meant that U.S. officials focused on African affairs could sometimes express hostility to Rhodesia without sparking rebuke from their bureaucratic opponents. In June 1965, Williams received the White House's blessing to announce an embargo on arms sales to Rhodesia, formalizing a policy that was already in effect. The administration also approved a series of public statements and diplomatic démarches condemning UDI and pledging full support of Britain. Some of these communications had a strikingly aggressive tone. In May 1965, for instance, the State Department instructed U.S. diplomats in Salisbury to convey U.S. "shock, regret and irritation at the inaccuracies, unrealistic tone, intemperate and undiplomatic phrasing and offensive lecturing" in a Rhodesian diplomatic note protesting Washington's refusal to sell military aircraft. The Smith government must have "no further illusions" about the U.S. attitude, the State Department insisted.[29] In Pretoria, meanwhile, Ambassador Satterthwaite felt sufficiently empowered by Washington's attitude to warn the South African government, a potentially important supporter of an independent Rhodesia, against any illusions that the deepening American preoccupation in Vietnam would deter Washington from strong action in southern Africa.[30]

Disagreements within the bureaucracy led to clashes on specific issues, however, highlighting the potential for a major clash over policy as circumstances evolved. One area of discord emerged in spring 1965, when China showed interest in helping Zambia reduce its economic dependence on Rhodesia by building a railroad line through Tanzania that would link Zambia to the sea. Williams and his allies in the Bureau of African Affairs feared that the scheme would be a major step toward Chinese penetration of southern Africa and insisted that Washington respond with a rail-building plan of its own to help Zambia export its copper. Although Williams admitted that a railroad would take years to construct and would therefore offer Zambia no early relief from Rhodesian economic warfare, he insisted that a quick U.S. counteroffer would be an "important part of whatever temporizing influence we can exert on the situation" in southern Africa.[31] Averell Harriman concurred and pressed the British government in May 1965 to team up on a joint U.S.-British construction plan. Other officials, however, opposed the effort as a monumental drain on U.S. resources (Komer estimated the cost at about $400 million) that Congress would never approve at a time of growing commitments in Vietnam. Moreover, the Chinese threat seemed manageable to some Americans. Rusk and Ball, backed by the president, regarded worries about Chinese activism in Africa as "nonsense," as Komer put it.[32] The Bureau of African Affairs had to settle for administration support of a feasibility study for highway improvements as an alternative to the rail line.[33]

Discord within the Johnson administration bubbled up far more vigorously in September and October 1965 as Rhodesia's declaration of independence became increasingly imminent. Unquestionably, advocates of a proactive U.S. policy watched with satisfaction as LBJ readily agreed to Prime Minister Wilson's requests that Washington back British policy by communicating its strong disapproval directly to Ian Smith. They largely shared Wilson's hope that U.S. influence might prove the "decisive factor" in leading Smith to back down and saw value in disabusing Salisbury of any lingering thought that the U.S. break from Britain in 1776 would make Washington sympathetic to the Rhodesian cause.[34] On October 29, Johnson dispatched a letter warning the Rhodesian government that the United States would not back down from its policy of "firm support for the position of the British Government."[35] But the Bureau of African Affairs and the NSC feared nonetheless that Washington was being too complacent in the face of crisis and wanted the administration to go much further by issuing a public condemnation of the UDI and specifying the sanctions that Washington had in mind. To Williams, there was little reason to believe that a private missive, even if sternly worded, would have much effect in Rhodesia. A public statement was, in Haynes's view, "our last remaining deterrent trump card." When Rusk backed Ball's refusal to authorize the public statement, the African Bureau appears to have tried a new tactic: a leak to the *St. Louis Post-Dispatch*. The day after Rusk's decision, the newspaper reported "deep division of sentiment" within the administration and called out Ball in particular for blocking a stronger U.S. policy on an issue of profound moral significance.[36]

Rusk and Ball's position discouraged Williams and the NSC staff, who feared that misleading statements by the government in Salisbury were creating a damaging public impression that Washington was inclined to tolerate UDI.[37] But their frustrations no doubt ran deeper than they expressed in connection with the controversy over the public declaration. Advocates of a stronger U.S. stance, dismayed by Britain's lack of specificity about the steps it would take following Rhodesian independence, proposed a range of proactive measures. With Rhodesia apparently "on the brink" of declaring its independence in mid-September, Komer and Haynes suggested a "unilateral approach" to Salisbury to drive home U.S. hostility to UDI. One possibility, they suggested, would be to send Harriman, whom the two officials regarded as an ally on the Rhodesia issue, to make the case.[38]

Two weeks later, Komer brought this idea to the president, suggesting that Washington send a "high-level delegation" to Salisbury to hold "full discussions" and call public attention to the U.S. position.[39] On October 8, Haynes tried again to spark urgent discussion of Rhodesia at the administration's highest levels, noting that the NSC and other arms of the bureaucracy were developing a range of possible responses to the UDI. The United States, he urged, must "preempt the field" with bold measure and thereby "stave off efforts to stir up more radical UN action." Only through strong action on the basis of its own principles, that is, could the United States channel the international response to UDI in a moderate, peaceful direction most likely to block communist inroads and secure Western interests. Among the initiatives under study in Washington were steps to safeguard the Zambian economy, impose sanctions on Rhodesia, and help Britain find alternative sources of tobacco and other goods that might cease to flow once economic sanctions had been imposed against Rhodesia.[40]

## UDI

The liberals' failure to generate support for U.S. activism became abundantly clear on November 11, 1965, when Prime Minister Ian Smith, touting his dedication to "justice, civilization and Christianity," finally proclaimed his nation's independence under a constitution that kept political and economic power in white hands.[41] Far from exuding the urgency and determination that Williams had hoped to inspire, the Johnson administration, apparently surprised by the precise timing of the UDI, responded with just the sort of caution that Ball had long advocated. Secretary Rusk told reporters only that the United States "deplored" the Rhodesian announcement and would recall its consul from Salisbury and terminate U.S. Information Agency programs in the country. Further sanctions would wait until "we see what Britain does," added Rusk, noting that Arthur Goldberg, the U.S. ambassador to the United Nations, would make a more complete statement of U.S. policy the next day. The secretary avowed that the administration was following the crisis with "deep concern," but the setting of his comments suggested that the president's attention was focused elsewhere. Rusk met with journalists on the front porch of LBJ's Texas ranch house during a break from high-level discussions focused on expanding military operations in Vietnam.[42]

In New York, Goldberg's promised declaration of U.S. policy heaped disapproval on Rhodesia. The ambassador threw U.S. support behind a Security Council resolution condemning the "illegal regime" in Salisbury and announced unilateral steps to punish Rhodesia going beyond the measures that Rusk had announced in the Texas Hill Country. The United States would, Goldberg specified, impose a comprehensive ban on arms shipments, suspend loans and credit guarantees, discourage Americans from traveling to Rhodesia, bar imports of Rhodesian sugar, and advise American firms against

FIGURE 8.2. Meeting at the Texas White House outside Austin, President Johnson (far right) consults with his top foreign policy aides on November 11, 1965, the day of Rhodesia's Unilateral Declaration of Independence. With his back to the camera is Defense Secretary Robert McNamara. To McNamara's left, moving clockwise around the room, are Secretary of State Dean Rusk, Undersecretary of State George Ball, and National Security Adviser McGeorge Bundy. LBJ Library photo by Frank Wolfe.

investing in the country.[43] In key respects, however, the announcement reflected the same caution that Rusk had demonstrated the day before. The ban on arms deliveries essentially reasserted a policy that the Johnson administration had followed for months, and there was little possibility of stopping a large shipment of sugar already underway from Rhodesia. The other measures held minor significance at best. Meanwhile, the Security Council resolution, crafted by London with U.S. input, stopped well short of demands by African governments for a blockade and military intervention against Rhodesia if punitive steps failed to achieve their objective. Neither the resolution nor Goldberg's statement of U.S. policy said anything about the use of force or the possibility of more meaningful economic sanctions. All in all, the administration clearly aimed, as it had for many months, to leave Rhodesia as much as possible to the British government, which set the tone for Washington by unveiling selective economic sanctions on November 11. Laying down an approach mimicked by the United States, these measures entailed bans on imports of Rhodesian export crops (sugar and tobacco, together accounting for about one-third of British imports from the territory), along with a ban on arms deliveries, suspension of Commonwealth trade preferences, and implementation of controls on currency exchanges.[44]

Prime Minister Wilson expressed confidence that these steps, perhaps supplemented by bans on imports of additional Rhodesian commodities, would achieve a "quick economic kill." That assertion was no doubt gratifying to U.S. decision makers who shared the president's preference to "give firm support to the British but not get out in front," as one official put it.[45] But Americans in the State Department's African Bureau and on the NSC staff had little confidence in either Wilson's promise or the cautious approach crafted at the Texas White House. Diplomatic reporting from Salisbury during the second half of November consistently noted that the Smith regime faced little internal opposition and could probably survive the effects of international economic sanctions for at least several months, largely due to economic support from Portugal and South Africa.[46] The State Department's Policy Planning Staff went further, speculating that sanctions might heighten the "unity and toughness" of the white Rhodesian population, making a negotiated solution less likely.[47]

Such a prolonged crisis could be disastrous for multiple reasons, warned proponents of stronger U.S. action. For one thing, mounting frustration among Black African governments might lead them to press harder, inside or outside of UN forums, for military action against the Smith regime, making a violent conflagration more likely. By the end of November, noted one U.S. report, Zambian leader Kenneth Kaunda already faced pressure to allow his territory to be used as a base from which military operations could be launched against Rhodesia.[48] In the diplomatic arena, meanwhile, several governments belonging to the OAU pledged to break diplomatic relations with Britain if the UDI had not been reversed by December 15, raising anew the specter of the Commonwealth's collapse. American fears also focused on the possibility that Rhodesia would fall into South Africa's "clutches" as economic sanctions pinched harder, thus expanding the "white redoubt" in southern Africa and further radicalizing racial tensions throughout the region.[49] No matter how hard Washington tried to avoid deep embroilment, British weakness seemed certain to leave the United States holding the bag, a possibility amplified on December 3 when Kaunda used a press conference to float the idea of requesting U.S. troops to help guard the crucial Kariba Dam on the Zambian-Rhodesian border.[50]

These considerations led advocates of an assertive U.S. policy to press their case anew in the weeks following UDI. At times, such officials focused on merely implementing the announced sanctions as stringently as possible. For instance, Goldberg and the African Bureau insisted that Washington refuse to allow the ship carrying the 1965 quota of Rhodesian sugar to dock in the United States. Allowing that cargo to be unloaded would, in Goldberg's view, raise questions in the Afro-Asian world about the sincerity of U.S. efforts to bring down the Smith regime.[51] But Goldberg and like-minded officials also entertained bolder steps going beyond implementation of the program already announced. On December 6, Robert Komer sent the president a memorandum laying out some possibilities. The goal, Komer wrote in a covering note to McGeorge Bundy, was to show LBJ that there was "more than one option" available to the United States. Komer acknowledged that no one wanted to bother the president with difficult decisions during his convalescence from gall bladder surgery back in September, the reason why LBJ was holed up at the Texas White House during this period. The NSC aide conceded, too, that the president probably wanted to stay "as far away from yet another mess as he can" at a time of critical decisions regarding Vietnam. Yet he also expressed concern that the State Department's "Seventh Floor"—a reference to Rusk and Ball—had never given Johnson the "whole picture" about Rhodesia, instead offering just "piecemeal tactical requests." Komer proposed to provide "the other side of the story" by pointing out the logic of U.S. activism.[52]

The memorandum to the president began by summarizing the stakes of the Rhodesia crisis. Komer allowed that the country was not very important to the United States in any tangible way and that Washington had enough problems "on its plate." But he hastened to add that Rhodesia was "critical" to Africans, who were watching anxiously to see whether the West lived up to its commitments to self-determination and racial justice. Much as Washington might want to leave the whole issue to London, the United States was already deeply implicated. And, advised Komer, it would become even more so as pressure mounted among Black Africans for the forceful overthrow of Smith's government. Given the almost certain failure of Wilson's strategy of political isolation and economic punishment, the United States would inevitably have to act at some point in order to head off intervention by the Soviet Union, China, or African forces sympathetic to Nasser's radical brand of Third World politics. The key question, of course, was what precisely the administration could do. Komer observed that tougher economic sanctions might help, as might the Wilson government's plan, announced on November 29, to dispatch British forces to Zambia in hopes of boosting Kaunda's confidence and discouraging him from accepting troops from other places. But Komer also proposed that the United States prod Britain to consider the use of force against Rhodesia and prepare its own military contribution, scenarios that had received little close attention up to that point due to pervasive hope that sanctions alone would do the trick.[53]

He acknowledged that a British-led military operation would be "highly painful" to Wilson, who had explicitly ruled out that step. Wilson's Labour Party held a small margin in Parliament and faced persistent criticism from Conservatives, who worried about British economic interests throughout southern Africa, blamed Wilson for mishandling negotiations with Smith, and staunchly opposed military action against "kith and kin" in white Africa. For the United States, though, Komer saw significant advantages to military action, whether a limited seizure of economic assets along the border with Zambia or a larger attack to overthrow Smith. For one thing, an early British-led operation would close off the possibility of military interventions led by Moscow, Beijing, or the OAU. For another, the cost of such an operation would, in Komer's view, be far lower than the cost of keeping Zambia's economy alive over an extended period. This consideration held particular appeal for the United States, asserted Komer, who speculated that the U.S. contribution to a military operation would be limited to an airlift of British troops into the region. Even if military action failed, he added, Washington and London would be in no worse shape than if they'd never attempted it since the worst Rhodesia could do to retaliate would be to cut economic links with Zambia, a step Salisbury was almost certain to take in any case. All of the biggest dangers lay in inactivity, concluded Komer, averring, "We can't stand aloof from the Rhodesia crisis—events won't let us."[54]

Komer's arguments had no appreciable impact on U.S. policy. In the first half of December, in fact, the contrary point of view largely prevailed in Washington. To be sure, administration officials met with executives of U.S. companies that imported Rhodesian goods—especially lithium, asbestos, and chrome—to explore the possibility of extending sanctions. Revealingly, however, U.S. officials pursued only voluntary restrictions in an effort to bring the overall reduction of American imports into line with the level achieved by Britain (an 80 percent cut to pre-UDI levels).[55] Indeed, the administration remained wedded to the principle of following the British lead. Even as U.S. officials studied the possibilities of supporting mandatory oil sanctions through the United Nations and participating in an airlift to keep the Zambian economy functioning, they closely coordinated their planning with British counterparts and cautioned London against unrealistic expectations of what the United States could provide. President Johnson made the point in a December 8 letter to Wilson, telling the British prime minister that the United States intended to provide its "utmost" support but "within the limits imposed on us by Vietnam."[56] Through the first half of December, Washington avoided new sanctions on Rhodesia and set aside just $600,000 to support British-led efforts to bolster the Zambian economy over the next two months. Rusk informed U.S. diplomats that the assistance was not "an open-ended undertaking" and that Zambia remained "a British concern."[57]

Johnson also made clear to both Wilson and his own bureaucracy that George Ball would be his point man on Rhodesia, a clear indication of his caution. The UDI did nothing to change Ball's sense that the Johnson administration should proceed warily in southern Africa since a proactive policy would put Washington on a slippery slope toward deep embroilment in a part of the world where the United States had few interests. In fact, the UDI and its immediate aftermath only affirmed Ball's sense that the Wilson government, facing conflicting pressures in southern Africa, had no coherent policy toward Rhodesia and was unlikely to provide strong leadership worthy of U.S. support. In this way, Ball's aversion to commitments in remote parts of the world and his particular doubts about the Labour government muted his usual affinity for European preferences. The United States, he believed, should back Britain but only distantly and with little expectation of success. More than any other U.S. official, Ball dragged his feet on sanctions by insisting that the administration lacked the legal authority and congressional support to comply with British requests for additional U.S. backing.[58] He also revealed his outlook on Rhodesia through his behavior in connection with the interagency "working group" that Johnson established immediately after UDI to cope with the problem. At first glance, the committee, which included representatives from the White House as well as the Commerce, Treasury, and Defense departments and various offices within the State Department, may have seemed a useful forum for airing conflicting views. In practice, however, Ball ensured tight control over the group's work by appointing Washington lawyer William D. Rogers as chair. According to Anthony Lake's account, Rogers, who later handled Latin American affairs in Henry Kissinger's State Department, agreed to serve as a "lid on the rest of the bureaucracy" in order to squelch the "harder policy" that Ball opposed.[59]

Unsurprisingly, Rogers worked assiduously to kill what stood out as the most ambitious element of that "harder" approach—the proposal to push for a British military operation. Rogers informed British officials in mid-December that the use of force would likely be "ineffective," but he and other U.S. officials worried as well about the political consequences for the Johnson administration if the United States provided logistical support, which London would plainly expect. (British officials were making inquiries, for instance, about the availability of U.S. fuel supplies on Ascension Island in the South Atlantic.) Johnson, Rusk, and Ball had been stung in earlier months by conservative criticism for supporting UN military operations in the Congo, and they had no desire to invite a similar response by deploying U.S. power on behalf of Black Africa, recalled Lake.[60] Mail to the White House gave the president some reason for such caution. For the week ending on November 25, only five pieces of mail supported the administration's efforts to tighten the economic noose around Rhodesia, whereas 181 opposed it.[61] In light of growing controversies connected to foreign affairs, recalled Lake, few senior officials had any enthusiasm for "a military drama" in Africa. "The Johnson administration was having enough trouble at home, as a result of Vietnam and the intervention in the Dominican Republic the previous spring, without helping to make Rhodesia any more of a front-page issue than it had to be," wrote Lake.[62]

Also weighing against the possibility of military action was the U.S. military's opposition to a potentially draining operation at a time when American forces were already stretched thin. The Joint Chiefs of Staff concluded that the three-thousand-strong Rhodesian army, which had another six thousand troops in reserve, was sufficiently large and well led to defeat any conceivable African force. But the Chiefs had no doubt that two British divisions, supplemented by fighter squadrons and various support forces, would be able to overcome Rhodesian resistance, secure key economic assets, and overthrow the Smith government. Still, none of this was an attractive prospect to the JCS. A study submitted to Secretary McNamara on December 16 observed that existing global obligations would make it difficult for London to muster adequate forces, that fighting would probably result in the destruction of the vital Kariba Dam and valuable coal fields, and that even a successful British operation would generate guerrilla resistance in the Rhodesian countryside. Worst of all from Washington's perspective, a British operation would depend on U.S. support that, if provided, would come at the expense of U.S. commitments elsewhere, especially Vietnam. In that theater alone, the African operation would mean canceling the dispatch of three squadrons of Air Force troop-carrier aircraft and air transport to support deployment of a tactical fighter squadron. In sum, the Chiefs judged U.S. backing for the use of force in Rhodesia "unsound" and "strongly" recommended rejection of any proposal to use U.S. military power in connection with Rhodesia. "Present major military commitments in NATO, Korea, Southeast Asia, and the Dominican Republic do not permit an additional significant military commitment wherein the depth of involvement is impossible to predict with any degree of accuracy," the Chiefs advised.[63]

The variety of opinions emanating from Washington confused British officials, who were uncertain whether the Johnson administration favored an incremental approach or stronger steps to "nip the rebellion in the bud."[64] In retrospect, though, it is easy to see that proponents of a cautious U.S. approach held the upper hand due to their superior positions in the bureaucracy. The "seventh floor," backed by the Pentagon, simply exerted more influence than the lower-ranking officials who urged strong pressure on the British or even unilateral U.S. action. Under these circumstances, only one scenario was likely to yield policy initiatives favored by Williams, Komer, and the other liberals: a decision by the British government itself to apply stronger pressure on Rhodesia. This is indeed what happened in the middle of December 1965, when Harold Wilson, concerned that he was rapidly losing any opportunity to overturn the UDI quickly and jeopardizing British influence throughout Africa, surprised many of his American critics by calling for sharper sanctions on the Smith government and even seemed to reopen the possibility of using force.[65] This British turn toward activism momentarily empowered U.S. advocates of those same steps, especially when LBJ himself, sensitive as usual to the proclivities of fellow heads of government, showed support for the turn in British policy. (Komer noted in January that the president was "more sympathetic than the rest of the [U.S. government]" to the British position, whatever approach London took.)[66] The United States, it seemed, could expand its own involvement in Rhodesia while remaining safely behind London's leadership.

The turning point in U.S. policy came on December 16, when Johnson and Wilson met in Washington, a warm encounter that boosted the president's confidence in British leadership on the Rhodesia question. Johnson indicated his willingness to follow London's policy no matter what form it took, "the zigs as well as the zags," in Lake's words.[67] More specifically, the two leaders agreed to a significant expansion of sanctions, embracing an embargo on oil deliveries to Rhodesia. Following Wilson's announcement of the embargo on December 17, the Johnson administration publicly endorsed the decision and instructed U.S. oil companies to comply. Although U.S. officials worried that such an embargo would fail since South Africa would offset any cutoff, Wilson struck a note of optimism. The Pretoria government was capable of "some very evil things," said the prime minister, but it was also "very law-abiding" and might obey restrictions embraced by the United Nations. One of Wilson's top aides predicted that the new pressure would bring Smith's regime down "in a matter of weeks."[68]

Meanwhile, Wilson and Johnson agreed to a sharply expanded program of support for Zambia, which was bound to face intensified economic pressure from Rhodesia as soon as the oil measure was announced. Amid the new tone of optimism and Anglo-American harmony, LBJ mentioned no specific limits on the U.S. contribution, telling the British only that Washington would "reinforce and supplement what you do."[69] The administration dutifully followed through in the weeks that followed. Starting in early January 1966, the United States began airlifting oil and gasoline to Zambia, a huge undertaking that delivered more than 3.6 million gallons of gas over four months. As historian Thomas Noer observes, the U.S. airlift burned through more fuel than it carried to Zambia, but it succeeded in preventing the nation's economic collapse. During the weeks after Wilson's visit, the Johnson administration also announced a series of new voluntary import bans on asbestos, lithium, chrome, and tobacco and, in February 1966, a cutoff of most U.S. exports to Rhodesia.[70]

Still, the familiar debate within the bureaucracy continued to percolate. For his part, Williams contended that the new sanctions would do little to get rid of Smith while imposing "indeterminable but certainly high" expenses for the United States. The use of force, even on a limited basis, stood a much better chance of securing "rapid results" at "much lower cost," Williams urged.[71] On the other side, Thomas Mann, who had been promoted to Undersecretary of State for Economic Affairs, put his considerable influence behind Ball's point of view, insisting that the administration impress upon London the limits of American help in both the economic and military domains.[72] Yet British activism lowered the temperature of disagreement within the Johnson administration, giving way to a period of optimistic watching and waiting among U.S. decision makers. By embracing new economic measures, London created conditions within which the Johnson administration could undertake stronger initiatives of its own without danger of taking over the main political and economic burden from Britain. It was an approach that both Williams and Ball could live with. Whether that situation would endure depended on the flow of events in Africa.

## New Debate, Old Policy

Cautious optimism persisted within the Johnson administration during the first months of 1966. Unquestionably, American hopes did not rise anywhere close to the level of confidence expressed by British leaders, who claimed to see "visible cracks" in Rhodesia as early as January and predicted that sanctions would bring down the Smith regime by the late spring.[73] "Our assessment is much more pessimistic," noted NSC aide Ric Haynes.[74] Yet even Americans who had previously advocated force as the only way to topple Smith saw reason to believe that the new sanctions might do the job. Komer reported to the president in mid-January on "mildly encouraging signs" that sanctions were "beginning to bite," causing distress especially in Rhodesia's business community. State Department experts were, advised Komer, "coming around to the view that it's no longer a question of *whether* sanctions will work but of whether Smith will cave before Kaunda or other Africans do something foolish." The biggest reason for anxiety, in other words, was that Africans, in their desperation to overturn the UDI, would undercut Western economic sanctions by insisting on the use of force or other confrontational steps.[75] LBJ himself acknowledged this danger in a letter to Prime Minister Wilson, expressing worry that African governments would not "sit still long enough" to permit sanctions to work.[76]

That danger seemed to ebb in the first weeks of 1966, providing another reason for optimism. U.S. diplomats reported that numerous African governments had gotten cold feet about their earlier pledges to break diplomatic relations with Britain if Smith had not been ousted by the middle of December. The "early rush" to condemn London in this way had passed, noted Haynes, with only nine nations following through on the threat.[77] On the whole, advised Haynes, pressure on London had "weakened considerably" as African governments consistently failed to settle on a unified policy. Komer confirmed the trend following a meeting of Commonwealth nations in Lagos, Nigeria, in mid-January. Most of the assembled African governments had agreed to give Britain more time, and the pressures from even the radical nations "should be blunted for a while," Komer informed LBJ.[78] Wilson emphasized the same point in a note to LBJ after the Lagos meeting. Although a few governments still favored the use of force, the meeting had decided to give sanctions a "fair run," Wilson wrote. "All in all," he added, "commonsense and realism prevailed" and African governments were "quiescent at least for the time being."[79]

Yet U.S. policymakers had ample reasons to worry that a policy of staying behind British leadership might not be sustainable for long. For one thing, the Rhodesia issue started to weigh more heavily in American domestic politics as 1966 advanced. Although mail to the White House suggested a disquieting degree of sympathy for the Smith regime in the weeks following the UDI, public discussion of the crisis mostly affirmed the administration's choices. Civil rights and university organizations voiced consistent approval of U.S. sanctions. A few editorials—like the one published by the *Chicago Tribune* expressing doubt about the worrying expansion of U.S. commitments around the world—offered criticism, but they did so obliquely, rarely raising doubts about the essential justice of U.S. efforts to overturn the illegal regime in Salisbury. As the crisis dragged on with no end in sight, however, public discussion of Rhodesia began to heat up, exposing the administration to increasingly strong criticism and conflicting pressures to do more—or less—to pressure Salisbury.

On one side, civil rights leaders and allied political forces urged Johnson to take additional steps to punish Smith. On the other side, conservatives increasingly assailed British policy and voiced sympathy for the Salisbury government. Typical of such critics was Representative H. R. Gross, a

Republican from Iowa who used a January 1966 speech on the House floor to denounce American support for Britain's economic pressure on Rhodesia at the same time Britain was defying U.S. policy by trading with both North Vietnam and Cuba. Administration spokesmen pointed out that London did not allow shipments of strategic materials to either nation, but LBJ and his aides were unable to squelch an essentially accurate accusation that would bedevil them over the months to come. But the core of Gross's critique was that the administration was engaging in "outrageous" efforts to overturn a "friendly government."[80]

This sort of criticism gained ground with the American public at a time of shifting attitudes about race relations, a transformation with heavy implications for LBJ's policymaking in both the domestic and international spheres. As numerous scholars have observed, 1965 marked a watershed for the Johnson presidency, dividing the early years of liberal triumph from the later period of disillusionment and social discord. This shift was especially pronounced in the arena of race relations. Criticism by civil rights leaders of the American embroilment in Vietnam strained the relationship between the White House and the movement. Meanwhile, intensifying urban unrest reflected Black disillusionment with the slow pace of change and enabled the president's critics to attack him for coddling irresponsible radicals. By 1966, in the words of historian Thomas Borstelmann, "the dominant image of African Americans in the national media had changed from the hymn-singing, flag-bearing marchers of Selma willing to suffer for the cause of justice to uncontrolled hooligans reveling in random violence."[81] Abundant evidence points to changing attitudes among whites. A Gallup poll in 1964 found that 72 percent of non-southern whites believed that Johnson's pace in promoting civil rights for Black Americans was either about right or too slow. By the end of 1966, more than half of all whites believed that Johnson and the Democrats were pushing civil rights too far, too quickly. The "number one concern" of most Americans had become fear that Black gains would come at the expense of whites, observed journalist Tom Wicker.[82]

Amid this shifting domestic milieu, the Rhodesia crisis became a rallying point for segregationists and alerted the administration to the dangers of pressing a pro-Black position too hard. For some of LBJ's critics, Ian Smith stood out as a hero who, in contrast to the president, was willing to act in defense of order and stability in the face of radicalism. The Smith regime worked hard to encourage this view. In public statements as well as private encounters with U.S. diplomats, Smith consistently chastised Washington for failing to back a nation trying to emulate America's own break with Britain two centuries before and resolutely committed to the fight against communism in Africa.

In his New Year's message on January 1, 1966, he called on the United States and Britain to stop the "march of communism" through Africa and to consider whether their actions against Rhodesia were "consistent with [their] avowed policy of combating communism."[83] A few members of Congress picked up the theme. In April 1966, Representative Joe Waggoner, a Democrat from Louisiana, went so far as to call Rhodesia "a cornerstone of this nation's tenuous foothold in the entire Afro-Asian world."[84] Liberals in the U.S. Congress challenged these claims, but Komer, for one, worried that such efforts would not suffice. Already, he warned in February 1966, the Rhodesian Information Office in Washington, a bureaucracy that remained open while the Johnson administration studied the legality of forcing its closure, was forming effective connections with "extreme right-wing groups" in the United States eager to end Washington's sanctions.[85]

A more immediate consideration—the leakiness of the oil embargo against Rhodesia—also caused doubt about whether the policy of following the British lead would achieve anything useful. British optimism about ending the Rhodesia crisis in 1966 rested on the assumption that Smith's nation would run out of fuel sometime in the spring. But numerous U.S. assessments pointed out that South Africa and Portugal, which had not signed on to the embargo, would likely keep Rhodesia supplied indefinitely. The white governments in Pretoria and Lorenço Marques (Maputo) had obvious interests in resisting the use of economic pressure to force political change. Another part of the problem was British unwillingness to apply meaningful pressure on South Africa to comply with international sanctions. Since the start of the crisis over the UDI, American officials had worried that British economic entanglement with South Africa would prevent London from taking any steps against Rhodesia that might entail new tensions with Pretoria or provoke Black African nations to seek sanctions against all of the white regimes in the southern part of the continent. In the first half of 1966, American officials watched with frustration as the British government looked the other way while British oil companies continued to supply South African firms, which in turn delivered the fuel to Rhodesia. In mid-March, the State Department estimated that nearly two hundred thousand gallons of gasoline were finding their way to Rhodesia each day, well above Rhodesia's minimal needs.[86]

If British passivity worried American officials, so too did Britain's effort to crack down on the flow of fuel into Rhodesia—a paradox that reveals the cross-cutting pressures operating within American decision-making circles. This curious situation became clear in April 1966, when reports surfaced that a Greek tanker, the *Manuela,* would soon dock in Mozambique with a load of oil destined for Rhodesia, a blatant act of defiance against international sanctions. Many U.S. officials were relieved when the Wilson government, bolstered by its victory in British general elections at the end of March, indicated that it would soon seek a UN resolution authorizing the use of force to intercept the tanker. Advocates of tough sanctions clearly welcomed London's gesture of determination, but so did Rusk, who saw bold British action as the best way to guard against demands for stronger U.S. involvement. Virtually the entire array of U.S. policymakers was therefore disappointed by events that neither increased pressure on the Smith government nor demonstrated London's competence in handling the Rhodesia crisis.

The problem was not the lack of British action against the tanker. In fact, HMS *Berwick* prevented the ship from docking at Beira on April 10, forcing it to sail on to South Africa. Rather, the problem was the way in which London went about obtaining UN approval for this action. First, British authorities crafted a UN resolution so narrowly worded as to leave no doubt that London would do nothing to challenge South Africa's support for Rhodesia. It then turned out, however, that Britain had inadvertently left the door open to much more severe UN action against Rhodesia by calling the situation in Rhodesia "a threat to peace." Under UN procedures, that phrasing automatically opened the door to an array of mandatory multilateral sanctions against Rhodesia and possibly the other white-governed territories in southern Africa, a sharp escalation of the crisis that the British government and most U.S. officials had sought to avoid.[87]

This series of events unraveled the rough consensus that had prevailed within the Johnson administration since mid-December 1965, when officials of differing outlooks had come together around a policy of supporting Britain that seemed to stand a chance of ending the crisis without the use of force. Now it seemed that the problem might be heading toward a nightmare scenario: an open-ended crisis in the hands of an irresolute British government prone to escalatory steps even as it lacked an overall strategy to defeat the Smith regime. Americans wanted a clear plan leading to a moderate outcome; what they saw instead was inconsistency and ineffectiveness likely to radicalize the Rhodesia controversy and pull the United States deeper into the region, whether Washington liked it or not. Two contradictory dangers stirred particular worry among U.S. officials. First, further use of naval power to enforce the oil embargo seemed to risk a larger military conflict in southern Africa. The Portuguese ambassador to the United States raised that specter in May, warning President Johnson that any British use of force against port areas in Mozambique would result in a "conflagration" that would inevitably involve South Africa.[88] Increasingly, however, Americans worried that Britain, in its desperation to escape the crisis, might veer in the other direction by opting for a negotiated settlement with Smith that would offer substantial concessions to white demands. Such a deal promised to put the United States in a dangerous position by causing outrage among Black African governments against both London and Washington. Rusk urged the president to be wary of any deal between London and Salisbury and to avoid any commitments of U.S. support before the details could be studied.[89]

But if Washington was rapidly losing confidence in London, what should U.S. policy be? There were no easy answers. Getting out from behind the British and adopting a distinct U.S. policy unencumbered by London's erratic choices held unmistakable appeal for officials as different as Ball and Williams, both of whom increasingly doubted London's ability to play an effective global role. The *Christian Science Monitor* captured the new reality in March 1966, reporting that administration "hawks" and "doves," for all their disagreements over Rhodesia, could readily agree that Britain was failing.[90] The American decision-making record over the remainder of the year reveals a persistent groping for alternatives. London's deficiencies and Washington's ambivalence had resulted in a U.S. policy that was "inconsistent," "inconclusive," and "contradictory," noted one State Department study of U.S. policy toward the region. The report revealed the extent of American uncertainty by laying out a wide spectrum of possibilities ranging from "disengagement" to new efforts to find common ground with the white regimes.[91]

As they weighed their options, however, U.S. officials discovered again and again that every possibility had major flaws. Total disengagement was a nonstarter given the extent to which Britain and numerous African governments had staked themselves to a resolution. Open-ended stalemate only heightened the chances of disastrous outcomes such as the collapse of the Commonwealth, the evisceration of British influence in Africa, or the revival of African demands for military action, all of which seemed to open the door to greater communist activity.[92] At home, meanwhile, inaction seemed likely to invite criticism from African American activists, who were taking a deeper interest in the issue.[93] Yet bolder U.S. action—certainly the use of force but also backing for tougher, mandatory economic sanctions through the United Nations—also held little appeal. "We think that economic sanctions have reached a level beyond which further escalation would not be profitable," concluded a committee of senior officials representing various agencies.[94] Besides doubts about the effectiveness of such sanctions and the damage they might do to Zambia by encouraging Rhodesia to retaliate against its neighbor, administration officials noted that Congress, increasingly irritated by British trade with North Vietnam, would inevitably balk at a policy that carried even the whiff of support for London's strategy of economic pressure.[95] LBJ probably shared that sense of anger as the Wilson government made clear its unwillingness to support the U.S.-led war in Vietnam in any tangible way.

Uncertainty about the best course of action in Rhodesia left space for freelancing. Secretary of Defense McNamara used a speech in Montreal to hint at his support for disengagement, a view consistent with his growing doubts about the ability of the United States to use its massive power to good effect throughout the developing world. "The United States has no mandate on high to police the world," he averred. Sometimes, he mused "deliberate nonaction was the wisest action of all."[96] Out of public view, Ball made the same suggestion with more explicit reference to Rhodesia, though he emphasized Britain's failure to chart any effective course rather than the intractability of political problems in postcolonial nations. Meanwhile, other officials toyed with the idea of using American diplomatic clout with South Africa and Portugal to chart a course independent of London. "Constructive reinvolvement" with the white regimes of southern Africa would, according to the proposal's architects in the State Department's Policy Planning Council, entail easing Western efforts to isolate South Africa in return for that country's cooperation on Rhodesia and other regional issues, including the increasingly bitter dispute over Pretoria's claims to South West Africa (Namibia).[97]

As the months passed, however, all of these alternatives faded and U.S. policy settled back where it had been at the start of the year. Washington would back Britain despite London's lackluster performance. The momentum behind existing policy and the unattractiveness of the alternatives was clear as early as May, when the president delivered his first major address on African affairs. The speech reverberated with aspirations to promote political and economic change on the continent and, crafted at a moment of maximum consternation about the British role in Rhodesia, might have been used as an opportunity to chart a new course. Yet LBJ could hardly have been clearer about U.S. deference to British leadership, faltering though it may have been. "We are giving every encouragement and support to the efforts of the United Kingdom and the United Nations to restore legitimate government in Rhodesia," Johnson declared before a White House audience that included thirty-six African ambassadors. "Only when this is accomplished can steps be taken to open the full power and responsibility of nationhood to all the people of Rhodesia—not just 6 percent of them," added the president, who insisted that his administration would not deviate abroad from the principles of justice and equality that it sought at home.[98] Unquestionably, the president's advisers crafted the speech in order to serve the president's immediate tactical needs. The implication of American activism in support of Britain served as a rejoinder to McNamara's appeal just a few days before for U.S. disengagement from Africa. In this way, the speech would reassure civil rights leaders—or, as presidential aide Bill Moyers put it in a moment of exasperation, provide a "cheap way to keep them quiet on at least one issue." Moyers also noted that LBJ's recommitment to Africa would preempt a major political rival, Robert F. Kennedy, who was expected to emphasize the theme of racial justice during a trip to South Africa the following week.[99]

Yet the speech was no mere exercise in political posturing. On the contrary, it laid out a policy—essentially a continuation of the stay-behind-Britain approach—that guided the administration's behavior until its end. LBJ and senior officials repeatedly reassured British counterparts of this intention, with the president even offering his most fulsome praise of London since the UDI. In a letter, LBJ lauded Wilson as a "great force for good" on the Rhodesia matter and commended him for "doing Africa and the world a great service."[100] To be sure, U.S. officials remained keenly aware of the familiar drawbacks of relying on Britain's leadership. In particular, they worried that the Wilson government, now tacking back toward a tough stand in renewed negotiations with Smith, would confront Washington with unwanted decisions, including whether to support any UN initiative entailing not only mandatory sanctions against Rhodesia but also sanctions against Pretoria if it refused to comply. The latter possibility raised the distinctly unappealing specter of intensified economic warfare across the entire region. Still, the administration clung to Britain's leadership.

The clearest test came in December 1966, when direct negotiations between Wilson and Smith—a dramatic encounter aboard the British warship *Tiger* on stormy seas off the coast of Gibraltar—collapsed following momentary optimism that a deal lay at hand. Berating Smith for his "very devious and schizophrenic personality," Wilson immediately threw British support behind selective but mandatory UN sanctions against Rhodesia, precisely as Americans anticipated.[101] LBJ had already informed Wilson that the United States would offer "full support" for such sanctions, which both sides understood would apply narrowly to Rhodesia and not to other white-ruled territories in southern Africa, despite the obvious limitations of that approach.[102] Ambassador Goldberg followed through on December 16, joining Britain in voting for a Security Council resolution adopted eleven to zero with four abstentions. The measure had little practical meaning for the United States since most American companies doing business in Rhodesia had already discontinued their activities in observance of the earlier voluntary sanction. Yet the Johnson administration, which had often expressed wariness if not outright opposition to the notion of mandatory sanctions, appreciated the political value of the gesture and left no doubt of its intention to back Britain. On January 5, 1967, Johnson signed an executive order criminalizing trade in several commodities critical to the Rhodesian economy, including oil, chrome, sugar, tobacco, and copper.[103]

## The Long Haul

The events of December 1966—the *Tiger* negotiations and then the UN resolution—captured headlines and stirred a flurry of new international attention to the Rhodesia issue. Reports pointed out the unprecedented nature of the UN action, the first time the organization had ever imposed mandatory sanctions and just the second time any world body had done so.[104] (The League of Nations had sanctioned Italy in this way in response to its invasion of Ethiopia in the 1930s.) Meanwhile, Ambassador Goldberg's rhetoric soared. Invoking the "great moral implications" at stake in Rhodesia, Goldberg praised Britain's "record of substantial achievement" in bringing about peaceful decolonization throughout Africa and the "strenuous efforts" it had made to reach an agreement with Ian Smith. The United States was, he added, prepared to "apply the full force of our law" to implement the new sanctions.[105]

Yet Washington's embrace of the new sanctions was not as bold or decisive a move as it may have appeared. For one thing, U.S. support for the UN resolution—a British initiative—reflected the Johnson administration's retreat from its flirtation with a more independent U.S. policy earlier in the year. Confronted with London's failings, Washington had mulled the alternatives, albeit never in a sustained or thorough way, and arrived back where it had started. Moreover, the Johnson administration backed mandatory sanctions despite its certainty that they would be no more effective in forcing a resolution to the Rhodesia problem than had the earlier voluntary measures. Due mostly to South African and Portuguese noncompliance, the voluntary program had cut Rhodesia's gross national product by only 15 percent, and British economists forecast that the new sanctions would trim only another 5 to 10 percent, according to one State Department assessment.[106] The department's European division worried, in fact, that the main effect of the new sanctions would be to sow frustration elsewhere by highlighting the inability of Britain, backed by the United States, to oust Smith. That scenario, wrote one European-focused official, John M. Leddy, amounted to the "worst of both worlds—growing ire in the black African states and no progress toward a Rhodesian settlement."[107] The Wilson government, which had tacked between relatively assertive and passive approaches ever since the UDI, offered only half-hearted assurances that sanctions might eventually work. London was "prepared for the long haul," a senior member of Parliament told U.S. officials in 1968.[108]

Even in the face of such gloomy predictions, though, the Johnson administration saw no reasonable alternative to the approach it had chosen. If the bureaucracy had actively contemplated charting a new course during 1966—an independent U.S. approach or at least application of pressure on London to take a more assertive line—it dropped any such ambitions in the last two years of Johnson's presidency, a period of complacency with respect to Rhodesia and dramatically declining confidence in the United Nations as a key to resolving problems in southern Africa or, for that matter, anywhere else.[109] As historian Thomas Noer observes, the administration enforced sanctions rigorously and effectively all the way to its end in January 1969.[110] It also backed one more British-led expansion of UN sanctions in May 1968. But that move reflected an attitude of deference to London, rooted in hope that Britain would steer a course that avoided the pitfalls at either extreme: capitulation to the Rhodesian whites and the use of force. The administration's approach became evident in the weeks after the adoption of the 1966 mandatory sanctions, a period when Washington might have worked harder for a solution to the Rhodesia impasse or at least pressed London for clarity about its intentions if mandatory sanctions failed. Instead, senior administration officials left no doubt that they sought a back seat as Britain drove policymaking on the issue. "This is first a UK problem, then a UN problem, and only then is it a U.S. problem," asserted Rusk at a crucial NSC discussion of the issue in late January 1967. Even more revealing were comments from senior administration officials suggesting both resignation and passivity. "We are not egging anyone on," noted Goldberg, denying any interest in encouraging African governments that favored the use of force. Washington officials had already taken "our lumps" for the administration's unwillingness to take a bolder stand, said Rusk, and no one saw any option but to brace for more of the same. "We will have to take current criticism," lamented Goldberg.[111]

Besides the sheer intractability of the Rhodesia problem, three trends between 1966 and 1968 contributed to American inactivity. First, personnel changes in the Johnson administration eliminated the most powerful and persistent voices that had argued for a more independent policy in earlier months. This trend was already evident in 1966 thanks to Williams's resignation as assistant secretary of state for African affairs in March of that year in order to run for the U.S. Senate. Although speculation had abounded since the start of LBJ's presidency about Williams's declining influence, he had continued his outspoken advocacy of racial justice in Africa down to the end of his tenure in the State Department. He had, in fact, earned South African prime minister Hendrik Verwoerd's condemnation as "that bull in the Africa China shop" just a few days before his resignation.[112] The *New York Times* captured the significance of Williams's departure in a news story noting that the African Bureau had consistently shown a "liberal and understanding attitude" toward Black Africa during his tenure and, in the process, "tried the Administration's patience considerably from time to time."[113] To fill the vacancy, LBJ appointed not Williams's deputy, Wayne Fredericks, who had shared his boss's outlook, but Joseph Palmer II, a consensus-oriented career diplomat who had served as an ambassador during the Eisenhower administration and would do so during the Nixon presidency as well.

A similar trend played out in the other epicenter of activism on the Rhodesia problem, the National Security Council. McGeorge Bundy's departure in early 1966 was followed by Komer's reassignment to the Vietnam portfolio. Nearly as significant was the resignation of Ulric Haynes, who had taken a deep interest in the Rhodesia crisis and had provided a steady stream of information and argumentation deployed at higher levels by Bundy and Komer. Into this void stepped Walt Rostow, who followed Bundy as national security adviser, and Edward K. Hamilton, an NSC staffer specializing in African and South Asian affairs. To be sure, Rostow and Hamilton neither called for nor carried out any abrupt transformation of U.S. policy toward Africa generally or Rhodesia in particular. Both men, in fact, scorned Ian Smith and consistently spoke in favor of racial equality. Yet there was a difference. Rostow's detached intellectualism contrasted with the energy that Komer and Haynes brought to bear. One keen observer of the American decision-making scene, the South African ambassador to Washington, noted in November 1966 that the new national security adviser did "not seem to react emotionally," a characteristic Pretoria could count on as a "safeguard" against American activism in southern Africa.[114] Additionally, Rostow had little interest in bucking the dominant currents of thinking in the State Department and the Oval Office, as Bundy and Komer had often done. Rostow understood that LBJ expected loyalty from his new appointee as well as willingness to put his prodigious intellect to work on behalf of the president's priorities at a time of rapidly mounting criticism.[115]

At the same time, a critical personnel change in the State Department squelched the most powerful voice urging that the United States assert its independence on the Rhodesia question by disengaging. George Ball had lost influence during 1965 and early 1966 as a consequence of his persistent criticism of U.S. escalation in Vietnam. Consistent with his broad outlook on southern Africa, Ball doubted the value of Vietnam to the United States and feared that a major commitment there would divert U.S. prestige and resources from far more important priorities around the world. Some colleagues praised Ball for taking a courageous stand. He was "extremely articulate and utterly fearless," recalled Clark Clifford, who came to appreciate many of Ball's reservations after becoming defense secretary in 1968.[116] Virtually all the senior officials who surrounded him in 1965 and 1966, however, rejected his views, either on their merits or out of resentment about Ball's willingness to exploit his personal links to Rusk and LBJ to get a hearing. In any case, Ball left the administration on September 30, 1966. He did so in part due to exhaustion and a desire to earn a higher salary in the private sector. But he also felt increasingly marginalized as the administration pressed ahead with escalation in Vietnam, even though he remained on good personal terms with LBJ.[117] To the extent that Rhodesia figured into his decision making, he could hardly have failed to see that the administration, whatever its frustrations with British leadership, would continue to back London.

Revealing of the overall drift besetting U.S. policy, however, Ball had the last laugh. When he returned to the Johnson administration in June 1968 as ambassador to the United Nations, he replaced the strongest remaining advocate of American activism in southern Africa, Arthur Goldberg, and found opportunities to show that nothing had changed in his basic outlook on Rhodesia. By seeming to accept "only what was ineffectual" in southern Africa, asserted Ball in one encounter with British counterparts, the United States was fueling the chances of violence and political upheaval that would damage American interests. He conceded that his criticism of sanctions was not the "official view" of the Johnson White House but noted nonetheless that his opinions had "some currency" in the United States and might yet lead to a review of U.S. policy, presumably in a new presidential administration.[118]

The second trend that discouraged bold moves on Rhodesia during the last years of the Johnson presidency was precisely the one that caused Ball so much distress: the deepening morass in Vietnam. Ball, of course, feared mostly that the war would diminish American attention to key U.S. alliance commitments, especially in Europe. But his diagnosis of the problem created by the escalating war—that it would suck resources away from other concerns—proved valid with respect to any number of parts of the world. Indeed, U.S. attention to sub-Saharan Africa, which clearly ranked near the bottom of American priorities, was certain to diminish disproportionately as the Johnson administration fixated on Vietnam and reckoned with declining congressional willingness to fund its priorities elsewhere. In practical terms, Washington's preoccupation with Southeast Asia meant not that the United States would abandon its interests in southern Africa but that it would try to maintain them at lower material and political cost.

This impulse is readily apparent in U.S. wariness of significant initiatives toward Africa in 1967 or 1968, when the Johnson administration jettisoned the small burst of enthusiasm for Africa that LBJ had demonstrated through his speech in March 1966. The change was clear by October of the following year, when NSC aide Ed Hamilton cautioned against the idea of a presidential trip to Africa to demonstrate Washington's ongoing commitment to political and economic development. At a time when Congress was likely to "mutilate" existing aid programs by cutting as much as 46 percent of U.S. assistance, wrote Hamilton, such a visit would only set up the United States for a "long hard fall" in African eyes by raising expectations that would never be met.[119] In keeping with its global approach to foreign aid, the administration aimed to shift more U.S. assistance into multilateral programs under the aegis of the World Bank, an approach strongly backed by an interdepartmental task force charged with studying U.S. aid for Africa.[120] Yet there could be no doubt that no matter how it was distributed, less would be available for Africa at a moment when the Johnson administration was already "down well below the bone" in delivering on aid promises to high-priority recipients such as India, Pakistan, Turkey, and Korea. "We must live and deal with the cold truth that the overwhelming theme of current U.S. relations with most of Africa is that we have promised much and delivered little," asserted Hamilton.[121]

The documentary record contains no explicit mention of the ways in which the expanding war in Vietnam narrowed Washington's options with respect to Rhodesia specifically. Yet, just as the war affected U.S. policy toward Africa as a whole, it undoubtedly reinforced Washington's wariness of taking steps independent of Britain or applying pressure on London to behave more assertively. By January 1967, as the largest U.S. military operation to date in Vietnam gathered momentum, U.S. officials with a range of perspectives on the Rhodesia problem agreed wholeheartedly on the impossibility of any action entailing a U.S. military commitment to southern Africa—an "appalling" prospect, as Rusk put it.[122] The subject never arose again at high levels of the administration. Indeed, debate within the administration often centered in 1967 and 1968 on the question of how far Washington could go in accepting a negotiated deal between London and Salisbury that granted significant concessions to the white Rhodesian position. Following this path, American officials acknowledged, might stir fierce criticism among African nationalists and radicalize the political situation throughout the continent. Yet it would also carry the advantage of ending the immediate crisis and bolstering the forces of stability in a volatile region. The Johnson administration never arrived at a clear position on the matter. The British ambassador in Washington, Patrick Dean, may have been correct, however, when he surmised in late 1967 that the Johnson administration would probably accept a deal that stopped short of immediate majority rule in order to put an end to a draining controversy. In the "overall context of U.S. foreign policy," Rhodesia hardly loomed large enough to lead Washington to oppose a deal that promised to ease the risks of a larger confrontation and remove a persistent source of tension between the Johnson administration and Congress, Dean wrote.[123]

Finally, the Johnson administration's retreat into passive support for British policy in Rhodesia flowed from the shifting political landscape within the United States. As during 1965 and 1966, many white liberals and African

American activists continued to applaud U.S. sanctions against Rhodesia. Yet, in keeping with the broad trajectory of race relations in the second half of the 1960s, attitudes about Rhodesia grew increasingly polarized as time passed, shrinking the base of support for resolving the problem through pressure on the Smith regime. On one side were radical activists who grew increasingly frustrated with the failure to dislodge the white regime in Salisbury and increasingly urged Blacks—both African and African American—to take matters into their own hands. Stokely Carmichael, who had recently resigned as chairman of the Student Non-Violent Coordinating Committee, made the case in no uncertain terms during his travels to Cuba and Africa in the second half of 1967. In an interview with a Tanzanian newspaper, Carmichael berated African leaders and the OAU for failing to forge common ground on the Rhodesia issue and to act boldly. "African leaders disgust me," he stated. "The only solution for the Africans," he continued, "was to get guns and fight."[124] A month later, SNCC leaders declared their intention to do exactly that, telling reporters they would soon begin recruiting Black volunteers to fight in Rhodesia.[125]

On the other side, the administration faced steadily mounting opposition from an array of voices hostile to its steps to punish Rhodesia. One source of criticism was the American business community. Some companies opposed the very idea of sanctions, bemoaning lost business and often chastising the Johnson administration for hypocrisy by forbidding relations with Rhodesia while allowing trade with communist nations. The bigger criticism among U.S. firms, though, was that Washington was enforcing sanctions strictly while other governments around the world, including London, often turned a blind eye to evasions. The Johnson administration was increasingly "under attack" on this issue by the spring of 1968 and abandoned interest in new sanctions, preferring that the United Nations limit itself to enforcing the ones that had already been adopted, noted Joseph Sisco, the assistant secretary of state for International Organization Affairs.[126]

Even more striking was the criticism from a growing array of grassroots organizations sympathetic to Smith. By one scholar's estimate, the largest of those groups, the Friends of Rhodesian Independence, had 122 branches and 25,000 members in the United States as early as 1967, dwarfing parallel efforts to defend South Africa's white regime. This pro-Rhodesian lobby drew strength from the growth of right-wing organizations such as the John Birch Society and the Liberty Lobby, the mounting backlash against the civil rights reforms of 1964 and 1965, and strong currents of Anglophobia that flowed in some pockets of American society.[127] All of this created fertile conditions for the outpouring of pamphlets and books that condemned American support for sanctions and sought to implicate American whites in the survival of Smith's government. "Rhodesia is no distant, isolated African episode; it reaches into your very home, however far away you may be," insisted a news release by the American–South African Council, which warned of the growing probability of a "third world war" if Washington did not bolster reliable forces of anticommunism around the world. "Rhodesia means you, from Whitehall to Washington, Wisconsin to Worcestershire, Wigan to Wilmington to Winnipeg."[128] The tone of such material grew even more apocalyptic following the first significant clashes between Rhodesian security units and guerrilla forces in August 1967. While most Americans were focused on Vietnam, warned the American–South African Council, the Johnson administration and the United Nations were weakening the "most stable and prosperous nations in Africa"—South Africa and Rhodesia.[129]

Meanwhile, the administration faced a steady stream of criticism from members of Congress, some of whom drew information and support from the grassroots activists. Democrat Richard Russell, chair of the Senate Armed Services Committee and once a close confidant of LBJ, spoke for many of his fellow Dixiecrats in blasting the Johnson administration for presiding over a "new low" in U.S. foreign relations by embracing mandatory sanctions against a "peaceful, independent country" while looking the other way as Britain continued to trade with North Vietnam.[130] Jesse Helms, a media commentator and radio executive from North Carolina who would win a Senate seat in 1972, charged that U.S. officials were being "played for suckers" by the British government, while one of the state's sitting senators, Sam Ervin, charged that any UN-sanctioned military action against Rhodesia would be akin to a foreign attack on Texas.[131] By the British embassy's count in late 1967, members of Congress had introduced twenty separate measures aimed at abolishing U.S. sanctions—so far without success. But a different story was unfolding at the state level. Legislatures in Louisiana, Alabama, Oklahoma, and Arizona had already adopted resolutions demanding an end to sanctions and recognition of Smith's government.[132] Another escalation of the pro-Rhodesian effort came in the form of visits to Rhodesia by prominent conservative Americans. Church leaders did much to blaze the trail in 1966, but members of Congress showed interest as well. No less a figure than Senator Barry Goldwater of Arizona, LBJ's Republican opponent for the presidency in 1964, held friendly meetings with Smith in late 1967. The Rhodesian had shown that a leader committed to "principle and purpose" might get "kicked around" but could bring success in the long run, Goldwater exulted in an interview with a Rhodesian radio station.[133]

For Lyndon Johnson, perhaps the most galling criticism of all came from men whose judgment he had valued in connection with other policy issues. At a time when LBJ was growing increasingly bitter toward liberal allies who took him to task on Vietnam, he could not have been pleased by the views of Joseph P. Roche, a high-profile political scientist and newspaper columnist who served as a presidential adviser from 1966 to the end of the Johnson presidency. Roche left no doubt of either his support for the administration's civil rights priorities or his hostility to white rule in southern Africa, describing the leaders of South Africa as a "savage crowd of neo-Nazis." Yet he advised LBJ that the United States had allowed itself to be "mousetrapped" by the British and urged that the administration study ways to extricate itself from its commitment to back London's policy.[134] Undoubtedly far more annoying to LBJ were the bluntly hostile opinions of Dean Acheson, the onetime secretary of state who had served as a high-profile adviser to John F. Kennedy and enjoyed the reputation as a foreign policy "wise man." As early as May 1966, Acheson blasted sanctions and defended the legitimacy of independent Rhodesia, which he regarded as a welcome source of stability in a sea of political turmoil. He also used his access to the White House to try to persuade Johnson on the matter. When he got nowhere, he grew increasingly strident in his denunciations of the administration and publicly speculated that LBJ had struck a deal with Wilson to back London in Rhodesia in return for a British promise not to criticize U.S. policy toward Vietnam, an idea popular with white Rhodesians insistent that U.S. opposition sprang from calculation rather than principle.[135] Sanctions were rooted in the "most reprehensible misrepresentation and hypocrisy," Acheson wrote on one occasion, lamenting that the war in Vietnam seemed to "absorb all our capacity for governmental leadership or public concern."[136] He held out hope that LBJ would see the light all the way until the administration's last days. Following Richard Nixon's victory over Hubert Humphrey, Acheson publicly urged LBJ to abandon failed policies pressed on him by liberals within his administration and to end sanctions before he left office.[137]

The Johnson administration made some efforts to push back against all of this criticism during its final two years in office. In March 1967, the State Department published a lengthy defense of U.S. policy in the *State Department Bulletin,* describing Washington's reaction to the UDI as a "measured response" and laying out the legal and moral rationale for sanctions.[138] Meanwhile, Goldberg and Palmer worked to rebut pro-Rhodesian arguments in a series of speeches during 1967. Both men labored especially to refute the idea that Washington had too readily fallen in line behind failing British policies and abandoned its own interests. "Contrary to propaganda assertions, we have not been engaged in pulling British chestnuts out of the fire," contended Goldberg in a speech to the American Negro Leadership Conference on Africa. Instead, Goldberg asserted, the United States had acted "for good American reasons of our own."[139]

Yet there could be little doubt that these initiatives, for all the bold rhetoric, were designed to defend the status quo, not to prepare the way for any new American initiatives on the Rhodesia issue. The administration had no interest in stirring new criticism in Congress by calling sustained attention to the controversy, much less by proposing anything bold. As the British embassy observed in November 1967, most liberals had grown "notably quiet" about Rhodesia in recent months. In Congress, "the main body of middle-of-the-road Senators and Congressmen" were no longer interested in the issue and wanted to avoid getting involved in a no-win situation if possible. While unwilling to abandon sanctions, many liberals, wrote embassy aide R. J. R. Owen, had become "demoralized and likely to remain pretty silent" on the issue, partly because the administration had achieved so little and partly because their support of Black African causes had "been having unwelcome repercussions for them in their electoral districts." Only at the extremes did Rhodesia remain a matter of lively debate, especially as the traumas of 1968 dominated political discourse and focused the administration's attention on Vietnam as never before. A few liberals advocated new sanctions, while a far larger block of conservatives agitated for abolishing sanctions altogether.[140] But neither of those options appealed to a president increasingly besieged by criticism and anxious to avoid new arenas of contention.

The LBJ administration's decision in May 1968 to line up behind a British initiative for additional UN sanctions—a relatively straightforward move that lacked the contentiousness of earlier American policymaking—made abundantly clear that dramatic change in the U.S. posture would be possible only when a new president had been elected. Sisco, for instance, predicted that the obvious failure of international sanctions to resolve the Rhodesia problem would inevitably lead a new president, whether Democrat or Republican, to undertake a "pretty thorough rethinking" of U.S. policy.[141] Change in the final months of LBJ's term would come only if the British themselves did something bold, most likely a compromise deal with Ian Smith. That outcome seemed momentarily possible in the fall of 1968. In a rerun of their 1966 negotiating effort, Smith and Wilson met once again aboard a British warship, this time HMS *Fearless,* at Gibraltar. American officials worried both that Wilson would get a deal and that he would not. Any deal would likely involve substantial British concessions to white demands, an outcome that would only inflame Black African opinion. But a failure to reach a settlement was hardly more appealing since prolongation of the crisis would underscore the ineffectiveness of sanctions and fuel that notion that violence alone could end the standoff.[142] The failure of the *Fearless* talks did little to ease American anxieties about the vice in which they were caught. But it enabled the administration to slide back into the relatively comfortable posture it had occupied for many months: low-profile efforts to stay behind the British in confidence there would be no dramatic turns demanding increased American attention or resources.

# Conclusion

LATE JULY 1969 witnessed two of the signature moments of Richard Nixon's presidency. On July 24, Nixon helicoptered aboard the USS *Hornet*, where he welcomed the astronauts of Apollo 11—the first expedition to land humans on the moon—back to earth. The exultant president appeared on television screens around the world, lauding Neil Armstrong and his crewmates for demonstrating that humanity could "reach for the stars." The dramatic splashdown and the astronauts' safe return, added Nixon, ended nothing less than "the greatest week in the history of the world since the Creation."[1] A day later, Nixon struck a different tone when he made a bold statement about the Cold War in Asia, a démarche that reporters, eager to grasp the outlines of U.S. foreign policy under a new administration that had promised innovation, dubbed the Nixon Doctrine. Speaking informally before the traveling press corps during a stopover in Guam, the president exuded a sense of cool realism about U.S. capabilities once the Vietnam War was over. He reaffirmed Washington's fidelity to its treaty commitments but hastened to add that the United States aimed to reduce its military presence and to avoid direct interventions like the one that had brought unbearable burdens in Indochina. Asked how the United States would cope with nations facing communist subversion in the future, Nixon asserted he would "help them fight the war but not fight the war for them." He pledged that the United States would learn from the Vietnam imbroglio and "must avoid that kind of involvement in the future."[2]

What made the declaration plausible as a full-blown "doctrine" was Nixon's suggestion that the approach he outlined for Asia—support for American allies to help them fight their own battles—would be applied globally in order to rein in American commitments at a time of dangerous overstretch. The president's most sweeping assertions of this point came in extemporaneous comments in response to journalists' questions, but it was clear he had given the matter considerable thought. Helping nations uphold their own security "is a good general principle, one which we would hope would be our policy generally throughout the world," Nixon declared. "I want to be sure that our policies in the future, all over the world, in Asia, Latin America, Africa, and the rest, reduce American involvement," explained the president, adding that U.S. policy would channel material assistance to help Third World nations "solve their own problems."[3]

If Nixon or his chief foreign policy aide, National Security Adviser Henry Kissinger, had any qualms about the media's eagerness to see these statements as a seminal articulation of administration policy, those concerns quickly dropped away. Kissinger was using the term in memorandums to his boss by the end of August.[4] The president, meanwhile, worked behind the scenes to encourage the media to abandon any flirtation with the label "Guam Doctrine" in favor of "Nixon Doctrine" and proudly invoked the latter in a major speech on November 3, 1969.[5] Describing a "new direction in American foreign policy," Nixon told a nationwide television audience that the United States would henceforth fight communist subversion not by deploying its own forces but by looking to any nation under threat "to assume the primary responsibility of providing the manpower for its defense."[6]

A statement of the administration's foreign policy objectives submitted to Congress in February 1970, later published as a 160-page book grandly titled *United States Foreign Policy for the 1970s: A New Strategy for Peace,* also trumpeted the Nixon Doctrine and developed the concept more broadly than before. For two decades after 1945, asserted the report, American leaders had made policy on the assumption that only the United States possessed the resources and know-how to construct and maintain a new international order. "The United States conceived programs and ran them," the report added. "We devised strategies, and proposed them to our allies. We discerned dangers, and acted directly to combat them." Now, things had changed. "We deal now with a world of stronger allies, a community of independent developing nations, and a Communist world still hostile but now divided." In an altered environment, the administration asserted, the United States could no longer "conceive *all* the plans, design *all* the programs, execute *all* the decisions and undertake *all* the defense of free nations of the world." America's "foreign friends" must do more for their own defense and economic progress as well as international stability more generally.[7]

The meaning of these words grew clearer as the new administration settled into office. Although Nixon and Kissinger promised to use American assistance to bolster friendly governments that they judged likely to serve U.S. geopolitical purposes, congressional skepticism and the administration's own relative indifference to development aid meant that the Nixon Doctrine's promise of expanded economic aid amounted to little in practice. Although economic assistance could still be valuable, the whole system of bilateral aid was "failing" due to political opposition, concluded the State Department's Policy Planning Council in December 1968.[8] Nixon and Kissinger readily accepted that judgment. Keenly aware of how much had changed since the early 1960s, the administration looked to multilateral aid institutions and private investment to advance its economic objectives. Nixon and Kissinger also faced congressional opposition to expanded military aid, but they showed more determination in this arena.[9] If overall levels of military assistance never climbed as high as they would have liked, they succeeded in channeling weaponry to certain nations that stood out as especially likely to advance American geopolitical interests.

At the same time, well aware of the limits on the material assistance they could provide, they deepened American political support for such nations, abandoning any remaining reservations about the drift from democracy in the Third World and embracing collaborations with nations they considered useful partners for Washington. The Nixon Doctrine came to mean, first and foremost, an emphasis on cultivating sources of stability in the Third World in order to reduce burdens on U.S. resources and to enable the administration to focus anew on U.S. relations with the Soviet Union and China, where Nixon and Kissinger aimed to make their mark. The corollary was that the United States would no longer cultivate nations and movements that did not share American priorities.

Even while acknowledging the extent to which practice differed from rhetoric, journalists, memoirists, and historians have often described the Nixon Doctrine and its implementation as a momentous, even landmark, departure in the history of U.S. foreign relations, crafted by an unusually creative administration determined to shore up American global influence and refocus attention on superpower relations. In early August 1969, syndicated newspaper columnists Roscoe and Geoffrey Drummond set the tone by praising the president not only for introducing a "radically changed Asian policy" but also for bringing about "a major turning point in American foreign policy."[10] Journalistic accounts of Nixonian foreign policy published in the 1970s often struck the same note. In a study published in 1978, *New York Times* reporter Tad Szulc, though no admirer of Nixon and Kissinger, described the Nixon Doctrine as a central component of policies that set the United States "on a wholly new course in its foreign relations."[11] Many later historians arrived at similar judgments. Jussi Hanhimäki's magisterial 2004 study of Henry Kissinger's foreign policy leadership notes, for example, that the Nixon Doctrine, coming at just the moment when the new administration began drawing down the number of U.S. troops in Vietnam, held "far-reaching significance" by indicating Washington's decision to pursue its interests in the Third World by bolstering regional powers inclined to serve U.S. interests. The doctrine was, writes Hanhimäki, a "key ingredient" in the administration's "global architecture of limiting American commitments in disparate regions."[12]

Nixon and Kissinger deserve credit for articulating the new U.S. approach to the Third World in a succinct and consistent manner. Starting in the mid-1960s, in fact, the two men had been urging precisely the innovations they would try to implement after they took office in 1969. In a speech to the exclusive Bohemian Club in July 1967, more than a year before his nomination as the Republican candidate for president, for example, Nixon had called for a "complete overhaul" of U.S. foreign aid, suggesting greater reliance on private assistance but urging especially that Washington use aid "to reward our friends and discourage our enemies." The time had also come, Nixon insisted, to lower American expectations about democratization. "Much as we like our own political system, American style democracy is not necessarily the best form of government for people in Asia, Africa and Latin America with entirely different backgrounds," insisted Nixon.[13]

Characteristically, Kissinger made the same point in a more philosophical manner. In the first twenty years after the Second World War, he wrote in a 1968 essay, the United States was well suited both materially and intellectually to the major problems of creating international order. Now, though, the situation had grown more complicated due to declining American resources and a burgeoning array of problems that had proven impervious to American solutions. "The United States is no longer in a position to operate programs globally; it has to encourage them," Kissinger asserted. "It can no longer impose its preferred solution; it must seek to evoke it." Going forward, he added, "our role will have to be to contribute to a structure that will foster the initiative of others." He did not refer specifically to the Third World, as Nixon had, but it was impossible to miss the implications for countries like Brazil and Iran. The United States must continue to contribute to defense and economic development programs around the world, Kissinger wrote, but it must "seek to encourage and not stifle a sense of local responsibility" and avoid "expecting too much" from the power that it exerted abroad. U.S.-supported "regional groupings" would have to take over "major responsibility for their immediate areas, with the United States being concerned more with the overall framework of order than with the management of every regional enterprise."[14]

Eloquence and analytical incisiveness should not, however, be confused with originality. As this book has demonstrated, the ideas at the core of the Nixon Doctrine had circulated for years within the Johnson presidency and produced a distinct shift toward precisely the policies that Nixon and Kissinger advocated both before and during their period in high office.[15] Just like the moon landing, the Nixon Doctrine was less a distinct achievement of the new administration than the visible culmination of trends that originated in earlier years. Regarding the Third World, the difference after the new Republican administration took office lay in the rhetorical boldness with which the new leaders articulated their vision. Johnson could go only so far in abandoning John F. Kennedy's high-minded assertions of liberal ambition in the Third World. Although LBJ had never come close to Kennedy's enthusiasm for development and democratization in Asia, Africa, the Middle East, and Latin America, the pressures of party affiliation and Johnson's own pledges of international activism, especially early in his presidency, constrained him from acknowledging publicly what occurred during his presidency. As the war in Vietnam consumed the administration's attention and commanded the nation's resources, Johnson increasingly prioritized stability over political and socioeconomic progress in the Third World and looked to rising regional powers to lighten American burdens. Nixon and Kissinger declared these steps among their core objectives, but Johnson and his aides had arrived at the same underlying analysis and did much to reorient U.S. foreign policy from 1964 to 1968. In this sense, LBJ, though the quintessence of the liberal president in the domestic arena, presided over a transformation that cut decisively against JFK's declared preferences and started the United States in a new direction.

To be sure, the change occurred in fits and starts and stoked discord—sometimes fierce—within the U.S. bureaucracy. That contention reflected one of the most significant points of this study: even in its heyday between 1961 and 1965, American liberalism—the belief that humanity, and the United States in particular, could use its vast resources and know-how to solve virtually any problem—not only coexisted with more skeptical views but also was itself riddled with uncertainties about methods and objectives. Numerous scholars have made this observation with respect to the domestic arena; the latter half of the 1960s has long been understood as a time when liberalism, so sturdy at the start of the decade, crumbled under pressure from both a dissatisfied left that aimed for faster, more thoroughgoing change and a resurgent conservative movement. One objective of this book is to show how a similar dynamic played out in the realm of foreign policy, particularly in the branch of international affairs where liberal ambitions ran highest in the early 1960s: policymaking toward the increasingly assertive Third World. Behind the rhetoric of paying "any price" lay substantial uncertainty about how to balance development and democratization of these regions against other American priorities, which American tools were most appropriate to the task, and especially how much risk the United States should run in the short term in order to align itself in the long run with profound sociopolitical changes occurring in what a later generation would call the Global South.

The assassination of John F. Kennedy in November 1963 eliminated a president who welcomed an ambitious, risk-tolerant approach to the Third World in favor of a man whose desire to leave his mark in the domestic sphere, combined with a less nuanced sense of the sea change occurring in the Third World, leaned the other way. The proclivities of the individual in the Oval Office, it turned out, mattered a great deal even as the Democratic Party's dominance held steady. Lyndon Johnson's arrival in the White House empowered advisers such as Dean Rusk, George Ball, and Thomas Mann, all skeptics of the New Frontier ethos. Some enthusiasts for a transformative policy in the Third World held onto senior positions for months or even years under the new president but experienced mounting frustration as the administration steadily reoriented U.S. policy under the pressure of the Vietnam War and a rapidly changing domestic political landscape. That reorientation did not go as far as some traditionally minded critics within the Democratic sphere would have liked. Most strikingly, Dean Acheson, once an icon of the Democratic Party, blasted LBJ for his ostensible unwillingness to scrap ambitions that the former secretary of state considered counterproductive by the time Nixon stepped into the presidency. It requires no leap of the imagination to conclude that Acheson's 1969 complaint about the "swinish, bullying boorishness" that made LBJ's final years "unbearable" reflected not just personal disgust but also a sense that Nixon and Kissinger would better promote the sort of international stability that the former secretary of state had long advocated.[16]

On the other end of the spectrum, the liberals who had espoused what this book has called "globalist" ideals were just as disappointed. Unquestionably, ambitious liberals who had pinned their hopes on Kennedy appreciated later in the decade that their expectations had run too high. "It is difficult if not impossible to order the internal affairs of even a small nation," South Dakota senator George McGovern, a rising voice in liberal circles, conceded in August 1968, referring to Vietnam but also generalizing about American frustrations worldwide.[17] Perhaps concluding that they had all shared to some extent in the failure, few liberals attacked Lyndon Johnson personally. But McGovern and other like-minded officials believed that the administration had abandoned worthy ideas and squandered America's opportunity to recast its foreign policy for a new era of progress and uplift. Disappointment on this score contributed to decisions by "Soapy" Williams, Arthur Schlesinger Jr., Ted Sorensen, John Kenneth Galbraith, and others to leave the Johnson administration. Howard Palfrey Jones, the former ambassador to Jakarta who had been replaced in April 1965, captured the general feeling in his 1971 memoir reflecting on his diplomatic career. Most American leaders had failed to realize, Jones contended, that political independence was not enough for the rising peoples of the Third World. "Archaic societal systems, too, had to be overthrown if the aspirations of the common man were to be realized." Although he acknowledged that this view was often dismissed as "highly idealistic and unrealistic," Jones insisted that the United States still had a strong interest in "positive policies" aimed at supporting change in the Third World.[18] Most of the internationalists gravitated toward the presidential campaigns of Robert F. Kennedy in 1968 and George McGovern in 1972, candidates who espoused policy ideas that faded from the Johnson administration by its end.

For many officials who occupied key posts in 1967 and 1968, however, the metamorphosis of policy toward the Third World made eminent sense. By its end, in this view, the administration had reckoned sensibly with the strains imposed by the struggle in Vietnam, embraced a reasonable sense of limits on American power, and rightly prioritized stability over promoting social and political progress. In doing so, contended supporters of this shift, Washington had pointed the way toward a durable foreign policy that rolled back the excessive promises of the early 1960s and bolstered U.S. power despite a changing global order that increasingly defied American control. Asked in January 1969 to reflect on nearly eight years as secretary of state, Dean Rusk told reporters he was "optimistic" about the position of the United States in the "long run." He denied that the nation had ever aspired to be the "world's policeman" but, in any case, expressed satisfaction that the Johnson administration was now sensibly committed only "to those situations which are considered to be in the vital interests of the United States" or where the United States was bound by treaty commitments.[19]

Predictably, Walt Rostow, the president's closest foreign policy adviser in the administration's final years, was even more enthusiastic about the changes that had taken place under his watch. Rostow's enthusiasm undoubtedly grew partly from his sense that U.S. foreign policy had moved in the direction he had advocated all along. To be sure, he conceded that foreign societies had grown less susceptible to American power as the decade advanced and now wrote favorably of pursuing U.S. objectives through international partnerships and regional groupings, a significant shift away from the vision of nation-building he had espoused earlier in the decade. Yet reliance on authoritarian regimes, whether or not those regimes readily submitted to U.S. power or the extent to which those nations exerted their influence via regional groupings, meshed well with his long-standing belief that anticommunist development in the Third World depended first and foremost on fostering robust nation-states with strong central institutions. Rostow's attitude also probably stemmed from his personal loyalty to LBJ and the desire that the two men shared to highlight positive achievements in the international arena despite the Vietnam debacle. If U.S. policy had evolved toward a more regional conception of how the United States should promote its interests, they were inclined to tout that outcome as an advance reflecting a sober assessment of how the United States could exert influence in a new era of setbacks and limits.

Unsurprisingly, Rostow especially extolled America's accomplishments in Asia, where, he assured LBJ, the U.S. commitment in Vietnam had bought time for the consolidation of a "cooperative Asian structure" that included democratic societies such as Australia and Japan but also authoritarian nations like Indonesia and South Korea.[20] Although the United States must contribute enough bilateral aid for Indonesia to ensure that Suharto could pull his country "out of the swamp," Rostow expressed confidence that the Association of Southeast Asian Nations (ASEAN), established in 1967, secured significant economic cooperation without direct U.S. involvement. The key, he added, anticipating the logic that would underpin the Nixon Doctrine, was that the United States led "on the security side" while avoiding new treaty commitments and leaving to Washington's Asian partners to provide the ground forces. In the Persian Gulf, meanwhile, Rostow enthused about the "latent possibility" of an Iranian-Saudi partnership at the core of a regional grouping that might eventually pull in Turkey. The Johnson administration had been "nursing along" this possibility and looked to the Nixon team to carry on with the project, Rostow wrote in a memorandum for the new president's designee as national security advisor, Henry Kissinger. As for Latin America, Rostow exuded satisfaction with the region's political reorientation during the mid-1960s, declaring that the main challenges now lay in promoting regional integration and private investment.[21] Nixon and Kissinger could hardly have said it better themselves.

---

Strong continuity between the Johnson and Nixon eras is evident in each of the five relationships examined in this book. In the case of Brazil, U.S. officials had settled into an enduring pattern of behavior long before LBJ left the White House. Starting with the 1964 coup, policymakers had voiced alarm at each step by the junta to tighten its grip. But each time, the most influential voices within the administration came to terms with the Brazilian government's actions, reasoning that repression was necessary to cope with the country's chaotic situation and that the United States needed to show support for a regime that clearly served U.S. interests. On this reasoning, the United States tightened its relationship with the Brazilian government even as the generals turned their backs on democracy and social progress. The same pattern played out in the first few months of the Nixon presidency. In response to the regime's

Fifth Institutional Act, promulgated on December 13, 1968, the Johnson administration had suspended U.S. aid even as it subtly signaled its enduring sympathy for the regime. The new administration picked up where Johnson's team had left off. Despite the regime's further crackdown on political dissidents in the first months of 1969, Nixon restored U.S. aid programs in May.

The new president's support for the Brazilian regime stemmed partly from the logic of his broader policy toward Latin America. In public statements and private utterances, Nixon voiced eagerness to lower U.S. ambitions in the region and forge productive partnerships with nations regardless of their commitments to democratic ideals. "The great contribution of the Nixon administration," NSC aide Robert E. Osgood wrote in October 1969, "should be the deflation of rhetoric, the dismantlement of Grand Designs, and the reestablishment of American policy on the more solid foundation of candor, realism, and a more modest conception of what the United States can achieve."[22] These ideas fed directly into a major address on Latin American affairs that Nixon delivered on Halloween 1969. Promising to shed the "grandiose promises" of earlier years, the president called for a "more mature partnership." He expressed a "preference" for democracy in other nations but showed little inclination to anguish, as Kennedy had done, over the question of whether to recognize authoritarian governments. "On the diplomatic level," Nixon averred, "we must deal realistically with governments in the inter-American system as they are."[23] Apparently concerned that these benign-seeming words might conceal his meaning, he told Kissinger the day before his speech that he really did "favor dictatorships."[24]

Nixon derived satisfaction from one dictatorship—Brazil's—more than any other. For one thing, the military regime produced impressive economic results and provided a fertile field for U.S. private investment that totaled more than $1.6 billion by 1969.[25] Characteristically, though, Nixon and Kissinger paid closer attention to geostrategic than to economic considerations. In this arena, Brazil was the centerpiece of the new administration's hopes to block leftist inroads and preserve stability across the hemisphere. It was, as one NSC paper put it, "the key nation of Latin America" due to its huge population, economic potential, and presumed influence throughout the hemisphere.[26] If other NSC studies allowed that Mexico and Argentina might also qualify as "chief pillars" of U.S. strategy in Latin America, as one 1971 paper put it, Nixon was often quick to single out Brazil as Washington's most dependable partner.[27] In contrast to the rest of Latin America, he exclaimed on one occasion in 1971, "Brazil is a country that matters."[28] He marveled that Brazil would have two hundred million people by the end of the century. "It's going to be a hell of a place," Nixon remarked on another occasion. "It's going; it's booming." He acknowledged that Brazil was a dictatorship but hastened to add that "it should be" in order to cope with disorder internally and throughout its region.[29]

The Nixon administration's partnership with Brazil remained strong even as the junta veered toward its most brutal phase and criticism of the generals mounted within the United States. Under General Emílio Garrastazú Médici, who came to power following a debilitating stroke suffered by Costa e Silva in August 1969, the nation had what historian Thomas E. Skidmore calls "the hardest-line government Brazil had seen."[30] The generals continued to constrict what remained of Brazil's political system through new repressive measures and consolidated the regime's partnership with technocratic elites who produced impressive economic growth at the cost of widening social inequality. But what really set the new government apart was the ferocity with which it cracked down on political dissidents and embraced the use of torture, a practice that persisted even after the government largely succeeded in crushing Brazil's modest urban guerrilla movement in 1971.[31]

Evidence of widespread abuses trickled out of Brazil, stirring an increasingly vocal international outcry in the early 1970s. In the United States, Frank Church, chair of the Senate subcommittee on U.S. relations with Latin America, convened hearings that brought redoubled attention to the issue through extensive media coverage. The syndicated columnist Jack Anderson wrote of the junta's "bestial practices" and described gruesome torture techniques.[32] But the Nixon administration showed little interest in changing course. True, U.S. aid for Brazil shrunk during the Nixon years, and in 1974 U.S. assistance totaled only $69.9 million, of which three-quarters was military aid.[33] Yet the reduction stemmed from the administration's global approach to foreign aid and soaring confidence in Brazilian self-sufficiency rather than any doubts about the regime.

The health of the U.S.-Brazilian partnership was especially clear in December 1971, when Médici paid a visit to Washington. As when Costa e Silvia had visited LBJ back in 1967, U.S. officials expressed squeamishness about visible displays of cooperation with the regime, resisting Brazilian insistence that Médici be invited to address a joint session of Congress.[34] They had no doubt, however, about the value of fostering partnership with a "staunch ally," as Secretary of State William P. Rogers put it, that shared U.S. interests throughout the hemisphere.[35] Indeed, senior officials viewed the meeting as an opportunity not only to show support for Médici's domestic reforms but also to coordinate policies toward other parts of South America at a time when the Brazilian government sought a more active international role consistent with what Kissinger called "the Nixon Doctrine concept."[36]

In the event, the talks could hardly have done more to affirm U.S. support for Médici or Washington's desire that Brazil take an active role beyond its borders. For his part, Médici proposed that his country and the United States "do everything in their power" to help other South American countries resist communist inroads.[37] Documents declassified in 2009 reveal just how far the two presidents went in assigning Brazil a leading role. Nixon, who closely resembled LBJ in his respect for powerful leaders with whom he could do business, assured Médici he hoped "we could cooperate closely, as there were many things that Brazil as a South American country could do that the US could not." Moreover, Nixon proposed that the two leaders establish a diplomatic backchannel to promote frank discussion of their joint efforts, a suggestion that Médici accepted. The presidents discussed cooperation to overthrow Fidel Castro in Cuba, but the most urgent concern for both men was undoubtedly Chile, where the leftist Salvador Allende had been elected president a year earlier. After Médici indicated his government was actively encouraging Chilean military officers to overthrow Allende, Nixon urged U.S. and Brazilian officials to "work closely" to promote a coup and offered Médici U.S. funding or other "discreet aid" to bolster covert Brazilian invention in Chile.[38]

U.S.-Brazilian comity contrasted starkly with the near disintegration of Washington's relationship with India at virtually the same moment in 1971. On December 16, as Nixon's effigy burned in several Indian cities, Indira Gandhi deplored U.S. passivity in the face of Pakistani aggression on the subcontinent. The war that had broken out on December 3 could have been avoided, she seethed in a letter to Nixon, if only the United States had taken meaningful action to uphold human rights and justice. Instead, Americans had leaned shamefully toward autocratic Pakistan while failing to take "a single worthwhile step" to promote peace.[39] Nixon lashed back in a letter of his own, charging that India "spurned" international peacemaking efforts and "chose" war.[40] Thus did U.S.-Indian ties hit what historians have called the "nadir" and "low ebb" of their relationship.[41] But, as chapter 4 showed, Washington and New Delhi had been heading in that direction since at least 1965, dissolving the optimism that had inspired John F. Kennedy and many of his aides to seek a new relationship with the world's largest democracy. By the time LBJ left office, Washington had curtailed economic aid, cut off military assistance, and lost confidence in both India and Pakistan as useful partners in pursuing U.S. objectives in Asia.

Upon assuming the presidency, Nixon and Kissinger possessed no plan to deviate from the policy of disengagement from the subcontinent that they inherited from their predecessors. Like the Johnson presidency, the new administration readily recognized a need to maintain the flow of U.S. food aid and development assistance and to consult on geostrategic problems. India and Pakistan were simply too powerful and populous to downgrade below a certain level. Yet the administration's goal in the region was, Kissinger wrote in his memoir, "quite simply, to avoid adding another complication to our agenda."[42] This was not, in short, a part of the world where the Nixon Doctrine would be implemented. As the months passed, however, various trends converged to disrupt U.S. apathy and to accelerate the deterioration of U.S.-Indian relations that had played out in the Johnson period. For one thing, the Indian government veered to the left as Prime Minister Gandhi, having prevailed in a bitter dispute that broke apart her Congress Party, postured more than ever as the defender of India's common people and cultivated communist support.[43] Gandhi's socialist inclinations in the domestic arena hardly pleased Washington, but her foreign policies did most damage in the eyes of the Nixon administration. U.S. officials watched with alarm as New Delhi and Moscow, bonded by rising hostility to China, set aside recent disagreements and reaffirmed their once-close relationship. The two nations negotiated a twenty-year treaty of friendship and cooperation, though Gandhi's fear of criticism for abandoning her country's non-alignment caused her to balk at signing the deal. Americans were upset as well by persistent Indian sniping about the war in Vietnam. U.S. diplomats took solace in Indian worries that a precipitate U.S. withdrawal from Southeast Asia might open the door to rapid Chinese advances, but they saw New Delhi's apparent determination to move forward with full diplomatic recognition of North Vietnam—a provocative step that India had so far resisted—as a slap in the face. That move, Kissinger warned L. K. Jha, the Indian ambassador to Washington, would be "taken very ill" in the United States.[44]

Just as important a cause of U.S.-Indian tensions was Washington's renewed preference for Pakistan. That nation, it is true, did not reclaim the pivotal position it had played in U.S. strategy for South Asia in the 1950s. Yet Nixon consistently displayed a visceral predilection for Pakistan—a "bias," he confessed in 1971—that harkened back to the era of close U.S.-Pakistani relations during his vice presidency. Whereas Nixon praised the Pakistanis as levelheaded and dependable friends, he dismissed the Indians as "a slippery, treacherous people" and their American admirers as the quintessence of "liberal softheadedness."[45] Nixon's partiality took tangible form in October 1970, when the administration departed from LBJ's 1967 ban on arms deliveries to the subcontinent by selling Pakistan armored personnel carriers and aircraft worth $50 million. Washington officials described the sale as a "one-time exception" to the U.S. policy, but many observers, not least the Indian government, had little difficulty discerning a deeper meaning. Easily the most important reason for the Nixon administration's pro-Pakistani leanings, however, was a calculation that had little to do with regional rivalries. Eager to explore a rapprochement with China—a central element of Nixon and Kissinger's project to remake great power relations—the president needed a go-between trusted by both

Washington and Beijing. For this role, the Americans pinned their hopes on Pakistan, above all President Agha Mohammad Yahya Khan, whose importance to Washington grew immeasurably as the Nixon administration and Mao Zedong's communist regime gradually warmed to each other, culminating in Kissinger's headline-making trip to Beijing in July 1971. If cultivating Pakistan's help with this initiative damaged U.S.-Indian ties, it was a price Nixon and Kissinger were willing to pay.

All of these factors weighed heavily in U.S. decision making as the Nixon administration confronted a major crisis on the subcontinent during 1971. The upheaval that would plunge relations between Washington and New Delhi to their low point had its roots in long-simmering regional tensions. At its founding in 1947, Pakistan had been divided into two parts, East and West Pakistan, separated by a thousand miles of Indian territory. The challenge of holding the nation together despite substantial ethnic and cultural differences became suddenly more acute at the end of 1970, when the Awami League, a political movement dedicated to Bengali autonomy, scored a sweeping election victory. With secessionists championing creation of a new nation called Bangladesh, the regime in Karachi launched a brutal military crackdown in the East. Hundreds of thousands died in ensuing blood-soaked weeks, while millions of refugees swept into eastern India.

Humanitarian catastrophe on an epic scale, along with the growing risk of Indian intervention and large-scale war, provoked demands from human rights organizations, op-ed pages around the world, members of the U.S. Congress, and even some State Department officials for American action to stop the Pakistani onslaught and find a peaceful resolution. But Nixon and Kissinger refused to act, instructing instead that the United States "tilt" toward Pakistan.[46] Indira Gandhi's decision in August to sign the friendship treaty with the Soviet Union that had been negotiated back in 1969 drove another nail in the coffin of U.S.-Indian ties, as did an icy Gandhi-Nixon summit meeting in November that one U.S. official called a "dialogue of the deaf."[47] Nixon dismissed Gandhi as "that bitch, that whore"—strong words even by the president's standards.[48] When India and Pakistan finally went to war in December, Nixon assumed the worst of Gandhi's intentions, anticipating, contrary to the advice of virtually all U.S. experts, that New Delhi would initiate an even bigger conflagration by attacking the West Pakistani heartland. India intended no such escalation, but nothing demonstrated the state of U.S.-Indian relations so well as Nixon's decision to send the nuclear aircraft carrier USS *Enterprise* and nine other warships to the Bay of Bengal to deter India and its Soviet patron. John F. Kennedy had dispatched the same ship to Indian waters in 1962 to show support for India in its war against China; this time, the intent was to send a wholly different message.[49]

If events on the subcontinent in 1971 sent U.S.-Indian relations to rock bottom, they revealed something very different about the relationship between the United States and Iran. Even as the Nixon administration leaned openly toward Pakistan, it remained wary of the fierce public criticism is would invite by sending U.S. weaponry to Yahya Khan's government. But their caution did not foreclose the possibility that Iran might do U.S. bidding by covertly sending American-made weaponry to Pakistan. Mohammad Reza Pahlavi backed Pakistan out of a desire to minimize Chinese influence there, but he also relished an opportunity to show Washington what a valuable role Iran could play in serving U.S. interests in a volatile part of the world—what a useful partner Tehran could be, in short, in fulfilling the vision at the heart of the Nixon Doctrine. Yet the agreement to send arms, worked out secretly in the first days of December 1971, was the logical outcome of policy decisions going back to the mid-1960s. The Johnson administration had abandoned many of the qualms that had once made Americans wary of the shah's regime and come to see Iran as a reliable regional power that could defend American interests at a time of diminished U.S. capabilities. Just as in the case of Brazil, Nixon picked up where LBJ had left off and carried the policy innovations of the later 1960s to their logical conclusion.

Nixon's admiration for the shah, which exceeded even LBJ's high opinion, meant that U.S.-Iranian relations grew even closer after 1968. The new president detected "an inner strength" in the Iranian leader upon their first meeting in 1953 and later praised him as a "decisive, confident, strong, kind, thoughtful" man who shared many ideas about geopolitics.[50] Personal affinity offers only a partial explanation, however, of Nixon-era decision making toward Iran. Indeed, when Nixon took office in 1969, he showed no inclination to depart from the policies developed by the Johnson administration in 1967 and 1968. For one thing, Nixon and Kissinger had higher priorities elsewhere in the world. But they also understood that Johnson's approach meshed neatly with their own predilections for the Persian Gulf more generally as British withdrawal drew closer. Just like LBJ and his advisers, Nixon and Kissinger aimed to build stability in the region by nurturing partnerships with both Iran and Saudi Arabia and fostering cooperation between the two. Just like Johnson, moreover, Nixon and Kissinger were wary of incessant Iranian demands to facilitate increased Iranian oil revenue—a demand that now took the form of insistence on a special quota for expanded sales to the United States—and to use the proceeds to buy ever larger quantities of U.S. military equipment. Although Kissinger acknowledged that the shah was "genuinely committed to the West," he advised against any new promises at a time of limited American capabilities and skepticism in the United States about arms sales.[51] The Nixon administration conceded little when the shah visited Washington in October 1969.

What moved U.S.-Iranian relations further down the road to partnership was not Nixon's relationship with the shah but the same thing that had driven closer ties over the previous years—mounting evidence that Iran was uniquely positioned to secure American interests in an area that was growing increasingly worrisome. The shah understood the logic of the Nixon Doctrine and pressed American interlocutors to view Iran as the prototype of a regional power that would act on Washington's behalf. He assured U.S. officials in October 1969 that Iran was eager to "take more responsibility for the region," where too many nations were led by "unprincipled bandits."[52] Events in 1970 and 1971 led Americans to see things in the same way. Iran's economic performance and political stability continued to impress Washington, as did growing indications that the shah—once belittled as a self-absorbed tyrant—had matured into a shrewd statesman. The shah's staunch support of U.S. policy in Vietnam, extending even as far as loaning ninety of his F-4 jets back to the United States for use in Vietnam in the fall of 1972, also pleased Washington.[53]

The shah won additional points with U.S. leaders through other gestures. He demonstrated statesmanship in May 1970 by peacefully giving up Iranian claims to Bahrain, a move that eased tensions with nearby Arab nations. He also contributed to regional stability by reestablishing diplomatic relations with Egypt in August and maintaining constructive links to Israel. When he used force, he did so effectively, notably when Iranian units seized three small islands in the Persian Gulf just as the British military departed in 1971. This performance stood out sharply against a deteriorating regional backdrop. U.S. officials worried that Saudi Arabia, beset by political intrigue and energetically committed to the Arab struggle against Israel, could no longer act as a reliable source of pro-American stability. Even more alarming, the revolutionary Ba'athist regime in Iraq, having come to power via a coup in July 1968, steadily expanded its economic and military ties to the Soviet Union, stirring new fears of a communist drive toward the Persian Gulf.[54]

The confluence of these trends led the Nixon administration to view Iran no longer as one of two pillars but as Washington's principal partner in the region, the final step in the evolution of American attitudes toward Iran that had begun in the mid-1960s. As historian Roham Alvandi observes, U.S. officials continued to pay "lip service" to Washington's partnership with the Saudi regime, but, for all intents and purposes, Iran was in a category by itself among Middle Eastern nations (or possibly, Alvandi notes, in a class that included Israel but not Saudi Arabia).[55] It was in this context that the shah and Nixon agreed to send U.S. weapons to Pakistan in December 1971. But the full meaning of Iran's evolving position in the Nixon administration's global strategy became even clearer in May 1972, when the president visited Tehran following his triumphant summit with Soviet leader Leonid Brezhnev in Moscow. During extensive talks, Nixon and the shah acknowledged the Nixon Doctrine more explicitly than ever before. With new weapon purchases at the top of his agenda, the shah insisted the Iran "must be able to stand alone" in defending its interests—and, by implication, Washington's. Remarkably, Nixon acknowledged Iran's leadership position in its region on behalf of the United States, urging the shah to use American equipment to "protect me."[56] Nixon ensured that Iran could play that role by promising that the United States would sell Iran highly sophisticated F-14 and F-15 fighters. In the following days, it became clear that the administration had lifted all restrictions on the shah's ability to buy weapons from the United States. The door was open to the sevenfold increase in the value of U.S. arms sales to Iran that would play out over the Nixon presidency, peaking at $682.8 million in 1974, and ultimately rising to a breathtaking $2.55 billion in 1977.[57]

U.S. support for Indonesia never approached the intensity of Washington's relationship with Iran during the Nixon years, and the reasons are not difficult to discern. Even after the dramatic rupture in 1965 that eviscerated Indonesia's communist party, the country remained wedded to non-alignment. Aversion to the United States, cultivated so assiduously by Sukarno, remained powerful within Indonesian society, so much so that the Nixon administration, like its predecessor, saw value in maintaining a "low profile" by tightly limiting the number of U.S. personnel stationed there.[58] U.S. economic assistance remained substantial, with Washington contributing $265 million in food and other forms of assistance during Nixon's first full year in office.[59] Yet the new administration clung to the effort pioneered in earlier years to limit direct engagement with Indonesia by channeling aid through multilateral mechanisms. In the military realm, meanwhile, the Jakarta regime, focused inwardly and generally satisfied with its large stocks of Soviet-made gear left over from the Sukarno period, applied only intermittent pressure on the new Nixon presidency to go beyond the modest $15 million annual aid program aimed at helping with noncombat functions like road building.

These methods of engagement did not mean, however, that the Nixon administration discounted Indonesia as a regional partner. To the contrary, Nixon and Kissinger built steadily on the foundation that LBJ had laid and carefully nurtured Indonesian partnership as the withdrawal of U.S. forces from Vietnam loomed closer in the early 1970s. Indonesian leaders reciprocated, making the Nixon years "the apex of the bilateral relationship" between Washington and Jakarta, as the American diplomat Paul F. Gardner put it.[60] Ever closer partnership resulted in part from Nixon and Suharto's personal affinity, developed in reciprocal state visits during Nixon's first two years in office. But it flowed most of all from a clear-eyed sense of shared interests. U.S.

officials lauded Suharto for political and economic stability achieved under the New Order but also, in the arena of foreign affairs, for Indonesian leadership within ASEAN and for Jakarta's helpful attitude toward the war in Vietnam. Americans were especially impressed by Suharto's support for U.S. bombing of North Vietnam, wariness of any quick U.S. disengagement, and professed willingness to insert an Indonesian peacekeeping force to buttress a peace settlement preserving an independent South Vietnam.[61] Indonesia's dedication to resisting communist expansion, combined with the archipelago's sheer size and economic potential, made the country "the key to at least South and Southeast Asia," Nixon exulted during a meeting with Suharto in July 1969.[62] In Kissinger's eyes, Suharto deftly blended two qualities that the United States sought under the Nixon Doctrine: a commitment to "national self-help" and dedication to "regional cooperation" in defense of Western interests.[63]

American expectations escalated as Jakarta showed mounting signs of playing the regional role that Washington hoped for as the United States pulled back. In 1969, the Indonesian regime gratified U.S. officials by handling a potentially controversial issue left over from the Kennedy period—the final incorporation of West Irian into Indonesia—without burdening the United States in any significant way.[64] Suharto impressed Americans still more the following year by throwing Indonesian political and military support behind Lon Nol, the military officer who came to power in Cambodia through a U.S.-backed coup d'état in March 1970. Indonesian hostility to the previous Cambodian leader, Prince Norodom Sihanouk, for allowing Vietnamese communist forces to operate in Cambodian territory aligned closely with Washington's outlook, and Suharto's support for Lon Nol remained steadfast even after Nixon ordered a wildly controversial U.S. military incursion into Cambodia at the end of April. Suharto sent Indonesian military assistance to the new regime in Phnom Penh and, in May, risked its non-aligned credentials by convening an urgent meeting of Southeast Asian governments aimed at bolstering Cambodia's anticommunists. These moves impressed Kissinger, who welcomed signs of Jakarta's growing capacity for "organization and leadership" in the region.[65] He and Nixon were also pleased later in the year when Suharto, eager to push back against radical African and Arab regimes, led an Indonesian delegation to a non-aligned summit meeting in Lusaka, Zambia. In a speech that garnered praise in Washington, Suharto joined the chorus condemning Western colonialism but stood out for emphasizing the danger of "foreign subversion" by communist powers bent on exploiting instability in Third World nations.[66] The U.S. ambassador, Francis J. Galbraith, spoke for many U.S. officials in praising the "great self-assurance" with which Suharto now spoke out on global matters.[67]

Unquestionably, the Nixon administration's efforts to restore relations with China in 1971 and 1972 caused friction in the U.S. relationship with the Indonesian regime, which remained fervently anti-Chinese. Yet Washington and Jakarta managed the problem without serious disruption and grew still closer, bonded by a common desire to promote regional stability following the end of the war in Vietnam. Indeed, as historian Wen-Qing Ngoei astutely observes, the American withdrawal and the ultimate communist victory in Vietnam coincided with the solidification of a strongly pro-American "arc of containment" consisting of Malaysia, Thailand, and the Philippines but centered on the vast Indonesian archipelago.[68] Perhaps the most striking evidence of American confidence in—and deference to—Indonesia came in 1975, when President Gerald Ford, with Secretary of State Henry Kissinger at his side, condoned the Suharto regime's brutal military takeover of East Timor, a piece of the rapidly disintegrating Portuguese empire adjacent to Indonesian territory. American leaders were all too willing to overlook Indonesia's questionable claims to East Timor in order to solidify relations with Jakarta, where the principal U.S. goal was, in Kissinger's words, to encourage the regime's "sense of self-reliance commensurate with its importance in the region."[69] The Nixon administration's growing determination to bolster Jakarta had, however, been clear for years before that dramatic event. Food and economic aid remained steady despite overall cuts in the U.S. foreign aid budget. "Whatever aid monies the U.S. had would go first to those that supported the U.S.," Treasury Secretary John Connally assured Suharto in November 1971.[70] In the military realm, meanwhile, Suharto's appeals for expanded American aid, including combat arms, fell on increasingly fertile soil by 1972. The administration, breaking the old $15 million cap, promised $25 million worth of gear in its next budget and indicated more might flow in the years to come.[71]

The gradualness with which Nixon and Kissinger intensified LBJ's relationship with Suharto contrasted with the new administration's approach to southern Africa. In that part of the world, Nixon significantly altered U.S. policy by deciding in early 1970 to open new contacts with the white regimes and to relax American sanctions, including those that had been slapped on Rhodesia in earlier years. It is easy, however, to exaggerate the extent or abruptness of Nixon's departure. As with the other cases examined in this book, the new administration's approach represented not a sharp break but a tactical "tilt," as journalist Jack Anderson called it, in the U.S. effort to bolster sources of stability in a turbulent part of the world.[72] The new openings to racist regimes stirred outrage at the time, as they have in the judgments of many historians, but, viewed in a geopolitical context, they represented an incremental change in policies developed during the Johnson presidency.[73] Following Southern Rhodesia's Unilateral Declaration of Independence in November 1965, LBJ had rejected proposals for strong American action against the Smith regime and fallen in line behind the British government, which aimed to resolve the crisis through negotiations. While hardly confident of British leadership, LBJ and the advisers who shared his outlook saw London as a reliable partner that stood a chance of settling the problem but at least would enable the United States to avoid embroilment in a dangerous conflict at a time when its resources were committed elsewhere. The new administration also sought to avoid entanglement in an area that Nixon called a "peripheral interest" but made a different judgment about the most likely source of stability.[74] It would come not strictly from the British, who were failing at the task, or from Black regimes, which were making little headway in rolling back white rule, but also from the white regimes themselves. Like LBJ, Nixon and Kissinger aimed at racial justice over the long term but concluded that engagement with Rhodesia, along with South Africa and the Portuguese territories, was most likely to encourage political moderation in the region while serving U.S. strategic and economic interests.

Some American officials, especially Africa specialists within the State Department, preferred to stick with LBJ's policy, fearing that the new administration would invite heightened unrest in southern Africa and damage to U.S. prestige by moving toward normalization of relations with the white regimes. NSC aide Winston Lord worried, meanwhile, that any shift in that direction might provoke sharp domestic criticism once the wind-down of the war in Vietnam led the administration's critics to focus on other issues.[75] Proposals to ease relations with the white regimes carried the day, however, in the interagency review of U.S. policy that culminated with Nixon's decisions in late 1969 and early 1970 to relax U.S. arms embargoes against South Africa and the Portuguese territories, oppose further sanctions against the white governments, permit certain types of economic engagement with Rhodesia, and lower the U.S. "profile" on African issues within the United Nations by avoiding strong positions.[76] Pressure from American companies resentful of sanctions routinely flouted by other countries contributed to the administration's decision making, as some historians have emphasized.[77] It may be, too, that Nixon's determination to cultivate political support among whites in the American South and warmer personal relations between senior U.S. officials and representatives of white Africa contributed to the evolution of U.S. policy. The South African ambassador in Washington, Harald Taswell, hailed a new "cordial and relaxed" atmosphere in his dealings with the United States, noting the new administration took a "less selfrighteous and less aggressive" attitude than had the Johnson presidency.[78] But the Nixon administration's new approach stemmed mostly from a belief that isolation of the white regimes had failed to promote change in the region and was, in fact, probably contributing to radicalization on both sides of the Black-white divide that would ultimately benefit only the communists. For evidence of such polarization, Americans looked no further than escalating combat between Rhodesian security forces and Black guerrillas and tighter military cooperation among South Africa, Portugal, and the Smith regime.[79]

Unquestionably, South Africa's large population, abundant resources, regional influence, and strategic location made it easily the most important country in U.S. calculations, even if its egregious racial policies placed limits on how close Pretoria's relationship with Washington could ever grow. By comparison, Rhodesia was a minor consideration—"something of a tail on the South African dog," as diplomat (and U.S. National Security Adviser in the 1990s) Anthony Lake put it in his 1976 critique of U.S. decision making.[80] Yet the new U.S. approach, which the Nixon administration worked strenuously to keep out of public view, became especially conspicuous with respect to Rhodesia from 1970 to 1972. The administration defied its critics by maintaining the U.S. consulate in Salisbury—by the early 1970s more a symbol of American tolerance of white rule than of Washington's hopes to mediate a settlement—until March 1970, when Rhodesia's adoption of a new constitution changed the consulate's legal status and forced the administration's hand. Around the same time, Nixon showed his willingness to ease U.S. enforcement of economic sanctions by allowing American companies to sell assets in Rhodesia and permitting the Union Carbide Corporation to take possession of 150,000 tons of chromium ore it had purchased before trade restrictions had been imposed. Meanwhile, U.S. authorities looked the other way while the Smith regime's propaganda arm in Washington, the Rhodesian Information Office, continued to help prominent American segregationists travel to Africa and to churn out pro-Salisbury commentary warning of another "Vietnam-style" guerrilla war in southern Africa if white governments were not bolstered.[81]

These steps prefigured the most flagrant expression of the Nixon administration's tilt toward white Africa, the White House's acceptance of the so-called Byrd Amendment, approved by Congress in 1971. Named for the Dixiecrat senator Henry F. Byrd of Virginia, the measure gutted U.S. adherence to UN sanctions by permitting import of chrome and other "strategic" commodities from Rhodesia. Dixiecrat members of Congress, fervently supportive of the Smith regime on both racial and geopolitical grounds, had urged that step ever since the Johnson administration backed UN sanctions. They finally prevailed in November 1971 by contending that the embargo made the United States dangerously dependent on chrome from the Soviet Union, the world's other major supplier. The Nixon administration voiced pro forma objections to the amendment, and some officials pushed for stronger condemnation. Yet the president signed the bill immediately after its passage and did little to support repeated efforts within Congress to repeal it, even though the measure placed the United States conspicuously alongside South Africa and Portugal as the only nations failing to uphold international sanctions.[82] The key objective, wrote NSC aide Melvin H. Levine, was to avoid responsibility as much as possible and to "put the monkey squarely on Congress' back."[83] As time passed without repeal, however, critics inevitably focused on the executive branch. The *New York Times* captured the mood in June 1972, charging that the administration had refused to provide the "minimal White House initiative" that would have been needed if the latest repeal effort had any chance of prevailing in the Senate. Nixon was, charged the *Times,* playing a "double game" by paying lip service to the sanctions while undermining them in practice.[84]

---

The transformation of U.S. foreign policy encapsulated in these five stories was in many ways a rational adjustment by American leaders at a time of national crisis. Liberal ambitions in the early sixties had outstripped American resources, expertise, and ideological appeal and lacked precision with respect to either goals or the tools needed to bring democracy and development to the Third World. Many parts of the Third World itself, moreover, evolved in ways that made them less tractable to American power. These problems became obvious as the United States grew ever more deeply committed to Vietnam, which cast a long shadow over every dimension of foreign affairs. The war diverted resources from other priorities and, along with mounting domestic unrest and polarization in the Third World, soured the American public on an expansive agenda of global solidarity and uplift that had seemed ascendant in the late 1950s and early 1960s. As chaos and disappointment increasingly shrouded both domestic and foreign policy, American leaders understandably shifted away from grand aspirations and instead prioritized order and stability. Washington distanced itself from India and other nations that demanded American largesse without catering to U.S. geopolitical purposes. Meanwhile, the United States embraced partnerships with nations that, in return for American political support and military assistance, promised to uphold American interests in their regions, enabling the United States to lower its profile and its expenditures of blood and treasure.

The rationality of American choices did not, however, mean that the transformation served the United States well in the long term. Nations outside Washington's orbit continued to create problems for the United States, as when India defied the Nixon administration and much of the rest of the international community in 1974 by testing a nuclear weapon. Meanwhile, many of the governments on which U.S. leaders depended proved to be less reliable than Washington hoped. Already in the late 1960s, as the case studies in this book demonstrate, Americans were sometimes frustrated by nationalist currents that led authoritarian regimes in Brazil, Pakistan, Iran, and Indonesia, for example, to bridle against U.S. influence. Washington's attraction to those nations ultimately attested more to the limits of U.S. power in the 1960s and 1970s than to the ability of the United States to respond creatively to changing circumstances. Rather than using regional proxies to impose its conception of security and order on the world, the United States often found itself hitched to regimes that brought headaches, liabilities, and setbacks. The ascendant regional powers defied American leadership as they exercised power unimaginable in earlier phases of the Cold War. In a few instances, American partners crumbled under the weight of internal resistance fueled by popular hostility to leaders associated too closely with Washington. Most spectacularly, the shah's regime collapsed amid Iran's Islamic revolution of 1979.

Even in cases where the United States managed to bolster stability, its achievements came with profound costs. Frank Church was surely correct in October 1971 when he lamented in a speech before his Senate colleagues that a "decade of disillusionment" had banished the optimism from U.S. policymaking toward the Third World and saddled Washington with an embarrassing set of friends who seemed to care little about the ordinary people under their rule. Stability was an "antiseptic" concept, as Church put it, that "reveals nothing about how individual people live and die." In the name of preserving the status quo, he complained, authoritarian regimes tortured and terrorized their own populations, sometimes delivering economic advances but almost always at the cost of rising inequality and the outflow of wealth to the West.[85] Indeed, the 1960s, so often understood as a time of human liberation, had witnessed numerous authoritarian coups, many supported directly or indirectly by Washington, and a dramatic ebbing of democracy on a global scale. By one count, thirteen governments in the world in 1962 had come to power via coups; by 1975, the number was thirty-eight.[86] The repressiveness of these governments sparked Church and innumerable other critics of the Johnson and Nixon administrations to bemoan the abandonment of cherished American principles.

Left-wing revolutionary governments and movements stretching from Havana to Hanoi by way of the Palestinian Liberation Organization and South Africa's African National Congress increasingly forged networks of mutual support, but so too did their right-wing counterparts. In South America, Brazil and other military regimes launched Operation Condor to suppress the left, while Indonesia made common cause with its authoritarian neighbors in Southeast Asia and the Smith regime in Rhodesia cooperated with other white regimes in southern Africa to block racial progress and political change. Similarly, the shah's Iran played a central role in efforts to prop up the existing social and political order in the Persian Gulf, the Middle East, and the Horn of Africa in the years before the regime's overthrow.[87] The rapprochement between the United States and China in the early 1970s muted Chinese ambitions in the Third World, blunting one major source of anti-Western activism in the previous decade. Still, polarization accelerated in the Third World, not least because of soaring confidence among Soviet leaders and other governments hostile to the United States following Washington's final defeat in Vietnam in 1975.

This polarization gutted the middle of the global political spectrum, the space where the Kennedy administration had once hoped to construct a new partnership between the United States and the rising Third World. JFK and many of his aides, that is, had aimed to transcend the Manichean mindset of the Cold War and forge cooperation with nations like Nehru's India that eschewed alliances but sought cooperation with the West to promote economic development and political moderation at home and internationally. So too did JFK and like-minded advisers hope to align the United States with the new African nations on the basis of a shared commitment to racial equality, decolonization, and development.

The disintegration of this vision opened space for a new liberal movement in the early 1970s aimed at building U.S. foreign policy around respect for human rights. Advocates contended that the United States could best ensure its global influence by living up to American principles of freedom, democracy, and due process. Culminating in Jimmy Carter's election to the presidency in 1976, the movement explicitly rebuked the stark amorality of the Nixon Doctrine. A parallel drive within the Republican Party to remoralize foreign policy in the late 1970s suggested that a rough consensus in favor of democratization and development in the post-Vietnam era might be at hand. That possibility faded as well by 1980, however, amid renewed political divisiveness and competing visions of U.S. foreign affairs. Just as the 1960s sowed social divisions that would shape American politics and society for many years to come, the decade generated enduring discord over foreign policy.

The ups and downs of the American struggle for a new foreign policy contrasted with the endurance of political and economic arrangements in much of the Third World. Even as Americans moved on from the 1960s, that is, the order they had fostered during that decade persisted for a remarkably long time in many places. The Brazilian generals remained in power until 1985, while Suharto lasted until his downfall in 1998. The 1980 Lancaster House Agreement brought Ian Smith's regime in Rhodesia to an end, though apartheid in South Africa persisted for another decade. The United States was not, of course, solely responsible for these regimes or their staying power. Nor was the United States uniquely responsible for the distance between Washington and New Delhi, or other governments skeptical of American leadership, in the last decades of the twentieth century. Soaring expectations of American resources and activism made disappointment and disgruntlement virtually inevitable. But the U.S. failure to cope more constructively with the rise of the Third World in the 1960s—to balance its impulse to promote change with a sensible awareness of the limits of its power—engendered anti-Americanism, sowed the seeds of future turmoil, and limited the prospects of success when American ambitions to promote development and democracy surged anew in the years to come.[88] A decade that started with grand visions of progress led instead to an era of diminished ambitions and unfulfilled hopes that lasted to the end of the Cold War and beyond.

# NOTES

## Introduction

1. Church keynote, July 11, 1960, Pre-Presidential Papers, Presidential Campaign Files, 1960, Democratic National Committee Press Releases, box 1034, JFKL.

2. "A Farewell to Foreign Aid: A Liberal Takes Leave," October 29, 1971, Symington Papers, vol. 3724.

3. Inaugural address, January 20, 1961, in *Public Papers of the Presidents: John F. Kennedy, 1961* (Washington, DC: Government Printing Office, 1962), 1.

4. "Remarks at the Annual Meeting of the Inter American Press Association," October 31, 1969, in *Public Papers of the Presidents: Richard Nixon, 1969* (Washington, DC: Government Printing Office, 1971), 894.

5. Recording of Nixon and Donald Rumsfeld, March 8, 1971, Nixon Tapes, conversation 463–6, www.whitehousetapes.org/pages/listen_tapes_rmn.htm.

6. Kissinger to Nixon, October 20, 1969, *FRUS 1969–1976*, vol. 1, doc. 41.

7. Two valuable exceptions are H. W. Brands, *The Wages of Globalism: Lyndon Johnson and the Limits of American Power* (New York: Oxford University Press, 1995) and Robert B. Rakove, *Kennedy, Johnson, and the Nonaligned World* (New York: Cambridge University Press, 2013), to which the present study is indebted. Still, neither of these studies does precisely what the present book aims to accomplish. Brands sweeps across the entire globe rather than focus on the Third World. Rakove delves mostly into the Kennedy years while focusing on American relations with non-aligned nations, indisputably a crucial set of countries but, in fact, only part of the larger Third World. Other helpful studies that touch on U.S. policymaking toward the Third World in the 1960s are H. W. Brands, *The Specter of Neutralism: The United States and the Emergence of the Third World, 1947–1960* (New York: Columbia University Press, 1989); Gabriel Kolko, *Confronting the Third World: United States Foreign Policy, 1945–1980* (New York: Pantheon, 1988); Robert J. McMahon, ed., *The Cold War in the Third World* (New York: Oxford University Press, 2013); and Odd Arne Westad, *The Global Cold War: Third World Interventions and the Making of Our Times* (New York: Cambridge University Press, 2005).

8. Nick Turse, *Kill Anything That Moves: The Real American War in Vietnam* (New York: Metropolitan, 2013), 257.

9. Francis J. Gavin and Mark Atwood Lawrence, eds., *Beyond the Cold War: Lyndon Johnson and the New Global Challenges of the 1960s* (New York: Oxford University Press, 2014), 1–12.

10. Rakove's *Kennedy, Johnson, and the Nonaligned World* stands out for its interest in this subject. The general paucity of work contrasts with the abundance of studies exploring the effect of the war on American relationships with Canada and Western Europe. See, for example,

Eugenie M. Blang, *Allies at Odds: America, Europe, and Vietnam, 1961–1968* (Lanham, MD: Rowman & Littlefield, 2011); Andreas Daum et al., eds., *America, the Vietnam War, and the World: Comparative and International Perspectives* (New York: Cambridge University Press, 2003); and Fredrik Logevall, *Choosing War: The Lost Chance for Peace and the Escalation of War in Vietnam* (Berkeley: University of California Press, 1999).

11. George W. Ball, *The Past Has Another Pattern: Memoirs* (New York: Norton, 1982), 336.

12. Thomas J. Noer, *Cold War and Black Liberation: The United States and White Rule in Africa, 1948–1968* (Columbia: University of Missouri Press, 1985), 236.

13. H. W. Brands, *India and the United States: The Cold Peace* (Boston: Twayne, 1990), 122; Barry Gewen, *The Inevitability of Tragedy: Henry Kissinger and His World* (New York: Norton, 2020), 237; and Stephen R. Graubard, *Kissinger: Portrait of a Mind* (New York: Norton, 1973), 226.

14. See chapters 1 and 3 for discussion of the scholarship related to each of the three presidencies.

15. My analysis draws loosely on the "bureaucratic politics" theory of decision making by noting that policymakers sometimes advanced positions that served the interests of their agencies. But I assign as much explanatory power to officials' personal outlooks and experiences while acknowledging that presidents exerted substantial power. On the bureaucratic politics school, see J. Garry Clifford, "Bureaucratic Politics," in *Explaining the History of American Foreign Relations*, 2nd ed., ed. Michael J. Hogan and Thomas G. Paterson (New York: Cambridge University Press, 2004). A few scholars have examined cases studied in this book through the bureaucratic-politics lens. See Carl Watts, "G. Mennen Williams and Rhodesian Independence: A Case Study in Bureaucratic Politics," *Michigan Academician* 36 (2004): 225–246, and Ben Offiler, *U.S. Foreign Policy and the Modernization of Iran: Kennedy, Johnson, Nixon, and the Shah* (London: Palgrave Macmillan, 2015).

16. Outstanding examples of scholarship highlighting the rise of conservatism in the 1960s include Mary C. Brennan, *Turning Right in the Sixties: The Conservative Capture of the GOP* (Chapel Hill: University of North Carolina Press, 1995), and Matthew D. Lassiter, *The Silent Majority: Suburban Politics in the Sunbelt South* (Princeton, NJ: Princeton University Press, 2006). For the impact of this trend on the Johnson administration, see Randall B. Woods, *Prisoners of Hope: Lyndon B. Johnson, the Great Society, and the Limits of Liberalism* (New York: Basic Books, 2016).

17. "Antecedents and Objectives of the Movement of Solidarity of the Peoples of Africa, Asia and Latin America," in *First Solidarity Conference of the Peoples of Africa, Asia and Latin America* (Havana: General Secretariat of the OSPAAAL, 1966), 23.

18. On this vast subject, see Gregg A. Brazinsky, *Winning the Third World: Sino-American Rivalry during the Cold War* (Chapel Hill: University of North Carolina Press, 2017); Jeremy Friedman, *Shadow Cold War: The Sino-Soviet Competition for the Third World* (Chapel Hill: University of North Carolina Press, 2015); and Lorenz M. Lüthi, *The Sino-Soviet Split: Cold War in the Communist World* (Princeton, NJ: Princeton University Press, 2008).

19. In this way, my analysis bolsters the growing call among some diplomatic and international historian for a return to the study of the U.S. policy process and domestic politics as the wellsprings of U.S. foreign relations. See Daniel Bessner and Fredrik Logevall, "Recentering the United States in the Historiography of American Foreign Relations," *Texas National Security Review* 3, no. 2 (Spring 2020): 39–55.

20. U.S. relationships with these nations during the sixties have been subjected to superb analysis, as the ensuing chapters, especially the footnotes, make clear. But key studies deserve mention here since they have done so much to shape this book: James A. Bill, *The Eagle and the Lion: The Tragedy of American-Iranian Relations* (New Haven, CT: Yale University Press, 1988); Ruth Leacock, *Requiem for Revolution: The United States and Brazil, 1961–1969* (Kent, OH: Kent State University Press, 1990); Robert J. McMahon, *The Cold War on the Periphery: The United States, India, and Pakistan* (New York: Columbia University Press, 1994); Bradley R. Simpson, *Economists with Guns: Authoritarian Development and U.S.-Indonesia Relations, 1960–1968* (Stanford, CA: Stanford University Press, 2008); Carl Peter Watts, *Rhodesia's Unilateral Declaration of Independence: An International History* (New York: Palgrave, 2012). India and Indonesia are deftly examined in Rakove, *Kennedy, Johnson, and the Nonaligned World.*

21. For analysis of the term, see Jason C. Parker, *Hearts, Minds, Voices: U.S. Cold War Public Diplomacy and the Formation of the Third World* (New York: Oxford University Press, 2016), 8–9; Arturo Escobar, *Encountering Development: The Making and Unmaking of the Third World* (Princeton, NJ: Princeton University Press, 1995); and B. R. Tomlinson, "What Was the Third World?," *Journal of Contemporary History* 38, no. 2 (April 2003): 307–321.

22. On the oddities of the terminology, see William Easterly, *The Tyranny of Experts: Economics, Dictators, and the Forgotten Rights of the Poor* (New York: Basic Books, 2013), 118–119.

23. Parker, *Hearts, Minds, Voices.*

24. Vijay Prashad, *The Darker Nations: A People's History of the Third World* (New York: New Press, 2007), xv.

25. Easterly, *Tyranny of Experts*, 119.

26. On the ways in which these nations straddled the communist and Third World movements, see Pierre Asselin, *Vietnam's American War: A History* (New York: Cambridge University Press, 2017); James G. Blight and Philip Brenner, *Sad and Luminous Days: Cuba's Struggle with the Superpowers after the Missile Crisis* (Lanham, MD: Rowman & Littlefield, 2002); and Brazinsky, *Winning the Third World.*

## Chapter 1

1. "President Johnson," *New York Times*, November 23, 1963, 27.

2. "Johnson Was Esteemed Highly by President," *Los Angeles Times*, November 23, 1963, 2.

3. Ormsby-Gore to Foreign Office, November 24, 1963, FO371/168411, NAUK.

4. Johnson speech, November 27, 1963, American Presidency Project, http://www.presidency.ucsb.edu/ws/?pid=25988.

5. "Europe's First Reaction to Talk Is Air of Relief," *Washington Post*, November 28, 1963, A19.

6. For example, John Dumbrell, "LBJ and the Cold War," in *A Companion to Lyndon Johnson*, ed. Mitchell B. Lerner (Malden, MA: Wiley-Blackwell, 2012), 243. See also Jennifer W. See, "An Uneasy Truce: John F. Kennedy and Soviet-American Détente, 1963," *Cold War History* 2, no. 2 (January 2002): 161–194.

7. Thomas Alan Schwartz, *Lyndon Johnson and Europe: In the Shadow of Vietnam* (Cambridge, MA: Harvard University Press, 2003).

8. Debate transcript, October 13, 1960, Commission on Presidential Debates, www.debates.org/index.php?page=october-13-1960-debate-transcript.

9. Kennedy speech, Alexandria, VA, August 24, 1960, www.presidency.ucsb.edu/ws/index.php?pid=74188.

10. Kennedy speech, Los Angeles, July 15, 1960, http://www.presidency.ucsb.edu/ws/index.php?pid=25966.

11. Study by Louis Harris and Associates, "A Survey of the Race for President in 1960 in the State of California," March 1958, Pre-Presidential Files, box 815, JFKL.

12. Study by Louis Harris and Associates, "A Study of the 1960 Presidential Election in New York State," September 19, 1960, Pre-Presidential Files, box 816, JFKL.

13. Speech to Massachusetts Federation of Taxpayers, April 21, 1951, Pre-Presidential Papers, House of Representatives Files, Boston Office Speech Files, box 95, JFKL.

14. Elizabeth N. Saunders, *Leaders at War: How Presidents Shape Military Interventions* (Ithaca, NY: Cornell University Press, 2011), 96.

15. Kennedy speech, July 2, 1957, https://www.jfklibrary.org/Research/Research-Aids/JFK-Speeches/United-States-Senate-Imperialism_19570702.aspx.

16. Inaugural address, January 20, 1961, http://www.presidency.ucsb.edu/ws/index.php?pid=8032.

17. Polls showed, for example, that a huge majority (71 percent in favor, 18 percent opposed, and 11 percent with no opinion) backed establishment of the Peace Corps, one of JFK's signature proposals connected to the Third World. Gallup Poll 640K, "Peace Corps," in George H. Gallup, *The Gallup Poll: Public Opinion, 1935–1971* (New York: Random House, 1972), 3:1704.

18. See, for example, James G. Blight et al., eds, *Vietnam: If Kennedy Had Lived* (Lanham, MD: Rowman & Littlefield, 2009); Thurston Clarke, *JFK's Last Hundred Days: The Transformation of a Man and the Emergence of a Great President* (New York: Penguin, 2013); and Lawrence Freedman, *Kennedy's Wars: Berlin, Cuba, Laos, and Vietnam* (New York: Oxford University Press, 2000).

19. For memoirs, see Richard D. Mahoney, *JFK: Ordeal in Africa* (New York: Oxford University Press, 1983); Arthur M. Schlesinger Jr., *A Thousand Days: John F. Kennedy in the White House* (New York: Fawcett, 1965); and Ted Sorensen, *Kennedy* (New York: Harper & Row, 1965). Scholarly works include Philip E. Muehlenbeck, *Betting on the Africans: John F. Kennedy's Courting of African Nationalist Leaders* (New York: Oxford University Press, 2012), and Rakove, *Kennedy, Johnson, and the Nonaligned World.*

20. Journalistic accounts include Seymour M. Hersh, *The Dark Side of Camelot* (Boston: Little, Brown, 1997), and Victor Lasky, *J.F.K.: The Man and the Myth* (New York: Macmillan, 1963). Scholarly works include Thomas G. Paterson, ed., *Kennedy's Quest for Victory: American Foreign Policy, 1961–1963* (New York: Oxford University Press, 1989); and David F. Schmitz, *The United States and Right-Wing Dictatorships* (New York: Cambridge University Press, 2006).

21. See esp. Clarke, *JFK's Last Hundred Days.*

22. Robert Dallek, *An Unfinished Life: John F. Kennedy, 1917–1963* (Boston: Little, Brown, 2003), chaps. 2–3 and 231–239.

23. James MacGregor Burns, *John Kennedy: A Political Profile* (New York: Harcourt Brace, 1959), 247.

24. Norman Mailer, "Superman Comes to the Supermarket," *Esquire*, November 1960, reprinted in Mailer, *The Presidential Papers* (New York: Putnam, 1963), 47.

25. Clarke, *JFK's Last Hundred Days*, xii, 6.

26. Clarke, *JFK's Last Hundred Days*, 7.

27. David Halberstam, *The Best and the Brightest*, new ed. (New York: Random House, 1992), 362.

28. Pierre Salinger, *With Kennedy* (Garden City, NY: Doubleday, 1966), 64.

29. Robert Dallek, *Camelot's Court: Inside the Kennedy White House* (New York: HarperCollins, 2013), 111.

30. Ball oral history, April 12, 1965, JFKL, 22, 24.

31. Rostow oral history, April 11, 1964, JFKL, 12–13.

32. Burns, *John Kennedy*, x.

33. Kennan oral history, March 23, 1965, JFKL, 33.

34. Andrew Preston, *The War Council: McGeorge Bundy, the NSC, and Vietnam* (Cambridge, MA: Harvard University Press, 2006), 38.

35. Kai Bird, *The Color of Truth: McGeorge Bundy and William Bundy: Brothers in Arms* (New York: Simon & Schuster, 2000), 7.

36. David Dellinger, *From Yale to Jail: The Life Story of a Moral Dissenter* (New York: Pantheon, 1993), 192.

37. Komer oral history, no. 5, December 22, 1969, JFKL, 6.

38. Andrew Preston, "The Little State Department: McGeorge Bundy and the National Security Council Staff, 1961–1965," *Presidential Studies Quarterly* 31, no. 4 (December 2001): 641–648.

39. Frank Leith Jones, *Blowtorch: Robert Komer, Vietnam, and American Cold War Strategy* (Annapolis, MD: Naval Institute Press, 2013), 39. See also Rakove, *Kennedy, Johnson, and the Nonaligned World*, 36–41.

40. Michael Lumbers, "The Irony of Vietnam: The Johnson Administration's Tentative Bridge Building to China, 1965–1966," *Journal of Cold War Studies* 6, no. 3 (Summer 2004): 71–73.

41. See also Rakove, *Kennedy, Johnson, and the Nonaligned World*, 45–51.

42. "Report to the Honorable John F. Kennedy from Adlai Stevenson," November 1960, Pre-Presidential Files, box 1074, JFKL.

43. "Report to the President-Elect of the Task Force on Immediate Latin American Problems," January 4, 1961, Pre-Presidential Files, box 1074, JFKL.

44. For example, "Report to the Honorable John F. Kennedy by the Task Force on Africa," December 31, 1960, Pre-Presidential Files, box 1073, JFKL.

45. Library of Congress Legislative Reference Service, "A Concise History of U.S. Foreign Aid," June 13, 1968, Symington Papers, vol. 3742.

46. For example, Michael E. Latham, *Modernization as Ideology: American Social Science and "Nation Building" in the Kennedy Era* (Chapel Hill: University of North Carolina Press, 2000).

47. For biographical sketches of Rostow and other enthusiasts for nation-building, see David Ekbladh, *The Great American Mission: Modernization and the Construction of an American World Order* (Princeton, NJ: Princeton University Press, 2010), 173–174; Latham, *Modernization as Ideology*; and David Milne, *America's Rasputin: Walt Rostow and the Vietnam War* (New York: Hill & Wang, 2008), 24, 40.

48. W.W. Rostow, *The Stages of Economic Growth: A Non-communist Manifesto*, 3rd ed. (Cambridge: Cambridge University Press, 1990), chap. 2.

49. Milne, *America's Rasputin*, 60.

50. "Guerrilla Warfare in the Underdeveloped Areas," *Department of State Bulletin* 34, no. 1154 (August 7, 1961): 234. See also Nils Gilman, *Mandarins of the Future: Modernization Theory in Cold War America* (Baltimore: Johns Hopkins University Press, 2003), esp. chap. 5; Mark Haefele, "Walt Rostow's Stages of Economic Growth: Ideas and Action," in *Staging Growth: Modernization, Development, and the Global Cold War*, ed. David C. Engerman et al. (Amherst: University of Massachusetts Press, 2003), 81–97; and Latham, *Modernization as Ideology*, chap. 2.

51. Rostow, *Stages of Economic Growth*, 143.

52. Bowles speech, Georgetown University, March 10, 1959, Church Papers, Foreign Relations Committee Files, box 8.

53. "Guerrilla Warfare in the Underdeveloped Areas," *Department of State Bulletin* 34, no. 1154 (August 7, 1961): 236.

54. For example, "Guerrilla Warfare in the Underdeveloped Areas," 235.

55. Christian G. Appy, *Patriots: The Vietnam War Remembered from All Sides* (New York: Viking, 2003), 82.

56. Rostow, *Stages of Economic Growth*, esp. 50–58. See also Edward S. Mason, *Economic Planning and the Underdeveloped Areas* (New York: Fordham University Press, 1958), chap. 3, and *Promoting Economic Development: The United States and Southeast Asia* (Claremont, CA: Claremont College, 1955), chaps. 1–2. On the pervasive view among Western economists that development could best be achieved by nondemocratic societies, see Easterly, *Tyranny of Experts*.

57. This terminology is inspired by John Lewis Gaddis's argument that U.S. grand strategy after 1945 was shaped by debate between officials who believed that the United States should concentrate its resources on key "strongpoints" at either end of the Eurasian landmass and others who advocated a "perimeter" approach demanding that the United States deploy its strength wherever communism threatened to expand. See John Lewis Gaddis, *Strategies of Containment: A Critical Appraisal of American National Security Policy during the Cold War*, rev. ed. (New York: Oxford University Press, 2005), esp. 56–57.

58. Robert L. Beisner, *Dean Acheson: A Life in the Cold War* (New York: Oxford University Press, 2006); James A. Bill, *George Ball: Behind the Scenes in U.S. Foreign Policy* (New Haven, CT: Yale University Press, 1997); and Walter Isaacson and Evan Thomas, *The Wise Men: Six Friends and the World They Made* (New York: Simon & Schuster, 1986).

59. Dallek, *Camelot's Court*, 99, and Richard Aldous, *Schlesinger: The Imperial Historian* (New York: Norton, 2017), 276.

60. For similar analysis of Rusk, see Rakove, *Kennedy, Johnson, and the Nonaligned World*, 51–53.

61. Ball, *Past Has Another Pattern*, 180.

62. Isaacson and Thomas, *Wise Men*, 590.

63. Beisner, *Dean Acheson*, 525.

64. Beisner, *Dean Acheson*, 630.

65. Halberstam, *Best and the Brightest*, 334.

66. Howard B. Schaffer, *Chester Bowles: New Dealer in the Cold War* (Cambridge, MA: Harvard University Press, 1993), 229.

67. Halberstam, *Best and the Brightest*, 309, 327.

68. Ball, *Past Has Another Pattern*, 183.

69. George W. Ball, *The Discipline of Power: Essentials of a Modern World Structure* (Boston: Little, Brown, 1968), 222.

70. Thomas J. Noer, "New Frontiers and Old Priorities in Africa," in Paterson, *Kennedy's Quest for Victory*, 265.

71. Halberstam, *Best and the Brightest*, 493.

72. Gareth Porter, *Perils of Dominance: Imbalance of Power and the Road to War in Vietnam* (Berkeley: University of California Press, 2005), chap. 5.

73. For similar analysis, see Tim Weiner, *Legacy of Ashes: The History of the CIA* (New York: Anchor, 2007), 189–194.

74. Maxwell D. Taylor, *The Uncertain Trumpet* (New York: Harper & Row, 1960).

75. On Dulles and LeMay, see Andrew J. Bacevich, *Washington Rules: America's Path to Permanent War* (New York: Metropolitan, 2010), 36–55.

76. Memorandum of conversation, February 21, 1961, *FRUS 1961–1963*, vol. 8, doc. 18.

77. John Nagl, *Learning to Eat Soup with a Knife: Counterinsurgency Lessons from Malaya to Vietnam* (Chicago: University of Chicago Press, 2005), 124.

78. Schlesinger, *Thousand Days*, 189–190.

79. Peter Grose, *Gentleman Spy: The Life of Allen Dulles* (Boston: Houghton Mifflin, 1994), 410.

80. David Halberstam, *The Fifties* (New York: Villard, 1993), 373–374.

81. Halberstam, *Best and the Brightest*, 21–22.

82. H. R. McMaster, *Dereliction of Duty: Lyndon Johnson, Robert McNamara, the Joint Chiefs of Staff, and the Lies That Led to Vietnam* (New York: HarperCollins, 1997), 15.

83. Dallek, *Camelot's Court*, 204–205. See also Beisner, *Dean Acheson*, 628–630.

84. Dallek, *Camelot's Court*, 103.

85. Townsend Hoopes, *The Limits of Intervention* (New York: McKay, 1973), 21. See also Halberstam, *Best and the Brightest*, 158–169.

86. Freedman, *Kennedy's Wars*, 400.

## Chapter 2

1. CIA report, "Brazil as an Instrument of Western Influence in Africa," March 1, 1961, CIA Electronic Reading Room, https://www.cia.gov/library/readingroom/document/0000293353.

2. Memo by C. F. Marotta, "Establishing Relations with New Brazilian Administration," February 1, 1961, NSF, box 12, JFKL.

3. Jonathan C. Brown, *Cuba's Revolutionary World* (Cambridge, MA: Harvard University Press, 2017), 239.

4. Schlesinger to Kennedy, "Brazil Briefing Book," March 31, 1962, NSF, box 12a, JFKL.

5. Schlesinger to Bundy and Rostow, March 15, 1961, NSF, box 215, JFKL.

6. CIA report, "Brazil as an Instrument of Western Influence in Africa," March 1, 1961, CIA Electronic Reading Room, document 0000293353, https://www.cia.gov/library/readingroom/document/0000293353.

7. Leacock, *Requiem for Revolution*, 2–4, and Steven G. Rabe, *The Killing Zone: The United States Wages Cold War in Latin America* (New York: Oxford University Press, 2012), 104.

8. For superb analysis of Brazil's economic condition and the growing appeal of Cuba, see Brown, *Cuba's Revolutionary World*, 242–244.

9. Thomas E. Skidmore, *Politics in Brazil, 1930–1964: An Experiment in Democracy* (New York: Oxford University Press, 1967), 218.

10. Schlesinger to Kennedy, March 10, 1961, NSF, Regional Security Files, box 215, JFKL.

11. Schlesinger to Kennedy, March 10, 1961.

12. For an overview, see Jeffrey F. Taffet, *Foreign Aid as Foreign Policy: The Alliance for Progress in Latin America* (New York: Routledge, 2007).

13. For U.S. gloom about the Brazilian economy in the first months of the alliance, see State Department report, "Latin America—Current Stage of Progress in Key Socio-Economic Reforms, by Country," September 28, 1961, NSF, box 215a, JFKL, and NSC memo, "Indices of Latin American Social Development," n.d., NSF, box 216, JFKL.

14. James G. Hershberg, "'High-Spirited Confusion': Brazil, the 1961 Belgrade Non-Aligned Conference, and the Limits of an 'Independent' Foreign Policy during the High Cold War," *Cold War History* 7, no. 3 (August 2007): 373–388.

15. Renata Keller, "The Latin American Missile Crisis," *Diplomatic History* 39, no. 2 (April 2015): 212–221.

16. For example, CIA report, "Economic Deterioration and Leftist Gains in Brazil," May 3, 1963, NSF, box 14, JFKL.

17. Memorandum of conversation, December 13, 1962, NSF, box 13a, JFKL.

18. James G. Hershberg, "The United States, Brazil, and the Cuban Missile Crisis (Part 2)," *Journal of Cold War Studies* 6, no. 3 (Summer 2004): 11.

19. Gordon to State Department, December 19, 1962, NSF, box 13a, JFKL.

20. Leacock, *Requiem for Revolution*, 161.

21. Leacock, *Requiem for Revolution*, 127–128.

22. Draper Commission report, November 3, 1962, NSF, box 13, JFKL.

23. Kennedy speech, March 13, 1961, NSF, box 215, JFKL.

24. Rostow to Edwin Martin, November 14, 1962, RG59, PPC, Subject Files, 1954–1962, box 213, NARA.

25. Memorandum of conversation, "Prevention of Bloc Intervention in the Hemisphere," May 21, 1963, NSF, box 216, JFKL. On Kennedy's attitude toward Cuba, see Freedman, *Kennedy's Wars*, 233–237.

26. For analysis of this line of thinking, see Simpson, *Economists with Guns*, 67–74.

27. Gordon (Rio de Janeiro) to State Department, August 21, 1962, NSF, box 13, JFKL.

28. CIA telegram, "View of San Tiago Dantas," February 11, 1963, NSF, box 13a, JFKL.

29. Meeting transcript, Kennedy with Gordon, et al., March 8, 1963, National Security Archive, http://nsarchive.gwu.edu/NSAEBB/NSAEBB465/docs/Document%206%20brazil-jfk%20tapes-030863-revised.pdf.

30. Gordon to Martin, "Political Trends and Contingencies in Brazil," August 22, 1963, NSF, box 14, JFKL.

31. Excerpts from Kennedy conversation with Gordon, McNamara, et al., October 7, 1963, National Security Archive, http://nsarchive.gwu.edu/NSAEBB/NSAEBB465/docs/Document%209%20brazil-jfk%20tapes-100763-revised.pdf.

32. State Department circular telegram to Latin American posts, October 5, 1963, NSF, Regional Security Files, box 216, JFKL.

33. Kennedy press conference, October 9, 1963, American Presidency Project, http://www.presidency.ucsb.edu/ws/?pid=9460.

34. This chapter concurs with historian Anthony W. Pereira, whose review of scholarship on U.S. support for the 1964 coup argues that scholars have often overstated the extent to which the Kennedy administration committed itself firmly to a coup. Pereira, "The U.S. Role in the 1964 Coup in Brazil: A Reassessment," *Bulletin of Latin American Research* 37, no. 1 (June 2016): 5–17, http://onlinelibrary.wiley.com/doi/10.1111/blar.12518/full.

35. Kennedy speech, "The Choice in Asia—Democratic Development in India," March 25, 1958, Pre-Presidential Papers, Senate Files, Speech Files, 1953–1960, JFKL.

36. Kennedy speech, "Choice in Asia."

37. John M. Leddy to Rostow, June 1, 1961, NSF, India, box 106, JFKL.

38. Rakove, *Kennedy, Johnson, and the Nonaligned World*, 186–188, and Dennis Kux, *India and the United States: Estranged Democracies* (Washington, DC: National Defense University Press, 1992), 188–189.

39. Quoted in McMahon, *Cold War on the Periphery*, 276.

40. Johnson to Kennedy, May 23, 1961, NSF, India, box 106, JFKL.

41. Briefing book, "Prime Minister Nehru's Visit, November 6–10, 1961," President's Office Files, box 118a, JFKL.

42. Schlesinger, *Thousand Days*, 485.

43. Schlesinger, *Thousand Days*, 484.

44. Mark Atwood Lawrence, "The Limits of Peacemaking: India and the Vietnam War, 1962–67," *India Review* 1, no. 3 (January 2002): 45.

45. Memcon, Bowles with Nehru, August 8–9, 1961, RG59, PPC, Subject Files, 1954–1962, box 141, NARA.

46. Andrew J. Rotter, *Comrades at Odds: The United States and India, 1947–1964* (Ithaca, NY: Cornell University Press, 2000), 182–186.

47. Paper by the Bureau of Near Eastern and South Asian Affairs, "United States Relations with South Asia: Major Issues and Recommended Courses of Action," n.d., *FRUS 1961–1963*, vol. 19, doc. 88.

48. Komer to Bundy, January 6, 1962, *FRUS 1961–1963*, vol. 19, doc. 87.

49. McMahon, *Cold War on the Periphery*, 287.

50. Sarvepalli Gopal, *Jawaharlal Nehru: A Biography*, vol. 3, *1956–1964* (London: Jonathan Cape, 1984), 223.

51. Rotter, *Comrades at Odds*, 73.

52. John Kenneth Galbraith, *Ambassador's Journal: A Personal Account of the Kennedy Years* (Boston: Houghton Mifflin, 1969), 495.

53. Author's interview with Rostow, October 3, 2000, Austin, TX.

54. Quoted in Kux, *India and the United States*, 212.

55. Kux, *India and the United States*, 213–214.

56. Tanvi Madan, "With an Eye to the East: The China Factor and the U.S.-India Relationship, 1949–1979" (PhD diss., University of Texas at Austin, 2012), 319.

57. Bowles to Bundy, October 5, 1963, NSF, Komer Files, box 418, JFKL.

58. Komer to Kennedy, November 12, 1963, NSF, Komer Files, box 418, JFKL, and Komer to William Bundy, November 14, 1963, *FRUS 1961–1963*, vol. 19, doc. 338.

59. Komer to Kennedy, November 12, 1963.

60. Chester Bowles, *Promises to Keep: My Years in Public Life, 1941–1969* (New York: Harper & Row, 1971), 481. My analysis is informed by Kux, *India and the United States*, 215–218.

61. Komer to William Bundy, November 14, 1963, *FRUS 1961–1963*, vol. 19, doc. 338.

62. Joint Chiefs of Staff to Secretary McNamara, January 26, 1961, *FRUS 1961–1963*, vol. 17, doc. 4.

63. Telcon, Rostow and Ball, May 8, 1961, Ball Papers, box 5, JFKL.

64. "Comments on Iran Task Force Paper on Contingency Planning," October 20, 1961, NSF, Komer files, box 425, JFKL.

65. National Intelligence Estimate, "Prospects for Iran," February 28, 1961, *FRUS 1961–1963*, vol. 17, doc. 16.

66. Mark J. Gasiorowski, *U.S. Foreign Policy and the Shah: Building a Client State in Iran* (Ithaca, NY: Cornell University Press, 1991), 96–98.

67. Report by Bureau of Near Eastern and South Asian Affairs, "The Current Internal Political Situation in Iran," March 27, 1961, *FRUS 1961–1963*, vol. 17, doc. 27.

68. CIA study, "Outlook for the Shah of Iran," August 15, 1958, CIA Electronic Reading Room, https://www.cia.gov/library/readingroom/document/cia-rdp79r00904a000400030025-0.

69. Report by Bureau of Near Eastern and South Asian Affairs, "The Current Internal Political Situation in Iran," March 27, 1961, *FRUS 1961–1963*, vol. 17, doc. 27.

70. Other scholars have written about the division over policy toward Iran. For analysis similar to my own and a survey of the relevant scholarship, see Offiler, *U.S. Foreign Policy*, 26–30.

71. Offiler, *U.S. Foreign Policy*.

72. Bill, *Eagle and the Lion*, 137.

73. Bowles to Holmes, June 3, 1961, *FRUS 1961–1963*, vol. 17, doc. 61.

74. Komer to Kennedy, May 18, 1961, *FRUS 1961–1963*, vol. 17, doc. 50.

75. Bill, *Eagle and the Lion*, 137, and Armin Meyer, *Quiet Diplomacy: From Cairo to Tokyo in the Twilight of Imperialism* (New York: iUniverse, 2003), 134.

76. Gasiorowski, *U.S. Foreign Policy and the Shah*, 112, and Taylor to Kennedy, March 14, 1962, NSF, box 117, JFKL.

77. Memo on State Department–Joint Chiefs of Staff meeting, March 31, 1961, *FRUS 1961–1963*, vol. 17, doc. 29.

78. Holmes to State Department, August 27, 1961, *FRUS 1961–1963*, vol. 17, doc. 102.

79. Report by Talbot, January 18, 1962, *FRUS 1961–1963*, vol. 17, doc. 168, and Holmes to Rusk, January 22, 1962, *FRUS 1961–1963*, vol. 17, doc. 172.

80. Komer to Kennedy, August 4, 1961, NSF, box 116, JFKL.

81. Hansen to Talbot, October 18, 1961, *FRUS 1961–1963*, vol. 17, doc. 130.

82. Telcon, Robert F. Kennedy and Ball, January 29, 1962, Ball Papers, box 5, JFKL.

83. Komer to Kaysen, January 19, 1962, *FRUS 1961–1963*, vol. 17, doc. 170.

84. Hansen to Komer, November 7, 1962, NSF, Komer Files, box 424, JFKL.

85. Memorandum of conversation, April 13, 1962, *FRUS 1961–1963*, vol. 17, doc. 246.

86. Memorandum of conversation, April 13, 1962, *FRUS 1961–1963*, vol. 17, doc. 247.

87. Memorandum of conversation, April 13, 1962, *FRUS 1961–1963*, vol. 17, doc. 246.

88. Battle to Bundy, May 4, 1962, *FRUS 1961–1963*, vol. 17, doc. 246.

89. Gasiorowski, *U.S. Foreign Policy and the Shah*, 185–187.

90. Yatsevitch to Holmes, September 18, 1962, NSF, Komer files, box 424, JFKL.

91. Brubeck to Bundy, January 21, 1963, *FRUS 1961–1963*, vol. 18, doc. 136.

92. Rusk to Kennedy, April 20, 1963, *FRUS 1961–1963*, vol. 18, doc. 218. Rusk's memo should be compared to the more mixed assessment in the document on which he obviously based his assessment: Special National Intelligence Estimate, "The Iranian Situation," April 10, 1963, *FRUS 1961–1963*, vol. 18, doc. 212.

93. Polk to Phillips Talbot, December 18, 1962, Komer files, box 424, JFKL.

94. CIA report, "Memorandum for the Director," August 16, 1962, Komer files, box 424, JFKL.

95. Report by Komer, October 20, 1962, *FRUS 1961–1963*, vol. 18, doc. 85.

96. Komer to Bundy, April 30, 1963, President's Weekend Reading file, box 8, JFKL.

97. Memorandum for the Record, May 2, 1963, *FRUS 1961–1963*, vol. 18, doc. 235.

98. V. H. Krulak to Chairman of the Joint Chiefs of Staff, June 13, 1963, *FRUS 1961–1963*, vol. 18, doc. 271.

99. Memorandum on State Department–Joint Chiefs of Staff meeting, December 6, 1963, *FRUS 1961–1963*, vol. 18, doc. 382.

100. Talbot to Rusk, October 5, 1963, *FRUS 1961–1963*, vol. 18, doc. 333.

101. Polk to Rostow, December 17, 1963, *FRUS 1961–1963*, vol. 18, doc. 387.

102. Komer to O'Donnell, November 18, 1963, NSF, Komer files, box 424, JFKL.

103. Komer to Bundy, December 3, 1963, *FRUS 1961–1963*, vol. 18, doc. 377.

104. Jones to State Department, January 25, 1961, *FRUS 1961–1963*, vol. 23, doc. 143.

105. David Webster, "Regimes in Motion: The Kennedy Administration and Indonesia's New Frontier, 1960–1962," *Diplomatic History* 33, no. 1 (January 2009): 99.

106. Jones to State Department, January 25, 1961, *FRUS 1961–1963*, vol. 23, doc. 143.

107. Rusk to Kennedy, April 3, 1961, *FRUS 1961–1963*, vol. 23, doc. 158.

108. Bissell to Bundy, March 27, 1961, *FRUS 1961–1963*, vol. 23, doc. 155.

109. Komer to Rostow, April 19, 1961, *FRUS 1961–1963*, vol. 23, doc. 167. See also Komer to Bundy, March 27, 1961, *FRUS 1961–1963*, vol. 23, doc 156.

110. For analysis of U.S. deliberations, see Rakove, *Kennedy, Johnson, and the Nonaligned World*, 111–121. See also Simpson, *Economists with Guns*, 39–43.

111. Bundy to Kennedy, December 1, 1961, *FRUS 1961–1963*, vol. 23, doc. 205.

112. Komer to Rostow, November 30, 1961, *FRUS 1961–1963*, vol. 23, doc. 206.

113. Robert H. Johnson to Bundy, December 12, 1961, *FRUS 1961–1963*, vol. 23, doc. 212.

114. Rakove, *Kennedy, Johnson, and the Nonaligned World*, 112.

115. Rostow to Kennedy, November 30, 1961, *FRUS 1961–1963*, vol. 23, doc. 205.

116. Matthew Jones, *Conflict and Confrontation in South East Asia, 1961–1965: Britain, the United States, Indonesia, and the Creation of Malaysia* (Cambridge: Cambridge University Press, 2002), 46–48.

117. RFK speech, University of Gadja Mada, February 15, 1962, https://www.justice.gov/sites/default/files/ag/legacy/2011/01/20/02-15-1962.pdf.

118. Memorandum of conversation, March 2, 1962, *FRUS 1961–1963*, vol. 23, doc. 244.

119. Komer to Bundy, May 12, 1962, *FRUS 1961–1963*, vol. 23, doc. 265. For detailed accounts of the talks, see Jones, *Conflict and Confrontation in South East Asia*, 39–54, and Simpson, *Economists with Guns*, 52–60.

120. Jones, *Conflict and Confrontation in South East Asia*, 52–54.

121. Komer to Kennedy, August15, 1962, *FRUS 1961–1963*, vol. 23, doc. 286.

122. Jones to State Department, March 1, 1963, *FRUS 1961–1963*, vol. 23, doc. 302.

123. CIA report, "Investigation of CIA Involvement in Plans to Assassinate Foreign Leaders," June 5, 1975, Richard B. Cheney Files, box 7, Gerald R. Ford Presidential Library, https://www.fordlibrarymuseum.gov/library/document/0005/7324009.pdf. The report does not specify the timing of CIA activities regarding Sukarno.

124. NSAM 179, August 16, 1962, *FRUS 1961–1963*, vol. 23, doc. 287.

125. JCS to McNamara, September 5, 1962, *FRUS 1961–1963*, vol. 23, doc. 288.

126. Ball to Kennedy, October 10, 1962, NSF, Komer Files, box 423, JFKL. See also Jones, *Conflict and Confrontation in South East Asia*, 55–57, and Simpson, *Economists with Guns*, 82–86.

127. Simpson, *Economists with Guns*, 88–90.

128. Komer to Kennedy, July 23, 1963, *FRUS 1961–1963*, vol. 23, doc. 312.

129. Russell speech, May 1, 1962, Russell Papers, series III, speeches/media, box 61, Russell Library.

130. Simpson, *Economists with Guns*, 104.

131. Jones, *Conflict and Confrontation in South East Asia*, pt. II, and Rakove, *Kennedy, Johnson, and the Nonaligned World*, 145–149.

132. Simpson, *Economists with Guns*, 82.

133. Jones to State Department, November 4, 1963, *FRUS 1961–1963*, vol. 23, doc. 319.

134. NSC memo, "Current Status of U.S. Aid Program in Indonesia," November 8, 1963, NSF, Country File, box 246, JFKL.

135. Memorandum of conversation, November 19, 1963, *FRUS 1961–1963*, vol. 23, doc. 320.

136. Thomas J. Noer, "'Non-Benign Neglect': The United States and Black Africa in the Twentieth Century," in *American Foreign Relations: A Historiographical Review*, ed. Gerald Haines and J. Samuel Walker (Westport, CT: Greenwood, 1981), 272.

137. Quoted in Thomas Borstelmann, *The Cold War and the Color Line: American Race Relations in the Global Arena* (Cambridge, MA: Harvard University Press, 2001), 145.

138. William H. Attwood oral history, November 8, 1965, JFKL, 7.

139. Muehlenbeck, *Betting on the Africans*, 42–43, 47–49.

140. Press release, Press Office of Senator John F. Kennedy, Williams Papers, box 7, Bentley Library.

141. Muehlenbeck, *Betting on the Africans*, 50.

142. Roger Hilsman, *To Move a Nation: The Politics of Foreign Policy in the Administration of John F. Kennedy* (Garden City, NY: Doubleday, 1967), 233.

143. Mahoney, *JFK*, 63.

144. The extent of CIA involvement in the assassination is a matter of controversy. For different views, see Weiner, *Legacy of Ashes*, 188–189, and Ludo De Witte, *The Assassination of Lumumba*, trans. Ann Wright and Renée Fenby (New York: Verso, 2001), xxii.

145. Lise Namikas, *Battleground Africa: Cold War in the Congo, 1960–1965* (Stanford, CA: Stanford University Press, 2013), 187.

146. On the dissolution of the federation, see Filipe Ribeiro de Meneses and Robert McNamara, *The White Redoubt, the Great Powers, and the Struggle for Southern Africa, 1960–1980* (London: Palgrave Macmillan, 2018), 33–43.

147. State Department paper by William R. Duggan and William Lewis, "The White Redoubt," June 28, 1962, National Security Archive, https://nsarchive.files.wordpress.com/2013/07/sapaper.pdf.

148. Policy Planning Council study, "A U.S. Foreign Policy for Africa over the Next Decade," May 22, 1961, RG59, PPC, Subject Files, 1954–1962, box 120, NARA.

149. Alex Thomson, *U.S. Foreign Policy toward Apartheid South Africa, 1948–1994* (New York: Palgrave Macmillan, 2008), 42–43, and Borstelmann, *Cold War and the Color Line*, 153.

150. JCS memo for McNamara, "U.S. Policy toward Portugal and the Republic of South Africa," July 10, 1963, NSF, box 159, JFKL.

151. JCS memo for McNamara, "U.S. Policy toward Portugal," and McNamara to Rusk, July 11, 1963, NSF, box 159, JFKL.

152. Rusk to heads of department, June 15, 1963, RG59, PPC, Subject and Country Files, 1965–1969, box 310, NARA.

153. Church comments, Naval Academy Foreign Affairs Conference, April 27, 1961, Church Papers, series 8.1, box 8.

154. Bundy to Kennedy, July 13, 1963, NSF, box 159, JFKL.

155. Ryan M. Irwin, *Gordian Knot: Apartheid and the Unmaking of the Liberal World Order* (New York: Oxford University Press, 2012), 69–70; Borstelmann, *Cold War and the Color Line*, 154–155; and Muehlenbeck, *Betting on the Africans*, 112–121.

156. Rusk to U.S. Mission at the United Nations, January 11, 1962, *FRUS 1961–1963*, vol. 21, doc. 324.

157. State Department to London embassy, October 5, 1962, *FRUS 1961–1963*, vol. 21, doc. 332.

158. Quoted in Noer, *Cold War and Black Liberation*, 189.

159. State Department to London embassy, January 7, 1963, *FRUS 1961–1963*, vol. 21, doc. 335.

160. State Department to London embassy, January 7, 1963; Memorandum for the President by William H. Brubeck, "Meeting with Sir Roy Welensky," October 7, 1963, NSF, box 155A, JFKL; and Salisbury to State Department, October 25, 1963, NSF, box 155A, JFKL.

161. Salisbury to State Department, December 6, 1962, NSF, box 155A, JFKL, and Borstelmann, *Cold War and the Color Line*, 146.

162. Williams to Rusk, June 15, 1963, *FRUS 1961–1963*, vol. 21, doc. 340; State Department to U.S. Mission to the United Nations, September 6, 1963, *FRUS 1961–1963*, vol. 21, doc. 342; and Noer, *Cold War and Black Liberation*, 190.

163. State Department memo for Bundy, "Situation Report on Southern Rhodesia," April 6, 1963, NSF, box 155A, JFKL.

164. Statement by Yates, March 25, 1963, Williams Papers, box 10, and U.S. Mission to the United Nations to State Department, April 9, 1963, NSF, box 155A, JFKL.

165. Brubeck to Bundy, October 29, 1963, *FRUS 1961–1963*, vol. 21, doc. 319.

166. Robert F. Kennedy to Bundy, November 20, 1963, NSF, box 76 [1 of 2], JFKL.

## Chapter 3

1. Johnson speech, January 8, 1964, American Presidency Project, https://www.presidency.ucsb.edu/ws/?pid=26787.

2. ". . . and of Foreign Policy," *New York Times*, January 9, 1964, 30.

3. Jenkins oral history, LBJL.

4. Ormsby-Gore to Michael Stewart, March 15, 1965, FO371/179558, NAUK.

5. Waldo Heinrichs, "Lyndon B. Johnson: Change and Continuity," in *Lyndon Johnson Confronts the World: American Foreign Policy, 1963–1968*, ed. Warren I. Cohen and Nancy Bernkopf Tucker (New York: Cambridge University Press, 1994), 26.

6. Brands, *Wages of Globalism*, 29.

7. Halberstam, *Best and the Brightest*, 440.

8. Lumbers, "Irony of Vietnam."

9. Saunders, *Leaders at War*, 92–102.

10. Saunders, *Leaders at War*, 134–148.

11. Johnson speech, December 17, 1963, Sorensen Papers, box 77, JFKL.

12. Mark Atwood Lawrence, "LBJ and the New Global Challenges," in Lerner, *Companion to Lyndon B. Johnson*, 450–465.

13. Saunders, *Leaders at War*, 143.

14. Johnson speech at Holy Cross College, June 10, 1964, https://www.presidency.ucsb.edu/documents/commencement-address-holy-cross-college.

15. Komer to Horace Busby, July 9, 1965, NSF, Komer File, box 10, LBJL.

16. Mark K. Updegrove, *Indomitable Will: LBJ in the Presidency* (New York: Skyhorse, 2012), 93.

17. Ted Sorensen, *Counselor: A Life at the Edge of History* (New York: Harper, 2008), 388.

18. Halberstam, *Best and the Brightest*, 438–439, 444.

19. Halberstam, *Best and the Brightest*, 438.

20. Randall B. Woods, *LBJ: Architect of American Ambition* (New York: Free Press, 2006), 120.

21. Daniel Sargent, "Lyndon Johnson and the Challenges of Economic Globalization," in Gavin and Lawrence, *Beyond the Cold War*, 22.

22. Updegrove, *Indomitable Will*, 220.

23. Patrick O. Cohrs, "Towards a New Deal for the World: Lyndon Johnson's Aspirations to Renew the Twentieth Century's Pax Americana," in Gavin and Lawrence, *Beyond the Cold War*, 44.

24. Doris Kearns Goodwin, *Lyndon Johnson and the American Dream* (New York: St. Martin's, 1976), 95.

25. Goodwin, *Lyndon Johnson and the American Dream*, 95.

26. Saunders, *Leaders at War*, 135.

27. Saunders, *Leaders at War*, 136.

28. For astute analysis of LBJ's advisory team in connection with domestic policy, see Joshua Zeitz, *Building the Great Society: Inside Lyndon Johnson's White House* (New York: Viking, 2018), esp. chaps. 1 and 6.

29. Preston, *War Council*, 49.

30. Richard E. Neustadt and Ernest R. May, *Thinking in Time: The Uses of History for Decision Makers* (New York: Free Press, 1986), 79, and Heinrichs, "Lyndon B. Johnson," 23.

31. Blema S. Steinberg, *Shame and Humiliation: Presidential Decision Making on Vietnam* (Pittsburgh: University of Pittsburgh Press, 1996), 76.

32. Kearns Goodwin, *Lyndon Johnson and the American Dream*, 122.

33. Memorandum by G. E. Hall, May 27, 1965, FO371/179567, NAUK.

34. Merle Miller, *Lyndon: An Oral Biography* (New York: Putnam, 1980), 386.

35. Robert A. Caro, *The Passage to Power: The Years of Lyndon Johnson* (New York: Knopf, 2012), 82.

36. Updegrove, *Indomitable Will*, 85. See also Robert Caro, *The Years of Lyndon Johnson: Means of Ascent* (New York: Knopf, 1990), 114–117.

37. Updegrove, *Indomitable Will*, 81–85.

38. Milne, *America's Rasputin*, 203.

39. Caro, *Passage to Power*, 409–414.

40. On these relationships, see Aldous, *Schlesinger*, chap. 17; Schaffer, *Chester Bowles*, chap. 16; and Sorensen, *Counselor*, chap. 28.

41. "The Big Three," *Time* 85, no. 18 (April 30, 1965): 37.

42. "The Big Three," 37.

43. Halberstam, *Best and the Brightest*, 627.

44. Thomas Tunstall Allcock, *Thomas C. Mann: President Johnson, the Cold War, and the Restructuring of Latin American Foreign Policy* (Lexington: University Press of Kentucky, 2018), 74–75.

45. Thomas A. Reinstein, "The Way a Drunk Uses a Lamp Post: Intelligence and Policy during the Vietnam War, 1962–1968" (PhD diss., Temple University, 2018), 112, 157, 223–224.

46. Mark Atwood Lawrence, "Exception to the Rule? The Johnson Administration and the Panama Canal," in *Looking Back at LBJ: White House Politics in a New Light*, ed. Mitchell B. Lerner (Lawrence: University Press of Kansas, 2005): 20–52.

47. Telcons, Johnson and Richard Russell, January 10, 1964, WH6401.10, and WH6401.11, LBJL.

48. Michael L. Conniff, *Panama and the United States: The Forced Alliance* (Athens: University of Georgia Press, 1992), 119.

49. Scammon to Ralph Dungan, January 17, 1964, Central File, Panama, LBJL.

50. Gallup poll, February 12, 1964, in Gallup, *Gallup Poll*, 1864.

51. State Department to Panama City, January 11, 1964, box 2560, State Department Central Files, NARA.

52. United Press International dispatch, "Goldwater Lays Crisis in Panama to Yielding," *Washington Post*, January 16, 1964.

53. William J. Jorden, *Panama Odyssey* (Austin: University of Texas Press, 1984), 74.

54. J. E. Killick to Foreign Office, December 4, 1963, FO371/168411, NAUK.

55. Humphrey to Johnson, February 17, 1965, *FRUS 1964–1968*, vol. 2, doc. 134.

56. Arnold A. Offner, *Hubert Humphrey: The Conscience of the Country* (New Haven, CT: Yale University Press, 2018), 228–229.

57. Lawrence, "Exception to the Rule?"

58. Lumbers, "Irony of Vietnam," 104–112.

59. Telcon, Johnson and Russell, June 11, 1964, WH6406.10, no. 3680, LBJL.

60. Robert D. Putnam with Shaylyn Romney Garrett, *The Upswing: How America Came Together a Century Ago and How We Can Do It Again* (New York: Simon & Schuster, 2020), 298.

61. Julian E. Zelizer, *The Fierce Urgency of Now: Lyndon Johnson, Congress, and the Battle for the Great Society* (New York: Penguin, 2015), 259, 277–278.

62. James T. Patterson, *Grand Expectations: The United States, 1945–1974* (New York: Oxford University Press, 1996), 649.

63. Jeff Woods, *Black Struggle, Red Scare: Segregation and Anti-communism in the South, 1948–1968* (Baton Route: Louisiana State University Press, 2004), 233.

64. Zelizer, *Fierce Urgency of Now*, 276.

65. Burton I. Kaufman, "Foreign Aid and the Balance-of-Payments Problem: Vietnam and Lyndon Johnson's Foreign Economic Policy," in *The Johnson Years*, vol. 2: *Vietnam, the Environment, and Science*, ed. Robert A. Divine (Lawrence: University Press of Kansas, 1987), 83, 98.

66. Organisation for Economic Co-operation and Development, Query Wizard for International Development Statistics, https://stats.oecd.org/qwids/.

67. Institute for International Social Research, "Hopes And Fears," October 1964, USGALLUP.637POS.Q10; Opinion Research Corporation, ORC Public Opinion Index, August 1967, USORC.67SEP2.R10; Gallup Poll, February 1966, USGALLUP.66–274.R06A; Louis Harris & Associates, Harris Survey, August 1964, USHARRIS.082464.R2H; Louis Harris & Associates, Harris Survey, July 1966, USHARRIS.HA071866.R2R; Louis Harris & Associates, Harris Survey, December 1967, USHARRIS.012268.R2C, Roper Center for Public Opinion Research, iPOLL Databank, Cornell University, https://ropercenter.cornell.edu.

68. Schaffer, *Chester Bowles*, 283.

69. J. William Fulbright, *The Arrogance of Power* (New York: Random House, 1966).

70. Rakove, *Kennedy, Johnson, and the Nonaligned World*, 224–230.

71. Declaration of the Conference of Heads of State or Government of Non-Aligned Countries, October 10, 1964, http://cns.miis.edu/nam/documents/Official_Document/2nd_Summit_FD_Cairo_Declaration_1964.pdf.

72. Lawrence, "Limits of Peacemaking," 55.

73. Friedman, *Shadow Cold War*, 128–131, and Mark Atwood Lawrence, "The Rise and Fall of Nonalignment," in McMahon, *Cold War in the Third World*, 148–152.

74. "General Resolution on Vietnam," in *First Solidarity Conference of the Peoples of Africa, Asia, and Latin America* (Havana: General Secretariat of the OSPAAAL, 1966), 129.

75. Eric Gettig, "'A Propaganda Boon for Us': The Havana Tricontinental Conference and the United States Response," in *The Tricontinental Revolution: Third World Radicalism and the Cold War*, ed. R. Joseph Parrott and Mark Atwood Lawrence (New York: Cambridge University Press, forthcoming).

76. Johnson speech, January 12, 1966, https://www.presidency.ucsb.edu/documents/annual-message-the-congress-the-state-the-union-27.

77. King speech, "A Time to Break Silence," April 4, 1967, in *The Vietnam War: An International History in Documents*, ed. Mark Atwood Lawrence (New York: Oxford University Press, 2014), 104.

78. For LBJ's budgetary calculations, see Irving Bernstein, *Guns or Butter: The Presidency of Lyndon Johnson* (New York: Oxford University Press, 1996), esp. chap. 14, and Jeffrey W.

Helsing, *Johnson's War / Johnson's Great Society: The Guns and Butter Trap* (Westport, CT: Praeger, 2000), esp. chaps. 9–10.

79. *Congressional Quarterly Almanac, 1966* (Washington, DC: Congressional Quarterly News Features, 1967), 408.

80. Johnson news conference, April 23, 1964, American Presidency Project, https://www.presidency.ucsb.edu/documents/the-presidents-news-conference-1046.

81. For U.S. frustration, see Department of State Research Memorandum, "Third Country Assistance to South Vietnam," August 28, 1964, NSF, CF, box 7, LBJL.

82. Edward J. Drea, *McNamara, Clifford and the Burdens of Vietnam, 1965–1969* (Washington, DC: Government Printing Office, 2011), 391–397.

83. Minutes of Executive Sessions of the Senate Foreign Relations Committee, May 23, 1967, 90th Congress, 1st session (Washington, DC: Government Printing Office, 2007), https://fas.org/irp/congress/2007_hr/1967executive.html.

84. M. S. Daoudi and M. S. Dajani, *Economic Diplomacy: Embargo Leverage and World Politics* (Boulder, CO: Westview, 1985), 56; Ethan B. Kapstein, *The Insecure Alliance: Energy Crises and Western Politics since 1944* (New York: Oxford University Press, 1990), 144; and Mark Atwood Lawrence, "America's Case of 'Tonkin Gulfitis,'" *New York Times*, March 7, 2017, https://www.nytimes.com/2017/03/07/opinion/americas-case-of-tonkin-gulfitis.html.

85. Minutes of Executive Sessions of the Senate Foreign Relations Committee, May 23, 1967, 90th Congress, 1st session (Washington, DC: Government Printing Office, 2007), https://fas.org/irp/congress/2007_hr/1967executive.html.

## Chapter 4

1. Rostow to Johnson, January 25, 1967, NSF, CF, box 9, LBJL.

2. Rusk to Rio de Janeiro embassy, January 13, 1967, RG59, PPC, Subject-Numeric Files, 1963–1973, box 1903, NARA.

3. Rusk to Johnson, December 19, December1966, NSF, CF, box 9, LBJL.

4. Rusk to Johnson, December 19, 1966.

5. Associated Press, "Johnson Tells Brazilian of Will to Aid," January 27, 1967, *New York Times*, A13. The *Post* ran a brief preview of the meeting on January 26 but did not report on the meeting itself. "Johnson, Brazil's Costa e Silva Confer Today," January 26, 1967, *Washington Post*, A10.

6. Gordon OH, May 30, 1964, JFKL.

7. Gordon to State Department, December 13, 1963, NSF, Special Head of State Correspondence File, box 5, LBJL.

8. Gordon to State Department, December 21, 1963, White House Confidential File, CO29, box 7 [1/2], LBJL.

9. Ball to Rio de Janeiro embassy, December 19, 1963, NSF, Special Head of State Correspondence File, box 5, LBJL.

10. Mein to State Department, December 27, 1963, NSF, CF, box 9, LBJL.

11. Gordon to Rusk, March 27, 1964, NSF, CF, box 9, LBJL.

12. CIA report, "Survey of Latin America," April 1, 1964, NSF, CF, box 1, LBJL.

13. CIA report, "Survey of Latin America."

14. CIA report, "Survey of Latin America."

15. Telephone conversation with James Farley, November 29, 1963, in *The Presidential Recordings: Lyndon B. Johnson, November 22–30, 1963*, ed. Max Holland (New York: Norton, 2005), 255.

16. Telephone conversation with Mansfield and John Pastore, December 20, 1963, in *The Presidential Recordings: Lyndon B. Johnson, December 1963*, ed. Robert David Johnson and David Shreve (New York: Norton, 2005), 603.

17. Memo by I. J. M. Sutherland, December 4, 1963, FO371/168415, NAUK.

18. See Allcock's astute discussion of this issue in *Thomas C. Mann*, esp. 76–77.

19. Mann OH, March 13, 1968, JFKL.

20. Allcock, *Thomas C. Mann*, 79–80.

21. Allcock, *Thomas C. Mann*, 80.

22. Leacock, *Requiem for Revolution*, 199.

23. Thomas Tunstall Allcock, "Becoming 'Mr. Latin America': Thomas C. Mann Reconsidered," *Diplomatic History* 38, no. 5 (2014): 1017.

24. Allcock, "Becoming 'Mr. Latin America,'" 79.

25. Mann speech, "The Experience of the United States in Economic Development: Its Relevance for Latin America," September 25, 1962, *Department of State Bulletin* 47, no. 1221 (November 19, 1962): 772–773.

26. Tad Szulc, "U.S. May Abandon Effort to Deter Latin Dictators," *New York Times*, March 19, 1964, A2.

27. Leacock, *Requiem for Revolution*, 208–213.

28. Gordon to State Department, March 31, 1964, NSF, CF, box 9, LBJL.

29. Transcript of telephone conversation, March 31, 1964, Ball Papers, LBJL.

30. Rusk to Gordon, March 30, 1964, *FRUS 1964–1968*, vol. 31, doc. 194.

31. Transcript of telephone conversation, March 31, 1964, Ball Papers, LBJL.

32. Transcript of telephone conversation, March 31, 1964; State Department to Rio, March 31, 1964, NSF, CF, box 9, LBJL; Memorandum for the Record, April 1, 1964, Office Files of Bill Moyers, box 81, LBJL.

33. For the dynamics of the coup, see Thomas E. Skidmore, *The Politics of Military Rule in Brazil, 1964–1985* (New York: Oxford University Press, 1990), chaps. 1–2.

34. Transcript of telephone call between Ball and McCone, April 1, 1964, Ball Papers, LBJL.

35. Rusk to Rio, April 2, 1964, NSF, CF, box 10 [1/2], LBJL.

36. Rusk to Rio, March 31, 1964, NSF, CF, box 9, LBJL.

37. For example, a large plurality of Americans favored a "firm" policy toward Panama. Gallup, *Gallup Poll*, 3:1864. On Fulbright's opinions, see Memorandum for the Record, April 1, 1964, McCone Memos, box 1, LBJL.

38. Gordon Chase to McGeorge Bundy, April 2, 1964, NSF, CF, box 10 [1/2], LBJL.

39. Transcript of telephone call between Ball and Johnson, April 2, 1964, Ball Papers, LBJL.

40. Johnson note to Mazzilli, April 2, 1964, NSF, Special Head of State Correspondence File, box 5, LBJL.

41. Leacock, *Requiem for Revolution*, 215.

42. Gordon to State Department, April 2, 1964, NSF, NSC Meetings File, box 1, LBJL.

43. CIA telegram, "Plans of the Revolutionary Leaders Once President Goulart Had Been Overthrown," April 4, 1964, NSF, CF, box 10 [1/2], LBJL.

44. "Brazil: The Spirit of '32," *Time* 83, no. 14 (April 3, 1964): 30–31.

45. Martha K. Huggins, *Political Policing: The United States and Latin America* (Durham, NC: Duke University Press, 1998), 120–123.

46. Leacock, *Requiem for Revolution*, 222–223.

47. Gordon to State Department, April 8, 1964, NSF, CF, box 10 [1/2], LBJL.

48. State Department to Gordon, June 9, 1964, NSF, CF, box 10 [2/2], LBJL.

49. Gordon to State Department, April 8, 1964, NSF, CF, box 10 [1/2], LBJL.

50. Gordon to State Department, April 10, 1964, NSF, CF, box 10 [1/2], LBJL.

51. CIA Directorate of Intelligence report, "Effects of the Brazilian Revolution," July 29, 1964, NSF, CF, box 10 [2/2], LBJL.

52. Gordon to State Department, October 15, 1964, NSF, CF, box 10 [2/2], LBJL.

53. Bureau of Intelligence and Research report, "Impact of Brazilian Coup on Communist Country Presence," April 9, 1964, NSF, CF, box 10 [1/2], LBJL.

54. E. Bradford Burns, "Tradition and Variation in Brazilian Foreign Policy," *Journal of Inter-American Studies* 9, no. 2 (April 1967): 207.

55. Johnson to Castelo Branco, August 25, 1964, NSF, Special Head of State Correspondence File, box 5, LBJL.

56. State Department Intelligence and Research report, "Third Country Assistance to South Vietnam," August 28, 1964, NSF, CF, box 7, LBJL.

57. For example, "EUA Quer Apoio do Brasil no Vietnam," August 6, 1964, *Correio da Manhã*, issue 21883, 2; Hermano Alves, "C'est La Guerre," August 8, 1964, *Correio da Manhã*, issue 21885, 6; and "Expediçao Armada ao Vietnam," August 12, 1964, *Correio da Manhã*, issue 21888.

58. See esp. Leacock, *Requiem for Revolution*, 231–232.

59. Robert M. Sayre to Bundy, June 15, 1964, NSF, CF, box 10 [2/2], LBJL.

60. Skidmore, *Politics of Military Rule in Brazil*, 29–37.

61. Mann to Gordon, April 2, 1964, NSF, CF, box 10 [1/2], LBJL.

62. CIA report, "Effects of the Brazilian Revolution," July 29, 1964, NSF, CF, box 10 [2/2], LBJL.

63. Bundy to Hubert Humphrey, August 31, 1964, NSF, CF, box 2 [1/2], LBJL.

64. See James N. Green, *We Cannot Remain Silent: Opposition to the Brazilian Military Dictatorship in the United States* (Durham, NC: Duke University Press, 2010), 22–23, and Skidmore, *Politics of Military Rule in Brazil*, 21–23, 29.

65. CIA report, "Effects of the Brazilian Revolution," July 29, 1964, NSF, CF, box 10 [2/2], LBJL.

66. Hal Brands, *Latin America's Cold War* (Cambridge, MA: Harvard University Press, 2010), 73–78, and Leacock, *Requiem for Revolution*, 228–229.

67. State Department to Rio de Janeiro, September 16, 1966, Office Files of Bill Moyers, box 81, LBJL.

68. Skidmore, *Politics of Military Rule in Brazil*, 42–43.

69. For detailed narratives of these events, see Green, *We Cannot Remain Silent*, 56–57; Leacock, *Requiem for Revolution*, 236–238; and Skidmore, *Politics of Military Rule in Brazil*, 40–45.

70. Gordon to State Department, October 27, 1965, NSF, CF, box 10 [2/2], LBJL.

71. Bundy to Johnson, "Brazilian Political-Military Crisis," October 27, 1965, NSF, CF, box 10 [2/2], LBJL.

72. Memorandum for Bundy, October 27, 1965, NSF, CF, box 10 [2/2], LBJL.

73. Gordon to State Department, November 14, 1965, NSF, CF, box 10 [2/2], LBJL.

74. Gordon to State Department, November 14, 1965.

75. NSC memorandum, "A United States Assistance Strategy for Brazil," November 10, 1965, NSF, CF, box 10 [2/2], LBJL.

76. CIA study, "The Political Situation in Brazil: The Meaning of the Second Institutional Act," November 29, 1965, NSF, CF, box 11, LBJL.

77. Freeman to Johnson, April 27, 1966, NSF, CF, box 2 [2/2], LBJL.

78. CIA study, "The Political Situation in Brazil: The Meaning of the Second Institutional Act," November 29, 1965, NSF, CF, box 11, LBJL.

79. Gordon to State Department, February 18, 1966, NSF, CF, box 11, LBJL.

80. Gallup, *Gallup Poll*, 1942.

81. Green, *We Cannot Remain Silent*, 55, 74.

82. Rio de Janeiro embassy to State Department, August 7, 1965, NSF, CF, box 9, LBJL.

83. Office of the Secretary of Defense to U.S. Defense Attaché in Rio de Janeiro, May 24, 1966, NSF, CF, box 11, LBJL.

84. Senate Foreign Relations Committee, "Nomination of Lincoln Gordon to Be Assistant Secretary of State for Inter-American Affairs," February 7, 1966 (Washington, DC: Government Printing Office, 1966), 21, 44, 64.

85. Gordon to State Department, November 14, 1965, NSF, CF, box 10 [2/2], LBJL.

86. Senate Foreign Relations Committee, "Nomination of Lincoln Gordon," 8.

87. NSC memorandum, "A United States Assistance Strategy for Brazil," November 10, 1965, NSF, CF, box 10 [2/2], LBJL.

88. CIA report, "Latin American Communist Developments," March 15, 1966, NSF, CF, box 2 [2/2], LBJL.

89. See Harlan Cleveland to Undersecretary of State, "Doctrinal Fallout of the Dominican Republic," May 20, 1965, RG59, Records of the PPC, State Department Central Files, 1965–1969, box 311, NARA; W. G. Bowdler to Bundy, September 16, 1965, NSF, CF, box 2 [2/2], LBJL; and W. G. Bowdler to Bill Moyers, September 20, 1965, NSF, CF, box 2 [2/2], LBJL.

90. Embassy in Rio de Janeiro to State Department, June 17, 1965, NSF, CF, box 10 [2/2], LBJL, and Gordon to State Department, September 22, 1965, NSF, CF, box 10 [2/2], LBJL.

91. For example, Mein to State Department, June 7, 1965, NSF, CF, box 10 [2/2], LBJL.

92. W. G. Bowdler to Bundy, "Proposal for a Public Statement Regretting Events in Brazil," October 27, 1965, NSF, CF, box 10 [2/2], LBJL.

93. "Governo Nega ida de Tropas a Asia," January 26, 1965, *Correio da Manhã*, issue 22028.

94. Harriman to Rio de Janeiro, December 11, 1965, NSF, CF, box 11, LBJL, and State Department to Rio de Janeiro, December 13, 1965, NSF, CF, box 11, LBJL.

95. Bowdler to Bundy, "Brazilian Program Loan," December 13, 1965, NSF, CF, box 11, LBJL.

96. "Nota: Labaredas," March 13, 1965, *Correio da Manhã*, issue 22066, p. 6.

97. "Governo Envolve Brasil no Conflito do Vietnam," March 8, 1965, *Correio da Manhã*, issue 22061, and "Envio de Tropas é com o Presidente," March 9, 1965, *Correio da Manhã*, issue 22062, p. 3.

98. Gordon to State Department, November 23, 1965, NSF, CF, box 10 [2/2], LBJL.

99. U.S. translation of letter from Castelo Branco to Johnson, July 21, 1966, NSF, Special Head of State Correspondence File, box 6, LBJL.

100. State Department memo, "Visit of President-Elect Costa e Silva of Brazil, Background Paper, Brazil and Viet Nam," January 23, 1967, NSF, CF, box 9, LBJL. For comparison with other Latin American nations, see Stanley Robert Larson and James Lawton Collins Jr., *Allied Participation in Vietnam* (Washington, DC: Government Printing Office, 1975), 168–169.

101. Carlos Lacerda, "O Brasil no Vietnã . . . ," February 27, 1967, *Tribuna da Imprensa*, Conselho de Seguranca Nacional files, N8-PRO-CSS-18.1, 472–473, National Archives of Brazil, http://sian.an.gov.br/sianex/Consulta/resultado_pesquisa_pdf.asp.

102. Skidmore, *Politics of Military Rule in Brazil*, 44, 55–56.

103. Draft memo by Gordon, "Aid Presentation on Brazil," November 4, 1965, NSF, CF, box 10 [2/2], LBJL.

104. Rusk to Johnson, "Memorandum for the President," November 13, 1965, NSF, CF, box 11, LBJL.

105. Skidmore, *Politics of Military Rule in Brazil*, 37.

106. Green, *We Cannot Remain Silent*, 56.

107. Skidmore, *Politics of Military Rule in Brazil*, 56.

108. National Intelligence Estimate, "The Outlook for Brazil," August 18, 1966, NSF, National Intelligence Estimates, box 9, LBJL.

109. Memcon, Costa e Silva, Tuthill, and Walters, August 4, 1966, NSF, CF, box 11, LBJL.

110. Tuthill to State Department, June 27, 1967, NSF, CF, box 11, LBJL.

111. Rostow to Johnson, February 16, 1968, NSF, CF, box 12, LBJL.

112. Fulbright, *Arrogance of Power*, 83.

113. Church comments, "The Case for Cutting Military Assistance," 1967 (no specific date), Church Papers, series 8.1, box 14.

114. Green, *We Cannot Remain Silent*, 59.

115. Tuthill to State Department, April 6, 1967, NSF, CF, box 11, LBJL.

116. Rio de Janeiro to State Department, April 21, 1967, NSF, CF, box 11, LBJL.

117. Tuthill to State Department, September 8, 1967, NSF, CF, box 11, LBJL.

118. Rostow to Johnson, June 14, 1967, NSF, CF, box 11, LBJL.

119. Tuthill to State Department, April 6, 1967, NSF, CF, box 11, LBJL.

120. Tuthill to State Department, April 6, 1967, NSF, CF, box 11, LBJL, and CIA report, "Brazil Under Costa e Silva," May 24, 1968, NSF, CF, box 12, LBJL.

121. For example, Summary Notes of the 581st Meeting of the National Security Council, February 7, 1968, *FRUS 1964–1968*, vol. 9, doc. 73.

122. "Talking Points," July 20, 1967, NSF, CF, box 11, LBJL.

123. Memcon, Leitao da Cunha, Johnson, et al., August 29, 1967, NSF, CF, box 12, LBJL.

124. State Department to Rio de Janeiro, December 6, 1968, NSF, CF, box 12, LBJL.

125. Report by State-Defense Study Group, "Latin America: A Recommended U.S. National Strategy," April 1968, RG59, Records of the PPC, State Department Central Files, 1965–1969, box 311, NARA.

126. Tuthill to State Department, June 20, 1967, NSF, CF, box 11, LBJL, and Leacock, *Requiem for Revolution*, 241–242.

127. McPherson to Rostow, March 18, 1968, NSF, CF, box 5, LBJL.

128. *Life International*, quoted in Tuthill to State Department, December 8, 1966, NSF, CF, box 11, LBJL.

129. Gallup poll, February 7, 1968, in Gallup, *Gallup Poll*, 2104–2105.

130. "Report by State-Defense Study Group, "Latin America: A Recommended U.S. National Strategy," April 1968, RG59, Records of the PPC, State Department Central Files, 1965–1969, box 311, NARA.

131. Skidmore, *Politics of Military Rule in Brazil*, 66–68.

132. Skidmore, *Politics of Military Rule in Brazil*, 103.

133. Skidmore, *Politics of Military Rule in Brazil*, 90.

134. State Department Intelligence and Research report, "Attacks upon US Installations in Latin America," May 24, 1968, NSF, CF, box 4, LBJL.

135. For example, "Proceedings against Francisco de Assis Chaves Bastos, 1969," Conselho de Seguranca Nacional files, N8-PRO-CSS-0613; "Proceedings against Jose Santilli Sobrinho, 1969," N8-PRO-CSS-1116; and "Proceedings against Iaperi Soares de Araújo," N8-PRO-CSS-0798, National Archives of Brazil, http://sian.an.gov.br/sianex/Consulta/resultado_pesquisa_pdf.asp.

136. CIA report, "The Military in Brazil," November 29, 1968, NSF, CF, box 12, LBJL.

137. Skidmore, *Politics of Military Rule in Brazil*, 81–104.

138. "Retreat in Brazil," *New York Times*, December 18, 1968, 46.

139. "Crisis in Brazil," *Washington Post*, December 17, 1968, A20.

140. Tuthill to State Department, December 28, 1968, NSF, CF, box 12, LBJL.

141. Tuthill to State Department, December 19, 1968, NSF, CF, box 12, LBJL.

142. Tuthill to State Department, December 28, 1968.

143. Tuthill to State Department, December 28, 1968.

144. State Department to Rio de Janeiro, December 19, 1968, *FRUS 1964–1968*, vol. 31, doc. 239.

145. Rostow to Johnson, January 13, 1969, NSF, CF, box 12, LBJL.

146. Johnson to Costa e Silva, January 17, 1969, NSF, Special Head of State Correspondence File, box 6, LBJL.

147. CIA Report, "The Road to Dictatorship," December 23, 1968, NSF, CF, box 12, LBJL.

## Chapter 5

1. Bundy to Johnson, December 31, 1965, *FRUS 1964–1968*, vol. 31, doc. 225.

2. Rusk to Humphrey, February 10, 1966, *FRUS 1964–1968*, vol. 25, doc. 293.

3. Komer to Johnson, February 26, 1964, *FRUS 1964–1968*, vol. 25, doc. 20.

4. McMahon, *Cold War on the Periphery*, 305–306, and Dennis Kux, *The United States and Pakistan: Disenchanted Allies, 1947–2000* (Washington, DC: Woodrow Wilson Center Press, 2001).

5. Komer to Bundy, November 23, 1963, NSC Histories, NSF, box 24, LBJL.

6. National Security Action Memorandum 279, February 8, 1964, *FRUS 1964–1968*, vol. 25, doc. 13.

7. Johnson to Bowles, January 21, 1964, *FRUS 1964–1968*, vol. 25, doc. 7.

8. National Security Action Memorandum 279, February 8, 1964, *FRUS 1964–1968*, vol. 25, doc. 13.

9. Madan, "With an Eye to the East," 321–322.

10. Madan, "With an Eye to the East," 324, and Komer to Johnson, February 26, 1964, *FRUS 1964–1968*, vol. 25, doc. 20.

11. National Security Action Memorandum 279, February 8, 1964, *FRUS 1964–1968*, vol. 25, doc. 13.

12. Komer to Bundy, June 2, 1964, *FRUS 1964–1968*, vol. 25, doc. 51.

13. Bundy to Bowles, March 9, 1964, *FRUS 1964–1968*, vol. 25, doc. 24.

14. Editorial Note, *FRUS 1964–1968*, vol. 25, doc. 47, and "Excerpts from a Poll of Four Indian Cities," April 1964, NSF, CF, box 128, LBJL.

15. Memcon, Taylor and Ayub, December 20, 1963, doc. 346, U.S. Department of State online archive, https://2001-2009.state.gov/r/pa/ho/frus/kennedyjf/46456.htm.

16. Kux, *United States and Pakistan*, 151.

17. Memcon, Johnson with McConaughy, et al., *FRUS 1964–1968*, vol. 25, doc. 65.

18. McConaughy to State Department, August 11, 1964, *FRUS 1964–1968*, vol. 25, doc. 67.

19. National Intelligence Estimate, "The Prospects for India," December 10, 1964, *FRUS 1964–1968*, vol. 25, doc. 78.

20. Madan, "With an Eye to the East," 319.

21. Madan, "With an Eye to the East."

22. Komer to Bundy, June 23, 1964, *FRUS 1964–1968*, vol. 25, doc. 59.

23. Karachi to State Department, March 11, 1964, *FRUS 1964–1968*, vol. 25, doc. 27.

24. Memcon, Johnson with McConaughy, et al., July 16, 1964 *FRUS 1964–1968*, vol. 25, doc. 65.

25. Karachi to State Department, August 11, 1964, *FRUS 1964–1968*, vol. 25, doc. 67.

26. Rusk to Karachi, August 16, 1964, *FRUS 1964–1968*, vol. 25, doc. 68. On Sino-Pakistani relations, see Brazinsky, *Winning the Third World*, 196–199.

27. Rusk to Tehran, April 6, 1965, *FRUS 1964–1968*, vol. 25, doc. 97.

28. "China Silent Ayub Asks Vietnam Talks," *New York Times*, March 8, 1965, 2, and Kux, *United States and Pakistan*, 153.

29. Madan, "With an Eye to the East," 341, and Dennis Merrill, *Bread and the Ballot: The United States and India's Economic Development, 1947–1963* (Chapel Hill: University of North Carolina Press, 1990), 180.

30. Bowles to State Department, May 20, 1965, State Department Central Files, 1964–1966, POL 7, box 2283, NARA.

31. Bowles to State Department, December 27, 1965, NSF, CF, box 130, LBJL.

32. Bowles to State Department, April 16, 1965, *FRUS 1964–1968*, vol. 25, doc. 104.

33. Bowles to State Department, March 15, 1965, NSF, CF, box 129, LBJL; Bowles to State Department, May 4, 1965, NSF, CF, box 129, LBJL; and New Delhi (Greene) to State Department, August 3, 1965, State Department Central Files, 1964–1966, POL 7, box 2283, NARA.

34. State Department to New Delhi, February 13, 1965, NSF, CF, box 129, LBJL.

35. New Delhi to State Department, April 26, 1965, NSF, CF, box 129, LBJL.

36. Rusk to New Delhi, April 14, 1965, *FRUS 1964–1968*, vol. 25, doc. 99.

37. Hohler (Saigon) to Foreign Office, January 17, 1963, FO371/170118, NAUK. On the broader history of Indian activity within the ICC, see Lawrence, "Limits of Peacemaking," and Peter Busch, *All the Way with JFK? Britain, the US, and the Vietnam War* (New York: Oxford University Press, 2003), 51–63.

38. Cox (Saigon) to Ministry of External Affairs, May 4, 1964, Record Group 25, vol. 10122, file 21–13-VIET-ICSC, Part 1.2, Library and Archives Canada, Ottawa.

39. Interview with Rostow, October 3, 2000, Austin, TX.

40. U.S. Consulate in Madras to State Department, July 9, 1965, State Department Central Files, 1964–1966, POL 1, box 2281, NARA.

41. Shastri to Johnson, May 23, 1965, *FRUS 1964–1968*, vol. 25, doc. 123.

42. Rusk to Bowles, April 14, 1965, *FRUS 1964–1968*, vol. 25, doc. 99.

43. Bowles to State Department, April 16, 1965, *FRUS 1964–1968*, vol. 25, doc. 104.

44. Johnson to Shastri, June 5, 1965, *FRUS 1964–1968*, vol. 25, doc. 127.

45. Memcon, Johnson with B. K. Nehru, et al., July 13, 1965, *FRUS 1964–1968*, vol. 25, doc. 149.

46. Delhi to State Department, July 26, 1965, NSF, CF, box 129, LBJL.

47. Bundy to Bowles, April 28, 1965, *FRUS 1964–1968*, vol. 25, doc. 113.

48. McMahon, *Cold War on the Periphery*, 324.

49. Intelligence memorandum, "Likelihood of Indian Development of Nuclear Weapons," February 25, 1965, *FRUS 1964–1968*, vol. 25, doc. 90.

50. Memcon, Rusk with Nehru, et al., May 8, 1965, *FRUS 1964–1968*, vol. 25, doc. 117.

51. McMahon, *Cold War on the Periphery*, 325.

52. McMahon, *Cold War on the Periphery*, and Komer to Johnson, June 21, 1965, *FRUS 1964–1968*, vol. 25, doc. 134.

53. Komer to Johnson, June 21, 1965, *FRUS 1964–1968*, vol. 25, doc. 134.

54. Transcript of telephone conversation, Johnson and Mann, June 28, 1965, *FRUS 1964–1968*, vol. 25, doc. 135.

55. Rusk to Bowles, June 15, 1965, *FRUS 1964–1968*, vol. 25, doc. 133.

56. Editorial note, *FRUS 1964–1968*, vol. 25, doc. 172.

57. Memcon, Johnson with Rusk, et al., September 2, 1965, *FRUS 1964–1968*, vol. 25, doc. 178.

58. Memcon, Foreign Secretary Stewart and Ball, et al., September 8, 1965, DO196/382, file 6998628, NAUK.

59. Rusk to Johnson, September 9, 1965, *FRUS 1964–1968*, vol. 25, doc. 196.

60. State Department to New Delhi, Sept 19, 1964, *FRUS 1964–1968*, vol. 25, doc. 216.

61. McMahon, *Cold War on the Periphery*, 329.

62. *Congressional Record—Senate*, 87th Congress, 1st session (September 8, 1965): 23060.

63. Bundy and Komer to Johnson, December 1, 1965, *FRUS 1964–1968*, vol. 25, doc. 256.

64. Special National Intelligence Estimate, December 7, 1965, *FRUS 1964–1968*, vol. 25, doc. 259.

65. Memcon, Ayub with Ball, et al., December 14, 1965, *FRUS 1964–1968*, vol. 25, doc. 265.

66. "President's Comments to US Advisers Concerning Private Meeting with President Ayub," December 15, 1965, *FRUS 1964–1968*, vol. 25, doc. 267.

67. Komer to Johnson, January 12, 1966, *FRUS 1964–1968*, vol. 25, doc. 279.

68. New Delhi to State Department, March 9, 1966, State Department Central File, 1964–1966, POL 7, box 2283, NARA.

69. Memcon, Johnson and Gandhi, March 28, 1966, *FRUS 1964–1968*, vol. 25, doc. 307.

70. Madan, "With an Eye to the East," 348.

71. Robert S. McNamara, *In Retrospect: The Tragedy and Lessons of Vietnam* (New York: Times Books, 1995), 218.

72. Katzenbach to Karachi, October 21, 1966, *FRUS 1964–1968*, vol. 25, doc. 382.

73. Komer to Johnson, February 4, 1966, *FRUS 1964–1968*, vol. 25, no. 290.

74. Editorial Note, *FRUS 1964–1968*, vol. 25, doc. 288.

75. Humphrey to State Department, February 20, 1966, *FRUS 1964–1968*, vol. 25, doc. 297.

76. Kux, *India and the United States*, 241–242. On the origins of the "short-tether" policy, see also Kristin L. Ahlberg, *Transplanting the Great Society: Lyndon Johnson and Food for Peace* (Columbia: University of Missouri Press, 2008), chap. 2, and Nick Cullather, *The Hungry World: America's Cold War Battle Against Poverty in Asia* (Cambridge, MA: Harvard University Press, 2010), chap. 8.

77. Johnson speech, January 4, 1965, American Presidency Project, https://www.presidency.ucsb.edu/documents/annual-message-the-congress-the-state-the-union-26.

78. Kux, *India and the United States*, 243.

79. Rusk oral history, January 2, 1970, p. 26, LBJL.

80. Kux, *India and the United States*, 241–247, and Madan, "With an Eye to the East," 364–365.

81. This view is consistent with the conclusions of Kristin L. Ahlberg, who argues LBJ was motivated by both a desire to promote reform and eagerness to exert leverage over India's foreign policy. See Ahlberg, *Transplanting the Great Society*, 106–107.

82. Ball to New Delhi, February 21, 1964, *FRUS 1964–1968*, vol. 25, doc. 18.

83. Rusk to New Delhi, November 10, 1965, *FRUS 1964–1968*, vol. 25, doc. 244.

84. Editorial note on Johnson's conversation with Freeman, February 2, 1966, *FRUS 1964–1968*, vol. 25, doc. 288.

85. Telcon, Johnson with Goldberg, November 18, 1965, WH6511.07, LBJL.

86. Komer to Johnson, January 12, 1966, *FRUS 1964–1968*, vol. 25, doc. 279.

87. Komer to Johnson, March 27, 1966, *FRUS 1964–1968*, vol. 25, doc. 306.

88. Memcon, Rusk with Gandhi, et al., March 29, 1966, *FRUS 1964–1968*, vol. 25, doc. 308.

89. J. Anthony Lukas, "India Needs U.S. Aid—And Honor, Too," *New York Times*, March 6, 1966, E3.

90. "PM Wins Hearts of Americans," *Times of India*, March 30, 1966, 10.

91. Jason A. Kirk, *India and the World Bank: The Politics of Aid and Influence* (London: Anthem, 2011), 17.

92. "M.P. Criticises 'Fiscal indiscipline' of Govt.," *Times of India*, June 9, 1966, 6.

93. Bowles to Johnson, July 5, 1966, State Department Central Files, 1964–1966, POL 1, box 2281, NARA.

94. Bowles to State Department, July 8, 1966, NSF, CF, box 133, LBJL.

95. Bowles to State Department, July 18, 1966, State Department Central File, 1964–1966, POL 7, box 2284, NARA.

96. Australian diplomatic cable, Moscow to Canberra, July 19, 1966, State Department Central File, 1964–1966, POL 7, box 2284, NARA. The Australian government shared this document with the U.S. State Department.

97. J. Anthony Lukas, "India Is Recalling Consul in Saigon," *New York Times*, July 21, 1966, 12.

98. Bowles to State Department, July 18, 1966, State Department Central File, 1964–1966, POL 7, box 2284, NARA.

99. Kux, *India and the United States*, 255.

100. Johnson news conference, July 20, 1966, American Presidency Project, https://www.presidency.ucsb.edu/documents/the-presidents-news-conference-1169.

101. Pranay Gupte, *Mother India: A Political Biography of Indira Gandhi* (New York: Penguin, 2009), 293.

102. State Department to New Delhi, January 6, 1967, State Department Central Files, 1967–1969, POL 27–14, box 2739, NARA.

103. State Department to New Delhi, January 6, 1967.

104. New Delhi to State Department, February 2, 1967, State Department Central File, 1967–1969, POL 27–14, box 2739, NARA.

105. New Delhi to State Department, August 19, 1967, NSF, CF, box 132, LBJL.

106. New Delhi to State Department, August 19, 1967, and New Delhi to State Department, February 2, 1967, State Department Central File, 1967–1969, POL 27–14, box 2739, NARA.

107. Louis Harris & Associates, Harris Survey, October 1966, USHARRIS.101166.R1C, Roper Center for Public Opinion Research, iPOLL Databank, Cornell University, https://ropercenter.cornell.edu.

108. Jones, *Blowtorch*, 93–97.

109. Ramachandra Guha, *India after Gandhi: The History of the World's Largest Democracy* (New York: Harper, 2007), 416.

110. For a fair-minded assessment, see Kux, *India and the United States*, 259–260.

111. Guha, *India after Gandhi*, 420.

112. "For Freedom—Or Dollars?," *Blitz*, July 23, 1966.

113. H. R. Vohra, "India's Worry Is Limited Now," *Times of India*, February 4, 1967, 7.

114. Selig Harrison, *The Widening Gulf: Asian Nationalism and American Policy* (New York: Free Press, 1978), 178.

115. "Once a Week in a Calcutta Theater: U.S. 'Atrocities' in Vietnam," *New York Times*, December 21, 1966.

116. Guha, *India after Gandhi*, 423.

117. "Johnson Effigy Burned," *New York Times*, May 5, 1966, and Lukas, "India Is Recalling Consul in Saigon."

118. Foreign Office report, "Annual Report of IRD Work in India, 1967–1968," May 8, 1968, FCO37/43, http://www.archivesdirect.amdigital.co.uk.ezproxy.lib.utexas.edu/Documents/Images/FCO_37_43/2.

119. Jairam Ramesh, *Intertwined Lives: P.N. Haksar and Indira Gandhi* (New Delhi: Simon & Schuster, 2018), 95.

120. Rusk to Bowles, May 18, 1967, *FRUS 1964–1968*, vol. 25, doc. 445.

121. Ramesh, *Intertwined Lives*, 98–99.

122. Rostow to Johnson, August 2, 1967, *FRUS 1964–1968*, vol. 25, doc. 450.

123. Howard Unna, "Uproar over CIA Imperils Fund's Work in India," *Washington Post*, March 3, 1967, A3; CIA report, title and date redacted, FOIA Collection, CREST number 0001088617, CIA Electronic Reading Room, https://www.cia.gov/library/readingroom/docs/DOC_0001088617.pdf; Kux, *India and the United States*, 267.

124. Rusk to Bowles, September 7, 1967, *FRUS 1964–1968*, vol. 25, doc. 457.

125. Rostow to Johnson, July 28, 1967, *FRUS 1964–1968*, vol. 25, doc. 449.

126. Rusk to Bowles, March 16, 1968, *FRUS 1964–1968*, vol. 25, doc. 488.

127. Merrill, *Bread and the Ballot*, 4.

128. Notes of Johnson's meeting with McNamara, et al., August 8, 1967, *FRUS 1964–1968*, vol. 25, doc. 452.

129. Hamilton to Johnson, August 21, 1967, *FRUS 1964–1968*, vol. 25, doc. 455.

130. Kux, *India and the United States*, 260–261.

131. Rusk to Johnson, July 25, 1966, *FRUS 1964–1968*, vol. 25, doc. 359.

132. Kux, *India and the United States*, 263.

133. Rostow to Johnson, May 8, 1968, *FRUS 1964–1968*, vol. 25, doc. 494.

134. Bowles to Church, March 5, 1968, series 2.2, box 24, Church Papers.

135. Katzenbach to Johnson, August 8, 1968, *FRUS 1964–1968*, vol. 25, doc. 509.

136. Gandhi speech, October 14, 1968, proceedings of the 1693rd plenary meeting, U.N. General Assembly, 23rd Session, https://undocs.org/en/A/PV.1693, 14.

137. Rostow to Johnson, September 23, 1968, *FRUS 1964–1968*, vol. 25, doc. 512, and memcon, October 4, 1968, *FRUS 1964–1968*, vol. 25, doc. 514.

## Chapter 6

1. Johnson statement, November 29, 1967, NSF, CF, box 136 [2 of 2], LBJL.

2. Rostow to Johnson, November 28, 1967, NSF, CF, box 136 [2 of 2], LBJL.

3. "U.S. and Iran Celebrate the End of Aid Program," *New York Times*, November 30, 1967, 13.

4. Memcon, Johnson with Hoveyda, et al., December 5, 1968, *FRUS 1964–1968*, vol. 22, doc. 321.

5. Shah to Johnson, November 24, 1963, NSF, Special Head of State Correspondence File, box 24, LBJL.

6. Mitchell Lerner, "'A Big Tree of Peace and Justice': The Vice Presidential Travels of Lyndon Johnson," *Diplomatic History* 34, no. 2 (April 2010): 368–370.

7. Shah to Johnson, January 7, 1964, *FRUS 1964–1968*, vol. 22, doc. 2.

8. NSC memo, "Iran's Interest in the Persian Gulf Increases," March 4, 1964, NSF, Komer File, box 27, LBJL.

9. Shah to Johnson, January 7, 1964, *FRUS 1964–1968*, vol. 22, doc. 2.

10. Holmes to State Department, March 10, 1964, *FRUS 1964–1968*, vol. 22, doc. 7.

11. Shah to Johnson, January 7, 1964, *FRUS 1964–1968*, vol. 22, doc. 2.

12. Roham Alvandi, "The Shah's Détente with Khrushchev: Iran's 1962 Missile Base Pledge to the Soviet Union," *Cold War History* 14, no. 3 (August 2014): 423–444.

13. Shah to Johnson, January 7, 1964, *FRUS 1964–1968*, vol. 22, doc. 2.

14. Komer to Johnson, January 25, 1964, NSF, CF, box 136 [1 of 2], LBJL.

15. Komer to Johnson, March 14, 1964, NSF, Special Head of State Correspondence File, box 24, LBJL, and Komer to Johnson, March 19 ,1964, NSF, Special Head of State Correspondence File, box 24, LBJL.

16. Deputy Assistant Secretary of State Jernigan to Rusk, March 20, 1964, *FRUS 1964–1968*, vol. 24, doc. 9.

17. National Intelligence Estimate, "Iran," May 20, 1964, *FRUS 1964–1968*, vol. 22, doc. 23.

18. Holmes to State Department, January 28, 1964, *FRUS 1964–1968*, vol. 22, doc. 4.

19. State Department report, "Shah of Iran: Visit to Washington, June 5, 1964," May 27, 1964, *FRUS 1964–1968*, vol. 22, doc. 25.

20. NSC paper, "The 'New Men' and Their Challenge to American Policy in Iran," August 11, 1964, NSF, Komer Files, box 27, LBJL.

21. CIA report, "The Visit of the Shah of Iran," May 30, 1964, *FRUS 1964–1968*, vol. 22, doc. 29.

22. Lyndon Baines Johnson, *The Vantage Point: Perspectives on the Presidency, 1963–1969* (New York: Holt, Rinehart and Winston, 1971).

23. Bill, *Eagle and the Lion*, 155–156.

24. Meyer, *Quiet Diplomacy*, 137.

25. Johnson to shah, March 19, 1964, NSF, Special Head of State Correspondence File, box 24, LBJL.

26. State Department to Tehran embassy, June 8, 1964, *FRUS 1964–1968*, vol. 22, doc. 39.

27. Memcon, Harriman and other U.S. officials with the shah, June 6, 1964, *FRUS 1964–1968*, vol. 22, doc. 37.

28. State Department to Tehran embassy, July 2, 1964, *FRUS 1964–1968*, vol. 22, doc. 47.

29. Komer to Johnson, June 4, 1964, *FRUS 1964–1968*, vol. 22, doc. 33.

30. Saunders to Bundy, July 2, 1964, *FRUS 1964–1968*, vol. 22, doc. 46.

31. Bill, *Eagle and the Lion*, 173.

32. Rusk to Johnson, June 3, 1964, *FRUS 1964–1968*, vol. 22, doc. 31.

33. Report by Director of Intelligence and Research, "Third Country Assistance to South Vietnam," August 28, 1964, NSF, CF, box 7, LBJL.

34. Bill, *Eagle and the Lion*, 156–161.

35. Khomeini speech, October 26, 1964, in *Islam and Revolution: Writings and Declarations of Imam Khomeini*, ed. and trans. Hamid Algar (Berkeley, CA: Mizan Press, 1981), 181–182, 186, 188.

36. Rockwell to State Department, November 5, 1964, *FRUS 1964–1968*, vol. 22, doc. 58.

37. Bureau of Intelligence and Research study, "The Significance of Khomeini's Opposition to the Iranian Government," n.d., *FRUS 1964–1968*, vol. 22, doc. 64. The document clearly comes from the early weeks of 1965.

38. Holmes to State Department, January 21, 1965, NSF, CF, box 136 [1 of 2], LBJL.

39. Hughes to Rusk, January 28, 1965, *FRUS 1964–1968*, vol. 22, doc. 67.

40. Meyer to State Department, April 20, 1965, *FRUS 1964–1968*, vol. 22, doc. 78.

41. CIA report, "The Situation in Iran," April 23, 1965, *FRUS 1964–1968*, vol. 22, doc. 79.

42. Excerpt of Memorandum for the Record, May 20, 1965, *FRUS 1964–1968*, vol. 22, doc. 86.

43. Meyer to State Department, October 27, 1965, *FRUS 1964–1968*, vol. 22, doc. 104.

44. Meyer to State Department, April 27, 1965, *FRUS 1964–1968*, vol. 22, doc. 81, and Saunders to Komer, June 8, 1965, *FRUS 1964–1968*, vol. 22, doc. 87.

45. Rockwell to State Department, July 4, 1965, NSF, CF, box 136 [1 of 2], LBJL, and Meyer to State Department, September 9, 1965, *FRUS 1964–1968*, vol. 22, doc. 97.

46. Andrew L. Johns, "The Johnson Administration, the Shah of Iran, and the Changing Pattern of U.S.-Iranian Relations, 1965–1967," *Journal of Cold War Studies* 9, no. 2 (Spring 2007): 73–74.

47. Howison to Talbot, January 18, 1965, *FRUS 1964–1968*, vol. 22, doc. 65.

48. Komer to Johnson, September 16, 1965, NSF, CF, box 136 [1 of 2], LBJL.

49. Komer to Johnson, September 7, 1965, NSF, CF, box 136 [1 of 2], LBJL; Meyer to State Department, November 18, 1965, *FRUS 1964–1968*, vol. 22, doc. 106; Meyer to State Department, November 25, 1965, *FRUS 1964–1968*, vol. 22, doc. 109; Meyer to State Department, November 28, 1965, *FRUS 1964–1968*, vol. 22, doc. 110; Bundy to Johnson, December 4, 1965, *FRUS 1964–1968*, vol. 22, doc. 112.

50. State Department memo for Bundy, "Strong Reaction by Shah of Iran to Gudarzian Affair," February 18, 1965, NSF, CF, box 136 [1 of 2], LBJL, and Meyer to State Department, June 2, 1965, NSF, CF, box 136 [1 of 2], LBJL.

51. Meyer to State Department, November 18, 1965, *FRUS 1964–1968*, vol. 22, doc. 106.

52. Meyer to State Department, September 13, 1965, *FRUS 1964–1968*, vol. 22, doc. 100.

53. Bill, *Eagle and the Lion*, 178–179.

54. Meyer to State Department, November 25, 1965, *FRUS 1964–1968*, vol. 22, doc. 108.

55. Meyer to State Department, September 12, 1965, NSF, CF, box 136 [1 of 2], LBJL; Meyer to State Department, September 20, 1965, NSF, CF, box 136 [1 of 2], LBJL; Memorandum for the President, "Proposed Presidential Message to the Shah of Iran on Indo-Pakistani Conflict," October 1, 1965, NSF, Special Head of State Correspondence File, box 24, LBJL.

56. NSC Memorandum for the Record, "Guidance for Intelligence Team Visiting Tehran," September 20, 1965, NSF, CF, box 136 [1 of 2], LBJL.

57. Telcon, Johnson and shah, May 18, 1965, *FRUS 1964–1968*, vol. 22, doc. 85.

58. State Department to Tehran embassy, June 17, 1965, NSF, Special Head of State Correspondence File, box 24, LBJL.

59. Rakove, *Kennedy, Johnson, and the Nonaligned World*, 220–224, 236.

60. Memcon, Harriman and shah, et al., May 18, 1965, *FRUS 1964–1968*, vol. 22, doc. 84.

61. Rockwell to State Department, July 4, 1965, *FRUS 1964–1968*, vol. 22, doc. 93.

62. Rockwell to State Department, July 26, 1965, NSF, Special Head of State Correspondence File, box 24, LBJL.

63. Meyer to State Department, November 28, 1965, NSF, CF, box 136 [1 of 2], LBJL, and State Department to Tehran embassy, December 13, 1965, NSF, Special Head of State Correspondence File, box 24, LBJL.

64. Meyer to State Department, November 28, 1965, NSF, CF, box 136 [1 of 2], LBJL.

65. Meyer to State Department, September 13, 1965, *FRUS 1964–1968*, vol. 22, doc. 100; Meyer to State Department, November 25, 1965, *FRUS 1964–1968*, vol. 22, doc. 108; and Meyer to State Department, November 25, 1965, *FRUS 1964–1968*, vol. 22, doc. 109.

66. Meyer to State Department, November 28, 1965, *FRUS 1964–1968*, vol. 22, doc. 110.

67. Thomas F. Brady, "Shah Denies Iran Depends on U.S.," *New York Times*, December 12, 1965, 1.

68. Meyer to State Department, March 2, 1966, *FRUS 1964–1968*, vol. 22, doc. 121.

69. National Intelligence Estimate 34–66, "Iran," March 24, 1966, NSF, National Intelligence Estimates, box 6, LBJL.

70. Shah to Johnson, March 25, 1966, NSF, Special Head of State Correspondence File, box 24, LBJL, and Meyer to State Department, April 12, 1966, NSF, CF, box 136 [2 of 2], LBJL. See also shah to Johnson, March 7, 1966, *FRUS 1964–1968*, vol. 22, doc. 122.

71. Meyer to State Department, March 2, 1966, *FRUS 1964–1968*, vol. 22, doc. 121.

72. Gasiorowski, *U.S. Foreign Policy and the Shah*, 8–21.

73. Report by Bureau of Intelligence and Research for Ball, June 3, 1966, *FRUS 1964–1968*, vol. 22, doc. 147.

74. Meyer to State Department, June 29, 1966, *FRUS 1964–1968*, vol. 22, doc. 148.

75. Meyer to State Department, June 29, 1966, and Meyer to State Department, July 11, 1966, *FRUS 1964–1968*, vol. 22, doc. 153.

76. Meyer to State Department, July 11, 1966, *FRUS 1964–1968*, vol. 22, doc. 153.

77. Meyer to State Department, July 3, 1966, *FRUS 1964–1968*, vol. 22, doc. 149.

78. Meyer to State Department, July 3, 1966.

79. Meyer to State Department, July 7, 1966, *FRUS 1964–1968*, vol. 22, doc. 151.

80. Meyer to State Department, July 11, 1966, *FRUS 1964–1968*, vol. 22, doc. 153.

81. CIA report, "The Shah of Iran's Current Outlook," March 30, 1966, *FRUS 1964–1968*, vol. 22, doc. 127, and CIA report, "Iran, the Shah, and the Soviets," July 27, 1966, NSF, CF, box 138 [1 of 2], LBJL.

82. Meyer to State Department, October 22, 1966, *FRUS 1964–1968*, vol. 22, doc. 178.

83. Meyer to State Department, January 24, 1967, *FRUS 1964–1968*, vol. 22, doc. 185.

84. Alfred Friendly, "Liberal-Minded Shah Runs Tight Ship," *Washington Post*, July 5, 1966, A1.

85. Alfred Friendly, "Shah's Image Established, His Program Accepted," *Washington Post*, July 6, 1966, A14.

86. Meyer to State Department, July 11, 1966, *FRUS 1964–1968*, vol. 22, doc. 153.

87. Rostow to Johnson, July 19, 1966, *FRUS 1964–1968*, vol. 22, doc. 157.

88. Meyer to State Department, December 13, 1966, *FRUS 1964–1968*, vol. 22, doc. 183.

89. Meyer to State Department, October 5, 1966, NSF, CF, box 136 [2 of 2], LBJL.

90. Meyer to State Department, July 23, 1966, *FRUS 1964–1968*, vol. 22, doc. 160.

91. Meyer to State Department, August 21, 1966, *FRUS 1964–1968*, vol. 22, doc. 174.

92. Rostow to Johnson, August 31, 1966, *FRUS 1964–1968*, vol. 22, doc. 175.

93. Meyer, *Quiet Diplomacy*, 143.

94. CIA report, "The Arab Threat to Iran," May 21, 1966, *FRUS 1964–1968*, vol. 22, doc. 139.

95. Rostow to Johnson, July 19, 1966, *FRUS 1964–1968*, vol. 22, doc. 156.

96. For example, Rusk to Tehran embassy, October 15, 1966, *FRUS 1964–1968*, vol. 22, doc. 177.

97. Memorandum for the Record, May 12, 1966, *FRUS 1964–1968*, vol. 22, doc. 137.

98. Meyer to State Department, December 8, 1966, *FRUS 1964–1968*, vol. 22, doc. 182.

99. With the benefit of hindsight, Gasiorowski highlights the ways in which Iranian autonomy flowed from the successes of the "cliency" relationship, which strengthened Iran to the point where it was capable of challenging Washington. Gasiorowski, *U.S. Foreign Policy and the Shah*, chap. 1.

100. Rostow to Johnson, August 31, 1966, *FRUS 1964–1968*, vol. 22, doc. 175.

101. W. Howard Wriggins to Rostow, July 22, 1966, *FRUS 1964–1968*, vol. 22, doc. 159.

102. Shah to Johnson, August 31, 1966, *FRUS 1964–1968*, vol. 22, doc. 173, and Rostow to Johnson, August 31, 1966, *FRUS 1964–1968*, vol. 22, doc. 175.

103. Offiler, *U.S. Foreign Policy*, 113, and Bill, *Eagle and the Lion*, 172.

104. Meyer to State Department, January 24, 1967, *FRUS 1964–1968*, vol. 22, doc. 185.

105. CIA report, "Iran: The Impact of Soviet Arms," February 15, 1967, NSF, CF, box 138 [1 of 2], LBJL.

106. Meyer to State Department, May 10, 1967, NSF, CF, box 137, LBJL.

107. Rusk to Meyer, May 11, 1967, NSF, CF, box 137, LBJL.

108. Meyer, *Quiet Diplomacy*, 141.

109. Meyer to State Department, November 20, 1967, *FRUS 1964–1968*, vol. 22, doc. 246.

110. Meyer to State Department, September 4, 1968, NSF, CF, box 136 [2 of 2], LBJL.

111. Meyer to State Department, May 13, 1967, *FRUS 1964–1968*, vol. 22, doc. 196.

112. Meyer to State Department, February 27, 1968, NSF, CF, box 136 [2 of 2], LBJL.

113. CIA report for McNamara, "The Shah of Iran," May 16, 1967, NSF, CF, box 137, LBJL.

114. Saunders to Rostow, May 29, 1967, NSF, CF, box 137, LBJL.

115. State Department report, "Visit of the Shah of Iran," n.d., NSF, CF, box 137, LBJL.

116. Rusk to Meyer, May 19, 1967, *FRUS 1964–1968*, vol. 22, doc. 201.

117. Rostow to Johnson, May 17, 1967, *FRUS 1964–1968*, vol. 22, doc. 198.

118. State Department report, "Visit of the Shah of Iran," n.d., NSF, CF, box 137, LBJL.

119. Charles Bohlen (Paris) to State Department, June 5, 1967, *FRUS 1964–1968*, vol. 22, doc. 207.

120. Briefing paper, "Visit of the Shah of Iran," August 16, 1967, NSF, CF, box 137, LBJL.

121. Offiler, *U.S. Foreign Policy*, 117–121.

122. State Department briefing paper, "Visit of the Shah of Iran," August 16, 1967, NSF, CF, box 137, LBJL.

123. State Department briefing paper, "Visit of the Shah of Iran," August 15, 1967, NSF, CF, box 137, LBJL.

124. Rostow to Johnson, August 22, 1967, *FRUS 1964–1968*, vol. 22, doc. 228.

125. Saunders to Johnson, August 18, 1967, NSF, CF, box 137, LBJL.

126. Humphrey to Johnson, August 24, 1967, *FRUS 1964–1968*, vol. 22, doc. 235.

127. Meyer to Johnson, October 21, 1967, Special Head of State Correspondence File, box 25, LBJL.

128. "Salute for the Shah," *Washington Post*, August 26, 1967, A12.

129. "Iran's Shah Crowns Himself and Queen," *New York Times*, October 27, 1967, 10.

130. Johnson statement, November 29, 1967, NSF, CF, box 136 [2 of 2], LBJL.

131. Rusk to Tehran embassy, March 30, 1967, *FRUS 1964–1968*, vol. 22, doc. 275.

132. Rohan Alvandi, *Nixon, Kissinger, and the Shah: The United States and Iran in the Cold War* (New York: Oxford University Press, 2014), 33–35.

133. Briefing paper, "U.S. Military Assistance to Iran," June 8, 1968, NSF, CF, box 137, LBJL.

134. Rostow to Johnson, April 29, 1968, *FRUS 1964–1968*, vol. 22, doc. 281.

135. Briefing paper, "Iran's Foreign Policy Posture," June 7, 1968, NSF, CF, box 137, LBJL.

136. For example, Meyer to State Department, January 5, 1968, NSF, CF, box 136 [1 of 2], LBJL, and Meyer to State Department, March 14, 1968, NSF, CF, box 136 [2 of 2], LBJL.

137. Meyer to State Department, February 9, 1968, NSF, CF, box 136 [2 of 2], LBJL.

138. Meyer to State Department, July 27, 1968, NSF, CF, box 136 [2 of 2], LBJL; Meyer to State Department, December 13, 1967, NSF, CF, box 136 [2 of 2], LBJL; Meyer to State Department, December 18, 1967, NSF, CF, box 136 [box 2 of 2], LBJL; Saunders to Rostow, December 26, 1967, NSF, CF, box 136 [2 of 2], LBJL; Meyer to State Department, April 1, 1968, NSF, CF, box 136 [2 of 2], LBJL; Rusk to Tehran embassy, April 24, 1968, NSF, CF, box 136 [2 of 2], LBJL.

139. Rusk to Tehran embassy, February 28, 1968, NSF, CF, box 136 [2 of 2], LBJL.

140. On these understudied events, see Meyer, *Quiet Diplomacy*, 148–155.

141. Briefing paper, "Iran in the Middle East Setting," June 8, 1968, NSF, CF, box 137, LBJL, and Rostow to Johnson, June 11, 1968, NSF, CF, box 137, LBJL.

142. Rusk to Tehran embassy, February 3, 1968, NSF, CF, box 136 [1 of 2], LBJL, and Meyer to State Department, March 15, 1968, NSF, CF, box 136 [2 of 2], LBJL.

143. Meyer, *Quiet Diplomacy*, 152–154.

144. Meyer to State Department, August 3, 1968, NSF, CF, box 136 [2 of 2], LBJL.

145. Briefing paper for visit by Hoveyda, November 27, 1968, NSF, CF, box 138 [1 of 2], LBJL.

146. Memcon, Rostow with Central Bank Governor Mehdi Samii, June 13, 1968, NSF, CF, box 136 [2 of 2], LBJL.

147. Meyer to Johnson, July 15, 1968, NSF, CF, box 136 [2 of 2], LBJL.

148. Meyer, *Quiet Diplomacy*, 152.

149. "A Holy Struggle," *Harvard Alumni Bulletin*, July 1, 1968, 25, https://harvardmagazine.com/2011/05/shah-of-iran-proposes-universal-welfare-legion.

150. Saunders to Johnson, December 4, 1968, NSF, CF, box 138 [1 of 2], LBJL.

151. Read to Rostow, November 7, 1968, *FRUS 1964–1968*, vol. 22, doc. 314.

152. Meyer, *Quiet Diplomacy*, 148.

153. Rusk to Johnson, December 2, 1968, *FRUS 1964–1968*, vol. 22, doc. 320.

154. Memcon, Johnson with Hoveyda et al., *FRUS 1964–1968*, vol. 22, doc. 321.

## Chapter 7

1. Jones to State Department, April 18, 1965, NSF, CF, box 247, LBJL.

2. "Jakarta Aglow for Celebration of Bandung Talks' 10th Birthday," *New York Times*, April 18, 1965, 7.

3. Record of Cabinet Meeting, October 18, 1967, *FRUS 1964–1968*, vol. 26, doc. 246.

4. Telcon, Johnson and McNamara, January 2, 1965, *FRUS 1964–1968*, vol. 26, doc. 1.

5. Quoted in Simpson, *Economists with Guns*, 126.

6. CIA report, "The Power Position of Indonesia's President Sukarno," February 7, 1964, NSF, CF, box 246, LBJL.

7. Jones to Rostow, February 24, 1964, NSF, CF, box 246, LBJL.

8. Jones to State Department, January 3, 1964, NSF, CF, box 246, LBJL.

9. Forrestal to Bundy, January 6, 1964, NSF, CF, box 246, LBJL.

10. Record of the 521st NSC meeting, January 7, 1964, *FRUS 1964–1968*, vol. 26, doc. 8.

11. Memo for the president, January 6, 1964, NSF, NSC Meetings File, box 1, LBJL.

12. Rusk to Robert Kennedy (London), January 23, 1964, *FRUS 1964–1968*, vol. 26, doc. 25.

13. Forrestal to Bundy, January 18, 1964, *FRUS 1964–1968*, vol. 26, doc. 18.

14. Komer to Johnson, January 18, 1964, *FRUS 1964–1968*, vol. 26, doc. 20.

15. Forrestal to Hilsman, February 19, 1964, *FRUS 1964–1968*, vol. 26, doc. 31.

16. Memorandum for the Record, March 4, 1964, *FRUS 1964–1968*, vol. 26, doc. 31.

17. Rusk to Jakarta, March 3, 1964, *FRUS 1964–1968*, vol. 26, doc. 33.

18. Forrestal to Bundy, March 5, 1964, *FRUS 1964–1968*, vol. 26, doc. 35.

19. Komer to Bundy, February 25, 1964, NSF, CF, box 246, LBJL.

20. Halberstam, *Best and the Brightest*, 374–379.

21. Jones to State Department, May 9, 1964, *FRUS 1964–1968*, vol. 26, doc. 47.

22. Forrestal to William Bundy, May 8, 1964, NSF, CF, box 246, LBJL.

23. Telcon, Bundy with Johnson, May 1, 1964, *FRUS 1964–1968*, vol. 26, doc. 46.

24. Talmadge press release, April 8, 1964, Talmadge Papers, series H, Press Office Series, 1965 subseries, box 282, Russell Library, Athens, GA.

25. Daniel Wei Boon Chua, *U.S.-Singapore Relations, 1965–1975: Strategic Non-Alignment in the Cold War* (Singapore: National University of Singapore Press, 2017), 91.

26. Rusk circular to various U.S. embassies, October 22, 1964, NSF, CF, box 246, LBJL.

27. "Excerpts from Sukarno's Independence Day Speech," August 17, 1964, CIA Electronic Reading Room, https://www.cia.gov/library/readingroom/print/1358879, and CIA report, "Sukarno's Independence Day Speech," August 20, 1964, NSF, CF, box 246, LBJL.

28. Galbraith to State Department, August 18, 1964, NSF, CF, box 246, LBJL.

29. CIA report, "Sukarno's Independence Day Speech," August 20, 1964, NSF, CF, box 246, LBJL.

30. Komer to Bundy, August 18, 1964, NSF, Komer Files, box 27, LBJL.

31. Komer to Harriman, August 19, 1964, Komer Files, box 27, LBJL.

32. Komer to Johnson, August 19, 1964, Komer Files, box 27, LBJL, and Komer to Bundy, August 24, 1964, Komer Files, box 27, LBJL.

33. Komer to Bundy, August 18, 1964, NSF, Komer Files, box 27, LBJL.

34. Rusk to Johnson, "Assistance Programs for Indonesia," August 30, 1964, NSF, CF, box 246, LBJL.

35. Memorandum for the Record, "Meeting with the Leadership," September 9, 1964, NSF, McCone Memos, box 1, LBJL.

36. Simpson, *Economists with Guns*, 146. On the background of covert operations in Indonesia, see also Weiner, *Legacy of Ashes*, 164–178, and Greg Poulgrain, *The Incubus of Intervention: Conflicting Indonesia Strategies of John F. Kennedy and Allen Dulles* (Petaling Jaya, Malaysia: Strategic Information and Research Development Centre, 2015), esp. chaps. 4–5.

37. Jones to State Department, March 6, 1964, NSF, CF, box 246, LBJL.

38. Thomson to Bundy, August 25, 1964, *FRUS 1964–1968*, vol. 26, doc. 64.

39. CIA report, "Prospects for Covert Action," September 18, 1964, *FRUS 1964–1968*, vol. 26, doc. 76.

40. Political Action Paper," November 19, 1964, *FRUS 1964–1968*, vol. 26, doc. 86.

41. Memorandum Prepared for the 303 Committee, February 23, 1965, *FRUS 1964–1968*, vol. 26, doc. 110fn.

42. Political Action Paper," November 19, 1964, *FRUS 1964–1968*, vol. 26, doc. 86.

43. CIA report, "The Secession Problem in Indonesia," December 30, 1964, NSF, CF, box 246, LBJL.

44. Komer to Bundy, November 19, 1964, NSF, CF, box 246, LBJL.

45. Komer to William Bundy, November 17, 1964, NSF, Komer Files, box 27, LBJL.

46. For example, Thomson to Bundy, January 16, 1965, *FRUS 1964–1968*, vol. 26, doc. 99; Jones to Forrestal, February 25, 1965, White House Confidential File, CO 110, box 9 [1 of 2], LBJL; Cooper to Bundy, March 13, 1965, *FRUS 1964–1968*, vol. 26, doc. 116; and Jones to State Department, March 18, 1965, NSF, CF, box 247, LBJL.

47. Prime Minister Wilson to Johnson, January 29, 1965, PREM13/2718, NAUK.

48. Komer to Bundy, November 19, 1964, NSF, CF, box 246, LBJL.

49. State Department to U.S. mission to the United Nations, January 15, 1965, *FRUS 1964–1968*, vol. 26, doc. 98.

50. Simpson, *Economists with Guns*, 153.

51. John Roosa, *Pretext for Mass Murder: The September 30 Movement and Suharto's Coup d'État in Indonesia* (Madison: University of Wisconsin Press, 2006), 191.

52. Telcon, Bundy and Ball, March 2, 1965, *FRUS 1964–1968*, vol. 26, doc. 112.

53. Ball to Johnson, March 18, 1965, *FRUS 1964–1968*, vol. 26, doc. 118.

54. Bundy and Thomson to Johnson, March 24, 1965, *FRUS 1964–1968*, vol. 26, doc. 119.

55. Report by Bunker for Johnson, "Indonesian-American Relations, Part 2: Recommendations," n.d., NSF, CF, box 247, LBJL.

56. Report by Bunker for Johnson, "Indonesian-American Relations, Part 1: General Conclusions," n.d., NSF, CF, box 247, LBJL.

57. Editorial Note, *FRUS 1964–1968*, vol. 25, doc. 136.

58. Barber to McNaughton, August 11, 1965, *FRUS 1964–1968*, vol. 26, doc. 133.

59. Simpson, *Economists with Guns*, 197.

60. For instance, Jones to State Department, January 21, 1965, NSF, CF, box 246, LBJL, and Editorial Note, *FRUS 1964–1968*, vol. 26, doc. 120.

61. Memcon, Rusk and Ball with Senate leaders, August 18, 1965, *FRUS 1964–1968*, vol. 26, doc. 134.

62. National Intelligence Estimate 54, "Prospects for Indonesia and Malaysia," July 1, 1965, CIA Electronic Reading Room, https://www.cia.gov/library/readingroom/document/0000012243.

63. Bundy to Johnson, June 30, 1965, NSF, Special Head of State Correspondence File, box 23, LBJL.

64. Simpson, *Economists with Guns*, 173.

65. Paul Thomas Chamberlin, *The Cold War's Killing Fields: Rethinking the Long Peace* (New York: Harper, 2018), chap. 8.

66. Simpson, *Economists with Guns*, 157, and Roosa, *Pretext for Mass Murder*, 188–193.

67. Chamberlin, *Cold War's Killing Fields*, 227; Geoffrey B. Robinson, *The Killing Season: A History of the Indonesian Massacres, 1965–66* (Princeton, NJ: Princeton University Press, 2018), esp. chap. 7; Roosa, *Pretext for Mass Murder*, 193–201; and Simpson, *Economists with Guns*, chap. 7.

68. Rostow and William Bundy to Ball, October 2, 1965, RG59, PPC, Subject and Country Files, 1965–1969, box 304, NARA.

69. CIA report, "Indonesia—Major General Suharto," October 2, 1965, NSF, CF, box 247, LBJL.

70. Blouin to McNaughton, "Situation in Indonesia," October 4, 1965, *FRUS 1964–1968*, vol. 26, doc. 146.

71. Green to State Department, October 17, 1965, *FRUS 1964–1968*, vol. 26, doc. 156.

72. Cuthell to William Bundy, November 3, 1965, *FRUS 1964–1968*, vol. 26, doc. 167.

73. Cuthell to William Bundy, November 3, 1965, and Green to State Department, October 17, 1965, *FRUS 1964–1968*, vol. 26, doc. 156.

74. Green to State Department, October 9, 1965, NSF, CF, box 247, LBJL.

75. CIA report, "Indonesian Army Attitudes toward Communism," November 22, 1965, CIA Electronic Reading Room, https://www.cia.gov/library/readingroom/document/cia-rdp79t00472a000600040009-3.

76. President's Daily Brief, October 5, 1965, CIA Electronic Reading Room, https://www.cia.gov/library/readingroom/docs/DOC_0005967926.pdf.

77. Green to State Department, October 6, 1965, NSF, CF, box 247, LBJL, and CIA cable, October 7, 1965, NSF, CF, box 247, LBJL.

78. Green to State Department, October 9, 1965, NSF, CF, box 247, LBJL.

79. Green to State Department, October 19, 1965, NSF, CF, box 247, LBJL.

80. Rusk to Jakarta embassy, October 13, 1965, NSF, CF, box 247, LBJL.

81. Ball to various posts, October 6, 1965, NSF, CF, box 247, LBJL.

82. CIA report, "Covert Assistance to the Indonesian Armed Forces," November 9, 1965, *FRUS 1964–1968*, vol. 26, doc. 172.

83. Simpson, *Economists with Guns*, 178–179, 190–191.

84. Memcon, Cuthell with Colby, et al., December 4, 1965, *FRUS 1964–1968*, vol. 26, doc. 181.

85. Simpson, *Economists with Guns*, 186, 190.

86. "Memorandum for the 303 Committee," November 17, 1965, *FRUS 1964–1968*, vol. 26, doc. 181 and footnote.

87. Green to William Bundy, December 2, 1965, *FRUS 1964–1968*, vol. 26, doc. 179.

88. Simpson, *Economists with Guns*, 194.

89. Green to State Department, December 22, 1965, *FRUS 1964–1968*, vol. 26, doc. 186, and JCS to McNamara, December 30, 1965, *FRUS 1964–1968*, vol. 26, doc. 187.

90. Rusk to Jakarta, December 8, 1965, NSF, CF, box 248, LBJL; Rusk to Jakarta, January 20, 1966, *FRUS 1964–1968*, vol. 26, doc. 189; and Memcon, Rusk with Green, February 14, 1966, *FRUS 1964–1968*, vol. 26, doc. 191.

91. Komer to Johnson, February 15, 1966, *FRUS 1964–1968*, vol. 26, doc. 192, and memcon, Johnson with William Bundy, et al., February 15, 1966, NSF, CF, box 248, LBJL.

92. Green to State Department, March 4, 1966, *FRUS 1964–1968*, vol. 26, doc. 198.

93. R. E. Elson, *Suharto: A Political Biography* (Cambridge: Cambridge University Press, 2001), 128–139.

94. President's Daily Brief, March 16, 1966, CIA Electronic Reading Room, https://www.cia.gov/library/readingroom/document/0005968207.

95. Komer to Johnson, March 12, 1966, *FRUS 1964–1968*, vol. 26, doc. 201.

96. CIA report, "Peking's Setbacks in Indonesia," April 1, 1966, CIA Electronic Reading Room, https://www.cia.gov/library/readingroom/docs/CIA-RDP79-00927A005200080002-7.pdf.

97. Green to State Department, May 27, 1966, *FRUS 1964–1968*, vol. 26, doc. 209.

98. In his 1995 memoir, Robert S. McNamara criticized himself and his colleagues for failing to reappraise the U.S. commitment to Vietnam following the turn in Indonesia. McNamara, *In Retrospect*, 214–215.

99. Record of the 557th NSC meeting, May 10, 1966, *FRUS 1964–1968*, vol. 4, doc. 135.

100. State Department paper for the president, June 8, 1966, *FRUS 1964–1968*, vol. 26, doc. 210.

101. CIA report "The Indonesian Crisis and U.S. Determination in Vietnam," May 13, 1966, NSF, CF, box 248, LBJL.

102. For example, McNamara to Johnson, March 1, 1967, *FRUS 1964–1968*, vol. 26, doc. 232, and Notes of 578th NSC meeting, November 8, 1967, NSF, NSC Meetings File, box 2, LBJL.

103. Notes of NSC meeting, August 9, 1967, Tom Johnson's Notes of Meetings, box 1, LBJL.

104. State Department paper, "Indonesia," August 1, 1966, *FRUS 1964–1968*, vol. 26, doc. 215.

105. State Department report, "Indonesia," June 8, 1966, *FRUS 1964–1968*, vol. 26, doc. 210. See also Robinson, *Killing Season*, 183–207, and Simpson, *Economists with Guns*, 188–199.

106. State Department report, "Indonesia," June 8, 1966, *FRUS 1964–1968*, vol. 26, doc. 210.

107. Green to State Department, October 27, 1966, *FRUS 1964–1968*, vol. 26, doc. 225.

108. Notes of 563rd NSC meeting, August 4, 1966, NSF, NSC Meetings File, box 2, LBJL.

109. Ropa to Rostow, July 9, 1966, *FRUS 1964–1968*, vol. 26, doc. 212.

110. State Department report, "Indonesia," August 4, 1967, *FRUS 1964–1968*, vol. 26, doc. 241.

111. Jorden to Rostow, August 5, 1967, WHCF, CO 122, box 40, LBJL. See also Elson, *Suharto*, 148–151; Simpson, *Economists with Guns*, 218–221; Michael R. J. Vatikiotis, *Indonesian Politics under Suharto: Order, Development, and Pressure for Change* (London: Routledge, 1993), 47–48.

112. Peter Braestrup, "Indonesia: A Go-Slow Approach for Tough Problems," *New York Times*, December 3, 1967, 260.

113. Memcon, House members with Widjojo, June 28, 1967, NSF, CF, box 248, LBJL.

114. State Department report, "Indonesia," August 4, 1967, *FRUS 1964–1968*, vol. 26, doc. 241.

115. Green to State Department, February 21, 1968, *FRUS 1964–1968*, vol. 26, doc. 253.

116. Weiner, *Legacy of Ashes*, 298–300.

117. Jones, *Conflict and Confrontation in South East Asia*, 275–277, and Simpson, *Economists with Guns*, 214–215, 223–224.

118. State Department report, "Indonesia," August 1, 1966, *FRUS 1964–1968*, vol. 26, doc. 215.

119. State Department report, "Indonesia."

120. CIA report, "Prospects for Indonesia," February 15, 1967, NSF, National Intelligence Estimates, box 7, LBJL.

121. Humphrey to Johnson, September 25, 1966, *FRUS 1964–1968*, vol. 26, doc. 222.

122. Record of cabinet meeting, October 18, 1967, *FRUS 1964–1968*, vol. 26, doc. 246.

123. Notes of NSC meeting, August 9, 1967, NSF, Tom Johnson's Notes of Meetings, box 1, LBJL.

124. For example, CIA cable, May 27, 1967, NSF, CF, box 248, LBJL.

125. President's Daily Brief, March 29, 1966, CIA Electronic Reading Room, https://www.cia.gov/library/readingroom/docs/DOC_0005968229.pdf.

126. Green to State Department, February 21, 1968, *FRUS 1964–1968*, vol. 26, doc. 253.

127. Patrick Dean to Foreign Office, May 20, 1966, FO371/185003, NAUK.

128. Ropa to Rostow, April 18, 1966, NSF, CF, box 248, LBJL.

129. State Department report, August 1, 1966, *FRUS 1964–1968*, vol. 26, doc. 215, and Notes of 563rd NSC meeting, August 4, 1966, *FRUS 1964–1968*, vol. 26, doc. 217.

130. State Department report, August 4, 1967, *FRUS 1964–1968*, vol. 26, doc. 241.

131. Ropa to Rostow, July 9, 1966, NSF, CF, box 248, LBJL.

132. State Department report, "Indonesia," August 1, 1966, *FRUS 1964–1968*, vol. 26, doc. 215.

133. AID memo for the president, February 16, 1967, NSF, CF, box 248, LBJL.

134. Charles L. Schultze to Johnson, February 18, 1967, NSF, CF, box 248, LBJL.

135. AID memo for the president, October 14, 1968, NSF, CF, box 249, LBJL.

136. Rostow to Johnson, October 17, 1968, NSF, CF, box 249, LBJL.

137. For details of the Inter-Governmental Group on Indonesia, see G. A. Posthumus, *The InterGovernmental Group on Indonesia* (Rotterdam: Rotterdam University Press, 1971).

138. Record of cabinet meeting, October 18, 1967, *FRUS 1964–1968*, vol. 25, doc. 246.

139. McNamara to Johnson, March 1, 1967, NSF, CF, box 248, LBJL.

140. Jakarta embassy report, "Trends during 1967 and Problem Areas for 1968," January 12, 1968, RG59, PPC, Subject and Country Files, 1965–1969, box 304, NARA. See also Simpson, *Economists with Guns*, 227–229.

141. Bohlen to Warnke, March 19, 1968, *FRUS 1964–1968*, vol. 26, doc. 254.

142. Jakarta embassy report, "Trends during 1967 and Problem Areas for 1968," January 12, 1968, RG59, PPC, Subject and Country Files, 1965–1969, box 304, NARA.

143. AID study, "Indonesia's Current Development Position," October 7, 1968, NSF, CF, box 248, LBJL.

144. Jakarta embassy report, "Trends during 1967 and Problem Areas for 1968," January 12, 1968, RG59, PPC, Subject and Country Files, 1965–1969, box 304, NARA.

145. AID study, "Indonesia's Current Development Position," October 7, 1968, NSF, CF, box 248, LBJL.

146. Notes of 563rd NSC Meeting, August 4, 1966, *FRUS 1964–1968*, vol. 26, doc. 217.

147. Simpson, *Economists with Guns*, 246.

148. Green to State Department, August 22, 1968, NSF, CF, box 249, LBJL; J. D. Hittle to Rostow, September 16, 1968, NSF, CF, box 249, LBJL; and National Intelligence Estimate 55–68, December 31, 1968, NSF, CF, box 249, LBJL.

149. For the later period, see, for instance, Rostow to Johnson, July 22, 1967, *FRUS 1964–1968*, vol. 26, doc. 238.

150. Johnson to Suharto, October 5, 1967, NSF, Special Head of State Correspondence File, box 23, LBJL.

151. Notes of cabinet meeting, October 18, 1967, *FRUS 1964–1968*, vol. 26, doc. 246.

152. Kyle Longley, *LBJ's 1968: Power, Politics, and the Presidency in America's Year of Upheaval* (New York: Cambridge University Press, 2018), 5.

153. Johnson, *Vantage Point*, 357.

## Chapter 8

1. "Fireman for the World?," *Chicago Tribune*, December 22, 1965, Douglas Papers, box 587.

2. Summary of meeting with African Bureau staff, April 10, 1964, Williams Papers, box 7, Bentley Library.

3. Memcon, Beauveau Malle with Vladimir N. Porshakov, April 27, 1965, NSF, CF, box 76 [1 of 2], LBJL.

4. Anthony Lake, *The "Tar Baby" Option: American Policy toward Southern Rhodesia* (New York: Columbia University Press, 1976), 67.

5. Namikas, *Battleground Africa*, 186.

6. Carl T. Rowan to Johnson, July 21, 1964, NSF, CF, box 76 [1 of 2], LBJL.

7. Bill Brubeck to Bundy, September 28, 1964, NSF, CF, box 78, LBJL, and Thomas G. Wyman to Bundy, November 18, 1964, NSF, CF, box 78, LBJL.

8. CIA report, "Communist Potentialities in Tropical Africa," December 1, 1964, NSF, CF, box 76 [1 of 2], LBJL.

9. Harriman to Johnson, October 28, 1964, NSF, CF, box 76 [1 of 2], LBJL.

10. Bundy to Johnson, March 8, 1965, NSF, CF, box 76 [1 of 2], LBJL.

11. National Intelligence Estimate 60/70–65, "Problems and Prospects in Sub-Saharan Africa," April 22, 1965, NSF, NIEs, box 8, LBJL. See also CIA report, "Communist World's Economic Relations with Africa," April 16, 1965, NSF, CF, box 76 [1 of 2], LBJL.

12. Bundy to Johnson, March 8, 1965, NSF, CF, box 76 [1 of 2], LBJL.

13. NSC memo, "Bench Marks for New Africa Program," n.d., NSF, CF, box 76, LBJL.

14. Haynes to Bundy, September 13, 1965, *FRUS 1964–1968*, vol. 24, doc. 466.

15. Watts, *Rhodesia's Unilateral Declaration of Independence*, 165–168.

16. Williams to Rusk, May 21, 1964, NSF, CF, box 76 [1 of 2], LBJL.

17. Williams to chiefs of missions of Africa posts, October 19, 1964, RG59, PPC, Subject and Country Files, 1965–1969, box 310, NARA.

18. Harald Taswell to Foreign Secretary, "Talk with Mr. Rusk," BTS 1/33/3, vol. 5A, National Archives of South Africa.

19. Williams statement to House Foreign Affairs Committee, February 10, 1965, Williams Papers, box 7, Bentley Library.

20. Bundy to Johnson, March 8, 1965, NSF, CF, box 76 [1 of 2), LBJL; William R. Duggan to Rostow, June 10, 1965, RG59, PPC, Subject and Country Files, 1965–1969, box 310, NARA; and Haynes to Bundy, June 5, 1965, NSF, CF, box 76 [1 of 2], LBJL.

21. Consistent with Anthony Lake's analysis, Carl Watts contends that the Departments of Defense, Treasure, and Commerce, along with NASA, composed a distinct cluster of opinion by objecting to all efforts to punish Rhodesia. In the abstract, these bureaucracies leaned that way. As a practical matter, however, they offered no significant resistance to the idea that the United States should simply line up behind Britain, perhaps recognizing that the Johnson administration had no choice but to take some form of action in response to UDI. Lake, *"Tar Baby" Option*, 68–69, and Watts, "G. Mennen Williams and Rhodesian Independence," 233–234.

22. Memcon, Ball and Bundy, October 5, 1965, *FRUS 1964–1968*, vol. 24, doc. 475.

23. Noer, *Cold War and Black Liberation*, 194.

24. Lake, *"Tar Baby" Option*, 64.

25. Nairobi to State Department, June 1, 1964, NSF, CF, box 76 [1 of 2], LBJL.

26. Cape Town to State Department, June 24, 1964, NSF, CF, box 78, LBJL.

27. Haynes to Bundy, September 13, 1965, *FRUS 1964–1968*, vol. 24, doc. 466.

28. Botha to Foreign Secretary, January 21, 1965, BTS 1/33/3, vol. 4A, National Archives of South Africa.

29. State Department to Salisbury, May 6, 1965, *FRUS 1964–1968*, vol. 24, doc. 461.

30. Pretoria to State Department, August 13, 1965, NSF, CF, box 78, LBJL.

31. Watts, "G. Mennen Williams and Rhodesian Independence," 238.

32. Komer to Bundy, May 28, 1965, *FRUS 1964–1968*, vol. 24, doc. 463.

33. Andy DeRoche, "Non-Alignment on the Racial Frontier: Zambia and the USA, 1964–1968," in *Cold War in Southern Africa: White Power, Black Liberation*, ed. Susan Onslow (London: Routledge, 2009), 134.

34. Wilson to Johnson, October 2, 1965, *FRUS 1964–1968*, vol. 24, doc. 473.

35. Johnson to Smith, October 29, 1965, *FRUS 1964–1968*, vol. 24, doc. 486.

36. Noer, *Cold War and Black Liberation*, 195–196, and Watts, "G. Mennen Williams and Rhodesian Independence," 237.

37. Haynes to Bundy, October 13, 1965, NSF, CF, box 97, LBJL.

38. Haynes to Bundy, September 13, 1965, NSF, CF, box 97, LBJL.

39. Komer to Johnson, September 27, 1965, NSF, CF, box 76 [2 of 2], LBJL.

40. Haynes to Bundy, October 8, 1965, NSF, CF, box 97, LBJL, and Williams to Rusk, November 9, 1965, NSF, CF, box 97, LBJL.

41. Lawrence Fellows, "Rhodesia Asserts Independence," *New York Times*, November 12, 1965, 1.

42. "Washington Recalls Consul General—Ends Activities of Information Agency," *New York Times*, November 12, 1965, 1.

43. Louis B. Fleming, "U.N. Council Condemns Rhodesia," *Los Angeles Times*, November 13, 1965, 1.

44. Gene Sherman, "Rhodesia Secedes; Wilson Invokes Strong Sanctions," *Los Angeles Times*, November 12, 1965, 1.

45. Wilson to Johnson, November 29, 1965, *FRUS 1964–1968*, vol. 24, doc. 500, and Benjamin H. Read to Bundy, November 18, 1965, *FRUS 1964–1968*, vol. 24, doc. 497.

46. S. G. Gebelt (Salisbury) to State Department, November 29, 1965, *FRUS 1964–1968*, vol. 24, doc. 499.

47. Rostow to Ball, December 7, 1965, RG59, PPC, Subject and Country Files, 1965–1969, box 307, NARA.

48. Gebelt (Salisbury) to State Department, November 18, 1965, NSF, CF, box 97, LBJL.

49. Salisbury to State Department, November 29, 1965, *FRUS 1964–1968*, vol. 24, doc. 499.

50. Haynes to Bundy, December 3, 1965, NSF, CF, box 97, LBJL.

51. Read to Bundy, November 18, 1965, *FRUS 1964–1968*, vol. 24, doc. 497, and telcon, Johnson and Goldberg, November 18 1965, WH6511.07, LBJL.

52. Komer to Bundy, December 6, 1965, *FRUS 1964–1968*, vol. 24, doc. 502.

53. "Memorandum for the President," December 6, 1965, *FRUS 1964–1968*, vol. 24, doc. 502.

54. "Memorandum for the President," December 6, 1965.

55. State Department to London embassy, December 9, 1965, *FRUS 1964–1968*, vol. 24, doc. 506.

56. Johnson to Wilson, December 8, 1965, *FRUS 1964–1968*, vol. 24, doc. 504.

57. Noer, *Cold War and Black Liberation*, 204.

58. Memcon, Ball with Michael Stewart, et al., December 1, 1965, NSF, CF, box 97, LBJL.

59. Lake, *"Tar Baby" Option*, 82.

60. Lake, *"Tar Baby" Option*, 83–84.

61. Memos to the president, November-December 1965, WHCF, White House Administration, Gen WH5–1, box 12, LBJL.

62. Lake, *"Tar Baby" Option*, 85.

63. JCS to McNamara, December 16, 1965, *FRUS 1964–1968*, vol. 24, doc. 511.

64. Haynes to Komer, December 2, 1965, NSF, CF, box 97, LBJL.

65. CIA report, "Possible UK Military Intervention in Southern Rhodesia," December 21, 1965, NSF, CF, box 97, LBJL.

66. Komer to Johnson, January 14, 1966, NSF, CF, box 97, LBJL.

67. Lake, *"Tar Baby" Option*, 90.

68. Memcon, Johnson with Wilson, et al., December 16–17, 1965, *FRUS 1964–1968*, vol. 24, doc. 513.

69. Memcon, Johnson with Wilson, et al., December 16–17, 1965.

70. Noer, *Cold War and Black Liberation*, 205.

71. Memorandum by Wilson, n.d., NSF, CF, box 97, LBJL. Clues in the document indicate that it dates to the days after the British announcement of oil sanctions.

72. Mann to Johnson, December 22, 1965, White House Confidential File, CO 206, box 11 [1 of 2], LBJL.

73. Haynes to Bundy, January 6, 1966, NSF, CF, box 97, LBJL, and London embassy to State Department, January 5, 1966, NSF, CF, box 97, LBJL.

74. Haynes to Bundy, January 6, 1966, NSF, CF, box 97, LBJL.

75. Komer to Johnson, January 13, 1966, *FRUS 1964–1968*, vol. 24, doc. 527, emphasis in original.

76. Johnson to Wilson, January 7, 1966, *FRUS 1964–1968*, vol. 24, doc. 524.

77. Haynes to Bundy, January 6, 1966, NSF, CF, box 97, LBJL.

78. Komer to Johnson, January 14, 1966, NSF, CF, box 97, LBJL.

79. Wilson to Johnson, January 14, 1966, *FRUS 1964–1968*, vol. 24, doc. 528.

80. Remarks by Rep. Gross, January 12, 1966, *Congressional Record* 112, pt. 1 (Washington, DC: Government Printing Office, 1966), 9a3.

81. Borstelmann, *Cold War and the Color Line*, 194.

82. Tom Wicker, "Lyndon Johnson and the Roots of Contemporary Conservatism," in *Long Time Gone: Sixties America Then and Now*, ed. Alexander Bloom (New York: Oxford University Press, 2001), 106, 120.

83. Gebelt (Salisbury) to State Department, January 2, 1966, NSF, CF, box 97, LBJL.

84. Noer, *Cold War and Black Liberation*, 209.

85. Komer to Johnson, February 17, 1966, NSF, CF, box 97, LBJL.

86. Memorandum for Mann, "Rhodesia/Zambia Situation Report No. 35," March 11, 1966, NSF, CF, box 97, LBJL.

87. Noer, *Cold War and Black Liberation*, 210–213, and Lake, *"Tar Baby" Option*, 94–95.

88. Memcon, Ambassador Garin with Johnson, et al., May 16, 1966, *FRUS 1964–1968*, vol. 24, doc. 535.

89. Rusk to Johnson, n.d., NSF, CF, box 97, LBJL.

90. Noer, *Cold War and Black Liberation*, 215.

91. PPC study, "Southern Africa in the Next Decade: A Case for Constructive Reinvolvement," August 23, 1966, RG59, PPC, Subject and Country Files, 1965–1969, box 310, NARA.

92. PPC study, "An Assessment of British Commitments in Africa," October 25, 1966, RG59, PPC, Subject and Country Files, 1965–1969, box 310, NARA.

93. Haynes to Rostow, April 18, 1966, *FRUS 1964–1968*, vol. 24, doc. 533.

94. Record of meeting of Senior Interdepartmental Group, April 12, 1966, *FRUS 1964–1968*, vol. 24, doc. 532.

95. Memcon, Rusk with Foreign Secretary Brown, et al., October 14, 1966, *FRUS 1964–1968*, vol. 24, doc. 543. For congressional sentiment at the end of 1966, see letters from House members in WHCF, GEN, CO 237, box 65, LBJL.

96. McNamara speech, May 18, 1966, Public Statements of Robert S. McNamara, vol. 7, LBJL.

97. PPC study, "Southern Africa in the Next Decade: A Case for Constructive Reinvolvement," August 23, 1966, RG59, PPC, Subject and Country Files, 1965–1969, box 310, NARA.

98. Johnson speech, May 26, 1966, American Presidency Project, https://www.presidency.ucsb.edu/documents/remarks-reception-marking-the-third-anniversary-the-organization-african-unity.

99. Moyers to Johnson, May 26, 1966, NSF, CF, box 76 [2 of 2], LBJL.

100. Johnson to Wilson, October 18, 1966, *FRUS 1964–1968*, vol. 24, doc. 544.

101. Wilson to Johnson, December 4, 1966, *FRUS 1964–1968*, vol. 24, doc. 549.

102. Johnson to Wilson, October 18, 1966, *FRUS 1964–1968*, vol. 24, doc. 544.

103. Noer, *Cold War and Black Liberation*, 229.

104. For example, Drew Middleton, "U.N. Council Votes Mandatory Curbs on Rhodesia, 11–0," *New York Times*, December 17, 1966, 1.

105. Goldberg statement, December 12, 1966, *Department of State Bulletin* 56, no. 1437 (January 9, 1967): 74–76.

106. Henry Owen to Rusk, January 23, 1967, RG59, PPC, Subject and Country Files, 1965–1969, box 307, NARA.

107. Leddy to Rusk, February 9, 1967, RG59, PPC, Subject and Country Files, 1965–1969, box 307, NARA.

108. Memcon, Goronwy Roberts with Sisco, et al., May 16, 1968, May 16, 1968, FCO 7/813, NAUK.

109. On declining confidence in the United Nations, see Irwin, *Gordian Knot*, esp. chap. 5.

110. Noer, *Cold War and Black Liberation*, 237.

111. Notes of 567th NSC Meeting, January 25, 1967, *FRUS 1964–1968*, vol. 24, doc. 556.

112. Durban consulate to State Department, March 6, 1966, Williams Papers, box 10.

113. Richard Eder, "President Names Key Africa Aide," *New York Times*, March 16, 1966, 21.

114. Harald Taswell to Foreign Secretary, "United States-South Africa Relations: Talk with Mr. Walt Rostow," BTS 1/33/3, vol. 7, National Archives of South Africa.

115. Milne, *America's Rasputin*, 164–169.

116. Clark Clifford with Richard Holbrooke, *Counsel to the President: A Memoir* (New York: Random House, 1991), 408.

117. Bill, *George Ball*, 74–75, 162–164.

118. Memcon, Lord Caradon with Sisco, et al., July 11, 1968, FCO 36/194, file 4417830, NAUK.

119. Hamilton to Rostow, October 11, 1967, NSF, CF, box 76 [2 of 2], LBJL.

120. Rostow to Johnson, August 9, 1966, NSF, CF, box 76 [2 of 2], LBJL.

121. Hamilton to Rostow, October 11, 1967, NSF, CF, box 76 [2 of 2], LBJL.

122. Notes of 567th NSC Meeting, January 25, 1967, *FRUS 1964–1968*, vol. 24, doc. 556.

123. Dean to Malcolm MacDonald, December 9, 1967, FCO 36/193, file 6998628, NAUK.

124. T. E. F. Williams (Dar es Salaam) to R. H. Hobden (Foreign Office), November 1, 1967, FCO 7, file 859, NAUK.

125. "U.S. Negroes Ready to Fight in Africa," December 29, 1967, *Times* (London), FCO 36/193, file 4417823, NAUK.

126. Memcon, Goronwy Roberts with Sisco, et al., May 16, 1968, FCO 7/813, NAUK.

127. Gerald Horne, *From the Barrel of a Gun: The United States and the War against Zimbabwe, 1965–1980* (Chapel Hill: University of North Carolina Press, 2001), 101–102.

128. Release by the American-South African Council, n.d., John B. Trevor Jr. Papers, box 6, Bentley Library.

129. Solicitation letter from American-South African Council, January 1968, John B. Trevor Jr. Papers, box 6, Bentley Library.

130. Russell to constituent E. R. Lott, June 5, 1968, Russell Papers, Series XVI, International, Subject File, box 24, Russell Library.

131. Noer, *Cold War and Black Liberation*, 230.

132. R. J. R. Owen (Washington embassy) to Foreign Office, November 17, 1967, FCO 36/193, file 4417823, NAUK.

133. Text of Goldwater interview, December 13, 1967, FCO 36/353, NAUK.

134. Roche to Moyers, December 8, 1966, WHCF Confidential File, CO 1–1, Africa 1966, box 6, LBJL.

135. See Ian Smith, *The Great Betrayal: The Memoirs of Ian Douglas Smith* (London: Blake, 1997), 113.

136. Acheson to Roy Wellensky, July 11, 1968, Acheson Papers, reel 22, Sterling Library.

137. Douglas Brinkley, *Dean Acheson: The Cold War Years, 1953–1971* (New Haven, CT: Yale University Press, 1992), 320–321.

138. "Southern Rhodesia and the United Nations: The U.S. Position," *State Department Bulletin*, 56, no. 1445 (March 6, 1967): 366–377.

139. Goldberg speech, January 27, 1967, *State Department Bulletin* 56, no. 1443 (February 20, 1967): 291. On the administration's counteroffensive in 1967, see Noer, *Cold War and Black Liberation*, 231–233.

140. R. J. R. Owen (Washington embassy) to Foreign Office, November 17, 1967, FCO 36/193, file 4417823, NAUK.

141. Memcon, Lord Caradon with Sisco, et al., July 11, 1968, FCO 36/194, file 4417830, NAUK.

142. For instance, Roger Morris to Rostow, November 15, 1968, *FRUS 1964–1968*, vol. 24 doc. 572.

## Conclusion

1. James T. Wooten, "Astronauts Back from Moon; Begin 18 Days in Quarantine," *New York Times*, July 25, 1969, 1.

2. "Informal Remarks in Guam with Newsmen," July 25, 1969, in *Public Papers of the Presidents: Richard Nixon, 1969* (Washington, DC: Government Printing Office, 1971), 548–552.

3. "Informal Remarks in Guam with Newsmen," July 25, 1969.

4. Kissinger to Nixon, August 29, NSC Files, Subject Files, box 378, RNL.

5. Stephen E. Ambrose, *Nixon: The Triumph of a Politician, 1962–1972* (New York: Touchstone, 1989), 287.

6. Nixon speech, November 3, 1969, in *Public Papers of the Presidents: Richard Nixon, 1969*, 901–909.

7. Richard Nixon, *United States Foreign Policy for the 1970s: A New Strategy for Peace* (New York: Bantam, 1970), 4–6, emphasis original.

8. PPC study, "The Future of Foreign Aid," December 1968, NSF, Subject File, box 50, LBJL.

9. For discussion of these trends, see Daniel J. Sargent, *A Superpower Transformed: The Remaking of American Foreign Relations in the 1970s* (New York: Oxford University Press, 2015), 53–59.

10. Kissinger to Nixon, August 29, NSC Files, Subject Files, box 378, RNL.

11. Tad Szulc, *The Illusion of Peace: Foreign Policy in the Nixon Years* (New York: Viking, 1978), 7.

12. Jussi Hanhimäki, *The Flawed Architect: Henry Kissinger and American Foreign Policy* (Oxford: Oxford University Press, 2004), 54.

13. Nixon speech, July 29, 1967, *FRUS 1969–1976*, vol. 1, doc. 2.

14. Henry A. Kissinger, "Central Issues in American Foreign Policy," first published 1968, *FRUS 1969–1976*, vol. 1, doc. 4.

15. Jeffrey Kimball makes a similar point in "The Nixon Doctrine: A Saga of Misunderstanding," *Presidential Studies Quarterly* 36, no. 1 (March 2006): 60, 72.

16. Robert D. Schulzinger, *Henry Kissinger: Doctor of Diplomacy* (New York: Columbia University Press, 1989), 30.

17. Longley, *LBJ's 1968*, 197.

18. Howard P. Jones, *Indonesia: The Possible Dream* (New York: Harcourt Brace Jovanovich, 1971), 421.

19. Transcript of Rusk press conference, January 3, 1969, Rusk Papers, series II, Secretary of State Speeches, box 5, Russell Library.

20. Rostow to Johnson, December 23, 1968, NSF, Subject File, box 50 LBJL.

21. Rostow to Kissinger, December 23, 1968, NSF, Rostow file, box 14, LBJL.

22. Osgood to Kissinger, October 14, 1969, NSC Institutional Files, box H-134, RNL.

23. Nixon speech, October 31, 1969, White House Central File, Subject Categories: speeches, box 113, RNL.

24. Telephone transcript, Nixon and Kissinger, October 30, 1969, Kissinger Telcons, box 2, RNL.

25. Green, *We Cannot Remain Silent*, 103.

26. "Issues Raised by Brazil Program Analysis," July 14, 1970, NSC Institutional Files, NSC Meetings, box H-049, RNL.

27. Robert Finch to Nixon, December 2, 1971, *FRUS 1969–1976*, vol. E-10, doc. 52.

28. Transcript, Nixon, Attorney General Mitchell, and others, September 30, 1971, *FRUS 1969–1976, vol. E-10, doc. 50.*

29. Recording of Nixon's meeting with Donald Rumsfeld, March 8, 1971, Nixon Tapes, conversation 463-6, www.whitehousetapes.org/pages/listen_tapes_rmn.htm. On the administration's broader approach to Latin America, see Mark Atwood Lawrence, "History from Below: The United States and Latin America in the Nixon Years," in *Nixon in the World: American Foreign Relations, 1969–1977*, ed. Fredrik Logevall and Andrew Preston (New York: Oxford University Press, 2008), 269–288.

30. Skidmore, *Politics of Military Rule in Brazil*, 108.

31. Skidmore, *Politics of Military Rule in Brazil*, chap. 5.

32. Anderson, "Bestial Practices in Brazil," *Baltimore News-American*, September 30, 1970, Church Papers, series 2.2, box 45.

33. Skidmore, *Politics of Military Rule in Brazil*, 154.

34. Theodore L. Eliot to Kissinger, October 29, 1971, RG59, Subject-Numeric Files, 1970–1973, box 2130, NARA.

35. Rogers to Nixon, December 2, 1971, RG59, Subject-Numeric Files, 1970–1973, box 2130, NARA.

36. Kissinger to Nixon, December 6, 1971, NSC Files, VIP Visits, box 911, RNL.

37. NSC memo for the CIA, "President's Conversations with Brazilian President Médici," December 21, 1971, NSC Files, VIP Visits, box 911, RNL.

38. Memcon for the president, December 9, 1971, National Security Archive, https://nsarchive2.gwu.edu/NSAEBB/NSAEBB282/Document%20143%2012.9.71.pdf.

39. Fox Butterfield, "Indian Animosity Grows," *New York Times*, December 16, 1971, 1, and "Text of Prime Minister Gandhi's Letter to the President," *New York Times*, December 17, 1971, 17.

40. Nixon to Gandhi, December 18, 1971, NSC files, Presidential Correspondence, 1969–1974, box 755, RNL.

41. Madan, "With an Eye to the East," 451, and Kux, *India and the United States*, 307.

42. Henry Kissinger, *The White House Years* (Boston: Little, Brown, 1979), 848.

43. Guha, *India after Gandhi*, 435–444.

44. Memcon, Kissinger with Jha, et al., July 15, 1970, NSC Files, Country File, box 596, RNL.

45. Robert J. McMahon, "The Danger of Geopolitical Fantasies: Nixon, Kissinger, and the South Asia Crisis of 1971," in Logevall and Preston, *Nixon in the World*, 250–251, and Kissinger, *White House Years*, 848.

46. Christopher Van Hollen, "The Tilt Policy Revisited: Nixon-Kissinger Geopolitics and South Asia," *Asian Survey* 20, no. 4 (April 1980): 339.

47. McMahon, "Danger of Geopolitical Fantasies," 262.

48. Hanhimäki, *Flawed Architect*, 175.

49. Madan, "With an Eye to the East," 418.

50. Richard M. Nixon, *RN: The Memoirs of Richard Nixon* (New York: Grosset and Dunlap, 1978), 133, and Alvandi, *Nixon, Kissinger, and the Shah*, 62.

51. Kissinger to Nixon, October 21, 1969, *FRUS 1969–1976*, NSC Files, VIP Visits, box 920, RNL.

52. Memcon, Shah with Laird, et al., October 22, 1969, *FRUS 1969–1972*, vol. E-4, doc. 36, and memcon, shah with Secretary of State William Rogers, *FRUS 1969–1972*, vol. E-4, doc. 33.

53. Offiler, *U.S. Foreign Policy*, 154.

54. Alvandi, *Nixon, Kissinger, and the Shah*, 51–57; Bill, *Eagle and the Lion*, 197–200; and Offiler, *U.S. Foreign Policy*, 147–150.

55. Alvandi, *Nixon, Kissinger, and the Shah*, 51–53.

56. Memcon, Nixon, Kissinger, and shah, May 31, 1972, *FRUS 1969–1972*, vol. E-4, doc. 201.

57. Alvandi, *Nixon, Kissinger, and the Shah*, 64.

58. State Department paper, "Summary of NSSM-61 on Indonesia," n.d., *FRUS 1969–1976*, vol. 20, doc. 277.

59. Kissinger to Nixon, December 22, 1969, *FRUS 1969–1976*, vol. 20, doc. 278.

60. Paul F. Gardner, *Shared Hopes, Separate Fears: Fifty Years of U.S.-Indonesian Relations* (Boulder, CO: Westview, 1997), 265.

61. For example, Kissinger to Nixon, March 26, 1969, *FRUS 1969–1976*, vol. 20, doc. 266, and memorandum for the record, July 27, 1969, *FRUS 1969–1976*, vol. 20, doc. 271.

62. Galbraith (Jakarta) to State Department, July 29, 1969, *FRUS 1969–1976*, vol. 20, doc. 272.

63. Kissinger to Nixon, July 18, 1969, https://nsarchive2.gwu.edu/NSAEBB/NSAEBB242/.

64. Rogers to Nixon, November 16, 1969, RG59, Subject-Numeric Files, 1967–1969, box 2207, NARA.

65. Kissinger to Nixon, May 26, 1970, NSC Files, VIP Visits, box, 919, RNL.

66. Jakarta to State Department, October 15, 1970, RG59, Subject-Numeric Files, 1970–1973, box 1967, NARA.

67. Jakarta to State Department, September 17, 1970, RG59, Subject-Numeric Files, 1970–1973, box 1967, NARA.

68. Wen-Qing Ngoei, *Arc of Containment: Britain, the United States, and Anticommunism in Southeast Asia* (Ithaca, NY: Cornell University Press, 2019), 159–160.

69. Hanhimäki, *Flawed Architect*, 402.

70. Tokyo embassy to State Department, November 12, 1971, *FRUS 1969–1976*, vol. 20, doc. 323.

71. National Security Decision Memorandum, "Indonesian Military Assistance," n.d., NSC Institutional Files, NSDMs, box H-223, RNL.

72. Jack Anderson, "Henry Kissinger's First Big 'Tilt,'" *Washington Post*, October 11, 1974, D19.

73. The analysis here resembles that of Thomas J. Noer, who emphasizes continuity between the Johnson and Nixon presidencies. Noer, *Cold War and Black Liberation*, 238–239. For an interpretation stressing a sharp break, see Horne, *From the Barrel of a Gun*, 148–150.

74. Minutes of NSC Meeting, December 17, 1969, NSC Institutional Files, NSSMs, box H-145, RNL.

75. Lord to Kissinger, October 17, 1969, RG59, PPC files, Director's Files, box 339, NARA.

76. National Security Decision Memorandum, December 17, 1969, NSC Institutional Files, NSC Meetings, box H-025, RNL.

77. For example, Horne, *From the Barrel of a Gun*, 148–151.

78. Taswell to Foreign Secretary, October 3, 1969, BTS 1/33/3, vol. 13, Archives of the South African Ministry of Foreign Affairs.

79. Ribeiro de Meneses and McNamara, *White Redoubt*, 124–129.

80. Lake, *"Tar Baby" Option*, 127.

81. Lake, *"Tar Baby" Option*, 167–174, and Rhodesian Information Office, "Communist-Backed Terrorism in Southern Africa," *Rhodesian Viewpoint*, March 6, 1969, Acheson Papers, reel 44, Sterling Memorial Library.

82. Sarah B. Snyder, *From Selma to Moscow: How Human Rights Activists Transformed U.S. Foreign Policy* (New York: Columbia University Press, 2018), 56–59.

83. Levine to Kissinger, April 19, 1972, NSC Institutional Files, NSSMs, box H-188, RNL.

84. "Hypocrisy on Rhodesia," *New York Times*, June 7, 1972, 44.

85. "A Farewell to Foreign Aid: A Liberal Takes Leave," October 29, 1971, Symington Papers, vol. 3724.

86. Samuel P. Huntington, *The Third Wave: Democratization in the Late Twentieth Century* (Norman: University of Oklahoma Press, 1991), 21.

87. On right- and left-wing collaborations, see Kyle Burke, *Revolutionaries for the Right: Anticommunist Internationalism and Paramilitary Warfare in the Cold War* (Chapel Hill: University of North Carolina Press, 2018); Paul Thomas Chamberlin, *The Global Offensive: The United States, the Palestinian Liberation Organization, and the Making of the Post–Cold War Order* (New

York: Oxford University Press, 2012); John Dinges, *The Condor Years: How Pinochet and His Allies Brought Terrorism to Three Continents* (New York: New Press, 2004); Carl Forsberg, "A Diplomatic Counterrevolution: The Transformation of the U.S.-Middle East Alliance System in the 1970s" (PhD diss., University of Texas at Austin, 2019); and Ngoei, *Arc of Containment.*

88. On the ways in which U.S. policy choices have driven anti-Americanism, see, for example, Alan McPherson, *Yankee, No! Anti-Americanism in U.S.-Latin American Relations* (Cambridge, MA: Harvard University Press, 2006); Barry Rubin and Judith Colp Rubin, *Hating America: A History* (New York: Oxford University Press, 2004), esp. chaps. 5–7; Westad, *Global Cold War,* conclusion.

# BIBLIOGRAPHY

## Primary Sources

### *Brazil*

National Archives of Brazil (online)
  Files of the Conselho de Seguranca Nacional

### *Canada*

Library and Archives Canada, Ottawa
  Records of the Department of External Affairs (Record Group 25)

### *South Africa*

Archives of the South African Ministry of Foreign Affairs, Pretoria

### *United Kingdom*

National Archives, Kew, Surrey
  Cabinet Office Files (CAB 148)
  Dominions Office Files (DO 148)
  Foreign and Commonwealth Office Files (FCO 7, 15, 36; FO 371)
  Prime Minister Files (PREM 13)

### *United States*

Lyndon Baines Johnson Presidential Library, Austin, TX
  National Security Files
  White House Central Files
John F. Kennedy Presidential Library, Boston, MA
  National Security Files
  Oral Histories
  Pre-Presidential Files
National Archives and Records Administration, College Park, MD
  Record Group 59, General Records of the Department of State
  Policy Planning Council
  Subject-Numeric Files, 1963–1973

Richard M. Nixon Presidential Library, Yorba Linda, CA
National Security Council Files

## *Personal Paper Collections*

Dean G. Acheson (Sterling Memorial Library, Yale University)
George W. Ball (Lyndon Baines Johnson Library, Austin, TX)
Samuel E. Belk III (John F. Kennedy Library, Boston, MA)
Frank Church (Albertsons Library, Boise State University)
Paul H. Douglas (Chicago Historical Society, Chicago, IL)
J. William Fulbright (Mullins Library, University of Arkansas)
Henry M. Jackson (Allen Library, University of Washington)
Robert F. Kennedy (John F. Kennedy Library, Boston, MA)
Henry Cabot Lodge Jr. (Massachusetts Historical Society, Boston, MA)
Dean Rusk (Richard B. Russell Library, University of Georgia)
Richard B. Russell (Richard B. Russell Library, University of Georgia)
Gerald L. K. Smith (Bentley Library, University of Michigan)
Theodore C. Sorensen (John F. Kennedy Library, Boston, MA)
W. Stuart Symington (Ellis Library, University of Missouri–Columbia)
Herman E. Talmadge (Richard B. Russell Library, University of Georgia)
John B. Trevor, Jr. (Bentley Library, University of Michigan)
G. Mennen Williams (Bentley Library, University of Michigan)

## *Newspapers and Periodicals*

*Chicago Tribute*
*Correia da Manhã*
*Los Angeles Times*
*Newsweek*
*New York Times*
*Time*
*Times of India*
*Washington Post*

## *Published Document Collections*

Algar, Hamid, ed. and trans. *Islam and Revolution: Writings and Declarations of Imam Khomeini.* Berkeley, CA: Mizan Press, 1981.

Executive Secretariat of the Organization of Solidarity of the Peoples of Africa, Asia, and Latin America. *First Solidarity Conference of the Peoples of Africa, Asia, and Latin America.* Havana: General Secretariat of the OSPAAAL, 1966.

Germany, Kent B., and David C. Carter. *The Presidential Recordings of Lyndon B. Johnson, Volumes 7–8: Mississippi Burning and the Passage of the Civil Rights Act.* New York: Norton, 2011.

Lawrence, Mark Atwood, ed. *The Vietnam War: An International History in Documents.* New York: Oxford University Press, 2014.

Mokoena, Kenneth, ed. *South Africa and the United States: The Declassified History*. New York: New Press, 1993.

Posthumus, G. A. *The InterGovernmental Group on Indonesia*. Rotterdam: University of Rotterdam Press, 1971.

*Public Papers of the Presidents*. Multiple vols. Washington, DC: U.S. Government Printing Office.

U.S. Department of State. *Foreign Relations of the United States, 1961–1963*. Multiple vols. Washington, DC: U.S. Government Printing Office.

———. *Foreign Relations of the United States, 1964–1968*. Multiple vols. Washington, DC: U.S. Government Printing Office.

Zelikow, Philip, and Ernest May, eds. *The Presidential Recordings of John F. Kennedy, Volumes 1–3: The Great Crises*. New York: Norton, 2001.

Zelikow, Philip, Ernest May, and Timothy Naftali, eds. *The Presidential Recordings of Lyndon B. Johnson, Volumes 1–3: The Kennedy Assassination and the Transfer of Power*. New York: Norton, 2005.

## Secondary Sources and Published Memoirs

Ahlberg, Kristin L. *Transplanting the Great Society: Lyndon Johnson and Food for Peace*. Columbia: University of Missouri Press, 2008.

Aldous, Richard. *Schlesinger: The Imperial Historian*. New York: Norton, 2017.

Allcock, Thomas Tunstall. "Becoming 'Mr. Latin America': Thomas C. Mann Reconsidered." *Diplomatic History* 38, no. 5 (2014): 1017–1045.

———. *Thomas C. Mann: President Johnson, the Cold War, and the Restructuring of Latin American Foreign Policy*. Lexington: University Press of Kentucky, 2018.

Allison, Graham T., and Philip Zelikow. *Essence of Decision: Explaining the Cuban Missile Crisis*. 2nd ed. New York: Longman, 1999.

Alvandi, Roham. *Nixon, Kissinger, and the Shah: The United States and Iran in the Cold War*. New York: Oxford University Press, 2014.

———. "The Shah's Détente with Khrushchev: Iran's 1962 Missile Base Pledge to the Soviet Union." *Cold War History* 14, no. 3 (August 2014): 423–444.

Ambrose, Stephen E. *Nixon: The Triumph of a Politician, 1962–1972*. New York: Touchstone, 1989.

Andrew, Christopher, and Vasili Mitrokhin. *"The World Was Going Our Way": The KGB and the Battle for the Third World*. New York: Basic Books, 2005.

Appy, Christian G. *Patriots: The Vietnam War Remembered from All Sides*. New York: Viking, 2003.

Ashby, Leroy, and Rod Gramer. *Fighting the Odds: The Life of Senator Frank Church*. Pullman: Washington State University Press, 1994.

Asselin, Pierre. *Vietnam's American War: A History*. New York: Cambridge University Press, 2017.

Bacevich, Andrew J. *Washington Rules: America's Path to Permanent War*. New York: Metropolitan, 2010.

Ball, George W. *The Discipline of Power: Essentials of a Modern World Structure*. Boston: Little, Brown, 1968.

———. *The Past Has Another Pattern: Memoirs*. New York: Norton, 1982.

Bass, Warren. *Support Any Friend: Kennedy's Middle East and the Making of the U.S.-Israel Alliance*. New York: Oxford University Press, 2003.

Beisner, Robert L. *Dean Acheson: A Life in the Cold War*. New York: Oxford University Press, 2006.

Berg, Manfred, and Andreas Etges, eds. *John F. Kennedy and the "Thousand Days": New Perspectives on the Foreign and Domestic Policies of the Kennedy Administration*. Heidelberg: Universitätsverlag Winter, 2007.

Bernstein, Irving. *Guns or Butter: The Presidency of Lyndon Johnson*. New York: Oxford University Press, 1996.

Bessner, Daniel, and Fredrik Logevall, "Recentering the United States in the Historiography of American Foreign Relations." *Texas National Security Review* 3, no. 2 (Spring 2020): 39–55.

Biagi, Orivaldo Leme. *O Imaginário e as Guerras da Imprensa*. Rio de Janeiro: Papel Virtual, 2003.

Bill, James A. *The Eagle and the Lion: The Tragedy of American-Iranian Relations*. New Haven, CT: Yale University Press, 1988.

———. *George Ball: Behind the Scenes in U.S. Foreign Policy*. New Haven, CT: Yale University Press, 1997.

Bird, Kai. *The Color of Truth: McGeorge Bundy and William Bundy: Brothers in Arms*. New York: Simon & Schuster, 2000.

Blang, Eugenie M. *Allies at Odds: America, Europe, and Vietnam, 1961–1968*. Lanham, MD: Rowman & Littlefield, 2011.

Blight, James G., and Philip Brenner. *Sad and Luminous Days: Cuba's Struggle with the Superpowers after the Missile Crisis*. Lanham, MD: Rowman & Littlefield, 2002.

Blight, James G., et al., eds. *Vietnam: If Kennedy Had Lived*. Lanham, MD: Rowman & Littlefield, 2009.

Bloom, Alexander, ed. *Long Time Gone: Sixties America Then and Now*. New York: Oxford University Press, 2001.

Borstelmann, Thomas. *Apartheid's Reluctant Uncle: The United States and Southern Africa in the Early Cold War*. New York: Oxford University Press, 1993.

———. *The Cold War and the Color Line: American Race Relations in the Global Arena*. Cambridge, MA: Harvard University Press, 2001.

———. "'Hedging Our Bets and Buying Time': John Kennedy and Racial Revolutions in the American South and Southern Africa." *Diplomatic History* 24, no. 3 (Summer 2000): 435–463.

Bowles, Chester. *Promises to Keep: My Years in Public Life, 1941–1969*. New York: Harper & Row, 1971.

Brands, H. W. *India and the United States: The Cold Peace*. Boston: Twayne, 1990.

———. "The Limits of Manipulation: How the United States Didn't Topple Sukarno." *Journal of American History* 76, no. 3 (December 1989): 785–808.

———. *The Specter of Neutralism: The United States and the Emergence of the Third World, 1947–1960*. New York: Columbia University Press, 1989.

———. *The Wages of Globalism: Lyndon Johnson and the Limits of American Power*. New York: Oxford University Press, 1995.

Brands, Hal. *Latin America's Cold War*. Cambridge, MA: Harvard University Press, 2010.

Brazinsky, Gregg A. *Winning the Third World: Sino-American Rivalry during the Cold War*. Chapel Hill: University of North Carolina Press, 2017.

Brennan, Mary C. *Turning Right in the Sixties: The Conservative Capture of the GOP*. Chapel Hill: University of North Carolina Press, 1995.

Brinkley, Douglas. *Dean Acheson: The Cold War Years, 1953–1971*. New Haven, CT: Yale University Press, 1992.

Brown, Jonathan C. *Cuba's Revolutionary World*. Cambridge, MA: Harvard University Press, 2017.

Bunnell, Frederick. "American 'Low Posture' Policy toward Indonesia in the Months Leading Up to the 1965 Coup." *Indonesia* 50 (October 1990): 29–60.

Burke, Kyle. *Revolutionaries for the Right: Anticommunist Internationalism and Paramilitary Warfare in the Cold War*. Chapel Hill: University of North Carolina Press, 2018.

Burns, E. Bradford. "Tradition and Variation in Brazilian Foreign Policy." *Journal of Inter-American Studies* 9, no. 2 (April 1967): 195–212.

Burns, James MacGregor. *John Kennedy: A Political Profile*. New York: Harcourt Brace, 1959.

Busch, Peter. *All the Way with JFK? Britain, the US, and the Vietnam War*. New York: Oxford University Press, 2003.

Campagna, Anthony S. *The Economic Consequences of the Vietnam War*. New York: Praeger, 1991.

Caro, Robert A. *Means of Ascent: The Years of Lyndon Johnson*. New York: Knopf, 1990.

———. *The Passage to Power: The Years of Lyndon Johnson*. New York: Knopf, 2012.

Chamberlin, Paul Thomas. *The Cold War's Killing Fields: Rethinking the Long Peace*. New York: Harper, 2018.

———. *The Global Offensive: The United States, the Palestinian Liberation Organization, and the Making of the Post–Cold War Order*. New York: Oxford University Press, 2012.

Chen Jian. *Mao's China and the Cold War*. Chapel Hill: University of North Carolina Press, 2001.

Chua, Daniel Wei Boon. *U.S.-Singapore Relations, 1965–1975: Strategic Non-alignment in the Cold War*. Singapore: National University of Singapore Press, 2017.

Clarke, Thurston. *JFK's Last Hundred Days: The Transformation of a Man and the Emergence of a Great President*. New York: Penguin, 2013.

Clifford, Clark, with Richard Holbrooke. *Counsel to the President: A Memoir*. New York: Random House, 1991.

Cohen, Warren I., and Nancy Bernkopf Tucker, eds. *Lyndon Johnson Confronts the World: American Foreign Policy, 1963–1968*. New York: Cambridge University Press, 1994.

Colburn, Forrest D. *The Vogue of Revolution in Poor Countries*. Princeton, NJ: Princeton University Press, 1994.

Connelly, Matthew J. *A Diplomatic Revolution: Algeria's Fight for Independence and the Origins of the Post–Cold War Era*. New York: Oxford University Press, 2002.

Conniff, Michael L. *Panama and the United States: The Forced Alliance*. Athens: University of Georgia Press, 1992.

Cornejo, Robert M. "When Sukarno Sought the Bomb: Indonesian Nuclear Aspirations in the Mid-1960s." *Nonproliferation Review* 7, no. 2 (Summer 2000): 31–43.

Cullather, Nick. *The Hungry World: America's Cold War Battle Against Poverty in Asia* Cambridge, MA: Harvard University Press, 2010.

Dallek, Robert. *Camelot's Court: Inside the Kennedy White House*. New York: HarperCollins, 2013.

———. *Nixon and Kissinger: Partners in Power*. New York: HarperCollins, 2007.

Dallek, Robert. *An Unfinished Life: John F. Kennedy, 1917–1963*. Boston: Little, Brown, 2003.

Daoudi, M. S., and M. S. Dajani. *Economic Diplomacy: Embargo Leverage and World Politics*. Boulder, CO: Westview, 1985.

Daum, Andreas, et al., eds. *America, the Vietnam War, and the World: Comparative and International Perspectives*. New York: Cambridge University Press, 2003.

Dean, Robert D. *Imperial Brotherhood: Gender and the Making of Cold War Foreign Policy*. Amherst: University of Massachusetts Press, 2001.

Dellinger, David. *From Yale to Jail: The Life Story of a Moral Dissenter*. New York: Pantheon, 1993.

De Witte, Ludo. *The Assassination of Lumumba*. Trans. Ann Wright and Renée Fenby. London: Verso, 2001.

Dinges, John. *The Condor Years: How Pinochet and His Allies Brought Terrorism to Three Continents*. New York: New Press, 2004.

Divine, Robert A., ed. *The Johnson Years*, vol. 1: *Foreign Policy, the Great Society, and the White House*. Lawrence: University Press of Kansas, 1987.

———, ed. *The Johnson Years*, vol. 2: *Vietnam, the Environment, and Science*. Lawrence: University Press of Kansas, 1987.

Drea, Edward J. *McNamara, Clifford and the Burdens of Vietnam, 1965–1969*. Washington, DC: Government Printing Office, 2011.

Dudziak, Mary L. *Cold War Civil Rights: Race and the Image of American Democracy*. Princeton, NJ: Princeton University Press, 2000.

Easterly, William. *The Tyranny of Experts: Economics, Dictators, and the Forgotten Rights of the Poor*. New York: Basic Books, 2013.

Ekbladh, David. *The Great American Mission: Modernization and the Construction of an American World Order*. Princeton, NJ: Princeton University Press, 2010.

Elson, R. E. *Suharto: A Political Biography*. Cambridge: Cambridge University Press, 2001.

Engerman, David C., Nils Gilman, Mark H. Haefele, and Michael E. Lathan, eds. *Staging Growth: Modernization, Development, and the Global Cold War*. Amherst: University of Massachusetts Press, 2003.

Escobar, Arturo. *Encountering Development: The Making and Unmaking of the Third World*. Princeton, NJ: Princeton University Press, 1995.

Forsberg, Carl. "A Diplomatic Counterrevolution: The Transformation of the U.S.-Middle East Alliance System in the 1970s." PhD diss., University of Texas at Austin, 2019.

Freedman, Lawrence. *Kennedy's Wars: Berlin, Cuba, Laos, and Vietnam*. New York: Oxford University Press, 2000.

Friedman, Jeremy. *Shadow Cold War: The Sino-Soviet Competition for the Third World*. Chapel Hill: University of North Carolina Press, 2015.

Fulbright, J. William. *The Arrogance of Power*. New York: Random House, 1966.

Fursenko, Aleksandr, and Timothy Naftali. *Khrushchev's Cold War: The Inside Story of an American Adversary*. New York: Norton, 2006.

Gaddis, John Lewis. *Strategies of Containment: A Critical Appraisal of American National Security Policy during the Cold War*. Rev. ed. New York: Oxford University Press, 2005.

Galbraith, John Kenneth. *The Affluent Society*. 4th anniv. ed. Boston: Houghton Mifflin, 1998.

———. *Ambassador's Journal: A Personal Account of the Kennedy Years*. Boston: Houghton Mifflin, 1969.

Gallup, George H. *The Gallup Poll: Public Opinion, 1935–1971*. New York: Random House, 1972.
Gardner, Paul F. *Shared Hopes, Separate Fears: Fifty Years of U.S.-Indonesian Relations*. Boulder, CO: Westview, 1997.
Gasiorowski, Mark J. *U.S. Foreign Policy and the Shah: Building a Client State in Iran*. Ithaca, NY: Cornell University Press, 1991.
Gavin, Francis J. *Gold, Dollars, and Power: The Politics of International Monetary Relations, 1958–1971*. Chapel Hill: University of North Carolina Press, 2004.
Gavin, Francis J., and Mark Atwood Lawrence, eds. *Beyond the Cold War: Lyndon Johnson and the New Global Challenges of the 1960s*. New York: Oxford University Press, 2014.
Gewen, Barry. *The Inevitability of Tragedy: Henry Kissinger and His World*. New York: Norton, 2020.
Gilman, Nils. *Mandarins of the Future: Modernization Theory in Cold War America*. Baltimore: Johns Hopkins University Press, 2003.
Gleijeses, Piero. *Conflicting Missions: Havana, Washington, and Africa, 1959–1976*. Chapel Hill: University of North Carolina Press, 2003.
Goodwin, Doris Kearns. *Lyndon Johnson and the American Dream*. New York: St. Martin's, 1976.
Gopal, Sarvepalli. *Jawaharlal Nehru: A Biography*, vol. 3, *1956–1964*. London: Jonathan Cape, 1984.
Graubard, Stephen R. *Kissinger: Portrait of a Mind*. New York, Norton, 1973.
Green, James N. *We Cannot Remain Silent: Opposition to the Brazilian Military Dictatorship in the United States*. Durham, NC: Duke University Press, 2010.
Grose, Peter. *Gentleman Spy: The Life of Allen Dulles*. Boston: Houghton Mifflin, 1994.
Grow, Michael. *U.S. Presidents and Latin American Interventions: Pursuing Regime Change in the Cold War*. Lawrence: University Press of Kansas, 2008.
Guha, Ramachandra. *India after Gandhi: The History of the World's Largest Democracy*. New York: Harper, 2007.
Gupte, Pranay. *Mother India: A Political Biography of Indira Gandhi*. New York: Penguin 2009.
Haines, Gerald, and J. Samuel Walker, eds. *American Foreign Relations: A Historiographical Review*. Westport, CT: Greenwood, 1981.
Halberstam, David. *The Best and the Brightest*. New ed. New York: Random House, 1992.
———. *The Fifties*. New York: Villard, 1993.
Hanhimäki, Jussi. *The Flawed Architect: Henry Kissinger and American Foreign Policy*. Oxford: Oxford University Press, 2004.
Harrison, Selig. *The Widening Gulf: Asian Nationalism and American Policy*. New York: Free Press, 1978.
Helsing, Jeffrey W. *Johnson's War / Johnson's Great Society: The Guns and Butter Trap*. Westport, CT: Praeger, 2000.
Hersh, Seymour M. *The Dark Side of Camelot*. Boston: Little, Brown, 1997.
Hershberg, James G. "'High-Spirited Confusion': Brazil, the 1961 Belgrade Non-Aligned Conference, and the Limits of an 'Independent' Foreign Policy during the High Cold War." *Cold War History* 7, no. 3 (August 2007): 373–388.
———. "The United States, Brazil, and the Cuban Missile Crisis (Part 2)." *Journal of Cold War Studies* 6, no. 3 (Summer 2004): 5–67.
Hess, Gary R. "Accommodation and Discord: The United States, India, and the Third World," *Diplomatic History* 16, no. 1 (January 1992): 1–22.

Hilsman, Roger. *To Move a Nation: The Politics of Foreign Policy in the Administration of John F. Kennedy*. Garden City, NY: Doubleday, 1967.

Hogan, Michael J., and Thomas G. Paterson, eds. *Explaining the History of American Foreign Relations*. 2nd ed. New York: Cambridge University Press, 2004.

Holland, Max, ed. *The Presidential Recordings: Lyndon B. Johnson, November 22–30, 1963*. New York: Norton, 2005.

Hoopes, Townsend. *The Limits of Intervention*. New York: McKay, 1973.

Horne, Gerald. *From the Barrel of a Gun: The United States and the War against Zimbabwe, 1965–1980*. Chapel Hill: University of North Carolina Press, 2001.

Huggins, Martha K. *Political Policing: The United States and Latin America*. Durham, NC: Duke University Press, 1998.

Huntington, Samuel P. *The Third Wave: Democratization in the Late Twentieth Century*. Norman: University of Oklahoma Press, 1991.

Iriye, Akira. *Global Community: The Role of International Organizations in the Making of the Contemporary World*. Berkeley: University of California Press, 2002.

Irwin, Ryan M. *Gordian Knot: Apartheid and the Unmaking of the Liberal World Order*. New York: Oxford University Press, 2012.

Isaacson, Walter, and Evan Thomas. *The Wise Men: Six Friends and the World They Made*. New York: Simon & Schuster, 1986.

Isserman, Maurice, and Michael Kazin. *America Divided: The Civil War of the 1960s*. 2nd ed. New York: Oxford University Press, 2004.

Jackson, Henry F. *From the Congo to Soweto: U.S. Foreign Policy toward Africa since 1960*. New York: William Morrow, 1982.

Johns, Andrew L. "The Johnson Administration, the Shah of Iran, and the Changing Pattern of U.S.-Iranian Relations, 1965–1967." *Journal of Cold War Studies* 9, no. 2 (Spring 2007): 64–94.

Johnson, Lyndon Baines. *The Vantage Point: Perspectives on the Presidency*. New York: Holt, Rinehart and Winston, 1971.

Johnson, Robert David. *Congress and the Cold War*. Cambridge: Cambridge University Press, 2006.

Johnson, Robert David, and David Shreve, eds. *The Presidential Recordings: Lyndon B. Johnson, December 1963*. New York: Norton, 2005.

Jones, Frank Leith. *Blowtorch: Robert Komer, Vietnam, and American Cold War Strategy*. Annapolis, MD: Naval Institute Press, 2013.

Jones, Howard P. *Indonesia: The Possible Dream*. New York: Harcourt Brace Jovanovich, 1971.

Jones, Matthew. *Conflict and Confrontation in South East Asia, 1961–1965: Britain, the United States, Indonesia, and the Creation of Malaysia*. Cambridge: Cambridge University Press, 2002.

Jorden, William J. *Panama Odyssey*. Austin: University of Texas Press, 1984.

Kahin, Audrey R., and George McT. Kahin. *Subversion as Foreign Policy: The Secret Eisenhower and Dulles Debacle in Indonesia*. New York: New Press, 1995.

Kaplan, Fred. *1959: The Year That Changed Everything*. New York: Wiley, 2009.

Kapstein, Ethan B. *The Insecure Alliance: Energy Crises and Western Politics since 1944*. New York: Oxford University Press, 1990.

Keller, Renata. "The Latin American Missile Crisis." *Diplomatic History* 39, no. 2 (April 2015): 212–221.

Kimball, Jeffrey. "The Nixon Doctrine: A Saga of Misunderstanding." *Presidential Studies Quarterly* 36, no. 1 (March 2006): 59–74.

Kirk, Jason A. *India and the World Bank: The Politics of Aid and Influence.* London: Anthem, 2011.

Kirkendall, Andrew J. "Kennedy Men and the Fate of the Alliance for Progress in LBJ Era Brazil and Chile." *Diplomacy and Statecraft* 18 (2007): 745–772.

Kissinger, Henry. *The White House Years.* Boston: Little, Brown, 1979.

———. *Years of Renewal.* New York: Simon & Schuster, 1999.

Kolko, Gabriel. *Confronting the Third World: United States Foreign Policy, 1945–1980.* New York: Pantheon, 1988.

Kuklick, Bruce. *Blind Oracles: Intellectuals and War from Kennan to Kissinger.* Princeton, NJ: Princeton University Press, 2006.

Kunz, Diane B., ed. *The Diplomacy of the Crucial Decade: American Foreign Relations during the 1960s.* New York: Columbia University Press, 1994.

Kux, Dennis. *India and the United States: Estranged Democracies.* Washington, DC: National Defense University Press, 1992.

———. *The United States and Pakistan: Disenchanted Allies, 1947–2000.* Washington, DC: Woodrow Wilson Center Press, 2001.

LaFeber, Walter. *The Panama Canal: The Crisis in Historical Perspective.* New York: Oxford University Press, 1978.

Lake, Anthony. *The "Tar Baby" Option: American Policy toward Southern Rhodesia.* New York: Columbia University Press, 1976.

Larson, Stanley Robert, and James Lawton Collins Jr. *Allied Participation in Vietnam.* Washington, DC: Government Printing Office, 1975.

Lasky, Victor. *J.F.K.: The Man and the Myth.* New York: Macmillan, 1963.

Lassiter, Matthew D. *The Silent Majority: Suburban Politics in the Sunbelt South.* Princeton, NJ: Princeton University Press, 2006.

Latham, Michael E. *Modernization as Ideology: American Social Science and "Nation Building" in the Kennedy Era.* Chapel Hill: University of North Carolina Press, 2000.

Lawrence, Mark Atwood. "The Limits of Peacemaking: India and the Vietnam War, 1962–67." *India Review* 1, no. 1 (January 2002): 39–72.

Leacock, Ruth. *Requiem for Revolution: The United States and Brazil, 1961–1969.* Kent, OH: Kent State University Press, 1990.

Leffler, Melvin P. *For the Soul of Mankind: The United States, the Soviet Union, and the Cold War.* New York: Hill & Wang, 2007.

Lerner, Mitchell B. "'A Big Tree of Peace and Justice': The Vice Presidential Travels of Lyndon Johnson." *Diplomatic History* 34, no. 2 (April 2010): 357–393.

———, ed. *A Companion to Lyndon B. Johnson.* Malden, MA: Wiley-Blackwell, 2012.

———, ed. *Looking Back at LBJ: White House Politics in a New Light.* Lawrence: University Press of Kansas, 2005.

Little, Douglas. *American Orientalism: The United States and the Middle East since 1945.* Chapel Hill: University of North Carolina Press, 2002.

Litwak, Robert S. *Détente and the Nixon Doctrine: American Foreign Policy and the Pursuit of Stability, 1969–1976*. Cambridge: Cambridge University Press, 1984.

Logevall, Fredrik. *Choosing War: The Lost Chance for Peace and the Escalation of War in Vietnam*. Berkeley: University of California Press, 1999.

Logevall, Fredrik, and Andrew Preston, eds. *Nixon in the World: American Foreign Relations, 1969–1977*. New York: Oxford University Press, 2008.

Longley, Kyle. *LBJ's 1968: Power, Politics, and the Presidency in America's Year of Upheaval*. New York: Cambridge University Press, 2018.

Lorenzini, Sara. *Global Development: A Cold War History*. Princeton, NJ: Princeton University Press, 2019.

Lumbers, Michael. "The Irony of Vietnam: The Johnson Administration's Tentative Bridge Building to China, 1965–1966." *Journal of Cold War Studies* 6, no. 3 (Summer 2004): 68–114.

———. *Piercing the Bamboo Curtain: Tentative Bridge Building to China during the Johnson Years*. Manchester: Manchester University Press, 2008.

Lüthi, Lorenz M. *The Sino-Soviet Split: Cold War in the Communist World*. Princeton, NJ: Princeton University Press, 2008.

Macdonald, Douglas J. *Adventures in Chaos: American Intervention for Reform in the Third World*. Cambridge, MA: Harvard University Press, 1992.

Madan, Tanvi. "With an Eye to the East: The China Factor and the U.S.-India Relationship, 1949–1979." PhD diss., University of Texas at Austin, 2012.

Mahoney, Richard D. *JFK: Ordeal in Africa*. New York: Oxford University Press, 1983.

Mailer, Norman. *The Presidential Papers*. New York: Putnam, 1963.

Manela, Erez. *The Wilsonian Moment: Self-Determination and the International Origins of Anticolonial Nationalism*. New York: Oxford University Press, 2007.

Mason, Edward S. *Economic Planning and the Underdeveloped Areas*. New York: Fordham University Press, 1958.

———. *Promoting Economic Development: The United States and Southeast Asia*. Claremont, CA: Claremont College, 1955.

McMahon, Robert J., ed. *The Cold War in the Third World*. New York: Oxford University Press, 2013.

———. *The Cold War on the Periphery: The United States, India, and Pakistan*. New York: Columbia University Press, 1994.

McMaster, H. R. *Dereliction of Duty: Lyndon Johnson, Robert McNamara, the Joint Chiefs of Staff, and the Lies That Led to Vietnam*. New York: Harper, 1998.

McNamara, Robert S., with Brian VanDeMark. *In Retrospect: The Tragedy and Lessons of Vietnam*. New York: Times Books, 1995.

McPherson, Alan. *Yankee, No! Anti-Americanism in U.S.-Latin American Relations*. Cambridge, MA: Harvard University Press, 2006.

Meriwether, James H. *Proudly We Can Be Africans: Black Americans and Africa, 1935–1961*. Chapel Hill: University of North Carolina Press, 2002.

Merrill, Dennis. *Bread and the Ballot: The United States and India's Economic Development, 1947–1963*. Chapel Hill: University of North Carolina Press, 1990.

Meyer, Armin. *Quiet Diplomacy: From Cairo to Tokyo in the Twilight of Imperialism*. New York: iUniverse, 2003.

Milani, Abbas. *The Persian Sphinx: Amir Abbas Hoveyda and the Riddle of the Iranian Revolution*. Washington, DC: Mage, 2001.

Miller, Merle. *Lyndon: An Oral Biography*. New York: Putnam, 1980.

Milne, David. *America's Rasputin: Walt Rostow and the Vietnam War*. New York: Hill & Wang, 2008.

Mortimer, Robert A. *The Third World Coalition in International Politics*. New York: Praeger, 1980.

Muehlenbeck, Philip E. *Betting on the Africans: John F. Kennedy's Courting of African Nationalist Leaders*. New York: Oxford University Press, 2012.

Nagl, John. *Learning to Eat Soup with a Knife: Counterinsurgency Lessons from Malaya to Vietnam*. Chicago: University of Chicago Press, 2005.

Namikas, Lise. *Battleground Africa: Cold War in the Congo, 1960–1965*. Stanford, CA: Stanford University Press, 2013.

Neustadt, Richard E., and Ernest R. May. *Thinking in Time: The Uses of History for Decision Makers*. New York: Free Press, 1986.

Ngoei, Wen-Qing. *Arc of Containment: Britain, the United States, and Anticommunism in Southeast Asia*. Ithaca, NY: Cornell University Press, 2019.

Nixon, Richard M. *RN: The Memoirs of Richard Nixon*. New York: Grosset and Dunlap, 1978.

———. *United States Foreign Policy for the 1970s: A New Strategy for Peace*. New York: Bantam, 1970.

Noer, Thomas J. *Cold War and Black Liberation: The United States and White Rule in Africa, 1948–1968*. Columbia: University of Missouri Press, 1985.

Offiler, Ben. *U.S. Foreign Policy and the Modernization of Iran: Kennedy, Johnson, Nixon, and the Shah*. London: Palgrave Macmillan, 2015.

Offner, Arnold A. *Hubert Humphrey: The Conscience of the Country*. New Haven, CT: Yale University Press, 2018.

Onslow, Susan, ed. *Cold War in Southern Africa: White Power, Black Liberation*. London: Routledge, 2009.

Packenham, Robert A. *Liberal America and the Third World: Political Development Ideas in Foreign Aid and Social Science*. Princeton, NJ: Princeton University Press, 1973.

Painter, David S. "Research Note: Explaining U.S. Relations with the Third World." *Diplomatic History* 19, no. 1 (Summer 1995): 525–548.

Parker, Jason C. *Hearts, Minds, Voices: U.S. Cold War Public Diplomacy and the Formation of the Third World*. New York: Oxford University Press, 2016.

Parrott, R. Joseph, and Mark Atwood Lawrence, eds. *The Tricontinental Revolution: Third World Radicalism and the Cold War*. New York: Cambridge University Press, forthcoming.

Paterson, Thomas G., ed. *Kennedy's Quest for Victory: American Foreign Policy, 1961–1963*. New York: Oxford University Press, 1989.

Patterson, James T. *Grand Expectations: The United States, 1945–1974*. New York: Oxford University Press, 1996.

Pereira, Anthony W. "The U.S. Role in the 1964 Coup in Brazil: A Reassessment." *Bulletin of Latin American Research* 37, no. 1 (June 2016): 5–17.

Perlstein, Rick. *Nixonland: The Rise of a President and the Fracturing of America*. New York: Scribner, 2008.

Pike, Fredrick B. *The United States and the Andean Republicans: Peru, Bolivia, and Ecuador*. Cambridge, MA: Harvard University Press, 1977.

Plummer, Brenda Gayle. *Window on Freedom: Race, Civil Rights, and Foreign Affairs, 1945–1988*. Chapel Hill: University of North Carolina Press, 2003.

Porter, Gareth. *Perils of Dominance: Imbalance of Power and the Road to War in Vietnam*. Berkeley: University of California Press, 2005.

Poulgrain, Greg. *The Incubus of Intervention: Conflicting Indonesia Strategies of John F. Kennedy and Allen Dulles*. Petaling Jaya, Malaysia: Strategic Information and Research Development Centre, 2015.

Prashad, Vijay. *The Darker Nations: A People's History of the Third World*. New York: New Press, 2007.

Preston, Andrew. "The Little State Department: McGeorge Bundy and the National Security Council Staff, 1961–1965." *Presidential Studies Quarterly* 31, no. 4 (December 2001): 635–659.

———. *The War Council: McGeorge Bundy, the NSC, and Vietnam*. Cambridge, MA: Harvard University Press, 2006.

Putnam, Robert D., with Shaylyn Romney Garrett. *The Upswing: How America Came Together a Century Ago and How We Can Do It Again*. New York: Simon & Schuster, 2020.

Rabe, Steven G. *Eisenhower and Latin America: The Foreign Policy of Anti-communism*. Chapel Hill: University of North Carolina Press, 1988.

———. *The Killing Zone: The United States Wages Cold War in Latin America*. New York: Oxford University Press, 2012.

———. *"The Most Dangerous Area in the World": John F. Kennedy Confronts Communist Revolution in Latin America*. Chapel Hill: University of North Carolina Press, 1999.

———. *U.S. Intervention in British Guiana: A Cold War Story*. Chapel Hill: University of North Carolina Press, 2005.

Rakove, Robert B. *Kennedy, Johnson, and the Nonaligned World*. New York: Cambridge University Press, 2013.

Ramesh, Jairam. *Intertwined Lives: P.N. Haksar and Indira Gandhi*. New Delhi: Simon & Schuster, 2018.

Reinstein, Thomas A. "The Way a Drunk Uses a Lamp Post: Intelligence and Policy during the Vietnam War, 1962–1968." PhD diss., Temple University, 2018.

Ribeiro de Meneses, Filipe, and Robert McNamara. *The White Redoubt, the Great Powers, and the Struggle for Southern Africa, 1960–1980*. London: Palgrave Macmillan, 2018.

Robinson, Geoffrey B. *The Killing Season: A History of the Indonesian Massacres, 1965–66*. Princeton, NJ: Princeton University Press, 2018.

Rodman, Peter W. *More Precious Than Peace: The Cold War and the Struggle for the Third World*. New York: Scribner's, 1994.

Roosa, John. *Pretext for Mass Murder: The September 30th Movement and Suharto's Coup d'État in Indonesia*. Madison: University of Wisconsin Press, 2006.

Rostow, W. W. *The Stages of Economic Growth: A Non-communist Manifesto*. 3rd ed. Cambridge: Cambridge University Press, 1990.

Rotter, Andrew J. *Comrades at Odds: The United States and India, 1947–1964*. Ithaca, NY: Cornell University Press, 2000.

Rubin, Barry, and Judith Colp Rubin. *Hating America: A History*. New York: Oxford University Press, 2004.

Rubinstein, Alvin Z. *Moscow's Third World Strategy*. Princeton, NJ: Princeton University Press, 1988.

Salinger, Pierre. *With Kennedy*. Garden City, NY: Doubleday, 1966.

Sargent, Daniel J. *A Superpower Transformed: The Remaking of American Foreign Relations in the 1970s*. New York: Oxford University Press, 2015.

Saunders, Elizabeth N. *Leaders at War: How Presidents Shape Military Interventions*. Ithaca, NY: Cornell University Press, 2011.

Schaffer, Howard B. *Chester Bowles: New Dealer in the Cold War*. Cambridge, MA: Harvard University Press, 1993.

Schlesinger, Arthur M., Jr. *Journals, 1952–2000*. New York: Penguin, 2007.

———. *A Thousand Days: John F. Kennedy in the White House*. New York: Fawcett, 1965.

Schmitz, David F. *Thank God They're on Our Side: The United States & Right-Wing Dictatorships, 1921–1965*. Chapel Hill: University of North Carolina Press, 1999.

———. *The United States and Right-Wing Dictatorships*. New York: Cambridge University Press, 2006.

Schoultz, Lars. *Beneath the United States: A History of U.S. Policy toward Latin America*. Cambridge, MA: Harvard University Press, 1998.

Schraeder, Peter J. *United States Foreign Policy toward Africa: Incrementalism, Crisis, and Change*. Cambridge: Cambridge University Press, 1994.

Schulman, Bruce J. *Lyndon B. Johnson and American Liberalism: A Brief Biography with Documents*. Boston: Bedford, 1995.

Schulman, Bruce J., and Julian E. Zelizer, eds. *Rightward Bound: Making America Conservative in the 1970s*. Cambridge, MA: Harvard University Press, 2008.

Schulzinger, Robert D. *Henry Kissinger: Doctor of Diplomacy*. New York: Columbia University Press, 1989.

Schwartz, Thomas Alan. *Lyndon Johnson and Europe: In the Shadow of Vietnam*. Cambridge, MA: Harvard University Press, 2003.

Scott, Peter Dale. "The United States and the Overthrow of Sukarno." *Pacific Affairs* 58, no. 2 (Summer 1985): 240–264.

See, Jennifer W. "An Uneasy Truce: John F. Kennedy and Soviet-American Détente, 1963." *Cold War History* 2, no. 2 (January 2002): 161–194.

Sikkink, Kathryn. *Mixed Signals: U.S. Human Rights Policy and Latin America*. Ithaca, NY: Cornell University Press, 2004.

Simpson, Bradley R. *Economists with Guns: Authoritarian Development and U.S.-Indonesian Relations, 1960–1968*. Stanford, CA: Stanford University Press, 2008.

Skidmore, Thomas E. *Politics in Brazil, 1930–1964: An Experiment in Democracy*. New York: Oxford University Press, 1967.

———. *The Politics of Military Rule in Brazil, 1964–1985*. New York: Oxford University Press, 1990.

Smith, Ian. *The Great Betrayal: The Memoirs of Ian Douglas Smith*. London: Blake, 1997.

# INDEX

## A NOTE ON THE TYPE

This book has been composed in Arno, an Old-style serif typeface in the classic Venetian tradition, designed by Robert Slimbach at Adobe.